A
WHO'S
WHO
OF
BRITISH
FILM
ACTORS

by
Scott Palmer

1981

The Scarecrow Press, Inc.
Metuchen, N.J., & London

Library of Congress Cataloging in Publication Data

Palmer, Scott, 1958-
    A who's who of British film actors.

    Bibliography: p.
    1. Moving-picture actors and actresses--Great
Britain.   2. Moving-pictures--Great Britain--
Catalogs.   I.   Title.
PN1998.A2P365   791.43'028'0922 [B]   80-26016
ISBN 0-8108-1388-2

To Pam and Walt

AUTHOR'S NOTE

Having viewed some 20, 000 motion pictures, I have come to the conclusion that British films are of the highest quality. Even the Hollywood films that have been most memorable to me have had British players in them. With this love for British films and actors, I thought it would be useful to find a book that listed virtually every British film actor with a complete list of films in which he or she appeared. After years of searching, I discovered that no such book existed. I therefore thought that I would write one myself.

It is impossible, however, for any single volume to include all actors or every flim they appeared in, as many big stars began their careers in small roles; others played nothing other than minor roles. This book includes some 1, 400 actors and actresses, listed in alphabetical order. The majority of them are English, but also included are the Scottish, Irish, Welsh, Australian, Canadian, South African, and many other British Commonwealth personalities. Since this latter group is less common, they will be identified specifically. Actors born in other countries will also be mentioned providing that they did their main work in British films. Also, actors who were British-born but did films in Hollywood or outside the U. K. are included.

The films are listed chronologically, with the emphasis on the sound era. Silent films will also be mentioned, but actors whose careers only covered the silent era have been omitted. Due to the vast number of films and sources used, there may be some variations concerning dates. A film may appear under one person as 1955 and another as 1956. I have tried to give the year the film was completed, but in some cases releases were delayed, even for several years. I beg the indulgence of the reader on this point, and can only plead the impossibility of cross-checking every entry in a book of such length. (I have also attempted to give the original title of the film, which was also difficult, considering that a good many films can be seen under several titles.)

There is also a brief description of each actor along with the years of birth and death. Most of this information was easy to find, but there are a number of actors (mainly small-part players) included whose dates could not be verified.

There have been many film reference books, but this is the first attempt (as far as I know) to document the films of solely British film actors, from international stars down to minor small-part players. Even so, every player cannot be mentioned, and if one of your favorites is not included, please accept my apology. Any corrections, comments, or advice will also be welcome and should be addressed to me c/o the publisher.

Finally, I would like to thank the following individuals and organizations for their help and advice during the writing of this book: The British Film Institute, Gabe DeNunzio, John Monteverde, Robert Redding and Peter Seward.

Scott Palmer
San Diego, June 1980

BIBLIOGRAPHY

Aaronson, Charles S. , ed. <u>1969 International Television Almanac.</u>
New York: Quigley Publishing Company, 1968.

Gifford, Denis, ed. <u>The British Film Catalogue 1895-1970.</u> New
York: McGraw-Hill Book Company, 1973.

Gifford, Denis. <u>The Illustrated Who's Who in British Films.</u> London: B. T. Batsford, Ltd. , 1978.

Halliwell, Leslie. <u>The Filmgoer's Companion.</u> 6th ed. New York:
Avon Books, 1978.

Katz, Ephraim. <u>The Film Encyclopedia.</u> New York: Thomas Y.
Crowell, 1979.

<u>The New York Times Directory of the Film.</u> New York: Arno Press,
1974.

Vermilye, Jerry. <u>The Great British Films.</u> Secaucus, New Jersey:
Citadel Press, 1978.

Willis, John, ed. <u>Screen World.</u> Vols. 23-30. New York: Crown
Publishers, 1972-1979.

A WHO'S WHO
OF BRITISH FILM ACTORS

JOHN ABBOTT (1905-)
Goggle-eyed character actor, in
Hollywood from 1941. Specialized
in playing eccentrics or excitable
foreigners.

Conquest of the Air, 1936
Mademoiselle Docteur, 1938
Return of the Scarlet Pimpernel,
  1938
Ten Days in Paris, 1939
The Saint in London, 1939
The Shanghai Gesture, 1941
Mrs. Miniver, 1942
They Got me Covered, 1942
Joan of Paris, 1942
Get Hep to Love, 1942
Nightmare, 1942
This Above All, 1942
Secret Motive, 1943
Gorilla Man, 1943
Mission to Moscow, 1943
Jane Eyre, 1944
The Mask of Dimitrios, 1944
Cry of the Werewolf, 1944
Summer Storm, 1944
Abroad With Two Yanks, 1944
The Falcon in Hollywood, 1944
Saratoga Trunk, 1945
The Vampire's Ghost, 1945
Pursuit to Algiers, 1945
Deception, 1946
One More Tomorrow, 1946
The Notorious Lone Wolf, 1946
Humoresque, 1946
Bandit of Sherwood Forest, 1946
Anna and the King of Siam, 1946
Adventure Island, 1947
Time Out of Mind, 1947
Navy Bound, 1947
The Web, 1947

The Woman in White, 1948
Dream Girl, 1948
If Winter Comes, 1948
Madame Bovary, 1949
Her Wonderful Lie, 1950
Crosswinds, 1951
Thunder on the Hill, 1951
The Merry Widow, 1952
Rogue's March, 1952
Thunder in the East, 1953
Sombrero, 1953
Steel Lady, 1953
Public Pigeon Number One, 1957
Gigi, 1958
Who's Minding the Store?, 1963
The Greatest Story Ever Told,
  1965
Gambit, 1966
Three Guns For Texas, 1968
Two Thousand Years Later, 1969
The Black Bird, 1975
Sherlock Holmes in New York,
  1976

JOSS ACKLAND (1928-)
Large character actor of ambitious personality; also frequently
on television.

A Midsummer Night's Dream,
  1961
Rasputin the Mad Monk, 1965
Crescendo, 1969
The House That Dripped Blood,
  1970
Villain, 1971
England Made Me, 1972
Cry of the Penguins, 1972
The Happiness Cage, 1972
Penny Gold, 1973

3

Hitler: The Last Ten Days, 1973
The Black Windmill, 1974
S. P. Y. S. , 1974
The Little Prince, 1974
Operation Daybreak, 1975
Royal Flash, 1975
One of Our Dinosaurs is Missing,
   1975
Great Expectations, 1975
Silver Bears, 1978
Watership Down, 1978
Who's Killing the Great Chefs
   of Europe?, 1978
Rough Cut, 1980

RONALD ADAM (1896-1979)
Small-part character actor, typically played stuffy, educated
businessmen or other authoritar-
ian types; also author and playwright.

The Drum, 1938
Strange Boarders, 1938
Inspector Hornleigh, 1938
Q Planes, 1939
At the Villa Rose, 1939
The Lion Has Wings, 1939
The Missing People, 1939
Meet Maxwell Archer, 1939
Too Dangerous to Live, 1939
Hell's Cargo, 1940
The Foreman Went to France,
   1942
Escape to Danger, 1943
Green For Danger, 1946
The Phantom Shot, 1947
Take My Life, 1947
Bonnie Prince Charlie, 1948
Counterblast, 1948
All Over the Town, 1949
Under Capricorn, 1949
The Case of Charles Peace,
   1949
Diamond City, 1949
My Daughter Joy, 1950
Seven Days to Noon, 1950
The Hidden Room, 1950
Shadow of the Past, 1950
Angels One Five, 1951
The Lavender Hill Mob, 1951
Laughter in Paradise, 1951

The Adventurers, 1951
The Late Edwina Black, 1951
Captain Horatio Hornblower,
   1951
Circumstantial Evidence, 1952
Hindle Wakes, 1952
Flannelfoot, 1953
Front Page Story, 1954
Escape By Night, 1954
The Million Pound Note, 1954
Johnny on the Spot, 1954
To Dorothy a Son, 1954
Malta Story, 1954
The Black Knight, 1954
Lust For Life, 1956
Reach For the Sky, 1956
Private's Progress, 1956
Assignment Redhead, 1956
Tons of Trouble, 1956
The Surgeon's Knife, 1957
Seawife, 1957
Kill Me Tomorrow, 1957
Inside Information, 1957
The Golden Disc, 1958
Carry On Admiral, 1958
Carleton Browne of the F. O. ,
   1959
Please Turn Over, 1959
And the Same to You, 1960
Snowball, 1960
Shoot to Kill, 1961
Three on a Spree, 1961
Offbeat, 1961
Carry On Regardless, 1961
Two-Letter Alibi, 1962
Postman's Knock, 1962
The Golden Rabbit, 1962
Satan Never Sleeps, 1962
Cleopatra, 1962
The Haunting, 1963
Heavens Above, 1963
The Tomb of Ligeia, 1964
Who Killed the Cat?, 1966
Hell Boats, 1969
Song of Norway, 1970
Zeppelin, 1971

JILL ADAMS (1930-)
Former model who became leading lady in a few films of the
50s and 60s.

Forbidden Cargo, 1954
Young Lovers, 1955
Doctor at Sea, 1955
Value For Money, 1955
One Way Out, 1955
The Constant Husband, 1955
One Jump Ahead, 1955
Private's Progress, 1956
The Green Man, 1957
Brothers in Law, 1957
The Scamp, 1957
Death Over My Shoulder, 1958
Carry on Constable, 1960
Crosstrap, 1962
The Yellow Teddy Bears, 1963
Doctor in Distress, 1963
The Comedy Man, 1963
Promise Her Anything, 1966

TOM ADAMS (1938-)
Strong, burly leading man of
the 60s; on television in series
"Spy Trap."

This Is My Street, 1963
The Peaches, 1964
Licensed to Kill, 1965
Where the Bullets Fly, 1966
Fighting Prince of Donegal,
  1966
Fathom, 1967
Subterfuge, 1969
The House That Dripped Blood,
  1970
The Fast Kill, 1972

DAWN ADDAMS (1930-)
Intelligent, attractive leading
lady, also in Hollywood.   Films
generally undistinguished.

Night Into Morning, 1951
The Hour of Thirteen, 1952
The Plymouth Adventure, 1952
The Robe, 1953
The Moon is Blue, 1953
Young Bess, 1953
The Unknown Man, 1953
Riders to the Stars, 1953
Khyber Patrol, 1954
Singing in the Rain, 1954

Return to Treasure Island, 1954
Mizar, 1954
The Bed, 1955
Treasure of Rommel, 1955
Secret Professional, 1956
A King in New York, 1957
London Calling North Pole, 1957
The Silent Enemy, 1958
Temptation, 1959
The Treasure of San Teresa,
  1959
The Two Faces of Dr. Jekyll,
  1960
The Thousand Eyes of Dr. Ma-
  buse, 1960
Prisoner of the Volga, 1960
House of Intrigue, 1960
Come Dance With Me, 1960
Follow That Man, 1961
The Liars, 1961
Lesson in Love, 1962
Long Distance, 1962
Come Fly With Me, 1963
The Black Tulip, 1964
Ballad in Blue, 1965
Where the Bullets Fly, 1966
Zeta One, 1969
The Vampire Lovers, 1970
Sappho, 1970
The Vault of Horror, 1973

MAX ADRIAN (1903-1973)
Adaptable actor of stage (since
1926) and screen, highly successful in one-man show as George
Bernard Shaw; also on American
television.

The Primrose Path, 1934
Eight Cylinder Love, 1934
A Touch of the Moon, 1936
To Catch a Thief, 1936
Nothing Like Publicity, 1936
The Happy Family, 1936
When the Devil Was Well, 1937
Why Pick On Me?, 1937
Macushlah, 1938
Merely Mr. Hawkins, 1938
Kipps, 1941
Penn of Pennsylvania, 1941
The Young Mr. Pitt, 1942
Talk About Jacqueline, 1942

Henry V, 1944
Her Favourite Husband, 1950
Pool of London, 1951
The Pickwick Papers, 1952
Uncle Vanya, 1963
Dr. Terror's House of Horrors,
    1965
Funeral in Berlin, 1966
The Deadly Affair, 1966
The Terrornauts, 1967
Julius Caesar, 1970
The Music Lovers, 1970
The Devils, 1971
The Boy Friend, 1971

JENNY AGUTTER (1952-)
Leading actress, originally
trained for ballet, also in Hollywood.

East of Sudan, 1964
Gates to Paradise, 1968
Star!, 1968
I Start Counting, 1970
The Railway Children, 1971
Walkabout, 1971
The Snow Goose, 1971
A War of Children, 1972
Logan's Run, 1976
The Eagle Has Landed, 1977
Equus, 1977
China 9 Liberty 37, 1978
Sweet William, 1979
The Riddle of the Sands, 1979
Amy-On-the-Lips, 1980

BRIAN AHERNE (1902-)
Popular hero of silent films,
came to Hollywood in 1933 and
remained to play the typical,
kindly English gentleman.

The Eleventh Commandment,
    1924
King of the Castle, 1925
The Squire of Long Hadley, 1925
Safety First, 1926
A Woman Redeemed, 1927
Shooting Stars, 1928
Underground, 1929
The W Plan, 1930

Madame Guillotine, 1931
The Constant Nymph, 1933
I Was a Spy, 1933
Song of Songs, 1933
The Fountain, 1934
What Every Woman Knows,
    1934
I Live My Life, 1935
Sylvia Scarlett, 1936
Beloved Enemy, 1936
The Great Garrick, 1937
Merrily We Live, 1938
Juarez, 1939
Captain Fury, 1939
Vigil in the Night, 1940
My Son My Son, 1940
Hired Wife, 1940
The Woman in Question, 1940
Skylark, 1941
The Man Who Lost Himself,
    1941
Smilin' Through, 1941
My Sister Eileen, 1942
A Night to Remember, 1943
Forever and a Day, 1943
First Comes Courage, 1943
What a Woman, 1943
The Locket, 1946
Angel on the Amazon, 1948
Smart Woman, 1948
I Confess, 1953
Titanic, 1953
Prince Valiant, 1954
A Bullet is Waiting, 1954
The Swan, 1956
The Best of Everything, 1959
Susan Slade, 1961
Lancelot and Guinevere, 1963
The Cavern, 1965
The Waltz King, 1966
Rosie, 1968

PATRICK AHERNE (1901-1970)
Irish-born light leading man,
brother of Brian Aherne; also
frequently in Hollywood from
1936. Married to Renee Houston.

The Cost of Beauty, 1924
Blinkeyes, 1926
The Game Chicken, 1926

Thou Fool, 1926
Ball of Fortune, 1926
A Daughter in Revolt, 1927
The Silver Lining, 1927
Carry On, 1927
Huntingtower, 1927
Virginia's Husband, 1928
Love's Option, 1928
Double Dealing, 1928
The Inseperables, 1929
Auld Lang Syne, 1929
City of Play, 1929
Come Into My Parlour, 1932
Pride of the Force, 1933
Oh What a Duchess!, 1933
Outcast, 1934
The Return of Bulldog Drummond, 1934
Falling in Love, 1934
Eight Cylinder Love, 1934
The Stoker, 1935
Trouble Ahead, 1936
Polly's Two Fathers, 1936
Q Planes, 1939
Ask a Policeman, 1939
Thursday's Child, 1943
Warn That Man, 1943
Green Dolphin Street, 1947
The Paradine Case, 1948
Bwana Devil, 1952
The Court Jester, 1956

RICHARD AINLEY (1910-1967)
Character actor who came to
Hollywood during WWII, son of
silent film star Henry Ainley
(1879-1945).

As You Like It, 1936
The Frog, 1937
The Gang Show, 1937
Our Fighting Navy, 1937
Lily of Laguna, 1938
Old Iron, 1938
There Ain't No Justice, 1939
An Englishman's Home, 1939
A Stolen Life, 1939
Lady With Red Hair, 1940
The Smiling Ghost, 1941
Singapore Woman, 1941
Shining Victory, 1941
Bullets For O'Hara, 1941

White Cargo, 1942
Above Suspicion, 1943
I Dood It, 1943
Three Hearts For Julia, 1943
Passage to Hong Kong, 1949

MURIEL AKED (1887-1955)
Comedy character actress who
followed lengthy stage career
by appearing as prim and proper spinsters in a number of
films.

A Sister to Assist 'Er, 1922
Bindle's Cocktail, 1926
The Middle Watch, 1930
Bed and Breakfast, 1930
A Sister to Assist 'Er, 1931
Her First Affaire, 1932
Rome Express, 1932
Goodnight Vienna, 1932
The Mayor's Next, 1932
Indiscretions of Eve, 1932
Trouble, 1933
Yes Madam, 1933
No Funny Business, 1933
Friday the Thirteenth, 1933
The Good Companions, 1933
Autumn Crocus, 1934
Evensong, 1934
The Queen's Affair, 1934
Night of the Party, 1934
Josser on the Farm, 1934
Can You Hear Me Mother?,
   1935
Don't Rush Me, 1936
Fame, 1936
Royal Eagle, 1936
Public Nuisance Number One,
   1936
Mr. Stringfellow Says No, 1937
A Sister to Assist 'Er, 1938
The Girl Who Forgot, 1939
The Silent Battle, 1939
A Girl Must Live, 1939
Cottage to Let, 1941
Continental Express, 1942
Colonel Blimp, 1943
The Demi-Paradise, 1943
Two Thousand Women, 1944
The Wicked Lady, 1945
The Years Between, 1946

Just William's Luck, 1947
So Evil My Love, 1948
A Sister to Assist 'Er, 1948
It's Hard to Be Good, 1948
William Comes to Town, 1949
Happiest Days of Your Life,
   1950
Wonder Kid, 1951
Flesh and Blood, 1951
Gilbert and Sullivan, 1953

JOHN ALDERTON (1940-   )
Light leading actor of the 60s
and 70s; gained popularity on
television in series "Emergency
Ward Ten" and "Please Sir. "

Cleopatra, 1962
The System, 1964
Duffy, 1968
Hannibal Brooks, 1969
You Can't Win Them All, 1970
Please Sir, 1971
Zardoz, 1973
It Shouldn't Happen to a Vet,
   1976
All Things Bright and Beautiful,
   1978

TERENCE ALEXANDER
   (1923-   )
Urbane light leading man of
stage, screen and television.
Generally latterly seen as army
major. Notable in tv series "The
Palisers;" "The Forsyte Saga. "

Comin' Thro' the Rye, 1947
Death is a Number, 1951
The Woman With No Name, 1951
The Gentle Gunman, 1952
Glad Tidings, 1953
Dangerous Cargo, 1954
The Runaway Bus, 1954
Portrait of Alison, 1955
The One That Got Away, 1957
The Square Peg, 1958
Death Was a Passenger, 1958
The Doctor's Dilemma, 1958
Breakout, 1959
Danger Within, 1959

The League of Gentlemen, 1959
Don't Panic Chaps, 1959
The Bulldog Breed, 1960
The Price of Silence, 1960
Carry on Regardless, 1961
Man at the Carlton Tower, 1961
The Fast Lady, 1962
The Gentle Terror, 1962
She Always Gets Their Man,
   1962
On the Beat, 1962
The Mind Benders, 1963
Bitter Harvest, 1963
The Intelligence Men, 1965
Judith, 1966
The Long Duel, 1967
The Spare Tyres, 1967
Only When I Larf, 1968
What's Good For the Goose,
   1969
Run a Crooked Mile, 1969
The Magic Christian, 1970
Waterloo, 1970
All the Way Up, 1970
Day of the Jackal, 1973
The Vault of Horror, 1973
The Unpleasantness at the Bel-
   lona Club, 1973
The Internecine Project, 1974
Ike, 1979

DOROTHY ALISON (1925-   )
Australian film actress, long
resident in England.

Mandy, 1952
Turn the Key Softly, 1953
The Maggie, 1954
Child's Play, 1954
The Purple Plain, 1954
The Silken Affair, 1956
The Feminine Touch, 1956
Reach For the Sky, 1956
The Long Arm, 1956
The Scamp, 1957
Interpol, 1957
The Man Upstairs, 1959
Life in Emergency Ward Ten,
   1959
Two Living One Dead, 1961
The Prince and the Pauper,
   1962

Georgy Girl, 1966
Pretty Polly, 1968
See No Evil, 1971
The Amazing Mr. Blunden, 1972
Baxter, 1973

ELIZABETH ALLAN (1908-)
Slender, aristocratic leading
lady of stage (1927) and screen;
heroine of early talkies, later
popular on television.

Alibi, 1931
The Rosary, 1931
Black Coffee, 1931
Rodney Steps In, 1931
Chin Chin Chinaman, 1931
Michael and Mary, 1931
Many Waters, 1931
Reserved For Ladies, 1932
Insult, 1932
The Lodger, 1932
Down Our Street, 1932
Nine Till Six, 1932
The Chinese Puzzle, 1932
Service For Ladies, 1932
No Marriage Ties, 1933
Looking Forward, 1933
Ace of Aces, 1933
The Solitaire Man, 1933
The Shadow, 1933
The Lost Chord, 1933
Java Head, 1934
Outcast Lady, 1934
Men in White, 1934
The Mystery of Mr. X, 1934
Phantom Fiend, 1935
Mark of the Vampire, 1935
David Copperfield, 1935
A Tale of Two Cities, 1935
The Story of Papworth, 1936
A Woman Rebels, 1936
Camille, 1936
Michael Strogoff, 1937
Slave Ship, 1937
Dangerous Medicine, 1938
The Girl Who Forgot, 1939
Inquest, 1939
Saloon Bar, 1940
The Great Mr. Handel, 1942
Went the Day Well, 1942
He Snoops to Conquer, 1944

That Dangerous Age, 1949
No Highway, 1951
Folly to Be Wise, 1952
Twice Upon a Time, 1953
The Heart of the Matter, 1953
Front Page Story, 1954
The Brain Machine, 1955
Grip of the Strangler, 1958

ADRIENNE ALLEN (1907-)
Light leading actress, mainly
on stage. Formerly married
to Raymond Massey; mother of
Anna and Daniel Massey.

Loose Ends, 1930
The Stronger Sex, 1931
Black Coffee, 1931
The Woman Between, 1931
The Night of June Thirteenth,
    1932
Merrily We Go to Hell, 1932
The Morals of Marcus, 1935
The October Man, 1947
Bond Street, 1948
Vote For Huggett, 1948
The Final Test, 1953
Meet Mr. Malcolm, 1954

CHESNEY ALLEN (1893-)
Aloof light comedian, music
hall entertainer and partner of
Bud Flanagan. Also member
of "The Crazy Gang. "

The Bailiffs, 1932
They're Off, 1933
The Dreamers, 1933
Wild Boy, 1934
A Fire Has Been Arranged,
    1934
Okay For Sound, 1937
Underneath the Arches, 1937
Alf's Button Afloat, 1938
The Frozen Limits, 1939
Gasbags, 1940
We'll Smile Again, 1942
Theatre Royal, 1943
Dreaming, 1944
Here Comes the Sun, 1945
Judgement Deferred, 1952

Dunkirk, 1957
Life is a Circus, 1959
The Wild Affair, 1963

JACK ALLEN (1907-)
General-purpose light character
actor, also on stage.

The Four Feathers, 1939
Spy For a Day, 1940
Elizabeth of Ladymead, 1949
She Shall Have Murder, 1950
Conspirator, 1950
The Sound Barrier, 1952
It Started in Paradise, 1952
Radio Cab Murder, 1954
Impulse, 1955
The Man From Tangier, 1957
The Headless Ghost, 1959
Life in Danger, 1959
The White Trap, 1959
The Breaking Point, 1961
Bomb in the High Street, 1961
The Big Switch, 1968
The Confessional, 1976

PATRICK ALLEN (1927-)
Square-jawed actor usually cast
in aggressive or villainous roles.
Popular on television in the
"Crane" series.

Dial M For Murder, 1954
Cross Channel, 1955
Confession, 1955
Dead On Time, 1955
Wicked as They Come, 1956
1984, 1956
High Tide at Noon, 1957
The Long Haul, 1957
Dunkirk, 1957
Tread Softly Stranger, 1958
High Hell, 1958
I Was Monty's Double, 1958
Mark of the Hawk, 1958
The Man Who Wouldn't Talk,
   1958
Jet Storm, 1959
Never Take Sweets From a
   Stranger, 1960
The Sinister Man, 1961

Flight From Singapore, 1962
The Traitors, 1962
Captain Clegg, 1962
Night of the Generals, 1966
Night of the Big Heat, 1967
The Body Stealers, 1969
When Dinosaurs Ruled the
   Earth, 1969
Puppet On a Chain, 1971
Diamonds On Wheels, 1973
Island of the Burning Damned
   1973
Persecution, 1974
The Wilby Conspiracy, 1975
The Wild Geese, 1978

SARA ALLGOOD (1883-1950)
Kindly Irish character actress,
former star of the Abbey Theatre, in Hollywood from 1940.
Sister of Maire O'Niell.

Just Peggy, 1918
Blackmail, 1929
To What Red Hell, 1929
Juno and Paycock, 1929
The World the Flesh & the
   Devil, 1932
Lily of Killarney, 1934
The Fortunate Fool, 1934
Irish Hearts, 1934
Lazybones, 1935
Peg of Old Drury, 1935
Passing of the Third Floor
   Back, 1935
Riders to the Sea, 1936
Pot Luck, 1936
It's Love Again, 1936
Southern Roses, 1936
Kathleen Mavourneen, 1937
Storm in a Teacup, 1937
The Sky's the Limit, 1937
Londonderry Air, 1938
On the Night of the Fire, 1939
The Fugitive, 1940
That Hamilton Woman, 1941
How Green Was My Valley,
   1941
Dr. Jekyll and Mr. Hyde, 1941
Lydia, 1941
The War Against Mrs. Hadley,
   1942

Roxie Hart, 1942
This Above All, 1942
It Happened in Flatbush, 1942
Life Begins at 8:30, 1942
City Without Men, 1943
Jane Eyre, 1944
The Lodger, 1944
Between Two Worlds, 1944
The Keys of the Kingdom, 1944
Strange Affair of Uncle Harry,
  1945
Cluny Brown, 1946
Kitty, 1946
The Spiral Staircase, 1946
Mother Wore Tights, 1947
The Fabulous Dorseys, 1947
Ivy, 1947
Mourning Becomes Electra,
  1947
My Wild Irish Rose, 1947
One Touch of Venus, 1948
The Man From Texas, 1948
The Girl From Manhattan, 1948
The Accused, 1948
Challenge to Lassie, 1949
Sierra, 1950
Cheaper By the Dozen, 1950

CLAUDE ALLISTER (1891-1970)
Monocled, dandified character
comedian of stage (from 1910)
and screen, also Hollywood.
Former stock exchange clerk.

Charming Sinners, 1929
Bulldog Drummond, 1929
Three Live Ghosts, 1929
The Trial of Mary Dugan, 1929
The Floradora Girl, 1930
Czar of Broadway, 1930
Reaching For the Moon, 1930
Slightly Scarlet, 1930
Such Men Are Dangerous, 1930
In the Next Room, 1930
Murder Will Out, 1930
Ladies Love Brutes, 1930
Monte Carlo, 1931
I Like Your Nerve, 1931
Platinum Blonde, 1931
Two White Arms, 1932
Blame the Woman, 1932
Diamond Cut Diamond, 1932

The Return of Raffles, 1932
The Midshipmaid, 1932
Medicine Man, 1932
Private Wives, 1933
Excess Baggage, 1933
That's My Wife, 1933
The Sleeping Car, 1933
Private Life of Henry VIII,
  1933
Those Were the Days, 1934
The Lady is Willing, 1934
The Return of Bulldog Drum-
  mond, 1934
The Private Life of Don Juan,
  1934
The Dark Angel, 1935
Dracula's Daughter, 1936
Bulldog Drummond at Bay,
  1937
Let's Make a Night of It, 1937
The Awful Truth, 1937
Men Are Such Fools, 1938
Captain Fury, 1939
Arrest Bulldog Drummond,
  1939
Lillian Russell, 1940
Charley's Aunt, 1941
The Reluctant Dragon, 1941
Confirm or Deny, 1941
The Hundred Pound Window,
  1944
Kiss the Bride Goodbye, 1944
Don Chicago, 1945
Dumb Dora Discovers Tobacco
  1945
Gaiety George, 1946
Quartet, 1948
The First Gentleman, 1948
Adventures of Ichabod & Mr.
  Toad, 1950
Hong Kong, 1952
Kiss Me Kate, 1953

JOSS AMBLER (1900-1959)
Screen character actor frequently cast as doctors, lawyers, policemen, etc. Most
prolific in the 40s.

Captain's Orders, 1937
The Last Curtain, 1937
The Citadel, 1938

Meet Mr. Penny, 1938
The Claydon Treasure Mystery
  1938
Secret Journey, 1939
Come On George, 1939
Trouble Brewing, 1939
Fingers, 1940
Once a Crook, 1941
The Black Sheep of Whitehall,
  1941
Break the News, 1941
Penn of Pennsylvania, 1941
Flying Fortress, 1942
Next of Kin, 1942
The Big Blockade, 1942
The Peterville Diamond, 1942
Much Too Shy, 1942
Gert and Daisy Clean Up 1942
Happidrome, 1942
Headline, 1943
Rhythm Serenade, 1943
Somewhere in Civvies, 1943
The Silver Fleet, 1943
Battle For Music, 1943
Give Me the Stars, 1944
Candles at Nine, 1944
They Were Sisters, 1945
The Agitator, 1945
Here Comes the Sun, 1945
The Years Between, 1945
Mine Own Executioner, 1947
Who Goes There?, 1952
Ghost Ship, 1952
The Captain's Paradise, 1953
The Harassed Hero, 1954
The Long Arm, 1956

DAPHNE ANDERSON (1922-)
Effective actress of stage (since
1937) and screen.

Trottie True, 1949
Cloudburst, 1951
Laughing Anne, 1953
The Beggar's Opera, 1953
Hobson's Choice, 1954
A Kid For Two Farthings, 1955
The Prince and the Showgirl,
  1957
No Time For Tears, 1957
Snowball, 1960
Captain Clegg, 1962
Stork Talk, 1962

Bitter Harvest, 1963
The Flood, 1963

JEAN ANDERSON (1908-)
Sympathetic stage and screen
actress, usually seen in well-
meaning spinsterly roles.

The Mark of Cain, 1948
The Romantic Age, 1949
Elizabeth of Ladymead, 1949
Out of True, 1951
Life in Her Hands, 1951
White Corridors, 1951
The Franchise Affair, 1951
Street Corner, 1953
The Kidnappers, 1953
Johnny on the Run, 1953
Lease of Life, 1954
The Secret Tent, 1956
A Town Like Alice, 1956
Heart of a Child, 1957
Robbery Under Arms, 1957
Lucky Jim, 1957
The Barretts of Wimpole Street,
  1957
Solomon and Sheba, 1959
SOS Pacific, 1959
Spare the Rod, 1961
The Inspector, 1962
Waltz of the Toreadors, 1962
The Silent Playground, 1963
Three Lives of Thomasina, 1963
Half a Sixpence, 1967
Country Dance, 1969
Run a Crooked Mile, 1969
The Night Digger, 1971

DAME JUDITH ANDERSON
  (1898-)
Distinguished, formidable Australian actress of stage (since
1915), screen and television,
often cast in sinister parts.
Probably best remembered as
Mrs. Danvers in "Rebecca."

Madame of the Jury, 1930
Blood Money, 1933
Forty Little Mothers, 1940
Rebecca, 1940
Free and Easy, 1941

King's Row, 1941
Lady Scarface, 1941
All Through tne Night, 1942
Edge of Darkness, 1943
Stage Door Canteen, 1944
Laura, 1944
And Then There Were None,
   1945
Diary of a Chambermaid, 1946
Specter of the Rose, 1946
Strange Love of Martha Ivers,
   1946
Pursued, 1947
The Red House, 1947
Tycoon, 1947
The Furies, 1950
The Silver Chord, 1951
Come of Age, 1953
Jane Eyre, 1953
Salome, 1953
Black Chiffon, 1954
Christmas Story, 1954
Yesterday's Magic, 1954
Louise, 1955
Virtue, 1955
The Senora, 1955
Creative Impulse, 1955
Circular Staircase, 1956
The Ten Commandments, 1956
Cradle Song, 1956
Caesar and Cleopatra, 1956
The Clouded Image, 1957
Abbey, Julia, and the Seven
   Pet Cows, 1958
Cat on a Hot Tin Roof, 1958
Bridge of San Luis Rey,
   1958
The Moon and Sixpence, 1959
Second Happiest Day, 1959
Medea, 1959
Cinderfella, 1960
Macbeth, 1960
To the Sounds of Trumpets,
   1960
Millionaire's Might, 1960
Why Bother to Knock?, 1961
Macbeth, 1966
Elizabeth the Queen, 1968
The File On Devlin, 1969
Hamlet, 1970
A Man Called Horse, 1970
The Borrowers, 1973
Inn of the Damned, 1974

The Underground Man, 1974
The Chinese Prime Minister,
   1975

MICHAEL ANDERSON JR.
   (1943-   )
Youthful leading actor of the
60s, son of film director
Michael Anderson (1920-   ).
Also Hollywood.

The Moonraker, 1958
Tiger Bay, 1959
The Sundowners, 1960
Reach For Glory, 1961
In Search of the Castaways,
   1962
Play it Cool, 1962
The Greatest Story Ever Told,
   1965
Dear Heart, 1965
Major Dundee, 1965
The Glory Days, 1965
The Sons of Katie Elder, 1965
WUSA, 1969
The Last Movie, 1971
Logan's Run, 1975

RONA ANDERSON (1926-   )
Attractive Scottish actress of
stage (1945) and screen; married to Gordon Jackson.

Sleeping Car to Trieste, 1948
Floodtide, 1949
Poet's Pub, 1949
Torment, 1949
The 20 Questions Murder Mys-
   tery, 1950
The Cure For Love, 1950
Her Favourite Husband, 1950
Home to Danger, 1951
Scrooge, 1951
Whispering Smith Hits London,
   1952
Circumstantial Evidence, 1952
Noose For a Lady, 1953
Malta Story, 1953
Black 13, 1954
Double Exposure, 1954
Bang You're Dead, 1954

The Black Rider, 1954
Little Red Monkey, 1955
Shadow of a Man, 1955
The Flaw, 1955
Stock Car, 1955
Time to Kill, 1955
Soho Incident, 1956
Hideout, 1956
Man With a Gun, 1958
The Solitary Child, 1958
The Bay of St. Michel, 1963
Devils of Darkness, 1964
River Rivals, 1967
The Prime of Miss Jean
  Brodie, 1969

ANTHONY ANDREWS (1948-)
Leading man of the 70s who
made the transition from television into films.

QB VII, 1974
A War of Children, 1974
Take Me High, 1974
Percy's Progress, 1975
Operation Daybreak, 1976

HARRY ANDREWS (1911-)
Tall, stern-looking character
star, frequently appearing in
military or other authority
roles; on stage from 1933.
His son is the television director David Andrews.

The Red Beret, 1953
The Black Knight, 1954
The Man Who Loved Redheads,
  1955
A Hill in Korea, 1956
Moby Dick, 1956
Alexander the Great, 1956
Saint Joan, 1957
I Accuse, 1958
Ice Cold in Alex, 1958
Solomon and Sheba, 1959
The Devil's Disciple, 1959
A Touch of Larceny, 1959
In the Nick, 1960
Circle of Deception, 1961
Reach For Glory, 1962

The Inspector, 1962
Barabbas, 1962
Fifty-Five Days at Peking,
  1962
The Best of Enemies, 1962
The Snout, 1963
Nine Hours to Rama, 1963
The Informers, 1963
Nothing But the Best, 1963
The System, 1964
633 Squadron, 1964
The Truth About Spring, 1964
The Hill, 1965
Sands of the Kalahari, 1965
The Agony and the Ecstasy,
  1965
Modesty Blaise, 1966
The Deadly Affair, 1966
Night of the Generals, 1966
The Jokers, 1966
The Long Duel, 1967
I'll Never Forget Whatsisname,
  1967
Danger Route, 1967
A Dandy in Aspic, 1968
Play Dirty, 1968
The Charge of the Light Bri-
  gade, 1968
The Night They Raided Min-
  sky's, 1968
Southern Star, 1969
Too Late the Hero, 1969
The Battle of Britain, 1969
A Nice Girl Like Me, 1969
The Sea Gull, 1969
Country Dance, 1969
Wuthering Heights, 1970
Entertaining Mr. Sloane, 1970
Burke and Hare, 1971
Nicholas and Alexandra, 1971
The Nightcomers, 1971
I Know What I Want, 1971
Night Hair Child, 1971
The Ruling Class, 1972
Man of La Mancha, 1972
Theatre of Blood, 1973
The Final Programme, 1973
Man at the Top, 1973
The Mackintosh Man, 1973
The Internecine Project, 1974
Sky Riders, 1976
The Blue Bird, 1976
The Passover Plot, 1977

15   Andrews

Equus, 1977
The Four Feathers, 1978
The Big Sleep, 1978
Crossed Swords, 1978
The Medusa Touch, 1978
Death On the Nile, 1978
Superman, 1978
Watership Down, 1978
SOS Titanic, 1979
The Curse of King Tut's Tomb,
1980

JULIE ANDREWS (1934-)
Popular singing star of the 60s,
famous on Broadway as Eliza
Dolittle in "My Fair Lady."
Mainly on television in the 70s.
Married to director Blake Ed-
wards.

Mary Poppins, 1964
The Americanization of Emily,
1964
The Sound of Music, 1965
Torn Curtain, 1966
Hawaii, 1966
Think 20th, 1967
Thoroughly Modern Millie, 1967
Star!, 1968
Darling Lilli, 1969
The Tamarind Seed, 1974
10, 1979
Little Miss Marker, 1980

HEATHER ANGEL (1909-)
Ladylike star of the 30s, went
to Hollywood in 1933 and was
cast mainly in subsidiary parts.
Latterly on television, notably
in series "Peyton Place" and
"Family Affair."

City of Song, 1931
A Night in Montmartre, 1931
Frail Women, 1931
Hound of the Baskervilles, 1931
Self-Made Lady, 1932
Mr. Bill the Conqueror, 1932
Men of Steel, 1932
After Office Hours, 1932
Pilgrimage, 1932

Charlie Chan's Greatest Case,
1932
Early to Bed, 1933
Berkeley Square, 1933
Farewell to Love, 1933
Orient Express, 1934
Springtime For Henry, 1934
Murder in Trinidad, 1934
Romance in the Rain, 1934
It Happened in New York, 1935
The Informer, 1935
The Three Musketeers, 1935
The Perfect Gentleman, 1935
The Mystery of Edwin Drood,
1935
Last of the Mohicans, 1936
Daniel Boone, 1936
Portia On Trial, 1937
Bulldog Drummond Escapes,
1937
Army Girl, 1938
Bulldog Drummond in Africa,
1938
Arrest Bulldog Drummond,
1939
Bulldog Drummond's Secret
Police, 1939
Undercover Doctor, 1939
Bulldog Drummond's Bride,
1939
Pride and Prejudice, 1940
That Hamilton Woman, 1941
Suspicion, 1941
Singapore Woman, 1941
Time to Kill, 1942
The Undying Monster, 1942
Cry Havoc, 1943
Lifeboat, 1944
In the Meantime Darling, 1944
The Saxon Charm, 1948
Alice in Wonderland, 1951
Peter Pan, 1952
The Premature Burial, 1962

MURIEL ANGELUS (1909-)
Blonde Scottish star of the
30s, on stage as well from
1921. Went to Hollywood and
retired in 1940 after brief career. Formerly married to
John Stuart.

Sailors Don't Care, 1928
The Ringer, 1928
The Infamous Lady, 1928
Red Aces, 1929
Eve's Fall, 1930
No Exit, 1930
Night Birds, 1930
Let's Love and Laugh, 1931
The Ringer, 1931
My Wife's Family, 1931
Hindle Wakes, 1931
Lloyd of the C.I.D., 1931
Blind Spot, 1932
Don't Be a Dummy, 1932
So You Won't Talk, 1935
The Light That Failed, 1939
The Great McGinty, 1940
The Way of All Flesh, 1940
Safari, 1940

AVRIL ANGERS (1922-)
Comedy character actress,
mainly on stage, in films sporadically since 1948.

The Lucky Mascot, 1948
Skimpy in the Navy, 1949
Miss Pilgrim's Progress, 1950
The Six Men, 1951
Don't Blame the Stork, 1954
The Green Man, 1956
Women Without Men, 1956
Bond of Fear, 1956
Light Fingers, 1957
Dentist in the Chair, 1960
Devils of Darkness, 1964
Be My Guest, 1965
The Family Way, 1966
Three Bites of the Apple, 1967
Two a Penny, 1967
The Best House in London, 1969
There's a Girl in My Soup, 1970
Cry of the Penguins, 1972

EVELYN ANKERS (1918-)
Leading lady who came to Hollywood in 1940 and starred in a
number of B pictures, mainly
horror features. Married to
Richard Denning.

Rembrandt, 1936
The Bells of St. Mary's, 1937
Knight Without Armour, 1937
Fire Over England, 1937
Wings of the Morning, 1937
Coming of Age, 1938
Second Thoughts, 1938
The Claydon Treasure Mystery
1938
Murder in the Family, 1938
The Villiers Diamond, 1938
Over the Moon, 1939
Hold That Ghost, 1941
Bachelor Daddy, 1941
The Wolf Man, 1941
Hit the Road, 1941
Burma Convoy, 1941
Eagle Squadron, 1942
North to the Klondike, 1942
Pierre of the Plains, 1942
Sherlock Holmes & the Voice
of Terror, 1942
Ghost of Frankenstein, 1942
The Great Impersonation, 1942
The Mad Ghoul, 1943
Hers to Hold, 1943
His Butler's Sister, 1943
All By Myself, 1943
Captive Wild Woman, 1943
Son of Dracula, 1943
Pardon My Rhythm, 1944
Ladies Courageous, 1944
Weird Woman, 1944
The Invisible Man's Revenge,
1944
Jungle Woman, 1944
The Pearl of Death, 1944
Bowery to Broadway, 1944
The Frozen Ghost, 1945
The Fatal Witness, 1945
Flight to Nowhere, 1946
The French Key, 1946
Black Beauty, 1946
Queen of Burlesque, 1946
Last of the Redmen, 1947
The Lone Wolf in London, 1947
Parole Inc., 1949
Tarzan's Magic Fountain, 1949
The Texan Meets Calamity Jane,
1950
No Greater Love, 1960

FRANCESCA ANNIS (1944-)
Leading actress and second
lead who began as teenager.
Excellent on television as
"Lillie" (1978).

The Cat Gang, 1958
No Kidding, 1960
Young Jacobites, 1960
Cleopatra, 1962
Crooks in Cloisters, 1963
The Eyes of Annie Jones, 1963
Flipper and the Pirates, 1964
Saturday Night Out, 1964
Murder Most Foul, 1965
The Pleasure Girls, 1965
Run With the Wind, 1966
The Sky Pirate, 1970
The Walking Stick, 1970
Macbeth, 1971

SCOTT ANTONY (1950-)
Juvenile leading actor of the
70s in occasional films.

Baxter, 1972
Savage Messiah, 1973
Dead Cert, 1974
The Mutations, 1974

BERNARD ARCHARD (1922-)
This, distinctive actor, well-
known on television in "Spy-
catcher" series, also on stage.

Village of the Damned, 1960
Man Detained, 1961
Clue of the New Pin, 1961
Flat Two, 1962
Two-Letter Alibi, 1962
A Woman's Privilege, 1962
The Silent Playground, 1963
The List of Adrian Messenger,
   1963
Face of a Stranger, 1964
The Spy With a Cold Nose, 1966
Son of the Sahara, 1967
The Mini Affair, 1968
File of the Golden Goose, 1968
Play Dirty, 1968
Run a Crooked Mile, 1969

Fragment of Fear, 1970
Horror of Frankenstein, 1970
Song of Norway, 1970
Macbeth, 1970
The Day of the Jackal, 1973

ROBERT ARDEN (1921-)
American-born actor who for-
sook vocal career and went to
England to appear in films in
supporting parts.

Two Thousand Women, 1944
No Orchids For Miss Blandish,
   1948
Joe Macbeth, 1955
Confidential Report, 1956
Soho Incident, 1956
A King in New York, 1957
The Depraved, 1957
The Counterfeit Plan, 1957
The Child and the Killer, 1959
Never Take Sweets From a
   Stranger, 1960
Mr. Arkadin, 1962

GEORGE ARLISS (1868-1946)
Distinguished, popular actor of
stage (1886) and screen; spe-
cialized in portraying historical
characters in both U. S. and
British films.   Also author.
His son is writer/director
Leslie Arliss (b. 1901).

The Devil, 1921
Disraeli, 1921
The Ruling Passion, 1922
The Man Who Played God, 1922
The Green Goddess, 1923
Twenty Dollars a Week, 1924
Disraeli, 1929
The Green Goddess, 1930
Old English, 1930
The Millionaire, 1931
Alexander Hamilton, 1931
The Man Who Played God, 1932
Successful Calamity, 1932
The King's Vacation, 1933
The Working Man, 1933
Voltaire, 1933

The House of Rothschild, 1934
The Last Gentleman, 1934
Cardinal Richelieu, 1935
The Tunnel, 1935
The Iron Duke, 1935
The Guvnor, 1935
East Meets West, 1936
Man of Affairs, 1937
Dr. Syn, 1937

JULIA ARNALL (1931-)
Austrian film actress, long
resident in Britain.

Man of the Moment, 1954
Knights of the Round Table,
  1954
I Am a Camera, 1955
Value For Money, 1955
Lost, 1956
House of Secrets, 1956
Tears For Simon, 1957
Triple Deception, 1957
Man Without a Body, 1957
Model For Murder, 1959
Mark of the Phoenix, 1959
The Trunk, 1961
Carry on Regardless, 1961
The Quiller Memorandum, 1966
The Double Man, 1967

YVONNE ARNAUD (1892-1958)
Popular French actress of stage
(1906) and occasionally screen,
in Britain from 1920.   Also
former prize-winning pianist.

Desire, 1920
The Temptress, 1920
On Approval, 1930
Canaries Sometimes Sing,
  1930
Tons of Money, 1931
A Cuckoo in the Nest, 1933
Princess Charming, 1934
Lady in Danger, 1934
Widow's Might, 1935
Stormy Weather, 1935
The Gay Adventure, 1936
The Improper Duchess, 1936
Neutral Port, 1940
Tomorrow We Live, 1942

I Want to Be An Actress, 1944
Woman to Woman, 1946
Ghosts of Berkeley Square,
  1947
My Uncle, 1958

PETER ARNE (1922-)
Unsympathetic, often villainous
character star of films, also
quite often on television.

Mystery On Bird Island, 1954
The Purple Plain, 1954
You Know What Sailors Are,
  1954
Murder Anonymous, 1955
Cockleshell Heroes, 1955
The Dam Busters, 1955
Time Slip, 1955
Stranger's Meeting, 1957
Tarzan and the Lost Safari,
  1957
High Tide at Noon, 1957
The Moonraker, 1958
Ice Cold in Alex, 1958
Intent to Kill, 1958
Danger Within, 1959
Conspiracy of Hearts, 1960
Scent of Mystery, 1960
Sands of the Desert, 1960
The Story of David, 1960
The Treasure of Monte Cristo,
  1961
The Hellfire Club, 1961
The Pirates of Blood River,
  1962
The Victors, 1963
The Black Torment, 1964
The Model Murder Case, 1964
Khartoum, 1966
The Sandwich Man, 1966
Chitty Chitty Bang Bang, 1968
Battle Beneath the Earth, 1968
The Oblong Box, 1969
Straw Dogs, 1971
Murders in the Rue Morgue,
  1971
When Eight Bells Toll, 1971
Pope Joan, 1972
Antony and Cleopatra, 1972
Return of the Pink Panther,
  1974
Providence, 1977

DENIS ARUNDELL (1898-)
Character actor in occasional
films; former star of radio
(notably as Dr. Morelle).

The Show Goes On, 1937
The Return of Carol Deane,
  1938
Glamour Girl, 1938
Contraband, 1940
The Saint Meets the Tiger,
  1941
Pimpernel Smith, 1941
Breach of Promise, 1941
Penn of Pennsylvania, 1941
Colonel Blimp, 1943
Meet Sexton Blake, 1944
The Echo Murders, 1945
The Man From Morocco, 1945
Carnival, 1946
The End of the River, 1947
The History of Mr. Polly, 1949
Something Money Can't Buy,
  1952

DAME PEGGY ASHCROFT
  (1907-)
Distinguished actress mainly
on stage; film appearances un-
fortunately very rare.

The Wandering Jew, 1933
The Thirty-Nine Steps, 1935
Rhodes of Africa, 1936
Channel Incident, 1940
Quiet Wedding, 1941
The Nun's Story, 1959
Secret Ceremony, 1968
Tell Me Lies, 1968
Three Into Two Won't Go, 1969
Sunday Bloody Sunday, 1971
The Pedestrian, 1974
Joseph Andrews, 1977
My Brilliant Career, 1980

JANE ASHER (1946-)
Leading actress of television
and films who began as a child
performer.

Mandy, 1952
Dance Little Lady, 1954

Adventure in the Hop Fields,
  1954
Third Party Risk, 1955
The Quatermass Experiment,
  1955
Charley Moon, 1956
The Greengage Summer, 1961
The Prince and the Pauper,
  1962
Girl in the Headlines, 1963
Masque of the Red Death, 1964
Alfie, 1966
A Winter's Tale, 1968
The Buttercup Chain, 1970
Deep End, 1971
Henry VIII & His Six Wives,
  1972

RENEE ASHERSON (1920-)
Attractive, intelligent stage
and film actress; wife of
Robert Donat.

Henry V, 1944
The Way Ahead, 1944
The Way to the Stars, 1945
Caesar and Cleopatra, 1946
Once a Jolly Swagman, 1948
The Small Back Room, 1949
The Cure For Love, 1950
The Dark Man, 1951
Pool of London, 1951
The Magic Box, 1951
Malta Story, 1953
Time is My Enemy, 1954
The Day the Earth Caught
  Fire, 1961
Rasputin the Mad Monk, 1965
The Smashing Bird I Used to
  Know, 1967
Theatre of Blood, 1973
Hell House Girls, 1975
A Man Called Intrepid, 1979
Disraeli: Portrait of a Romantic,
  1980

EDWARD ASHLEY (1904-)
Australian leading actor of the
30s who went to Hollywood and
was given auxiliary parts.
Also on stage and (latterly)
television.

Men of Steel, 1932
Timbuctoo, 1933
Old Faithful, 1935
Under Proof, 1936
Saturday Night Revue, 1937
Underneath the Arches, 1937
The Villiers Diamond, 1938
Spies of the Air, 1939
Pride and Prejudice, 1940
Bitter Sweet, 1940
Sky Murder, 1940
Gallant Sons, 1940
Maisie Was a Lady, 1941
Come Live With Me, 1941
The Black Swan, 1942
Love Honor and Goodbye, 1945
Nocturne, 1946
Dick Tracy vs. Gruesome,
    1947
The Other Love, 1947
Tarzan and the Mermaids,
    1948
Macao, 1952
El Alamein, 1953
Elephant Walk, 1954
The Court Jester, 1956
King Rat, 1965
Herbie Rides Again, 1973
Won Ton Ton, 1976

ARTHUR ASKEY (1900-)
Small character comedian,
gained wide popularity on radio
during the 30s, frequently
teamed with Richard Murdoch.

Calling All Stars, 1937
Band Wagon, 1940
Charley's Big-Hearted Aunt,
    1940
The Ghost Train, 1941
I Thank You, 1941
Back Room Boy, 1942
King Arthur Was a Gentleman,
    1942
The Nose Has it, 1942
Miss London Ltd. , 1943
Bees in Paradise, 1944
The Love Match, 1955
Ramsbottom Rides Again, 1956
Make Mine a Million, 1958
Friends and Neighbours, 1959

The Alf Garnett Saga, 1972
End of Term, 1977

ROBIN ASKWITH (1950-)
Youthful leading actor of the
70s, latterly appearing in low-
budget films.

If, 1968
Bartleby, 1970
Cool it Carol, 1970
Scramble, 1970
Nicholas and Alexandra, 1971
The Four Dimensions of Great,
    1971
Bless This House, 1973
Horror Hospital, 1973
The Dirtiest Girl I Ever Met,
    1973
The Flesh and Blood Show,
    1974
Confessions of a Window
    Cleaner, 1974
Confessions of a Pop Per-
    former, 1975
Confessions of a Driving In-
    structor, 1976

GREGOIRE ASLAN (1908-)
Lugubrious Turkish character
actor, former drummer, in
British and international films,
typically cast in heavy or villainous roles.

Feu de Joie, 1938
Sleeping Car to Trieste, 1948
Occupe toi D'Amelie, 1949
Last Holiday, 1950
Cage of Gold, 1950
Cairo Road, 1950
Confidential Report, 1953
An Act of Love, 1954
The Red Inn, 1954
Joe Macbeth, 1955
He Who Must Die, 1956
The Snorkel, 1958
The Roots of Heaven, 1958
Windom's Way, 1958
Sea Fury, 1958
Killers of Kilimanjaro, 1959

Oasis, 1960
Our Man in Havana, 1960
Under Ten Flags, 1960
Three Worlds of Gulliver, 1960
The Criminal, 1960
The Rebel, 1961
King of Kings, 1961
The Happy Thieves, 1961
The Devil at Four O'Clock,
    1961
Invasion Quartet, 1961
Cleopatra, 1962
Mr. Arkadin, 1962
Village of Daughters, 1962
The Main Chance, 1964
The Yellow Rolls-Royce, 1964
Paris When it Sizzles, 1964
The High Bright Sun, 1965
A Man Could Get Killed, 1965
Moment to Moment, 1965
Marco the Magnificent, 1966
Our Man in Marrakesh, 1966
Lost Command, 1966
The 25th Hour, 1967
Marry Me Marry Me, 1968
A Flea in Her Ear, 1968
You Can't Win Them All, 1970
The Golden Voyage of Sinbad,
    1973
The Girl From Petrovka, 1974
Return of the Pink Panther,
    1974
Bon Baisers de Hong Kong,
    1975
The Killer Who Wouldn't Die,
    1976

ROSALIND ATKINSON (1900-1978)
Character actress long on stage,
films extremely rare but memorable.

Tomorrow We Live, 1936
Tom Jones, 1963
The Pumpkin Eater, 1964

SIR RICHARD ATTENBOROUGH
   (1923-   )
Distinguished stage and screen
star and latterly character actor who escaped early type-

casting as weakling to exhibit
a wide and ambitious range of
characterizations, equally adept
at kindliness or villainy. Also
producer (with Bryan Forbes)
and director ("Oh What a Lovely War," "Young Winston,"
"A Bridge Too Far," "Magic,"
etc.) Married to Sheila Sim.

In Which We Serve, 1942
Schweik's New Adventures,
    1943
The Hundred Pound Window,
    1944
Journey Together, 1945
A Matter of Life and Death,
    1946
School For Secrets, 1946
Dancing With Crime, 1947
The Man Within, 1947
Brighton Rock, 1947
The Guinea Pig, 1948
London Belongs to Me, 1948
The Lost People, 1949
Boys in Brown, 1949
Morning Departure, 1950
Hell is Sold Out, 1951
The Magic Box, 1951
The Gift Horse, 1952
Father's Doing Fine, 1952
Eight O'clock Walk, 1954
The Ship That Died of Shame,
    1955
The Baby and the Battleship,
    1956
Private's Progress, 1956
The Scamp, 1957
Brothers in Law, 1957
Dunkirk, 1957
Desert Patrol, 1958
The Man Upstairs, 1958
Jet Storm, 1959
Danger Within, 1959
I'm All Right, Jack, 1959
The League of Gentlemen, 1959
SOS Pacific, 1959
The Angry Silence, 1960
Talk of Many Things, 1962
Only Two Can Play, 1962
The Dock Brief, 1962
All Night Long, 1962
The Great Escape, 1963

Seance On a Wet Afternoon,
  1964
Guns at Batasi, 1964
The Third Secret, 1964
Flight of the Phoenix, 1965
The Sand Pebbles, 1966
Dr. Dolittle, 1967
Insurance Italian Style, 1967
The Walls Come Tumbling Down,
  1967
Think 20th, 1967
Only When I Larf, 1968
The Bliss of Mrs. Blossom,
  1968
David Copperfield, 1969
The Last Grenade, 1970
Private Life of Sherlock Holmes,
  1970
The Magic Christian, 1970
Don't Make Me Laugh, 1970
10 Rillington Place, 1971
A Severed Head, 1971
Loot, 1971
Brannigan, 1974
Rosebud, 1974
Conduct Unbecoming, 1975
Ten Little Indians, 1975
The Chess Players, 1978
The Human Factor, 1980

LIONEL ATWILL (1885-1946)
Imposing, often unemotional star
character actor; on stage from
1904, went to Hollywood in 1932
where he portrayed evil geniuses
and the like, especially in horror films.

For Sale, 1918
The Marriage Price, 1919
The Highest Bidder, 1921
Indiscretion, 1921
The Silent Witness, 1932
Doctor X, 1932
The Vampire Bat, 1933
The Secret of Madame Blanche,
  1933
Mystery of the Wax Museum,
  1933
Murders in the Zoo, 1933
The Sphynx, 1933
Song of Songs, 1933

Secret of the Blue Room, 1933
The Solitaire Man, 1933
Nana, 1934
Beggars in Ermine, 1934
Stamboul Quest, 1934
One More River, 1934
Age of Innocence, 1934
The Firebird, 1934
Man Who Reclaimed His Head,
  1935
Mark of the Vampire, 1935
The Devil is a Woman, 1935
The Murder Man, 1935
Rendezvous, 1935
Captain Blood, 1935
Lady of Secrets, 1936
Absolute Quiet, 1936
Till We Meet Again, 1936
The Road Back, 1937
Last Train From Madrid, 1937
The Great Garrick, 1937
Lancer Spy, 1937
Three Comrades, 1938
The Great Waltz, 1938
Son of Frankenstein, 1939
The Three Musketeers, 1939
Hound of the Baskervilles, 1939
The Gorilla, 1939
The Sun Never Sets, 1939
Mr. Moto Takes a Vacation,
  1939
The Secret of Dr. Kildare,
  1939
Balalaika, 1939
The Mad Empress, 1940
Johnny Apollo, 1940
Charlie Chan's Murder Cruise,
  1940
The Girl in 313, 1940
Boom Town, 1940
The Great Profile, 1940
Man Made Monster, 1941
The Mad Doctor of Market St.,
  1942
To Be Or Not to Be, 1942
Strange Case of Dr. RX, 1942
The Ghost of Frankenstein,
  1942
Pardon My Sarong, 1942
Cairo, 1942
Night Monster, 1942
Junior G-Men of the Air, 1942
Sherlock Holmes & the Secret

Weapon, 1942
Frankenstein Meets the Wolf
Man, 1943
House of Frankenstein, 1944
Captain America, 1944
Raiders of Ghost City, 1944
Lady in the Death House, 1944
Secrets of Scotland Yard, 1944
Fog Island, 1945
Genius at Work, 1945
Crime Inc., 1945
House of Dracula, 1945
Lost City of the Jungle, 1946

ANNE AUBREY (1937-)
Leading lady who made a number of films, chiefly in the adventure genre, during a brief
career.

High Flight, 1957
No Time to Die, 1958
The Man Inside, 1958
The Secret Man, 1958
Idol On Parade, 1959
Model For Murder, 1959
The Bandit of Zhobe, 1959
Killers of Kilimanjaro, 1959
Jazzboat, 1960
Let's Get Married, 1960
In the Nick, 1960
Date at Midnight, 1960
The Hellions, 1961

MAXINE AUDLEY (1923-)
Beautiful stage (from 1940) actress who had made a number
of films, usually in supporting
roles. Also on television.

The Sleeping Tiger, 1954
A King in New York, 1957
The Barretts of Wimpole Street,
1957
The Prince and the Showgirl,
1957
Dunkirk, 1957
The Vikings, 1958
Our Man in Havana, 1959
Trials of Oscar Wilde, 1960
Hell is a City, 1960

Peeping Tom, 1960
Man at the Carlton Tower,
1961
Petticoat Pirates, 1961
Vengeance, 1962
Riccochet, 1963
Never Mention Murder, 1964
A Jolly Bad Fellow, 1964
Battle of the Villa Fiorita,
1965
The Agony and the Ecstasy,
1965
Payment in Kind, 1967
Here We Go Round the Mul-
berry Bush, 1967
Sinful Davy, 1969
House of Cards, 1969
Frankenstein Must be Destroyed,
1969
The Looking Glass War, 1970

MARIE AULT (1870-1951)
Film and stage actress who
was mainly associated with
comedy character roles.

Class and No Class, 1921
A Prince of Lovers, 1922
The Wee MacGregor's Sweet-
heart, 1922
If Four Walls Told, 1922
The Monkey's Paw, 1922
Paddy the Next Best Thing,
1923
Woman to Woman, 1923
The Starlit Garden, 1923
The Prude's Fall, 1924
The Colleen Bawn, 1924
Children of the Night, 1925
The Rat, 1925
Triumph of the Rat, 1926
The Lodger, 1926
Mademoiselle From Armentieres,
1926
The Rolling Road, 1927
Roses of Picardy, 1927
Hindle Wakes, 1927
Madame Pompadour, 1927
A Daughter in Revolt, 1927
The Silver Lining, 1927
Troublesome Wives, 1928
Yellow Stockings, 1928

Life, 1928
Victory, 1928
Virginia's Husband, 1928
God's Clay, 1928
Dawn, 1928
Return of the Rat, 1929
Kitty, 1929
Fanny Hawthorn, 1929
Little Miss London, 1929
Downstream, 1929
The Alley Cat, 1929
Hobson's Choice, 1931
Third Time Lucky, 1931
Contraband Love, 1931
The Speckled Band, 1931
Peace and Quiet, 1931
Little Fella, 1932
Their Night Out, 1933
Daughters of Today, 1933
Money For Speed, 1933
Maid Happy, 1933
Windfall, 1935
Swinging the Lead, 1935
Lend Me Your Wife, 1935
Tropical Trouble, 1936
Major Barbara, 1941
Love On the Dole, 1941
The Missing Million, 1942
We Dive at Dawn, 1943
It Happened One Sunday, 1944
They Knew Mr. Knight, 1945
I See a Dark Stranger, 1946
Three Weird Sisters, 1948
Madness of the Heart, 1949
Cheer the Brave, 1951

SIR FELIX AYLMER (1889-1979)
Distinguished, prolific, outstanding character star of stage (1911)
and screen, usually seen as bis-
hops, schoolmasters, or other
assorted kindly gentlemen. Also
author of several plays.

Escape, 1930
The Temporary Widow, 1930
The World, the Flesh & the
   Devil, 1932
The Lodger, 1932
The Ghost Camera, 1932
Home Sweet Home, 1932
The Wandering Jew, 1933

Night Club Queen, 1933
Whispering Tongues, 1934
Path of Glory, 1934
My Old Dutch, 1934
Doctor's Orders, 1934
The Iron Duke, 1935
Ace of Spades, 1935
Price of a Song, 1935
Hello Sweetheart, 1935
The Divine Spark, 1935
Old Roses, 1935
The Clairvoyant, 1935
Checkmate, 1935
Her Last Affaire, 1935
She Shall Have Music, 1935
The Improper Duchess, 1936
Jack of All Trades, 1936
In the Soup, 1936
Tudor Rose, 1936
Royal Eagle, 1936
Seven Sinners, 1936
As You Like It, 1936
Dusty Ermine, 1936
Man in the Mirror, 1936
Sensation, 1937
The Mill On the Floss, 1937
Dreaming Lips, 1937
The Frog, 1937
Glamorous Night, 1937
The Vicar of Bray, 1937
Action For Slander, 1937
Victoria the Great, 1937
The Live Wire, 1937
The Rat, 1937
The Citadel, 1938
Bank Holiday, 1938
Just Like a Woman, 1938
Kate Plus Ten, 1938
Break the News, 1938
I've Got a Horse, 1938
Sixty Glorious Years, 1938
Spies of the Air, 1939
Young Man's Fancy, 1939
Doctor O'Dowd, 1940
The Briggs Family, 1940
Charley's Big-Hearted Aunt,
   1940
Night Train to Munich, 1940
Saloon Bar, 1940
Case of the Frightened Lady,
   1940
The Girl in the News, 1940
Spellbound, 1941

The Ghost of St. Michael's,
  1941
The Saint's Vacation, 1941
Quiet Wedding, 1941
Major Barbara, 1941
Atlantic Ferry, 1941
Once a Crook, 1941
I Thank You, 1941
The Seventh Survivor, 1941
The Black Sheep of Whitehall,
  1941
Hi Gang, 1941
South American George, 1941
Kipps, 1941
The Young Mr. Pitt, 1942
Sabotage at Sea, 1942
Uncensored, 1942
The Peterville Diamond, 1942
Thursday's Child, 1943
Colonel Blimp, 1943
Escape to Danger, 1943
The Demi-Paradise, 1943
Welcome to Britain, 1943
Time Flies, 1944
English Without Tears, 1944
Mr. Emmanuel, 1944
Henry V, 1944
The Way to the Stars, 1945
The Wicked Lady, 1945
Julius Caesar, 1945
Caesar and Cleopatra, 1945
The Years Between, 1946
The Laughing Lady, 1946
The Magic Bow, 1947
Green Fingers, 1947
The Man Within, 1947
A Man About the House, 1947
The October Man, 1947
Ghosts of Berkeley Square,
  1947
The Calendar, 1948
Hamlet, 1948
Alice in Wonderland, 1948
Quartet, 1948
Prince of Foxes, 1949
Edward My Son, 1949
Christopher Columbus, 1949
Your Witness, 1950
So Long at the Fair, 1950
Trio, 1950
She Shall Have Murder, 1950
Quo Vadis, 1951
Lady With a Lamp, 1951

The House in the Square, 1951
Ivanhoe, 1952
The Man Who Watched Trains
  Go By, 1953
The Master of Ballantrae, 1953
The Love Lottery, 1954
Knights of the Round Table,
  1954
The Angel Who Pawned Her
  Harp, 1955
Loser Take All, 1956
Anastasia, 1956
Saint Joan, 1957
I Accuse, 1958
Separate Tables, 1958
The Two-Headed Spy, 1958
The Doctor's Dilemma, 1958
The Mummy, 1959
Exodus, 1960
From the Terrace, 1960
The Hands of Orlac, 1960
Never Take Sweets From a
  Stranger, 1960
Macbeth, 1961
The Boys, 1962
The Road to Hong Kong, 1962
The Running Man, 1963
The Chalk Garden, 1964
Becket, 1964
Masquerade, 1965
Decline & Fall of a Bird
  Watcher, 1968
Hostile Witness, 1968

MAX BACON (-)
Character actor who is best
remembered for comedy roles;
also on stage.

Soft Lights and Sweet Music,
  1936
Calling All Stars, 1937
Kicking the Moon Around, 1938
King Arthur Was a Gentleman,
  1942
Miss London Ltd. , 1943
Give Us the Moon, 1944
Bees in Paradise, 1944
Pool of London, 1951
The Gambler and the Lady,
  1952
Take a Powder, 1953

The Entertainer, 1960
Crooks in Cloisters, 1963
The Eyes of Annie Jones, 1963
The Sandwich Man, 1966
Privilege, 1967
The Whisperers, 1967
Chitty Chitty Bang Bang, 1968
The Nine Ages of Nakedness,
  1969

ANGELA BADDELEY (1904-
  1976)
Character actress, mainly on
stage, sister of Hermione Baddeley. Well-known as Mrs.
Bridges, the cook on "Upstairs
Downstairs" (1971-75) on television.

The Speckled Band, 1931
The Ghost Train, 1931
Capture, 1932
Arms and the Man, 1932
The Safe, 1932
Those Were the Days, 1934
Quartet, 1948
Zoo Baby, 1957
No Time For Tears, 1957
Tom Jones, 1963

HERMIONE BADDELEY
  (1906-)
Blustery character comedienne
with stage experience since
childhood; latterly seen on
American TV, notably in series
"Maude." Sister: Angela Baddeley.

A Daughter in Revolt, 1927
The Guns of Loos, 1928
Caste, 1930
Love Life and Laughter, 1934
Royal Cavalcade, 1935
Kipps, 1941
Brighton Rock, 1947
It Always Rains on Sunday,
  1947
Quartet, 1948
No Room at the Inn, 1949
Dear Mr. Prohack, 1949

Passport to Pimlico, 1949
Scrooge, 1951
Tom Brown's School Days,
  1951
There is Another Sun, 1951
Hell is Sold Out, 1951
The Pickwick Papers, 1952
The Woman in Question, 1952
Wall of Death, 1952
Song of Paris, 1952
Cosh Boy, 1953
Time Gentlemen Please, 1953
Counterspy, 1953
The Belles of St. Trinian's,
  1954
Women Without Men, 1956
Jet Storm, 1959
Expresso Bongo, 1959
Room at the Top, 1959
Midnight Lace, 1960
Let's Get Married, 1960
Rag Doll, 1961
Information Received, 1961
The Unsinkable Molly Brown,
  1964
Mary Poppins, 1964
Harlow, 1965
Marriage On the Rocks, 1965
Do Not Disturb, 1965
The Happiest Millionaire, 1967
Adventures of Bullwhip Griffin,
  1967
Up the Front, 1972
The Black Windmill, 1974
C. H. O. M. P. S. , 1979

ALAN BADEL (1923-)
Sensitive leading man of stage
(1940) and character actor of
films. Married: Yvonne Owen.
Also Hollywood.

The Young Mr. Pitt, 1942
Salome, 1953
The Stranger Left No Card,
  1953
Will Any Gentleman, 1953
Three Cases of Murder, 1955
Magic Fire, 1956
Bitter Harvest, 1963
This Sporting Life, 1963
Children of the Damned, 1964

Arabesque, 1966
Otley, 1968
Where's Jack?, 1969
The Adventurers, 1970
Day of the Jackal, 1973
Luther, 1974
Telefon, 1977
The Medusa Touch, 1978
Force Ten From Navarone,
   1978
Nijinsky, 1979
Shogun, 1980

ROBIN BAILEY (1919-)
Well-mannered character actor
of stage, films, and television.

School For Secrets, 1946
Private Angelo, 1949
Portrait of Clare, 1950
His Excellency, 1952
The Gift Horse, 1952
Sailor of the King, 1953
For Better, For Worse, 1954
Folly to Be Wise, 1954
Hell Drivers, 1957
Just My Luck, 1957
The Diplomatic Corpse, 1958
Mouse On the Moon, 1963
Having a Wild Weekend, 1965
Catch Us if You Can, 1965
The Spy With a Cold Nose, 1966
The Whisperers, 1967
Danger Route, 1967
See No Evil, 1971
The Gathering Storm, 1974
Commuter Husbands, 1974
Murder Must Advertise, 1975
The Four Feathers, 1978

ANTONY BAIRD (-)
Lean character actor who has
made occasional films.

Dead of Night, 1945
The Hangman Waits, 1947
Night Comes Too Soon, 1948
Reluctant Heroes, 1951
Carry on Spying, 1964
The Ipcress File, 1965
The Christmas Tree, 1966

GEORGE BAKER (1929-)
Handsome, dependable leading
man of stage (from 1945) and
films, most popular in the 50s;
also on television.

The Intruder, 1953
The Ship That Died of Shame,
   1955
The Dam Busters, 1955
The Woman For Joe, 1955
The Feminine Touch, 1956
The Extra Day, 1956
A Hill in Korea, 1956
These Dangerous Years, 1957
No Time For Tears, 1957
The Moonraker, 1958
Tread Softly Stranger, 1958
Lancelot and Guinevere, 1963
Curse of the Fly, 1965
Mister Ten Per Cent, 1966
On Her Majesty's Secret Ser-
   vice, 1968
Justine, 1969
Goodbye Mr. Chips, 1969
The Executioner, 1970
A Warm December, 1972
Three For All, 1974
Because of the Cats, 1974
Intimate Games, 1976
The Spy Who Loved Me, 1977
Ffolkes, 1980
The Thirty Nine Steps, 1980

HYLDA BAKER (1909-)
North-country character comedienne with variety and music
hall experience; films infrequent.

Saturday Night and Sunday Morn-
   ing, 1960
She Knows Y'Know, 1962
Oliver, 1968
Up the Junction, 1968
Nearest and Dearest, 1973

SIR STANLEY BAKER (1927-
   1976)
Tough, virile Welsh leading actor who could portray heroes
or villains with equal skill; on

stage in the 40s, later much
on television.   Also Hollywood.

Undercover, 1943
All Over the Town, 1949
Your Witness, 1950
The Rossiter Case, 1951
Cloudburst, 1951
Home to Danger, 1951
Captain Horatio Hornblower,
    1951
Lilli Marlene, 1952
Whispering Smith Hits London,
    1952
The Cruel Sea, 1953
The Red Beret, 1953
The Telltale Heart, 1953
Hell Below Zero, 1954
The Good Die Young, 1954
Beautiful Stranger, 1954
Knights of the Round Table,
    1954
Richard III, 1955
Helen of Troy, 1955
Alexander the Great, 1956
A Child in the House, 1956
A Hill in Korea, 1956
Checkpoint, 1956
Hell Drivers, 1957
Campbell's Kingdom, 1957
Sea Fury, 1958
Violent Playground, 1958
The Angry Hills, 1959
Yesterday's Enemy, 1959
Jet Storm, 1959
Blind Date, 1959
Chance Meeting, 1960
Hell is a City, 1960
The Criminal, 1960
The Guns of Navarone, 1961
A Prize of Arms, 1962
The Man Who Finally Died,
    1962
Eva, 1962
Sodom and Gomorrah, 1962
In the French Style, 1963
Zulu, 1964
Sands of the Kalahari, 1965
Dingaka, 1965
One of Them is Brett, 1967
Accident, 1967
Robbery, 1967
Girl With a Pistol, 1968

Where's Jack?, 1969
Moon Zero Two, 1969
The Italian Job, 1969
The Games, 1970
The Last Grenade, 1970
Perfect Friday, 1970
Popsy Pop, 1971
Innocent Bystanders, 1972
Stiletto, 1972
A Lizard in a Woman's Skin,
    1973
Orzowei, 1975
How Green Was My Valley,
    1975
Zorro, 1976
Petita Jiminez, 1976

TOM BAKER (1941-)
Ambitious, prominent character
player of films of the 1970s.

I, a Man, 1967
Nicholas and Alexandra, 1971
Frankenstein: The True Story,
    1973
Vault of Horror, 1973
Luther, 1974
The Mutations, 1974
The Golden Voyage of Sinbad,
    1975
The Curse of King Tut's Tomb,
    1980

JILL BALCON (1925-)
Actress of the late 40s, daughter
of producer Sir Michael Balcon
(1896-1977).

Nicholas Nickleby, 1947
Good Time Girl, 1948
Saraband For Dead Lovers,
    1949
The Lost People, 1949
Highly Dangerous, 1951

BETTY BALFOUR (1903-)
Popular star comedienne of silent films, later in character
parts.   Also had production
company.

Nothing Else Matters, 1920
Squibs, 1921
Mary Finds the Gold, 1921
Mord Em'ly, 1922
The Wee MacGregor's Sweet-
heart, 1922
Squibs Wins the Calcutta Sweep,
1922
Love, Life and Laughter, 1923
Squibs MP, 1923
Squibs' Honeymoon, 1923
Reveille, 1924
Satan's Sister, 1925
Somebody's Darling, 1925
The Sea Urchin, 1926
Blinkeyes, 1926
A Little Bit of Fluff, 1928
Champagne, 1928
Paradise, 1928
Vagabond Queen, 1929
Raise the Roof, 1930
The Nipper, 1930
Paddy the Next Best Thing, 1933
Evergreen, 1934
My Old Dutch, 1934
Forever England, 1935
Squibs, 1935
Eliza Comes to Stay, 1936
29 Acacia Avenue, 1945

MICHAEL BALFOUR (1918-   )
American-born small-part character actor of British films;
usually cast as waiters, cab
drivers, porters, etc.

No Orchids For Miss Blandish,
1948
The Small Voice, 1948
Melody Club, 1949
Obsession, 1950
Her Favourite Husband, 1950
Prelude to Fame, 1950
The Quiet Woman, 1951
A Case For PC 49, 1951
13 East Street, 1952
Hot Ice, 1952
The Assassin, 1952
Genevieve, 1953
Johnny on the Run, 1953
Albert RN, 1953
Black Thirteen, 1953

Delayed Action, 1954
Devil's Point, 1954
The Delavine Affair, 1954
Secret Venture, 1955
Barbados Quest, 1955
The Steel Key, 1955
Breakaway, 1956
Secret of the Forest, 1956
Fiend Without a Face, 1958
The Monster of Highgate Ponds,
1961
Design For Loving, 1962
She Always Gets Their Man,
1962
The Rescue Squad, 1963
Beware of the Dog, 1964
Five Have a Mystery to Solve,
1964
Strangler's Web, 1966
Fahrenheit 451, 1966
The Oblong Box, 1969
The Undertakers, 1969
Hoverbug, 1970
The Adventurers, 1970
Macbeth, 1971
Candleshoe, 1978

VINCENT BALL (-)
Australian character of the 50s
and 60s, long in Britain.

Stop Press Girl, 1949
Warning to Wantons, 1949
Come Dance With Me, 1950
London Entertains, 1951
Talk of a Million, 1951
Dangerous Voyage, 1954
Devil's Point, 1954
The Dark Stairway, 1954
The Black Rider, 1954
The Blue Peter, 1955
Stolen Time, 1955
A Town Like Alice, 1956
Secret of the Forest, 1956
Face in the Night, 1957
Robbery Under Arms, 1957
Blood of the Vampire, 1958
Sea of Sand, 1958
Danger Within, 1959
Identity Unknown, 1960
Feet of Clay, 1960
Dead Lucky, 1960

Dentist in the Chair, 1960
The Middle Course, 1961
Highway to Battle, 1961
Very Important Person, 1961
A Matter of WHO, 1961
Carry On Cruising, 1962
Echo of Diana, 1963
The Mouse On the Moon, 1963
Where Eagles Dare, 1968
Oh What a Lovely War, 1969

LESLIE BANKS (1890-1952)
Distinguished star and character actor of stage (since 1911)
and screen with unique profile;
also in Hollywood.

The Most Dangerous Game, 1932
I Am Suzanne, 1933
Strange Evidence, 1933
The Fire Raisers, 1933
The Night of the Party, 1934
The Red Ensign, 1934
The Man Who Knew Too Much,
  1934
Sanders of the River, 1935
The Tunnel, 1935
Debt of Honour, 1936
The Three Maxims, 1936
Wings of the Morning, 1937
Fire Over England, 1937
Farewell Again, 1937
21 Days, 1938
Jamaica Inn, 1939
Dead Man's Shoes, 1939
The Arsenal Stadium Mystery,
  1939
Guide Dogs For the Blind, 1939
Sons of the Sea, 1940
The Door With Seven Locks, 1940
Busman's Honeymoon, 1940
Neutral Port, 1940
Cottage to Let, 1941
Ships With Wings, 1941
Give Us More Ships, 1941
The Big Blockade, 1942
Went the Day Well, 1942
Henry V, 1944
Mrs. Fitzherbert, 1947
The Small Back Room, 1948
Your Witness, 1940
Madeleine, 1950

IAN BANNEN (1928-)
Solid, effective Scots leading
man and character actor also
on stage (from mid-40s) and
television.

Private's Progress, 1956
The Long Arm, 1956
Yangtse Incident, 1957
Miracle in Soho, 1957
The Birthday Present, 1957
A Tale of Two Cities, 1958
Behind the Mask, 1958
She Didn't Say No, 1958
Carleton Browne of the F.O.,
  1959
A French Mistress, 1960
Suspect, 1960
On Friday at Eleven, 1961
Macbeth, 1961
The World in My Pocket, 1962
Station 6-Sahara, 1963
Psyche 59, 1963
Mister Moses, 1964
The Hill, 1965
Rotten to the Core, 1965
Flight of the Phoenix, 1965
Penelope, 1967
Sailor From Gibraltar, 1967
Lock Up Your Daughters, 1968
Too Late the Hero, 1969
Jane Eyre, 1970
Fright, 1971
The Deserter, 1971
The Offence, 1972
Doomwatch, 1972
The Mackintosh Man, 1973
The Gathering Storm, 1974
From Beyond the Grave, 1975
Terror From Within, 1975
The Driver's Seat, 1975
Bite the Bullet, 1975
The Voyage, 1977
Jesus of Nazareth, 1977
Sweeney, 1977
The Inglorious Bastards, 1978
A Watcher in the Woods, 1980
Tinker, Tailor, Soldier, Spy,
  1980

ERIC BARKER (1912-)
Character actor specializing in

comedy cameos, a popular pre-
war radio performer with wife
Pearl Hackney. Not to be confused with silent film actor of
the same name.

Carry On London, 1937
West End Frolics, 1937
Concert Party, 1937
On Velvet, 1938
Brothers in Law, 1957
Happy is the Bride, 1958
Blue Murder at St. Trinian's,
   1958
Carry On Sergeant, 1958
A Clean Sweep, 1958
Bachelor of Hearts, 1959
Left, Right and Centre, 1959
Carry On Constable, 1960
Dentist in the Chair, 1960
Watch Your Stern, 1960
The Pure Hell of St. Trinian's,
   1960
Nearly a Nasty Accident, 1961
Dentist On the Job, 1961
Raising the Wind, 1961
On the Fiddle, 1961
Carry On Cruising, 1962
The Fast Lady, 1962
On the Beat, 1962
Mouse On the Moon, 1963
Heavens Above, 1963
Father Came Too, 1963
The Bargee, 1964
Carry On Spying, 1964
Ferry Cross the Mersey, 1964
Three Hats For Lisa, 1965
Those Magnificent Men in Their
   Flying Machines, 1965
Doctor in Clover, 1965
The Great St. Trinian's Train
   Robbery, 1966
Maroc 7, 1966
Twinky, 1969
There's a Girl in My Soup,
   1970
Cool it Carol, 1970

RONNIE BARKER (1929-   )
Adaptable, rotund character
comedian, mainly seen on
television.

The Cracksman, 1963
Kill or Cure, 1963
Doctor in Distress, 1963
Father Came Too, 1963
The Bargee, 1964
A Home of Your Own, 1964
Runaway Railway, 1965
The Man Outside, 1967
Ghost of a Chance, 1968
Futtock's End, 1970
Robin and Marian, 1976

PETER BARKWORTH (1929-   )
Polished, polite comedy character actor, also seen on stage
and television.

A Touch of Larceny, 1959
No Love For Johnnie, 1961
No My Darling Daughter, 1961
Seven Keys, 1962
Play it Cool, 1962
Tiara Tahiti, 1963
Position of Trust, 1963
Downfall, 1964
Two a Penny, 1967
Where Eagles Dare, 1968
Patton, 1970
The Littlest Horse Thieves,
   1977
International Velvet, 1978

IVOR BARNARD (1887-1953)
Wily character of stage and
screen, seen to best advantage
in evil or slyly inquisitive roles.

The Skin Game, 1920
Sally in Our Alley, 1931
Blind Spot, 1932
The Crime at Blossom's, 1933
The Good Companions, 1933
The Sleeping Car, 1933
The Roof, 1933
Waltz Time, 1933
The Wandering Jew, 1933
Love, Life and Laughter, 1934
Princess Charming, 1934
Brides to Be, 1934
The Price of Wisdom, 1935
The 39 Steps, 1935

The Village Squire, 1935
Some Day, 1935
Foreign Affaires, 1935
Dreams Come True, 1936
House of the Spaniard, 1936
The Man Behind the Mask, 1936
What a Man, 1937
The Frog, 1937
Storm in a Teacup, 1937
The Mill On the Floss, 1937
Victoria the Great, 1937
Farewell to Cinderella, 1937
Double Exposures, 1937
Pygmalion, 1938
Everything Happens to Me, 1938
Eye Witness, 1939
Oh Dear Uncle, 1939
Cheer Boys Cheer, 1939
The Stars Look Down, 1939
The Saint's Vacation, 1941
The Silver Fleet, 1943
Undercover, 1943
Escape to Danger, 1943
Hotel Reserve, 1944
The Wicked Lady, 1945
Perfect Strangers, 1945
Appointment With Crime, 1946
Great Expectations, 1946
So Well Remembered, 1947
Mrs. Fitzherbert, 1947
Oliver Twist, 1948
Dulcimer Street, 1948
Don't Take it to Heart, 1948
Esther Waters, 1948
The Queen of Spades, 1949
Paper Orchid, 1949
Madeleine, 1950
Hot Ice, 1952
Time Gentlemen Please, 1952
Malta Story, 1953
Sea Devils, 1953
Beat the Devil, 1953

BARRY K. BARNES (1906-
     1965)
Stylish, educated leading man
of stage (1927) and films,
mainly in the action or adventure vein.

Dodging the Dole, 1936
Return of the Scarlet Pimper-

nel, 1937
This Man is News, 1938
Who Goes Next?, 1938
Prison Without Bars, 1938
You're the Doctor, 1938
The Ware Case, 1938
The Midas Touch, 1939
Spies of the Air, 1939
This Man in Paris, 1939
Two For Danger, 1940
The Girl in the News, 1940
Law and Disorder, 1940
Bedelia, 1946
Dancing With Crime, 1947

BINNIE BARNES (1905-)
Assiduous light character actress who went to Hollywood in
1934; former chorus girl and
nurse. Married to film executive Mike Frankovitch.

Phonofilm, 1929
A Night in Montmartre, 1931
Love Lies, 1931
Dr. Josser KC, 1931
Out of the Blue, 1931
Murder at Covent Garden, 1932
Partners Please, 1932
Innocents of Chicago, 1932
Down Our Street, 1932
Strip Strip Hooray, 1932
The Last Coupon, 1932
Old Spanish Customers, 1932
Taxi to Paradise, 1933
Counsel's Opinion, 1933
The Charming Deceiver, 1933
Their Night Out, 1933
Heads We Go, 1933
Private Life of Henry VIII,
     1933
The Silver Spoon, 1934
The Lady is Willing, 1934
Nine Forty-Five, 1934
There's Always Tomorrow,
     1934
No Escape, 1934
Private Life of Don Juan, 1934
Forbidden Territory, 1934
Rendezvous, 1935
Diamond Jim, 1935
Sutter's Gold, 1936

Small Town Girl, 1936
Last of the Mohicans, 1936
The Magnificent Brute, 1936
Breezing Home, 1937
Three Smart Girls, 1937
Adventures of Marco Polo,
   1938
Three Blind Mice, 1938
The Divorce of Lady X, 1938
Holiday, 1938
The First 100 Years, 1938
Always Goodbye, 1938
Tropic Holiday, 1938
Gateway, 1938
Thanks For Everything, 1938
Broadway Melody of 1938, 1938
The Three Musketeers, 1939
Daytime Wife, 1939
Frontier Marshal, 1939
Man About Town, 1939
Wife, Husband and Friend, 1939
Till We Meet Again, 1940
This Thing Called Love, 1941
Tight Shoes, 1941
Skylark, 1941
Three Girls About Town, 1941
Call Out the Marines, 1942
New Wine, 1942
In Old California, 1942
I Married an Angel, 1942
The Man From Down Under,
   1943
Barbary Coast Gent, 1944
Up in Mabel's Room, 1944
The Hour Before the Dawn,
   1944
It's in the Bag, 1945
Getting Gertie's Garter, 1945
The Spanish Main, 1945
The Time of Their Lives, 1946
Bedelia, 1946
If Winter Comes, 1947
My Own True Love, 1948
Pirates of Capri, 1949
Shadow of the Eagle, 1950
Fugitive Lady, 1951
Decameron Nights, 1953
Malaga, 1954
The Trouble With Angels, 1966
Where Angels Go Trouble
   Follows, 1968
40 Carats, 1972

PATRICK BARR (1908-)
Dependable star and latterly
character actor of films, stage
and television, usually seen as
policemen, lawyers, soldiers,
or other lawabiding citizens.
Former engineer.

The Merry Men of Sherwood,
   1932
Meet My Sister, 1933
Irish Hearts, 1934
Gay Old Dog, 1935
Wednesday's Luck, 1936
East Meets West, 1936
Midnight at Madame Tussaud's,
   1936
Things to Come, 1936
Cavalier of the Streets, 1937
The Show Goes On, 1937
Return of the Scarlet Pimper-
   nel, 1937
Incident in Shanghai, 1938
Sailing Along, 1938
Star of the Circus, 1938
Meet Mr. Penny, 1938
Yellow Sands, 1938
Marigold, 1938
The Gaunt Stranger, 1938
Let's Be Famous, 1939
Case of the Frightened Lady,
   1940
The Blue Lagoon, 1949
To Have and to Hold, 1951
The Lavender Hill Mob, 1951
Death of an Angel, 1952
The Story of Robin Hood, 1952
King of the Underworld, 1952
You're Only Young Twice, 1952
Murder at Scotland Yard, 1952
Murder at the Grange, 1952
A Ghost For Sale, 1952
The Black Orchid, 1953
Singlehanded, 1953
The Intruder, 1953
Black Thirteen, 1953
Duel in the Jungle, 1954
Escape By Night, 1954
Seagulls Over Sorrento, 1954
Time is My Enemy, 1954
The Brain Machine, 1954
All Living Things, 1955

The Dam Busters, 1955
Room in the House, 1955
It's Never Too Late, 1956
At the Stroke of Nine, 1957
Saint Joan, 1957
Lady of Vengeance, 1957
Next to No Time, 1958
Urge to Kill, 1960
The Valiant, 1962
The Longest Day, 1962
Billy Liar, 1963
On the Run, 1963
Ring of Spies, 1963
The Great Pony Raid, 1968
Guns in the Heather, 1969
The Flesh and Blood Show,
   1972
Satanic Rites of Dracula, 1973
House of Whipcord, 1974
The Black Windmill, 1974
Count Dracula and His Vampire
   Bride, 1978

JANE BARRETT (1923-1969)
Leading lady of stage and screen
whose film appearances were
sporadic.

The Captive Heart, 1946
Eureka Stockade, 1948
Colonel Bogey, 1948
Time Gentlemen Please, 1952
The Sword and the Rose, 1953
Bond of Fear, 1956
Change Partners, 1965

RAY BARRETT (1926-)
Australian leading man long
popular on British television;
films fairly rare.

The Sundowners, 1960
Jigsaw, 1962
Time to Remember, 1962
Touch of Death, 1962
Moment of Decision, 1962
To Have and to Hold, 1963
80,000 Suspects, 1963
Valley of the Kings, 1964
The Reptile, 1965
Thunderbirds Are Go, 1966

Revenge, 1971
Terror From Under the House,
   1976
Let the Balloon Go, 1977

NIGEL BARRIE (-)
Small-part character actor of
silent and early sound films;
also on stage.

Widow By Proxy, 1919
Charge It, 1921
Prince There Was, 1921
The Stranger's Banquet, 1923
Peg O' My Heart, 1923
Hogan's Alley, 1925
Steel Preferred, 1925
Amateur Gentleman, 1926
Climbers, 1927
Shield of Honour, 1927
The Lone Eagle, 1927
The Forger, 1928
The Ringer, 1928
Cocktails, 1928
Under the Greenwood Tree,
   1929
The Plaything, 1929
Old Soldiers Never Die, 1931
Dreyfus, 1931
Passenger to London, 1937
Anything to Declare?, 1938

WENDY BARRIE (1912-1978)
Pretty blonde star of stage and
films, went to Hollywood in
1934 but never achieved roles
that did her justice; also later
in radio and talk-show hostess
on television (1948).

Collision, 1931
Threads, 1932
It's a Boy, 1932
The Callbox Mystery, 1932
Wedding Rehearsal, 1932
The Barton Mystery, 1932
Where is the Lady?, 1932
Cash, 1933
The House of Trent, 1933
Private Life of Henry VIII,
   1933

This Acting Business, 1933
Murder at the Inn, 1934
Without You, 1934
The Man I Want, 1934
Freedom of the Seas, 1934
Give Her a Ring, 1934
There Goes Susie, 1934
For Love Or Money, 1934
A Feather in Her Hat, 1935
It's a Small World, 1935
College Scandal, 1935
Millions in the Air, 1935
Love On a Bet, 1936
Speed, 1936
Under Your Spell, 1936
Ticket to Paradise, 1936
Big Broadcast of 1936, 1936
Breezing Home, 1937
What Price Vengeance, 1937
Dead End, 1937
Wings Over Honolulu, 1937
A Girl With Ideas, 1938
I Am the Law, 1938
Pacific Liner, 1939
The Witness Vanishes, 1939
Hound of the Baskervilles, 1939
Five Came Back, 1939
Newsboy's Home, 1939
The Saint Strikes Back, 1939
Cross Country Romance, 1940
Men Against the Sky, 1940
Repent at Leisure, 1940
The Saint Takes Over, 1940
Who Killed Aunt Maggie?, 1940
The Gay Falcon, 1941
A Date With the Falcon, 1941
The Saint in Palm Springs,
   1941
Eyes of the Underworld, 1942
Women in War, 1942
Forever and a Day, 1943
It Could Happen to You, 1953

KEITH BARRON (1934-)
Stern leading actor and second
lead who began on stage, went
to television, and graduated to
films.

The Haunted Man, 1966
Baby Love, 1969
Melody, 1970

The Fire Chasers, 1970
Man Who Had Power Over
   Women, 1970
She'll Follow You Anywhere,
   1971
Nothing But the Night, 1973
The Land That Time Forgot,
   1975
Voyage of the Damned, 1976

JOAN BARRY (1903-)
Former stage actress who
gained brief popularity during
early sound film era.

The Card, 1922
The Happy Ending, 1925
The Rising Generation, 1928
Blackmail, 1929
Atlantic, 1929
The Outsider, 1931
Man of Mayfair, 1931
Rich and Strange, 1931
Ebb Tide, 1932
Women Who Play, 1932
The First Mrs. Fraser, 1932
Sally Bishop, 1932
Rome Express, 1932
Mrs. Dane's Defence, 1934

FREDDIE BARTHOLOMEW,
   (1924-)
Refined, impeccable child actor,
mainly associated with Hollywood films, on stage from 1927.
Retired and went into adver-
tising.

Fascination, 1930
Toyland, 1930
Lily Christine, 1932
Strip Strip Hooray, 1932
David Copperfield, 1935
Anna Karenina, 1935
Professional Soldier, 1935
Little Lord Fauntleroy, 1936
The Devil is a Sissy, 1936
Lloyds of London, 1936
Captains Courageous, 1937
Kidnapped, 1938
Lord Jeff, 1938

Listen Darling, 1938
Spirit of Culver, 1938
Two Bright Boys, 1939
The Swiss Family Robinson,
    1940
Tom Brown's Schooldays, 1940
Naval Academy, 1941
Cadets on Parade, 1942
A Yank at Eton, 1942
The Town Went Wild, 1944
Sepia Cinderella, 1947
St. Benny the Dip, 1951

DOROTHY BARTLAM (1908-)
Star of silent and early sound
films, former beauty contest
winner and novelist.

The Fake, 1927
The Woman Redeemed, 1927
A Little Bit of Fluff, 1928
Mine, 1928
Not Quite a Lady, 1928
Afterwards, 1928
The Flying Squad, 1929
The Ringer, 1931
Birds of a Feather, 1931
Fascination, 1931
Stranglehold, 1931
The Love Race, 1931
Immediate Possession, 1931
We Dine at Seven, 1931
Tin Gods, 1932
Her Night Out, 1932
Watch Beverly, 1932
The Fires of Fate, 1932
Call Me Mame, 1933
The Fear Ship, 1933
Up For the Derby, 1933
On Thin Ice, 1933

ALFIE BASS (1921-)
Small Cockney character comedian specializing in cheerful
cameos; on stage from 1939,
also made a number of army
training films.

Johnny Frenchman, 1945
Perfect Strangers, 1945
Brief Encounter, 1945

Holiday Camp, 1947
It Always Rains On Sunday,
    1947
Vice Versa, 1948
The Monkey's Paw, 1948
They Gave Him the Works,
    1948
The Hasty Heart, 1949
Boys in Brown, 1949
Stage Fright, 1950
Man On the Run, 1950
Pool of London, 1951
Talk of a Million, 1951
The Galloping Major, 1951
The Lavender Hill Mob, 1951
High Treason, 1952
The Planter's Wife, 1952
Derby Day, 1952
Treasure Hunt, 1952
Made in Heaven, 1952
Brandy For the Parson, 1952
Top of the Form, 1953
The Square Ring, 1953
To Dorothy a Son, 1954
Time is My Enemy, 1954
The Passing Stranger, 1954
Make Me An Offer, 1954
Svengali, 1954
The Night My Number Came
    Up, 1955
Murder By Proxy, 1955
A Kid For Two Farthings, 1955
The Bespoke Overcoat, 1955
King's Rhapsody, 1955
Tiger in the Smoke, 1956
Jumping For Joy, 1956
A Child in the House, 1956
Behind the Headlines, 1956
Sailor Beware, 1956
A Touch of the Sun, 1956
The Angel Who Pawned Her
    Harp, 1956
No Road Back, 1957
Carry On Admiral, 1957
Hell Drivers, 1957
A Tale of Two Cities, 1958
I Was Monty's Double, 1958
I Only Arsked, 1958
The Millionairess, 1960
Help!, 1965
Doctor in Clover, 1965
Alfie, 1966
The Sandwich Man, 1966

A Funny Thing Happened On
the Way to the Forum, 1966
Dance of the Vampires, 1967
Challenge For Robin Hood,
1967
Up the Junction, 1967
Bindle, 1967
The Fixer, 1968
Magnificent 7 Deadly Sins, 1971
The Chiffy Kids, 1976
Come Play With Me, 1976
Moonraker, 1979

ALAN BATES (1934-)
Aggressive, offbeat leading man
of the 60s and 70s; on stage
since 1955. Also Hollywood.
Formerly in the RAF.

The Entertainer, 1960
Whistle Down the Wind, 1961
A Kind of Loving, 1962
The Running Man, 1963
The Caretaker, 1963
Nothing But the Best, 1963
Zorba the Greek, 1964
Georgy Girl, 1966
King of Hearts, 1966
Far From the Madding Crowd,
1967
The Fixer, 1968
Women in Love, 1969
Three Sisters, 1970
The Go-Between, 1971
A Day in the Death of Joe Egg,
1971
Butley, 1973
Impossible Object, 1973
In Celebration, 1974
Royal Flash, 1975
An Unmarried Woman, 1977
The Rose, 1978
The Shout, 1978
Nijinsky, 1979

MICHAEL BATES (1920-1978)
Incisive character actor of
stage, films, and television,
often seen as policeman or
military officer.

The Stratford Adventure, 1953
Carrington VC, 1955
I'm All Right, Jack, 1959
Bedazzled, 1967
Here We Go Round the Mul-
berry Bush, 1967
Salt and Pepper, 1968
Don't Raise the Bridge Lower
the River, 1968
Hammerhead, 1968
Oh What a Lovely War, 1969
The Battle of Britain, 1969
Patton, 1970
The Rise & Rise of Michael
Rimmer, 1970
The Engagement, 1971
A Clockwork Orange, 1971
Frenzy, 1972
No Sex Please We're British,
1973
The Bawdy Adventures of Tom
Jones, 1975
Gulliver's Travels, 1977

RALPH BATES (1940-)
Young leading actor of the 70s,
also much on television; mainly
acts in horror films.

Taste the Blood of Dracula,
1970
Lust For a Vampire, 1970
Horror of Frankenstein, 1970
Dr. Jekyll and Sister Hyde,
1971
Fear in the Night, 1973
Persecution, 1974
The Devil Within Her, 1976

TIMOTHY BATESON (1926-)
Character actor mainly seen on
stage, in occasional films
mainly in comedy parts.

Nicholas Nickleby, 1947
The Guinea Pig, 1948
White Corridors, 1952
Richard III, 1955
The Mouse That Roared, 1959
Our Man in Havana, 1959

There Was a Crooked Man,
  1960
The Girl On the Boat, 1961
The Golden Rabbit, 1962
It's Trad, Dad, 1962
Nightmare, 1963
Father Came Too, 1963
70 Deadly Pills, 1964
The Knack, 1965
The Wrong Box, 1966
The Anniversary, 1967
1917, 1970

SIR ARCHIBALD BATTY
  (1887-)
Distinguished ex-soldier who
played military roles in a few
films of the 30s.

Discord, 1933
The Vulture, 1937
I See Ice, 1938
The Drum, 1938
The Four Feathers, 1939
The Lion Has Wings, 1939

JANE BAXTER (1909-)
Leading character actress of
stage (1925) and screen, also
in Hollywood.

Bedrock, 1930
Bed and Breakfast, 1930
Down River, 1931
Two White Arms, 1932
Flat No. 9, 1932
The Constant Nymph, 1933
The Night of the Party, 1934
The Double Event, 1934
Girls Please, 1934
Blossom Time, 1934
We Live Again, 1934
Royal Cavalcade, 1935
Drake of England, 1935
The Clairvoyant, 1935
Line Engaged, 1935
Enchanted April, 1935
The Man Behind the Mask,
  1936
Dusty Ermine, 1936
April Romance, 1937

Second Best Bed, 1938
The Ware Case, 1938
Confidential Lady, 1939
Murder Will Out, 1939
The Chinese Bungalow, 1940
The Briggs Family, 1940
Ships With Wings, 1941
The Flemish Farm, 1943
Death of an Angel, 1952
All Hallowe'en, 1953

KEITH BAXTER (1933-)
Leading actor long on stage,
film appearances extremely
rare.

The Barretts of Wimpole Street,
  1957
Chimes at Midnight, 1966
Ash Wednesday, 1973

STANLEY BAXTER (1928-)
Scotch character comedian and
impressionist, mainly on television and stage.

Geordie, 1955
Very Important Person, 1961
Crooks Anonymous, 1962
The Fast Lady, 1963
Father Came Too, 1963
Joey Boy, 1965

GEOFFREY BAYLDON
  (1924-)
Lean, rangy comedy character
actor of stage and films, revels in eccentric or forgetful
characterizations.

The Stranger Left No Card,
  1953
Dracula, 1958
A Night to Remember, 1958
The Two-Headed Spy, 1958
Libel, 1959
Whirlpool, 1959
Bomb in the High Street, 1961
The Webster Boy, 1962
55 Days at Peking, 1963

A Jolly Bad Fellow, 1964
King Rat, 1965
Sky West and Crooked, 1965
To Sir With Love, 1967
Assignment K, 1967
Two a Penny, 1967
Casino Royale, 1967
Otley, 1969
The Raging Moon, 1970
Scrooge, 1970
The House That Dripped Blood,
   1970
Frankenstein Must Be Destroyed,
   1970
Asylum, 1972
Tales From the Crypt, 1972
The Gathering Storm, 1974
The Slipper and the Rose, 1976
The Pink Panther Strikes Again,
   1976
Abide With Me, 1977

HILDA BAYLEY (-)
Popular star of stage (since
1913) and silent films, played
character roles in sound films.

Sisters in Arms, 1918
A Soul's Crucifixion, 1919
Under Suspicion, 1919
Mr. Wu, 1919
Guilda Louise, 1919
The Barton Mystery, 1920
Carnival, 1921
While London Sleeps, 1922
Flames of Passion, 1922
The Scandal, 1923
The Woman Who Obeyed, 1923
Head Office, 1936
Under a Cloud, 1937
Room For Two, 1940
Jeannie, 1941
Much Too Shy, 1942
I'll Walk Beside You, 1943
Madonna of the Seven Moons,
   1944
Give Me the Stars, 1944
Home Sweet Home, 1945
When You Come Home, 1947
My Brother Jonathan, 1948
School For Randle, 1949
Elizabeth of Ladymead, 1949

Three Men and a Girl, 1949
Madame Louise, 1951
Golden Arrow, 1952

ANN BEACH (1938-)
Character comedienne of stage
and films.

On the Fiddle, 1961
Horror Hotel, 1963
Hotel Paradiso, 1966
Sebastian, 1968
Under Milk Wood, 1971

ROBERT BEATTY (1909-)
Dependable Canadian leading
man and latterly character star,
on stage since 1938. Also former radio star of the 30s.
Long resident in Britain.

Murder in Soho, 1938
Mein Kampf My Crimes, 1939
Dangerous Moonlight, 1940
49th Parallel, 1941
One of Our Aircraft is Missing,
   1942
Suspected Person, 1942
San Demetrio-London, 1943
It Happened One Sunday, 1944
Appointment With Crime, 1946
Odd Man Out, 1947
Green Fingers, 1947
Against the Wind, 1948
Counterblast, 1948
Another Shore, 1948
Portrait From Life, 1948
The 20 Questions Murder Mys-
   tery, 1949
Her Favourite Husband, 1950
Calling Bulldog Drummond,
   1951
Captain Horatio Hornblower,
   1951
The Magic Box, 1951
Spotlight, 1951
Wings of Danger, 1952
Man On a Tightrope, 1952
The Gentle Gunman, 1952
The Figurehead, 1952
The Loves of Three Women,

1953
Devil's Plot, 1953
The Oracle, 1953
The Net, 1953
The Square Ring, 1953
The Broken Horseshoe, 1953
Albert RN, 1953
Out of the Clouds, 1954
Portrait of Alison, 1955
Something of Value, 1956
Time Lock, 1957
Tarzan and the Lost Safari,
  1957
The Horse's Mouth, 1959
The Shakedown, 1960
The Amorous Prawn, 1962
One Million Years B. C. , 1966
2001: A Space Odyssey, 1968
Where Eagles Dare, 1968
Pope Joan, 1972
Sitting Target, 1972
Man at the Top, 1973
The Spikes Gang, 1974
The Gathering Storm, 1974
Sleepwalker, 1975
The Pink Panther Strikes Again,
  1976
Jesus of Nazareth, 1977
The Martian Chronicles, 1980

SUSAN BEAUMONT (1936-)
Leading lady who retired after
a brief success during the 50s.

Jumping For Joy, 1955
Eyewitness, 1956
High Tide at Noon, 1957
On the Run, 1958
Innocent Sinners, 1958
The Spaniard's Curse, 1958
Web of Suspicion, 1959
No Safety Ahead, 1959
The Man Who Liked Funerals,
  1959
Carry On Nurse, 1959

TONY BECKLEY (1932-)
Star and second lead of films
who frequently appears in tough,
villainous roles.

Chimes at Midnight, 1966
The Penthouse, 1967
The Lost Continent, 1968
The Long Day's Dying, 1968
The Italian Job, 1969
Get Carter, 1971
Sitting Target, 1972
Beware of the Brethren, 1972
Gold, 1974
Diagnosis Murder, 1975
Revenge of the Pink Panther,
  1978

REGINALD BECKWITH (1908-
  1965)
Tubby, cherubic, delightful
character star of stage (1926),
screen and television, in prim
comedy roles. Also author,
playwright, film & theatre critic, and BBC War correspondant.

Freedom Radio, 1941
My Brother's Keeper, 1948
Scott of the Antarctic, 1948
Miss Pilgrim's Progress, 1949
The Body Said No, 1950
Mr. Drake's Duck, 1951
Circle of Danger, 1951
Another Man's Poison, 1951
Whispering Smith Hits London,
  1952
Brandy For the Parson, 1952
Penny Princess, 1952
You're Only Young Once, 1952
Genevieve, 1953
The Titfield Thunderbolt, 1953
Innocents in Paris, 1953
Don't Blame the Stork, 1953
The Million Pound Note, 1954
The Runaway Bus, 1954
Fast and Loose, 1954
Dance Little Lady, 1954
Lease of Life, 1954
Aunt Clara, 1954
Men of Sherwood Forest, 1954
Break in the Circle, 1955
They Can't Hang Me, 1955
A Yank in Ermine, 1955
The Lyons in Paris, 1955
Charley Moon, 1955

The March Hare, 1956
It's a Wonderful World, 1956
Carry On Admiral, 1957
These Dangerous Years, 1957
Lucky Jim, 1957
Night of the Demons, 1957
Up the Creek, 1958
Law and Disorder, 1958
Next to No Time, 1958
Rockets Galore, 1958
The Captain's Table, 1959
The Horse's Mouth, 1959
The 39 Steps, 1959
The Ugly Duckling, 1959
Upstairs and Downstairs, 1959
The Navy Lark, 1959
Friends and Neighbours, 1959
Desert Mice, 1959
Expresso Bongo, 1959
Bottoms Up, 1960
Dentist in the Chair, 1960
Doctor in Love, 1960
There Was a Crooked Man,
   1960
The Night We Got the Bird,
   1960
The Girl on the Boat, 1961
Five Golden Hours, 1961
Double Bunk, 1961
Dentist on the Job, 1961
Day the Earth Caught Fire,
   1961
Hair of the Dog, 1962
The Prince and the Pauper,
   1962
Night of the Eagle, 1962
The Password is Courage, 1962
The King's Breakfast, 1963
Just For Fun, 1963
Lancelot and Guinevere, 1963
Doctor in Distress, 1963
The VIPs, 1963
Never Put it in Writing, 1963
Mr. Moses, 1964
A Shot in the Dark, 1964
Gonks Go Beat, 1965
Moll Flanders, 1965
The Big Job, 1965
Thunderball, 1965
How to Undress in Public,
   1965

BRIAN BEDFORD (1935-)
Leading actor of the 60s,
mainly on stage, in occasional
films.

Miracle in Soho, 1958
The Angry Silence, 1960
Number Six, 1962
The Punch and Judy Man, 1963
The Pad, 1966
Grand Prix, 1966
Robin Hood, 1973

ARNOLD BELL (-)
Prolific character actor of
stage and screen, most active
in the 50s.

Convict 99, 1919
Dr. Josser KC, 1931
Josser in the Army, 1932
Doss House, 1933
OHMS, 1937
Beyond Price, 1947
The Greed of William Hart,
   1948
The Temptress, 1949
Murder at 3 A. M. , 1953
The Master Plan, 1954
The Golden Link, 1954
Profile, 1954
Star of India, 1954
One Jump Ahead, 1955
Three Crooked Men, 1958
Moment of Indiscretion, 1958
The Square Peg, 1958
Top Floor Girl, 1959
High Jump, 1959
An Honourable Murder, 1960
Sentenced For Life, 1960
Nothing Barred, 1961
Seance On a Wet Afternoon,
   1964

TOM BELL (1932-)
Emaciated leading man of films
and television, also with stage
experience; popular in the
1960s.

The Criminal, 1960
Echo of Barbara, 1961
The Kitchen, 1961
Payroll, 1961
HMS Defiant, 1962
The L-Shaped Room, 1962
A Prize of Arms, 1963
Rebels Against the Light, 1964
Ballad in Blue, 1965
He Who Rides a Tiger, 1966
Sands of Beersheba, 1966
In Enemy Country, 1968
The Long Day's Dying, 1968
Lock Up Your Daughters, 1969
All the Right Noises, 1969
The Violent Enemy, 1969
Quest For Love, 1971
The Spy's Wife, 1971
Royal Flash, 1975
The Sailor's Return, 1978

BERTHA BELMORE (1882-
1953)
Stately character comedienne,
the dignified foil of many comedians; sister of Lionel Belmore.

Going Gay, 1933
Are You a Mason?, 1934
Happy, 1934
Keep it Quiet, 1934
Give Her a Ring, 1934
Over the Garden Wall, 1934
Blossom Time, 1934
So You Won't Talk, 1935
Royal Cavalcade, 1935
Be Careful Mr. Smith, 1935
In the Soup, 1936
Broken Blossoms, 1936
Over She Goes, 1937
Please Teacher, 1937
Let's Make a Night of It, 1937
Yes Madam, 1938
Hold My Hand, 1938
Queer Cargo, 1938
Weddings Are Wonderful, 1938
Discoveries, 1939
The Midas Touch, 1939
She Couldn't Say No, 1939

LIONEL BELMORE (1867-1953)

Distinguished, portly star character actor of stage and films;
in Hollywood from early 30s.
Brother of Bertha Belmore.

The Antique Dealer, 1915
Madame X, 1920
Jes Call Me Jim, 1920
Moonlight Follies, 1921
Two Minutes to Go, 1921
Oliver Twist, 1921
Kindred of the Dust, 1922
Peg O' My Heart, 1922
Within the Law, 1923
Red Lights, 1923
A Boy of Flanders, 1924
The Sea Hawk, 1924
The Man Who Fights Alone,
1924
Eve's Secret, 1925
The Black Bird, 1925
Never the Twain Shall Meet,
1925
Bardelys the Magnificent, 1926
King of Kings, 1927
Sorrell and Son, 1927
Rose Marie, 1928
The Play Girl, 1928
Matinee Idol, 1928
Goodbye Kiss, 1928
The Circus Kid, 1929
The Redeeming Sin, 1929
Monte Carlo, 1930
Hell's Island, 1930
Sweet Kitty Bellairs, 1930
Boudoir Diplomat, 1930
The Rogue Sons, 1930
Captain of the Guards, 1930
Playing Around, 1930
The Love Parade, 1930
One Heavenly Night, 1931
Ten Nights in a Barroom, 1931
Frankenstein, 1931
Alexander Hamilton, 1931
Fame Street, 1932
So Big, 1932
The Warrior's Husband, 1932
The Vampire Bat, 1933
Oliver Twist, 1933
Vanessa, 1934
I Am Suzanne, 1934
The Count of Monte Cristo,
1934

Caravan, 1934
Cleopatra, 1934
Cardinal Richelieu, 1935
Mutiny on the Bounty, 1935
Mary of Scotland, 1936
Little Lord Fauntleroy, 1936
The Prince and the Pauper,
    1937
The Toast of New York, 1937
Adventures of Robin Hood, 1938
Tower of London, 1939
Diamond Frontiers, 1940
My Son My Son, 1940

HYWEL BENNETT (1944-)
Thoughtful, sensitive Welsh
leading man of the 60s and 70s,
also on stage.

The Family Way, 1966
Twisted Nerve, 1968
The Virgin Soldiers, 1970
The Buttercup Chain, 1970
Loot, 1971
Percy, 1971
Endless Night, 1972
Alice's Adventures in Wonder-
    land, 1972
The Love Ban, 1972
It's a 2' 6" Above the Ground
    World, 1972
Tinker, Tailor, Soldier, Spy,
    1980

JILL BENNETT (1930-)
Character actress and second
lead, also on stage. Frequently
plays nervous characters. Also
Hollywood. Married to playwright John Osborne (1929-).

Moulin Rouge, 1952
Hell Below Zero, 1954
Aunt Clara, 1954
Murder Anonymous, 1955
Lust For Life, 1956
The Extra Day, 1956
The Criminal, 1960
The Skull, 1965
The Nanny, 1965
Inadmissible Evidence, 1968

Charge of the Light Brigade,
    1968
Julius Caesar, 1970
I Know What I Want, 1971
Mr. Quilp, 1974
Full Circle, 1977

GEORGE BENSON (1911-)
Small-part character star of
stage and screen, adept at nervous or twitching comedy cameos.
TV series: "The Forsyte Saga. "

Holiday Lovers, 1932
Keep Fit, 1937
Convoy, 1940
The October Man, 1947
Highly Dangerous, 1950
Pool of London, 1951
The Man in the White Suit,
    1951
The Broken Horseshoe, 1953
The Captain's Paradise, 1953
Doctor in the House, 1954
Value For Money, 1955
The Naked Truth, 1957
Dracula, 1958
Left, Right and Centre, 1959
A Jolly Bad Fellow, 1964
A Home of Your Own, 1964
Great St. Trinian's Train Rob-
    bery, 1966
The Strange Affair, 1968
The Creeping Flesh, 1972

MARTIN BENSON (1918-)
Screen character adept at portraying sly, villainous roles
and other menacing continental
types. Also Hollywood.

The Blind Goddess, 1948
But Not in Vain, 1948
Trapped By the Terror, 1949
Adventures of PC 49, 1949
Night Without Stars, 1951
Assassin For Hire, 1951
Lucky Nick Cain, 1951
Mystery Junction, 1951
The Dark Light, 1951
Judgement Deferred, 1952

Wide Boy, 1952
Top of the Form, 1953
Wheel of Fate, 1953
Recoil, 1953
West of Zanzibar, 1954
Passage Home, 1955
The King and I, 1956
23 Paces to Baker Street, 1956
Soho Incident, 1956
The Man From Tangier, 1957
Interpol, 1957
Istanbul, 1957
Doctor at Large, 1957
The Flesh is Weak, 1957
Windom's Way, 1958
The Cosmic Monster, 1958
The Two-Headed Spy, 1958
Killers of Kilimanjaro, 1959
Make Mine a Million, 1959
Exodus, 1960
Once More With Feeling, 1960
Sands of the Desert, 1960
Oscar Wilde, 1960
The Three Worlds of Gulliver, 1960
The Gentle Trap, 1960
Five Golden Hours, 1961
Gorgo, 1961
Cleopatra, 1962
Captain Clegg, 1962
The Silent Invasion, 1962
The Fur Collar, 1962
Satan Never Sleeps, 1962
A Matter of WHO, 1962
Behold a Pale Horse, 1963
A Shot in the Dark, 1964
Goldfinger, 1964
The Secret Door, 1964
The Secret of My Success, 1965
A Man Could Get Killed, 1965
Mozambique, 1966
The Magnificent Two, 1967
Battle Beneath the Earth, 1968
Pope Joan, 1972
Tiffany Jones, 1976
The Omen, 1976
Mohammed Messenger of God, 1977
Jesus of Nazareth, 1977

MICHAEL BENTINE (1922-   )
Anglo-Peruvian comedian, long popular on stage and television for his loony, unique brand of humor.

Cookery Nook, 1951
Down Among the Z Men, 1952
Loonizoo, 1953
Force's Sweetheart, 1953
Raising a Riot, 1955
Fun at the Movies, 1957
I Only Arsked, 1958
Climb Up the Wall, 1960
We Joined the Navy, 1962
The Sandwich Man, 1966
Bachelor of Arts, 1969

JOHN BENTLEY (1916-   )
Stage and radio star of the 30s who entered films and became the hero of low-budget crime and adventure dramas. Also on tv.

The Hills of Donegal, 1947
Calling Paul Temple, 1948
Torment, 1949
Happiest Days of Your Life, 1950
She Shall Have Murder, 1950
Bait, 1950
Paul Temple's Triumph, 1951
Salute the Toff, 1952
Hammer the Toff, 1952
The Woman's Angle, 1952
Paul Temple Returns, 1952
Tread Softly, 1952
Lost Hours, 1952
The Black Orchid, 1953
Men Against the Sun, 1953
River Beat, 1954
The Scarlet Spear, 1954
Double Exposure, 1954
Profile, 1954
Final Appointment, 1954
Golden Ivory, 1954
Confession, 1955
The Flaw, 1955
Stolen Assignment, 1955
Dial 999, 1955
Flight From Vienna, 1956
Escape in the Sun, 1956

Deadliest Sin, 1956
Istanbul, 1957
Way Out, 1958
Submarine Seahawk, 1959
The Girl On the Boat, 1961
An Helligen Wassern, 1961
The Singer Not the Song, 1961
Mary Had a Little, 1961
The Sinister Man, 1961
Stranglehold, 1962
The Fur Collar, 1962
The Shadow of Treason, 1963
Blind Man's Bluff, 1967

HARRY BERESFORD (1864-
   1944)
General-purpose character of
stage and screen, long in Hollywood.

The Quarterback, 1926
Finn and Hattie, 1931
Up Pops the Devil, 1931
The Secret Call, 1931
Sob Sister, 1931
Heaven On Earth, 1931
Mississippi, 1931
Charlie Chan Carries On, 1931
So Big, 1932
Dr. X, 1932
The Sign of the Cross, 1932
Dance Team, 1932
High Pressure, 1932
Scandal For Sale, 1932
Strange Love of Molly Louvain,
   1932
Forgotten Commandments, 1932
Night Flight, 1933
College Coach, 1933
Murders in the Zoo, 1933
Dinner at Eight, 1933
Cleopatra, 1934
The Little Minister, 1934
Friends of Mr. Sweeney, 1934
I Found Stella Parrish, 1935
I'll Love You Always, 1935
Page Miss Glory, 1935
Seven Keys to Baldpate, 1935
David Copperfield, 1935
Klondike Annie, 1936
Grand Jury, 1936
In His Steps, 1936

Follow the Fleet, 1936
The Prince and the Pauper,
   1937
They Won't Forget, 1937
Anna Karenina, 1937
The Go-Getter, 1937
She's No Lady, 1937

BALLARD BERKELEY
   (1904-   )
Light actor and latterly equally
light character actor of stage
and films.

London Melody, 1930
The Chinese Bungalow, 1930
White Ensign, 1934
East Meets West, 1936
Jennifer Hale, 1937
The Last Adventurers, 1937
The Outsider, 1938
The Saint in London, 1939
In Which We Serve, 1942
Quiet Weekend, 1946
They Made Me a Fugitive,
   1947
Third Time Lucky, 1949
Stage Fright, 1950
The Long Dark Hall, 1951
Circumstantial Evidence, 1952
The Night Won't Talk, 1952
The Blue Parrot, 1953
Three Steps to the Gallows,
   1953
Operation Diplomat, 1953
Dangerous Cargo, 1954
Delayed Action, 1954
Child's Play, 1954
White Fire, 1954
See How They Run, 1955
The Stolen Airliner, 1955
Passport to Treason, 1956
Bullet From the Past, 1957
The Betrayal, 1958
Chain of Events, 1958
Impact, 1963
A Matter of Choice, 1963
The Murder Game, 1965
The Night Caller, 1965
Star!, 1968
Weekend Murders, 1972

EDNA BEST (1900-1974)
Early romantic lead and later
character star of stage (since
1917) and films, in Hollywood
from 1939. At one time married to Herbert Marshall.

Tilly of Bloomsbury, 1921
A Couple of Down and Outs,
1923
Tilly of Bloomsbury, 1930
Sleeping Partners, 1930
Loose Ends, 1930
Beyond the Cities, 1930
Escape, 1930
Michael and Mary, 1931
The Calendar, 1931
The Faithful Heart, 1932
The Key, 1934
The Man Who Knew Too Much,
1934
Sleeping Partners, 1937
South Riding, 1938
Prison Without Bars, 1938
Escape to Happiness, 1939
Intermezzo, 1939
Swiss Family Robinson, 1940
A Dispatch From Reuters, 1940
The Late George Apley, 1947
The Ghost and Mrs. Muir, 1947
The Iron Curtain, 1948

MARTINE BESWICK (1941-)
Attractive second lead and supporting actress of occasional
films.

From Russia With Love, 1962
Thunderball, 1965
Slave Girls, 1966
One Million Years B.C., 1966
The Penthouse, 1967
Dr. Jekyll and Sister Hyde,
1971
Seizure, 1974
The Happy Hooker Goes Holly-
wood, 1980

RODNEY BEWES (1937-)
Tubby character actor, mainly
seen in comedy roles; also

much on television, notably in
series "The Likely Lads,"
"Dear Mother Love Albert,"
and "Whatever Happened to the
Likely Lads?"

Billy Liar, 1963
San Ferry Ann, 1965
Decline and Fall, 1968
Spring and Port Wine, 1970
Alice's Adventures in Wonder-
land, 1972
The Likely Lads, 1976
Jabberwocky, 1977

JOHN BIRD (1936-)
Character actor who is mainly
seen on stage, popular in films
of the late 60s.

Red and Blue, 1967
30 is a Dangerous Age Cynthia,
1968
A Dandy in Aspic, 1968
Take a Girl Like You, 1969
A Promise of Bed, 1969
The Best House in London,
1969

NORMAN BIRD (1920-)
Comedy character actor of
stage, screen and television,
often seen as police sergeant
or in sympathetic or downtrod-
den roles.

An Inspector Calls, 1954
The League of Gentlemen, 1959
The Angry Silence, 1960
The Secret Partner, 1961
Very Important Person, 1961
Man in the Moon, 1961
Victim, 1961
Whistle Down the Wind, 1961
Cash on Demand, 1962
Night of the Eagle, 1962
Term of Trial, 1962
Maniac, 1962
The Mind Benders, 1962
The Cracksman, 1963
The Punch and Judy Man, 1963

Bitter Harvest, 1963
80,000 Suspects, 1963
Hot Enough For June, 1963
The Bargee, 1964
The Beauty Jungle, 1964
The Black Torment, 1964
The Hill, 1965
Sky West and Crooked, 1965
The Wrong Box, 1966
A Dandy in Aspic, 1968
The Limbo Line, 1968
All at Sea, 1969
Run a Crooked Mile, 1969
The Virgin and the Gypsy, 1970
The Raging Moon, 1970
Rise & Rise of Michael Rim-
    mer, 1970
Hands of the Ripper, 1971
The Slipper and the Rose, 1976
The Medusa Touch, 1978

RICHARD BIRD (1894-   )
Friendly light character actor,
popular in the 30s; also occasional director.

Tilly of Bloomsbury, 1930
Number Please, 1931
The Professional Guest, 1931
Fires of Fate, 1931
The Water Gypsies, 1932
Nine Till Six, 1932
Impromptu, 1932
A Letter of Warning, 1932
Whiteface, 1932
The Right to Live, 1933
The Warren Case, 1934
The Great Defender, 1934
What Happened Then?, 1934
Night Mail, 1935
Royal Cavalcade, 1935
Mimi, 1935
The Crouching Beast, 1935
Invitation to the Waltz, 1935
Sensation, 1937
Bulldog Drummond at Bay, 1937
The Terror, 1938
The Door With Seven Locks,
    1940
The Girl in the News, 1940
I'll Walk Beside You, 1943
Halfway House, 1944

Don't Take it to Heart, 1944
Forbidden, 1949
Death Trap, 1962
Return to Sender, 1963

JACQUELINE BISSET (1944-   )
Attractive, dark-haired leading
lady, latterly seen in Hollywood
and international productions.

The Knack, 1965
Cul de Sac, 1966
Casino Royale, 1967
Two For the Road, 1967
The Capetown Affair, 1967
The Detective, 1968
The Sweet Ride, 1968
Bullitt, 1968
The First Time, 1969
Secret World, 1969
L'Echelle Blanche, 1969
Airport, 1970
The Grasshopper, 1970
The Mephisto Waltz, 1971
Believe in Me, 1971
Secrets, 1971
Stand Up and Be Counted, 1972
Life & Times of Judge Roy
    Bean, 1972
The Thief Who Came to Dinner,
    1973
La Nuit Americaine, 1973
Day For Night, 1974
Le Magnifique, 1974
Murder On the Orient Express,
    1974
End of the Game, 1975
The Sunday Woman, 1976
St. Ives, 1976
The Deep, 1977
The Greek Tycoon, 1978
Who is Killing the Great Chefs
    of Europe?, 1978
Amo non Amo, 1979
The Day the World Ended, 1979
Inchon, 1980

HONOR BLACKMAN (1926-   )
Popular leading lady of films
and television, best remembered for tv series "The

Avengers. " Wife of Maurice Kaufmann.

Fame is the Spur, 1947
Daughter of Darkness, 1948
Quartet, 1948
A Boy a Girl and a Bike, 1949
Diamond City, 1949
Conspirator, 1950
So Long at the Fair, 1950
Set a Murderer, 1951
Green Grow the Rushes, 1951
Come Die My Love, 1953
The Rainbow Jacket, 1954
The Delavine Affair, 1954
Outsiders, 1954
Diplomatic Passport, 1955
The Glass Cage, 1955
The Three Musketeers, 1955
Breakaway, 1956
Homecoming, 1956
Suspended Alibi, 1957
You Pay Your Money, 1957
Account Rendered, 1957
Danger List, 1957
A Night to Remember, 1958
The Square Peg, 1959
A Matter of WHO, 1961
Serena, 1962
A Sense of Belonging, 1962
Jason and the Argonauts, 1963
Goldfinger, 1964
The Secret of My Success, 1965
Moment to Moment, 1965
Life at the Top, 1965
A Twist of Sand, 1968
Shalako, 1968
Twinky, 1969
The Last Grenade, 1970
The Virgin and the Gypsy, 1970
Fright, 1971
Something Big, 1971
To the Devil a Daughter, 1976
Age of Innocence, 1977
The Cat and the Canary, 1977

COLIN BLAKELEY (1930-)
Stocky Irish character star of stage (1958) and films, also in Hollywood; former salesman. Married: Margaret Whiting.

Saturday Night and Sunday Morning, 1960
The Hellions, 1961
The Password is Courage, 1962
This Sporting Life, 1963
The Informers, 1963
Never Put it in Writing, 1963
The Long Ships, 1964
A Man For All Seasons, 1966
The Spy With a Cold Nose, 1966
The Day the Fish Came Out, 1967
Decline and Fall of a Bird-watcher, 1968
The Vengeance of She, 1968
Charlie Bubbles, 1968
Alfred the Great, 1969
Private Life of Sherlock Holmes, 1970
Something to Hide, 1971
Young Winston, 1972
The National Health, 1973
Murder On the Orient Express, 1974
Galileo, 1975
Love Among the Ruins, 1975
It Shouldn't Happen to a Vet, 1976
The Pink Panther Strikes Again, 1976
Equus, 1977
The Big Sleep, 1978
Nijinsky, 1979
Antony and Cleopatra, 1980
The Day Christ Died, 1980
Meetings With Remarkable Men, 1980

NEWTON BLICK (-)
Craggy character actor specializing in playing judges, doctors, and other stately old men.

Carrington VC, 1955
The Long Arm, 1956
The Feminine Touch, 1956
Charley Moon, 1956
Bachelor of Hearts, 1958
The Gypsy & the Gentleman, 1958

Man in the Moon, 1960
Flame in the Streets, 1961
Term of Trial, 1962
Ring of Spies, 1963
70 Deadly Pills, 1964
Lord Jim, 1965
Morgan, 1966

DEREK BLOMFIELD (1920-
  1964)
Character actor of stage and
screen, popular in juvenile
roles in the 30s.

Emil and the Detectives, 1935
Turn of the Tide, 1935
Shipmates O'Mine, 1936
John Smith Wakes Up, 1940
The Ghost of St. Michael's,
  1941
Alibi, 1942
Night and the City, 1950
The Floating Dutchman, 1953
Hobson's Choice, 1954
It's Great to Be Young, 1956
It's a Wonderful World, 1956
Carry On Admiral, 1957
Escort For Hire, 1960
East of Sudan, 1964

CLAIRE BLOOM (1931-)
Attractive, intelligent leading
lady of stage, screen and television; also in Hollywood. Formerly married to Rod Steiger.

The Blind Goddess, 1948
Limelight, 1952
Innocents in Paris, 1953
The Man Between, 1953
Richard III, 1955
Alexander the Great, 1956
The Buccaneer, 1958
The Brothers Karamazov, 1958
Look Back in Anger, 1959
Brainwashed, 1960
The Royal Game, 1961
The Chapman Report, 1962
Wonderful World of the
  Brothers Grimm, 1962

The Haunting, 1963
80,000 Suspects, 1963
The Maestro of Vigueano, 1963
The Outrage, 1964
The Spy Who Came in From
  the Cold, 1965
High Infidelity, 1965
Charley, 1968
Three Into Two Won't Go, 1968
The Illustrated Man, 1969
Red Sky at Morning, 1971
A Severed Head, 1971
A Doll's House, 1973
Islands in the Stream, 1977
Backstairs at the White House,
  1979
Hamlet, 1980

ERIC BLORE (1887-1959)
Distinctive character actor of
stage and screen; former insurance agent. Specialized in
portraying eccentric butlers,
waiters, etc. In Hollywood
from 1923.

A Night Out and a Day In,
  1920
The Great Gatsby, 1926
The Gay Divorcee, 1934
Top Hat, 1935
Behold My Wife, 1935
Folies Bergere, 1935
The Casino Murder Case, 1935
Diamond Jim, 1935
I Live My Life, 1935
To Beat the Band, 1935
I Dream Too Much, 1935
Seven Keys to Baldpate, 1935
Two in the Dark, 1936
Sons O' Guns, 1936
The Ex-Mrs. Bradford, 1936
Swing Time, 1936
Piccadilly Jim, 1936
Quality Street, 1937
Shall We Dance, 1937
Michael Strogoff, 1937
It's Love I'm After, 1937
Breakfast For Two, 1937
Hitting a New High, 1937
The Joy of Living, 1938

Swiss Miss, 1938
$1000 a Touchdown, 1939
A Gentleman's Gentleman, 1939
Music in My Heart, 1940
The Boys From Syracuse, 1940
Till We Meet Again, 1940
The Man Who Wouldn't Talk,
  1940
The Lone Wolf Strikes, 1940
The Lone Wolf Meets a Lady,
  1940
South of Suez, 1940
Sullivan's Travels, 1941
The Lady Eve, 1941
The Lone Wolf Keeps a Date,
  1941
The Road to Zanzibar, 1941
The Lone Wolf Takes a Chance,
  1941
Lady Scarface, 1941
New York Town, 1941
Confirm or Deny, 1941
The Shanghai Gesture, 1941
The Moon and Sixpence, 1942
Counter Espionage, 1942
Holy Matrimony, 1943
The Sky' the Limit, 1943
San Diego I Love You, 1944
Men in Her Diary, 1945
Abie's Irish Rose, 1946
Kitty, 1946
The Lone Wolf in London, 1947
Romance on the High Seas,
  1948
Fancy Pants, 1950
Love Happy, 1950
Babes in Bagdad, 1952
Bowery to Bagdad, 1954

JOHN BLYTHE (1921-)
Stage and screen character actor who frequently plays petty
criminals, race track touts and
the like.

This Happy Breed, 1944
Holiday Camp, 1947
Dear Murderer, 1947
Crime Reporter, 1947
River Patrol, 1948
Good Time Girl, 1948
Here Come the Huggetts, 1948

Portrait From Life, 1948
Vote For Huggett, 1949
The Huggetts Abroad, 1949
A Boy, a Girl and a Bike,
  1949
Diamond City, 1949
It's a Wonderful Day, 1949
Boys in Brown, 1949
Worm's Eye View, 1951
The Frightened Man, 1952
Lilli Marlene, 1953
Out of the Bandbox, 1953
It's a Grand Life, 1953
Three Steps to the Gallows,
  1953
White Fire, 1954
The Gay Dog, 1954
Meet Mr. Malcolm, 1954
Doublecross, 1956
They Never Learn, 1956
1984, 1956
A Foxhole in Cairo, 1960
Gaolbreak, 1962
A Stitch in Time, 1964
The Bed Sitting Room, 1969
Love Among the Ruins, 1975

DIRK BOGARDE (1920-)
Superb, versatile leading actor
of stage (1939) and screen, latterly seen in complex characterizations in international motion pictures.

Come On George, 1939
Dancing With Crime, 1947
Esther Waters, 1947
Quartet, 1948
Once a Jolly Swagman, 1949
Dear Mr. Prohack, 1949
Boys in Brown, 1949
The Blue Lamp, 1950
So Long at the Fair, 1950
The Woman in Question, 1950
Blackmailed, 1951
Penny Princess, 1952
Hunted, 1952
The Gentle Gunman, 1952
Appointment in London, 1953
Desperate Moment, 1953
They Who Dare, 1954
Doctor in the House, 1954

The Sleeping Tiger, 1954
For Better, For Worse, 1954
The Sea Shall Not Have Them,
  1955
Simba, 1955
Doctor at Sea, 1955
Cast a Dark Shadow, 1955
The Spanish Gardener, 1956
Ill Met By Moonlight, 1957
Doctor at Large, 1957
Campbell's Kingdom, 1957
A Tale of Two Cities, 1958
The Wind Cannot Read, 1958
The Doctor's Dilemma, 1959
Libel, 1959
Song Without End, 1960
The Angel Wore Red, 1960
The Singer Not the Song, 1960
Victim, 1961
HMS Defiant, 1962
The Password is Courage, 1962
The Mind Benders, 1962
We Joined the Navy, 1962
I Could Go On Singing, 1962
Doctor in Distress, 1963
Hot Enough For June, 1963
The Servant, 1963
King and Country, 1964
The High Bright Sun, 1964
Darling, 1965
Modesty Blaise, 1966
Accident, 1967
Our Mother's House, 1967
Sebastian, 1968
The Fixer, 1968
The Damned, 1969
Justine, 1969
Oh What a Lovely War, 1969
Death in Venice, 1970
Upon This Rock, 1970
The Serpent, 1972
The Night Porter, 1973
Permission to Kill, 1975
A Bridge Too Far, 1977
Providence, 1977
Despair, 1978

VERA BOGETTI (-)
Character actress most active
in the 30s, often in comedy
pictures.

Mannequin, 1933
To Be a Lady, 1934
The Girl in the Flat, 1934
The Life of the Party, 1934
Crazy People, 1934
Borrow a Million, 1934
Seeing is Believing, 1934
Say it With Diamonds, 1935
Gentleman's Agreement, 1935
Inside the Room, 1935
Handle With Care, 1935
Get Off My Foot, 1935
The Mad Hatters, 1935
Excuse My Glove, 1936
Eliza Comes to Stay, 1936
Everything in Life, 1936
Intimate Relations, 1937
The Singing Cop, 1938
Thistledown, 1938
Special Edition, 1938
Confidential Lady, 1939
Two For Danger, 1940
The Prime Minister, 1941
This Was Paris, 1942
Thursday's Child, 1943
It's in the Bag, 1943
Candles at Nine, 1944

DEREK BOND (1919-)
Good-looking Scottish leading
man and character player, on
stage from 1937.   Awarded
Military Cross in WW II.

The Captive Heart, 1946
Nicholas Nickleby, 1947
Uncle Silas, 1947
The Loves of Joanna Godden,
  1947
Broken Journey, 1948
The Weaker Sex, 1948
Scott of the Antarctic, 1948
Marry Me, 1949
Poet's Pub, 1949
Christopher Columbus, 1949
Tony Draws a Horse, 1950
The Quiet Woman, 1951
Distant Trumpet, 1952
Love's a Luxury, 1952
The Hour of Thirteen, 1952
Trouble in Store, 1953

Stranger From Venus, 1954
Svengali, 1954
The High Terrace Behind the
  Screen, 1956
Rogue's Yarn, 1956
Gideon's Day, 1958
Stormy Crossing, 1958
The Hand, 1960
Saturday Night Out, 1964
Wonderful Life, 1964
Secrets of a Windmill Girl,
  1965
Press For Time, 1966
When Eight Bells Toll, 1971
Intimate Relations, 1975
Hijack, 1975

GARY BOND (1940-)
Light leading man of stage and
screen; films rare but memorable.

Zulu, 1964
Anne of the Thousand Days,
  1970
Outback, 1971

ANTHONY BOOTH (1937-)
Adaptable character actor of
stage and screen, also on television in series "Till Death Us
Do Part." (1967-71).

The Risk, 1961
Pit of Darkness, 1961
Mix Me a Person, 1962
The L-Shaped Room, 1962
The Hi-Jackers, 1963
The Partner, 1963
Of Human Bondage, 1964
Till Death Us Do Part, 1968
Corruption, 1968
Girl With a Pistol, 1969
Alf 'n Family, 1972
The Alf Garnett Saga, 1972
Brannigan, 1974
Neither the Sea Nor the Sand,
  1974
Confessions of a Window
  Cleaner, 1974

JAMES BOOTH (1930-)
Star character actor of stage
(from 1950) and screen, equally
good in dramatic or comedy
roles. Also Hollywood.

Jazzboat, 1959
In the Nick, 1959
Let's Get Married, 1959
The Trials of Oscar Wilde,
  1960
The Hellions, 1961
In the Doghouse, 1962
Sparrows Can't Sing, 1963
French Dressing, 1963
Zulu, 1964
The Secret of My Success,
  1965
Ninety Degrees in the Shade,
  1965
Robbery, 1967
Fraulein Doktor, 1967
The Bliss of Mrs. Blossom,
  1968
Man Who Had Power Over
  Women, 1970
Adam's Woman, 1970
Darker Than Amber, 1970
Macho Callahan, 1971
Revenge, 1971
Rentadick, 1972
Penny Gold, 1973
That'll Be the Day, 1973
Brannigan, 1974
I'm Not Feeling Myself Today,
  1975
Airport '77, 1977

CHILI BOUCHIER (1909-)
Leading lady of the 30s and latterly character actress of stage
and screen. Known as Dorothy
Bouchier 1931-35. Former
model and typist.

A Woman in Pawn, 1927
Maria Marten, 1928
Dawn, 1928
Chick, 1928
Warned Off, 1928
Palais de Danse, 1928

Shooting Stars, 1928
You Know What Sailors Are,
    1928
City of Play, 1929
The Silver King, 1929
Downstream, 1929
Call of the Sea, 1930
Kissing Cup's Race, 1930
Enter the Queen, 1930
Carnival, 1931
Brown Sugar, 1931
The Blue Danube, 1932
Ebb Tide, 1932
Summer Lightning, 1933
The King's Cup, 1933
Purse Strings, 1933
To Be a Lady, 1934
The Office Wife, 1934
It's a Cop, 1934
Lucky Days, 1935
The Mad Hatters, 1935
Royal Cavalcade, 1935
Death Drives Through, 1935
Honours Easy, 1935
Mr. Cohen Takes a Walk, 1935
Get Off My Foot, 1935
Where's Sally?, 1936
Southern Roses, 1936
The Ghost Goes West, 1936
Faithful, 1936
Gypsy, 1937
Mayfair Melody, 1937
The Minstrel Boy, 1937
Change For a Sovereign, 1937
Mr. Satan, 1938
Everything Happens to Me,
    1938
The Singing Cop, 1938
The Dark Stairway, 1938
The Return of Carol Deane,
    1938
The Mind of Mr. Reeder, 1939
Facing the Music, 1941
My Wife's Family, 1941
Murder in Reverse, 1945
The Laughing Lady, 1946
Mrs. Fitzherbert, 1947
Old Mother Riley's New Ven-
    ture, 1949
The Case of Charles Peace,
    1949
The Wallet, 1952

The Counterfeit Plan, 1957
The Boy and the Bridge, 1959
Dead Lucky, 1960

PETER BOWLES (-)
Leading character comedy star
of screen and television, sometimes cast as the moustachioed
cad.

Three Hats For Lisa, 1965
Dead Man's Chest, 1965
Blow Up, 1966
Charge of the Light Brigade,
    1968
The Assassination Bureau,
    1969
Taste of Excitement, 1969
Eyewitness, 1970
A Day in the Death of Joe Egg,
    1972
The Offence, 1972
The Legend of Hell House,
    1973
Murder Must Advertise, 1975
For the Love of Benji, 1977

JOHN BOXER (1909-)
Character actor of stage, in
occasional films, often in official or military roles.

George and Margaret, 1940
The Foreman Went to France,
    1942
Millions Like Us, 1943
San Demetrio-London, 1943
The Demi-Paradise, 1943
The October Man, 1947
My Brother's Keeper, 1948
The Blue Lagoon, 1949
Mr. Drake's Duck, 1950
Secret Venture, 1955
The Bridge On the River Kwai,
    1957
The Tommy Steele Story, 1957
The Haunted Man, 1966
Frenzy, 1972

STEPHEN BOYD (1928-1977)
Irish leading man of stage and
screen who rose to international
stardom in the 60s; best remembered in evil or villainous
roles.

An Alligator Named Daisy,
   1955
A Hill in Korea, 1956
The Man Who Never Was, 1956
Seven Waves Away, 1957
Island in the Sun, 1957
Seven Thunders, 1957
Heaven Fell That Night, 1957
The Bravados, 1958
Ben Hur, 1959
Woman Obsessed, 1959
The Best of Everything, 1959
Les Bijoutiers du Clair de
   Lune, 1960
The Big Gamble, 1961
The Inspector, 1962
Jumbo, 1962
Imperial Venus, 1963
The Third Secret, 1964
Fall of the Roman Empire,
   1964
Genghis Khan, 1965
The Bible, 1966
The Oscar, 1966
Fantastic Voyage, 1966
The Poppy is Also a Flower,
   1966
Assignment K, 1967
Caper of the Golden Bulls, 1967
Shalako, 1968
Slaves, 1969
Carter's Army, 1971
The Hands of Cormac Joyce,
   1971
The Big Game, 1972
A Man Called Noon, 1973
The Manipulator, 1973
Kill Kill Kill, 1974
Marta, 1974
Those Dirty Dogs, 1974
La Polizia Interviene, 1975
Potato Fritz, 1976
Evil in the Deep, 1976
The Squeeze, 1977
The Devil Has Seven Faces,
   1977

Impossible Love, 1977
One Man Against the Organiza-
   tion, 1977

WILFRED BRAMBELL (1912-)
Character actor who revels in
grotesquery or eccentricity, famous on television in "Steptoe
and Son." Autobiography: All
Above Board.

The Thirty-Nine Steps, 1935
Another Shore, 1948
Dry Rot, 1956
The Long Hot Summer, 1958
Serious Charge, 1958
Flame in the Streets, 1961
What a Whopper, 1961
The Boys, 1962
In Search of the Castaways,
   1962
The Fast Lady, 1963
The Three Lives of Thomasina,
   1963
The Small World of Sammy Lee,
   1963
Crooks in Cloisters, 1963
A Hard Day's Night, 1964
Go Kart Go!, 1964
San Ferry Ann, 1965
Where the Bullets Fly, 1966
Witchfinder General, 1968
Cry Wolf, 1968
Lionheart, 1968
The Undertakers, 1968
Carry On Again Doctor, 1969
Some Will, Some Won't, 1970

SARAH BRANCH (1938-)
Leading lady of stage and occasional films of the early 60s.

The Night We Dropped a
   Clanger, 1959
Sands of the Desert, 1960
Hell is a City, 1961
The Sword of Sherwood Forest,
   1961

MICHAEL BRENNAN (1912-)
Masculine character actor of
stage and films, often seen as
tough crook.

Cardboard Cavalier, 1949
The Clouded Yellow, 1950
Morning Departure, 1950
They Were Not Divided, 1950
Waterfront, 1950
Blackout, 1950
No Trace, 1950
Circle of Danger, 1951
Tom Brown's School Days,
  1951
13 East Street, 1952
Made in Heaven, 1952
Ivanhoe, 1952
Trouble in Store, 1953
It's a Grand Life, 1953
Up to His Neck, 1954
See How They Run, 1955
The Big Money, 1956
Not Wanted on Voyage, 1957
The Day They Robbed the Bank
  of England, 1960
Johnny Nobody, 1961
Ambush in Leopard Street, 1961
The Devil's Agent, 1962
Three Hats For Lisa, 1965
Thunderball, 1965
Cuckoo Patrol, 1965
The Great Pony Raid, 1968
Lust For a Vampire, 1970
Fright, 1971
Doomwatch, 1972

EDMOND BREON (1882-1951)
Scottish character star of stage
(since 1906) and screen, usually portrayed well-meaning
bumblers or monocled friends.
Also Hollywood.

A Little Bit of Fluff, 1928
On Approval, 1930
The Dawn Patrol, 1930
I Like Your Nerve, 1931
Born to Love, 1931
Chances, 1931
The Love Habit, 1931
Uneasy Virtue, 1931

Women Who Play, 1932
Wedding Rehearsal, 1932
Leap Year, 1932
No Funny Business, 1933
Waltz Time, 1933
Three Men in a Boat, 1933
The Private Life of Don Juan,
  1934
Mr. Cinders, 1934
The Scarlet Pimpernel, 1935
Night Mail, 1935
The Divine Spark, 1935
She Shall Have Music, 1935
Love in Exile, 1936
Strangers On a Honeymoon,
  1936
French Leave, 1937
Keep Fit, 1937
Return of the Scarlet Pimpernel,
  1937
Owd Bob, 1938
Almost a Honeymoon, 1938
A Yank at Oxford, 1938
Dangerous Medicine, 1938
Crackerjack, 1938
Luck of the Navy, 1938
Premiere, 1938
Many Tanks Mr. Atkins, 1938
Goodbye Mr. Chips, 1939
The Outsider, 1939
Gentleman of Virtue, 1940
Gaslight, 1944
The Hour Before the Dawn,
  1944
Casanova Brown, 1944
The White Cliffs of Dover, 1944
The Woman in the Window,
  1945
The Man in Half Moon Street,
  1945
Devotion, 1946
Dressed to Kill, 1946
Forever Amber, 1947
The Imperfect Lady, 1947
Enchantment, 1948
The Hills of Home, 1948
Challenge to Lassie, 1950
At Sword's Point, 1951

BERNARD BRESSLAW (1933-)
Large comic actor most famous
on television, notable in series

"The Army Game" during the
mid-late 50s.

Men of Sherwood Forest, 1954
Up in the World, 1956
I Only Arsked, 1957
High Tide at Noon, 1957
Blood of the Vampire, 1958
Too Many Crooks, 1958
The Ugly Duckling, 1959
It's All Happening, 1963
Carry On Cowboy, 1965
Carry On Screaming, 1966
Morgan, 1966
Carry On Up the Khyber, 1968
Carry On Camping, 1969
Moon Zero Two, 1969
Up Pompeii, 1970
Carry On Loving, 1970
Carry On Up the Jungle, 1970
Spring and Port Wine, 1970
Vampira, 1974
Old Dracula, 1975
One of Our Dinosaurs is Miss-
   ing, 1976
Jabberwocky, 1977

JEREMY BRETT (1935-)
Handsome light leading man of
stage and television, in occasional films.

War and Peace, 1956
Macbeth, 1961
The Wild and the Willing, 1961
The Very Edge, 1963
My Fair Lady, 1964
The Model Murder Case, 1964
One Deadly Owner, 1973
No Longer Alone, 1978
Rebecca, 1980

SHANE BRIANT (1946-)
Youthful general purpose actor
of the early 70s.

Demons of the Mind, 1970
Straight On Till Morning, 1971
Captain Kronos, 1972
Frankenstein & the Monster
   From Hell, 1972

RSM RONALD BRITTAIN (-)
Regimental sergeant-major who
appeared in military roles in
films, sometimes with a twinge
of comedy.

They Were Not Divided, 1950
Carrington VC, 1955
You Lucky People, 1955
The Missing Note, 1961
The Inspector, 1962
The Amorous Prawn, 1962
55 Days at Peking, 1963
Joey Boy, 1965
The Spy With a Cold Nose,
   1966

TONY BRITTON (1924-)
Quiet, refined leading actor
and character actor of stage
(1942) screen and television.

Salute the Toff, 1952
Loser Takes All, 1956
The Birthday Present, 1957
Behind the Mask, 1957
Operation Amsterdam, 1958
Heart of a Man, 1959
The Rough and the Smooth,
   1959
Suspect, 1960
The Horsemasters, 1961
Stork Talk, 1962
The Break, 1962
Dr. Syn Alias the Scarecrow,
   1963
There's a Girl in My Soup,
   1970
Sunday Bloody Sunday, 1971
Cry of the Penguins, 1972
Day of the Jackal, 1973
Night Watch, 1973
The People That Time Forgot,
   1977

DOROTHY BROMILEY (1935-)
Leading lady with very brief
career, also in Hollywood.

The Girls of Pleasure Island,
   1953

It's Great to Be Young, 1956
A Touch of the Sun, 1956
Zoo Baby, 1957
The Criminal, 1960
The Servant, 1963
Jemima and Johnny, 1966

ELEANOR BRON (1934-   )
Light character actress and
revue star, also on television
and in U. S.

Help!, 1965
Alfie, 1966
Bedazzled, 1967
Two For the Road, 1967
Sailor From Gibraltar, 1967
Women in Love, 1969
A Touch of Love, 1969
Thank You All Very Much,
   1969
The Day Christ Died, 1980

CLIVE BROOK (1887-1974)
Distinguished, sophisticated
star of stage (1919), screen
and occasionally latterly television, very popular in Hollywood and Britain alike.   Children: Faith and Lyndon Brook.

Trent's Last Case, 1920
Kissing Cup's Race, 1920
Her Penalty, 1921
The Loudwater Mystery, 1921
Daniel Deronda, 1921
A Sportsman's Wife, 1921
Sonia, 1921
Christie Johnstone, 1921
Shirley, 1922
Married to a Mormon, 1922
Stable Companions, 1922
The Experiment, 1922
Vanity Fair, 1922
A Tale of Two Cities, 1922
Whispering, 1922
La Traviata, 1922
The Sheik, 1922
Rigoletto, 1922
Sir Rupert's Wife, 1922
The Parson's Fight, 1922

Debt of Honour, 1922
Love and a Whirlwind, 1922
The Reverse of the Medal,
   1923
Through Fire and Water, 1923
This Freedom, 1923
Out to Win, 1923
Royal Oak, 1923
Woman to Woman, 1923
The Money Habit, 1924
The White Shadow, 1924
The Wine of Life, 1924
The Passionate Adventure,
   1924
Human Desires, 1924
Recoil, 1924
Enticement, 1925
Declasse, 1925
Seven Sinners, 1925
Playing With Souls, 1925
If Marriage Fails, 1925
The Home Maker, 1925
Compromise, 1925
You Never Know Women, 1926
For Alimony Only, 1926
The Popular Sin, 1926
Afraid to Love, 1926
Hula, 1927
Barbed Wire, 1927
French Dressing, 1927
Underworld, 1927
The Devil Dancer, 1927
Forgotten Faces, 1928
The Yellow Lily, 1928
The Perfect Crime, 1928
Interference, 1928
A Dangerous Woman, 1929
Charming Sinners, 1929
Return of Sherlock Holmes,
   1929
Four Feathers, 1930
Slightly Scarlet, 1930
The Laughing Lady, 1930
Anybody's Woman, 1930
Paramount on Parade, 1930
Sweethearts and Wives, 1930
Scandal Sheet, 1931
East Lynne, 1931
Tarnished Lady, 1931
The Lawyer's Secret, 1931
Silence, 1931
24 Hours, 1931
Husband's Holiday, 1931

Shanghai Express, 1932
The Night of June 13th, 1932
Sherlock Holmes, 1932
The Midnight Club, 1933
Cavalcade, 1933
Gallant Lady, 1933
If I Were Free, 1934
Let's Try Again, 1934
Where Sinners Meet, 1934
For Love of a Queen, 1935
Love Affair of a Dictator, 1935
Love in Exile, 1936
The Lonely Road, 1937
Action For Slander, 1938
The Ware Case, 1939
Return to Yesterday, 1939
Convoy, 1940
Freedom Radio, 1941
Breach of Promise, 1942
The Flemish Farm, 1943
The Shipbuilders, 1944
On Approval, 1945
The List of Adrian Messenger,
   1963

FAITH BROOK (1922-   )
Light leading actress of stage,
films and television; daughter
of Clive Brook.

Suspicion, 1941
The Jungle Book, 1942
Uneasy Terms, 1948
Wicked as They Come, 1956
The Intimate Stranger, 1956
Man in the Shadow, 1957
Chase a Crooked Shadow, 1957
Across the Bridge, 1957
The 39 Steps, 1959
We Shall See, 1964
The Heroes of Telemark, 1965
To Sir With Love, 1967
The Smashing Bird I Used to
   Know, 1969
Walk a Crooked Path, 1970
Ffolkes, 1980
The Curse of King Tut's Tomb,
   1980

LESLEY BROOK (1916-   )
Dark-haired leading lady of

stage (from 1934) and films,
often seen in sentimental dramatic second features.

The Man Who Made Diamonds,
   1937
The Vulture, 1937
Side Street Angel, 1937
Patricia Gets Her Man, 1937
The Viper, 1938
Dead Men Tell No Tales, 1938
Quiet Please, 1938
It's in the Blood, 1938
The Return of Carol Deane,
   1938
Dark Stairway, 1938
Glamour Girl, 1938
Night Alone, 1938
The Nursemaid Who Disap-
   peared, 1939
The Briggs Family, 1940
Rose of Tralee, 1942
Variety Jubilee, 1943
I'll Walk Beside You, 1943
When We Are Married, 1943
The Bells Go Down, 1943
Twilight Hour, 1944
For You Alone, 1945
The Trojan Brothers, 1946
House of Darkness, 1948
The Fool and the Princess,
   1948
The Gypsy and the Gentleman,
   1958

LYNDON BROOK (1926-   )
Stage and screen character
actor, also frequently on television; son of Clive Brook.

Train of Events, 1949
The Purple Plain, 1954
The Passing Stranger, 1954
One Way Out, 1955
Reach For the Sky, 1956
The Spanish Gardener, 1956
The Surgeon's Knife, 1957
Innocent Sinners, 1958
Violent Moment, 1959
Surprise Package, 1960
Song Without End, 1960
Clue of the Silver Key, 1961

Invasion, 1966
Pope Joan, 1972

ELWYN BROOK-JONES (1911-
  1962)
Versatile, heavy-set character
actor, adept at playing everything from policemen to crooks.

Dangerous Moonlight, 1941
Tomorrow We Live, 1942
Odd Man Out, 1947
The Three Weird Sisters, 1948
Good Time Girl, 1948
Bonnie Prince Charlie, 1948
It's Hard to Be Good, 1948
Life in Her Hands, 1951
I'll Get You For This, 1951
The Wonder Kid, 1951
Judgement Deferred, 1952
The Night Won't Talk, 1952
Three Steps in the Dark, 1953
The Harassed Hero, 1954
Beau Brummell, 1954
The Gilded Cage, 1955
Assignment Redhead, 1956
Rogue's Yarn, 1956
The Duke Wore Jeans, 1958
Passport to Shame, 1959
The Ugly Duckling, 1959
Mystery in the Mine,   1959
The Pure Hell of St. Trinian's,
  1961

RAY BROOKS (1939-   )
Youthful star and second lead
of the 60s and 70s, also on
stage and tv.

HMS Defiant, 1962
Play it Cool, 1962
Some People, 1963
The Knack, 1965
Daleks Invasion Earth 2150 AD,
  1966
The Last Grenade, 1970
Alice's Adventures in Wonder-
  land, 1972
House of Whipcord, 1974
The Flesh and Blood Show, 1974
Tiffany Jones, 1976

GEORGIA BROWN (1933-   )
Cabaret singer and stage actress, also in U.S.   Films infrequent.

Murder Reported, 1957
A Study in Terror, 1966
The Fixer, 1968
Lock Up Your Daughters, 1969
The Raging Moon, 1970
Nothing But the Night, 1973
Tales That Witness Madness,
  1973
Galileo, 1975
Bawdy Adventures of Tom
  Jones, 1975
The Seven Percent Solution,
  1976

PAMELA BROWN (1917-1975)
Aristocratic leading lady and
character actress of stage
(from 1936) and screen, often
in eccentric roles.   Films
relatively few but impressive.
Also excellent on television as
"Victoria Regina," for which
she won an Emmy.

One of Our Aircraft is Missing,
  1942
I Know Where I'm Going, 1945
Alice in Wonderland, 1951
Tales of Hoffman, 1951
The Second Mrs. Tanqueray,
  1952
Personal Affair, 1953
Richard III, 1955
Lust For Life, 1956
Now and Forever, 1956
The Scapegoat, 1959
Cleopatra, 1962
Becket, 1964
A Funny Thing Happened on the
  Way to the Forum, 1966
Half a Sixpence, 1967
Secret Ceremony, 1968
Wuthering Heights, 1970
Figures in a Landscape, 1970
On a Clear Day You Can See
  Forever, 1970
The Night Digger, 1971

Lady Caroline Lamb, 1972
Dracula, 1973

ROBERT BROWN (1918-   )
Stout, sturdy character actor
of stage, screen and television.

Time Gentlemen Please, 1952
The Large Rope, 1953
Helen of Troy, 1955
Passage Home, 1955
A Hill in Korea, 1956
Kill Me Tomorrow, 1957
Steel Bayonet, 1957
The Abominable Snowman, 1957
Campbell's Kingdom, 1957
Ben Hur, 1959
Shake Hands With the Devil, 1959
Passport to Shame, 1959
A Story of David, 1960
The Challenge, 1960
Sink the Bismarck, 1960
The 300 Spartans, 1962
Billy Budd, 1962
Masque of the Red Death, 1964
Operation Crossbow, 1965
One Million Years B.C., 1966
Private Road, 1971
Mohammed Messenger of God,
    1977
Warlords of Atlantis, 1978
Henry IV Part 1, 1980

CORAL BROWNE (1913-   )
Australian character actress,
mainly on stage, often seen in
wealthy or sophisticated parts.
Married to Vincent Price.

Charing Cross Road, 1935
Line Engaged, 1935
Guilty Melody, 1936
The Amateur Gentleman, 1936
We're Going to Be Rich, 1938
Black Limelight, 1938
Yellow Sands, 1938
The Nursemaid Who Disap-
    peared, 1939
Let George Do It, 1940
Piccadilly Incident, 1946
The Courtneys of Curzon

Street, 1947
Kathy's Love Affair, 1952
Beautiful Stranger, 1954
Auntie Mame, 1958
Roman Spring of Mrs. Stone,
    1961
Go To Blazes, 1962
Tamahine, 1963
Dr. Crippen, 1964
Night of the Generals, 1966
The Legend of Lylah Clare,
    1968
The Killing of Sister George,
    1968
The Ruling Class, 1972
Theatre of Blood, 1973
The Drowning Pool, 1975

IRENE BROWNE (1891-1965)
Character actress mainly associated with the stage, often
cast in aristocratic or superior
roles.

After Many Days, 1919
The Letter, 1929
Cavalcade, 1933
Berkeley Square, 1933
Christopher Strong, 1933
Peg O' My Heart, 1933
My Lips Betray, 1933
The Amateur Gentleman, 1936
Pygmalion, 1938
The Prime Minister, 1941
Kipps, 1941
Meet Me at Dawn, 1947
Quartet, 1948
The Red Shoes, 1948
The Bad Lord Byron, 1949
Madeleine, 1950
The House in the Square, 1951
All at Sea, 1957
Rooney, 1958
Serious Charge, 1959
The Wrong Arm of the Law,
    1962

BRENDA BRUCE (1918-   )
Star and supporting player
mainly on stage and television;
popular in the 40s.

Millions Like Us, 1943
They Came to a City, 1945
Piccadilly Incident, 1946
Carnival, 1946
I See a Dark Stranger, 1946
Night Boat to Dublin, 1946
While the Sun Shines, 1947
When the Bough Breaks, 1947
My Brother's Keeper, 1948
Marry Me, 1949
Don't Ever Leave Me, 1949
Two On the Tiles, 1951
The Final Test, 1953
Law and Disorder, 1958
Behind the Mask, 1958
Peeping Tom, 1960
Nightmare, 1963
The Uncle, 1965
That'll Be the Day, 1974
All Creatures Great and Small,
    1975
Swallows and Amazons, 1977
Henry IV Part 1, 1980
Henry IV Part 2, 1980
Henry V, 1980

NIGEL BRUCE (1895-1953)
Chubby star of stage and screen,
mainly in Hollywood. Generally
played the bumbling but well-
meaning aristocrat, but is best
and most fondly remembered as
Dr. Watson to Basil Rathbone's
Sherlock Holmes (1939-46).

Red Aces, 1929
Escape, 1930
The Squeaker, 1931
The Calendar, 1931
Lord Camber's Ladies, 1932
The Midshipmaid, 1932
Channel Crossing, 1932
I Was a Spy, 1933
Springtime For Henry, 1934
Stand Up and Cheer, 1934
A Coming Out Party, 1934
Murder in Trinidad, 1934
The Lady is Willing, 1934
Treasure Island, 1934
The Scarlet Pimpernel, 1935
Becky Sharp, 1935
Jalna, 1935

She, 1935
The Man Who Broke the Bank
    at Monte Carlo, 1935
Trail of the Lonesome Pine,
    1936
Under Two Flags, 1936
The White Angel, 1936
Charge of the Light Brigade,
    1936
Follow Your Heart, 1936
Make Way For a Lady, 1936
The Man I Married, 1936
Thunder in the City, 1937
The Last of Mrs. Cheyney,
    1937
The Baroness and the Butler,
    1938
Kidnapped, 1938
Suez, 1938
Hound of the Baskervilles, 1939
The Adventures of Sherlock
    Holmes, 1939
The Rains Came, 1939
Rebecca, 1940
Susan and God, 1940
Adventure in Diamonds, 1940
The Bluebird, 1940
A Dispatch From Reuters, 1940
Hudson's Bay, 1940
Lillian Russell, 1940
Playgirl, 1941
Free and Easy, 1941
The Chocolate Soldier, 1941
This Woman is Mine, 1941
Suspicion, 1941
Roxie Hart, 1942
This Above All, 1942
Eagle Squadron, 1942
Sherlock Holmes and the Voice
    of Terror, 1942
Sherlock Holmes and the Secret
    Weapon, 1942
Journey For Margaret, 1942
Forever and a Day, 1943
Crazy House, 1943
Sherlock Holmes in Washington,
    1943
Sherlock Holmes Faces Death,
    1943
Follow the Boys, 1944
Gypsy Wildcat, 1944
Frenchman's Creek, 1944
The Scarlet Claw, 1944

The Pearl of Death, 1944
The Spider Woman, 1944
The House of Fear, 1945
The Woman in Green, 1945
Pursuit to Algiers, 1945
Son of Lassie, 1945
The Corn is Green, 1945
Terror By Night, 1946
Dressed to Kill, 1946
The Two Mrs. Carrolls, 1947
The Exile, 1947
Julia Misbehaves, 1948
Vendetta, 1950
Hong Kong, 1951
Limelight, 1952
Bwana Devil, 1953
World For Ransom, 1953

TONI EDGAR BRUCE (-)
Character actress of silent and
sound films, also on stage,
sometimes seen in comedy
pictures. Popular in the early
30s.

The Duke's Son, 1920
Charles Augustus Milverton,
 1922
A Warm Corner, 1930
Tell England, 1931
Lucky Girl, 1932
Diamond Cut Diamond, 1932
Mr. Bill the Conqueror, 1932
Brother Alfred, 1932
Falling For You, 1933
Letting in the Sunshine, 1933
Leave it to Me, 1933
Heads We Go, 1933
As Good as New, 1933
The Melody Maker, 1933
Broken Melody, 1934
Whispering Tongues, 1934
Lilies of the Field, 1934
Captain Bill, 1935
Mr. What's His Name, 1935
Handle With Care, 1935
Night Mail, 1935
The Last Waltz, 1936
Behind Your Back, 1937
Boys Will Be Girls, 1937
Scruffy, 1938
The First of the Few, 1942

Gert and Daisy Clean Up, 1942
Somewhere On Leave, 1942
Heaven is Round the Corner,
 1944
Waltz Time, 1945

DORA BRYAN (1924-)
Comedy character actress of
stage (1935) and screen specializing in friendly, warmhearted cockney characters.

Odd Man Out, 1947
The Fallen Idol, 1948
No Room at the Inn, 1948
Once Upon a Dream, 1949
Now Barabbas, 1949
Adam and Evalyne, 1949
Traveller's Joy, 1949
Interrupted Journey, 1949
The Cure For Love, 1950
The Blue Lamp, 1950
No Trace, 1950
Something in the City, 1950
Files From Scotland Yard,
 1951
The Quiet Woman, 1951
Circle of Danger, 1951
Scarlet Thread, 1951
High Treason, 1951
No Highway, 1951
Lady Godiva Rides Again, 1951
Whispering Smith Hits London,
 1952
13 East Street, 1952
The Gift Horse, 1952
Time Gentlemen Please, 1952
Mother Riley Meets the Vam-
 pire, 1952
Made in Heaven, 1952
Women of Twilight, 1952
The Ringer, 1952
Miss Robin Hood, 1952
Street Corner, 1953
The Fake, 1953
The Intruder, 1953
Harmony Lane, 1954
You Know What Sailors Are,
 1954
Fast and Loose, 1954
The Crowded Day, 1954
Mad About Men, 1954

As Long As They're Happy,
   1955
See How They Run, 1955
You Lucky People, 1955
Cockleshell Heroes, 1955
Child in the House, 1956
The Green Man, 1956
The Man Who Wouldn't Talk,
   1958
Carry On Sergeant, 1958
Hello London, 1958
Operation Bullshine, 1959
Desert Mice, 1959
Follow That Horse, 1960
Night We Got the Bird, 1960
A Taste of Honey, 1961
The Great St. Trinian's Train
   Robbery, 1966
The Sandwich Man, 1966
Two a Penny, 1967
Hands of the Ripper, 1971
Up the Front, 1972

MICHAEL BRYANT (1928-   )
Stage, screen and television
actor adept at portraying foreigners.

Life For Ruth, 1962
The Mind Benders, 1963
The Deadly Affair, 1966
Torture Garden, 1967
Goodbye Mr. Chips, 1969
Mumsy, Nanny, Sonny and
   Girly, 1969
Nicholas and Alexandra, 1971
The Ruling Class, 1972
Caravan to Vaccares, 1976

JACK BUCHANAN (1891-1957)
Tall, carefree Scottish-born
song and dance man, also in
Hollywood; on stage from 1912.
Also producer and director.

Auld Lang Syne, 1917
Her Heritage, 1919
The Audacious Mr. Squire,
   1923
The Happy Ending, 1925
Settled Out of Court, 1925

Bulldog Drummond's Third
   Round, 1925
Confetti, 1927
Toni, 1928
Paris, 1929
Show of Shows, 1929
Monte Carlo, 1930
Man of Mayfair, 1931
Goodnight Vienna, 1932
Yes Mr. Brown, 1933
That Girl, 1934
Sons O' Guns, 1935
Brewster's Millions, 1935
Come Out of the Pantry, 1935
That's a Good Girl, 1935
Limelight, 1936
When Knights Were Bold, 1936
Smash and Grab, 1937
This'll Make You Whistle, 1937
The Sky's the Limit, 1937
Sweet Devil, 1938
Break the News, 1938
Cavalcade of the Stars, 1938
Alias the Bulldog, 1939
The Gang's All Here, 1939
The Middle Watch, 1940
Bulldog Sees it Through,
   1940
Some Like it Rough, 1944
Giselle, 1952
The Band Wagon, 1953
As Long As They're Happy,
   1953
Josephine and Men, 1955
The Diary of Major Thompson,
   1956
The French They Are a Funny
   Race, 1957

PETER BULL (1912-   )
Corpulent character star of
stage (since 1933) and screen,
specializing in supercillious
comedy roles.

As You Like It, 1936
Sabotage, 1936
Dreaming Lips, 1937
The Ware Case, 1938
Dead Man's Shoes, 1939
Contraband, 1940
The Grand Escapade, 1946

The Turners of Prospect Road,
 1947
Saraband For Dead Lovers,
 1948
Oliver Twist, 1948
The African Queen, 1951
I'll Get You For This, 1951
The Six Men, 1951
The Lavender Hill Mob, 1951
The Second Mrs. Tanqueray,
 1952
Strange Stories, 1953
The Malta Story, 1953
The Captain's Paradise, 1953
Beau Brummell, 1954
Footsteps in the Fog, 1955
The Green Man, 1956
Tom Thumb, 1958
The Scapegoat, 1959
The Three Worlds of Gulliver,
 1960
The Girl on the Boat, 1961
Goodbye Again, 1961
Follow That Man, 1961
The Rebel, 1961
The Old Dark House, 1963
Tom Jones, 1963
Dr. Strangelove, 1964
Licensed to Kill, 1965
The Intelligence Men, 1965
Dr. Dolittle, 1967
Lock Up Your Daughters, 1969
The Executioner, 1970
Up the Front, 1972
Alice's Adventures in Wonder-
 land, 1972
Lady Caroline Lamb, 1972
Great Expectations, 1975
Joseph Andrews, 1977

AVIS BUNNAGE (-)
Character actress of stage; occasional but excellent films.

Expresso Bongo, 1959
Saturday Night and Sunday
 Morning, 1960
Loneliness of the Long Dis-
 tance Runner, 1962
The L-Shaped Room, 1962
Sparrows Can't Sing, 1963
What a Crazy World, 1963

Tom Jones, 1963
Rotten to the Core, 1965
The Wrong Box, 1966
The Whisperers, 1967
Mrs. Brown, You've Got a
 Lovely Daughter, 1968
Day of Rest, 1970

HUGH BURDEN (1913-)
General-purpose character actor, also on stage.

Death Croons the Blues, 1937
Ships With Wings, 1941
One of Our Aircraft is Missing,
 1942
The Way Ahead, 1944
Fame is the Spur, 1947
Sleeping Car to Trieste, 1948
Ghost Ship, 1952
The Malta Story, 1953
The Secret Partner, 1961
No Love For Johnnie, 1961
Funeral in Berlin, 1966
The Inn Way Out, 1967
The Best House in London,
 1969
The Statue, 1971
Blood From the Mummy's Tomb,
 1971
The Ruling Class, 1972
The House in Nightmare Park,
 1973

ALFRED BURKE (1918-)
Character actor of stage and
screen; mainly seen in dispas-
sionate roles. Also on television in series "The Public
Eye."

Touch and Go, 1956
No Time To Die, 1958
The Man Upstairs, 1958
The Angry Silence, 1960
Moment of Danger, 1960
Dead Lucky, 1960
Man at the Carleton Tower,
 1961
Backfire, 1962
The Pot Carriers, 1962

Mix Me a Person, 1962
The £20,000 Kiss, 1963
Farewell Performance, 1963
The Small World of Sammy
   Lee, 1963
Children of the Damned, 1964
The Nanny, 1965
The Night Caller, 1965
Guns in the Heather, 1969
A Day in the Life of Ivan
   Denisovitch, 1971
The House On Garibaldi Street,
   1979

MARIE BURKE (1894-   )
Star and character actress with
long and distinguished stage career; films sporadic.

Little Miss Rebellion, 1920
The Heart Raider, 1923
Little Old New York, 1923
Three Miles Out, 1924
After the Ball, 1932
Madness of the Heart, 1949
Warning to Wantons, 1949
The Man From Yesterday, 1949
Odette, 1950
The Lavender Hill Mob, 1951
The Flanagan Boy, 1953
The Constant Husband, 1955
The Green Man, 1956
Miracle in Soho, 1957
The Snorkel, 1958
Terror of the Tongs, 1961
Girl in the Headlines, 1963
Rattle of a Simple Man, 1964
Vendetta For the Saint, 1968

PATRICIA BURKE (1917-   )
Character actress, also on
stage; daughter of Marie Burke.

Ship's Concert, 1937
Love Story, 1946
The Trojan Brothers, 1946
Lisbon Story, 1946
While I Live, 1947
Forbidden, 1949
The Happiness of Three Women,
   1954

The Desperate Man, 1959
Spider's Web, 1960
Marriage of Convenience, 1960
The Impersonator, 1961
Dilemma, 1962
Daylight Robbery, 1964
Strangler's Web, 1965
The Day the Fish Came Out, 1967
Soft Beds Hard Battles, 1973

DAVY BURNABY (1881-1949)
Portly, monocled character
comedian and entertainer of
stage (from 1902) and screen.

The Devil's Maze, 1929
The Co-Optimists, 1929
Just My Luck, 1933
The Wishbone, 1933
That's My Wife, 1933
Cleaning Up, 1933
Three Men in a Boat, 1933
The Right to Live, 1933
Strike it Rich, 1933
A Shot in the Dark, 1933
Screen Vaudeville Number One,
   1934
On the Air, 1934
Murder at the Inn, 1934
The Man I Want, 1934
Keep it Quiet, 1934
How's Chances, 1934
Are You a Mason?, 1934
Radio Parade of 1935, 1935
Equity Musical Revue, 1935
Dandy Dick, 1935
We've Got to Have Love, 1935
When the Cat's Away, 1935
Boys Will Be Boys, 1935
While Parents Sleep, 1935
The Marriage of Corbal, 1936
Song of the Road, 1937
Feather Your Nest, 1937
Calling All Stars, 1937
Song of the Forge, 1937
Talking Feet, 1937
Leave it to Me, 1937
Second Best Bed, 1938
Chips, 1938
Kicking the Moon Around, 1938
Many Tanks Mr. Atkins, 1938
Come On George, 1939

MARK BURNS (1936-)
Leading man and second lead
of films of the 60s and 70s,
also on stage.

Tunes of Glory, 1960
Exodus, 1960
A Prize of Arms, 1961
Life at the Top, 1965
The Jokers, 1966
Death is a Woman, 1966
I'll Never Forget Whatsisname,
    1967
Charge of the Light Brigade,
    1968
The Virgin and the Gypsy, 1970
The Adventures of Gerard, 1970
A Day on the Beach, 1970
Death in Venice, 1970
A Time For Loving, 1972
Ludwig, 1972
Juggernaut, 1974
The Maids, 1975
House of the Living Dead, 1977

RICHARD BURTON (1925-)
Dark-haired Welsh leading actor of stage (1943) and screen,
also in Hollywood. Married
Elizabeth Taylor and made a
number of films with her in the
60s.

The Last Days of Dolwyn, 1948
Now Barabbas, 1949
Waterfront, 1950
The Woman With No Name,
    1950
Green Grow the Rushes, 1951
My Cousin Rachel, 1952
The Robe, 1953
The Desert Rats, 1953
Prince of Players, 1954
Thursday's Children, 1954
The Rains of Ranchipur, 1955
Alexander the Great, 1956
Seawife, 1957
Bitter Victory, 1958
The Bramble Bush, 1959
Look Back in Anger, 1959
Ice Palace, 1960
The Longest Day, 1962

Cleopatra, 1962
The VIPs, 1963
Zulu (voice), 1964
The Inheritance, 1964
Becket, 1964
Night of the Iguana, 1964
The Spy Who Came in From
    the Cold, 1965
The Sandpiper, 1965
Who's Afraid of Virginia Woolf?,
    1966
Dr. Faustus, 1967
The Taming of the Shrew, 1967
The Comedians, 1967
Boom!, 1968
Where Eagles Dare, 1968
Candy, 1969
Staircase, 1969
Anne of the Thousand Days,
    1970
Villain, 1971
Under Milk Wood, 1971
Sujeska, 1971
Raid On Rommel, 1971
Hammersmith is Out, 1972
The Assassination of Trotsky,
    1972
Bluebeard, 1972
A Wall in Jerusalem, 1972
Divorce His Divorce Hers,
    1973
Massacre in Rome, 1974
The Gathering Storm, 1974
The Klansman, 1974
The Voyage, 1974
Brief Encounter, 1975
Volcano, 1977
Exorcist II: The Heretic, 1977
Equus, 1977
The Medusa Touch, 1978
The Wild Geese, 1978
Breakthrough, 1979
Tristan and Isolde, 1980

FREDERICK BURTWELL
    (-)
Character actor of the 30s and
40s, also on stage. Popular in
comedy films.

Down Our Street, 1932
Just My Luck, 1933

Path of Glory, 1934
Inside the Room, 1935
Midshipman Easy, 1935
Twelve Good Men, 1936
Laburnum Grove, 1936
Educated Evans, 1936
Rembrandt, 1936
Dr. Syn, 1937
The Vulture, 1937
Feather Your Nest, 1937
It's Not Cricket, 1937
Gypsy, 1937
French Leave, 1937
I See Ice, 1938
Almost a Honeymoon, 1938
Everything Happens to Me,
    1938
Many Tanks Mr. Atkins, 1938
A Girl Must Live, 1939
His Brother's Keeper, 1939
Murder Will Out, 1939
The Stars Look Down, 1939
Confidential Lady, 1939
This Was Paris, 1942
Much Too Shy, 1942
The Silver Fleet, 1943
The Dark Tower, 1943
We Dive at Dawn, 1943
I'll Be Your Sweetheart, 1945
They Knew Mr. Knight, 1945
Gaiety George, 1946
The Laughing Lady, 1946
Nicholas Nickleby, 1947
Uncle Silas, 1947

ANTHONY BUSHELL (1904-   )
Distinguished star of stage
(1924) and screen, also in Hollywood. Latterly also producer,
director, and much on television.

Disraeli, 1929
Show of Shows, 1929
Journey's End, 1930
Three Faces East, 1930
Lovin' the Ladies, 1930
The Flirting Widow, 1930
Five Star Final, 1931
The Royal Bed, 1931
Born to Love, 1931
Chances, 1931
Expensive Women, 1931

A Woman Commands, 1932
Vanity Fair, 1932
Escapade, 1932
The Silver Greyhound, 1932
Sally Bishop, 1932
The Midshipmaid, 1932
Soldiers of the King, 1933
The Ghoul, 1933
I Was a Spy, 1933
Channel Crossing, 1933
Crime on the Hill, 1933
Red Wagon, 1934
Love at Second Sight, 1934
Lilies of the Field, 1934
Forbidden Territory, 1934
The Scarlet Pimpernel, 1935
Admirals All, 1935
Dusty Ermine, 1936
Dark Journey, 1937
Farewell Again, 1937
The Angelus, 1937
Return of the Scarlet Pimper-
    nel, 1937
Rebel Son, 1938
The Lion Has Wings, 1939
The Arsenal Stadium Mystery,
    1939
The Small Back Room, 1948
The Angel With the Trumpet,
    1950
The Miniver Story, 1950
The Long Dark Hall, 1951
High Treason, 1951
Who Goes There?, 1952
The Red Beret, 1953
The Black Knight, 1954
The Purple Plain, 1954
The Black Tent, 1955
Battle of the River Plate, 1956
Bhowani Junction, 1956
Bitter Victory, 1957
The Wind Cannot Read, 1958
A Night to Remember, 1958
Desert Mice, 1959
The Queen's Guards, 1960
Terror of the Tongs, 1961
A Woman's Privilege, 1962

ERNEST BUTCHER (1885-
    1965)
Character actor of stage and
screen who made a career of

portraying ineffectual or harmless characters.

Key to Harmony, 1935
Wedding Eve, 1935
The Small Man, 1935
Lieutenant Daring RN, 1935
Talking Feet, 1937
Song of the Road, 1937
Overcoat Sam, 1937
Stepping Toes, 1938
Meet My Pal, 1939
Pack Up Your Troubles, 1940
Old Mother Riley in Business, 1940
Variety Jubilee, 1943
It's in the Bag, 1943
When We Are Married, 1943
Candles at Nine, 1944
It Happened One Sunday, 1944
Tawny Pipit, 1944
Men of the Mines, 1945
Appointment With Crime, 1946
The Years Between, 1946
Dear Murderer, 1947
While I Live, 1947
My Brother Jonathan, 1948
Meet Simon Cherry, 1949
Time Bomb, 1953
The Desperate Man, 1959

PETER BUTTERWORTH
   (1923-   )
Comedy character of films who
generally plays good-natured
buffoons or bunglers.

William Comes to Town, 1949
The Adventures of Jane, 1949
Murder at the Windmill, 1949
Mr. Drake's Duck, 1950
The Body Said No, 1950
Miss Pilgrim's Progress, 1950
The Case of the Missing Scene, 1951
Old Mother Riley's Jungle
   Treasure, 1951
Appointment With Venus, 1951
Saturday Island, 1952
Penny Princess, 1952
Watch Out, 1953
A Good Pull-Up, 1953

Will Any Gentleman, 1953
Five O'clock Finish, 1954
The Gay Dog, 1954
Playground Express, 1955
Black in the Face, 1955
That's an Order, 1955
Fun at St. Fanny's, 1956
Blow Your Own Trumpet, 1958
Tom Thumb, 1958
The Spider's Web, 1960
Escort For Hire, 1960
Murder She Said, 1962
Fate Takes a Hand, 1962
The Prince and the Pauper, 1962
She'll Have to Go, 1962
Live Now Pay Later, 1962
Kill or Cure, 1963
Horse Without a Head, 1963
The Rescue Squad, 1963
Doctor in Distress, 1963
Never Mention Murder, 1964
A Home of Your Own, 1964
Moll Flanders, 1965
Carry on Cowboy, 1965
Carry on Screaming, 1966
Carry on Don't Lose Your
   Head, 1967
Carry on Follow That Camel, 1967
Danny and the Dragon, 1967
Ouch!, 1967
Carry on Doctor, 1968
Prudence and the Pill, 1968
Carry on Up the Khyber, 1968
Carry on Camping, 1969
Carry on Again Doctor, 1969
Carry on Henry VIII, 1970
The Ritz, 1976
Robin and Marian, 1976

MAX BYGRAVES (1922-   )
Cockney comedian and stage
entertainer who matured into
a fine character star.

Nitwits On Parade, 1949
Bless 'Em All, 1949
Skimpy in the Navy, 1949
Tom Brown's School Days, 1951
Harmony Lane, 1954

Charley Moon, 1956
A Cry From the Streets, 1958
Bobbikins, 1959
Spare the Rod, 1961
The Alf Garnett Saga, 1972

EDDIE BYRNE (1911-   )
Versatile Irish character of
stage and films who is adept
at portraying characters on
either side of the law.

I See a Dark Stranger, 1946
Hungry Hill, 1947
Odd Man Out, 1947
Captain Boycott, 1947
Saints and Sinners, 1949
Lady Godiva Rides Again, 1951
The Gentle Gunman, 1952
Time Gentlemen Please, 1953
The Square Ring, 1953
Albert RN, 1953
Children Galore, 1954
Aunt Clara, 1954
Beautiful Stranger, 1954
Tonight's the Night, 1954
The Sea Shall Not Have Them,
   1955
A Kid For Two Farthings, 1955
Three Cases of Murder, 1955
Trouble in the Glen, 1955
The Divided Heart, 1955
Stolen Assignment, 1955
One Way Out, 1955
The Extra Day, 1956
Reach For the Sky, 1956
It's Great to Be Young, 1956
Seven Waves Away, 1957
Zarak, 1957
The Admirable Crichton, 1957
Man in the Sky, 1957
The Face in the Night, 1957
Wonderful Things, 1958
These Dangerous Years, 1958
Rooney, 1958
Dunkirk, 1958
The Mummy, 1959
The Bridal Path, 1959
Floods of Fear, 1959
The Scapegoat, 1959
Jack the Ripper, 1960
The Shakedown, 1960

The Bulldog Breed, 1960
The Mark, 1961
Johnny Nobody, 1961
Jackpot, 1961
Mutiny On the Bounty, 1962
The Break, 1962
The Pot Carriers, 1962
The Cracksman, 1963
The Punch and Judy Man, 1964
Locker 69, 1964
Devils of Darkness, 1965
Island of Terror, 1966
Mr. Ten Percent, 1966
Gold is Where You Find It,
   1967
Where's Jack?, 1969
Guns in the Heather, 1969
Sinful Davy, 1969
The Mackintosh Man, 1973
Star Wars, 1977

KATHLEEN BYRON (1922-   )
Leading actress of the forties
and latterly character star,
also long stage experience.

The Young Mr. Pitt, 1942
The Silver Fleet, 1943
A Matter of Life and Death,
   1946
Black Narcissus, 1947
The Small Back Room, 1948
Madness of the Heart, 1949
Prelude to Fame, 1949
The Reluctant Widow, 1950
Tom Brown's School Days,
   1951
The Scarlet Thread, 1951
Life in Her Hands, 1951
Hell is Sold Out, 1951
Four Days, 1951
The House in the Square, 1951
My Death is a Mockery, 1952
The Gambler and the Lady,
   1952
Young Bess, 1953
Star of My Night, 1954
Profile, 1954
Night of the Full Moon, 1954
Secret Venture, 1955
Hand in Hand, 1960
Night of the Eagle, 1962

Hammerhead, 1968
Twins of Evil, 1971
Private Road, 1971
Nothing But the Night, 1972
Craze, 1973
The Abdication, 1974
One of Our Dinosaurs is Miss-
    ing, 1976

SEBASTIAN CABOT (1918-
    1977)
Rotound, often bearded character
actor of stage, films and tv.
Often portrayed either kindly or
pompous characters. Popular
in television programs "Checkmate" and as Mr. French on
"Family Affair" in U.S.

Secret Agent, 1936
Love On the Dole, 1941
Pimpernel Smith, 1941
The Agitator, 1945
Othello, 1946
Teheran, 1947
Dual Alibi, 1947
They Made Me a Fugitive, 1947
Third Time Lucky, 1949
Dick Barton Strikes Back, 1949
The Spider and the Fly, 1949
The Adventures of Jane, 1949
Old Mother Riley's New Ven-
    ture, 1949
Old Mother Riley's Jungle
    Treasure, 1950
Midnight Episode, 1950
Laughter in Paradise, 1951
Wonder Kid, 1951
Ivanhoe, 1952
Babes in Bagdad, 1952
Heights of Danger, 1953
The Captain's Paradise, 1953
Always a Bride, 1953
Romeo and Juliet, 1954
The Love Lottery, 1954
Kismet, 1955
Dragoon Wells Massacre, 1957
Johnny Tremain, 1957
Black Patch, 1958
Terror in a Texas Town, 1958
In Love and War, 1958
Say One For Me, 1959

The Angry Hills, 1959
The Time Machine, 1960
Seven Thieves, 1960
Twice Told Tales, 1963
The Family Jewels, 1965

JEAN CADELL (1884-1967)
Dry, sharp-featured Scottish
character actress with long
career on stage and screen,
often seen in vitriolic roles.

David Garrick, 1912
The Man Who Stayed at Home,
    1915
Anna the Adventuress, 1920
Alf's Button, 1920
The Naked Man, 1923
The Loves of Robert Burns,
    1930
Fires of Fate, 1932
Two White Arms, 1932
Timbuctoo, 1933
Little Friend, 1934
Luck of a Sailor, 1934
David Copperfield, 1935
Whom the Gods Love, 1936
Love From a Stranger, 1937
Pygmalion, 1938
Confidential Lady, 1939
Quiet Wedding, 1941
The Young Mr. Pitt, 1942
Dear Octopus, 1943
I Know Where I'm Going, 1945
Jassy, 1947
Whiskey Galore, 1948
That Dangerous Age, 1949
Marry Me, 1949
Madeleine, 1950
No Place For Jennifer, 1950
The Reluctant Widow, 1950
The Late Edwina Black, 1951
I'm a Stranger, 1953
Meet Mr. Lucifer, 1953
Keep it Clean, 1956
The Surgeon's Knife, 1957
Rockets Galore, 1957
The Little Hut, 1957
Let's Be Happy, 1957
Serious Charge, 1959
Upstairs and Downstairs,
    1959

A Taste of Money, 1960
Very Important Person, 1962

MICHAEL CAINE (1933-)
Tall, versatile cockney star of
stage, films and television,
now popular in international
films.

A Hill in Korea, 1956
How to Murder a Rich Uncle,
   1957
The Key, 1958
Blind Spot, 1958
Danger Within, 1959
The Bulldog Breed, 1960
The Day the Earth Caught Fire,
   1961
Solo For Sparrow, 1962
Hamlet, 1964
Zulu, 1964
The Ipcress File, 1965
Alfie, 1966
Gambit, 1966
The Wrong Box, 1966
Funeral in Berlin, 1966
Think 20th, 1967
Billion Dollar Brain, 1967
Woman Times Seven, 1967
Hurry Sundown, 1967
Tonite Let's All Make Love in
   London, 1967
Deadfall, 1968
The Magus, 1968
Play Dirty, 1968
Too Late the Hero, 1969
The Italian Job, 1969
The Battle of Britain, 1969
Simon Simon, 1970
Get Carter, 1970
The Last Valley, 1971
Zee and Co., 1971
Kidnapped, 1971
Pulp, 1972
Sleuth, 1972
The Marseille Contract, 1974
The Black Windmill, 1974
The Destructors, 1974
The Wilby Conspiracy, 1975
The Man Who Would Be King,
   1975
The Romantic Englishwoman,

1975
Peeper, 1976
Harry and Walter Go to New
   York, 1976
A Bridge Too Far, 1977
The Eagle Has Landed, 1977
Silver Bears, 1978
California Suite, 1978
The Swarm, 1978
Ashanti, 1978
Beyond the Poseidon Adventure,
   1979
The Island, 1980
The Hand, 1980
Dressed to Kill, 1980
Escape to Victory, 1980

RICHARD CALDICOT (1908-)
Mild-mannered character actor
of stage, screen and television.

One Good Turn, 1954
The Horse's Mouth, 1958
Clue of the Twisted Candle,
   1960
Court Martial of Major Keller,
   1961
Dentist On the Job, 1961
The Durant Affair, 1962
The Battleaxe, 1962
Weekend Murders, 1972
Eskimo Nell, 1977
Firepower, 1979

KAY CALLARD (-)
Second lead and supporting
player of films, active in the
50s.

They Who Dare, 1954
The Stranger Came Home, 1954
Stolen Assignment, 1955
The Reluctant Bride, 1955
Joe Macbeth, 1955
Find the Lady, 1956
West of Suez, 1957
The Hypnotist, 1957
Man in the Shadow, 1957
Cat Girl, 1957
The Flying Scot, 1957
Undercover Girl, 1958

Escapement, 1958
Intent to Kill, 1958
A Woman Possessed, 1958
The Links of Justice, 1959
The Great Van Robbery, 1959
Top Floor Girls, 1959
Freedom to Die, 1962

DONALD CALTHROP (1888-
   1940)
Prominent character star of
stage (1906) and screen, typically cast in twitching, nasty
or villainous roles.

Wanted a Widow, 1916
The Altar Chains, 1916
Masks and Faces, 1917
The Gay Lord Quex, 1917
Goodbye, 1918
Nelson, 1918
Shooting Stars, 1928
The Flying Squad, 1929
Clue of the New Pin, 1929
Blackmail, 1929
Atlantic, 1929
Juno and the Paycock, 1929
Up the Poll, 1929
The Cockney Spirit in War,
   1930
Elstree Calling, 1930
Song of Soho, 1930
The Night Porter, 1930
Loose Ends, 1930
Two Worlds, 1930
Murder, 1930
Spanish Eyes, 1930
We Take Off Our Hats, 1930
Almost a Honeymoon, 1930
Star Impersonations, 1930
Love Storm, 1931
Cape Forlorn, 1931
Uneasy Virtue, 1931
The Ghost Train, 1931
The Bells, 1931
Many Waters, 1931
Number Seventeen, 1931
Money For Nothing, 1932
F. P. One, 1933
Orders is Orders, 1933
Rome Express, 1933
Fires of Fate, 1933

Early to Bed, 1933
I Was a Spy, 1933
Sorrell and Son, 1933
Friday the 13th, 1933
The Red Ensign, 1934
It's a Cop, 1934
Nine Forty-Five, 1934
This Acting Business, 1934
The Phantom Light, 1935
The Divine Spark, 1935
The Clairvoyant, 1935
Scrooge, 1935
The Man of the Moment, 1935
The Man Behind the Mask,
   1936
Broken Blossoms, 1936
The Man Who Changed His
   Mind, 1936
Love From a Stranger, 1937
Fire Over England, 1937
Cafe Colette, 1937
Dreaming Lips, 1937
Shadow of Death, 1939
The Band Wagon, 1940
Let George Do It, 1940
Charley's Big-Hearted Aunt,
   1940
Major Barbara, 1941

PHYLLIS CALVERT (1915-)
Well-bred leading lady of the
40s, usually seen in romantic
dramas. On stage as dancer
from 1925; also Hollywood.
Married: Peter Murray-Hill.

Two Days to Live, 1939
They Came By Night, 1940
Charley's Big-Hearted Aunt,
   1940
Let George Do It, 1940
Neutral Port, 1940
Inspector Hornleigh Goes to It,
   1941
Kipps, 1941
Uncensored, 1942
The Young Mr. Pitt, 1942
The Man in Grey, 1943
Fanny By Gaslight, 1944
Two Thousand Women, 1944
Madonna of the Seven Moons,
   1945

They Were Sisters, 1945
Men of Two Worlds, 1946
The Magic Bow, 1947
The Root of All Evil, 1947
Time Out of Mind, 1947
My Own True Love, 1948
Broken Journey, 1948
Appointment With Danger, 1949
The Golden Madonna, 1949
The Woman With No Name,
1950
Mr. Denning Drives North,
1951
Mandy, 1952
The Net, 1953
It's Never Too Late, 1956
A Child in the House, 1956
Indiscreet, 1958
A Lady Mislaid, 1958
The Young and the Guilty, 1959
Oscar Wilde, 1960
Battle of the Villa Fiorita,
1965
Twisted Nerve, 1968
Oh What a Lovely War, 1969
The Walking Stick, 1970

EARL CAMERON (1925-)
Jamaican-born star and character actor long in Britain.

Pool of London, 1950
There is Another Sun, 1951
Emergency Call, 1952
The Heart of the Matter, 1953
The Woman For Joe, 1955
Simba, 1955
Dollars For Sale, 1955
Odongo, 1956
Safari, 1956
Accused, 1957
The Heart Within, 1957
Sapphire, 1957
Killers of Kilimanjaro, 1959
No Kidding, 1960
Tarzan the Magnificent, 1960
Flame in the Streets, 1961
Term of Trial, 1962
Guns at Batasi, 1964
Thunderball, 1965
The Sandwich Man, 1966
Two a Penny, 1967

Battle Beneath the Earth, 1968
The Revolutionary, 1970
A Warm December, 1973
Mohammed Messenger of God,
1977
Cuba, 1979

BEATRICE CAMPBELL
(1923-)
Attractive Irish leading actress
of stage and screen, married
to Nigel Patrick.

Wanted For Murder, 1946
Meet Me at Dawn, 1947
The Hangman Waits, 1947
My Brother Jonathan, 1948
Things Happen at Night, 1948
Silent Dust, 1949
No Place For Jennifer, 1950
Last Holiday, 1950
The Mudlark, 1950
Laughter in Paradise, 1951
The House in the Square, 1951
Grand National Night, 1953
The Master of Ballantrae, 1953
Cockleshell Heroes, 1955

JUDY CAMPBELL (1916-)
Leading actress, mainly on
stage (from 1935) and television,
in occasional pictures, primarily of the 40s.

Now You're Talking, 1940
Convoy, 1940
Saloon Bar, 1940
East of Piccadilly, 1941
Breach of Promise, 1941
The World Owes Me a Living,
1945
Green For Danger, 1946
Bonnie Prince Charlie, 1948
There's a Girl in My Soup,
1970
Cry of the Penguins, 1972

ESMA CANNON (-1972)
Tiny character actress seen for
many years in spinsterish roles.

The £5 Man, 1937
The Last Adventurers, 1937
It's in the Air, 1938
Trouble Brewing, 1939
I Met a Murderer, 1939
The Years Between, 1946
Jassy, 1947
Holiday Camp, 1947
Don't Take it to Heart, 1948
The Huggetts Abroad, 1949
Guilt is My Shadow, 1950
Last Holiday, 1950
Double Confession, 1950
The Dam Busters, 1955
Sailor Beware, 1956
No Kidding, 1960
Carry On Regardless, 1961
What a Carve Up!, 1961
Raising the Wind, 1961
Over the Odds, 1961
In the Doghouse, 1961
We Joined the Navy, 1962
The Fast Lady, 1962
On the Beat, 1962
Carry on Cruising, 1962
Nurse On Wheels, 1963
Hide and Seek, 1963
Call Me a Cab, 1963

JAMES CAREW (1876-1938)
Dramatic character actor of
stage (since 1890) and screen,
primarily known for silent films.
Married to Ellen Terry.

The Fool, 1913
The Suffragette, 1913
The Corner House Burglary,
 1914
The Rajah's Tiara, 1914
The Flight of Death, 1914
The Polo Champion, 1915
Justice, 1917
The Profit and the Loss, 1917
Spinner O' Dreams, 1918
Victory and Peace, 1918
Twelve Ten, 1919
The Kinsmen, 1919
The Nature of the Beast, 1919
Sunken Rocks, 1919
Sheba, 1919
The Forest on the Hill, 1919

Anna and the Adventuress, 1920
Alf's Button, 1920
Helen of Four Gates, 1920
Mrs. Erricker's Reputation,
 1920
Wild Heather, 1921
The Narrow Valley, 1921
Dollars in Surrey, 1921
Tansy, 1922
Mr. Justice Raffles, 1922
Mist in the Valley, 1923
Strangling Threads, 1923
The Naked Man, 1923
Comin' Thro' the Rye, 1923
Eugene Aram, 1924
The Wine of Life, 1924
The Drum, 1924
Love Story of Aliette Brunton,
 1924
Owd Bob, 1924
Satan's Sister, 1925
Children of the Night, 1925
One Colombo Night, 1926
A Woman Redeemed, 1927
The King's Highway, 1927
One of the Best, 1927
Love's Option, 1928
A Window in Piccadilly, 1928
The Lady of the Lake, 1928
High Treason, 1929
High Seas, 1929
City of Play, 1929
Guilt, 1931
To Oblige a Lady, 1931
Mischief, 1931
Brother Alfred, 1932
Mayfair Girl, 1932
You Made Me Love You, 1933
Too Many Millions, 1934
Freedom of the Seas, 1934
Oh What a Night, 1935
Who's Your Father?, 1935
Royal Cavalcade, 1935
Love Affair of the Dictator,
 1935
All at Sea, 1935
The Tunnel, 1935
Mystery of the Mary Celeste,
 1935
Come Out of the Pantry, 1935
The Improper Duchess, 1936
Living Dangerously, 1936
Midnight at Madame Tussaud's,

1936
Not Wanted on Voyage, 1936
Wings Over Africa, 1936
You Must Get Married, 1936
Murder at the Cabaret, 1936
David Livingstone, 1936
Strange Experiment, 1937
Thunder in the City, 1937
Jericho, 1937
Rhythm Racketeer, 1937
Glamour Girl, 1938
Dark Sands, 1938

JOYCE CAREY (1898-)
Character actress of stage and
screen, often latterly cast in
snobbish parts.   Also playwright.
Daughter of Lillian Braithwaite.

God and the Man, 1918
Because, 1918
Colonel Newcome the Perfect
   Gentleman, 1921
The Newcomes, 1925
In Which We Serve, 1942
Blithe Spirit, 1945
The Way to the Stars, 1945
Brief Encounter, 1945
The October Man, 1947
London Belongs to Me, 1948
It's Hard to Be Good, 1948
The Chiltern Hundreds, 1949
The Astonished Heart, 1950
Happy Go Lovely, 1951
Cry the Beloved Country, 1952
Street Corner, 1953
Stolen Assignment, 1955
The End of the Affair, 1955
Loser Take All, 1956
Alive and Kicking, 1958
Libel, 1959
The Rough and the Smooth, 1959
Let's Get Married, 1960
Greyfriar's Bobby, 1960
The Naked Edge, 1961
Nearly a Nasty Accident, 1961
Portrait of a Sinner, 1961
The VIPs, 1963
The Eyes of Annie Jones, 1963
A Nice Girl Like Me, 1969
The Black Windmill, 1974
Only a Scream Away, 1974

PATRICK CARGILL (1918-)
Veteran actor of stage and
screen, faultless in character
comedy roles.   Excellent on
tv in series "Father Dear
Father" (1969-75).

Carry On Regardless, 1961
Clue of the Silver Key, 1961
Carry On Jack, 1963
The Hi-Jackers, 1963
The Cracksman, 1963
This is My Street, 1963
A Stitch in Time, 1964
Help!, 1965
The Wrong Box, 1966
A Countess From Hong Kong,
   1967
Inspector Clouseau, 1968
Hammerhead, 1968
Every Home Should Have One,
   1970
The Magic Christian, 1970
Up Pompeii, 1970
Father Dear Father, 1973

VERONICA CARLSON (1944-)
Leading actress of the 60s and
70s, chiefly in horror films.

Smashing Time, 1967
Hammerhead, 1968
Dracula Has Risen From the
   Grave, 1968
Crossplot, 1969
Frankenstein Must be Destroyed,
   1969
The Horror of Frankenstein,
   1970
Pussycat Pussycat I Love You,
   1970
Vampira, 1974
The Ghoul, 1975
Old Dracula, 1975

IAN CARMICHAEL (1920-)
Light leading actor of stage
(since 1939) and screen, adept
at nervous or innocent comedy
roles.   Also outstanding on

television as Dorothy Sayers'
fictional detective Lord Peter
Wimsey.

Bond Street, 1948
Trottie True, 1949
Dear Mr. Prohack, 1949
Betrayed, 1951
The Ghost Ship, 1952
Time Gentlemen Please, 1953
Meet Mr. Lucifer, 1953
The Colditz Story, 1954
Storm Over the Nile, 1955
Simon and Laura, 1955
Private's Progress, 1956
Brothers In Law, 1957
Lucky Jim, 1957
Happy is the Bride, 1958
The Big Money, 1958
I'm All Right, Jack, 1959
Left, Right and Centre, 1959
School For Scoundrels, 1960
Light Up the Sky, 1960
Double Bunk, 1961
The Amorous Prawn, 1962
Heavens Above, 1963
Hide and Seek, 1963
Smashing Time, 1967
The Magnificent 7 Deadly Sins,
   1971
From Beyond the Grave, 1973
Clouds of Witness, 1973
Unpleasantness at the Bellona
   Club, 1973
The Nine Tailors, 1974
Murder Must Advertise, 1975
Five Red Herrings, 1975
The Lady Vanishes, 1980

GEORGE CARNEY (1887-1947)
Character player and occasional
lead of stage and screen adept
at portraying the average man.

Some Waiter, 1916
Television Follies, 1933
Commissionaire, 1933
Say it With Flowers, 1934
Night Club Queen, 1934
Music Hall, 1934
Lest We Forget, 1934
Easy Money, 1934

A Glimpse of Paradise, 1934
Hyde Park, 1934
Flood Tide, 1934
A Real Bloke, 1935
The Small Man, 1935
Variety, 1935
City of Beautiful Nonsense,
   1935
Cock O' the North, 1935
Windfall, 1935
It's in the Bag, 1936
Land Without Music, 1936
Tomorrow We Live, 1936
Beauty and the Barge, 1937
Dreaming Lips, 1937
Father Steps Out, 1937
Little Miss Somebody, 1937
Lancashire Luck, 1937
Easy Riches, 1938
Paid in Error, 1938
Kicking the Moon Around, 1938
Weddings Are Wonderful, 1938
Consider Your Verdict, 1938
Miracles Do Happen, 1938
The Divorce of Lady X, 1938
Young Man's Fancy, 1939
Where's That Fire?, 1939
A Window in London, 1939
Come on George, 1939
The Stars Look Down, 1939
The Briggs Family, 1940
Convoy, 1940
Kipps, 1941
Love On the Dole, 1941
The Common Touch, 1941
Hard Steel, 1942
Lady in Distress, 1942
Unpublished Story, 1942
Rose of Tralee, 1942
Thunder Rock, 1942
In Which We Serve, 1942
The Night Invader, 1943
When We Are Married, 1943
Schweik's New Adventures,
   1943
Tawny Pipit, 1944
Welcome Mr. Washington, 1944
Soldier Sailor, 1944
Waterloo Road, 1945
The Agitator, 1945
I Know Where I'm Going, 1945
Wanted For Murder, 1946
Spring Song, 1946

Woman to Woman, 1946
The Root of All Evil, 1947
The Little Ballerina, 1947
Brighton Rock, 1947
Fortune Lane, 1947
Good Time Girl, 1948

Date at Midnight, 1960
Dr. Crippen, 1962
Panic, 1963
Call Me Bwana, 1963
The Beauty Jungle, 1964
First Men in the Moon, 1964

PAUL CARPENTER (1921-
1964)
Canadian star and character
actor long in Britain; former
singer. Appeared chiefly in
secondary features.

School For Secrets, 1946
Uneasy Terms, 1948
Landfall, 1949
Albert RN, 1953
Johnny On the Spot, 1954
The Weak and the Wicked, 1954
Face the Music, 1954
The House Across the Lake,
1954
The Unholy Four, 1954
Night People, 1954
Five Days, 1954
Duel in the Jungle, 1954
The Stranger Came Home, 1954
The Young Lovers, 1954
Diplomatic Passport, 1955
Shadow of a Man, 1955
The Sea Shall Not Have Them,
1955
One Jump Ahead, 1955
Hornet's Nest, 1955
Doctor at Sea, 1955
Stock Car, 1955
Women Without Men, 1956
Reach For the Sky, 1956
The Narrowing Circle, 1956
Fire Maidens From Outer Space,
1956
Behind the Headlines, 1956
The Iron Petticoat, 1956
No Road Back, 1957
Murder Reported, 1957
The Hypnotist, 1957
Hi-Jack, 1957
Black Ice, 1957
Undercover Girl, 1958
Intent to Kill, 1958
Jet Storm, 1959

JANE CARR (1909-1957)
Leading lady of stage and films,
popular in the thirties.

Love Me, Love My Dog, 1932
Let Me Explain Dear, 1932
Orders is Orders, 1933
Dick Turpin, 1933
Taxi to Paradise, 1933
Lord Edgware Dies, 1934
On the Air, 1934
Oh No Doctor, 1934
Murder at the Inn, 1934
Night Club Queen, 1934
Keep it Quiet, 1934
Those Were the Days, 1934
The Outcast, 1934
The Church Mouse, 1934
Youthful Folly, 1934
The Triumph of Sherlock
Holmes, 1935
Annie Leave the Room, 1935
The Lad, 1935
The Ace of Spades, 1935
Night Mail, 1935
Hello Sweetheart, 1935
Get Off My Foot, 1935
Interrupted Honeymoon, 1936
Million, 1936
Little Miss Somebody, 1937
Captain's Orders, 1937
The Lilac Domino, 1937
The Seventh Survivor, 1941
Alibi, 1942
Lady From Lisbon, 1942
Sabotage at Sea, 1942
It's Not Cricket, 1949
The Saint's Return, 1953
36 Hours, 1954

LEO G. CARROLL (1892-1972)
Distinguished, wry character
star of stage (1911), screen and
television, usually seen as pro-

fessional men. Notable in tv
programs "Topper," "Going My
Way," and as Mr. Waverly in
"The Man From UNCLE. "
Films mainly in Hollywood.

Sadie McGee, 1934
Outcast Lady, 1934
The Right to Live, 1934
The Barretts of Wimpole Street,
  1934
Clive of India, 1935
Stamboul Quest, 1935
Murder On a Honeymoon, 1935
The Casino Murder Case, 1935
London By Night, 1937
A Christmas Carol, 1938
Elizabeth the Queen, 1939
Wuthering Heights, 1939
Tower of London, 1939
Bulldog Drummond's Secret
  Police, 1939
Charlie Chan's Murder Cruise,
  1939
Charlie Chan in City in Dark-
  ness, 1939
Rebecca, 1940
Waterloo Bridge, 1940
Scotland Yard, 1941
Suspicion, 1941
This Woman is Mine, 1941
Bahama Passage, 1942
Spellbound, 1945
The House On 92nd Street,
  1945
Forever Amber, 1947
Song of Love, 1947
Time Out of Mind, 1947
So Evil My Love, 1948
The Paradine Case, 1948
Enchantment, 1948
The Happy Years, 1950
Father of the Bride, 1950
The First Legion, 1951
Strangers on a Train, 1951
Rommel-Desert Fox, 1951
The Snows of Kilimanjaro, 1952
Rogue's March, 1953
The Bad and the Beautiful,
  1953
Young Bess, 1953
Treasure of the Golden Con-
  dor, 1953

Tarantula, 1955
The Swan, 1956
We're No Angels, 1958
North By Northwest, 1959
The Parent Trap, 1961
One Plus One, 1961
The Prize, 1963
One Spy Too Many, 1966
The Spy With My Face, 1966
The Karate Killers, 1967
From Nashville With Music,
  1969

MADELEINE CARROLL
  (1906-)
Beautiful blonde leading lady of
stage (since 1927) and screen,
generally cast in well-bred,
ladylike roles. In Hollywood
from 1936.

The Guns of Loos, 1928
The First Born, 1928
What Money Can Buy, 1928
The Crooked Billet, 1929
The American Prisoner, 1929
Atlantic, 1929
The W Plan, 1930
Young Woodley, 1930
French Leave, 1930
Escape, 1930
Kissing Cup's Race, 1930
School For Scandal, 1930
Madame Guillotine, 1930
Fascination, 1931
The Written Law, 1931
Peace or War, 1933
Speeding Car, 1933
I Was a Spy, 1933
The World Moves On, 1934
Love Affair of the Dictator,
  1935
The Thirty-Nine Steps, 1935
Secret Agent, 1936
The Story of Papworth, 1936
The Case Against Mrs. Ames,
  1936
The General Died at Dawn,
  1936
Lloyds of London, 1936
On the Avenue, 1937
The Prisoner of Zenda, 1937

It's All Yours, 1938
Blockade, 1938
Honeymoon in Bali, 1939
Cafe Society, 1939
My Son My Son, 1940
Safari, 1940
Northwest Mounted Police,
    1940
Virginia, 1941
One Night in Lisbon, 1941
Bahama Passage, 1942
My Favorite Blonde, 1942
White Cradle Inn, 1947
Don't Trust Your Husband,
    1948
The Fan, 1949

CHARLES CARSON (1885-)
Distinguished, prolific character star of stage and screen
who had been portraying elderly
gentlemen in films for nearly
50 years.

Dreyfus, 1931
Ariane, 1931
Many Waters, 1931
The Chinese Puzzle, 1932
Marry Me, 1932
Leap Year, 1932
There Goes the Bride, 1932
The Blarney Stone, 1933
Trouble in Store, 1934
Whispering Tongues, 1934
The Perfect Flaw, 1934
No Escape, 1934
Father and Son, 1934
Blossom Time, 1934
Hyde Park, 1934
Blind Justice, 1934
Broken Melody, 1934
D'Ye Ken John Peel?, 1935
Sanders of the River, 1935
Invitation to the Waltz, 1935
Men of Tomorrow, 1935
Scrooge, 1935
Abdul the Damned, 1935
Moscow Nights, 1935
Head Office, 1936
Secret Agent, 1936
Forget Me Not, 1936
Talk of the Devil, 1936

Beloved Vagabond, 1936
Once in a Million, 1936
Things to Come, 1936
Dark Journey, 1937
Victoria the Great, 1937
The Frog, 1937
Cafe Colette, 1937
The Angelus, 1937
Dreaming Lips, 1937
Fire Over England, 1937
Glamorous Night, 1937
Old Mother Riley, 1937
Saturday Night Revue, 1937
We're Going to Be Rich, 1938
Sixty Glorious Years, 1938
Oh Boy, 1938
No Parking, 1938
Return of the Frog, 1938
The Saint in London, 1939
The Gang's All Here, 1939
Quiet Wedding, 1940
Penn of Pennsylvania, 1941
The Common Touch, 1941
They Flew Alone, 1942
Battle For Music, 1943
The Dummy Talks, 1943
Pink String & Sealing Wax,
    1945
Cry the Beloved Country, 1952
The Master of Ballantrae, 1953
Beau Brummell, 1954
The Dam Busters, 1955
The Silken Affair, 1956
Reach For the Sky, 1956
Bobbikins, 1959
A Touch of Larceny, 1959
The Trials of Oscar Wilde,
    1960
A Story of David, 1960
Macbeth, 1961
Curse of the Fly, 1965
Lady Caroline Lamb, 1972

JEANNIE CARSON (1928-)
Ebullient star of stage, films
and television who retired after
short career. On tv in series
"Hey Jeannie!" (1956). Infrequent films.

Love in Pawn, 1953
As Long as They're Happy,

1954
An Alligator Named Daisy,
1955
Rockets Galore, 1957
Seven Keys, 1962

GERALD CASE (-)
Classical character actor of
stage and, occasionally, films.

Museum Mystery, 1937
In Which We Serve, 1942
Henry V, 1944
Jean's Plan, 1946
Night Boat to Dublin, 1946
The Dancing Years, 1950
Assassin For Hire, 1951
Home at Seven, 1952
The Fake, 1953
Candlelight Murder, 1953
Night Plane to Amsterdam,
1955
The Flying Scot, 1957
The Carringford School Mystery,
1958
Accidental Death, 1963
The Third Secret, 1964

SIR LEWIS CASSON (1875-
1969)
Distinguished actor and manager, mainly on stage, long
married to Dame Sybil Thorndike.

The Merchant of Venice, 1927
Escape, 1930
Crime On the Hill, 1933
Night Club Queen, 1934
Little Friend, 1934
Midshipman Easy, 1935
Rhodes of Africa, 1936
Calling the Tune, 1936
Victoria the Great, 1937
South Riding, 1938
Sixty Glorious Years, 1938
The Winslow Boy, 1948
Shake Hands With the Devil,
1959

ROY CASTLE (1933-)
Stage entertainer in very occasional films.

Hello London, 1959
Dr. Terror's House of Horrors,
1965
Dr. Who and the Daleks, 1966
Carry On Up the Khyber, 1968
Legend of the Werewolf, 1975

PAUL CAVANAGH (1895-1964)
Debonair star and character
player of stage and screen, in
Hollywood from the late 20s.
Played villains and titled aris-
tocrats with equal skill.

Tesha, 1928
Two Little Drummer Boys,
1928
A Woman in the Night, 1929
The Runaway Princess, 1929
Grumpy, 1930
The Storm, 1930
The Devil to Pay, 1930
Strictly Unconventional, 1930
Unfaithful, 1931
Born to Love, 1931
Always Goodbye, 1931
Transgression, 1931
Heartbreak, 1931
Menace, 1931
The Squaw Man, 1931
The Devil's Lottery, 1932
A Bill of Divorcement, 1932
The Crash, 1932
Tonight is Ours, 1933
The Kennel Murder Case, 1933
Tarzan and His Mate, 1934
The Notorious Sophie Lang,
1934
The Sin of Nora Moran, 1934
Shoot the Works, 1934
Goin' to Town, 1935
Splendor, 1935
Champagne Charlie, 1936
Crime Over London, 1936
Cafe Colette, 1937
A Romance in Flanders, 1937
Reno, 1939
Within the Law, 1939

The Under-Pup, 1939
I Take This Woman, 1940
The Case of the Black Parrot, 1940
Maisie Was a Lady, 1941
Captains of the Clouds, 1942
Eagle Squadron, 1942
The Strange Case of Dr. RX, 1942
Pacific Rendezvous, 1942
The Hard Way, 1943
The Gorilla Man, 1943
Maisie Goes to Reno, 1944
Marriage is a Private Affair, 1944
The Scarlet Claw, 1944
The House of Fear, 1945
The Woman in Green, 1945
The Man in Half Moon Street, 1945
Night in Paradise, 1946
Night and Day, 1946
The Verdict, 1946
Humoresque, 1946
Ivy, 1947
Dishonored Lady, 1947
Secret Beyond the Door, 1948
The Babe Ruth Story, 1948
The Black Arrow, 1948
You Gotta Stay Happy, 1948
The Iroquois Trail, 1950
Hollywood Story, 1951
Son of Dr. Jekyll, 1951
The Strange Door, 1951
The Golden Hawk, 1952
Mississippi Gambler, 1952
The Plymouth Adventure, 1952
Port Sinister, 1953
House of Wax, 1953
Bandits of Corsica, 1953
All American, 1953
The Iron Glove, 1954
The Raid, 1954
Khyber Patrol, 1954
Magnificent Obsession, 1954
Casanova's Big Night, 1954
The Scarlet Coat, 1955
The King's Thief, 1955
The Purple Mask, 1955
The Prodigal, 1956
Francis in the Haunted House, 1956
Diane, 1957

The Four Skulls of Jonathan Drake, 1959

JONATHAN CECIL (1939-   )
Comedy actor in occasional films, generally seen in bumbling or ineffectual characterizations.

The Yellow Rolls-Royce, 1964
Otley, 1968
The Private Life of Sherlock Holmes, 1970
Barry Lyndon, 1975

FRANK CELLIER (1884-1948)
Character actor of stage and screen, often portrayed frowning, cold, or unsympathetic types.

Her Reputation, 1931
Tin Gods, 1932
Hearts of Oak, 1933
The Fire Raisers, 1933
The Golden Cage, 1933
Doss House, 1933
Soldiers of the King, 1933
Colonel Blood, 1934
The Woman in Command, 1934
Love Affair of the Dictator, 1935
Lorna Doone, 1935
The Guvnor, 1935
The Thirty-Nine Steps, 1935
Passing of the Third Floor Back, 1936
Rhodes of Africa, 1936
Tudor Rose, 1936
The Man Who Changed His Mind, 1936
OHMS, 1937
Action For Slander, 1937
Take My Tip, 1937
Non-Stop New York, 1937
Sixty Glorious Years, 1938
The Ware Case, 1938
Kate Plus Ten, 1938
A Royal Divorce, 1938
The Spider, 1939
The Midas Touch, 1939

Cottage to Let, 1941
The Black Sheep of Whitehall, 1941
Quiet Wedding, 1941
Love On the Dole, 1941
Ships With Wings, 1941
The Big Blockade, 1942
Give Us the Moon, 1944
Quiet Weekend, 1946
The Magic Bow, 1947
The Blind Goddess, 1948
Easy Money, 1948

CYRIL CHAMBERLAIN (1909-   )
Veteran character actor of stage and screen, usually cast as the common man or other small roles.

This Man in Paris, 1939
Poison Pen, 1939
Jailbirds, 1939
What Would You Do Chums?, 1939
Old Mother Riley in Business, 1940
Night Watch, 1941
The Upturned Glass, 1947
Dancing With Crime, 1947
London Belongs to Me, 1948
Stop Press Girl, 1949
Boys in Brown, 1949
Blackmailed, 1951
Old Mother Riley's Jungle Treasure, 1951
The Lavender Hill Mob, 1951
Scarlet Thread, 1951
Sing Along With Me, 1952
The Net, 1953
Out of the Bandbox, 1953
Trouble in Store, 1953
The Diamond, 1954
The Embezzler, 1954
Impulse, 1955
Tiger By the Tail, 1955
Windfall, 1955
Simon and Laura, 1955
Wall of Death, 1956
Up in the World, 1956
The Green Man, 1956
The Tommy Steele Story, 1957

Carry On Sergeant, 1958
A Night to Remember, 1958
Wonderful Things, 1958
Man With a Gun, 1958
Blue Murder at St. Trinian's, 1958
Carry On Nurse, 1959
Carry On Teacher, 1959
Carry On Constable, 1960
No Kidding, 1960
Two-Way Stretch, 1960
The Dover Road Mystery, 1960
Carry On Regardless, 1961
Dentist on the Job, 1961
Nearly a Nasty Accident, 1961
Pure Hell of St. Trinian's, 1961
Flame in the Streets, 1961
Carry On Cruising, 1962

NAOMI CHANCE (1930-   )
Distinctive leading lady of the fifties, also on stage.

Wings of Danger, 1952
It Started in Paradise, 1952
The Gambler and the Lady, 1952
Blood Orange, 1953
The Saint's Return, 1953
Strange Stories, 1953
Dangerous Voyage, 1954
End of the Road, 1954
A Touch of the Sun, 1956
Suspended Alibi, 1957
The Man Inside, 1958
Operation Bullshine, 1959
The Trials of Oscar Wilde, 1960
The Comedy Man, 1963
He Who Rides a Tiger, 1965

EDWARD CHAPMAN (1901-1977
Tough, dependable star character player of stage and screen, often seen as bulldog types. Portrayed northerners and sometimes villains as well.

Juno and the Paycock, 1929

Murder, 1930
Caste, 1930
The Skin Game, 1931
Tilly of Bloomsbury, 1931
The Flying Squad, 1932
Happy Ever After, 1932
The Queen's Affair, 1933
Guest of Honour, 1934
The Church Mouse, 1934
Blossom Time, 1934
Girls Will Be Boys, 1934
Mr. Cinders, 1934
The Divine Spark, 1935
Things to Come, 1936
Someone at the Door, 1936
The Man Who Could Work
    Miracles, 1936
Rembrandt, 1936
Who Killed John Savage?, 1937
April Romance, 1937
I've Got a Horse, 1938
Marigold, 1938
Premiere, 1938
The Citadel, 1938
The Nursemaid Who Disappeared,
    1939
The Four Just Men, 1939
There Aint No Justice, 1939
Poison Pen, 1939
Inspector Hornleigh on Holiday,
    1939
The Proud Valley, 1940
Now You're Talking, 1940
The Briggs Family, 1940
Law and Disorder, 1940
Convoy, 1940
Goofer Trouble, 1940
Inspector Hornleigh Goes to It,
    1941
Eating Out With Tommy, 1941
Turned Out Nice Again, 1941
Jeannie, 1941
Ships With Wings, 1941
They Flew Alone, 1942
Journey Together, 1945
The Wild Heart, 1947
The October Man, 1947
It Always Rains on Sunday,
    1947
Man on the Run, 1949
The Spider and the Fly, 1949
Mr. Perrin and Mr. Traill,
    1949

The History of Mr. Polly, 1949
Trio, 1950
Madeleine, 1950
Night and the City, 1950
Gone to Earth, 1950
The Magic Box, 1951
His Excellency, 1952
The Card, 1952
Mandy, 1952
The Ringer, 1952
Folly to Be Wise, 1952
A Day to Remember, 1953
The Intruder, 1953
Point of No Return, 1953
The Crowded Day, 1954
End of the Road, 1954
The Love Match, 1955
A Yank in Ermine, 1955
Lisbon, 1956
Bhowani Junction, 1956
X The Unknown, 1956
Doctor at Large, 1957
Just My Luck, 1957
Innocent Sinners, 1958
Young and the Guilty, 1958
The Square Peg, 1958
Rough and the Smooth, 1959
School For Scoundrels, 1960
Oscar Wilde, 1960
The Bulldog Breed, 1960
Hide and Seek, 1963
A Stitch in Time, 1963
The Early Bird, 1965
Joey Boy, 1965
The Man Who Haunted Himself,
    1970

JOHN CHARLESWORTH (1935-
    1960)
Juvenile supporting player of
the 50s.

The Magic Box, 1951
Tom Brown's School Days, 1951
Scrooge, 1951
John of the Fair, 1952
The Oracle, 1953
Blue Peter, 1955
Yangtse Incident, 1957
Five on a Treasure Island,
    1957
Blonde Sinner, 1957

The Adventures of Hal, 1958
The Man Upstairs, 1959
No Safety Ahead, 1959
The Angry Silence, 1960
So Evil So Young, 1960
Dead Lucky, 1960
Date at Midnight, 1960

HELEN CHERRY (1915-)
Beautiful, dignified actress
mainly on stage (since 1938),
married to Trevor Howard.

The Courtneys of Curzon Street,
   1947
The Mark of Cain, 1948
For Them That Trespass, 1949
Adam and Evalyn, 1949
Morning Departure, 1950
They Were Not Divided, 1950
Last Holiday, 1950
The Woman With No Name,
   1950
Young Wives' Tale, 1951
His Excellency, 1952
Castle in the Air, 1952
Three Cases of Murder, 1955
High Flight, 1957
The Naked Edge, 1961
Tomorrow at Ten, 1962
The Devil's Agent, 1962
Flipper's New Adventure, 1964
Charge of the Light Brigade,
   1968
Hard Contract, 1969
11 Harrowhouse, 1974
Conduct Unbecoming, 1975
No Longer Alone, 1978

ERIK CHITTY (-)
Aged, small-part character actor of the 60s and 70s.

The Devil's Disciple, 1959
Day They Robbed the Bank of
   England, 1960
The Horror of it All, 1964
First Men in the Moon, 1964
Dr. Zhivago, 1965
Ouch!, 1967
A Nice Girl Like Me, 1969

Twinky, 1969
Anne of the Thousand Days,
   1970
Lust For a Vampire, 1970
The Statue, 1970
The Railway Children, 1971
Vault of Horror, 1973
Great Expectations, 1975
The Seven Percent Solution,
   1976
A Bridge Too Far, 1977

JULIE CHRISTIE (1941-)
Beautiful blonde leading lady of
stage (1957) and screen, popular in the 60s. Also in Hollywood.

Crooks Anonymous, 1962
The Fast Lady, 1962
Billy Liar, 1963
Young Cassidy, 1964
Darling, 1965
Dr. Zhivago, 1965
Fahrenheit 451, 1966
Far From the Madding Crowd,
   1967
Tonite Let's All Make Love in
   London, 1967
Petulia, 1968
In Search of Gregory, 1970
The Go-Between, 1971
McCabe and Mrs. Miller, 1971
Don't Look Now, 1973
Shampoo, 1975
The Demon Seed, 1977
Heaven Can Wait, 1978
Memoirs of a Survivor, 1980

BELLE CHRYSTALL (1910-)
Dark-haired leading lady of the
thirties.

A Warm Corner, 1930
Hindle Wakes, 1931
Hobson's Choice, 1931
The Frightened Lady, 1932
Friday the Thirteenth, 1933
Youthful Folly, 1934
The Scotland Yard Mystery,
   1934

The Girl in the Flat, 1934
Key to Harmony, 1935
Edge of the World, 1937
Follow Your Star, 1938
Yellow Sands, 1938
Breakers Ahead, 1938
Anything to Declare, 1938
Poison Pen, 1939
House of the Arrow, 1940

DIANA CHURCHILL (1913-)
Leading actress of the thirties,
mainly on stage; married to
Mervyn Johns.

Sally Bishop, 1932
Foreign Affaires, 1935
Pot Luck, 1936
Dishonour Bright, 1936
Sensation, 1937
The Dominant Sex, 1937
School For Husbands, 1937
Housemaster, 1938
Jane Steps Out, 1938
Yes Madam, 1938
The Spider, 1939
Law and Disorder, 1940
The Flying Squad, 1940
The House of the Arrow, 1940
Eagle Squadron, 1942
Scott of the Antarctic, 1948
The History of Mr. Polly, 1949
A Winter's Tale, 1968
Nashville, 1975

DONALD CHURCHILL
   (1930-)
Light actor, usually seen in
nervous, secondary roles; films
very occasional. Also television writer.

Victim, 1961
The Wild Affair, 1964
Spaceflight IC1, 1965
The Space Tyres, 1967

SARAH CHURCHILL (1914-)
Pretty stage (from 1936) and
screen actress, also in Holly-

wood. Daughter of Sir Winston
Churchill; also author of poetry
books.

Who's Your Lady Friend?,
   1937
Spring Meeting, 1941
He Found a Star, 1941
Daniele Cortis, 1947
All Over Town, 1949
Royal Wedding, 1951
When in Rome, 1952
Serious Charge, 1959
Churchill the Man, 1973

DIANE CILENTO (1933-)
Attractive, adaptable Australian
actress of stage (since 1949)
and films, also novelist. Formerly married to Sean Connery.

Wings of Danger, 1952
All Hallowe'en, 1953
The Passing Stranger, 1954
The Angel Who Pawned Her
   Harp, 1955
Passage Home, 1955
A Woman For Joe, 1955
The Admirable Crichton, 1957
The Truth About Women, 1958
Jet Storm, 1959
The Full Treatment, 1961
The Naked Edge, 1961
I Thank a Fool, 1962
The Breaking Point, 1962
Tom Jones, 1963
The Third Secret, 1964
Rattle of a Simple Man, 1964
The Agony and the Ecstasy,
   1965
Hombre, 1966
Once Upon a Tractor, 1967
You Only Live Twice, 1967
Negatives, 1968
Z. P. G. , 1972
The Wicker Man, 1973
Hitler: The Last Ten Days,
   1973
Tiger Lily, 1975

MARY CLARE (1894-1970)
Dominant character star of
stage (from 1910) and screen,
used to best advantage in evil
or overbearing roles.

The Black Spider, 1920
The Skin Game, 1920
The Prince of Lovers, 1922
Foolish Monte Carlo, 1922
The Gypsy Cavalier, 1922
The Lights of London, 1923
Becket, 1924
Packing Up, 1927
The Constant Nymph, 1928
The Princess in the Tower,
   1928
The Feather, 1929
Shadows, 1931
The Outsider, 1931
Keepers of Youth, 1931
Hindle Wakes, 1931
Gypsy Blood, 1931
Many Waters, 1931
Bill's Legacy, 1931
The Constant Nymph, 1933
Say it With Flowers, 1933
Night Club Queen, 1934
Jew Suss, 1934
Lorna Doone, 1935
A Real Bloke, 1935
The Clairvoyant, 1935
Passing of the 3rd Floor Back,
   1935
The Guvnor, 1936
Line Engaged, 1936
The Mill on the Floss, 1937
The Rat, 1937
Young and Innocent, 1937
Our Royal Heritage, 1937
The Challenge, 1938
The Lady Vanishes, 1938
Climbing High, 1938
The Citadel, 1938
A Girl Must Live, 1939
There Aint No Justice, 1939
Mrs. Pym of Scotland Yard,
   1939
On the Night of the Fire, 1939
The Briggs Family, 1940
Miss Grant Goes to the Door,
   1940
Old Bill and Son, 1940

The Fugitive, 1940
This Man is Dangerous, 1941
The Night Has Eyes, 1942
Next of Kin, 1942
The Hundred Pound Window,
   1944
One Exciting Night, 1944
Fiddlers Three, 1944
London Town, 1946
Mrs. Fitzherbert, 1947
The Three Weird Sisters, 1948
My Brother Jonathan, 1948
Oliver Twist, 1948
Esther Waters, 1948
Cardboard Cavalier, 1949
Portrait of Clare, 1950
The Black Rose, 1950
Penny Princess, 1952
Hindle Wakes, 1952
Moulin Rouge, 1952
The Beggar's Opera, 1953
Mambo, 1955
The Price of Silence, 1960

O. B. CLARENCE (1870-1955)
Character actor with long stage
experience; generally seen in
kindly, senile or eccentric
parts.

Liberty Hall, 1914
London Pride, 1920
The Little Hour of Peter Wells,
   1920
The Man From Chicago, 1930
Keepers of Youth, 1931
The Bells, 1931
Where is This Lady?, 1932
The Barton Mystery, 1932
The Flag Lieutenant, 1932
Goodnight Vienna, 1932
Discord, 1933
Excess Baggage, 1933
Soldiers of the King, 1933
The Only Girl, 1933
Falling For You, 1933
His Grace Gives Notice, 1933
A Shot in the Dark, 1933
I Adore You, 1933
Eyes of Fate, 1933
Perfect Understanding, 1933
Friday the 13th, 1933

Heart Song, 1934
The Silver Spoon, 1934
The Double Event, 1934
Song at Eventide, 1934
Father and Son, 1934
The Great Defender, 1934
The King of Paris, 1934
Lady in Danger, 1934
The Feathered Serpent, 1934
The Scarlet Pimpernel, 1935
The Private Secretary, 1935
Squibs, 1935
Barnacle Bill, 1935
Captain Bill, 1935
No Monkey Business, 1935
All In, 1936
Seven Sinners, 1936
King of Hearts, 1936
The Cardinal, 1936
East Meets West, 1936
Return of the Scarlet Pimpernel,
   1937
The Mill On the Floss, 1937
Pygmalion, 1938
It's in the Air, 1938
Old Iron, 1938
Me and My Pal, 1939
Saloon Bar, 1940
Return to Yesterday, 1940
Spy For a Day, 1940
Black Eyes, 1940
Old Mother Riley in Business,
   1940
Inspector Hornleigh Goes to It,
   1941
Penn of Pennsylvania, 1941
Quiet Wedding, 1941
Turned Out Nice Again, 1941
Old Mother Riley's Circus,
   1941
Front Line Kids, 1942
On Approval, 1944
A Place of One's Own, 1944
Great Expectations, 1946
Uncle Silas, 1947
Meet Me at Dawn, 1947
While the Sun Shines, 1947

ERNEST CLARK (1912-)
Character star of stage, screen
and television, often portrays
unsympathetic or stern characters.

Private Angelo, 1949
Father Brown, 1954
Doctor in the House, 1954
Beau Brummell, 1954
The Dam Busters, 1955
1984, 1956
The Baby and the Battleship, 1956
Time Without Pity, 1957
Man in the Sky, 1957
The Safecracker, 1958
A Tale of Two Cities, 1958
Woman of Mystery, 1958
Blind Spot, 1958
A Touch of Larceny, 1959
Sink the Bismarck, 1960
Partners in Crime, 1961
Three On a Spree, 1961
Time to Remember, 1962
Tomorrow at Ten, 1962
A Woman's Privilege, 1962
Master Spy, 1963
A Stitch in Time, 1963
Devil Ship Pirates, 1964
Boy With a Flute, 1964
Nothing But the Best, 1964
Cuckoo Patrol, 1965
Finders Keepers, 1966
Arabesque, 1966
It, 1966
Attack on the Iron Coast, 1968
Salt and Pepper, 1968
Run a Crooked Mile, 1969
The Executioner, 1970

JAMESON CLARK (-)
Scotch character actor of stage
and films, often in cameo roles.

Whiskey Galore, 1948
The Brave Don't Cry, 1952
Laxdale Hall, 1953
The Kidnappers, 1953
The Maggie, 1954
Geordie, 1955
The High Terrace, 1956
Bond of Fear, 1956
X The Unknown, 1956
The Key, 1957
The 39 Steps, 1959
Beyond This Place, 1959
Battle of the Sexes, 1959
A Pair of Briefs, 1962
Ring of Bright Water, 1969

PETULA CLARK (1932-)
Former radio performer (1941)
and actress of films and television who became a popular
singer during the 60s and 70s.

Medal For the General, 1944
Murder in Reverse, 1945
I Know Where I'm Going, 1945
Strawberry Roan, 1945
Trouble at Townsend, 1946
London Town, 1946
Vice Versa, 1947
Easy Money, 1948
Here Come the Huggetts, 1948
Vote For Huggett, 1949
The Huggetts Abroad, 1949
Don't Ever Leave Me, 1949
The Romantic Age, 1949
Dance Hall, 1950
White Corridors, 1951
Madame Louise, 1951
The Card, 1952
Made in Heaven, 1952
The Runaway Bus, 1954
The Gay Dog, 1954
The Happiness of Three Women,
   1954
Track the Man Down, 1955
That Woman Opposite, 1957
The 6. 5 Special, 1958
Daggers Drawn, 1964
Finian's Rainbow, 1968
Goodbye Mr. Chips, 1969

D. A. CLARKE-SMITH (1888-
   1959)
Popular character star of the
30s, also on stage.

Atlantic, 1929
Shadows, 1931
Bracelets, 1931
The Old Man, 1931
Peace and Quiet, 1931
Michael and Mary, 1931
A Letter of Warning, 1932
A Voice Said Goodnight, 1932
Help Yourself, 1932
Illegal, 1932
White Face, 1932
The Frightened Lady, 1932

Friday the 13th, 1933
The Laughter of Fools, 1933
Head of the Family, 1933
Mayfair Girl, 1933
Skipper of the Osprey, 1933
Turkey Time, 1933
The Thirteenth Candle, 1933
I'm an Explosive, 1933
High Finance, 1933
Follow the Lady, 1933
Smithy, 1933
The Good Companions, 1933
Waltz Time, 1933
The Ghoul, 1933
Warn London, 1934
The Man Who Knew Too Much,
   1934
Menace, 1934
Flat No. 3, 1934
Keep it Quiet, 1934
Designing Women, 1934
A Cup of Kindness, 1934
Passing Shadows, 1934
The Perfect Flaw, 1934
Money Mad, 1934
The Feathered Serpent, 1934
Royal Cavalcade, 1935
Lorna Doone, 1935
Key to Harmony, 1935
Sabotage, 1936
The Happy Family, 1936
Murder by Rope, 1936
Southern Roses, 1936
Cafe Colette, 1937
Splinters in the Air, 1937
Little Miss Somebody, 1937
Dangerous Fingers, 1937
I've Got a Horse, 1938
The Flying Fifty-Five, 1939
Freida, 1947
Quo Vadis, 1951
Something Money Can't Buy,
   1952
The Sword and the Rose, 1953
The Baby & the Battleship,
   1956

JOHN CLEESE (1939-)
Tall comedian, primarily on
television, member of the
"Monty Python" gang.

Interlude, 1968
The Bliss of Mrs. Blossom, 1968
The Best House in London, 1969
The Magic Christian, 1970
The Rise & Rise of Michael
    Rimmer, 1970
The Statue, 1970
And Now For Something Com-
    pletely Different, 1971
The Love Ban, 1972
Monty Python and the Holy
    Grail, 1975
Monty Python Meets Beyond
    the Fringe, 1978
The Life of Brian, 1979
The Taming of the Shrew, 1980

SIR JOHN CLEMENTS (1910-)
Distinguished actor, mainly on
stage (since 1930), married to
Kay Hammond.

No Quarter, 1934
Once in a New Moon, 1935
The Divine Spark, 1935
Things to Come, 1936
Ticket of Leave, 1936
Rembrandt, 1936
I Claudius, 1937
Knight Without Armour, 1937
South Riding, 1938
Star of the Circus, 1938
The Four Feathers, 1939
The Housemaster, 1939
Convoy, 1940
This England, 1941
Ships With Wings, 1941
Tomorrow We Live, 1942
Undercover, 1943
They Came to a City, 1944
Call of the Blood, 1948
Train of Events, 1949
The Silent Enemy, 1958
The Mind Benders, 1962
Oh What a Lovely War, 1969

LADDIE CLIFF (1891-1937)
Songwriter and light character
comedian of the 30s, in very
occasional films.

The Co-Optimists, 1929
The Sleeping Car, 1933
Happy, 1934
Sporting Love, 1936
Over She Goes, 1937

COLIN CLIVE (1889-1937)
Star and character player,
former soldier, also in Hollywood. Specialized in deep or
involved character studies.

Journey's End, 1930
Frankenstein, 1931
The Stronger Sex, 1931
Lily Christine, 1932
Christopher Strong, 1933
Looking Forward, 1933
The Key, 1934
Jane Eyre, 1934
One More River, 1934
Clive of India, 1935
The Right to Live, 1935
Bride of Frankenstein, 1935
The Girl From Tenth Avenue,
    1935
Mad Love, 1935
The Man Who Broke the Bank
    at Monte Carlo, 1935
History is Made at Night, 1937
The Woman I Love, 1937

E. E. CLIVE (1879-1940)
Welsh character actor of stage
and screen, long in Hollywood
where he specialized in portraying sullen or gloomy characters.

The Invisible Man, 1933
One More River, 1934
Bulldog Drummond Strikes Back,
    1934
Charlie Chan in London, 1934
The Mystery of Edwin Drood,
    1935
The Bride of Frankenstein,
    1935
Stars Over Broadway, 1935
A Tale of Two Cities, 1935

Captain Blood, 1935
Clive of India, 1935
Little Lord Fauntleroy, 1936
The Unguarded Hour, 1936
The Golden Arrow, 1936
Dracula's Daughter, 1936
Trouble For Two, 1936
Ticket To Paradise, 1936
Piccadilly Jim, 1936
Cain and Mabel, 1936
Libeled Lady, 1936
Charge of the Light Brigade,
    1936
Tarzan Escapes, 1936
Lloyds of London, 1936
Camille, 1937
On the Avenue, 1937
Maids of Salem, 1937
Ready Willing and Able, 1937
Personal Property, 1937
Night Must Fall, 1937
The Emperor's Candlesticks,
    1937
Love Under Fire, 1937
Bulldog Drummond Comes Back,
    1937
It's Love I'm After, 1937
Live Love and Learn, 1937
Beg Borrow or Steal, 1937
Danger-Love at Work, 1937
Bulldog Drummond's Revenge,
    1937
Arsene Lupin Returns, 1938
Bulldog Drummond's Peril,
    1938
The First Hundred Years, 1938
Kidnapped, 1938
Gateway, 1938
Bulldog Drummond in Africa,
    1938
Submarine Patrol, 1938
The Last Warning, 1938
Arrest Bulldog Drummond, 1939
The Little Princess, 1939
I'm From Missouri, 1939
Hound of the Baskervilles, 1939
Bulldog Drummond's Secret
    Police, 1939
Rose of Washington Square,
    1939
Man About Town, 1939
Bachelor Mother, 1939
Bulldog Drummond's Bride, 1939

Adventures of Sherlock Holmes,
    1939
The Honeymoon's Over, 1939
Raffles, 1939
Congo Maisie, 1940
The Earl of Chicago, 1940
Pride and Prejudice, 1940
Foreign Correspondent, 1940

ALEC CLUNES (1912-1970)
Prominent character star of
stage, occasionally in films.

Convoy, 1940
Saloon Bar, 1940
Sailors Three, 1940
One of Our Aircraft is Missing,
    1942
Now Barabbas, 1949
Melba, 1953
Quentin Durward, 1955
Richard III, 1955
Tiger in the Smoke, 1957
Tomorrow at Ten, 1962

CHARLES COBORN (1852-1945)
Longevous stage entertainer in
rare but memorable films, well-
remembered for "The Man Who
Broke the Bank at Monte Carlo."
Not to be confused with American actor Charles Coburn (1877-
1961).

Say it With Flowers, 1934
Music Hall, 1935
Pictorial Revue, 1936
Old Times, 1936
Variety Jubilee, 1943

GEORGE COLE (1925-)
Comic actor of stage (since
1939) and screen, usually cast
as nervous novices.

Cottage to Let, 1941
Those Kids From Town, 1942
The Demi-Paradise, 1943
Henry V, 1944
My Brother's Keeper, 1948

Quartet, 1948
The Spider and the Fly, 1949
Morning Departure, 1950
Gone to Earth, 1950
Flesh and Blood, 1951
Laughter in Paradise, 1951
Scrooge, 1951
Lady Godiva Rides Again, 1951
The Happy Family, 1952
Folly to Be Wise, 1952
Who Goes There?, 1952
Top Secret, 1952
Clue of the Missing Ape, 1953
Will Any Gentleman, 1953
The Intruder, 1953
Our Girl Friday, 1953
Happy Ever After, 1954
The Belles of St. Trinian's,
   1954
An Inspector Calls, 1954
Where There's a Will, 1955
A Prize of Gold, 1955
The Constant Husband, 1955
Quentin Durward, 1955
It's a Wonderful World, 1956
The Weapon, 1956
The Green Man, 1956
Blue Murder at St. Trinian's,
   1957
Too Many Crooks, 1958
Don't Panic Chaps, 1959
The Bridal Path, 1959
Pure Hell of St. Trinian's,
   1960
Cleopatra, 1962
Dr. Syn Alias the Scarecrow,
   1963
One Way Pendulum, 1964
The Legend of Young Dick Tur-
   pin, 1965
The Great St. Trinian's Train
   Robbery, 1966
The Green Shoes, 1968
The Vampire Lovers, 1970
Fright, 1971
Take Me High, 1973
Gone in 60 Seconds, 1974
The Blue Bird, 1976
Double Nickels, 1978

SYLVIA COLERIDGE (1909-)
Character actress mainly asso-

ciated with the stage, films
few.

Cross My Heart, 1937
I Met a Murderer, 1939
Jailbirds, 1939
Rebecca, 1980

IAN COLIN (-)
Small-part character player
mainly active during the 30s.

A Moorland Tragedy, 1933
The Small Man, 1935
Cross Currents, 1935
Late Extra, 1935
Blue Smoke, 1935
Born That Way, 1936
Blind Man's Bluff, 1936
Servants All, 1936
Men of Yesterday, 1936
Wings Over Africa, 1936
Toilers of the Sea, 1936
It's Never Too Late to Mend,
   1937
A Dream of Love, 1938
Darts Are Trumps, 1938
The Life of Chopin, 1938
The Outsider, 1939
The Last Load, 1948
Trapped By the Terror, 1949
The Adventures of Jane, 1949
The Big Chance, 1957
Witness in the Dark, 1959
Dangerous Afternoon, 1961
Strongroom, 1962

JEAN COLIN (1905-)
Leading stage and screen actress of the 1930s.

A Dear Liar, 1925
Wreck of the Hesperus, 1926
The Hate Ship, 1930
Compromising Daphne, 1930
Lord Babs, 1932
Charing Cross Road, 1935
Such is Life, 1936
Mad About Money, 1937
The Mikado, 1939
Laugh it Off, 1940

Bob's Your Uncle, 1941
Eating Out With Tommy, 1941
Surprise Broadcast, 1941
Last Holiday, 1950
Laxdale Hall, 1953

BONAR COLLEANO JR.   (1924-
    1958)
American actor, former acrobat; went to England in 1936
and remained to portray villainous or wise-cracking roles in
a number of films.   Also on
radio and stage.   Was married
to Susan Shaw.

Starlight Serenade, 1944
The Way to the Stars, 1945
Wanted For Murder, 1946
A Matter of Life and Death,
    1946
While the Sun Shines, 1947
Merry-Go-Round, 1947
Broken Journey, 1948
Good Time Girl, 1948
One Night With You, 1948
Sleeping Car to Trieste, 1948
Once a Jolly Swagman, 1949
Give Us This Day, 1949
Dance Hall, 1950
Pool of London, 1950
A Tale of Five Cities, 1951
Eight Iron Men, 1952
Is Your Honeymoon Really
    Necessary?, 1953
The Flame and the Flesh, 1954
Time is My Enemy, 1954
The Sea Shall Not Have Them,
    1955
Joe Macbeth, 1955
Zarak, 1956
Stars in Your Eyes, 1956
Interpol, 1957
Fire Down Below, 1957
No Time To Die, 1958
Them Nice Americans, 1958
The Man Inside, 1958
Death Over My Shoulder, 1958

CONSTANCE COLLIER   (1878-
    1955)

Eminant stage actress who appeared as eccentric dowagers
and the like for many years in
Hollywood films.

Intolerance, 1916
The Code of Marcia Gray,
    1916
Macbeth, 1916
Bleak House, 1920
The Bohemian Girl, 1922
Our Betters, 1933
Dinner at Eight, 1933
Peter Ibbetson, 1934
Shadow of Doubt, 1935
Anna Karenina, 1936
Girl's Dormitory, 1936
Professional Soldier, 1936
Little Lord Fauntleroy, 1936
Clothes and the Woman, 1937
Thunder in the City, 1937
Wee Willie Winkie, 1937
Stage Door, 1937
She Got What She Wanted, 1937
A Damsel in Distress, 1937
Zaza, 1939
Susan and God, 1940
Half a Sinner, 1940
Weekend at the Waldorf, 1945
Kitty, 1946
Monsieur Beaucaire, 1946
The Dark Corner, 1946
The Perils of Pauline, 1947
An Ideal Husband, 1948
Rope, 1948
Girl From Manhattan, 1948
Whirlpool, 1950

JOHN COLLIN   (1931-   )
Stage and screen character
player of the 60s and 70s.

The Devil's Own, 1967
Star!, 1968
Before Winter Comes, 1969
Innocent Bystanders, 1972
Man at the Top, 1973
All Creatures Great and Small,
    1975
The Porn Brokers, 1977

JOAN COLLINS (1933-)
Passionate, sultry leading lady
of stage (1946) and films, also
in Hollywood. Formerly married to Maxwell Reed & Anthony
Newley.

I Believe in You, 1952
The Woman's Angle, 1952
Judgement Deferred, 1952
Decameron Nights, 1952
Cosh Boy, 1953
Turn the Key Softly, 1953
The Square Ring, 1953
Our Girl Friday, 1953
The Good Die Young, 1954
Land of the Pharaohs, 1955
The Virgin Queen, 1955
Girl in the Red Velvet Swing,
    1955
The Opposite Sex, 1956
The Wayward Bus, 1957
Island in the Sun, 1957
Seawife, 1957
Stopover Tokyo, 1957
The Bravados, 1958
Rally Round the Flag Boys,
    1958
Seven Thieves, 1960
Esther and the King, 1960
The Road to Hong Kong, 1962
Warning Shot, 1966
Subterfuge, 1968
Can Heironymous Merkin ... ,
    1969
Up in the Cellar, 1970
Drive Hard Drive Fast,
    1970
The Executioner, 1970
Quest For Love, 1971
Revenge, 1971
Fear in the Night, 1972
Tales From the Crypt,
    1972
Dark Places, 1973
Tales That Witness Madness,
    1973
Alfie Darling, 1975
Bawdy Adventures of Tom
    Jones, 1975
The Great Adventure, 1976
The Devil Within Her, 1976
Empire of the Ants, 1977

Zero to Sixty, 1978
The Stud, 1978
The Big Sleep, 1978
The Bitch, 1979
Sunburn, 1979
Game For Vultures, 1979

RONALD COLMAN (1891-1958)
Suave, elegant leading man of
stage (from 1916) and screen,
long in Hollywood, usually portraying aristocratic, gentlemanly or romantic heroes.
Married to Benita Hume.

The Toilers, 1919
A Son of David, 1919
Daughter of Eve, 1919
Snow in the Desert, 1919
Anna the Adventuress, 1920
The Black Spider, 1920
Handcuffs or Kisses, 1921
The Eternal City, 1923
The White Sister, 1923
$20 a Week, 1924
Tarnish, 1924
Romola, 1924
Her Night of Romance, 1924
A Thief in Paradise, 1924
His Supreme Moment, 1925
The Sporting Venus, 1925
Her Sister From Paris, 1925
The Dark Angel, 1925
Stella Dallas, 1925
Lady Windermere's Fan, 1925
Kiki, 1926
Beau Geste, 1926
The Winning of Barbara Worth,
    1926
The Night of Love, 1927
The Magic Flame, 1927
The Lovers, 1928
The Rescue, 1929
Bulldog Drummond, 1929
Condemned, 1929
Handsome Gigolo, Poor Gigolo,
    1930
Raffles, 1930
The Devil to Pay, 1930
The Unholy Garden, 1931
Arrowsmith, 1931
Cynara, 1932

The Masquerader, 1933
Bulldog Drummond Strikes
   Back, 1934
Clive of India, 1935
The Man Who Broke the Bank
   at Monte Carlo, 1935
A Tale of Two Cities, 1935
Under Two Flags, 1936
Lost Horizon, 1937
The Prisoner of Zenda, 1937
If I Were King, 1938
The Light That Failed, 1939
Lucky Partners, 1940
My Life With Caroline, 1941
Talk of the Town, 1942
Random Harvest, 1942
Kismet, 1944
The Late George Apley, 1947
A Double Life, 1947
Champagne For Caesar, 1950
Around the World in 80 Days,
   1956
The Story of Mankind, 1957

FAY COMPTON (1894-1978)
Distinguished actress of stage
(from 1906) and screen, latterly
in character parts.   Also on tv
in "The Forsyte Saga." Her
fourth husband was Ralph
Michael.

She Stoops to Conquer, 1914
One Summer's Day, 1917
The Labour Leader, 1917
Judge Not, 1920
A Woman of No Importance,
   1921
The Old Wives' Tale, 1921
House of Peril, 1922
Diana of the Crossways, 1922
A Bill of Divorcement, 1922
This Freedom, 1923
The Loves of Mary Queen of
   Scots, 1923
Claude Duval, 1924
The Eleventh Commandment,
   1924
The Happy Ending, 1925
Settled Out of Court, 1925
London Love, 1926
Robinson Crusoe, 1926

Somehow Good, 1927
Zero, 1928
Fashions in Love, 1929
Love Storm, 1931
Cape Forlorn, 1931
Uneasy Virtue, 1931
Tell England, 1931
Waltzes From Vienna, 1933
Autumn Crocus, 1934
Song at Eventide, 1934
Wedding Group, 1936
The Mill On the Floss, 1937
Cavalcade of the Stars, 1938
So This is London, 1939
The Prime Minister, 1940
Odd Man Out, 1947
Nicholas Nickleby, 1947
London Belongs to Me, 1948
Esther Waters, 1948
Britannia Mews, 1949
Blackmailed, 1950
Laughter in Paradise, 1951
Othello, 1952
Lady Possessed, 1952
Aunt Clara, 1954
Doublecross, 1956
Town On Trial, 1957
The Story of Esther Costello,
   1957
The Haunting, 1963
Uncle Vanya, 1963
I Start Counting, 1969
The Virgin and the Gypsy,
   1970

SEAN CONNERY (1930-)
Manly Scots star of stage (1953),
screen and television, now in international films.   Gained popularity as Ian Fleming's James
Bond in several films; now getting more ambitious roles.

No Road Back, 1956
Action of the Tiger, 1957
Time Lock, 1957
Hell Drivers, 1957
Another Time Another Place,
   1958
Tarzan's Greatest Adventure,
   1959
Darby O'Gill and the Little

People, 1959
The Frightened City, 1961
On the Fiddle, 1961
Dr. No, 1962
The Longest Day, 1962
From Russia With Love, 1963
Woman of Straw, 1964
Goldfinger, 1964
Marnie, 1964
The Hill, 1965
Thunderball, 1965
A Fine Madness, 1966
You Only Live Twice, 1967
Shalako, 1968
The Molly Maguires, 1970
The Red Tent, 1971
The Anderson Tapes, 1971
Diamonds Are Forever, 1971
The Offence, 1972
Zardoz, 1973
Ransom, 1974
Murder On the Orient Express, 1974
The Wind and the Lion, 1975
The Man Who Would Be King, 1975
Robin and Marian, 1976
The Next Man, 1976
A Bridge Too Far, 1977
The Great Train Robbery, 1978
Cuba, 1979
Meteor, 1979
Warhead, 1980
Tai-Pan, 1980

EDRIC CONNOR (1915-1968)
West Indian-born actor of films and television, in Britain from 1944. Also singer and music/script writer. Former engineer.

Cry the Beloved Country, 1952
West of Zanzibar, 1954
Moby Dick, 1956
Fire Down Below, 1957
Seven Thunders, 1957
The Vikings, 1958
Virgin Island, 1958
The Roots of Heaven, 1958
Four For Texas, 1963
Only When I Larf, 1968
Nobody Runs Forever, 1968

KENNETH CONNOR (1918-   )
Radio and film comedian, popular in bashful or inexperienced roles; in the "Carry On" series.

Never Say Die, 1950
Elstree Story, 1952
Marilyn, 1953
There Was a Young Lady, 1953
The Ladykillers, 1955
The Black Rider, 1955
Davy, 1957
Carry On Sergeant, 1958
Carry On Nurse, 1959
Makes Mine a Million, 1959
Dentist in the Chair, 1960
Carry On Constable, 1960
Dentist on the Job, 1961
What a Carve Up!, 1961
A Weekend With Lulu, 1961
His and Hers, 1961
Watch Your Stern, 1961
Carry On Regardless, 1961
Nearly a Nasty Accident, 1962
Call Me a Cab, 1963
A Hard Day's Night, 1964
Gonks Go Beat, 1965
Carry On Cleo, 1965
How to Undress in Public, 1965
Cuckoo Patrol, 1965
Danny the Dragon, 1967
Captain Nemo and the Underwater City, 1969
Carry On Henry VIII, 1970
Carry On Up the Jungle, 1970
Rhubarb, 1970
Carry On England, 1976

JESS CONRAD (1940-   )
Pop singer and occasional light actor of the sixties.

Too Young to Love, 1959
Friends and Neighbours, 1959
The Queen's Guards, 1960
Rag Doll, 1961
Konga, 1961
The Boys, 1962
Kil-1, 1962
The Golden Head, 1965
Moll Flanders, 1965
Hell is Empty, 1967

The Assassination Bureau, 1969
The Dirtiest Girl I Ever Met,
   1973

FRANK CONROY (1890-1964)
Actor of stage and screen who
went to Hollywood in 1930 and
remained to play a number of
tyrannical or dominant roles.

The Royal Family of Broadway,
   1930
Bad Company, 1931
Possessed, 1931
Hell Divers, 1931
Manhattan Parade, 1931
Disorderly Conduct, 1932
Grand Hotel, 1932
Ann Carver's Profession, 1933
Midnight Mary, 1933
Night Flight, 1933
The Kennel Murder Case, 1933
Ace of Aces, 1933
Frontier Marshal, 1934
The Cat and the Fiddle, 1934
Little Miss Marker, 1934
The White Parade, 1934
The Little Minister, 1934
Call of the Wild, 1935
West Point of the Air, 1935
Charlie Chan in Egypt, 1935
I Live My Life, 1935
The Last Days of Pompeii,
   1935
Show Them No Mercy, 1935
Nobody's Fool, 1936
The White Angel, 1936
Meet Nero Wolfe, 1936
The Gorgeous Hussy, 1936
Charlie Chan at the Opera,
   1936
Wells Fargo, 1937
Stolen Holiday, 1937
Love is News, 1937
Nancy Steele is Missing, 1937
That I May Live, 1937
This is My Affair, 1937
Big Business, 1937
The Emperor's Candlesticks,
   1937
Music For Madame, 1937
The Last Gangster, 1937

This Woman is Mine, 1941
Adventures of Martin Eden,
   1942
Crossroads, 1942
The Loves of Edgar Allan Poe,
   1942
Crash Dive, 1943
Lady of Burlesque, 1943
The Ox-Bow Incident, 1943
That Hagen Girl, 1947
All My Sons, 1948
For the Love of Mary, 1948
Sealed Verdict, 1948
Rogue's Regiment, 1948
The Snake Pit, 1948
The Naked City, 1948
The Threat, 1949
Lightning Strikes Twice, 1951
Day the Earth Stood Still, 1951
The Young Philadelphians, 1959
The Last Mile, 1959
The Bramble Bush, 1960

TOM CONWAY (1904-1967)
Light leading actor who followed
his brother George Sanders to
Hollywood in 1940 and remained
to play heroes in a number of
B-pictures. Popular as "The
Falcon" (whom Sanders had
previously portrayed).

Sky Murder, 1940
The Trial of Mary Dugan, 1941
Free and Easy, 1941
The Bad Man, 1941
The People vs. Dr. Kildare,
   1941
Lady Be Good, 1941
Tarzan's Secret Treasure, 1941
Checkered Coat, 1941
Bungalow 13, 1942
Rio Rita, 1942
Mr. and Mrs. North, 1942
Grand Central Murder, 1942
The Falcon's Brother, 1942
Cat People, 1942
Triple Cross, 1943
The Falcon in Danger, 1943
I Walked With a Zombie, 1943
The Falcon Strikes Back, 1943
The Seventh Victim, 1943

The Great Plane Robbery, 1944
A Night of Adventure, 1944
The Falcon in Mexico, 1944
The Falcon in Hollywood, 1944
The Falcon Out West, 1944
The Falcon in San Francisco,
    1945
Two O'clock Courage, 1945
Criminal Court, 1946
Whistle Stop, 1946
The Falcon's Alibi, 1946
The Falcon's Adventure, 1946
Lost Honeymoon, 1947
Repeat Performance, 1947
One Touch of Venus, 1948
Painting the Clouds With Sun-
    shine, 1951
Confidence Girl, 1952
Park Plaza 505, 1953
Paris Model, 1953
Tarzan and the She-Devil, 1953
Prince Valiant, 1954
Norman Conquest, 1954
Barbados Quest, 1955
Three Stops to Murder, 1956
Death of a Scoundrel, 1956
The Last Man to Hang, 1956
The She-Creature, 1956
Operation Murder, 1957
Atomic Submarine, 1959
Twelve to the Moon, 1960
What a Way to Go!, 1964

PETER COOK (1937-   )
Tall comedy star and writer,
often teamed with Dudley Moore.

The Wrong Box, 1966
Bedazzled, 1967
Think 20th, 1967
A Dandy in Aspic, 1968
Monte Carlo or Bust, 1969
The Bed Sitting Room, 1969
Rise and Rise of Michael Rim-
    mer, 1970
Hound of the Baskervilles, 1978
Monty Python Meets Beyond the
    Fringe, 1978

FREDERICK COOPER (-)
Character actor of the 40s,
mainly on stage.

Dark Sands, 1937
Jericho, 1937
Unpublished Story, 1942
The Great Mr. Handel,
    1942
Thunder Rock, 1942
Warn That Man, 1943
Escape to Danger, 1943
Henry V, 1944
They Knew Mr. Knight,
    1945

GEORGE A. COOPER
    (1916-   )
Dramatic character actor specializing in mean or vindictive
parts.

The Passing Stranger, 1954
Miracle in Soho, 1956
The Secret Place, 1957
Violent Playground, 1958
Hell is a City, 1961
Vengeance, 1962
The Cracksman, 1963
Tom Jones, 1963
Nightmare, 1963
The Bargee, 1964
Ferry Cross the Mersey, 1964
Life at the Top, 1965
The Strange Affair, 1968
Dracula Has Risen From the
    Grave, 1968
Rise and Rise of Michael Rim-
    mer, 1970
The Black Windmill, 1974

DAME GLADYS COOPER
    (1888-1971)
Distinguished, dignified star
and character actress of stage
(since 1904), screen and television, in Hollywood from 1940.

The Eleventh Commandment,
    1913
Dandy Donovan, 1914
The Real Thing at Last,
    1916
The Sorrows of Satan, 1917
Masks and Faces, 1917
My Lady's Dress, 1917

Unmarried, 1920
Bohemian Girl, 1922
Bonnie Prince Charlie, 1923
The Iron Duke, 1935
Rebecca, 1940
Kitty Foyle, 1940
That Hamilton Woman, 1941
The Black Cat, 1941
The Gay Falcon, 1941
This Above All, 1942
Eagle Squadron, 1942
Now Voyager, 1942
Forever and a Day, 1943
Mr. Lucky, 1943
Princess O'Rourke, 1943
The Song of Bernadette, 1943
The White Cliffs of Dover,
    1944
Mrs. Parkington, 1944
The Valley of Decision, 1945
Love Letters, 1946
The Green Years, 1946
The Cockeyed Miracle, 1946
Beware of Pity, 1946
Green Dolphin Street, 1947
The Bishop's Wife, 1947
Homecoming, 1948
The Pirate, 1948
The Secret Garden, 1949
Madame Bovary, 1949
Thunder on the Hill, 1951
At Sword's Point, 1952
The Man Who Loved Redheads,
    1954
Separate Tables, 1958
The List of Adrian Messenger,
    1963
My Fair Lady, 1964
The Happiest Millionaire, 1967
A Nice Girl Like Me, 1969

MELVILLE COOPER (1896-
    1973)
Character star of stage (from
1914) and screen, long in Hollywood; generally played ostentatious or pompous characters.

All Riot on the Western Front,
    1930
Black Coffee, 1931
The Calendar, 1931

Two White Arms, 1932
Leave it To Me, 1933
Forging Ahead, 1933
To Brighton With Gladys, 1933
The Private Life of Don Juan,
    1934
The Scarlet Pimpernel, 1935
The Bishop Misbehaves, 1935
The Gorgeous Hussy, 1936
The Last of Mrs. Cheyney,
    1937
Tovarich, 1937
Thin Ice, 1937
The Great Garrick, 1937
Women Are Like That, 1938
Gold Diggers in Paris, 1938
Four's a Crowd, 1938
Garden of the Moon, 1938
Hard to Get, 1938
Dramatic School, 1938
Comet Over Broadway, 1938
Adventures of Robin Hood,
    1938
The Dawn Patrol, 1938
The Sun Never Sets, 1939
I'm From Missouri, 1939
Blind Alley, 1939
Two Bright Boys, 1939
Rebecca, 1940
Pride and Prejudice, 1940
Too Many Husbands, 1940
The Lady Eve, 1941
Submarine Zone, 1941
Scotland Yard, 1941
The Flame of New Orleans,
    1941
You Belong to Me, 1941
This Above All, 1942
Life Begins at 8:30, 1942
Random Harvest, 1942
Holy Matrimony, 1943
Immortal Sergeant, 1943
Hit Parade of 1943, 1943
My Kingdom For a Crook,
    1943
Heartbeat, 1946
13 Rue Madeleine, 1947
The Imperfect Lady, 1947
Enchantment, 1948
The Red Danube, 1949
And Baby Makes Three, 1949
Love Happy, 1950
Father of the Bride, 1950

Underworld Story, 1950
The Petty Girl, 1950
Let's Dance, 1950
It Should Happen to You, 1953
Moonfleet, 1955
The King's Thief, 1955
Diane, 1956
Bundle of Joy, 1956
Around the World in 80 Days,
  1956
The Story of Mankind, 1957
From the Earth to the Moon,
  1958

RICHARD COOPER (1893-1947)
Character actor of the thirties,
typically cast in weak-minded,
absurd or lacklustre roles.

At the Villa Rose, 1930
House of the Arrow, 1930
Bed and Breakfast, 1930
The Last Hour, 1930
Enter the Queen, 1930
Lord Richard in the Pantry,
  1930
Kissing Cup's Race, 1930
The Officer's Mess, 1931
Rodney Steps In, 1931
Black Coffee, 1931
The Other Mrs. Phipps, 1931
Once Bitten, 1932
The First Mrs. Fraser, 1932
Double Dealing, 1932
Home Sweet Home, 1933
Mannequin, 1933
Lord Edgware Dies, 1934
The Black Abbot, 1934
Four Masked Men, 1934
Annie Leave the Room, 1935
The Ace of Spades, 1935
Three Witnesses, 1935
That's My Uncle, 1935
Stepping Toes, 1938
Shipyard Sally, 1939

ROBERT COOTE (1909-)
Humorous, friendly character
star, on stage from 1925; also
in Hollywood. On tv in series
"The Rogues."

Sally in Our Alley, 1931
Personal Column, 1935
A Yank at Oxford, 1938
Gunga Din, 1939
The Girl Downstairs, 1939
Mr. Moto's Last Warning, 1939
Bad Lands, 1939
Nurse Edith Cavell, 1939
Vigil in the Night, 1940
You Can't Fool Your Wife, 1940
Commandos Strike at Dawn,
  1943
Forever and a Day, 1943
A Matter of Life and Death,
  1946
The Ghost and Mrs. Muir,
  1947
Forever Amber, 1947
Bonnie Prince Charlie, 1948
The Three Musketeers, 1948
Berlin Express, 1948
The Red Danube, 1949
The Elusive Pimpernel, 1949
Soldiers Three, 1951
Rommel-Desert Fox, 1951
The Prisoner of Zenda, 1952
Scaramouche, 1952
The Merry Widow, 1952
The Constant Husband, 1955
Othello, 1955
The Swan, 1956
Merry Andrew, 1958
The Horse's Mouth, 1958
Hello London, 1958
The League of Gentlemen, 1959
The VIPs, 1963
The Golden Head, 1965
A Man Could Get Killed, 1965
The Swinger, 1966
The Cool Ones, 1967
Prudence and the Pill, 1968
Kenner, 1969
Up the Front, 1972
Theatre of Blood, 1973
Institute For Revenge, 1979

KENNETH COPE (1931-)
Comic actor of the sixties,
popular on television.

These Dangerous Years, 1957
Dunkirk, 1958

The Lady is a Square, 1959
Naked Fury, 1959
The Criminal, 1960
The Unstoppable Man, 1960
Jungle Street, 1961
Tomorrow at Ten, 1962
The Damned, 1962
Death Trap, 1962
Father Came Too, 1963
Change Partners, 1965
Dateline Diamonds, 1965
Genghis Khan, 1965
Night of the Big Heat, 1967
Hammerhead, 1968
A Touch of the Other, 1970
She'll Follow You Anywhere,
   1971
Island of the Burning Damned,
   1973
Juggernaut, 1974

PETER COPLEY (1915-   )
Character star of stage, screen
and television who is generally
cast in oppressed or ominous
parts.   Former husband of
Pamela Brown.   Tv series:
"The Forstye Saga. "

Tell Me If It Hurts, 1934
The Golden Salamander, 1950
The Card, 1952
The Sword and the Rose, 1953
Peril For the Guy, 1956
Foreign Intrigue, 1956
Time Without Pity, 1957
Man Without a Body, 1957
Just My Luck, 1957
Mystery in the Mine, 1959
Follow That Horse, 1960
Victim, 1961
The Third Secret, 1964
King and Country, 1964
Help!, 1965
The Knack, 1965
Quatermass and the Pit, 1967
The Shoes of the Fisherman,
   1968
Frankenstein Must Be Destroyed,
   1969
All at Sea, 1969
Walk a Crooked Path, 1970

The Engagement, 1970
Jane Eyre, 1970
What Became of Jack and Jill?,
   1972
Hennessy, 1975
Shout at the Devil, 1976

HARRY H. CORBETT (1925-   )
Stage and screen actor whose
greatest success came from
television series "Steptoe and
Son. "   Formerly cast as
crooks, gangsters, etc.; now
mainly in comedy parts.   Not
to be confused with puppeteer
Harry Corbett.

The Passing Stranger, 1954
Floods of Fear, 1958
Nowhere to Go, 1958
In the Wake of a Stranger,
Shake Hands With the Devil,
   1959
Shakedown, 1960
Cover Girl Killer, 1960
The Big Day, 1960
The Unstoppable Man, 1960
Marriage of Convenience, 1960
Wings of Death, 1961
Time to Remember, 1962
Some People, 1962
A Boy Ten Feet Tall, 1963
Sparrows Can't Sing, 1963
Sammy Going South, 1963
Ladies Who Do, 1963
What a Crazy World, 1963
The Bargee, 1964
Rattle of a Simple Man, 1964
Joey Boy, 1965
Carry On Screaming, 1966
The Sandwich Man, 1966
Crooks and Coronets, 1969
The Magnificent 7 Deadly Sins,
   1971
Steptoe and Son, 1972
Steptoe and Son Ride Again,
   1973
Percy's Progress, 1974
Hardcore, 1976
Adventures of a Private Eye,
   1977
Jabberwocky, 1977

LEONORA CORBETT (1907-
1960)
Stage actress popular in films
of the thirties.

Heart's Delight, 1932
Love On Wheels, 1932
The Constant Nymph, 1933
Friday the 13th, 1933
Wild Boy, 1934
Warn London, 1934
Lady in Danger, 1934
Royal Cavalcade, 1935
Heart's Desire, 1935
Living Dangerously, 1936
The Happy Family, 1936
The Price of Folly, 1937
Farewell Again, 1937
Night Alone, 1938
Anything to Declare?, 1938
Fingers, 1940
Under Your Hat, 1940

RONNIE CORBETT (1930-)
Diminutive comedian mainly on
television; films few.

Rockets Galore, 1957
Casino Royale, 1967
Some Will, Some Won't, 1970
Rise & Rise of Michael Rim-
mer, 1970
No Sex Please We're British,
1973

HARRY CORDING (-)
Bluff, burly, often bearded character actor, long in Hollywood.
Mainly portrayed villainous or
no-nonsense characters.

The Knockout, 1925
The Patriot, 1928
The Rescue, 1929
Sins of the Fathers, 1929
Christina, 1929
The Squall, 1929
Captain of the Guard, 1930
Bride of the Regiment, 1930
Rough Romance, 1930
The Conquering Horde, 1931

Honor of the Family, 1931
File No. 113, 1932
The World and the Flesh, 1932
Forgotten Commandments, 1932
Cabin in the Cotton, 1932
Viva Villa, 1934
Captain Blood, 1935
Mutiny On the Bounty, 1935
The Crusades, 1935
Les Miserables, 1935
Anna Karenina, 1935
Road Gang, 1936
Sutter's Gold, 1936
White Angel, 1936
Daniel Boone, 1936
Prince and the Pauper, 1937
Crime School, 1938
Adventures of Robin Hood,
1938
Valley of the Giants, 1938
Painted Desert, 1938
Each Dawn I Die, 1939
Passport to Alcatraz, 1940
The Great Plane Robbery, 1940
Lady From Cheyenne, 1941
Mutiny in the Arctic, 1941
Arabian Nights, 1942
Sherlock Holmes and the Secret
Weapon, 1942
Ali Baba & the 40 Thieves,
1944
Gypsy Wildcat, 1944
Mrs. Parkington, 1944
The House of Fear, 1945
Sudan, 1945
Dressed to Kill, 1946
A Woman's Vengeance, 1948
Lady in Ermine, 1948
The Fighting O'Flynn, 1949
Fortunes of Captain Blood,
1950
Last of the Buccaneers,
1950
Mask of the Avenger, 1951
The Big Trees, 1952
Against All Flags, 1952
Titanic, 1953

ADRIENNE CORRI (1930-)
Attractive red-haired Scottish
leading actress of stage, films,
and television.

The Romantic Age, 1949
The River, 1950
Quo Vadis, 1951
The Kidnappers, 1953
Devil Girl From Mars, 1954
Lease of Life, 1954
Meet Mr. Callaghan, 1954
Make Me an Offer, 1954
The Feminine Touch, 1956
Behind the Headlines, 1956
Shield of Faith, 1956
Three Men in a Boat, 1956
Second Fiddle, 1957
The Big Chance, 1957
The Surgeon's Knife, 1957
Corridors of Blood, 1958
The Rough and the Smooth,
1959
The Tell-Tale Heart, 1960
Doctor of Seven Dials, 1960
The Hellfire Club, 1961
Sword of Lancelot, 1963
Dynamite Jack, 1964
Dr. Zhivago, 1965
Bunny Lake is Missing, 1965
A Study in Terror, 1965
Africa-Texas Style, 1967
Woman Times Seven, 1967
The Viking Queen, 1967
File of the Golden Goose, 1968
Cry Wolf, 1968
Moon Zero Two, 1969
A Clockwork Orange, 1971
Vampire Circus, 1971
Madhouse, 1974
Rosebud, 1974

ERNEST COSSART (1876-1951)
Portly character comedian, on
stage from 1896. Mainly in
Hollywood where he was typically
cast as the supercilious butler.

Strange Case of Mary Page,
1916
Accent On Youth, 1935
Two For Tonight, 1935
The Scoundrel, 1935
Desire, 1936
The Great Ziegfeld, 1936
My American Wife, 1936
Murder With Pictures, 1936

Angel, 1937
Three Smart Girls, 1937
Champagne Waltz, 1937
As Good as Married, 1937
Letter of Introduction, 1938
Never Say Die, 1938
Zaza, 1939
The Light That Failed, 1939
Three Smart Girls Grow Up,
1939
The Magnificent Fraud, 1939
Lady of the Tropics, 1939
Tower of London, 1939
A Bill of Divorcement, 1940
Kitty Foyle, 1940
Tom Brown's Schooldays, 1940
Charley's Aunt, 1941
One Foot in Heaven, 1941
Skylark, 1941
King's Row, 1942
Casanova Brown, 1944
Knickerbocker Holiday, 1944
Tonight and Every Night, 1945
Cluny Brown, 1946
Love Letters, 1946
The Jolson Story, 1946
Love From a Stranger, 1947
John Loves Mary, 1949

JAMES COSSINS (1932-   )
Character player generally seen
in nervous or ostentatious roles.

Darling, 1965
Privilege, 1967
How I Won the War, 1967
Otley, 1968
The Anniversary, 1968
Lost Continent, 1968
Melody, 1970
Wuthering Heights, 1970
Rise & Rise of Michael Rim-
mer, 1970
Villain, 1971
Hitler: The Last Ten Days,
1973
Raw Meat, 1973
The Man With the Golden Gun,
1974

GEORGE COULOURIS (1903-)
Character star, on stage from
1926; also Hollywood. Adept
at both villainous and comedic
characters.

Christopher Bean, 1933
All This and Heaven Too, 1940
The Lady in Question, 1940
Citizen Kane, 1941
This Land is Mine, 1943
Assignment in Brittany, 1943
For Whom the Bell Tolls,
  1943
Watch On the Rhine, 1943
Between Two Worlds, 1944
Mr. Skeffington, 1944
The Master Race, 1944
None But the Lonely Heart,
  1944
A Song to Remember, 1945
Hotel Berlin, 1945
Lady On a Train, 1945
Confidential Agent, 1945
Nobody Lives Forever, 1946
The Verdict, 1946
California, 1946
Mr. District Attorney, 1947
Where There's Life, 1947
Sleep My Love, 1947
Beyond Glory, 1948
Joan of Arc, 1948
A Southern Yankee, 1948
An Outcast of the Islands, 1951
Appointment With Venus, 1951
The Venetian Bird, 1952
A Day to Remember, 1953
The Dog and the Diamonds,
  1953
The Heart of the Matter, 1953
The Runaway Bus, 1954
Doctor in the House, 1954
Duel in the Jungle, 1954
The Teckman Mystery, 1954
Mask of Dust, 1954
Doctor at Sea, 1955
Private's Progress, 1956
The Big Money, 1956
Doctor at Large, 1957
Man Without a Body, 1957
Kill Me Tomorrow, 1957
Seven Thunders, 1957
Tarzan and the Lost Safari,

1957
I Accuse, 1958
Woman Eater, 1958
No Time to Die, 1958
Son of Robin Hood, 1958
Law and Disorder, 1958
Conspiracy of Hearts, 1960
Bluebeard's Ten Honeymoons,
  1960
Surprise Package, 1960
Fury at Smuggler's Bay, 1961
The Boy Who Stole a Million,
  1961
King of Kings, 1961
The Crooked Road, 1964
The Skull, 1965
Arabesque, 1966
The Assassination Bureau,
  1969
No Blade of Grass, 1970
Blood From the Mummy's
  Tomb, 1971
Tower of Evil, 1972
Clouds of Witness, 1973
Papillon, 1973
The Final Programme, 1973
Percy's Progress, 1974
Murder On the Orient Express,
  1974
Mahler, 1975
The Antichrist, 1975
Shout at the Devil, 1976
The Ritz, 1976
The Tempter, 1978

HAZEL COURT (1926-)
Attractive leading redhead of
films, latterly of the horror
genre. Also Hollywood. Married: Dermot Walsh.

Champagne Charlie, 1944
Dreaming, 1944
Gaiety George, 1946
Carnival, 1946
Meet Me at Dawn, 1947
The Root of All Evil, 1947
Dear Murderer, 1947
Holiday Camp, 1947
My Sister and I, 1948
Bond Street, 1948
Forbidden, 1949

It's Not Cricket, 1949
Ghost Ship, 1952
Counterspy, 1953
The Scarlet Web, 1954
Devil Girl From Mars, 1954
Behind the Headlines, 1956
The Narrowing Circle, 1956
Curse of Frankenstein, 1957
The Hour of Decision, 1957
Woman of Mystery, 1958
Model For Murder, 1958
Breakout, 1958
The Man Who Could Cheat
    Death, 1959
The Shakedown, 1960
The Man Who Was Nobody,
    1960
Dr. Blood's Coffin, 1961
Mary Had a Little 1961
The Premature Burial, 1962
The Raven, 1963
Masque of the Red Death, 1964

TOM COURTENAY (1937-)
Gaunt star of stage (1959) and
screen, usually seen in offbeat
or underprivileged roles.

The Loneliness of the Long
    Distance Runner, 1962
Private Potter, 1962
Billy Liar, 1963
King and Country, 1964
King Rat, 1965
Dr. Zhivago, 1965
Operation Crossbow, 1965
Night of the Generals, 1966
The Day the Fish Came Out,
    1967
A Dandy in Aspic, 1968
Otley, 1968
Catch Me a Spy, 1971
One Day in the Life of Ivan
    Denisovitch, 1971
Keep Your Fingers Crossed,
    1971

DAME CICELY COURTNEIDGE
    (1893-1980)
Distinguished, vivacious comedienne and entertainer of stage

(1901) and screen; revels in
eccentricity. Long married
to Jack Hulbert, with whom
she frequently appeared.

Elstree Calling, 1930
The Ghost Train, 1931
Jack's the Boy, 1932
Happy Ever After, 1932
Soldiers of the King, 1933
Falling For You, 1933
Night and Day, 1933
Aunt Sally, 1934
The Woman in Command, 1934
Things Are Looking Up, 1935
Me and Marlborough, 1935
The Perfect Gentleman, 1935
Everybody Dance, 1936
Take My Tip, 1937
The Imperfect Lady, 1937
Under Your Hat, 1940
The Spider's Web, 1960
The L-Shaped Room, 1962
Those Magnificent Men in Their
    Flying Machines, 1965
The Wrong Box, 1966
Not Now Darling, 1972

SIR NOEL COWARD (1899-
    1973)
Distinguished playwright, director, composer and wit, also
occasional actor. On stage
from 1911, latterly in films in
eccentric parts. Also in Hollywood.

Hearts of the World, 1918
The Scoundrel, 1935
In Which We Serve, 1942
The Astonished Heart, 1950
Around the World in 80 Days,
    1956
Our Man in Havana, 1959
Surprise Package, 1960
Paris When it Sizzles, 1964
Bunny Lake is Missing, 1965
Pretty Polly, 1967
Boom!, 1968
The Italian Job, 1969

ALEC CRAIG (1878-1945)
Diminutive, bald-headed Scotch
character actor long in Hollywood; often cast in sympathetic
as well as miserly roles.

Mutiny On the Bounty, 1935
Mary of Scotland, 1936
Winterset, 1936
That Girl From Paris, 1937
China Passage, 1937
The Woman I Love, 1937
There Goes My Girl, 1937
Super Sleuth, 1937
Hideaway, 1937
Crashing Hollywood, 1938
Wise Guy, 1938
She's Got Everything, 1938
Vivacious Lady, 1938
Abe Lincoln in Illinois, 1939
Tom Brown's Schooldays, 1940
Phantom Raiders, 1940
Golden Gloves, 1940
Stranger On the Third Floor,
   1940
Shining Victory, 1941
A Date With the Falcon, 1941
Mrs. Miniver, 1942
Random Harvest, 1942
Night Before the Divorce, 1942
Cat People, 1942
Holy Matrimony, 1943
Lassie Come Home, 1943
Tennessee Johnson, 1943
Appointment in Berlin, 1943
Northern Pursuit, 1943
Calling Dr. Death, 1944
Gaslight, 1944
The Spider Woman, 1944
The White Cliffs of Dover,
   1944
Kitty, 1946

MICHAEL CRAIG (1928-)
Handsome hero of stage (since
1949) and screen, latterly at-
taining more worthy roles.
Former merchant seaman.

Malta Story, 1954
The Love Lottery, 1954
Svengali, 1954

Passage Home, 1955
The Black Tent, 1955
Eyewitness, 1956
Yield to the Night, 1956
House of Secrets, 1956
High Tide at Noon, 1957
Campbell's Kingdom, 1957
The Silent Enemy, 1958
Nor the Moon by Night, 1958
Sea of Sand, 1958
Life in Emergency Ward 10,
   1959
Sapphire, 1959
Upstairs and Downstairs, 1959
The Angry Silence, 1960
Cone of Silence, 1960
Doctor in Love, 1960
Payroll, 1961
No My Darling Daughter, 1961
Mysterious Island, 1961
Life For Ruth, 1962
The Iron Maiden, 1962
A Pair of Briefs, 1962
The Stolen Hours, 1963
Captive City, 1963
Summer Flight, 1964
Of a Thousand Delights, 1965
Life at the Top, 1965
Modesty Blaise, 1966
Sandra, 1966
Walk in the Shadow, 1966
Star!, 1968
Twinky, 1969
The Royal Hunt of the Sun,
   1969
Country Dance, 1969
A Town Called Bastard, 1971
Vault of Horror, 1973
Ride a Wild Pony, 1974
The Irishman, 1978

WENDY CRAIG (1934-)
Actress mainly on stage and
television; occasional films
during the 60s.

The Mind Benders, 1963
The Servant, 1964
The Nanny, 1965
Just Like a Woman, 1966
I'll Never Forget Whatsisname,
   1967

ANDREW CRAWFORD (1917-)
Scottish character player and
supporting star of the 40s.

Jassy, 1947
The Brothers, 1947
Dear Murderer, 1947
Love in Waiting, 1948
Broken Journey, 1948
London Belongs to Me, 1948
Trottie True, 1949
Boys in Brown, 1949
Diamond City, 1949
Morning Departure, 1950
One Wild Oat, 1951
Bitter Victory, 1958
The Queen's Guards, 1960
Shadow of the Cat, 1961
80,000 Suspects, 1963
Julius Caesar, 1970

ANNE CRAWFORD (1920-1956)
Amiable, well-bred blonde leading actress of stage (1940) and
films; popular in the 40s.

They Flew Alone, 1942
The Peterville Diamond, 1942
The Dark Tower, 1943
Millions Like Us, 1943
The Night Invader, 1943
Headline, 1943
The Hundred Pound Window, 1944
Two Thousand Women, 1944
They Were Sisters, 1945
Caravan, 1946
Bedelia, 1946
The Master of Bankdam, 1947
Daughter of Darkness, 1948
Night Beat, 1948
The Blind Goddess, 1948
It's Hard to Be Good, 1948
Tony Draws a Horse, 1950
Trio, 1950
Thunder on the Hill, 1951
Street Corner, 1953
Knights of the Round Table,
1954
Mad About Men, 1954

MICHAEL CRAWFORD

(1942-)
Energetic light comedy star of
all media, former child actor.
Also Hollywood.

Soap Box Derby, 1958
Blow Your Own Trumpet, 1958
A French Mistress, 1960
Two Living One Dead, 1961
Two Left Feet, 1962
The War Lover, 1963
The Knack, 1965
A Funny Thing Happened On
the Way to the Forum, 1966
The Jokers, 1966
How I Won the War, 1967
The Games, 1969
Hello Dolly, 1969
Hello Goodbye, 1970
Alice's Adventures in Wonder-
land, 1972

BERNARD CRIBBINS (1928-)
Comedy character star and recording artist, popular on television ("The Bernard Cribbins
Show").

Make Mine a Million, 1959
Tommy the Toreador, 1959
Visa to Canton, 1960
Two-Way Stretch, 1960
The World of Suzie Wong, 1960
The Girl On the Boat, 1961
Nothing Barred, 1961
The Wrong Arm of the Law,
1962
Carry On Jack, 1963
The Mouse On the Moon, 1963
Crooks in Cloisters, 1963
Carry On Spying, 1964
A Home of Your Own, 1964
The Counterfeit Constable,
1964
She, 1965
You Must Be Joking!, 1965
Cup Fever, 1965
The Sandwich Man, 1966
Daleks Invasion Earth 2250
A.D., 1966
Casino Royale, 1967
Ghost of a Chance, 1968

Don't Raise the Bridge Lower
  the River, 1968
The Undertakers, 1969
The Railway Children, 1970
Frenzy, 1972
The Water Babies, 1979

DONALD CRISP (1880-1974)
Distinguished, versatile, kindly
Scottish character star and di-
rector; on stage from 1906, in
Hollywood from 1908.

The French Maid, 1908
The Primal Call, 1911
Musketeers of Pig Alley, 1912
Battle of the Sexes, 1914
The Escape, 1914
Home Sweet Home, 1914
Tavern of Tragedy, 1914
Their First Acquaintance, 1914
The Never Woman, 1914
The Mysterious Shot, 1914
Birth of a Nation, 1915
Broken Blossoms, 1919
The Bonnie Briar Bush, 1921
Don Q, Son of Zorro, 1925
The Black Pirate, 1926
River Pirate, 1928
The Viking, 1928
The Pagan, 1928
Return of Sherlock Holmes,
  1929
Scotland Yard, 1930
Svengali, 1931
Kick In, 1931
Passport to Hell, 1932
Red Dust, 1932
Broadway Bird, 1933
Crime Doctor, 1934
The Key, 1934
Life of Vergie Winters, 1934
What Every Woman Knows,
  1934
The Little Minister, 1934
Vanessa, 1935
Laddie, 1935
Oil For the Lamps of China,
  1935
Mutiny On the Bounty, 1935
The White Angel, 1936
Mary of Scotland, 1936

A Woman Rebels, 1936
Charge of the Light Brigade,
  1936
Beloved Enemy, 1936
The Great O'Malley, 1937
Parnell, 1937
The Life of Emile Zola, 1937
Confession, 1937
That Certain Woman, 1937
Jezebel, 1938
Beloved Brat, 1938
The Amazing Dr. Clitterhouse,
  1938
Valley of the Giants, 1938
The Sisters, 1938
Comet Over Broadway, 1938
The Dawn Patrol, 1938
Oklahoma Kid, 1939
Wuthering Heights, 1939
Juarez, 1939
Daughters Courageous, 1939
Elizabeth the Queen, 1939
Dr. Ehrlich's Magic Bullet,
  1940
Brother Orchid, 1940
The Sea Hawk, 1940
City For Conquest, 1940
Knute Rockne-All American,
  1940
Shining Victory, 1941
How Green Was My Valley,
  1941
Dr. Jekyll and Mr. Hyde, 1941
The Gay Sisters, 1942
Forever and a Day, 1943
Lassie Come Home, 1943
The Uninvited, 1944
Adventures of Mark Twain,
  1944
National Velvet, 1944
The Valley of Decision, 1945
Son of Lassie, 1945
Ramrod, 1947
The Hills of Home, 1948
Whispering Smith, 1949
Challenge to Lassie, 1950
Bright Leaf, 1950
Prince Valiant, 1954
The Long Grey Line, 1955
Man From Laramie, 1955
Saddle the Wind, 1958
The Last Hurrah, 1958
A Dog of Flanders, 1960

Pollyanna, 1960
Greyfriars Bobby, 1961
Spencer's Mountain, 1963

SYD CROSSLEY (1885-1960)
Music hall comedian and singer
(1900) and supporting player of
films; in Hollywood as well in
the 20s.

Keep Smiling, 1925
The Unknown Soldier, 1926
The Gorilla, 1927
Fangs of the Wild, 1928
Atlantic, 1929
The Hate Ship, 1929
Pride of Donegal, 1929
Just For a Song, 1929
Suspense, 1930
The Middle Watch, 1930
The Man From Chicago, 1930
The Musical Beauty Shop, 1930
Never Trouble Trouble, 1931
The Flying Fool, 1931
The Professional Guest, 1931
Men Like These, 1931
Tonight's the Night, 1932
The Mayor's Nest, 1932
High Society, 1932
On the Air, 1932
Lucky Ladies, 1932
For the Love of Mike, 1932
The Last Coupon, 1932
The King's Cup, 1933
Letting in the Sunshine, 1933
Leave it to Me, 1933
The Medicine Man, 1933
Excess Baggage, 1933
The Umbrella, 1933
Meet My Sister, 1933
You Made Me Love You, 1933
The Bermondsey Kid, 1933
Night Club Queen, 1934
Master and Man, 1934
Those Were the Days, 1934
Gay Love, 1934
It's a Bet, 1934
Eighteen Minutes, 1934
Dandy Dick, 1934
Bagged, 1934
Over the Garden Wall, 1934
Give Her a Ring, 1934

Radio Parade of 1935, 1935
The Deputy Drummer, 1935
Honeymoon For Three, 1935
Me and Marlborough, 1935
Royal Cavalcade, 1935
Jimmy Boy, 1935
Music Hath Charms, 1935
The Ghost Goes West, 1935
One Good Turn, 1935
Public Nuisance Number One,
  1935
Everything is Rhythm, 1935
Cheer Up, 1936
Queen of Hearts, 1936
Two's Company, 1936
Paybox Adventure, 1936
Full Speed Ahead, 1936
The Man in the Mirror, 1937
Silver Blaze, 1937
Sensation, 1937
The Gang Show, 1937
Lucky Jade, 1937
Feather Your Nest, 1937
Pearls Bring Tears, 1937
Boys Will Be Girls, 1937
Old Mother Riley, 1937
Young and Innocent, 1937
Sweet Devil, 1938
The Return of Carol Deane,
  1938
Everything Happens to Me,
  1938
His Lordship Goes to Press,
  1938
Peter's Pence, 1938
Save a Little Sunshine, 1938
Little Dolly Daydream, 1938
We're Going to Be Rich, 1938
Penny Paradise, 1938
Oh Dear Uncle, 1939
Meet Maxwell Archer, 1939
Come On George, 1939
Old Mother Riley's Circus,
  1941

ANDREW CRUICKSHANK
  (1907-)
Scottish actor of stage and
screen, usually seen as professional man. Became famous
on tv in "Dr. Finlay's Case-
book." (1965-71).

Auld Lang Syne, 1937
The Mark of Cain, 1948
Idol of Paris, 1948
Forbidden, 1949
Paper Orchid, 1949
Your Witness, 1950
The Angel With the Trumpet,
   1950
The Reluctant Widow, 1950
The Cruel Sea, 1953
Richard III, 1955
John and Julie, 1956
The Secret Tent, 1956
The Battle of the River Plate,
   1956
The Story of Esther Costello,
   1957
Innocent Sinners, 1958
A Question of Adultery, 1958
The 39 Steps, 1959
Stranglers of Bombay, 1959
Kidnapped, 1959
There Was a Crooked Man,
   1960
Greyfriars Bobby, 1961
El Cid, 1961
Live Now Pay Later, 1962
We Joined the Navy, 1962
Come Fly With Me, 1963
Murder Most Foul, 1965

ROSALIE CRUTCHLEY
   (1921-   )
Lean, conspicuous character
actress of stage and screen.

Take My Life, 1947
Give Us This Day, 1949
Prelude to Fame, 1950
Lady With a Lamp, 1951
Quo Vadis, 1951
Malta Story, 1953
The Sword and the Rose, 1953
Make Me An Offer, 1954
The Flame and the Flesh, 1954
The Spanish Gardener, 1956
The Gamma People, 1956
Miracle in Soho, 1957
Seven Thunders, 1957
No Time For Tears, 1957
A Tale of Two Cities, 1958
Beyond This Place, 1959

The Nun's Story, 1959
Sons and Lovers, 1960
Frederic Chopin, 1961
No Love For Johnnie, 1961
Freud, 1962
The Girl in the Headlines,
   1963
The Haunting, 1963
Behold a Pale Horse, 1964
Wuthering Heights, 1970
Creatures the World Forgot,
   1971
Blood From the Mummy's
   Tomb, 1971
Whoever Slew Auntie Roo?,
   1971
Man of La Mancha, 1972
Au Pair Girls, 1973
And Now the Screaming Starts,
   1973
Mahler, 1975
Mohammed Messenger of God,
   1977

FREDERICK CULLEY (-)
Character star of adventure
films of the thirties.

Enter the Queen, 1930
Madame Guillotine, 1931
The Private Life of Henry VIII,
   1933
Once a Thief, 1935
Talk of the Devil, 1936
Annie Laurie, 1936
Conquest of the Air, 1936
The Rat, 1937
Knight Without Armour, 1937
Mr. Smith Carries On, 1937
Our Fighting Navy, 1937
The Drum, 1938
Special Edition, 1938
The Four Feathers, 1939
Sword of Honour, 1939
The Young Mr. Pitt, 1942
Uncensored, 1942
The Bells Go Down, 1943

ROLAND CULVER (1900-   )
Distinguished actor and character star of stage and screen,

often cast in upper-crust comedy or gentlemanly parts. Also in Hollywood. Also excellent on television in "The Pallisers."

77 Park Lane, 1931
Flat No. 9, 1931
Fascination, 1931
C. O. D. , 1932
A Voice Said Goodnight, 1932
Love On Wheels, 1932
There Goes the Bride, 1932
Her First Affaire, 1932
Puppets of Fate, 1933
Head of the Family, 1933
Mayfair Girl, 1933
Her Imaginary Lover, 1933
Lucky Loser, 1934
Two Hearts in Waltz Time, 1934
Father and Son, 1934
Scoop, 1934
Borrow a Million, 1934
Nell Gwyn, 1935
Oh What a Night, 1935
Accused, 1936
Paradise For Two, 1937
The Gaiety Girls, 1938
French Without Tears, 1939
Blind Folly, 1939
Dangerous Comment, 1940
Night Train to Munich, 1940
Old Bill and Son, 1940
Fingers, 1940
This England, 1941
Quiet Wedding, 1941
Unpublished Story, 1942
One of Our Aircraft is Missing, 1942
Talk About Jacqueline, 1942
The Day Will Dawn, 1942
The First of the Few, 1942
Secret Mission, 1942
Colonel Blimp, 1943
Dear Octopus, 1943
On Approval, 1944
English Without Tears, 1944
Give Us the Moon, 1944
Dead of Night, 1945
Perfect Strangers, 1945
Wanted For Murder, 1946
To Each His Own, 1947
Down to Earth, 1947

Singapore, 1947
The Emperor Waltz, 1948
Isn't it Romantic, 1948
The Great Lover, 1949
Trio, 1950
The Late Edwina Black, 1951
Hotel Sahara, 1951
The Magic Box, 1951
Encore, 1951
The Holly and the Ivy, 1952
The Hour of Thirteen, 1952
Obsessed, 1952
Folly to Be Wise, 1952
Rough Shoot, 1953
Betrayed, 1954
The Teckman Mystery, 1954
The Man Who Loved Redheads, 1955
Ship That Died of Shame, 1955
Touch and Go, 1955
An Alligator Named Daisy, 1955
Safari, 1956
Light Fingers, 1957
The Hypnotist, 1957
Vicious Circle, 1957
The Truth About Women, 1958
My Friend Charles, 1958
Bonjour Tristesse, 1958
Next to No Time, 1958
Rockets Galore, 1958
The Iron Maiden, 1962
Term of Trial, 1962
A Pair of Briefs, 1962
The Yellow Rolls-Royce, 1964
A Man Could Get Killed, 1965
Thunderball, 1965
Fragment of Fear, 1970
The Magic Christian, 1970
In Search of Gregory, 1970
Rise & Rise of Michael Rimmer, 1970
The Legend of Hell House, 1973
The Nelson Affair, 1973
The Mackintosh Man, 1973
The Uncanny, 1977
The Greek Tycoon, 1978
No Longer Alone, 1978
Rough Cut, 1980

CONSTANCE CUMMINGS
(1910-   )
Light leading American-born
actress of stage (since 1926)
and screen, in England from
1932.

The Criminal Code, 1931
The Guilty Generation, 1931
Traveling Husbands, 1931
The Last Parade, 1931
Lover Come Back, 1931
Movie Crazy, 1932
Behind the Mask, 1932
The Last Man, 1932
American Madness, 1932
Attorney For the Defense,
1932
Washington Merry-Go-Round,
1932
Billion Dollar Scandal, 1933
The Mind Reader, 1933
The Charming Deceiver, 1933
Channel Crossing, 1933
Broadway Thro' a Keyhole,
1933
Glamour, 1934
Looking For Trouble, 1934
This Man is Mine, 1934
Doomed Cargo, 1935
Remember the Night, 1935
Seven Sinners, 1936
Strangers On a Honeymoon,
1936
Busman's Honeymoon, 1940
The Outsider, 1940
This England, 1941
The Foreman Went to France,
1942
Blithe Spirit, 1945
Into the Blue, 1950
Man in the Dinghy, 1951
The Scream, 1953
John and Julie, 1955
The Intimate Stranger, 1956
Battle of the Sexes, 1959
Sammy Going South, 1962
In the Cool of the Day,
1963
Jane Eyre, 1970

PEGGY CUMMINS (1925-   )

Attractive Welsh leading actress of stage (from 1938) and
screen, also in Hollywood.
Former teenage star.

Dr. O'Dowd, 1940
Salute John Citizen, 1942
Old Mother Riley Detective,
1943
Welcome Mr. Washington, 1944
English Without Tears, 1944
The Late George Apley, 1947
Moss Rose, 1947
Gun Crazy, 1948
Green Grass of Wyoming, 1948
Escape, 1948
That Dangerous Age, 1949
My Daughter Joy, 1950
Who Goes There?, 1952
Street Corner, 1953
Always a Bride, 1953
Meet Mr. Lucifer, 1953
The Love Lottery, 1954
To Dorothy a Son, 1954
The March Hare, 1956
Carry On Admiral, 1957
Hell Drivers, 1957
Night of the Demon, 1958
The Captain's Table, 1959
Your Money or Your Wife,
1959
Dentist in the Chair, 1960
In the Doghouse, 1961

FINLAY CURRIE (1878-1968)
Prolific Scottish character star
of stage (1898) and screen,
also in Hollywood.   Portrayed
kindliness and villainy with
equal gusto.   Best remembered
as Magwitch, the convict in
"Great Expectations."

The Old Man, 1931
The Frightened Lady, 1932
Rome Express, 1932
Excess Baggage, 1933
The Good Companions, 1933
Orders is Orders, 1933
Princess Charming, 1934
Little Friend, 1934
Gay Love, 1934

Mr. Cinders, 1934
My Old Dutch, 1935
In Town Tonight, 1935
The Big Splash, 1935
The Improper Duchess, 1936
The Gay Adventure, 1936
Wanted, 1937
Glamourous Night, 1937
Catch as Catch Can, 1937
Edge of the World, 1937
Command Performance, 1937
Paradise For Two, 1937
The Claydon Treasure Mystery,
  1938
Around the Town, 1938
Follow Your Star, 1938
Hospital Hospitality, 1939
49th Parallel, 1941
The Day Will Dawn, 1942
Thunder Rock, 1942
The Bells Go Down, 1943
Theatre Royal, 1943
Undercover Girl, 1943
They Met in the Dark, 1943
Warn That Man, 1943
The Shipbuilders, 1944
Don Chicago, 1945
I Know Where I'm Going, 1945
The Trojan Brothers, 1946
Spring Song, 1946
Woman to Woman, 1946
School For Secrets, 1946
Great Expectations, 1946
The Brothers, 1947
My Brother Jonathan, 1948
So Evil My Love, 1948
Mr. Perrin and Mr. Traill,
  1948
Sleeping Car to Trieste, 1948
Bonnie Prince Charlie, 1948
Whiskey Galore, 1948
The History of Mr. Polly,
  1949
Treasure Island, 1950
My Daughter Joy, 1950
Trio, 1950
The Black Rose, 1950
Quo Vadis, 1951
The Mudlark, 1951
People Will Talk, 1952
Ivanhoe, 1952
Walk East on Beacon, 1952
Kangaroo, 1952

Rob Roy, 1953
Stars and Stripes Forever,
  1953
Treasure of the Golden Condor,
  1953
Beau Brummell, 1954
Make Me an Offer, 1954
The End of the Road, 1954
Third Party Risk, 1955
Footsteps in the Fog, 1955
King's Rhapsody, 1955
Around the World in 80 Days,
  1956
Zarak, 1956
The Little Hut, 1957
Seven Waves Away, 1957
Saint Joan, 1957
Campbell's Kingdom, 1957
Dangerous Exile, 1957
6. 5 Special, 1958
Rockets Galore, 1958
The Naked Earth, 1958
The Tempest, 1959
Ben Hur, 1959
Corridors of Blood, 1959
Solomon and Sheba, 1959
Adventures of Huckleberry
  Finn, 1960
The Angel Wore Red, 1960
Kidnapped, 1960
Hand in Hand, 1960
Francis of Assisi, 1961
Five Golden Hours, 1961
Clue of the Silver Key, 1961
Joseph and His Brethren,
  1962
Go to Blazes, 1962
The Inspector, 1962
The Amorous Prawn, 1962
Cleopatra, 1962
Murder at the Gallop, 1963
Billy Liar, 1963
The Cracksman, 1963
West Eleven, 1963
The Three Lives of Thomasina,
  1963
Who Was Maddox?, 1964
Fall of the Roman Empire,
  1964
Battle of the Villa Fiorita,
  1965
Bunny Lake is Missing, 1965
Vendetta For the Saint, 1968

PATRIC CURWEN (-)
Character player of the 30s
and 40s, usually seen as doctors, lawyers, etc.

The Ringer, 1931
Loyalties, 1934
Department Store, 1935
The Gap, 1937
Two Minutes, 1939
Bringing it Home, 1940
Yellow Canary, 1943
The Man in Grey, 1943
Medal For the General, 1944
Give Me the Stars, 1944
Don't Take it to Heart, 1944
The Echo Murders, 1945
The Grand Escapade, 1946
Nothing Venture, 1948

GEORGE CURZON (1898-1976)
Actor of stage (1924) and
screen, often cast in threatening
roles. Former naval officer.
Popular in the thirties.

Escape, 1930
The Impassive Footman, 1932
Woman in Chains, 1932
Her First Affaire, 1932
After the Ball, 1932
Murder at Covent Garden, 1932
Strange Evidence, 1933
Trouble, 1933
Scotland Yard Mystery, 1934
Java Head, 1934
The Man Who Knew Too Much,
   1934
Lorna Doone, 1935
The Widow's Might, 1935
Admirals All, 1935
Sexton Blake and the Bearded
   Doctor, 1935
Sexton Blake & the Mademoi-
   selle, 1935
Two Hearts in Harmony, 1935
The White Angel, 1936
Whom the Gods Love, 1936
Young and Innocent, 1937
Sexton Blake and the Hooded
   Terror, 1938
Strange Boarders, 1938

A Royal Divorce, 1938
The Mind of Mr. Reeder, 1939
Q Planes, 1939
Jamaica Inn, 1939
Uncle Silas, 1947
The First Gentleman, 1948
For Them That Trespass,
   1949
That Dangerous Age, 1949
Sing Along With Me, 1952
The Cruel Sea, 1953
The Final Test, 1953
Harry Black, 1958
Woman of Straw, 1964

CYRIL CUSACK (1910-)
Diminutive Irish actor of stage
(since 1917) and screen, very
adept at portraying evil or
kindly parts alike. Formerly
with the Abbey Theatre; also
in Hollywood.

Knocknagow, 1922
The Man Without a Face, 1935
Servants All, 1936
Once a Crook, 1941
Odd Man Out, 1947
Esther Waters, 1948
Escape, 1948
Once a Jolly Swagman, 1948
The Small Back Room, 1948
All Over Town, 1949
The Blue Lagoon, 1949
Gone to Earth, 1950
The Elusive Pimpernel, 1950
The Blue Veil, 1951
Soldiers Three, 1951
The Wild Heart, 1952
Secret of Convict Lake, 1953
Saadia, 1954
Passage Home, 1955
The Man Who Never Was,
   1956
The Man in the Road, 1956
The March Hare, 1956
Jacqueline, 1956
The Spanish Gardener, 1956
Ill Met By Moonlight, 1957
The Rising of the Moon, 1957
Miracle in Soho, 1957
Gideon's Day, 1958

Night Ambush, 1958
Floods of Fear, 1958
Shake Hands With the Devil,
 1959
A Terrible Beauty, 1960
Johnny Nobody, 1961
Waltz of the Toreadors, 1962
The Breaking Point, 1962
Lawrence of Arabia, 1962
I Thank a Fool, 1962
80,000 Suspects, 1963
Passport to Oblivion, 1964
Where the Spies Are, 1965
The Spy Who Came In From
 the Cold, 1965
I Was Happy Here, 1965
Fahrenheit 451, 1966
Oedipus the King, 1967
The Taming of the Shrew, 1967
Galileo, 1968
Country Dance, 1969
David Copperfield, 1969
King Lear, 1970
Harold and Maude, 1971
Sacco and Vanzetti, 1971
Tam Lin, 1971
The Homecoming, 1973
Day of the Jackal, 1973
All the Way Boys, 1973
The Italian Connection, 1973
Run Run Joe, 1974
The Abdication, 1974
Children of Rage, 1975
The Last Circus Show, 1975
Execution Squad, 1976
Jesus of Nazareth, 1977
An Eye For an Eye, 1978
Pointin', 1979
Cry of the Innocent, 1980

PETER CUSHING (1913-   )
Thin, distinctive star of stage,
screen and television. A popular star of horror films, especially when teamed with Christopher Lee. Also in Hollywood.

Man in the Iron Mask, 1939
A Chump at Oxford, 1939
Vigil in the Night, 1940
Laddie, 1940
They Dare Not Love, 1941

Women in War, 1942
Hamlet, 1948
Moulin Rouge, 1952
The Black Knight, 1954
The End of the Affair, 1955
Magic Fire, 1956
Alexander the Great, 1956
Time Without Pity, 1957
The Curse of Frankenstein,
 1957
The Abominable Snowman,
 1957
Violent Playground, 1957
Dracula, 1958
Revenge of Frankenstein, 1958
Hound of the Baskervilles,
 1959
The Mummy, 1959
John Paul Jones, 1959
Cone of Silence, 1960
Flesh and the Fiends, 1960
The Brides of Dracula, 1960
Sword of Sherwood Forest,
 1960
Suspect, 1960
The Hellfire Club, 1961
Fury at Smuggler's Bay, 1961
The Naked Edge, 1961
Cash on Demand, 1961
The Devil's Agent, 1961
Captain Clegg, 1962
The Man Who Finally Died,
 1962
The Evil of Frankenstein, 1964
The Gorgon, 1964
Dr. Terror's House of Hor-
 rors, 1965
She, 1965
Dr. Who and the Daleks, 1965
The Skull, 1965
Island of Terror, 1966
Daleks Invasion Earth 2250 AD,
 1966
Frankenstein Created Woman,
 1967
Some May Live, 1967
Night of the Big Heat, 1967
Torture Garden, 1967
Death Head's Moth, 1968
Blood Beast Terror, 1968
Corruption, 1968
Frankenstein Must Be De-
 stroyed, 1969

Scream and Scream Again,
   1969
The Vampire Lovers, 1970
The House That Dripped Blood,
   1970
Incense For the Damned, 1970
One More Time, 1970
I Monster, 1970
Twins of Evil, 1971
Fear in the Night, 1972
Asylum, 1972
Tales From the Crypt, 1972
Dr. Phibes Rises Again, 1972
Dracula AD 1972, 1972
The Creeping Flesh, 1972
Nothing But the Night, 1972
Horror Express, 1972
Island of the Burning Damned,
   1973
The Satanic Rites of Dracula,
   1973
Frankenstein & the Monster
   From Hell, 1973
From Beyond the Grave, 1973
And Now the Screaming Starts,
   1973
The Beast Must Die, 1974
Legend of the 7 Golden Vam-
   pires, 1974
Madhouse, 1974
Legend of the Werewolf, 1974
Shatter, 1974
The Ghoul, 1975
Tender Dracula, 1975
La Grande Trouille, 1975
Dirty Knight's Work, 1976
The Great Houdinis, 1976
Trial By Combat, 1976
At the Earth's Core, 1976
The Devil's Men, 1976
The Uncanny, 1977
Die Standarte, 1977
Star Wars, 1977
Shock Waves, 1977
Land of the Minotaur, 1977
Count Dracula and His Vampire
   Bride, 1978
Arabian Adventure, 1979

ALLAN CUTHBERTSON
   (1921-   )
Australian actor, long in

Britain, usually seen in unsympathetic, weakling, or slightly
haughty roles. Also on television.

The Million Pound Note, 1954
Carrington VC, 1955
Portrait of Alison, 1955
The Man Who Never Was, 1956
Anastasia, 1956
Eyewitness, 1956
Doublecross, 1956
Dick Turpin-Highwayman, 1956
Cloak Without Dagger, 1956
A Novel Affair, 1957
The Passionate Stranger, 1957
Law and Disorder, 1958
Ice Cold in Alex, 1958
I Was Monty's Double, 1958
The Crowning Touch, 1959
Shake Hands With the Devil,
   1959
Stranglers of Bombay, 1959
Killers of Kilimanjaro, 1959
Room at the Top, 1959
Tunes of Glory, 1960
The Guns of Navarone, 1961
On the Double, 1961
The Malpas Mystery, 1961
Man at the Carlton Tower,
   1961
The Boys, 1962
Solo For Sparrow, 1962
The Fast Lady, 1962
Term of Trial, 1962
Vengeance, 1962
Tamahine, 1963
The Informers, 1963
Bitter Harvest, 1963
Mouse On the Moon, 1963
The Running Man, 1963
The Seventh Dawn, 1964
Life at the Top, 1965
Operation Crossbow, 1965
Game For Three Losers, 1965
Press For Time, 1966
Half a Sixpence, 1967
Rocket to the Moon, 1967
The Trygon Factor, 1967
The Body Stealers, 1969
Captain Nemo and the Under-
   water City, 1969
The Adventurers, 1970

The Firechasers, 1970
One More Time, 1970
Performance, 1970
The Railway Children, 1971
In the Devil's Garden, 1974
Hopscotch, 1980

PATRICIA CUTTS (1926-1974)
Attractive actress, popular in
the 40s and 50s, daughter of
silent film director Graham
Cutts (1885-1958). Also Hollywood.

Self-Made Lady, 1932
Flying With Prudence, 1946
Just William's Luck, 1948
Bond Street, 1948
Madness of the Heart, 1949
Adventures of PC 49, 1949
Your Witness, 1950
The Long Dark Hall, 1951
Those People Next Door, 1953
The Happiness of Three Women,
   1954
The Man Who Loved Redheads,
   1955
Merry Andrew, 1958
The Tingler, 1958
No Place Like Home, 1959
The Cad, 1960
Private Road, 1971

PATRICIA DAINTON (1930-)
Leading actress of films, former teenage star.

Don't Ever Leave Me, 1949
The Dancing Years, 1950
Castle in the Air, 1952
Tread Softly, 1952
Hammer the Toff, 1952
Operation Diplomat, 1953
The Passing Stranger, 1957
At the Stroke of Nine, 1957
No Road Back, 1957
Witness in the Dark, 1960
The House in Marsh Road, 1960
Ticket to Paradise, 1961
The Third Alibi, 1961

AMY DALBY (1888-1969)
Aged character actress of
stage and screen, usually in
cameo roles.

The Wicked Lady, 1945
The Straw Man, 1953
The Man Upstairs, 1958
The Lamp in Assassin Mews,
   1962
The Secret of My Success,
   1965
Who Killed the Cat?, 1966
The Spy With a Cold Nose,
   1966

JIM DALE (1935-)
Pop singer and light comedian
of stage (1951), radio, screen
and television. Also frequently
in the "Carry On" series.

6. 5 Special, 1958
Raising the Wind, 1961
The Iron Maiden, 1962
Nurse On Wheels, 1963
Carry On Jack, 1963
Carry On Cabby, 1963
Carry On Cleo, 1964
Carry On Spying, 1964
The Big Job, 1965
Carry On Cowboy, 1965
Carry On Screaming, 1966
Carry On Don't Lose Your
   Head, 1966
Carry On Follow That Camel,
   1967
Carry On Doctor, 1967
The Plank, 1967
The Winter's Tale, 1968
Lock Up Your Daughters, 1969
Carry On Again Doctor, 1969
Adolf Hitler-My Part in His
   Downfall, 1972
The National Health, 1973
Digby-the Biggest Dog in the
   World, 1973
Joseph Andrews, 1977
Pete's Dragon, 1977
Hot Lead and Cold Feet, 1978

AUDREY DALTON (1934-   )
Light leading actress, primarily
in Hollywood.

My Cousin Rachel, 1952
Girls of Pleasure Island, 1953
Titanic, 1953
Casanova's Big Night, 1954
Drum Beat, 1954
Confession, 1955
The Prodigal, 1956
Deadliest Sin, 1956
Hold Back the Night, 1956
Monster That Challenged the
    World, 1957
Separate Tables, 1958
This Other Eden, 1960
Mr. Sardonicus, 1961
Kitten With a Whip, 1964
The Bounty Killer, 1965

TIMOTHY DALTON (1944-   )
Gloomy, taciturn star of stage,
in occasional films of the 70s.

The Lion in Winter, 1968
Wuthering Heights, 1970
Cromwell, 1970
Mary Queen of Scots, 1971
Lady Caroline Lamb, 1972
Permission to Kill, 1975
El Hombre Que Supo Amar, 1976
Sextette, 1978
Centennial, 1978
Agatha, 1979

MARK DALY (1887-1957)
Cheerful character actor of
stage (since 1906) and screen,
most active in the 30s.

East Lynne, 1931
The Beggar Student, 1931
The Third String, 1932
Up For the Derby, 1933
Doss House, 1933
Private Life of Henry VIII,
    1933
A Cuckoo in the Nest, 1933
Say it With Flowers, 1934
River Wolves, 1934

Bypass to Happiness, 1934
Music Hall, 1934
There Goes Susie, 1934
Flood Tide, 1934
That's My Uncle, 1935
The Small Man, 1935
A Real Bloke, 1935
Jubilee Window, 1935
The Ghost Goes West, 1936
Shipmates O'Mine, 1936
The Captain's Table, 1936
Wanted, 1937
Good Morning Boys, 1937
Command Performance, 1937
Captain's Orders, 1937
Wings of the Morning, 1937
Follow Your Star, 1938
Lassie From Lancashire, 1938
Hoots Mon, 1939
Break the News, 1941
Next of Kin, 1942
The Voyage of Peter Joe, 1946
Stage Frights, 1947
Bonnie Prince Charlie, 1948
Three Bags Full, 1949
The Romantic Age, 1949
Alf's Baby, 1953
The Delavine Affair, 1954
Lease of Life, 1954
Don't Blame the Stork, 1954
The Shiralee, 1957
The Tommy Steele Story, 1957
Soapbox Derby, 1958

CLAUDE DAMPIER (1879-
    1955)
Character comedian of stage
and screen with music hall experience from 1896; generally
seen as the bespectacled country bumpkin.

Claude Deputises, 1930
Boys Will Be Boys, 1935
Radio Parade of 1935, 1935
So You Won't Talk, 1935
White Lilac, 1935
She Shall Have Music, 1935
No Monkey Business, 1935
All In, 1936
Such is Life, 1936
She Knew What She Wanted,

1936
Public Nuisance Number One,
1936
Kings of the Castle, 1936
Mr. Stringfellow Says No,
1937
Riding High, 1937
Wanted, 1937
Sing As You Swing, 1937
The Backyard Front, 1940
Don't Take it to Heart, 1944
Meet Mr. Malcolm, 1954
Climb Up the Wall, 1960

PAUL DANEMAN (1930-)
Light leading actor primarily
on stage and tv, in occasional
films. Television series:
"Spy Trap."

Time Without Pity, 1957
The Clue of the New Pin, 1961
The Fourth Square, 1961
Locker 69, 1962
Zulu, 1964
How I Won the War, 1967
Oh What a Lovely War, 1969

HENRY DANIELL (1894-1963)
Suave, penetrating character
star, long in Hollywood where
he was memorable in villainous
roles.

Jealousy, 1929
The Unguarded Hour, 1930
Path of Glory, 1934
Camille, 1936
The Thirteenth Chair, 1937
Madame X, 1937
The Awful Truth, 1937
Under Cover of Night, 1937
The Firefly, 1937
Marie Antoinette, 1938
Holiday, 1938
We Are Not Alone, 1939
Elizabeth the Queen, 1939
All This and Heaven Too,
1940
The Great Dictator, 1940
The Sea Hawk, 1940

The Philadelphia Story, 1940
Dressed to Kill, 1941
A Woman's Face, 1941
The Feminine Touch, 1941
Nightmare, 1942
Sherlock Holmes and the Voice
of Terror, 1942
Sherlock Holmes in Washington,
1943
Watch On the Rhine, 1943
Reunion in France, 1943
Mission to Moscow, 1943
Jane Eyre, 1944
The Suspect, 1945
Hotel Berlin, 1945
The Body Snatcher, 1945
The Woman in Green, 1945
Captain Kidd, 1945
Bandit of Sherwood Forest,
1946
Song of Love, 1947
The Exile, 1947
Wake of the Red Witch, 1948
Siren of Atlantis, 1949
Buccaneer's Girl, 1950
The Egyptian, 1954
Man in the Grey Flannel Suit,
1956
Diane, 1956
The Prodigal, 1956
Lust For Life, 1956
Les Girls, 1957
Mr. Corey, 1957
The Sun Also Rises, 1957
The Story of Mankind, 1957
Witness For the Prosecution,
1957
From the Earth to the Moon,
1958
The Comancheros, 1961
Notorious Landlady, 1962
Five Weeks in a Balloon, 1962
Madison Avenue, 1962
The Chapman Report, 1962
My Fair Lady, 1964

A. BROMLEY DAVENPORT
(-)
Old-time character actor, popular in silent films and sound
films alike; most active in the
thirties.

The Great Gay Road, 1920
The Bigamist, 1921
Running Water, 1922
Boy Woodburn, 1922
The Persistent Lovers, 1922
Fox Farm, 1922
Maid of the Silver Sea, 1922
Bonnie Prince Charlie, 1923
Sally Bishop, 1923
Eugene Aram, 1924
What the Butler Saw, 1924
The Impatient Patient, 1925
Somebody's Darling, 1925
Roses of Picardy, 1927
A Sister to Assist 'Er, 1927
Flight Commander, 1927
The Glad Eye, 1927
The Fake, 1927
Glorious Youth, 1928
Spangles, 1928
The Blue Peter, 1928
The American Prisoner, 1929
Too Many Crooks, 1930
Leave it to Me, 1930
Captivation, 1931
Glamour, 1931
When London Sleeps, 1932
The Face at the Window, 1932
The Marriage Bond, 1932
Self-Made Lady, 1932
Mr. Bill the Conqueror, 1932
Flat No. 9, 1932
The Return of Raffles, 1932
Lord Camber's Ladies, 1932
Money Means Nothing, 1932
Little Miss Nobody, 1933
The Wishbone, 1933
The Stolen Necklace, 1933
Enemy of the Police, 1933
A Shot in the Dark, 1933
The Iron Stair, 1933
The Melody Maker, 1933
The Pointing Finger, 1933
Lily of Killarney, 1934
Lost in the Legion, 1934
Love, Life and Laughter, 1934
The Warren Case, 1934
So You Won't Talk, 1935
Vintage Wine, 1935
The Crouching Beast, 1935
Mysterious Mr. Davis, 1936
The Cardinal, 1936
Owd Bob, 1938

Second Thoughts, 1938
To the Victor, 1938
Jamaica Inn, 1939
The Farmer's Wife, 1941
Love On the Dole, 1941
Old Mother Riley's Ghosts,
    1941
Those Kids From Town, 1942
The Young Mr. Pitt, 1942
When We Are Married, 1943

NIGEL DAVENPORT (1928-)
Likable, masculine actor of
stage, screen, and television,
often seen in strong or important roles.

Desert Mice, 1959
Look Back in Anger, 1959
The Entertainer, 1960
Peeping Tom, 1960
Lunch Hour, 1962
Return to Sender, 1963
In the Cool of the Day, 1963
Ladies Who Do, 1963
The Third Secret, 1964
The Verdict, 1964
Life at the Top, 1965
A High Wind in Jamaica, 1965
Where the Spies Are, 1965
Sands of the Kalahari, 1965
A Man For All Seasons, 1966
Red and Blue, 1967
Sebastian, 1967
The Strange Affair, 1968
Play Dirty, 1968
Sinful Davy, 1969
The Virgin Soldiers, 1969
The Mind of Mr. Soames, 1969
The Royal Hunt of the Sun,
    1969
No Blade of Grass, 1970
The Last Valley, 1970
Villain, 1971
Mary Queen of Scots, 1971
Living Free, 1972
Charley One-Eye, 1972
Dracula, 1973
Phase IV, 1974
Stand Up Virgin Soldiers, 1977
The Island of Dr. Moreau,
    1977

Black Trash, 1978
An Eye For An Eye, 1978
The London Affair, 1979
Cry of the Innocent, 1980
Zulu Dawn, 1980
Hawks, 1980
The Ordeal of Dr. Mudd, 1980

BETTY ANN DAVIES (1910-
    1955)
Stage and screen actress frequently cast in strained or rigid
roles.

Oh What a Duchess, 1933
Death at Broadcasting House,
    1934
Youthful Folly, 1934
Joy Ride, 1935
Play Up the Band, 1935
Chick, 1936
Excuse My Glove, 1936
She Knew What She Wanted,
    1936
Tropical Trouble, 1936
Radio Lover, 1936
Lucky Jade, 1937
Under a Cloud, 1937
Merry Comes to Town, 1937
Silver Top, 1938
Mountains O'Mourne, 1938
Kipps, 1941
It Always Rains On Sunday,
    1947
Escape, 1948
The Passionate Friends, 1948
To the Public Danger, 1948
Which Will You Have?, 1949
Now Barabbas, 1949
The History of Mr. Polly, 1949
Trio, 1950
An Outcast of the Islands, 1951
Cosh Boy, 1952
Grand National Night, 1953
Tonight at 8:30, 1953
The Belles of St. Trinian's,
    1954
Blackout, 1954
Murder By Proxy, 1955
Alias John Preston, 1956

JOHN HOWARD DAVIES
    (1939-   )
Fine child actor whose films
were very occasional but very
memorable.   Now television
director.

Oliver Twist, 1948
The Rocking Horse Winner,
    1950
The Magic Box, 1951
Tom Brown's School Days,
    1951

RUPERT DAVIES (1916-1976)
Character actor of stage and
screen, often in cameo roles,
most popular on television in
the "Maigret" series (1970).

The Traitors, 1957
Next to No Time, 1957
Sea Fury, 1958
The Key, 1958
Sapphire, 1959
Breakout, 1959
John Paul Jones, 1959
Life in Emergency Ward 10,
    1959
Violent Moment, 1959
Devil's Bait, 1959
Idol On Parade, 1959
The Criminal, 1960
Danger Tomorrow, 1960
Bobbikins, 1960
Death and Butter, 1962
Witness to Murder, 1962
Spy Who Came in From the
    Cold, 1965
The Uncle, 1965
Five Golden Dragons, 1966
Brides of Fu Manchu, 1966
House of a Thousand Dolls,
    1967
Curse of the Crimson Altar,
    1968
Dracula Has Risen From the
    Grave, 1968
Witchfinder General, 1968
Submarine X-1, 1969
The Oblong Box, 1969
The Firechasers, 1970

Waterloo, 1970
Zeppelin, 1971
The Night Visitor, 1971
Frightmare, 1976

STRINGER DAVIS (1896-1973)
Cheerful comedy character actor of stage and screen, generally seen in small parts,
often with his wife Dame Margaret Rutherford.

The Happiest Days of Your
    Life, 1950
Curtain Up, 1953
The Runaway Bus, 1954
The Smallest Show On Earth,
    1957
Murder She Said, 1962
Murder at the Gallop, 1963
The VIPs, 1963
Murder Ahoy, 1964
Murder Most Foul, 1965

ANTHONY DAWSON (1916-)
Character star of stage, screen
and television who is quite good
at portraying evil or menacing
roles.   Also in Hollywood.

The Way to the Stars, 1945
School For Secrets, 1946
Beware of Pity, 1949
The Queen of Spades, 1949
The Woman in Question, 1950
The Wooden Horse, 1950
The Long Dark Hall, 1951
Valley of the Eagles, 1951
Dial M For Murder, 1954
That Lady, 1955
Action of the Tiger, 1957
The Hour of Decision, 1957
The Haunted Strangler, 1958
Tiger Bay, 1959
Libel, 1959
Midnight Lace, 1960
Curse of the Werewolf, 1961
Offbeat, 1961
Dr. No, 1962
Seven Seas to Calais, 1963
Change Partners, 1965

Moll Flanders, 1965
Triple Cross, 1967
Hell is Empty, 1967
Cool Million 1971
The Battle of Neretva, 1971
The Big Game, 1972
The Count of Monte Cristo, 1975

FRANCES DAY (1908-)
Blonde German-Russian ac-
tress of stage and screen, long
in Britain; popular in the 30s.

The Price of Divorce, 1928
Big Business, 1930
O. K. Chief, 1930
The First Mrs. Fraser, 1932
The Girl From Maxim's, 1933
Two Hearts in Waltz Time,
    1934
Temptation, 1934
Oh Daddy, 1935
Public Nuisance Number One,
    1936
Dreams Come True, 1936
You Must Get Married, 1936
Who's Your Lady Friend?,
    1937
The Girl in the Taxi, 1937
Room For Two, 1940
Fiddlers Three, 1944
Tread Softly, 1952
There's Always a Thursday,
    1957
Climb Up the Wall, 1960

VERA DAY (1939-)
Blonde leading and supporting
actress of the fifties, normally
seen in humorous, absent-
minded roles.

Dance Little Lady, 1952
The Crowded Day, 1954
A Kid For Two Farthings,
    1955
It's a Great Day, 1956
Fun at St. Fanny's, 1956
Stars in Your Eyes, 1956
Hell Drivers, 1957
Quatermass II, 1957

The Prince and the Showgirl, 1957
The Flesh is Weak, 1957
A Clean Sweep, 1958
Woman Eater, 1958
Up the Creek, 1958
Them Nice Americans, 1958
Grip of the Strangler, 1958
I Was Monty's Double, 1958
Too Many Crooks, 1959
And The Same to You, 1960
The Trouble With Eve, 1960
The Trunk, 1961
Watch it Sailor, 1961
A Stitch in Time, 1963
Saturday Night Out, 1964

BRENDA DE BANZIE
   (1915-   )
Character actress and occasional leading lady of stage (since 1935), screen and television. Also in Hollywood.

The Long Dark Hall, 1951
I Believe in You, 1952
Private Information, 1952
Never Look Back, 1952
A Day to Remember, 1953
Hobson's Choice, 1954
The Purple Plain, 1954
As Long As They're Happy, 1954
What Every Woman Wants, 1954
A Kid For Two Farthings, 1955
Doctor at Sea, 1955
The Man Who Knew Too Much, 1956
House of Secrets, 1956
Too Many Crooks, 1959
The 39 Steps, 1959
Passport to Shame, 1959
Come September, 1960
The Entertainer, 1960
The Mark, 1961
Flame in the Streets, 1961
I Thank a Fool, 1962
A Pair of Briefs, 1962
The Pink Panther, 1963
Pretty Polly, 1967

NIGEL DE BRULIER (1878-1948)
Character actor with long career in Hollywood, primarily seen in silent films.

Intolerance, 1916
The Mystery of Thirteen, 1919
Sahara, 1919
Virgin of Stamboul, 1920
The Three Musketeers, 1921
Four Horsemen of the Apocalypse, 1921
Without Benefit of Clergy, 1921
A Doll's House, 1922
Omar the Tentmaker, 1922
Rupert of Hentzau, 1923
Salome, 1923
The Hunchback of Notre Dame, 1923
Wild Oranges, 1924
Three Weeks, 1924
A Boy of Flanders, 1924
Mademoiselle Midnight, 1924
A Regular Fellow, 1925
The Greater Glory, 1926
Ben Hur, 1926
Don Juan, 1926
Surrender, 1927
The Gaucho, 1927
Wings, 1927
Soft Cushions, 1927
Beloved Rogue, 1927
Loves of An Actress, 1928
Me Gangster, 1928
Two Lovers, 1928
Noah's Ark, 1929
The Iron Mask, 1929
Thru Different Eyes, 1929
The Wheel of Life, 1929
The Green Goddess, 1930
Moby Dick, 1931
Son of India, 1931
Ben Hur, 1931
Rasputin and the Empress, 1932
Miss Pinkerton, 1932
I'm No Angel, 1933
Viva Villa, 1934
Charlie Chan in Egypt, 1935
The Three Musketeers, 1935
Down Under the Sea, 1936

Mary of Scotland, 1936
The Garden of Allah, 1936
Zorro Rides Again, 1937
Hound of the Baskervilles,
 1939
One Million B. C. , 1940
Viva Cisco Kid, 1940
The Mad Empress, 1940
Adventures of Captain Marvel,
 1941
Tonight We Raid Calais, 1943

JEANNE DE CASALIS (1896-
 1966)
Character actress of stage
(1919) and screen, generally
seen in flighty or scatterbrained
roles.   Also famous on radio
as "Mrs. Feather. "   Married
to Colin Clive.

Settled Out of Court, 1925
The Glad Eye, 1927
The Arcadians, 1927
Zero, 1928
Infatuation, 1930
Knowing Men, 1930
Nine Till Six, 1932
Radio Parade, 1933
Mixed Doubles, 1933
Nell Gwyn, 1934
Just Like a Woman, 1938
Jamaica Inn, 1939
The Girl Who Forgot, 1939
Sailors Three, 1940
Charley's Big-Hearted Aunt,
 1940
Cottage to Let, 1941
The Fine Feathers, 1941
Pathetone Parade of 1941, 1941
Pathetone Parade of 1942, 1942
Those Kids From Town, 1942
They Met in the Dark, 1943
Medal For the General, 1944
This Man is Mine, 1946
The Turners of Prospect Road,
 1947
Woman Hater, 1948
The 20 Questions Murder
 Mystery, 1950

DERRICK DE MARNEY   (1906-
 1978)
Handsome leading man of stage
(from 1926) and screen, brother of Terence De Marney.

Two Little Drummer Boys,
 1928
Adventurous Youth, 1928
The Forger, 1928
Valley of the Ghosts, 1928
Shadows, 1930
Stranglehold, 1931
The Laughter of Fools, 1933
Music Hall, 1934
Once in a New Moon, 1935
Immortal Gentleman, 1935
Windfall, 1935
Things to Come, 1936
Land Without Music, 1936
Cafe Mascot, 1936
Born That Way, 1936
Blonde Cheat, 1937
Victoria the Great, 1937
Young and Innocent, 1937
Pearls of the Crown, 1938
Sixty Glorious Years, 1938
Flying Fifty-Five, 1939
The Lion Has Wings, 1939
The Spider, 1939
The Second Mr. Bush, 1940
Three Silent Men, 1940
Dangerous Moonlight, 1941
The First of the Few, 1942
Latin Quarter, 1945
Uncle Silas, 1947
Sleeping Car to Trieste, 1948
She Shall Have Murder, 1950
No Way Back, 1951
Meet Mr. Callaghan, 1954
Private's Progress, 1956
The March Hare, 1956
Doomsday at Eleven, 1963
The Projected Man, 1966

TERENCE DE MARNEY   (1909-
 1971)
Sinewy, vigorous character
star, on stage since 1923,
brother of Derrick De Marney.
Also in Hollywood.

The Eternal Feminine, 1931
Heroes of the Mine, 1932
The Merry Men of Sherwood,
    1932
Little Napoleon, 1933
Eyes of Fate, 1933
The Unholy Quest, 1934
Immortal Gentleman, 1935
Mystery of the Mary Celeste,
    1935
Born That Way, 1936
House of Silence, 1937
I Killed the Count, 1939
Dual Alibi, 1947
No Way Back, 1949
Uneasy Terms, 1949
The Silver Chalice, 1954
Desert Sands, 1955
Target Zero, 1955
23 Paces to Baker Street, 1956
Wreck of the Mary Deare,
    1959
Spartacus, 1960
On the Double, 1961
Monster of Terror, 1965
Death is a Woman, 1966
Hand of Night, 1966
Son of the Sahara, 1967
Separation, 1968
The Strange Affair, 1968
All Neat in Black Stockings,
    1969

EDWARD DE SOUZA (1933-)
Dark-haired leading man, mainly
seen on stage.

The Roman Spring of Mrs.
    Stone, 1961
The Phantom of the Opera, 1962
Kiss of the Vampire, 1963
The Main Chance, 1964
Rocket to the Moon, 1967
Spell of Evil, 1973
The Spy Who Loved Me, 1977
The Thirty Nine Steps, 1980

FRANCIS DE WOLFF (1913-)
Bluff, bearded character star
of films and television, often
seen in surly or menacing roles.

Flame in the Heather, 1935
Fire Over England, 1937
Adam and Evalyn, 1948
Trottie True, 1949
Under Capricorn, 1949
Treasure Island, 1950
The Naked Earth, 1950
Scrooge, 1951
Tom Brown's School Days,
    1951
Ivanhoe, 1952
The Master of Ballantrae,
    1953
Miss Robin Hood, 1953
The Kidnappers, 1953
The Seekers, 1954
The Diamond, 1954
Geordie, 1955
King's Rhapsody, 1955
The Naked Heart, 1955
Moby Dick, 1956
The Smallest Show On Earth,
    1957
Saint Joan, 1957
Odongo, 1957
Sea Fury, 1958
The Roots of Heaven, 1958
Corridors of Blood, 1958
Hound of the Baskervilles,
    1959
Tommy the Toreador, 1959
The Man Who Could Cheat
    Death, 1959
House of Fright, 1960
Clue of the Twisted Candle,
    1960
The Silent Invasion, 1962
The Durant Affair, 1962
The World Ten Times Over,
    1963
Seige of the Saxons, 1963
The Devil Doll, 1963
From Russia With Love, 1963
The Three Lives of Thomasina,
    1963
The Black Torment, 1964
Carry On Cleo, 1964
Licensed to Kill, 1965
The Liquidator, 1966
Triple Cross, 1967
Sinful Davy, 1969
Clouds of Witness, 1973
Jesus of Nazareth, 1977

ISABEL DEAN (1918-)
Stage actress in occasional
films since the late 40s, generally seen in patrician roles.

The Passionate Friends, 1948
24 Hours in a Woman's Life,
  1952
The Last Page, 1952
The Woman's Angle, 1952
Twice Upon a Time, 1953
Gilbert and Sullivan, 1953
Out of the Clouds, 1955
Davy, 1957
Virgin Island, 1958
Light in the Piazza, 1962
A High Wind in Jamaica, 1965
A Man Could Get Killed, 1965
Inadmissible Evidence, 1968
Oh What a Lovely War, 1969
Catch Me a Spy, 1971
The Terrorists, 1975
The Bawdy Adventures of Tom
  Jones, 1975
Rough Cut, 1980

IVOR DEAN (1917-1974)
Character actor of the 60s,
also on television.

The Sorcerers, 1966
Theatre of Death, 1967
Stranger in the House, 1967
Where Eagles Dare, 1968
File of the Golden Goose, 1968
The Oblong Box, 1969
Dr. Jekyll and Sister Hyde,
  1972

DIANA DECKER (1926-)
Attractive, intelligent American
leading lady; in Britain from
late 1930s. Also on television.

San Demetrio-London, 1943
Fiddlers Three, 1944
The Gong Cried Murder, 1946
Meet Me at Dawn, 1947
When You Come Home, 1947
A Man's Affair, 1949
Murder at the Windmill, 1949

Saturday Island, 1952
It Started in Paradise, 1952
Is Your Honeymoon Really
  Necessary?, 1953
Will Any Gentleman, 1953
Knave of Hearts, 1954
A Yank in Ermine, 1955
The Betrayal, 1958
Lolita, 1962
Devils of Darkness, 1964

EUGENE DECKERS (1917-)
French character player, long
in Britain where he normally
is cast as policemen or other
kindly officials, often foreign.

Dual Alibi, 1946
Woman to Woman, 1946
Mrs. Fitzherbert, 1947
Against the Wind, 1948
Sleeping Car to Trieste, 1948
The Elusive Pimpernel, 1950
The Golden Salamander, 1950
Highly Dangerous, 1950
Madeleine, 1950
The Lavender Hill Mob, 1951
Tony Draws a Horse, 1951
So Long at the Fair, 1951
Hotel Sahara, 1952
Night Without Stars, 1953
The Love Lottery, 1954
Father Brown, 1954
The Colditz Story, 1955
House of Secrets, 1956
Port Afrique, 1956
Seven Thunders, 1957
Northwest Frontier, 1959
A Weekend With Lulu, 1961
Lady L, 1966
The Last Safari, 1967
Hell is Empty, 1967
The Limbo Line, 1968
The Assassination Bureau,
  1969

MAUREEN DELANEY (-)
Irish character actress in films
of the 40s and 50s.

Odd Man Out, 1947

Captain Boycott, 1947
The Mark of Cain, 1948
Another Shore, 1948
Under Capricorn, 1949
Saints and Sinners, 1949
The Holly and the Ivy, 1952
The Long Arm, 1956
The March Hare, 1956
Jacqueline, 1956
The Rising of the Moon, 1957
The Scamp, 1957
The Story of Esther Costello, 1957
Tread Softly Stranger, 1958
The Doctor's Dilemma, 1959

CYRIL DELEVANTI (1887-1976)
Character actor of stage and screen, long in Hollywood where he played old men in occasional films.

Devotion, 1931
Night Monster, 1942
Phantom of the Opera, 1943
The House of Fear, 1945
The Emperor Waltz, 1948
D-Day, the Sixth of June, 1956
Dead Ringer, 1964
Mary Poppins, 1964
Night of the Iguana, 1964
The Greatest Story Ever Told, 1965
Oh Dad Poor Dad, 1966
Counterpoint, 1968
The Killing of Sister George, 1968
Bedknobs and Broomsticks, 1971
Black Eye, 1973
Soylent Green, 1973

JUDI DENCH (1934-)
Stage actress who made occasional but impressive films.

The Third Secret, 1964
A Study in Terror, 1965
He Who Rides a Tiger, 1966
Four in the Morning, 1966

A Midsummer Night's Dream, 1968
Luther, 1973
Dead Cert, 1974

MAURICE DENHAM (1909-)
Versatile character star of stage (from 1934), radio (1939) and films; often cast in official capacity.

Home and School, 1946
Daybreak, 1946
The Man Within, 1947
Take My Life, 1947
Dear Murderer, 1947
The Upturned Glass, 1947
Holiday Camp, 1947
Jassy, 1947
Captain Boycott, 1947
End of the River, 1947
Easy Money, 1948
Blanche Fury, 1948
Escape, 1948
Miranda, 1948
My Brother's Keeper, 1948
London Belongs to Me, 1948
The Blind Goddess, 1948
Oliver Twist, 1948
Quartet, 1948
Look Before You Love, 1948
Here Come the Huggetts, 1948
Once Upon a Dream, 1949
The Blue Lagoon, 1949
It's Not Cricket, 1949
A Boy, a Girl and a Bike, 1949
Poet's Pub, 1949
Madness of the Heart, 1949
Don't Ever Leave Me, 1949
Landfall, 1949
The Spider and the Fly, 1949
Traveller's Joy, 1950
No Highway, 1951
The Net, 1953
Time Bomb, 1953
Street Corner, 1953
Eight O'clock Walk, 1954
The Million Pound Note, 1954
The Purple Plain, 1954
Carrington VC, 1955
Simon and Laura, 1955

Doctor at Sea, 1955
Animal Farm, 1955
23 Paces to Baker Street,
  1956
Checkpoint, 1956
Night of the Demon, 1957
Barnacle Bill, 1957
Man With a Dog, 1958
The Captain's Table, 1959
Our Man in Havana, 1959
Ali and the Camel, 1960
Two-Way Stretch, 1960
Sink the Bismarck, 1960
The Mark, 1961
Invasion Quartet, 1961
The Greengage Summer, 1961
HMS Defiant, 1962
Penang, 1963
The Setup, 1963
Paranoiac, 1963
The King's Breakfast, 1963
The Very Edge, 1963
Downfall, 1964
The Seventh Dawn, 1964
Hysteria, 1964
The Uncle, 1965
Legend of Young Dick Turpin,
  1965
Operation Crossbow, 1965
Those Magnificent Men in
  Their Flying Machines, 1965
The Nanny, 1965
The Alphabet Murders, 1965
The Heroes of Telemark, 1966
After the Fox, 1966
The Night Caller, 1966
The Eliminator, 1967
The Long Duel, 1967
Torture Garden, 1967
Danger Route, 1967
Attack on the Iron Coast, 1968
Negatives, 1968
Some Girls Do, 1969
Midas Run, 1969
The Best House in London,
  1969
A Touch of Love, 1969
The Virgin and the Gypsy,
  1970
Countess Dracula, 1970
Sunday Bloody Sunday, 1971
Nicholas and Alexandra, 1971
Day of the Jackal, 1973

Luther, 1974
Shout at the Devil, 1976
Julia, 1977

MICHAEL DENISON (1915-   )
Gentle-mannered leading actor
of stage and screen, married
to Dulcie Gray.

Tilly of Bloomsbury, 1940
Hungry Hill, 1946
My Brother Jonathan, 1948
The Blind Goddess, 1948
The Glass Mountain, 1948
Landfall, 1949
The Franchise Affair, 1950
The Magic Box, 1951
Angels One Five, 1952
The Tall Headlines, 1952
The Importance of Being
  Earnest, 1952
There Was a Young Lady,
  1953
Contraband Spain, 1955
The Truth About Women, 1958
Faces in the Dark, 1960

REGINALD DENNY (1891-
  1967)
Kindly, debonair character
star of stage and screen, long
in Hollywood.   Latterly in the
aviation business.

49 East, 1920
Footlights, 1921
Escape to Burma, 1921
The Iron Trail, 1921
The Leather Pushers, 1922
The Abysmal Brute, 1923
Sporting Youth, 1924
The Reckless Age, 1924
The Fast Worker, 1924
Skinner's Dress Suit, 1925
I'll Show You the Town, 1925
Where Was I?, 1925
Oh Doctor, 1926
What Happened to Jones, 1926
Rolling Home, 1926
Take it From Me, 1926
California Straight Ahead, 1927

The Cheerful Fraud, 1927
Fast and Furious, 1927
Out All Night, 1927
On Your Toes, 1928
That's My Daddy, 1928
Good Morning Judge, 1928
The Night Bird, 1928
Red Hot Speed, 1929
Clear the Decks, 1929
Embarassing Moments, 1929
Madam Satan, 1930
What a Man!, 1930
Those Three French Girls,
   1930
A Lady's Morals, 1930
Kiki, 1931
Parlor, Bedroom and Bath,
   1931
Strange Justice, 1932
Private Lives, 1932
The Iron Master, 1933
The Barbarian, 1933
Only Yesterday, 1933
The Lost Patrol, 1934
Of Human Bondage, 1934
The World Moves On, 1934
Dancing Men, 1934
One More River, 1934
We're Rich Again, 1934
Richest Girl in the World,
   1934
The Little Minister, 1934
Vagabond Lady, 1935
Anna Karenina, 1935
No More Ladies, 1935
Here's to Romance, 1935
Remember Last Night, 1935
Romeo and Juliet, 1936
The Preview Murder Mystery,
   1936
Two in a Crowd, 1936
More Than a Secretary, 1936
Women of Glamour, 1937
The Great Gambini, 1937
Bulldog Drummond Comes Back,
   1937
Beg, Borrow Or Steal, 1937
Bulldog Drummond's Revenge,
   1937
Bulldog Drummond's Peril,
   1938
Four Men and a Prayer, 1938
Blockade, 1938

Bulldog Drummond in Africa,
   1938
Arrest Bulldog Drummond,
   1939
Bulldog Drummond's Secret
   Police, 1939
Bulldog Drummond's Bride,
   1939
Spring Parade, 1940
Seven Sinners, 1940
Rebecca, 1940
One Night in Lisbon, 1941
Appointment for Love, 1941
International Squadron, 1941
Captains of the Clouds, 1942
Eyes in the Night, 1942
Thunderbirds, 1942
Over My Dead Body, 1942
Sherlock Holmes and the Voice
   of Terror, 1942
Song of the Open Road, 1944
Love Letters, 1945
Tangier, 1946
The Locket, 1946
The Macomber Affair, 1947
Secret Life of Walter Mitty,
   1947
My Favorite Brunette, 1947
Escape Me Never, 1947
Christmas Eve, 1947
Mr. Blandings Builds His
   Dream House, 1948
Iroquois Trail, 1951
Abbott and Costello Meet Dr.
   Jekyll and Mr. Hyde, 1953
World For Ransom, 1954
Sabaka, 1956
Around the World in 80 Days,
   1956
Fort Vengeance, 1959
Cat Ballou, 1965
Batman, 1966

FLORENCE DESMOND
   (1905-)
Actress of stage (from 1916)
and screen, also dancer and
impersonator; popular in the
30s. Also Hollywood.

The Road to Fortune, 1930
Sally in Our Alley, 1931

Murder On the Second Floor,
  1932
The Marriage Bond, 1932
Nine Till Six, 1932
Impromptu, 1932
High Society, 1932
The River House Ghost, 1932
Mr. Skitch, 1933
Long Live the King, 1933
Radio Parade, 1933
My Lucky Star, 1933
Gay Love, 1934
No Limit, 1935
Accused, 1936
Keep Your Seats Please, 1936
Kicking the Moon Around, 1938
Hoots Mon, 1939
Three Came Home, 1950
Charley Moon, 1956
Some Girls Do, 1969

JERRY DESMONDE (1908-
  1967)
Stage and screen character
player who served as a straight
man to a number of different
comedians.

London Town, 1946
Cardboard Cavalier, 1949
Trouble in Store, 1953
Alf's Baby, 1953
The Malta Story, 1953
The Angel Who Pawned Her
  Harp, 1955
Man of the Moment, 1955
Ramsbottom Rides Again, 1956
Up in the World, 1956
A King in New York, 1957
Follow a Star, 1959
Carry On Regardless, 1961
A Kind of Loving, 1962
The Switch, 1963
Stolen Hours, 1963
A Stitch in Time, 1963
The Beauty Jungle, 1964
The Early Bird, 1965
Gonks Go Beat, 1965

TAMARA DESNI (1913-)
Dark-haired Russian-born

leading actress, long in Britain; married to Raymond
Lovell.   Films mainly in the
30s.

Der Schrecken Der Garmison,
  1932
Falling For You, 1933
Jack Ahoy, 1934
Bypass to Happiness, 1934
How's Chances, 1934
Forbidden Territory, 1934
McGlusky the Sea Rover, 1935
Dark World, 1935
Blue Smoke, 1935
Love in Exile, 1936
Fire Over England, 1937
The Squeaker, 1937
His Brother's Keeper, 1939
Traitor Spy, 1939
Flight From Folly, 1945
Send For Paul Temple, 1946
The Hills of Donegal, 1947
Dick Barton at Bay, 1950

ANTON DIFFRING (1918-)
German character star of British and latterly international
films, generally seen as nazi
officer or other villainous characters.

State Secret, 1950
Appointment With Venus, 1951
The Woman's Angle, 1952
Hotel Sahara, 1952
The Red Beret, 1953
Albert RN, 1953
Park Plaza 605, 1953
Operation Diplomat, 1953
Betrayed, 1954
The Sea Shall Not Have Them,
  1955
The Colditz Story, 1955
The Crooked Sky, 1955
I Am a Camera, 1956
Doublecross, 1956
The Black Tent, 1956
The Traitors, 1957
Triple Deception, 1957
The Man Who Could Cheat
  Death, 1959

Circus of Horrors, 1960
Enter Inspector Duval,
    1960
Lady of Vengeance, 1960
A Question of Adultery,
    1961
Incident at Midnight, 1963
The Heroes of Telemark,
    1965
Fahrenheit 451, 1966
The Blue Max, 1966
The Double Man, 1967
Counterpoint, 1968
Where Eagles Dare, 1968
Zeppelin, 1971
Dead Pigeon on Beethoven
    Street, 1972
Little Mother, 1973
The Beast Must Die, 1974
The Swiss Conspiracy, 1975
Call Him Mr. Shatter, 1975
Mark of the Devil Part II,
    1975
Operation Daybreak, 1976
Potato Fritz, 1976
Vanessa, 1977
Valentino, 1977
Les Indiens Sont Encore Loin,
    1977
L'Imprecateur, 1977

DUDLEY DIGGES (1879-1947)
Irish actor popular in Hollywood
in the 30s; formerly with the
Abbey Theatre.

Condemned, 1929
Outward Bound, 1930
Upper Underworld, 1930
The Maltese Falcon, 1931
The Ruling Voice, 1931
Alexander Hamilton, 1931
Devotion, 1931
The Honorable Mr. Wong, 1931
The Hatchet Man, 1932
Strange Case of Clara Deane,
    1932
Roar of the Dragon, 1932
The First Year, 1932
Tess of the Storm Country,
    1932
The King's Vacation, 1933

Mayor of Hell, 1933
Silk Express, 1933
The Narrow Corner, 1933
The Invisible Man, 1933
The Emperor Jones, 1933
Before Dawn, 1933
Fury of the Jungle, 1934
Caravan, 1934
The World Moves On, 1934
Massacre, 1934
What Every Woman Knows, 1934
I Am a Thief, 1934
Notorious Gentleman, 1935
Mutiny On the Bounty, 1935
China Seas, 1935
The Bishop Misbehaves, 1935
Three Live Ghosts, 1936
The Voice of Bugle Ann, 1936
The Unguarded Hour, 1936
The General Died at Dawn, 1936
Valiant is the Word For Car-
    rie, 1936
Love is News, 1937
The Light That Failed, 1939
The Fight For Life, 1940
Raffles, 1940
Son of Fury, 1942
The Searching Wind, 1946

BASIL DIGNAM (1905-)
Small-part character player,
generally seen as doctors,
lawyers, etc. Brother of Mark
Dignam.

Hammer the Toff, 1952
His Excellency, 1952
Touch and Go, 1955
They Can't Hang Me, 1955
The Narrowing Circle, 1956
The Intimate Stranger, 1956
Three Sundays to Live, 1957
Son of a Stranger, 1957
Brothers In Law, 1957
Carry On Sergeant, 1958
Corridors of Blood, 1958
Them Nice Americans, 1958
The Spaniard's Curse, 1958
A Touch of Larceny, 1959
Toom at the Top, 1959
I'm All Right, Jack, 1959
Sentenced For Life, 1960

Spider's Web, 1960
Court Martial of Major Keller,
    1961
The Fourth Square, 1961
The Silent Partner, 1961
Victim, 1961
Suspect, 1961
Fate Takes a Hand, 1962
Life For Ruth, 1963
80,000 Suspects, 1963
Rotten to the Core, 1965
Cuckoo Patrol, 1965
The Jokers, 1966
Naked Evil, 1966
Walk in the Shadow, 1966
Laughter in the Dark, 1969
The Games, 1970
10 Rillington Place, 1971

MARK DIGNAM (1909-)
Small-part character player
cast in much the same fashion
as his brother Basil Dignam.

Jim the Penman, 1947
Train of Events, 1949
Murder in the Cathedral, 1952
The Maggie, 1954
Beau Brummell, 1954
The Passing Stranger, 1954
The Prisoner, 1955
Carrington VC, 1955
Sink the Bismarck, 1960
Conscience Bay, 1960
No Love For Johnnie, 1961
Lancelot and Guinevere, 1963
Siege of the Saxons, 1963
Tom Jones, 1963
The Eyes of Annie Jones, 1963
Clash By Night, 1963
A Jolly Bad Fellow, 1964
Game For Three Losers, 1965
Charge of the Light Brigade,
    1968
Isadora, 1968
Hamlet, 1970
Disraeli: Portrait of a Ro-
    mantic, 1980

VERNON DOBTCHEFF (- -)
Character actor of television

and films who is at his best
in evil or menacing characterizations.

The Hidden Face, 1965
The Taming of the Shrew,
    1967
The Assassination Bureau,
    1969
Anne of the Thousand Days,
    1970
The Beast in the Cellar, 1970
Mary Queen of Scots, 1971
The Horsemen, 1971
Nicholas and Alexandra, 1971
Fiddler on the Roof, 1971
Day of the Jackal, 1973
The Destructors, 1974
Murder on the Orient Express,
    1974
Galileo, 1975
The Spy Who Loved Me, 1977
March Or Die, 1977
Nijinsky, 1979

GUY DOLEMAN (1923-)
Australian actor of films and
tv who mostly plays unruffled
or no-nonsense characters.

Kangaroo, 1952
Phantom Stockade, 1953
His Majesty O'Keefe, 1954
Smiley, 1956
The Shiralee, 1957
Smiley Gets a Gun, 1958
On the Beach, 1958
The Partner, 1963
The System, 1964
Boy With a Flute, 1964
Thunderball, 1965
The Ipcress File, 1965
The Idol, 1966
Funeral in Berlin, 1966
Twist of Sand, 1967
Billion Dollar Brain, 1967
The Deadly Bees, 1967

JAMES DONALD (1917-)
Scottish star of stage (from
1935), screen and television,

also in Hollywood. Usually
seen in good-natured, deep-
thinking roles.

The Missing Million, 1941
In Which We Serve, 1942
San Demetrio-London, 1943
Went the Day Well, 1943
The Way Ahead, 1944
Broken Journey, 1948
The Small Voice, 1948
Edward My Son, 1949
Trottie True, 1949
Cage of Gold, 1950
White Corridors, 1951
Brandy For the Parson, 1952
The Gift Horse, 1952
The Pickwick Papers, 1952
The Net, 1953
Beau Brummell, 1954
Lust For Life, 1956
The Bridge On the River Kwai,
1957
The Vikings, 1958
Third Man On the Mountain,
1959
The Great Escape, 1963
King Rat, 1965
The Jokers, 1966
Cast a Giant Shadow, 1966
Quatermass and the Pit, 1967
Hannibal Brooks, 1969
The Royal Hunt of the Sun,
1969
David Copperfield, 1969
Destiny of a Spy, 1969
Conduct Unbecoming, 1975
The Big Sleep, 1978

ROBERT DONAT (1905-1958)
Distinguished, outstanding, gentlemanly star of stage (1921)
and screen, also in Hollywood.
Married to Renee Asherson.

Men of Tomorrow, 1932
That Night in London, 1932
Cash, 1933
Private Life of Henry VIII,
1933
The Count of Monte Cristo,
1934

The Thirty-Nine Steps, 1935
The Ghost Goes West, 1936
Knight Without Armour, 1937
The Citadel, 1938
Goodbye Mr. Chips, 1939
The Young Mr. Pitt, 1942
The Adventures of Tartu, 1943
Perfect Strangers, 1945
Captain Boycott, 1947
The Winslow Boy, 1948
The Cure For Love, 1949
The Magic Box, 1951
Royal Heritage, 1953
Lease of Life, 1954
Stained Glass at Fairford, 1956
Inn of the Sixth Happiness,
1958

YOLANDE DONLAN (1920-)
Blonde, American-born leading
actress of stage (1938); in occasional films since 1940.
Long in Britain, married to
director Val Guest (1911-).

Turnabout, 1940
Traveller's Joy, 1949
Miss Pilgrim's Progress, 1950
The Body Said No, 1950
Mr. Drake's Duck, 1951
Penny Princess, 1952
They Can't Hang Me, 1955
Tarzan and the Lost Safari,
1957
Expresso Bongo, 1959
Jigsaw, 1962
80,000 Suspects, 1963
The Adventurers, 1970
Seven Nights in Japan, 1976

PATRIC DOONAN (1925-1958)
Stage and screen actor generally cast as honest, good-
natured fellows. Son of comedian George Doonan.

Once a Jolly Swagman, 1948
Train of Events, 1949
A Run For Your Money, 1949
All Over Town, 1949
The Blue Lamp, 1950

Blackout, 1950
Highly Dangerous, 1950
Calling Bulldog Drummond,
   1951
The Lavender Hill Mob, 1951
The Man in the White Suit,
   1951
High Treason, 1951
Appointment With Venus, 1951
I'm a Stranger, 1952
The Gift Horse, 1952
The Gentle Gunman, 1952
Wheel of Fate, 1953
The Red Beret, 1953
The Net, 1953
Seagulls Over Sorrento, 1954
What Every Woman Wants, 1954
John and Julie, 1955
Cockleshell Heroes, 1955

SANDRA DORNE (1925-)
Attractive leading lady of stage
(from 1944) and screen, primarily in second features.
Married to Patrick Holt.

Eyes That Kill, 1947
Saraband For Dead Lovers,
   1948
Once a Jolly Swagman, 1948
A Piece of Cake, 1949
All Over Town, 1949
The Golden Arrow, 1949
The Miniver Story, 1950
Never Say Die, 1950
The Clouded Yellow, 1950
Happy Go Lovely, 1951
13 East Street, 1952
Hindle Wakes, 1952
The Yellow Balloon, 1952
Alf's Baby, 1953
Wheel of Fate, 1953
The Beggar's Opera, 1953
Marilyn, 1953
Roadhouse Girl, 1954
The Weak and the Wicked,
   1954
The Good Die Young, 1954
Police Dog, 1955
The Gelignite Gang, 1956
Alias John Preston, 1956
The Iron Petticoat, 1956

Operation Murder, 1957
Three Sundays to Live, 1957
Orders to Kill, 1958
Portrait of a Matador, 1958
The Bank Raiders, 1958
Not a Hope in Hell, 1960
House in Marsh Road, 1960
The Malpas Mystery, 1960
The Amorous Prawn, 1962
Devil Doll, 1963
The Secret Door, 1964
All Coppers Are, 1971
Joseph Andrews, 1977

DIANA DORS (1931-)
Buxom blonde leading actress
of stage and films, often seen
in brash characterizations.
Also in Hollywood.

The Shop at Sly Corner, 1946
Holiday Camp, 1947
Dancing With Crime, 1947
Oliver Twist, 1948
The Calendar, 1948
Good Time Girl, 1948
My Sister and I, 1948
Penny and the Pownall Case,
   1948
Here Come the Huggetts, 1948
Vote For Huggett, 1949
It's Not Cricket, 1949
A Boy, a Girl and a Bike,
   1949
Diamond City, 1949
Dance Hall, 1950
Worm's Eye View, 1951
Lady Godiva Rides Again, 1951
The Last Page, 1952
My Wife's Lodger, 1952
The Great Game, 1953
Is Your Honeymoon Really
   Necessary?, 1953
It's a Grand Life, 1953
The Weak and the Wicked, 1954
As Long as They're Happy,
   1954
Miss Tulip Stays the Night,
   1955
A Kid For Two Farthings,
   1955
Value For Money, 1955

An Alligator Named Daisy,
1955
Yield to the Night, 1956
The Unholy Wife, 1957
The Long Haul, 1957
I Married a Woman, 1958
Tread Softly Stranger, 1958
Passport to Shame, 1959
Ladies May, 1960
Scent of Mystery, 1960
The Love Specialist, 1961
On the Double, 1961
King of the Roaring Twenties,
1961
Mrs. Gibbons' Boys, 1962
West Eleven, 1963
Allez France, 1964
The Counterfeit Constable,
1964
The Sandwich Man, 1966
Berserk, 1967
Danger Route, 1967
Hammerhead, 1968
Baby Love, 1969
Deep End, 1970
There's a Girl in My Soup,
1970
Hannie Caulder, 1971
The Pied Piper, 1971
The Amazing Mr. Blunden,
1972
Nothing But the Night, 1972
Theatre of Blood, 1973
A Taste of Blood, 1973
Steptoe and Son Ride Again,
1973
From Beyond the Grave, 1973
Craze, 1973
The Amorous Milkman, 1974
Bedtime With Rosie, 1974
Three For All, 1974
Keep it Up Downstairs, 1976
Adventures of a Taxi Driver,
1976
Confessions of a Driving In-
structor, 1976
Adventures of a Private Eye,
1977
The Groove Room, 1977
The David Galaxy Affair, 1979

ROY DOTRICE (1923-)

Stage actor adept at doddering
characterizations, films infrequent.

The Heroes of Telemark, 1965
A Twist of Sand, 1968
Lock Up Your Daughters, 1969
One of Those Things, 1971
Nicholas and Alexandra, 1971

ROBERT DOUGLAS (1909-)
Actor of stage (1927) and
screen, seen as hero or villain alike. Also Hollywood;
also television director.

P. C. Josser, 1931
Many Waters, 1931
The Blarney Stone, 1933
Death Drives Through, 1935
The Street Singer, 1936
London Melody, 1937
Our Fighting Navy, 1937
Over the Moon, 1937
The Challenge, 1938
The Lion Has Wings, 1939
The Chinese Bungalow, 1940
End of the River, 1947
New Adventures of Don Juan,
1948
Decision of Christopher Blake,
1948
The Fountainhead, 1949
Homicide, 1949
The Lady Takes a Sailor,
1949
Barricade, 1950
The Flame and the Arrow,
1950
Spy Hunt, 1950
Kim, 1950
Mystery Submarine, 1950
This Side of the Law, 1950
Buccaneer's Girl, 1950
Sons of the Musketeers, 1951
Target Unknown, 1951
Thunder On the Hill, 1951
The Prisoner of Zenda, 1952
Ivanhoe, 1952
At Sword's Point, 1952
Fair Wind to Java, 1953
The Desert Rats, 1953

Flight to Tangier, 1953
Saskatchewan, 1954
King Richard and the Crusaders,
  1954
The Virgin Queen, 1955
The Scarlet Coat, 1955
Good Morning Miss Dove, 1955
Helen of Troy, 1955
The Young Philadelphians, 1959

JOAN DOWLING (1929-1954)
Supporting actress of the 40s
and 50s, often seen as teenager. Married to Harry Fowler.

Hue and Cry, 1946
No Room at the Inn, 1948
Bond Street, 1948
Train of Events, 1949
Landfall, 1949
For Them That Trespass, 1949
A Man's Affair, 1949
Murder Without Crime, 1950
Pool of London, 1951
The Magic Box, 1951
Women of Twilight, 1952
24 Hours of a Woman's Life,
  1952

LESLEY ANN DOWN (1954-)
Dark-haired leading actress of
television and films, popular on
the "Upstairs Downstairs" series.

Countess Dracula, 1970
All the Right Noises, 1971
Pope Joan, 1972
Scalawag, 1973
From Beyond the Grave, 1973
In the Devil's Garden, 1974
Brannigan, 1974
The Pink Panther Strikes Again,
  1976
A Little Night Music, 1978
The Betsy, 1978
The Great Train Robbery, 1979
Hanover Street, 1979
Rough Cut, 1980

VERNON DOWNING (-)
Character actor long in Hollywood, adept at nervous or
twitching parts.

The Barretts of Wimpole Street,
  1934
Clive of India, 1935
Les Miserables, 1935
Mutiny On the Bounty, 1935
Romeo and Juliet, 1936
Wuthering Heights, 1939
Suspicion, 1941
Sherlock Holmes Faces Death,
  1943
The Spider Woman, 1944

KENNETH DOWNY (-)
Small-part actor adept at supercilious roles, films very rare.

Oliver Twist, 1948
Dulcimer Street, 1948
The Happiest Days of Your
  Life, 1950

CHARLIE DRAKE (1925-)
Diminutive slapstick comedian,
mainly on television (since
1950).

The Golden Link, 1954
Sands of the Desert, 1960
Petticoat Pirates, 1961
The Cracksman, 1963
Mister Ten Per Cent, 1966
Professor Popper's Problems,
  1974

FABIA DRAKE (1904-)
Character actress of stage and
films, generally seen in domineering roles.

Masks and Faces, 1917
Meet Mr. Penny, 1938
Poet's Pub, 1949
All Over Town, 1949
White Corridors, 1951
Young Wives' Tale, 1951

The Hour of Thirteen, 1952
Isn't Life Wonderful?, 1953
Fast and Loose, 1954
All For Mary, 1955
My Wife's Family, 1956
Man in the Shadow, 1957
The Good Companions, 1957
Not Wanted On Voyage, 1957
Girls at Sea, 1958
Operation Bullshine, 1959
What a Whopper, 1961
Seven Keys, 1962
Dead End Creek, 1964
Tam Lin, 1971

ALFRED DRAYTON (1881-
    1949)
Bald-pated character star of
stage (from 1908) and screen,
latterly in villainous comedy
parts.

Iron Justice, 1915
A Little Bit of Fluff, 1919
Honeypot, 1920
The Temporary Gentleman,
    1920
Love Maggy, 1921
A Scandal in Bohemia, 1921
The Squeaker, 1930
The W Plan, 1931
Brown Sugar, 1931
The Happy Ending, 1931
The Calendar, 1931
Lord Babs, 1932
The Little Damozel, 1933
It's a Boy, 1933
Falling For You, 1933
Friday the Thirteenth, 1933
Jack Ahoy, 1934
Red Ensign, 1934
Lady in Danger, 1934
Radio Parade of 1935, 1935
Love Affair of the Dictator,
    1935
Oh Daddy, 1935
Look Up and Laugh, 1935
Me and Marlborough, 1935
First a Girl, 1935
The Crimson Circle, 1936
Tropical Trouble, 1936
Aren't Men Beasts?, 1937

A Spot of Bother, 1938
So This is London, 1939
Banana Ridge, 1941
The Big Blockade, 1942
Women Aren't Angels, 1942
Halfway House, 1944
Don't Take it to Heart, 1944
They Knew Mr. Knight, 1944
Nicholas Nickleby, 1947
Things Happen at Night, 1948

SONIA DRESDEL (1909-1976)
Dominant actress, mainly on
stage, outstanding in authoritative or slightly sinister roles.
Also on television, notably in
"The Pallisers." (1976). Occasional but memorable films.

The World Owes Me a Living,
    1945
While I Live, 1947
This Was a Woman, 1948
The Fallen Idol, 1948
The Clouded Yellow, 1950
The Third Visitor, 1951
The Secret Tent, 1956
Now and Forever, 1956
Death Over My Shoulder, 1958
The Trials of Oscar Wilde,
    1960
The Break, 1962
Lady Caroline Lamb, 1972

PENELOPE DUDLEY-WARD
    (1919-)
Leading actress of the 40s,
married to Sir Carol Reed.

Moscow Nights, 1935
Escape Me Never, 1935
The Citadel, 1938
Hell's Cargo, 1939
Dangerous Comment, 1940
Convoy, 1940
Case of the Frightened Lady,
    1940
Major Barbara, 1941
The Demi-Paradise, 1943
The Way Ahead, 1944
English Without Tears, 1944

ARCHIE DUNCAN (1914-)
Sturdy Scotch actor of films
and television, famous as Little John in the "Robin Hood"
television show.   Active in the
50s.

Operation Diamond, 1947
The Bad Lord Byron, 1949
Floodtide, 1949
The Gorbals Story, 1950
Green Grow the Rushes, 1951
The Lavender Hill Mob, 1951
The Brave Don't Cry, 1952
Rob Roy, 1953
Robin Hood, 1953
Counterspy, 1953
The Maggie, 1953
Street Corner, 1953
Trouble in the Glen, 1954
Laxdale Hall, 1954
Johnny On the Run, 1956
The Devil's Pass, 1957
Saint Joan, 1957
Harry Black, 1958
John Paul Jones, 1959
Postman's Knock, 1962
Lancelot and Guinevere, 1963
The Horror of it All, 1964
Ring of Bright Water, 1969
The Wilby Conspiracy, 1975

EMMA DUNN (1875-1966)
Character actress, long in
Hollywood, first on stage and
then in films where she played
mostly mothers, aunts, house-
keepers, etc.

Old Lady 31, 1920
Pied Piper Malone, 1923
Side Street, 1929
The Texan, 1930
Manslaughter, 1930
Bad Sister, 1931
Too Young to Marry, 1931
The Prodigal, 1931
This Modern Age, 1931
Compromised, 1931
Bad Company, 1931
Morals For Women, 1931
The Guilty Generation, 1931

Under Eighteen, 1931
The Man I Killed, 1932
Hell's House, 1932
It's Tough to Be Famous, 1932
The Cohens and Kellys in
    Hollywood, 1932
The Wet Parade, 1932
Letty Lynton, 1932
Blessed Event, 1932
Grand Slam, 1933
Hard to Handle, 1933
Private Jones, 1933
Elmer the Great, 1933
It's Great to Be Alive, 1933
Dark Hazard, 1934
The Quitter, 1934
Dr. Monica, 1934
George White's Scandals, 1935
Keeper of the Bees, 1935
Little Big Shot, 1935
The Glass Key, 1935
Seven Keys to Baldpate, 1935
The Harvester, 1936
Second Wife, 1936
When You're in Love, 1936
Mr. Deeds Goes to Town, 1936
The Emperor's Candlesticks,
    1937
Varsity Show, 1937
Hideaway, 1937
Madame X, 1937
Lord Jeff, 1938
Thanks For the Memory, 1938
Cowboy From Brooklyn, 1938
Three Loves Has Nancy, 1938
Young Dr. Kildare, 1938
The Cowboy and the Lady, 1938
The Duke of West Point, 1938
Calling Dr. Kildare, 1939
Son of Frankenstein, 1939
Each Dawn I Die, 1939
The Secret of Dr. Kildare,
    1939
The Great Dictator, 1940
Dr. Kildare's Strange Case,
    1940
You Can't Fool Your Wife,
    1940
One Crowded Night, 1940
Dr. Kildare Goes Home, 1940
Mr. and Mrs. Smith, 1941
Ladies in Retirement, 1941
Scattergood Baines, 1941

The Penalty, 1941
Dr. Kildare's Wedding Day,
    1941
Rise and Shine, 1941
I Married a Witch, 1942
Babes On Broadway, 1942
Talk of the Town, 1942
When Johnny Comes Marching
    Home, 1943
Bridge of San Luis Rey,
    1944
It Happened Tomorrow, 1944
Are These Our Parents?, 1944
The Hoodlum Saint, 1946
Life With Father, 1947
Mourning Becomes Electra,
    1947
The Woman in White, 1948

GEOFFREY DUNN (1903-   )
Character actor of stage; very
rare film appearances.

Quo Vadis, 1951
The Leather Boys, 1963
Doomsday at Eleven, 1963
Lancelot and Guinevere, 1963

RUTH DUNNING (1911-   )
Character actress in occasional
pictures, mainly on stage.

Save a Little Sunshine, 1938
The Woman in the Hall, 1947
Intimate Relations, 1953
It's a Great Day, 1956
Urge to Kill, 1960
And Women Shall Weep, 1960
Dangerous Afternoon, 1961
Hoffman, 1970

FRED DUPREZ (-)
Popular thirties film personality
and entertainer.

Heads We Go, 1933
Oh What a Duchess!, 1933
Meet My Sister, 1933
Without You, 1934
Love, Life and Laughter, 1934

Danny Boy, 1934
Dance Band, 1935
No Monkey Business, 1935
Dark World, 1935
Ball at Savoy, 1936
A Wife Or Two, 1936
Queen of Hearts, 1936
The Big Noise, 1936
Gypsy Melody, 1936
International Revue, 1936
Hearts of Humanity, 1936
You Must Get Married, 1936
Reasonable Doubt, 1936
All That Glitters, 1936
Cafe Colette, 1937
Head Over Heels, 1937
Kathleen Mavourneen, 1937
Knights For a Day, 1937
Okay For Sound, 1937
Shooting Stars, 1937
Pearls of the Crown, 1938
Take Off That Hat, 1938
Hey Hey U.S.A., 1938

JUNE DUPREZ (1918-   )
Lovely leading lady of the thirties and forties, also in Hollywood.

The Cardinal, 1936
The Crimson Circle, 1936
The Spy in Black, 1938
The Lion Has Wings, 1939
The Four Feathers, 1939
The Thief of Bagdad, 1940
Little Tokyo, U.S.A., 1942
Don Winslow of the Navy, 1942
They Raid By Night, 1942
Forever and a Day, 1943
None But the Lonely Heart,
    1944
And Then There Were None,
    1945
The Brighton Strangler, 1945
That Brennan Girl, 1946
Tiger Fangs, 1946
Calcutta, 1947
The Last Tycoon, 1950
One Plus One, 1961

PAUL DUPUIS (1916-)
French-Canadian leading actor
and supporting player in British
films of the 40s.

Johnny Frenchman, 1945
The Laughing Lady, 1946
The White Unicorn, 1947
Sleeping Car to Trieste, 1948
Against the Wind, 1948
Madness of the Heart, 1949
The Romantic Age, 1949
Passport to Pimlico, 1949
The Reluctant Widow, 1950

HILARY DWYER (1935-)
Attractive young actress,
mainly seen in horror pictures.

Witchfinder General, 1968
File of the Golden Goose, 1968
The Body Stealers, 1969
The Oblong Box, 1969
Two Gentlemen Sharing, 1969
Cry of the Banshee, 1970
Wuthering Heights, 1970

LESLIE DWYER (1906-)
Cockney character star of
stage (since 1916) and screen,
also frequently on television.

Fifth Form at St. Dominic's,
   1921
The Flag Lieutenant, 1931
The Goose Steps Out, 1941
In Which We Serve, 1942
The Lamp Still Burns, 1943
The Way Ahead, 1944
Perfect Strangers, 1945
I See a Dark Stranger, 1946
Piccadilly Incident, 1946
Night Boat to Dublin, 1946
The Little Ballerina, 1947
When the Bough Breaks, 1947
Christmas Weekend, 1947
Bond Street, 1948
The Calendar, 1948
Temptation Harbour, 1949
The Bad Lord Byron, 1949
It's Not Cricket, 1949

Poet's Pub, 1949
Now Barabbas, 1949
A Boy, a Girl, and a Bike,
   1949
Lilli Marlene, 1950
Double Confession, 1950
Midnight Episode, 1950
Wall of Death, 1951
Laughter in Paradise, 1951
Smart Alec, 1951
There is Another Sun, 1951
My Wife's Lodger, 1952
Judgement Deferred, 1952
The Hour of Thirteen, 1952
Hindle Wakes, 1952
Marilyn, 1953
Act of Love, 1954
The Good Die Young, 1954
Road House Girl, 1955
Where There's a Will, 1955
Not So Dusty, 1955
Room in the House, 1955
Bless This House, 1955
The Black Rider, 1955
Death of a Ham, 1956
The Milkman, 1956
Cloak Without Dagger, 1956
Eyewitness, 1956
Face in the Night, 1957
Stormy Crossing, 1958
The 39 Steps, 1959
Left, Right and Centre, 1959
Rendezvous, 1961
70 Deadly Pills, 1964
I've Gotta Horse, 1965
House at the End of the World,
   1966
Lionheart, 1968
Up in the Air, 1969
Crooks and Coronets, 1969
A Hole Lot of Trouble, 1970

FRANKLIN DYALL (1874-1950)
Character star of stage (from
1894) and screen. Married to
Mary Merrall; father of Valentine Dyall.

Esther, 1916
The Garden of Resurrection,
   1919
Easy Virtue, 1927

Atlantic, 1929
A Safe Affair, 1931
Alibi, 1931
The Ringer, 1931
A Night in Montmartre, 1931
Creeping Shadows, 1931
Man of Steel, 1932
Called Back, 1933
Private Life of Henry VIII,
    1933
FP One, 1934
The Iron Duke, 1935
The Case of Gabriel Perry,
    1935
Conquest of the Air, 1936
Mr. Stringfellow Says No, 1937
Leave it To Me, 1937
Captain's Orders, 1937
Fire Over England, 1937
Mr. Satan, 1938
All at Sea, 1939
The Yellow Canary, 1943
Bonnie Prince Charlie, 1948

VALENTINE DYALL (1908-   )
Thin actor of stage and screen,
mainly in supporting roles.
Also well-known during the war
as "The Man in Black" on radio.   Son of Franklin Dyall and
Mary Merrall.

Life & Death of Colonel Blimp,
    1943
The Yellow Canary, 1943
The Silver Fleet, 1943
Henry V, 1944
Hotel Reserve, 1944
Latin Quarter, 1945
I Know Where I'm Going, 1945
Caesar and Cleopatra, 1945
Brief Encounter, 1945
Appointment With Fear, 1946
The White Unicorn, 1947
Corridor of Mirrors, 1948
The Story of Shirley Yorke,
    1948
Night Comes Too Soon, 1948
Woman Hater, 1948
My Brother's Keeper, 1948
Vengeance is Mine, 1949
The Queen of Spades, 1949

Helter Skelter, 1949
Dr. Morelle-The Case of the
    Missing Heiress, 1949
For Them That Trespass, 1949
The Case of Charles Peace,
    1949
Room to Let, 1950
Miss Pilgrim's Progress, 1950
The Man in Black, 1950
The Body Said No, 1950
Stranger at My Door, 1950
Ivanhoe, 1952
Hammer the Toff, 1952
Salute the Toff, 1952
Paul Temple Returns, 1952
The Final Test, 1953
The Devil's Jest, 1954
Johnny on the Spot, 1954
Suspended Alibi, 1957
Night Train For Inverness,
    1960
City of Dead, 1960
Identity Unknown, 1960
Fate Takes a Hand, 1962
Horror Hotel, 1963
The Haunting, 1963
The Horror of it All, 1964
The Wrong Box, 1966
Casino Royale, 1967
The Great McGonagall, 1975
The Slipper and the Rose,
    1976

PETER DYNELEY (1921-   )
Character actor in films since
mid-fifties; married to Jane
Hylton.

Hell Below Zero, 1954
Beau Brummel, 1954
The Young Lovers, 1954
Third Party Risk, 1955
The Stolen Airliner, 1955
The Strange Awakening, 1958
The Whole Truth, 1958
The Golden Disc, 1958
Deadly Record, 1959
The October Moth, 1960
The Split, 1960
House of Mystery, 1961
The Roman Spring of Mrs.
    Stone, 1961

Call Me Bwana, 1963
Thunderbirds Are Go, 1966
Thunderbird Six, 1968
The Executioner, 1970
Chato's Land, 1972
Color Him Dead, 1974
Black Trash, 1978

SHIRLEY EATON (1937-)
Beautiful blonde leading lady of
stage (since 1954) and screen,
also in Hollywood. Often in
comedy pictures.

You Know What Sailors Are,
    1954
Doctor in the House, 1954
The Belles of St. Trinian's,
    1954
The Love Match, 1955
Charley Moon, 1956
Sailor Beware, 1956
Doctor at Large, 1957
Three Men in a Boat, 1957
The Naked Truth, 1958
In the Wake of a Stranger, 1958
Carry On Sergeant, 1958
Further Up the Creek, 1958
Carry On Nurse, 1959
Life is a Circus, 1959
Carry On Constable, 1960
Our Man in the Caribbean,
    1960
A Weekend With Lulu, 1961
Nearly a Nasty Accident, 1961
Dentist On the Job, 1961
What a Carve Up!, 1961
Date With Disaster, 1962
Get On With It, 1962
The Girl Hunters, 1963
The Naked Brigade, 1964
Rhino!, 1964
Goldfinger, 1964
Ten Little Indians, 1965
The Scorpio Letters, 1966
Around the World Under the
    Sea, 1966
Eight On the Lam, 1967
Sumuru, 1967
The Blood of Fu Manchu,
    1968
Girl From Rio, 1968

WALLAS EATON (1917-)
Character actor mainly seen
on the stage, in occasional
films since the late 40s.

A Man's Affair, 1949
Up For the Cup, 1950
Dark Interval, 1950
Let's Go Crazy, 1951
Chelsea Story, 1951
Adventure in the Hopfields,
    1954
Alive On Saturday, 1957
A Clean Sweep, 1958
Operation Cupid, 1960
Johann Sebastian Bach, 1961
Victim, 1961
Inspector Clouseau, 1968
Isadora, 1968
Lock Up Your Daughters, 1969
O Lucky Man, 1973
Mad Dog, 1976
The Last Wave, 1978

DONALD ECCLES (1908-)
Actor of stage (primarily),
screen (very occasionally) and
television.

A Taste of Money, 1960
The Wicker Man, 1973
The Nine Tailors, 1974

MARK EDEN (-)
Light leading actor and supporting player of stage, films and
tv.

The Password is Courage, 1962
The L-Shaped Room, 1962
Heavens Above, 1963
The Partner, 1963
Blind Corner, 1963
Seance On a Wet Afternoon,
    1964
Dr. Zhivago, 1965
Man in the Dark, 1965
The Pleasure Girls, 1965
Game For Three Losers, 1965
I'll Never Forget Whatsisname,
    1967

Attack on the Iron Coast, 1968
Curse of the Crimson Altar,
1968
A Little of What You Fancy,
1968
Unpleasantness at the Bellona
Club, 1973
Clouds of Witness, 1973
The Nine Tailors, 1973
Murder Must Advertise,
1975
Jesus of Nazareth, 1977

GLYNN EDWARDS (-)
Character player of small but
telling roles, mainly on stage.

The Hi-Jackers, 1963
Smokescreen, 1964
Zulu, 1964
Robbery, 1967
Blood Beast Terror, 1968
Get Carter, 1970
Fragment of Fear, 1970
Shaft in Africa, 1973
11 Harrowhouse, 1974

HENRY EDWARDS (1882-1952)
Star of stage (from 1900) and
screen who began in silent
films as hero and graduated
into character parts. Also director. Married to silent film
star Chrissie White (1896-).

Clancarty, 1914
A Bachelor's Love Story, 1914
The Man Who Stayed at Home,
1915
Alone in London, 1915
My Old Dutch, 1915
Lost and Won, 1915
Far From the Madding Crowd,
1915
The Welsh Singer, 1915
Doorsteps, 1915
Grim Justice, 1916
East is East, 1916
The Cobweb, 1917
Merely Mrs. Stubbs, 1917
Dick Carson Wins Through,
1917
Nearer My God to Thee, 1917
Broken Threads, 1917
The Touch of a Child, 1918
The Hanging Judge, 1918
The Refugee, 1918
Tares, 1918
Towards the Light, 1918
A New Version, 1918
The Message, 1918
Against the Grain, 1918
Old Mother Hubbard, 1918
Anna, 1918
Her Savings Saved, 1918
The Poet's Windfall, 1918
The Inevitable, 1918
What's the Use of Grumbling,
1918
The Secret, 1918
Broken in the Wars, 1919
His Dearest Possession, 1919
The Kinsman, 1919
Possession, 1919
City of Beautiful Nonsense,
1919
A Temporary Vagabond, 1919
Amazing Quest of Ernest Bliss,
1920
Aylwin, 1920
John Forrest Finds Himself,
1920
The Lunatic at Large, 1921
The Bargain, 1921
Simple Simon, 1922
Tit For Tat, 1922
Lilly of the Alley, 1923
Boden's Boy, 1923
The Naked Man, 1923
The World of Wonderful Real-
ity, 1924
The Flag Lieutenant, 1926
The Fake, 1927
Fear, 1927
Further Adventures of a Flag
Lieutenant, 1927
Three Kings, 1929
Ringing the Changes, 1929
Call of the Sea, 1930
The Girl in the Night, 1931
Stranglehold, 1931
The Flag Lieutenant, 1932
General John Regan, 1933
The Man Who Changed His

Name, 1934
Are You a Mason?, 1934
Scrooge, 1935
Juggernaut, 1937
High Treason, 1937
Captain's Orders, 1937
East of Piccadilly, 1941
Spring Meeting, 1941
Green For Danger, 1946
The Magic Bow, 1947
Take My Life, 1947
London Belongs to Me, 1948
Oliver Twist, 1948
Woman Hater, 1948
Quartet, 1948
The Lucky Mascot, 1948
All Over Town, 1949
Dear Mr. Prohack, 1949
Elizabeth of Ladymead, 1949
Madeleine, 1950
Double Confession, 1950
Trio, 1950
The Golden Salamander, 1950
The Rossiter Case, 1951
White Corridors, 1951
Lady With a Lamp, 1951
The Magic Box, 1951
Never Look Back, 1952
Something Money Can't Buy,
  1952
The Long Memory, 1952
Trent's Last Case, 1952

HILTON EDWARDS (1903-)
Lugubrious character actor of
stage and screen, in occasional
films.

Call of the Blood, 1948
Cat and Mouse, 1958
The Big Gamble, 1961
Victim, 1961
The Quare Fellow, 1962
The Wrong Box, 1966
Half a Sixpence, 1967

JIMMY EDWARDS (1920-)
Mustachioed comedian of stage
(since 1946) and screen, also
popular on radio ("Take it
From Here").

Trouble in the Air, 1948
Helter Skelter, 1949
Murder at the Windmill, 1949
Treasure Hunt, 1952
Innocents in Paris, 1953
An Alligator Named Daisy,
  1955
Three Men in a Boat, 1957
Bottoms Up, 1960
Nearly a Nasty Accident, 1961
The Plank, 1967
Ghost of a Chance, 1968
Lionheart, 1968
The Bed Sitting Room, 1969
Rhubarb, 1970
Magnificent $6\frac{1}{2}$, 1971
Anoop and the Elephant, 1972

MEREDITH EDWARDS
  (1917-)
Welsh supporting actor of
stage and films, popular during the fifties.

A Run For Your Money, 1949
The Blue Lamp, 1950
Midnight Episode, 1950
The Magnet, 1950
There is Another Sun, 1951
The Lavender Hill Mob, 1951
Where No Vultures Fly, 1951
The Last Page, 1952
The Gambler and the Lady,
  1952
Girdle of Gold, 1952
The Gift Horse, 1952
The Cruel Sea, 1953
The Great Game, 1953
A Day to Remember, 1953
Meet Mr. Malcolm, 1954
Devil On Horseback, 1954
Burnt Evidence, 1954
Final Appointment, 1954
To Dorothy a Son, 1954
Mad About Men, 1954
Mask of Dust, 1954
Lost, 1956
The Long Arm, 1956
Peril For the Guy, 1956
Circus Friends, 1956
Town On Trial, 1957
Dunkirk, 1958

Law and Disorder, 1958
Escapement, 1958
The Supreme Secret, 1958
Tiger Bay, 1959
The Trials of Oscar Wilde,
  1960
Doctor in Love, 1960
Flame in the Streets, 1961
Mix Me a Person, 1962
Only Two Can Play, 1962
This is My Street, 1963

SAMANTHA EGGAR (1939-)
Leading lady of the sixties and
seventies; also on stage. On
television in "Anna and the
King" (1972). Now in international films.

The Wild and the Willing, 1961
Dr. Crippen, 1962
Doctor in Distress, 1963
Psyche '59, 1963
Return From the Ashes, 1965
The Collector, 1965
Walk Don't Run, 1966
Dr. Dolittle, 1967
The Walking Stick, 1970
The Molly Maguires, 1970
The Lady in the Car With
  Glasses and a Gun, 1970
Light at the Edge of the World,
  1971
The Dead Are Alive, 1972
Double Indemnity, 1973
The Seven Per Cent Solution,
  1976
Why Shoot the Teacher?, 1977
The Uncanny, 1977
Welcome to Blood City, 1977
The Brood, 1979
The Exterminator, 1980

AVRIL ELGAR (1932-)
Actress of stage and occasionally screen; films rare.

Room at the Top, 1959
She Always Gets Their Man, 1962
Ladies Who Do, 1963
Spring and Port Wine, 1970

DENHOLM ELLIOTT (1922-)
Suave, gentlemanly actor of
stage (from 1945) and screen,
former soldier. Also in Hollywood. Much on television too.

Dear Mr. Prohack, 1949
The Sound Barrier, 1952
The Holly and the Ivy, 1952
The Ringer, 1952
The Cruel Sea, 1953
The Heart of the Matter, 1953
They Who Dare, 1954
Lease of Life, 1954
The Man Who Loved Redheads,
  1954
The Night My Number Came
  Up, 1955
Pacific Destiny, 1956
The Lark, 1957
Scent of Mystery, 1959
Station Six-Sahara, 1963
Nothing But the Best, 1963
The High Bright Sun, 1964
King Rat, 1965
You Must Be Joking!, 1965
Alfie, 1966
Maroc 7, 1966
The Spy With a Cold Nose,
  1966
Here We Go Round the Mul-
  berry Bush, 1967
Dr. Jekyll and Mr. Hyde, 1968
The Night They Raided Min-
  sky's, 1968
Too Late the Hero, 1969
The Seagull, 1969
The Rise and Rise of Michael
  Rimmer, 1970
The House That Dripped Blood,
  1970
Percy, 1970
The Quest For Love, 1971
Madame Sin, 1972
A Doll's House, 1973
The Vault of Horror, 1973
Percy's Progress, 1974
Apprenticeship of Duddy
  Kravitz, 1974
Russian Roulette, 1975
Partners, 1976
Robin and Marian, 1976
To the Devil a Daughter, 1976

Voyage of the Damned, 1976
A Bridge Too Far, 1977
Sweeney, 1977
La Petite Fille en Velours
   Bleu, 1978
Watership Down, 1978
The Boys From Brazil, 1978
Saint Jack, 1978
Hound of the Baskervilles, 1978
Game For Vultures, 1979
Cuba, 1979
Zulu Dawn, 1980

DEREK ELPHINSTONE (-)
Small-part actor in occasional
films, also on stage.

The Four Feathers, 1939
In Which We Serve, 1942
The Red Shoes, 1948
Distant Trumpet, 1952
The Armchair Detective, 1952

ISOBEL ELSOM (1893-)
Silent film star and latterly
character actress, also in
Hollywood. On stage from
1911. Married to director
Maurice Elvey (1887-1967).

A Prehistoric Love Story, 1915
Milestones, 1916
The Way of an Eagle, 1918
Tinker Tailor Soldier Sailor,
   1918
The Elder Miss Blossom, 1918
God Bless Our Red White and
   Blue, 1918
Onward Christian Soldiers, 1918
The Man Who Won, 1918
Quinneys, 1919
In Bondage, 1919
Linked By Fate, 1919
A Member of Tattersalls, 1919
Edge O' Beyond, 1919
Mrs. Thompson, 1919
Nance, 1920
Aunt Rachel, 1920
For Her Father's Sake, 1921
The Game of Life, 1922
Dick Turpin's Ride to York,

1922
Debt of Honour, 1922
Harbour Lights, 1923
The Sign of Four, 1923
The Wandering Jew, 1923
Love of Ailette Brunton, 1924
Who is the Man?, 1924
The Last Witness, 1925
Glamis Castle, 1926
The Tower of London, 1926
Human Law, 1926
The Other Woman, 1931
Stranglehold, 1931
The Crooked Lady, 1932
Illegal, 1932
The Thirteenth Candle, 1933
The Primrose Path, 1934
Ladies in Retirement, 1941
Eagle Squadron, 1942
The War Against Mrs. Hadley,
   1942
You Were Never Lovelier, 1942
Seven Sweethearts, 1942
Forever and a Day, 1943
First Comes Courage, 1943
My Kingdom For a Crook,
   1943
Between Two Worlds, 1944
Casanova Brown, 1944
The Horn Blows at Midnight,
   1945
The Unseen, 1945
Two Sisters From Boston,
   1946
Of Human Bondage, 1946
Ivy, 1947
Love From a Stranger, 1947
Monseur Verdoux, 1947
The Two Mrs. Carrolls, 1947
The Ghost and Mrs. Muir,
   1947
Escape Me Never, 1947
The Paradine Case, 1948
The Secret Garden, 1949
Her Wonderful Lie, 1950
Deep in My Heart, 1954
Desire, 1954
The King's Thief, 1955
Love is a Many Splendored
   Thing, 1955
Over Exposed, 1956
Lust For Life, 1956
23 Paces to Baker St. , 1956

Rock a Bye Baby, 1958
The Miracle, 1959
Young Philadelphians, 1959
The Second Time Around, 1961
The Errand Boy, 1961
Who's Minding the Store, 1963
My Fair Lady, 1964
The Pleasure Seekers, 1965

ROY EMERTON (1892-1944)
Long-nosed, often villainous
Canadian character star of
stage and screen, long in Britain.

Shadows, 1931
That Night in London, 1932
The Sign of Four, 1932
Java Head, 1934
The Lash, 1934
Lorna Doone, 1935
Triumph of Sherlock Holmes,
1935
Everything is Thunder, 1936
Tudor Rose, 1936
Big Fella, 1937
The Gang Show, 1937
The Last Adventurers, 1937
Silent Barriers, 1937
Dr. Syn, 1937
The Drum, 1938
Convict 99, 1938
Home From Home, 1939
The Good Old Days, 1939
The Frightened Lady, 1940
The Thief of Bagdad, 1940
Busman's Honeymoon, 1940
Old Mother Riley's Circus,
1941
The Young Mr. Pitt, 1942
The Man in Grey, 1943
Time Flies, 1944
Welcome Mr. Washington, 1944
Henry V, 1944

DICK EMERY (1919-)
Tubby character comedian of
films, frequently seen in dis-
guised roles. Also much on tv.

Super Secret Service, 1953

The Case of the Mukkinese
Battlehorn, 1956
Light Up the Sky, 1960
A Taste of Money, 1960
Mrs. Gibbons' Boys, 1962
Crooks Anonymous, 1962
The Fast Lady, 1962
The Wrong Arm of the Law, 1963
Just For Fun, 1963
The Big Job, 1965
The Wrong Box, 1966
River Rivals, 1967
Baby Love, 1969
Loot, 1970
Ooh You Are Awful, 1972

GILBERT EMERY (1875-1945)
Character actor who generally
was cast as man of importance
or position; long in Hollywood.

Behind That Curtain, 1929
The Sky Hawk, 1929
The Royal Bed, 1930
Sarah and Son, 1930
Let Us Be Gay, 1930
A Lady's Morals, 1930
Scandal Sheet, 1931
Ladies' Man, 1931
Party Husband, 1931
The Ruling Voice, 1931
Rich Man's Folly, 1931
The Man Called Back, 1932
A Farewell to Arms, 1932
House of Rothschild, 1934
One More River, 1934
All of Me, 1934
A Coming Out Party, 1934
Where Sinners Meet, 1934
Whom the Gods Destroy, 1934
Grand Canary, 1934
Now and Forever, 1934
Clive of India, 1935
Magnificent Obsession, 1935
The Man Who Reclaimed His
Head, 1935
Night Life of the Gods, 1935
Let's Live Tonight, 1935
Goin to Town, 1935
Harmony Lane, 1935
Peter Ibbetson, 1935
Dracula's Daughter, 1936

Wife vs. Secretary, 1936
Bullets or Ballots, 1936
Girl On the Front Page, 1936
Souls at Sea, 1937
The Life of Emile Zola, 1937
Double or Nothing, 1937
Making the Headlines, 1938
A Man to Remember, 1938
Lord Jeff, 1938
Storm Over Bengal, 1938
The Saint Strikes Back, 1939
Nurse Edith Cavell, 1939
Raffles, 1939
The Lady's From Kentucky,
   1939
House of the Seven Gables,
   1940
Anne of Windy Poplars, 1940
Rage in Heaven, 1941
That Hamilton Woman, 1941
Scotland Yard, 1941
Singapore Woman, 1941
A Woman's Face, 1941
New Wine, 1942
The Remarkable Andrew, 1942
Loves of Edgar Allan Poe, 1942
Return of the Vampire, 1944
Between Two Worlds, 1944
The Brighton Strangler, 1945

FRED EMNEY (1900-   )
Heavyweight, monocled, cigar-
chewing character actor of stage
(since 1915) and screen, usually
in comedy roles.

Brewster's Millions, 1935
Come Out of the Pantry, 1935
Let's Make a Night of It, 1937
The Lilac Domino, 1937
Just Like a Woman, 1938
Jane Steps Out, 1938
Hold My Hand, 1938
Yes Madam, 1938
Just William, 1939
She Couldn't Say No, 1939
The Middle Watch, 1939
Goofer Trouble, 1940
Let the People Sing, 1942
Fun at St. Fanny's, 1956
The Fast Lady, 1962
Father Came Too, 1963

A Home of Your Own, 1964
I've Gotta Horse, 1965
San Ferry Ann, 1965
Bunny Lake is Missing, 1965
Those Magnificent Men in
   Their Flying Machines, 1965
The Sandwich Man, 1966
Oliver, 1968
Lock Up Your Daughters, 1969
The Italian Job, 1969
The Magic Christian, 1970
Doctor in Trouble, 1970
Under the Table You Must Go,
   1970
Up the Chastity Belt, 1971
Mistress Pamela, 1973
The Amorous Milkman, 1974
Adventures of a Private Eye,
   1977

JILL ESMOND (1908-   )
Leading lady of the thirties,
on stage from 1922, formerly
married to Laurence Olivier;
latterly in Hollywood as character actress.

The Chinese Bungalow, 1930
The Skin Game, 1931
Once a Lady, 1931
The Eternal Feminine, 1931
Ladies of the Jury, 1932
Is My Face Red?, 1932
State's Attorney, 1932
Thirteen Women, 1932
No Funny Business, 1933
F. P. One, 1933
This Above All, 1942
Random Harvest, 1942
The Pied Piper, 1942
Journey For Margaret, 1942
Eagle Squadron, 1942
The White Cliffs of Dover,
   1944
My Pal Wolf, 1944
Casanova Brown, 1944
Bedelia, 1946
The Bandit of Sherwood Forest,
   1946
Escape, 1948
Private Information, 1952
Night People, 1954
A Man Called Peter, 1955

ANTONY EUSTREL (1904-)
Dramatic character actor of
stage and screen, also in Hollywood.

Second Bureau, 1936
The Wife of General Ling, 1937
Under the Red Robe, 1937
Gasbags, 1940
The Silver Fleet, 1943
The Adventures of Tartu, 1943
Caesar and Cleopatra, 1945
Counterblast, 1948
The Story of Robin Hood, 1952
Devil's Plot, 1953
The Robe, 1953
Titanic, 1953
King Richard and the Crusaders,
  1954
The Unsinkable Molly Brown, 1964
Games, 1967
Fitzwilly, 1967

CLIFFORD EVANS (1912-)
Welsh star and latterly character player of stage (1930) and
screen, also known on television
in "Stryker of the Yard" and
"Power Game. "

The River House Mystery, 1935
Ourselves Alone, 1936
Calling the Tune, 1936
A Woman Alone, 1936
The Tenth Man, 1936
Mutiny of the Elsinore, 1937
Mademoiselle Docteur, 1937
Thirteen Men and a Gun, 1938
Luck of the Navy, 1938
His Brother's Keeper, 1939
At the Villa Rose, 1939
The Proud Valley, 1940
The Flying Squad, 1940
The House of the Arrow, 1940
Fingers, 1940
Freedom Radio, 1941
Love on the Dole, 1941
Penn of Pennsylvania, 1941
The Saint Meets the Tiger,
  1941
The Foreman Went to France,
  1942

Suspected Person, 1942
The Flemish Farm, 1943
The Silver Darlings, 1947
While I Live, 1947
A Run For Your Money, 1949
The 20 Questions Murder Mys-
  tery, 1950
Escape Route, 1953
Valley of Song, 1953
The Straw Man, 1953
Point of No Return, 1953
Solution By Phone, 1954
The Gilded Cage, 1955
Passport to Treason, 1956
At the Stroke of Nine, 1957
Face in the Night, 1957
The Heart Within, 1957
Violent Playground, 1958
Man With a Dog, 1958
SOS Pacific, 1959
Curse of the Werewolf, 1961
Kiss of the Vampire, 1962
The Long Ships, 1964
Twist of Sand, 1967
One Brief Summer, 1970

DAME EDITH EVANS (1888-
  1976)
Distinguished, inimitable, outstanding actress, mainly on
stage (from 1912); superb in
occasional films. Also in
Hollywood.

A Honeymoon For Three, 1915
A Welsh Singer, 1915
East is East, 1916
The Queen of Spades, 1948
The Last Days of Dolwyn, 1949
The Importance of Being Earn-
  est, 1952
Look Back in Anger, 1959
The Nun's Story, 1959
Tom Jones, 1963
The Chalk Garden, 1964
Young Cassidy, 1965
The Whisperers, 1967
Fitzwilly, 1967
Prudence and the Pill, 1968
Crooks and Coronets, 1969
The Madwoman of Chaillot,
  1969

David Copperfield, 1969
Scrooge, 1970
Upon This Rock, 1970
A Doll's House, 1973
Craze, 1973
QB VII, 1974
The Slipper and the Rose, 1976
Nasty Habits, 1976

MAURICE EVANS (1901-)
Forceful Welsh actor of stage
(since 1926), films and television, former singer. Also in
Hollywood. Tv series: "Bewitched" (1968-71).

White Cargo, 1929
Raise the Roof, 1930
Should a Doctor Tell?, 1930
Cupboard Love, 1931
Wedding Rehearsal, 1932
Marry Me, 1932
The Only Girl, 1933
Path of Glory, 1934
Bypass to Happiness, 1934
Scrooge, 1935
Checkmate, 1936
Kind Lady, 1951
Gilbert and Sullivan, 1953
Androcles and the Lion, 1953
Macbeth, 1960
The War Lover, 1965
Jack of Diamonds, 1967
Planet of the Apes, 1968
Rosemary's Baby, 1968
The Body Stealers, 1970
Beneath the Planet of the Apes,
  1970
Terror in the Wax Museum,
  1973
The Girl, the Gold Watch, and
  Everything, 1980

NORMAN EVANS (1901-1962)
Comedian of stage and screen,
best known as toothless music
hall character and female impersonator. Films rare.

Pathetone Parade of 1941, 1941
Demobbed, 1944

Under New Management, 1946
Over the Garden Wall, 1950

PEGGY EVANS (-)
Fair-haired supporting actress
of the 40s and 50s.

School For Secrets, 1946
Penny and the Pownall Case,
  1948
Love in Waiting, 1948
Look Before You Love, 1948
The Blue Lamp, 1950
Calling Bulldog Drummond,
  1951
Murder at 3 AM, 1953

REX EVANS (1903-1969)
Portly character actor, mainly
in Hollywood, generally cast as
butlers or the like.

Comets, 1930
Aunt Sally, 1933
Camille, 1936
Zaza, 1939
The Philadelphia Story, 1940
Adventure in Diamonds, 1940
Suspicion, 1941
The Shanghai Gesture, 1941
Frankenstein Meets the Wolf
  Man, 1943
Higher and Higher, 1944
Pursuit to Algiers, 1945
The Brighton Strangler, 1945
Till the Clouds Roll By, 1946
Dangerous Millions, 1947
Adam's Rib, 1949
It Should Happen to You, 1953
The Birds and the Bees, 1956
The Matchmaker, 1958
Merry Andrew, 1958
Midnight Lace, 1960
On the Double, 1961

TENNIEL EVANS (1926-)
Welsh actor seen chiefly on
stage, films most rare.

The Haunted Man, 1966

Walk a Crooked Path, 1970
10 Rillington Place, 1971

BARBARA EVEREST (1891-
    1967)
Actress of stage and screen,
often cast in matronly roles;
also in Hollywood.

The Hypocrites, 1916
Man Without a Soul, 1916
Whosoever Will Offend, 1919
Not Guilty, 1919
Till Our Ship Comes In, 1919
The Lady Clare, 1919
Cavalry, 1920
Joyous Adventures of Aristide
    Pujol, 1920
Testimony, 1920
The Bigamist, 1921
A Romance of Old Bagdad,
    1922
The Persistent Lovers, 1922
There Goes the Bride, 1932
When London Sleeps, 1932
The Lodger, 1932
Lily Christine, 1932
The World, the Flesh & the
    Devil, 1932
The Roof, 1933
Love's Old Sweet Song, 1933
The Wandering Jew, 1933
The Umbrella, 1933
She Was Only a Village Maiden,
    1933
Passing Shadows, 1934
Scrooge, 1935
Passing of the Third Floor
    Back, 1935
Love in Exile, 1936
Death Croons the Blues, 1937
Old Mother Riley, 1937
Jump For Glory, 1937
Discoveries, 1939
Inquest, 1939
Trunk Crime, 1939
Meet Maxwell Archer, 1939
Tilly of Bloomsbury, 1940
Bringing it Home, 1940
Telefootler, 1941
The Prime Minister, 1941
The Patient Vanishes, 1941

He Found a Star, 1941
Phantom of the Opera, 1943
Mission to Moscow, 1943
Jane Eyre, 1944
The Uninvited, 1944
Gaslight, 1944
Commandos Strike at Dawn,
    1945
The Valley of Decision, 1945
Wanted For Murder, 1946
Freida, 1947
Children of Chance, 1949
Madeleine, 1950
Tony Draws a Horse, 1950
An Inspector Calls, 1954
The Safecracker, 1958
The Damned, 1961
Dangerous Afternoon, 1961
The Man Who Finally Died,
    1962
Rotten to the Core, 1965

DEREK FARR (1912-   )
Leading actor of stage (from
1937), films and television;
former schoolmaster. Married
to Muriel Pavlow.

Q Planes, 1939
The Outsider, 1939
Black Eyes, 1939
Spellbound, 1940
Freedom Radio, 1941
Quiet Wedding, 1941
Quiet Weekend, 1945
Wanted For Murder, 1946
The Shop at Sly Corner, 1946
Teheran, 1947
Bond Street, 1948
The Noose, 1948
Silent Dust, 1948
Man on the Run, 1949
The Story of Shirley Yorke,
    1949
Double Confession, 1950
Murder Without Crime, 1950
Young Wives' Tale, 1951
Reluctant Heroes, 1951
Little Big Shot, 1952
Front Page Story, 1954
Bang You're Dead, 1954
Eight O'clock Walk, 1954

The Dam Busters, 1955
Value For Money, 1955
The Man in the Road, 1956
Town On Trial, 1956
Doctor at Large, 1957
Vicious Circle, 1957
The Truth About Women, 1958
Attempt to Kill, 1961
The Projected Man, 1966
30 Is a Dangerous Age Cynthia,
   1967
The Johnstown Monster, 1971
Pope Joan, 1972

DAVID FARRAR (1908-)
Tall, heroic star of stage
(since 1932) and screen, most
popular during the 40s; also in
Hollywood from the 50s. Former journalist.

Return of a Stranger, 1937
Silver Top, 1938
Sexton Blake and the Hooded
   Terror, 1938
A Royal Divorce, 1938
Danny Boy, 1941
Penn of Pennsylvania, 1941
Sheepdog of the Hills, 1941
Suspected Person, 1942
Went the Day Well, 1942
The Dark Tower, 1943
The Night Invader, 1943
They Met in the Dark, 1943
Headline, 1943
The Hundred Pound Window,
   1944
For Those in Peril, 1944
Meet Sexton Blake, 1944
The Echo Murders, 1945
The Trojan Brothers, 1945
The World Owes Me a Living,
   1945
Lisbon Story, 1946
Black Narcissus, 1947
Freida, 1947
The Small Back Room, 1948
Mr. Perrin and Mr. Traill,
   1948
Diamond City, 1949
Cage of Gold, 1950
Gone to Earth, 1950

The Golden Horde, 1951
Night Without Stars, 1951
The Late Edwina Black, 1951
The Woman and the Hunter,
   1953
Duel in the Jungle, 1954
Lilacs in the Spring, 1954
The Black Shield of Falworth,
   1954
The Sea Chase, 1955
Escape to Burma, 1955
Lost, 1955
Pearl of the South Pacific, 1955
Tears For Simon, 1957
I Accuse, 1958
Son of Robin Hood, 1958
John Paul Jones, 1959
Watusi, 1959
Solomon and Sheba, 1959
Middle of Nowhere, 1960
Beat Girl, 1960
The Webster Boy, 1962
The 300 Spartans, 1962

CHARLES FARRELL (1906-)
Irish character player of stage
and films, generally seen in
cameo roles. Not to be confused with American actor
Charles Farrell (1901-).

Song of Soho, 1930
The House Opposite, 1931
The Man at Six, 1931
The Flying Fool, 1931
Creeping Shadows, 1931
Tonight's the Night, 1932
Money For Nothing, 1932
The Spare Room, 1932
Jack's the Boy, 1932
A Tight Corner, 1932
Lucky Ladies, 1932
The Stolen Necklace, 1933
Taking Ways, 1933
Falling in Love, 1934
Boys Will Be Boys, 1935
The Lonely Road, 1936
Not Wanted On Voyage, 1936
The Flying Doctor, 1936
Under Proof, 1936
Moonlight Sonata, 1937
Midnight Menace, 1937

Meet Mr. Penny, 1938
Night Journey, 1939
Jailbirds, 1939
Convoy, 1940
Bell Bottom George, 1943
Meet Sexton Blake, 1944
Don Chicago, 1945
They Made Me a Fugitive, 1947
Night and the City, 1950
Madame Louise, 1951
There Was a Young Lady, 1953
Final Appointment, 1954
See How They Run, 1955
Stolen Assignment, 1955
Hornet's Nest, 1955
Morning Call, 1957
The Diplomatic Corpse, 1958
Death Over My Shoulder, 1958
The Sheriff of Fractured Jaw, 1958
Hidden Homicide, 1959
Operation Cupid, 1960
Oh What a Lovely War, 1969
Countess Dracula, 1970

JAMES FAULKNER (-)
Leading man and strong supporting player of the seventies; films very occasional.

The Great Waltz, 1972
The Abdication, 1974
Great Expectations, 1975
Conduct Unbecoming, 1975
Night of the Askari, 1978
Zulu Dawn, 1980

W. G. FAY (-)
Elderly character actor of the 30s and 40s, usually in kindly roles.

The Blarney Stone, 1933
General John Regan, 1933
Storm in a Teacup, 1937
The Last Curtain, 1937
Spellbound, 1940
Spring Meeting, 1941
The Patient Vanishes, 1941
London Town, 1946
Temptation Harbour, 1947
Odd Man Out, 1947

Oliver Twist, 1948

MARTY FELDMAN (1933-)
Bug-eyed, diminutive comedian of the 70s, former musician; also much on television. Tv series: "Marty" (1970).

Every Home Should Have One, 1969
The Bed Sitting Room, 1969
The Man Who Came to Dinner, 1972
Young Frankenstein, 1974
Adventures of Sherlock Holmes'
    Smarter Brother, 1976
Silent Movie, 1976
Sex With a Smile, 1976
The Last Remake of Beau
    Geste, 1977
In God We Trust, 1979

SHIRLEY ANN FIELD (1936-)
Attractive actress of the 50s with repertory experience; also in Hollywood.

All For Mary, 1955
It's Never Too Late, 1956
Lost, 1956
It's a Wonderful World, 1956
Dry Rot, 1956
Loser Takes All, 1956
Yield to the Night, 1956
The Good Companions, 1957
Seven Thunders, 1957
The Flesh is Weak, 1957
The Silken Affair, 1957
Horrors of the Black Museum,
    1959
Upstairs and Downstairs, 1959
And the Same to You, 1959
Peeping Tom, 1960
The Entertainer, 1960
Beat Girl, 1960
Once More With Feeling, 1960
Saturday Night and Sunday
    Morning, 1960
Man in the Moon, 1960
The Damned, 1961
The War Lover, 1962
Lunch Hour, 1962
Kings of the Sun, 1963

Doctor in Clover, 1965
Alfie, 1966
Hell is Empty, 1967
With Love in Mind, 1970
A Touch of the Other, 1970
House of the Living Dead,
    1977

VIRGINIA FIELD (1917-)
Second lead and supporting actress with stage experience, in
Hollywood from 1936. Married
to Willard Parker (1912-).

The Primrose Path, 1934
The Lady is Willing, 1934
Sing Baby Sing, 1936
Thank You Jeeves, 1936
Ladies in Love, 1936
Little Lord Fauntleroy, 1936
Lloyds of London, 1936
London By Night, 1937
Think Fast Mr. Moto, 1937
Ali Baba Goes to Town, 1937
Charlie Chan at Monte Carlo,
    1938
Lancer Spy, 1938
Bridal Suite, 1939
Mr. Moto's Last Warning, 1939
Captain Fury, 1939
The Sun Never Sets, 1939
Mr. Moto Takes a Vacation, 1939
Eternally Yours, 1939
Cisco Kid and the Lady, 1939
Dance Girl Dance, 1940
Waterloo Bridge, 1940
Hudson's Bay, 1940
Singapore Woman, 1941
Atlantic Convoy, 1942
The Crystal Ball, 1943
Stage Door Canteen, 1943
The Perfect Marriage, 1946
The Ladies' Man, 1947
The Imperfect Lady, 1947
Repeat Performance, 1947
Christmas Eve, 1947
Dream Girl, 1948
A Connecticut Yankee in King
    Arthur's Court, 1949
John Loves Mary, 1949
Dial 1119, 1950
The Lady Pays Off, 1951

Weekend With Father, 1951
Veils of Bagdad, 1953
The Big Story, 1958
Appointment With a Shadow, 1959
The Explosive Generation, 1962
The Earth Dies Screaming, 1965

MARJORIE FIELDING (1892-1956)
Stage and screen actress; usually portrayed firm, commanding, but kindly characters.

Second Thoughts, 1938
Quiet Wedding, 1941
Jeannie, 1941
The Demi-Paradise, 1943
The Yellow Canary, 1943
Quiet Weekend, 1945
Fame is the Spur, 1947
Easy Money, 1948
Spring in Park Lane, 1948
The Chiltern Hundreds, 1949
Trio, 1950
Conspirator, 1950
Portrait of Clare, 1950
The Mudlark, 1950
The Franchise Affair, 1951
The Lavender Hill Mob, 1951
Circle of Danger, 1951
The Magic Box, 1951
The Woman's Angle, 1952
Mandy, 1952
Rob Roy, 1953
The Net, 1953

DAME GRACIE FIELDS (1898-
    1979)
Inimitable comedienne of films,
stage and music halls; former
singer. Also latterly in Hollywood. At one time the world's
highest paid film star.

Sally in Our Alley, 1931
Looking On the Bright Side, 1932
This Week of Grace, 1933
Love, Life and Laughter, 1933
Sing As We Go, 1934
Look Up and Laugh, 1935
Queen of Hearts, 1936
The Show Goes On, 1937

We're Going to Be Rich, 1938
Keep Smiling, 1938
Shipyard Sally, 1939
Stage Door Canteen, 1943
Holy Matrimony, 1943
Molly and Me, 1945
Paris Underground, 1945
A Murder is Announced, 1956
The Old Lady Shows Her Medals,
  1956
Mrs 'Arris Goes to Paris, 1958

JON FINCH (1941-)
Leading actor of stage, screen
and television, latterly excellent in Shakespearian roles.

The Vampire Lovers, 1970
Horror of Frankenstein, 1970
Macbeth, 1971
Sunday Bloody Sunday, 1971
Frenzy, 1972
Lady Caroline Lamb, 1972
The Final Programme, 1973
Diagnosis Murder, 1975
El Segundo Poder, 1977
Death On the Nile, 1978
Richard II, 1979
Henry IV Part I, 1980
Henry IV Part II, 1980

PETER FINCH (1916-1977)
Outstanding, intelligent star of
stage (from 1935) and screen,
latterly in international films.
Also at one time a leading radio
performer (In Australia).

Dad and Dave Come to Town,
  1937
Red Sky at Morning, 1937
Mr. Chedworth Steps Out, 1938
The Rats of Tobruk, 1944
The Power and the Glory, 1945
A Son is Born, 1946
Eureka Stockade, 1948
Train of Events, 1949
The Wooden Horse, 1950
The Miniver Story, 1950
Robin Hood, 1952
Gilbert and Sullivan, 1953

The Heart of the Matter, 1953
Father Brown, 1954
Elephant Walk, 1954
Make Me An Offer, 1955
The Dark Avenger, 1955
Passage Home, 1955
Simon and Laura, 1955
Josephine and Men, 1955
Battle of the River Plate,
  1956
A Town Like Alice, 1956
The Shiralee, 1957
Robbery Under Arms, 1957
Windom's Way, 1957
Operation Amsterdam, 1958
A Far Cry, 1958
The Nun's Story, 1959
Kidnapped, 1959
The Trials of Oscar Wilde,
  1960
The Sins of Rachel Cade, 1960
Breaking Point, 1961
No Love For Johnnie, 1961
The Day, 1961
I Thank a Fool, 1962
In the Cool of the Day, 1963
Girl With Green Eyes, 1964
First Men in the Moon, 1964
The Pumpkin Eater, 1964
Judith, 1965
Flight of the Phoenix, 1965
10:30 PM Summer, 1966
Far From the Madding Crowd,
  1967
The Legend of Lylah Clare, 1968
The Red Tent, 1971
Sunday Bloody Sunday, 1971
Something to Hide, 1971
England Made Me, 1972
Lost Horizon, 1973
Bequest to the Nation, 1973
The Abdication, 1974
Network, 1976
Raid On Entebbe, 1977

FRANK FINLAY (1926-)
Prominent star and latterly
character star of stage (since
1957), films, and television.
Also in Hollywood.

Private Potter, 1962

The Loneliness of the Long Dis-
tance Runner, 1962
Life For Ruth, 1962
The Informers, 1963
Doctor in Distress, 1963
Hot Enough For June, 1963
The Comedy Man, 1963
Othello, 1965
A Study in Terror, 1965
The Sandwich Man, 1966
The Jokers, 1966
Robbery, 1967
The Deadly Bees, 1967
The Spare Tyres, 1967
I'll Never Forget Whatsisname,
1967
Inspector Clouseau, 1968
Twisted Nerve, 1968
The Shoes of the Fisherman, 1968
The Virgin Soldiers, 1969
The Molly Maguires, 1970
Assault, 1970
Cromwell, 1970
Gumshoe, 1971
The Body, 1971
Danny Jones, 1971
Sitting Target, 1972
Neither the Sea Nor the Sand,
1972
Shaft in Africa, 1973
The Three Musketeers, 1974
The Four Musketeers, 1975
The Wild Geese, 1978
Count Dracula, 1978
Murder By Decree, 1979

ALBERT FINNEY (1936-)
Dynamic star of stage (from
1956) and screen, also latterly
producer and recording artist.

The Entertainer, 1960
Saturday Night and Sunday
Morning, 1960
Tom Jones, 1963
The Victors, 1963
Night Must Fall, 1964
Two For the Road, 1967
Charlie Bubbles, 1967
The Picasso Summer, 1969
Scrooge, 1970
Gumshoe, 1971

Alpha Beta, 1973
Murder On the Orient Express,
1974
The Duellists, 1977
Annie, 1981

BARRY FITZGERALD (1888-1961)
Diminutive Irish character star
of stage and screen, long in
Hollywood where he was immensely popular, especially
during the 40s, for his roles
as generally lovable, roguish
characters.   Formerly with the
Abbey Theatre.   Brother:
Arthur Shields.

Juno and the Paycock, 1929
When Knights Were Bold, 1936
The Plough and the Stars, 1936
Ebb Tide, 1937
Marie Antoinette, 1938
Bringing Up Baby, 1938
Pacific Liner, 1938
The Dawn Patrol, 1938
Four Men and a Prayer, 1938
The Saint Strikes Back, 1939
Full Confession, 1939
The Long Voyage Home, 1940
How Green Was My Valley,
1941
Tarzan's Secret Treasure, 1941
The Sea Wolf, 1941
Forever Yours, 1942
Two Tickets to London, 1942
San Francisco Docks, 1943
Corvette K-225, 1943
The Amazing Mrs. Halliday,
1943
I Love a Soldier, 1944
None But the Lonely Heart,
1944
Going My Way, 1944
And Then There Were None,
1945
Incendiary Blonde, 1945
The Stork Club, 1945
Duffy's Tavern, 1945
Variety Girl, 1945
Two Years Before the Mast,
1946
Third Avenue, 1946

California, 1946
Easy Come, Easy Go, 1946
The Sainted Sisters, 1947
Welcome Stranger, 1947
The Naked City, 1948
Miss Tatlock's Millions, 1948
The White Steed, 1948
The Man Who Struck It Rich,
  1949
The Story of Seabiscuit, 1949
Top O' the Morning, 1949
Union Station, 1950
Silver City, 1951
The Quiet Man, 1952
Il Filo D'Erba, 1953
Tonight's the Night, 1954
The Cradle of Genius, 1955
The Catered Affair, 1956
Rooney, 1958
Broth of a Boy, 1959

Personal Affair, 1953
Front Page Story, 1954
Our Girl Friday, 1954
Lease of Life, 1954
Something of Value, 1955
The Green Scarf, 1955
Cockleshell Heroes, 1955
Around the World in 80 Days,
  1956
Man in the Sky, 1957
The Birthday Present, 1957
The Camp On Blood Island,
  1958
Third Man On the Mountain,
  1959
Darby O'Gill and the Little
  People, 1959
We Joined the Navy, 1962
Too Many Detectives, 1962
HMS Defiant, 1962

WALTER FITZGERALD (1896-
  1976)
Character star and occasional
lead of stage (1922) and screen;
typically portrayed likable characters.

Murder at Covent Garden, 1932
Q Planes, 1939
This England, 1941
In Which We Serve, 1942
Squadron Leader X, 1942
San Demetrio-London, 1943
Great Day, 1945
Strawberry Roan, 1945
Mine Own Executioner, 1947
Blanche Fury, 1948
This Was a Woman, 1948
Lost Illusion, 1948
The Small Back Room, 1948
The Winslow Boy, 1948
The Fallen Idol, 1948
Edward My Son, 1949
Treasure Island, 1950
Flesh and Blood, 1951
The Pickwick Papers, 1952
The Ringer, 1952
The Cruel Sea, 1953
Appointment in London, 1953
Twice Upon a Time, 1953
The Net, 1953

BUD FLANAGAN (1896-
  1968)
Friendly comedian and songwriter, on stage from 1908.
Teamed long with Chesney
Allen, subsequently member
of "The Crazy Gang."

The Bailiffs, 1932
They're Off, 1933
The Dreamers, 1933
Wild Boy, 1934
A Fire Has Been Arranged,
  1935
Underneath the Arches, 1937
Okay For Sound, 1937
Alf's Button Afloat, 1938
The Frozen Limits, 1939
Gasbags, 1940
We'll Smile Again, 1942
Theatre Royal, 1943
Here Comes the Sun, 1944
Judgement Deferred, 1952
Dunkirk, 1958
Life is a Circus, 1959
The Wild Affair, 1963

IAN FLEMING (1888-1969)
Australian character star who
was most often cast as pro-

fessional men, also well-
remembered as Dr. Watson to
Arthur Wontner's Sherlock
Holmes during the 30s. No
relation to Ian Fleming, (1906-
1964), creator of the James
Bond character.

Second to None, 1926
The Ware Case, 1928
The Devil's Maze, 1929
School For Scandal, 1930
The Sleeping Cardinal, 1931
The Missing Rembrandt, 1932
After Dark, 1932
Lucky Girl, 1932
Called Back, 1933
The Third Clue, 1934
Riverside Murder, 1935
School For Stars, 1935
Sexton Blake & the Mademoi-
    selle, 1935
The Crouching Beast, 1935
The Triumph of Sherlock
    Holmes, 1935
21 Today, 1936
Prison Breaker, 1936
Darby and Joan, 1937
Racing Romance, 1937
Jump For Glory, 1937
Silver Blaze, 1937
Almost a Honeymoon, 1938
Ghost Tales Retold, 1938
Dial 999, 1938
The Reverse Be My Lot, 1938
Quiet Please, 1938
Double Or Quits, 1938
If I Were Boss, 1938
Men Without Honour, 1939
The Lion Has Wings, 1939
The Nursemaid Who Disap-
    peared, 1939
Shadowed Eyes, 1939
Hatter's Castle, 1941
Sabotage at Sea, 1942
Up With the Lark, 1943
The Butler's Dilemma, 1943
I Didn't Do It, 1945
George in Civvy Street, 1946
Captain Boycott, 1947
A Matter of Murder, 1949
Murder Will Out, 1953
Recoil, 1953

It's a Grand Life, 1953
The Seekers, 1954
A Woman Possessed, 1958
Innocent Meeting, 1959
Web of Suspicion, 1959
Man Accused, 1959
Crash Drive, 1959
Your Money Or Your Wife,
    1960
The Trials of Oscar Wilde,
    1960
Return of a Stranger, 1962
The Lamp in Assassin Mews,
    1962
What Every Woman Wants,
    1962
70 Deadly Pills, 1964
The Return of Mr. Moto, 1965

ROBERT FLEMYNG (1912-)
Stately character star of stage
(1931), films, and television;
generally cast as man of prominence or importance. Awarded
Military Cross and O. B. E. for
service in WWII.

Head Over Heels, 1937
Bond Street, 1948
The Guinea Pig, 1948
Conspirator, 1950
The Blue Lamp, 1950
Blackmailed, 1951
The Magic Box, 1951
The Holly and the Ivy, 1952
Cast a Dark Shadow, 1955
The Man Who Never Was, 1956
Funny Face, 1956
Windom's Way, 1957
Let's Be Happy, 1957
Blind Date, 1959
A Touch of Larceny, 1959
Chance Meeting, 1959
Radius, 1961
The Terror of Dr. Hitchcock,
    1963
Mystery Submarine, 1963
The King's Breakfast, 1963
The Spy With a Cold Nose,
    1966
The Deadly Affair, 1966
The Quiller Memorandum, 1966

Blood Beast Terror, 1967
Deathhead Avenger, 1967
The Body Stealers, 1969
Oh What a Lovely War, 1969
The Battle of Britain, 1969
The Firechasers, 1970
Travels With My Aunt, 1972
Young Winston, 1972
The Darwin Adventure, 1972
The Medusa Touch, 1978
The Four Feathers, 1978
Rebecca, 1980
The Thirty-Nine Steps, 1980

BRAMWELL FLETCHER
   (1904-   )
Fair-haired lead and supporting player of stage (1927),
screen, and tv; specialized in
Shavian parts.   Also in Hollywood.

Chick, 1928
SOS, 1928
To What Red Hell, 1930
Raffles, 1931
Svengali, 1931
So This is London, 1931
The Millionaire, 1931
Daughter of the Dragon, 1931
Once a Lady, 1931
The Silent Witness, 1932
A Bill of Divorcement, 1932
The Mummy, 1932
Only Yesterday, 1932
Line Engaged, 1935
The Scarlet Pimpernel, 1935
Random Harvest, 1942
White Cargo, 1942
The Immortal Sergeant, 1942

CYRIL FLETCHER   (1913-   )
Stage and revue star and comedian, films infrequent.

The Yellow Canary, 1943
Nicholas Nickleby, 1947
A Piece of Cake, 1948

ERROL FLYNN   (1909-1959)

Swashbuckling Tasmanian-born
leadingman of Australian par-
entage; mainly in Hollywood.
Famous for being as much a
rogue off the screen as on.
Former shipping clerk and
sailor.

Murder at Monte Carlo, 1934
Case of the Curious Bride,
   1934
Don't Bet On Blondes, 1935
Captain Blood, 1935
Charge of the Light Brigade,
   1936
The Green Light, 1936
Another Dawn, 1937
The Perfect Specimen, 1937
The Prince and the Pauper,
   1937
Four's a Crowd, 1938
The Adventures of Robin Hood,
   1938
The Sisters, 1938
The Dawn Patrol, 1938
Dodge City, 1939
Virginia City, 1939
Elizabeth and Essex, 1939
The Sea Hawk, 1940
Santa Fe Trail, 1940
Footsteps in the Dark, 1941
Dive Bomber, 1941
They Died With Their Boots
   On, 1941
Gentleman Jim, 1942
Desperate Journey, 1942
Edge of Darkness, 1943
Northern Pursuit, 1943
Thank Your Lucky Stars, 1943
Uncertain Glory, 1944
Objective Burma, 1945
San Antonio, 1945
Never Say Goodbye, 1945
Cry Wolf, 1946
Escape Me Never, 1947
Silver River, 1947
New Adventures of Don Juan,
   1948
That Forsyte Woman, 1949
Montana, 1950
Rocky Mountain, 1950
Kim, 1951
Adventures of Captain Fabian,

1951
Mara Maru, 1952
Against All Flags, 1952
The Master of Ballantrae, 1953
Crossed Swords, 1954
Lilacs in the Spring, 1955
The Dark Avenger, 1955
King's Rhapsody, 1956
The Big Blockade, 1956
Istanbul, 1957
The Sun Also Rises, 1957
Too Much Too Soon, 1958
The Roots of Heaven, 1958
Cuban Rebel Girls, 1959
The Golden Shanty, 1959

BRYAN FORBES (1926-)
Small-part character and supporting player of stage (1942)
and screen who became an outstanding director, producer
and writer; formed film company with Sir Richard Attenborough. Married to Nanette
Newman.

The Small Back Room, 1948
All Over Town, 1949
Dear Mr. Prohack, 1949
The Wooden Horse, 1950
Green Grow the Rushes, 1951
The World in His Arms, 1952
Appointment in London, 1953
Sea Devils, 1953
Wheel of Fate, 1953
The Million Pound Note, 1954
An Inspector Calls, 1954
Up to the Neck, 1954
The Colditz Story, 1954
Passage Home, 1955
Now and Forever, 1955
The Quatermass Experiment,
1955
The Last Man to Hang, 1955
The Extra Day, 1956
It's Great to Be Young, 1956
The Baby and the Battleship,
1956
Satellite in the Sky, 1956
Quatermass II, 1957
The Key, 1958
I Was Monty's Double, 1958

The League of Gentlemen,
1959
Yesterday's Enemy, 1959
The Guns of Navarone, 1961
A Shot in the Dark, 1964

MARY FORBES (1882-1974)
Veteran character actress,
also on stage; mainly in Hollywood. Was generally cast in
supercilious, aristocratic parts.

Women Who Win, 1919
The Child Thou Gavest Me,
1921
Her Private Life, 1929
The Thirteenth Chair, 1929
The Tresspasser, 1929
Sunny Side Up, 1929
Abraham Lincoln, 1930
So This is London, 1930
Holiday, 1930
East is West, 1930
The Devil to Pay, 1930
Born to Love, 1931
The Man Who Came Back,
1931
Chances, 1931
The Brat, 1931
The Silent Witness, 1932
A Farewell to Arms, 1932
Stepping Sisters, 1932
Bombshell, 1933
You Can't Buy Everything,
1934
Blind Date, 1934
Cavalcade, 1934
Happiness Ahead, 1934
Anna Karenina, 1935
Captain Blood, 1935
Les Miserables, 1935
Laddie, 1935
The Perfect Gentleman, 1935
Another Dawn, 1937
Wee Willie Winkie, 1937
Women of Glamour, 1937
The Awful Truth, 1937
Everybody Sing, 1938
Always Goodbye, 1938
You Can't Take it With You,
1938
You Can't Cheat an Honest

Man, 1939
Risky Business, 1939
The Sun Never Sets, 1939
The Adventures of Sherlock
    Holmes, 1939
Private Affairs, 1940
South of Suez, 1940
Nothing But the Truth, 1941
Mrs. Miniver, 1942
This Above All, 1942
Two Tickets to London, 1943
Tender Comrade, 1944
Jane Eyre, 1944
Woman in Bondage, 1944
Earl Carroll's Vanities, 1945
The Picture of Dorian Gray,
    1945
Terror By Night, 1946
The Other Love, 1947
Ivy, 1947
The Exile, 1947
You Gotta Stay Happy, 1948
The Ten Commandments, 1956

MERIEL FORBES (1913-)
Leading and supporting actress,
mainly on stage; wife of Sir
Ralph Richardson.

Borrow a Million, 1934
Girls Please, 1934
The Case For the Crown, 1934
Vintage Wine, 1935
Mr. Cohen Takes a Walk,
    1935
The Bells of St. Clement's,
    1936
Come On George, 1939
Young Man's Fancy, 1939
The Gentle Sex, 1943
The Bells Go Down, 1943
The Captive Heart, 1946
The Long Dark Hall, 1951
Home at Seven, 1952
The Battle of Britain, 1969
Oh What a Lovely War, 1969

GEORGE FORMBY (1904-1961)
Grinning, ukulele-picking comedian, extremely popular during
the 30s and 40s. In music

halls from 1921; also famous
on radio.   Former boy jockey
(1915).

By the Shortest of Heads, 1915
Boots Boots, 1934
Off the Dole, 1935
No Limit, 1935
Keep Your Seats Please, 1936
Feather Your Nest, 1937
Keep Fit, 1937
I See Ice, 1938
Cavalcade of the Stars, 1938
It's in the Air, 1938
Trouble Brewing, 1939
Come On George, 1939
Spare a Copper, 1940
Let George Do It, 1940
South American George, 1941
Turned Out Nice Again, 1941
Much Too Shy, 1942
Get Cracking, 1943
Bell Bottom George, 1943
He Snoops to Conquer, 1944
I Didn't Do It, 1945
George in Civvy Street, 1946

BARRY FOSTER (1931-)
Light leading man and supporting actor, adept at comedy and
villainy alike.

Yangtse Incident, 1957
Sea of Sand, 1958
Yesterday's Enemy, 1959
Surprise Package, 1960
Playback, 1962
King and Country, 1964
The Family Way, 1966
Robbery, 1967
Twisted Nerve, 1968
Inspector Clouseau, 1968
The Battle of Britain, 1969
Ryan's Daughter, 1970
Frenzy, 1972
Divorce His Divorce Hers, 1973
The Wild Geese, 1978

JULIA FOSTER (1942-)
Pretty blonde leading lady of
films and television.

Term of Trial, 1962
The Loneliness of the Long
  Distance Runner, 1962
Two Left Feet, 1963
The Small World of Sammy
  Lee, 1963
The System, 1964
One Way Pendulum, 1964
The Bargee, 1964
Alfie, 1966
Half a Sixpence, 1967
Percy, 1970
Simon Simon, 1970
All Coppers Are, 1972
The Great McGonagall, 1974

HARRY FOWLER (1926-)
Cockney character player of
films, also on radio (from
1941), generally seen in small
roles. Former newsboy.
Married to Joan Dowling.

Went the Day Well, 1942
Salute John Citizen, 1942
Those Kids From Town, 1942
Get Cracking, 1943
The Demi-Paradise, 1943
Painted Boats, 1944
Champagne Charlie, 1944
Don't Take it To Heart, 1944
Hue and Cry, 1946
For Them That Trespass, 1948
A Piece of Cake, 1948
Now Barabbas, 1949
Once a Sinner, 1950
She Shall Have Murder, 1950
Scarlet Thread, 1951
The Dark Man, 1951
High Treason, 1951
Angels One Five, 1951
Madame Louise, 1951
I Believe In You, 1952
The Pickwick Papers, 1952
The Last Page, 1952
At Home With the Hardwickes,
  1952
A Day to Remember, 1953
Top of the Form, 1953
Conflict of Wings, 1954
Don't Blame the Stork, 1954
Up to His Neck, 1954

Stock Car, 1955
Blue Peter, 1955
Fire Maidens From Outer
  Space, 1956
Behind the Headlines, 1956
Town On Trial, 1956
Lucky Jim, 1957
Booby Trap, 1957
West Of Suez, 1957
Home and Away, 1957
The Birthday Present, 1957
The Diplomatic Corpse, 1958
Soapbox Derby, 1958
The Supreme Secret, 1958
Idol On Parade, 1959
Heart of a Man, 1959
The Dawn Killer, 1959
Don't Panic Chaps, 1960
The Golliwog, 1962
The Longest Day, 1962
Lawrence of Arabia, 1962
Flight From Singapore, 1962
Crooks Anonymous, 1962
Just For Fun, 1963
Clash By Night, 1963
Ladies Who Do, 1963
The Nanny, 1965
Life at the Top, 1965
Joey Boy, 1965
Doctor in Clover, 1965
Secrets of a Windmill Girl,
  1966

EDWARD FOX (1937-)
Leading man and supporting
actor of stage (1958), films,
and television, most effective
in amoral roles. Former
shop assistant. Married:
Tracy Reed; brother of James
Fox. Also in Hollywood. Excellent on television in "Edward & Mrs. Simpson. "

The Mind Benders, 1963
Morgan, 1966
The Jokers, 1966
I'll Never Forget Whatsisname,
  1967
The Naked Runner, 1967
The Frozen Dead, 1967
The Long Duel, 1967

The Battle of Britain, 1969
Oh What a Lovely War, 1969
Skullduggery, 1970
The Go-Between, 1971
The Breaking of Bumbo, 1971
Day of the Jackal, 1973
A Doll's House, 1973
Galileo, 1975
The Squeeze, 1977
A Bridge Too Far, 1977
The Duellists, 1977
The Cat and the Canary, 1977
Force Ten From Navarone,
   1978
The Big Sleep, 1978
Soldiers of Orange, 1979

JAMES FOX (1939-)
Slender leading man of stage
and screen, former child star.
Brother of Edward Fox. Also
in Hollywood.

The Magnet, 1950
The Miniver Story, 1950
Loneliness of the Long Dis-
   tance Runner, 1962
Tamahine, 1963
The Servant, 1963
King Rat, 1965
Those Magnificent Men in Their
   Flying Machines, 1965
The Chase, 1966
Arabella, 1967
Thoroughly Modern Millie,
   1967
Duffy, 1968
Isadora, 1969
Performance, 1970
No Longer Alone, 1978

C. V. FRANCE (1868-1949)
Dry, aged character player of
stage and films, mainly portraying lawyers or other characters of prominence. Active
in the 30s.

The Blue Bird, 1910
Eugene Aram, 1924
The Burgomaster of Stilemond,
   1928
The Loves of Robert Burns,
   1930
Black Coffee, 1931
These Charming People, 1931
The Skin Game, 1931
A Night Like This, 1932
Lord Edgware Dies, 1934
Scrooge, 1935
Royal Cavalcade, 1935
Broken Blossoms, 1936
Victoria the Great, 1937
A Yank at Oxford, 1938
Ten Days in Paris, 1939
Cheer Boys Cheer, 1939
The Ware Case, 1939
If I Were King, 1939
Night Train to Munich, 1940
Breach of Promise, 1941
Went the Day Well, 1942
It Happened One Sunday, 1944
Halfway House, 1944

RONALD FRANKAU (1894-1951)
Stage and screen character
comedian of the thirties, also
popular on radio.

The Calendar, 1931
The Skin Game, 1931
Potiphar's Wife, 1931
Let's Love and Laugh, 1931
The Other Mrs. Phipps, 1931
Pathetone Parade of 1934,
   1934
Radio Parade of 1935, 1935
International Revue, 1936
Pictorial Revue, 1936
Talking Hands, 1936
The Show's the Thing, 1936
Hands in Harmony, 1936
Two Men in a Box, 1938
Pathetone Parade of 1938,
   1938
His Brother's Keeper, 1939
Pathetone Parade of 1941, 1941
What Do We Do Now?, 1945
Wot! No Gangsters?, 1946
Dual Alibi, 1946
The Ghosts of Berkeley
   Square, 1947
Round Rainbow Corner, 1950

PAMELA FRANKLIN (1949-)
Child performer and latterly
leading lady of films and television. Originally intended for
ballet. Also in Hollywood.

The Innocents, 1961
The Lion, 1962
The Horse Without a Head, 1963
The Third Secret, 1964
A Tiger Walks, 1964
Flipper's New Adventure, 1964
The Nanny, 1965
Our Mother's House, 1967
Night of the Following Day,
  1968
The Prime of Miss Jean Brodie,
  1969
David Copperfield, 1969
Sinful Davy, 1969
And Soon the Darkness, 1970
Necromancy, 1972
The Legend of Hell House,
  1973
Ace Eli & Rodger of the Skies,
  1973
Terror From Within, 1975
Food of the Gods, 1976
Eleanor & Franklin, 1976

WILLIAM FRANKLYN (1926-)
Polished film actor, latterly
popular in comedy programs
on television.

Time is My Enemy, 1954
The Love Match, 1955
That Woman Opposite, 1957
Quatermass II, 1957
The Flesh is Weak, 1957
The Snorkel, 1958
Danger Within, 1959
The Big Day, 1960
Fury at Smuggler's Bay, 1961
Pit of Darkness, 1962
The Legend of Young Dick
  Turpin, 1965
The Intelligence Men, 1965
Cul De Sac, 1966
Satanic Rites of Dracula,
  1973
Get Charley Tully, 1977

BILL FRASER (1907-)
Small-part character actor of
stage, films and television,
popular in comedy cameos.
On tv as "Snudge. "

The Common Touch, 1941
Meet Me Tonight, 1952
The Captain's Paradise, 1953
Time Bomb, 1953
Orders Are Orders, 1954
The Barefoot Contessa, 1954
Charley Moon, 1956
Alias John Preston, 1956
Second Fiddle, 1957
Just My Luck, 1957
A Clean Sweep, 1958
The Man Who Liked Funerals,
  1959
What a Crazy World, 1963
A Home of Your Own, 1964
I've Gotta Horse, 1965
Masquerade, 1965
Joey Boy, 1965
The Americanization of Emily,
  1965
Diamonds For Breakfast, 1968
The Best House in London,
  1969
Captain Nemo and the Under-
  water City, 1969
All the Way Up, 1970
Up Pompeii, 1970
Up the Chastity Belt, 1971
That's Your Funeral, 1973
The Corn is Green, 1979

JOHN FRASER (1931-)
Scotch leading actor and supporting player of stage, films,
and television.

The Good Beginning, 1953
Valley of Song, 1953
Touch and Go, 1955
The Dam Busters, 1955
The Good Companions, 1957
The Wind Cannot Read, 1958
The Trials of Oscar Wilde,
  1960
Tunes of Glory, 1960
The Horsemasters, 1961

El Cid, 1961
Fury at Smuggler's Bay, 1961
Waltz of the Toreadors, 1962
Tamahine, 1963
Repulsion, 1965
Operation Crossbow, 1965
A Study in Terror, 1965
Doctor in Clover, 1966
Isadora, 1968
The Man and the Snake, 1972
Soup du Jour, 1975
Schizo, 1976
American Sex Fantasy, 1977

LIZ FRASER (1933-)
Buxom blonde supporting actress, usually seen in dumb
cockney characterizations.

Wonderful Things, 1958
I'm All Right Jack, 1959
The Night We Dropped a
    Clanger, 1959
Desert Mice, 1959
Two-Way Stretch, 1960
Doctor in Love, 1960
The Night We Got the Bird,
    1960
The Pure Hell of St. Trinian's,
    1960
The Bulldog Breed, 1960
Fury at Smuggler's Bay, 1961
Watch it Sailor, 1961
Double Bunk, 1961
The Rebel, 1961
Carry On Regardless, 1961
The Painted Smile, 1961
Carry On Cruising, 1962
The Amorous Prawn, 1962
Raising the Wind, 1962
Live Now Pay Later, 1963
Carry On Cabby, 1963
A Pair of Briefs, 1963
Every Day's a Holiday, 1964
Americanization of Emily,
    1965
The Family Way, 1966
Up the Junction, 1968
Dad's Army, 1970
Confessions of a Driving
    Instructor, 1976

MOYRA FRASER (1923-)
Australian comedy actress,
seen sporadically in films;
also on television.

Madeleine, 1950
The Dancing Years, 1950
The Man Who Loved Redheads,
    1955
Left, Right, and Centre, 1959
Here We Go Round the Mul-
    berry Bush, 1967
Prudence and the Pill, 1968
The Boy Friend, 1971

RONALD FRASER (1930-)
Stout, solid character actor of
films and television, typically
cast as complaining soldier.

The Sundowners, 1960
There Was a Crooked Man,
    1960
The Long & the Short & the
    Tall, 1961
Don't Bother to Knock, 1961
The Girl On the Boat, 1961
The Hellions, 1961
The Best of Enemies, 1961
Private Potter, 1962
In Search of the Castaways,
    1962
The Pot Carriers, 1962
Table Bay, 1963
The Punch and Judy Man, 1963
The VIPs, 1963
Daylight Robbery, 1964
The Model Murder Case, 1964
The Counterfeit Constable,
    1964
Crooks in Cloisters, 1964
The Beauty Jungle, 1964
Code 7 Victim 5, 1965
Flight of the Phoenix, 1965
The Whisperers, 1967
Fathom, 1967
Sebastian, 1968
The Killing of Sister George,
    1968
Sinful Davy, 1969
Too Late the Hero, 1969

The Bed Sitting Room, 1969
The Rise & Rise of Michael
    Rimmer, 1970
The Magnificent 7 Deadly Sins,
    1971
Rentadick, 1972
Ooh You Are Awful, 1972
Paper Tiger, 1975
Swallows and Amazons, 1977
Get Charley Tully, 1977
The Wild Geese, 1978

LESLIE FRENCH (1899-   )
Small film character player,
mostly seen as kindly, mild-
mannered characters.   Films
sporadic.

Peg of Old Drury, 1936
This England, 1941
Orders to Kill, 1958
The Scapegoat, 1959
The Malpas Mystery, 1960
The Singer Not the Song, 1961
The Leopard, 1963
Rescue Squad, 1963
More Than a Miracle, 1967
Death in Venice, 1970
Henry IV Part II, 1980

PHILIP FRIEND (1915-   )
Handsome leading man and
character star of stage (since
1935), screen and television,
also in Hollywood.

The Midas Touch, 1939
Inquest, 1939
Sheepdog of the Hills, 1941
Dangerous Moonlight, 1941
Pimpernel Smith, 1941
In Which We Serve, 1942
Back Room Boy, 1942
Next of Kin, 1942
The Day Will Dawn, 1942
We Dive at Dawn, 1943
The Bells Go Down, 1943
Warn That Man, 1943
The Flemish Farm, 1943
Great Day, 1945

Enchantment, 1948
My Own True Love, 1949
Sword in the Desert, 1949
Buccaneer's Girl, 1950
Spy Hunt, 1950
Panther's Moon, 1950
The Highwayman, 1951
Smuggler's Island, 1951
Thunder On the Hill, 1951
Desperate Moment, 1953
Background, 1953
The Diamond, 1954
Cloak Without Dagger, 1956
Dick Turpin the Highwayman,
    1956
Danger List, 1957
Betrayal, 1958
Son of Robin Hood, 1958
Web of Suspicion, 1959
The Solitary Child, 1959
Stranglehold, 1962
The Fur Collar, 1962
Manutara, 1964
The Vulture, 1967

LESLIE FULLER   (1889-1948)
Concert-party comedian who
became immensely popular during the 30s in expensive comedy features.

Not So Quiet On the Western
    Front, 1930
Why Sailors Leave Home, 1930
Kiss Me Sergeant, 1930
Old Soldiers Never Die, 1931
What a Night, 1931
Poor Old Bill, 1931
Bill's Legacy, 1931
Tonight's the Night, 1932
The Last Coupon, 1932
Old Spanish Customers, 1932
Hawleys of High Street, 1933
Pride of the Force, 1933
A Political Party, 1934
The Outcast, 1934
Lost in the Legion, 1934
Doctor's Orders, 1934
Strictly Illegal, 1935
The Stoker, 1935
Captain Bill, 1935

One Good Turn, 1936
Boys Will Be Girls, 1937
The Middle Watch, 1939
Two Smart Men, 1940
My Wife's Family, 1941
Front Line Kids, 1942
What Do We Do Now?, 1945

JUDITH FURSE (1912-)
Character actress generally seen
in small parts, often of the
comedy variety.

Goodbye Mr. Chips, 1939
English Without Tears, 1944
Johnny Frenchman, 1945
Quiet Weekend, 1946
While The Sun Shines, 1947
Black Narcissus, 1947
One Night With You, 1948
Dear Mr. Prohack, 1949
Helter Skelter, 1949
The Romantic Age, 1949
The Man in the White Suit, 1951
Mother Riley Meets the Vam-
    pire, 1952
Mad About Men, 1954
Doctor at Large, 1957
Blue Murder at St. Trinian's,
    1958
Serious Charge, 1959
Not a Hope in Hell, 1960
Scent of Mystery, 1960
Carry On Regardless, 1961
Live Now Pay Later, 1962
The Iron Maiden, 1962
Carry On Cabby, 1963
Carry On Spying, 1964
Sky West and Crooked, 1965
Twinky, 1969

WILL FYFFE (1885-1947)
Scotch comedy character star,
on stage from 1895, popular in
music halls (from 1916) for
song "I Belong to Glasgow."
Also in Hollywood.

Elstree Calling, 1930
Happy, 1934
Rolling Home, 1935

King of Hearts, 1936
Debt of Honour, 1936
Love in Exile, 1936
Men of Yesterday, 1936
Annie Laurie, 1936
Well Done Henry, 1937
Spring Handicap, 1937
Cotton Queen, 1937
Said O'Reilly to McNab, 1937
Owd Bob, 1938
Rulers of the Sea, 1938
To the Victor, 1938
The Mind of Mr. Reeder, 1939
The Missing People, 1939
They Came By Night, 1940
For Freedom, 1940
Neutral Port, 1941
The Prime Minister, 1941
Heaven is Round the Corner,
    1943
Give Me the Stars, 1945
The Brothers, 1947

RENEE GADD (1908-)
Blonde leading actress popular
in the 30s; former dancer.
Also in Hollywood.

Aren't We All, 1932
White Face, 1932
Money For Nothing, 1932
Women Who Play, 1932
Josser Joins the Navy, 1932
The Bad Companions, 1932
Maid of the Mountains, 1932
His Wife's Mother, 1932
Letting in the Sunshine, 1933
Skipper of the Osprey, 1933
Happy, 1934
The Love Captive, 1934
The Crimson Circle, 1936
Where's Sally?, 1936
The Man in the Mirror, 1936
Tomorrow We Live, 1936
The Man Who Made Diamonds,
    1937
Brief Ecstasy, 1937
Clothes and the Woman, 1937
Under a Cloud, 1937
Meet Mr. Penny, 1938
Murder in Soho, 1939
Unpublished Story, 1942

They Came to a City, 1944
Dead of Night, 1945
Frieda, 1947
Good Time Girl, 1948
The Blue Lamp, 1950

WARBURTON GAMBLE (-)
Character actor of stage and
films, also in Hollywood.

The Silver King, 1919
Society Exile, 1919
The Paliser Case, 1920
Tonight or Never, 1931
As You Desire Me, 1932
Fast Night, 1932
Tonight is Ours, 1933
Child of Manhattan, 1933
A Study in Scarlet, 1933
By Candlelight, 1934
The Lonely Road, 1936
Blind Man's Bluff, 1936
Spare a Copper, 1940

REGINALD GARDINER (1908-80)
Humourous, moustached character star of stage (from 1920)
and films, mainly in Hollywood.
Retired in 1967.

Bull Rushes, 1931
Aroma of the South Seas, 1931
My Old China, 1931
Flat No. 9, 1932
The Lovelorn Lady, 1932
Josser On the River, 1932
Radio Parade, 1933
Just Smith, 1933
How's Chances, 1934
Virginia's Husband, 1934
Borrow a Million, 1934
Opening Night, 1935
A Little Bit of Bluff, 1935
Royal Cavalcade, 1935
Born to Dance, 1936
A Damsel in Distress, 1937
Everybody Sing, 1937
Marie Antoinette, 1938
The Girl Downstairs, 1939
Flying Deuces, 1939
The Night of Nights, 1939

Sweethearts, 1939
The Great Dictator, 1940
The Doctor Takes a Wife, 1940
Dulcy, 1940
My Life With Caroline, 1941
The Man Who Came to Dinner,
   1941
Sundown, 1941
A Yank in the RAF, 1941
Captains of the Clouds, 1942
Immortal Sergeant, 1943
Sweet Rosie O'Grady, 1943
Claudia, 1943
The Horn Blows at Midnight,
   1945
Molly and Me, 1945
The Dolly Sisters, 1945
Christmas in Connecticut, 1945
Cluny Brown, 1946
One More Tomorrow, 1946
Do You Love Me?, 1946
I Wonder Who's Kissing Her
   Now, 1947
Fury at Furnace Creek, 1948
That Lady in Ermine, 1948
That Wonderful Urge, 1948
Wabash Avenue, 1950
Halls of Montezuma, 1951
Elopement, 1951
Androcles and the Lion, 1953
The Black Widow, 1954
Aint Misbehaving, 1955
The Birds and the Bees, 1956
The Story of Mankind, 1957
Rock a Bye Baby, 1958
Back Street, 1961
Mr. Hobbs Takes a Vacation,
   1962
What a Way to Go!, 1964
Sergeant Deadhead, 1965
Do Not Disturb, 1965

JOAN GARDNER (1914-)
Leading lady of the 30s, also
on stage (since 1931). Married
to director Zoltan Korda (1895-
1961).

Wedding Rehearsal, 1932
Men of Tomorrow, 1932
The Man Outside, 1933
The Private Life of Don

Juan, 1934
Catherine the Great, 1934
Love at Second Sight, 1934
Barnacle Bill, 1935
The Scarlet Pimpernel, 1935
The Man Who Could Work
    Miracles, 1936
Forget Me Not, 1936
Wings Over Africa, 1936
Dark Journey, 1937
Forever Yours, 1937
The Challenge, 1938
Rebel Son, 1939

JOHN GARRICK (1902-)
Second lead and supporting star
of the 30s, also in Hollywood.
Began as singer in 1920.

The Sky Hawk, 1929
Married in Hollywood, 1929
Song O' My Heart, 1930
Just Imagine, 1930
Charlie Chan Carries On, 1931
Always Goodbye, 1931
Bad Company, 1931
The Lottery Bride, 1931
Chu Chin Chow, 1934
Lily of Killarney, 1934
The Broken Melody, 1934
Too Many Millions, 1934
Anything Might Happen, 1934
D'Ye Ken John Peel, 1935
His Majesty and Co. , 1935
Street Song, 1935
The Turn of the Tide, 1935
The Rocks of Valpre, 1935
The Mother, 1936
A Touch of the Moon, 1936
Royal Eagle, 1936
Shipmates O' Mine, 1936
To Catch a Thief, 1936
A Woman Alone, 1936
Live Again, 1936
Sunset in Vienna, 1937
The Last Rose of Summer,
    1937
Remember When, 1937
The Bells of St. Mary's, 1937
Knights For a Day, 1937
Riding High, 1937
Two Who Dared, 1937

High Treason, 1937
Special Edition, 1938
The Great Victor Herbert,
    1939
Suicide Legion, 1940

GREER GARSON (1908-)
Attractive red-headed Irish
leading lady of stage (since
1932) and films, mainly in
Hollywood.

Goodbye Mr. Chips, 1939
Remember, 1939
Pride and Prejudice, 1940
Blossoms in the Dust, 1941
When Ladies Meet, 1941
Mrs. Miniver, 1942
Random Harvest, 1942
Madame Curie, 1943
The Youngest Profession, 1943
Mrs. Parkington, 1944
Valley of Decision, 1945
Adventure, 1945
Desire Me, 1947
Julia Misbehaves, 1948
That Forsyte Woman, 1949
The Miniver Story, 1950
The Law and the Lady, 1951
Scandal at Scourie, 1952
Julius Caesar, 1953
Her Twelve Men, 1954
Strange Lady in Town, 1954
Sunrise at Campobello, 1960
Pepe, 1960
The Singing Nun, 1966
The Happiest Millionaire, 1967
Crown Matrimonial, 1974

ALEXANDER GAUGE (1914-1960)
Obese character actor of the
fifties, also on television, notably in the "Robin Hood" series
(as Friar Tuck).

Interrupted Journey, 1949
Murder in the Cathedral, 1952
The Pickwick Papers, 1952
Penny Princess, 1952
Will Any Gentleman, 1953
Martin Luther, 1953

House of Blackmail, 1953
The Great Game, 1953
Counterspy, 1953
Fast and Loose, 1954
Double Exposure, 1954
Dance Little Lady, 1954
The Golden Link, 1954
Mystery On Bird Island, 1954
Before I Wake, 1955
Tiger By the Tail, 1955
The Reluctant Bride, 1955
Port of Escape, 1956
Breakaway, 1956
The Green Man, 1956
The Iron Petticoat, 1956
The Passionate Stranger, 1957
Nothing Barred, 1961

PETER GAWTHORNE (1884-
   1962)
Excellent thirties comedy actor
of stage and screen, primarily
cast as ostentatious military or
naval officer.

Behind That Curtain, 1929
Sunny Side Up, 1929
Temple Tower, 1930
Charlie Chan Carries On, 1931
The Man Who Came Back, 1931
Jack's the Boy, 1932
C. O. D. , 1932
His Lordship, 1932
The Lodger, 1932
The Flag Lieutenant, 1932
Night and Day, 1933
The Blarney Stone, 1933
Perfect Understanding, 1933
Just Smith, 1933
Prince of Arcadia, 1933
The House of Trent, 1933
Grand Prix, 1934
Girls Please, 1934
Something Always Happens,
   1934
The Camels Are Coming, 1934
Money Mad, 1934
My Old Dutch, 1934
Dirty Work, 1934
Two Hearts in Waltz Time,
   1934
The Iron Duke, 1935

Phantom Fiend, 1935
Who's Your Father?, 1935
Murder at Monte Carlo, 1935
Me and Marlborough, 1935
Crime Unlimited, 1935
Stormy Weather, 1935
The Crouching Beast, 1935
Man of the Moment, 1935
No Limit, 1935
Wolf's Clothing, 1936
Pot Luck, 1936
The Man Behind the Mask,
   1936
A Woman Alone, 1936
Everybody Dance, 1936
Gangway, 1937
Ticket of Leave Man, 1937
Good Morning Boys, 1937
Mr. Stringfellow Says No, 1937
Father Steps Out, 1937
Brief Ecstasy, 1937
Under a Cloud, 1937
The Last Adventurers, 1937
Remember When, 1937
Alf's Button Afloat, 1938
Easy Riches, 1938
George Bizet, 1938
Convict 99, 1938
Scruffy, 1938
Hey Hey USA, 1938
Ask a Policeman, 1939
Dead Men Are Dangerous, 1939
Home From Home, 1939
Flying Fifty-Five, 1939
Sword of Honour, 1939
Secret Journey, 1939
Where's That Fire?, 1939
What Would You Do Chums?,
   1939
Traitor Spy, 1939
Laugh it Off, 1940
Three Silent Men, 1940
Band Wagon, 1940
They Came By Night, 1940
Two For Danger, 1940
Gasbags, 1940
Inspector Hornleigh Goes To It,
   1941
Love On the Dole, 1941
Pimpernel Smith, 1941
Let the People Sing, 1942
Much Too Shy, 1942
Bell Bottom George, 1943

The Hundred Pound Window,
    1944
This Man is Mine, 1946
Nothing Venture, 1948
The Case of Charles Peace,
    1949
Hi Jinks in Society, 1949
Soho Conspiracy, 1950
Death is a Number, 1951
Paul Temple Returns, 1952
Five Days, 1954

EUNICE GAYSON (1931-)
Leading actress of the fifties,
also on stage.

Melody in the Dark, 1949
Dance Hall, 1950
To Have and To Hold, 1951
Miss Robin Hood, 1952
Street Corner, 1953
Dance Little Lady, 1954
Out of the Clouds, 1955
The Last Man to Hang, 1955
Zarak, 1956
Carry On Admiral, 1957
Revenge of Frankenstein, 1958
Dr. No, 1962
From Russia With Love, 1963

JUDY GEESON (1948-)
Pert, attractive leading actress
of the 60s and 70s, also on
stage and television. Sister:
Sally Geeson.

Wings of Mystery, 1963
Think 20th, 1967
To Sir With Love, 1967
Berserk!, 1967
Here We Go Round the Mulberry
    Bush, 1967
Prudence and the Pill, 1968
Hammerhead, 1968
Two Gentlemen Sharing, 1969
Three Into Two Won't Go,
    1969
Goodbye Gemini, 1970
The Executioner, 1970
One of Those Things, 1971
Who Killed the Mysterious

Mr. Foster, 1971
10 Rillington Place, 1971
Doomwatch, 1972
Fear in the Night, 1972
It Happened at Nightmare Inn,
    1973
Percy's Progress, 1974
Brannigan, 1974
Adventures of a Taxi Driver,
    1975
Diagnosis Murder, 1975
Murder On the Midnight Ex-
    press, 1975
Carry On England, 1976
The Eagle Has Landed, 1977

SALLY GEESON (1950-)
Juvenile actress of the sixties
and seventies, also on television in the fifties, sister of
Judy Geeson.

The Millionairess, 1960
Go To Blazes, 1962
The Great St. Trinian's Train
    Robbery, 1966
What's Good For the Goose,
    1969
The Oblong Box, 1969
Cry of the Banshee, 1970
Cry of the Penguins, 1972
Carry On Abroad, 1972
Bless This House, 1972
Carry On Girls, 1973

LEO GENN (1905-1978)
Distinguished, gentlemanly
actor of stage (from 1930),
screen and television with
resonant voice who gave up
law career to become a popular star on both sides of the
Atlantic.   Also colonel during
WW II who prosecuted at the
Nuremberg and Belsen War
Crimes trials.

Immortal Gentleman, 1935
Dream Doctor, 1936
Jump For Glory, 1937
The Rat, 1937

Cavalier of the Streets, 1937
Playgirl After Dark, 1937
Kate Plus Ten, 1938
The Drum, 1938
Pygmalion, 1938
Wainwright G. F. D. , 1938
Governor Bradford, 1938
Dangerous Medicine, 1938
Missing Ten Days, 1939
Contraband, 1940
Law and Disorder, 1940
The Young Mr. Pitt, 1942
Desert Victory (voice), 1943
Tunisian Victory (voice), 1944
The Way Ahead, 1944
Henry V, 1944
Julius Caesar, 1945
Theirs Was the Glory, 1945
Caesar and Cleopatra, 1945
Green For Danger, 1946
Green Fields, 1947
Mourning Becomes Electra,
    1947
The Velvet Touch, 1948
The Snake Pit, 1948
Blackmail, 1950
The Miniver Story, 1950
No Place For Jennifer, 1950
The Wooden Horse, 1950
The Undefeated (voice), 1950
The Magic Box, 1951
Quo Vadis, 1951
24 Hours of a Woman's Life,
    1952
Invitation to Monte Carlo, 1952
The Plymouth Adventure, 1952
Elizabeth is Queen (voice), 1952
Personal Affair, 1953
The Girls of Pleasure Island,
    1953
The Red Beret, 1953
Blackout, 1954
The Green Scarf, 1955
The Lowest Crime, 1955
Lady Chatterley's Lover, 1956
Beyond Mombasa, 1956
Moby Dick, 1956
Steel Bayonet, 1957
Titanic Incident, 1957
I Accuse, 1958
No Time to Die, 1958
Salome, 1958
You'll Never See Me Again,

1959
Too Hot to Handle, 1960
Mrs. Miniver, 1960
It Was Night in Rome, 1960
Escape By Night, 1960
The Life of Adolf Hitler, 1960
Give My Love a Gun, 1961
Wait For the Dawn, 1962
The Longest Day, 1962
55 Days at Peking, 1962
Death Rays of Dr. Mabuse,
    1963
The Strange Report, 1964
Ten Little Indians, 1965
Circus of Fear, 1966
Khartoum (voice), 1966
The Fifth Passenger, 1967
The Doctor's Dilemma, 1967
Vision and the Dream, 1967
The Gift, 1968
Cat's Cradle, 1968
The Case of Marie Stopes,
    1968
Dr. Jekyll and Mr. Hyde, 1968
Connecting Rooms, 1969
Howard's End, 1969
Expert, 1970
Saint Joan, 1970
Die Screaming Marianne, 1970
The Bloody Judge, 1971
Endless Night, 1971
Le Silencieux, 1971
Night of the Blood Monster,
    1972
Rebound, 1972
Ice Cream Man, 1972
Coventry Cathedral, 1972
The Silent One, 1972
The Mackintosh Man, 1973
A Lizard in a Woman's Skin,
    1973
Dr. Korckzak and His Children,
    1973
Edge of Noubere, 1974
Escape to Nowhere, 1974
Frightmare, 1975
The Dilke Case, 1975
The Martyr, 1976

MURIEL GEORGE (1883-1965)
Chubby character actress of
stage and screen, often seen as
landlady, maid, etc.

His Lordship, 1932
Yes Mr. Brown, 1933
Cleaning Up, 1933
My Song For You, 1934
Something Always Happens,
    1934
Nell Gwyn, 1934
Wedding Eve, 1935
Mr. What's His Name, 1935
Old Faithful, 1935
Limelight, 1936
Busman's Holiday, 1936
The Happy Family, 1936
Not So Dusty, 1936
Whom the Gods Love, 1936
King of Hearts, 1936
Song of the Road, 1937
Merry Comes to Town, 1937
Dr. Syn, 1937
Overcoat Sam, 1937
Talking Feet, 1937
Lancashire Luck, 1937
A Sister to Assist 'Er, 1938
Darts Are Trumps, 1938
Crackerjack, 1938
Who's Your Lady Friend?,
    1938
21 Days, 1939
Pack Up Your Troubles, 1940
Food For Thought, 1940
The Briggs Family, 1940
Quiet Wedding, 1941
Freedom Radio, 1941
Lady Be Kind, 1941
Telefootlers, 1941
Cottage to Let, 1941
Love On the Dole, 1941
Rush Hour, 1941
Unpublished Story, 1942
They Flew Alone, 1942
Alibi, 1942
Went the Day Well, 1942
The Bells Go Down, 1943
Dear Octopus, 1943
The Man From Scotland Yard,
    1944
Kiss the Bride Goodbye, 1944
For You Alone, 1945
I'll Be Your Sweetheart, 1945
Perfect Strangers, 1945
The Years Between, 1946
When the Bough Breaks, 1947
Last Holiday, 1950

The Dancing Years, 1950
Simon and Laura, 1955

SUSAN GEORGE (1950-)
Blonde leading actress, former
child actress, generally cast
in sexy roles. Also in Hollywood.

Cup Fever, 1965
Davy Jones' Locker, 1966
The Sorcerers, 1967
Billion Dollar Brain, 1967
The Strange Affair, 1968
Up the Junction, 1968
All Neat in Black Stockings,
    1968
Twinky, 1969
The Looking Glass War, 1970
Spring and Port Wine, 1970
Eyewitness, 1970
Die Screaming Marianne, 1970
Fright, 1971
Straw Dogs, 1971
Dirty Mary Crazy Larry, 1973
Sonny and Jed, 1974
Mandingo, 1975
Out of Season, 1975
A Small Town in Texas, 1976
Tintorera, 1977
Tomorrow Never Comes, 1977

MARY GERMAINE (1933-)
Leading actress of films during
a brief period in the 50s.

Laughter in Paradise, 1951
Cloudburst, 1951
Where's Charley?, 1952
Women of Twilight, 1952
Father's Doing Fine, 1952
The Night Won't Talk, 1952
Flannelfoot, 1953
The Floating Dutchman, 1953
House of Blackmail, 1953
Knights of the Round Table,
    1954
Devil's Point, 1954
The Green Buddha, 1954

GENE GERRARD (1892-1971)
Light musical comedy star and
director of the thirties, also
on stage (since 1911).

Let's Love and Laugh, 1931
My Wife's Family, 1931
Out of the Blue, 1931
Brother Alfred, 1932
Lucky Girl, 1932
Let Me Explain Dear, 1932
Leave It To Me, 1933
The Love Nest, 1933
There Goes Susie, 1934
It's a Bet, 1935
Joy Ride, 1935
Royal Cavalcade, 1935
The Guvnor, 1935
No Monkey Business, 1935
Faithful, 1936
Where's Sally?, 1936
Such is Life, 1936
Wake Up Famous, 1937
Glamour Girl, 1938
Dumb Dora Discovers Tobacco,
   1945

SIR JOHN GIELGUD (1904-)
Distinguished, outstanding actor
of stage (from 1921) and screen,
excellent in Shakespearian roles.
Also author.   Also in Hollywood.   His brother is mystery
writer Val Gielgud (1900-).

Who is the Man?, 1924
Clue of the New Pin, 1929
Insult, 1932
The Good Companions, 1933
Secret Agent, 1936
The Prime Minister, 1941
Hamlet (voice), 1948
Julius Caesar, 1953
Romeo and Juliet, 1954
Richard III, 1955
Around the World in 80 Days, 1956
The Barretts of Wimpole Street,
   1956
Saint Joan, 1957
The Browning Version, 1959
To Die in Madrid (voice), 1963
Becket, 1964
Hamlet, 1964

The Loved One, 1965
Chimes at Midnight, 1966
Sebastian, 1967
Charge of the Light Brigade, 1968
Assignment to Kill, 1968
The Shoes of the Fisherman, 1968
Oh What a Lovely War, 1969
Julius Caesar, 1970
Hamlet, 1970
Home, 1971
Eagle in a Cage, 1971
Search, 1972
Lost Horizon, 1973
Frankenstein: The True Story,
   1973
William, 1973
QB VII, 1974
Luther, 1974
Gold, 1974
11 Harrowhouse, 1974
Murder On the Orient Express,
   1974
Galileo, 1975
Aces High, 1976
Grand Inquisitor, 1976
Joseph Andrews, 1977
Providence, 1977
Caligula, 1977
No Man's Land, 1978
Portrait of the Artist as a
   Young Man, 1978
Richard II, 1979
Murder By Decree, 1979
The Formula, 1980
The Human Factor, 1980
Omar Mukhtar-Lion of the
   Desert, 1980
Why Didn't They Ask Evans?,
   1981

JEAN GILLIE (1915-1949)
Attractive thirties star, former
stage dancer (1931); also latterly in Hollywood.

His Majesty and Co. , 1935
Smith's Wives, 1935
Brewster's Millions, 1935
School For Stars, 1935
It Happened in Paris, 1935
While Parents Sleep, 1935
This'll Make You Whistle,
   1936

The Girl in the Taxi, 1937
The Live Wire, 1937
Sweet Devil, 1938
What Would You Do Chums?,
  1939
The Middle Watch, 1939
The Spider, 1939
Tilly of Bloomsbury, 1940
Sailors Don't Care, 1940
A Call For Arms, 1940
The Saint Meets the Tiger,
  1941
The Gentle Sex, 1943
Tawny Pipit, 1944
Flight From Folly, 1945
Decoy, 1946
The Macomber Affair, 1947

HERMIONE GINGOLD (1897-)
Comedy actress of stage (from
1908), screen and television;
specializes in eccentric, gro-
tesque, or outrageous characterizations. Also Hollywood.

Someone at the Door, 1936
Merry Comes to Town, 1937
Meet Mr. Penny, 1938
The Butler's Dilemma, 1943
Cosh Boy, 1952
The Pickwick Papers, 1952
Our Girl Friday, 1954
Around the World in 80 Days,
  1956
Bell, Book and Candle, 1958
Gigi, 1958
The Naked Edge, 1961
The Music Man, 1961
Gay Purr-ee, 1962
I'd Rather Be Rich, 1964
Harvey Middleman, Fireman,
  1965
Munster Go Home, 1966
Promise Her Anything, 1966
Rocket to the Moon, 1967
Banyon, 1967
A Little Night Music, 1976

PETER GLENVILLE (1913-)
Supporting actor of stage (from
1933) and films, also in Holly-

wood. Turned to directing in
1955.

His Brother's Keeper, 1939
Two For Danger, 1940
Uncensored, 1942
Heaven is Round the Corner,
  1944
Madonna of the Seven Moons,
  1944
Good Time Girl, 1948
Hotel Paradiso, 1966

JULIAN GLOVER (1935-)
Versatile supporting actor of
stage, films, and television.

Tom Jones, 1963
The Girl With Green Eyes,
  1964
I Was Happy Here, 1966
The Alphabet Murders, 1966
Theatre of Death, 1966
Quatermass and the Pit, 1967
The Magus, 1968
The Adding Machine, 1969
Alfred the Great, 1969
The Last Grenade, 1970
Wuthering Heights, 1970
Nicholas and Alexandra, 1971
Hitler: The Last Ten Days,
  1973
Antony and Cleopatra, 1973
Luther, 1974
Dead Cert, 1974
The Internecine Project, 1974
Juggernaut, 1974
Henry V, 1980

MARY GLYNNE (1898-1954)
Aristocratic leading lady of
stage and films, mainly seen
in well-bred roles.

A Cry For Justice, 1919
His Last Defence, 1919
Unmarried, 1920
The Call of Youth, 1920
The Hundredth Chance, 1920
The White Hen, 1921
Candytuft, I Mean Veronica,

1921
Appearances, 1921
The Princess of New York,
   1921
Dangerous Lies, 1921
Mystery Road, 1921
Beside the Bonnie Briar Bush,
   1922
Inquest, 1931
The Lost Chord, 1933
The Good Companions, 1933
Outcast, 1934
Flat No. 3, 1934
Emil and the Detectives, 1935
Scrooge, 1935
Royal Cavalcade, 1935
Grand Finale, 1936
The Heirloom Mystery, 1936
The Angelus, 1937
Cavalcade of the Stars, 1938

ALF GODDARD (1897-19)
Star of the 20s and 30s, typically cast in tough cockney
parts; former stuntman (1920)
and boxer.

The Sign of Four, 1923
Battling Bruisers, 1925
Every Mother's Son, 1926
White Heat, 1926
Mademoiselle From Armentieres,
   1926
Second to None, 1927
Downhill, 1927
Hindle Wakes, 1927
Remembrance, 1927
A Sister to Assist 'Er, 1927
The Flight Commander, 1927
Carry On, 1927
Sailors Don't Care, 1928
What Money Can Buy, 1928
Mademoiselle Parley Voo, 1928
Smashing Through, 1928
Balaclava, 1928
You Know What Sailors Are,
   1928
The Last Page, 1929
Down Channel, 1929
High Treason, 1929
Rough Seas, 1929
The Cockney Spirit in War,

1930
Alf's Button, 1930
The Brat, 1930
Bed and Breakfast, 1930
Old Soldiers Never Die, 1931
East Lynne, 1931
The Happy Ending, 1931
Splinters in the Navy, 1931
The Third String, 1932
Too Many Wives, 1933
Pride of the Force, 1933
Enemy of the Police, 1933
Lost in the Legion, 1934
Strictly Illegal, 1935
It's a Bet, 1935
No Limit, 1935
Song of Freedom, 1936
Amazing Quest of Ernest Bliss,
   1936
Farewell Again, 1937
The Squeaker, 1937
King Solomon's Mines, 1937
Non Stop New York, 1937
Bank Holiday, 1938
Owd Bob, 1938
The Drum, 1938
Convict 99, 1938
St. Martin's Lane, 1938
Luck of the Navy, 1938
Night Journey, 1938
The Ware Case, 1939
Murder in Soho, 1939
Young Man's Fancy, 1939
Let's Be Famous, 1939
A Window in London, 1939
Return to Yesterday, 1940
Spy For a Day, 1940
South American George, 1941
The Young Mr. Pitt, 1942
Lady in Distress, 1942
They Met in the Dark, 1943
The Way Ahead, 1944
The Way to the Stars, 1945
I'll Be Your Sweetheart, 1945
They Knew Mr. Knight, 1945
Perfect Strangers, 1945
Innocents in Paris, 1953

DEREK GODFREY (1924-)
Stage star who has appeared
in occasional films since 1962.

Guns of Darkness, 1962
The Vengeance of She, 1968
A Midsummer Night's Dream,
    1968
Julius Caesar, 1970
The Abominable Dr. Phibes,
    1971
Hands of the Ripper, 1971
Jesus of Nazareth, 1977
The Tempest, 1980

VANDA GODSELL (1919-)
Character actress of the 50s
and 60s, often seen in cameo
roles.

The Large Rope, 1953
Song of Norway, 1955
The Brain Machine, 1955
Wall of Death, 1956
Hour of Decision, 1957
Innocent Sinners, 1958
Hell is a City, 1960
The Man Who Was Nobody,
    1960
Sword of Sherwood Forest,
    1960
Shadow of the Cat, 1961
Payroll, 1961
Konga, 1961
Candidate For Murder, 1962
Waltz of the Toreadors, 1962
The Pot Carriers, 1962
Term of Trial, 1962
Night Without Pity, 1962
The Wrong Arm of the Law,
    1962
Bitter Harvest, 1963
80,000 Suspects, 1963
The Undesirable Neighbour,
    1963
Clash By Night, 1963
This Sporting Life, 1963
The Earth Dies Screaming,
    1964
A Shot in the Dark, 1964
Dateline Diamonds, 1965
The Wrong Box, 1966
Who Killed the Cat?, 1966
The Pink Panther Strikes
    Again, 1976

JIMMY GOLD (1886-1967)
Popular comedian and music
hall entertainer; partner of
Charlie Naughton and member
of "The Crazy Gang. "

Sign Please, 1933
My Lucky Star, 1933
Cock O' the North, 1935
Highland Fling, 1936
Wise Guys, 1937
Okay For Sound, 1937
Alf's Button Afloat, 1938
The Frozen Limits, 1939
Gasbags, 1940
Down Melody Lane, 1943
Life is a Circus, 1959

MICHAEL GOLDEN (1913-)
Character player of the fifties,
also on stage.

Send For Paul Temple, 1946
Hungry Hill, 1947
Escape, 1948
Another Shore, 1948
The Blue Lamp, 1950
Pool of London, 1951
Salute the Toff, 1952
The Gentle Gunman, 1952
36 Hours, 1954
The Black Rider, 1954
Murder By Proxy, 1955
Cross Channel, 1955
The Green Scarf, 1955
Josephine and Men, 1955
Man Without a Body, 1957
A Date With Disaster, 1957
Robbery With Violence, 1959
Murder She Said, 1962

CHARLES GOLDNER (1900-1955)
Austrian character star of
stage and films, in Britain
from the 30s. Equally skillful
at comedy or dramatic roles.

Room For Two, 1940
The Seventh Survivor, 1941
Mr. Emmanuel, 1944

Flight From Folly, 1945
The Laughing Lady, 1946
Brighton Rock, 1947
Bonnie Prince Charlie, 1948
One Night With You, 1948
Third Time Lucky, 1948
Bond Street, 1948
No Orchids For Miss Blandish,
  1948
Dear Mr. Prohack, 1949
The Rocking Horse Winner,
  1949
Give Us This Day, 1949
Black Magic, 1949
Shadow of the Eagle, 1950
I'll Get You For This, 1951
Top Secret, 1952
Secret People, 1952
South of Algiers, 1952
Encore, 1952
The Captain's Paradise, 1953
Always a Bride, 1953
The Master of Ballantrae,
  1953
The Golden Mask, 1954
Flame and the Flesh, 1954
Duel in the Jungle, 1954
The Racers, 1955
The End of the Affair, 1955

MICHAEL GOODLIFFE (1914-
  1976)
Likable, intelligent actor of
stage, films and television,
usually seen as professional
man or military officer.

The Small Back Room, 1948
Stop Press Girl, 1949
The Wooden Horse, 1950
Captain Horatio Hornblower,
  1951
Cry the Beloved Country, 1952
Sea Devils, 1953
Rob Roy, 1953
Front Page Story, 1954
The End of the Affair, 1955
Quentin Durward, 1955
Dial 999, 1955
Battle of the River Plate, 1956
Wicked As They Come, 1956
The One That Got Away, 1957

Fortune is a Woman, 1957
A Night to Remember, 1958
The Camp On Blood Island,
  1958
Carve Her Name With Pride,
  1958
Up the Creek, 1958
Further Up the Creek, 1958
Battle of the Sexes, 1959
The White Trap, 1959
The 39 Steps, 1959
Sink the Bismarck, 1960
The Trials of Oscar Wilde,
  1960
Peeping Tom, 1960
Conspiracy of Hearts, 1960
No Love For Johnnie, 1961
The Day the Earth Caught
  Fire, 1961
Number Six, 1962
Jigsaw, 1962
80,000 Suspects, 1963
The £20,000 Kiss, 1963
The Seventh Dawn, 1964
Man in the Middle, 1964
The Gorgon, 1964
Troubled Waters, 1964
633 Squadron, 1964
Von Ryan's Express, 1965
The Jokers, 1966
Cromwell, 1970
Hitler: The Last Ten Days,
  1973
The Man With the Golden Gun,
  1974

CAROL GOODNER (1904-)
American-born leading actress
of British films of the thirties.

Those Who Love, 1929
The Ringer, 1931
The Flying Squad, 1932
There Goes the Bride, 1932
Strange Evidence, 1933
The Fire Raisers, 1933
Just Smith, 1933
Red Ensign, 1934
What's in a Name?, 1934
Royal Cavalcade, 1935
Mimi, 1935
The Student's Romance, 1935

Music Hath Charms, 1935
The Dominant Sex, 1937
The Frog, 1937
A Royal Divorce, 1938

HAROLD GOODWIN (1917-)
Small-part character player of
the fifties and sixties, often in
Cockney characterizations.

The Happiest Days of Your
  Life, 1950
Dance Hall, 1950
The Magnet, 1951
The Man in the White Suit, 1951
Angels One Five, 1952
The Card, 1952
The Cruel Sea, 1953
The Harassed Hero, 1954
The Gay Dog, 1954
The Ship That Died of Shame,
  1955
The Dam Busters, 1955
The Ladykillers, 1955
Zarak, 1956
Barnacle Bill, 1957
The Prince and the Showgirl,
  1957
Bridge On the River Kwai, 19
  1957
Seawife, 1957
Law and Disorder, 1958
Sea of Sand, 1958
The Mummy, 1959
Wrong Number, 1959
Spartacus, 1960
Operation Cupid, 1960
The Bulldog Breed, 1960
On the Fiddle, 1961
The Traitors, 1962
Hair of the Dog, 1962
Number Six, 1962
Phantom of the Opera, 1962
The Hi-Jackers, 1963
The Comedy Man, 1963
Curse of the Mummy's Tomb,
  1964
Don't Raise the Bridge Lower
  the River, 1968
Frankenstein Must be De-
  stroyed, 1969
Jabberwocky, 1977

RICHARD GOOLDEN (1895-)
Character player of stage and
screen often seen in perplexed
or confused roles; famous on
radio as Old Ebenezer the
night watchman.

Once in a New Moon, 1935
Whom the Gods Love, 1936
School For Husbands, 1937
Television Talent, 1937
Meet Mr. Penny, 1938
Two Days to Live, 1939
Mistaken Identity, 1939
Headline, 1943
The Tell-Tale Taps, 1945
Vengeance is Mine, 1949
Heights of Danger, 1953
The Weapon, 1956
In the Doghouse, 1961
It's All Happening, 1963

COLIN GORDON (1911-1972)
Comedy character actor of
stage (since 1931) and screen;
typically cast as cynical or
doubtful official.

Jim the Penman, 1947
Bond Street, 1948
The Winslow Boy, 1948
Helter Skelter, 1949
Traveller's Joy, 1949
Three Men and a Girl, 1949
Edward My Son, 1949
The Third Visitor, 1951
The Long Dark Hall, 1951
Green Grow the Rushes, 1951
Circle of Danger, 1951
The Hour of Thirteen, 1951
The Man in the White Suit,
  1951
Mandy, 1952
Folly to Be Wise, 1952
The Heart of the Matter, 1953
Grand National Night, 1953
Innocents in Paris, 1953
Up to His Neck, 1954
Little Red Monkey, 1955
Escapade, 1955
Jumping For Joy, 1955
A Touch of the Sun, 1956

Up in the World, 1956
The Extra Day, 1956
Keep it Clean, 1956
The Green Man, 1956
The Key Man, 1957
The One That Got Away,
    1957
Alive and Kicking, 1958
The Safecracker, 1958
The Doctor's Dilemma, 1958
Virgin Island, 1958
The Mouse That Roared,
    1959
Please Turn Over, 1959
Bobbikins, 1959
The Crowning Touch, 1959
His and Hers, 1960
The Big Day, 1960
Carry On Constable, 1960
The Day They Robbed the Bank
    of England, 1960
Three On a Spree, 1961
The Horsemasters, 1961
House of Mystery, 1961
Don't Bother to Knock, 1961
In the Doghouse, 1961
Crooks Anonymous, 1962
Night of the Eagle, 1962
The Devil's Agent, 1962
The Boys, 1962
Strongroom, 1962
Seven Keys, 1962
Burn Witch Burn, 1962
Very Important Person, 1962
Bitter Harvest, 1963
The Running Man, 1963
Heavens Above, 1963
The Pink Panther, 1963
The Family Way, 1966
The Psychopath, 1966
The Liquidator, 1966
The Great St. Trinian's Train
    Robbery, 1966
The Trygon Factor, 1967
Casino Royale, 1967
Subterfuge, 1968
Don't Raise the Bridge Lower
    the River, 1968
Mischief, 1969

HAL GORDON (1894-   )
Amiable, good-natured come-

dian of stage and screen,
used to good advantage as a
foil for the star; most popular in the 30s.

Adam's Apple, 1928
When Knights Were Bold, 1929
The Windjammer, 1930
The Cockney Spirit in War,
    1930
Out of the Blue, 1931
Old Soldiers Never Die, 1931
Poor Old Bill, 1931
Bill and Coo, 1931
Up For the Cup, 1931
Money For Nothing, 1932
Tonight's the Night, 1932
Partners Please, 1932
The New Hotel, 1932
The Strangler, 1932
Old Spanish Customers, 1932
Help Yourself, 1932
Indiscretions of Eve, 1932
The Bad Companions, 1932
Brother Alfred, 1932
Strip Strip Hooray, 1932
Lucky Girl, 1932
The Last Coupon, 1932
Josser in the Army, 1932
His Wife's Mother, 1932
Money Talks, 1932
Sleepless Nights, 1932
For the Love of Mike, 1932
Lord Camber's Ladies, 1932
Let Me Explain, 1932
Their Night Out, 1933
Hawleys of High Street, 1933
Facing the Music, 1933
The Pride of the Force, 1933
Crime On the Hill, 1933
A Southern Maid, 1933
Master and Man, 1934
Happy, 1934
A Political Party, 1934
The Outcast, 1934
Sometimes Good, 1934
My Song Goes Round the World,
    1934
Lost in the Legion, 1934
Wishes, 1934
Captain Bill, 1935
Dance Band, 1935
Eighteen Minutes, 1935

Dandy Dick, 1935
Lend Me Your Wife, 1935
The Deputy Drummer, 1935
Invitation to the Waltz, 1935
Play Up the Band, 1935
No Escape, 1936
Queen of Hearts, 1936
The Man Behind the Mask,
  1936
One Good Turn, 1936
Amazing Quest of Ernest
  Bliss, 1936
Keep Your Seats Please, 1936
It's in the Bag, 1936
Dusty Ermine, 1936
Southern Roses, 1936
Keep Fit, 1937
East of Ludgate Hill, 1937
Father O'Mine, 1938
We're Going to Be Rich, 1938
It's in the Air, 1938
Come On George, 1939
Let George Do It, 1940
Food For Thought, 1940
Spare a Copper, 1940
Old Mother Riley Detective,
  1943
Give Me the Stars, 1945

MARY GORDON (1882-1963)
Delightful, diminutive Scottish
character actress of stage and
screen, long in Hollywood.
Perfectly cast as Mrs. Hudson,
the landlady in the Sherlock
Holmes films (1939-1946).

The Home Maker, 1925
Black Paradise, 1926
Naughty Nanette, 1927
Clancy's Kosher Wedding, 1927
Dynamite, 1929
Madam X, 1929
The Black Camel, 1931
The Little Minister, 1934
Mutiny On the Bounty, 1935
Bride of Frankenstein, 1935
Vanessa: Her Love Story,
  1935
The Irish in Us, 1935
The Plough and the Stars,
  1936

Laughing Irish Eyes, 1936
Forgotten Faces, 1936
Mary of Scotland, 1936
Great Guy, 1937
The Great O'Malley, 1937
Double Wedding, 1937
Lady Behave, 1938
Kidnapped, 1938
City Streets, 1938
Captain Fury, 1939
Parents On Trial, 1939
Rulers of the Sea, 1939
Hound of the Baskervilles,
  1939
Adventures of Sherlock Holmes,
  1939
Tear Gas Squad, 1940
Joe and Ethel Turp Call on
  the President, 1940
When the Daltons Rode, 1940
No No Nanette, 1940
Flight From Destiny, 1941
Pot O'Gold, 1941
Appointment For Love, 1941
The Mummy's Tomb, 1942
Bombay Clipper, 1942
Powder Town, 1942
Sherlock Holmes and the Voice
  of Terror, 1942
Sherlock Holmes and the Se-
  cret Weapon, 1942
Sherlock Holmes Faces Death,
  1943
Sherlock Holmes in Washing-
  ton, 1943
Sarong Girl, 1943
Two Tickets to London, 1943
The Hour Before the Dawn,
  1944
The Pearl of Death, 1944
The Scarlet Claw, 1944
The Spider Woman, 1944
The House of Fear, 1945
Pursuit to Algiers, 1945
The Woman in Green, 1945
See My Lawyer, 1945
Strange Confession, 1945
Sentimental Journey, 1946
The Hoodlum Saint, 1946
Terror By Night, 1946
Dressed to Kill, 1946
Little Giant, 1946
The Invisible Wall, 1947
West of Wyoming, 1950

MARIUS GORING (1912-)
Versatile actor of stage (since
1925) and films, typically seen
in neurotic or decadent roles.
Married to Lucy Mannheim.

Rembrandt, 1936
Dead Men Tell No Tales, 1938
Consider Your Verdict, 1938
The Spy in Black, 1939
Flying Fifty-Five, 1939
Pastor Hall, 1940
Case of the Frightened Lady,
  1940
The Big Blockade, 1942
Night Invader, 1943
Lilli Marlene, 1944
Night Boat to Dublin, 1946
A Matter of Life and Death,
  1946
Take My Life, 1947
The Red Shoes, 1948
Mr. Perrin and Mr. Traill,
  1948
Odette, 1950
Highly Dangerous, 1950
Pandora & the Flying Dutchman,
  1951
Circle of Danger, 1951
The Magic Box, 1951
So Little Time, 1952
Paris Express, 1953
Rough Shoot, 1954
The Barefoot Contessa, 1954
Break in the Circle, 1955
Quentin Durward, 1955
Ill Met By Moonlight, 1957
The Truth About Women, 1958
The Family Doctor, 1958
The Moonraker, 1958
I Was Monty's Double, 1958
Son of Robin Hood, 1958
Whirlpool, 1959
The Angry Hills, 1959
Treasure of San Teresa, 1959
Desert Mice, 1959
Exodus, 1960
Beyond the Curtain, 1960
The Unstoppable Man, 1960
The Devil's Daffodil, 1962
The Inspector, 1962
The Devil's Agent, 1962
Crooked Road, 1964

The 25th Hour, 1967
Girl On a Motorcycle, 1968
Subterfuge, 1968
First Love, 1970
Zeppelin, 1971
Holocaust, 1977
La Petite Fille en Velours
  Bleu, 1978

HELEN GOSS (-)
Small-part character player,
often cast as servants and the
like.

Important People, 1934
The Reverse Be My Lot, 1938
A Place of One's Own, 1944
The Wicked Lady, 1945
Pink String and Sealing Wax,
  1945
They Were Sisters, 1945
My Sister and I, 1948
The Planter's Wife, 1952
Hound of the Baskervilles, 1959
Jane Eyre, 1970

MICHAEL GOUGH (1917-)
Tall character star of stage
(since 1936) and films, also in
Hollywood. Latterly viewed in
horror films; also adept at evil
characterizations.

Blanche Fury, 1948
Anna Karenina, 1948
Saraband For Dead Lovers,
  1948
The Small Back Room, 1948
Blackmailed, 1950
No Resting Place, 1951
The Man in the White Suit, 1951
Night Was Our Friend, 1951
Twice Upon a Time, 1953
The Sword and the Rose, 1953
Rob Roy, 1953
Richard III, 1955
Reach For the Sky, 1956
Ill Met By Moonlight, 1957
Dracula, 1957
The House in the Woods, 1957
Model For Murder, 1958

The Horse's Mouth, 1959
Horrors of the Black Museum,
   1959
Konga, 1961
Mr. Topaze, 1961
What a Carve Up!, 1962
Candidate For Murder, 1962
Phantom of the Opera, 1962
Black Zoo, 1963
Tamahine, 1963
Dr. Terror's House of Horrors,
   1964
Game For Three Losers, 1965
The Skull, 1965
They Came From Beyond Space,
   1967
Berserk!, 1967
Curse of the Crimson Altar,
   1968
Women in Love, 1969
A Walk With Love and Death,
   1969
Trog, 1970
The Corpse, 1970
Julius Caesar, 1970
The Go-Between, 1971
Savage Messiah, 1972
Henry VIII & His Six Wives,
   1972
The Legend of Hell House, 1973
Horror Hospital, 1973
Galileo, 1975
Satan's Slave, 1976
The Boys From Brazil, 1978

GIBSON GOWLAND (1872-1951)
Leading actor and latterly supporting star, primarily in Hollywood. Also on stage.

Birth of a Nation, 1915
Macbeth, 1916
The Hawk, 1917
Blind Husbands, 1919
White Heather, 1919
The Fighting Shepherdess, 1920
The Right of Way, 1920
Behind the Door, 1920
Ladies Must Love, 1921
Shifting Sands, 1923
Harbor Lights, 1923
Greed, 1924

Border Legion, 1924
Love and Glory, 1924
The Red Lily, 1924
Phantom of the Opera, 1925
The Prairie Wife, 1925
The Outsider, 1926
Don Juan, 1926
Topsy and Eva, 1927
The First Auto, 1927
The Broken Gate, 1927
Night of Love, 1927
Isle of Forgotten Women, 1927
The Land Beyond the Law,
   1927
Rose Marie, 1928
Mysterious Island, 1929
Hell Harbor, 1930
The Sea Brat, 1930
Doomed Battalion, 1932
SOS Iceberg, 1933
Secret of the Loch, 1934
The Private Life of Don Juan,
   1934
Mystery of the Mary Celeste,
   1936
Cotton Queen, 1937
The Wife of General Ling,
   1937

MORLAND GRAHAM (1891-1949)
Solid Scotch character player of
stage and films of the 30s and
40s.

What Happened to Harkness?,
   1934
Get Off My Foot, 1935
Moscow Nights, 1935
The Scarlet Pimpernel, 1935
Twelve Good Men, 1936
Where's Sally?, 1936
Fair Exchange, 1936
Full Speed Ahead, 1939
Jamaica Inn, 1939
Old Bill and Son, 1940
Night Train to Munich, 1940
This England, 1941
Freedom Radio, 1941
The Ghost Train, 1941
Tower of Terror, 1941
Ships With Wings, 1941
The Big Blockade, 1942

The Shipbuilders, 1943
Henry V, 1944
Medal For the General, 1944
Gaiety George, 1944
The Brothers, 1946
The Upturned Glass, 1947
Bonnie Prince Charlie, 1948
Esther Waters, 1948
Whiskey Galore, 1948

MARGOT GRAHAME (1911-)
Luxurious blonde leading actress of the 30s, also in Hollywood. On stage as well from
1926.

Rookery Nook, 1930
Compromising Daphne, 1930
The Love Habit, 1931
Uneasy Virtue, 1931
The Rosary, 1931
Stamboul, 1931
Glamour, 1931
Creeping Shadows, 1931
Postal Orders, 1932
Letter of Warning, 1932
Innocents of Chicago, 1932
Illegal, 1932
Yes Mr. Brown, 1933
Forging Ahead, 1933
Timbuctoo, 1933
Prince of Arcadia, 1933
I Adore You, 1933
Sorrell and Son, 1933
Without You, 1934
The Broken Melody, 1934
Falling in Love, 1934
The Arizonan, 1935
The Informer, 1935
Crime Over London, 1936
The Three Musketeers, 1936
Two in the Dark, 1936
Counterfeit, 1936
Trouble Ahead, 1936
Make Way For a Lady, 1936
Night Waitress, 1936
Criminal Lawyer, 1937
Michael Strogoff, 1937
The Buccaneer, 1938
Fight For Your Lady, 1938
The Shipbuilders, 1944
Broken Journey, 1948

The Romantic Age, 1949
Black Magic, 1949
Lucky Nick Cain, 1951
Venetian Bird, 1952
The Crimson Pirate, 1952
The Beggar's Opera, 1953
Orders Are Orders, 1954
Saint Joan, 1957

STEWART GRANGER (1913-)
Tall, romantic leading man of
stage (1935), screen and television, also in Hollywood.
Latterly in international films.

A Southern Maid, 1933
Give Her a Ring, 1934
Mademoiselle Docteur, 1937
So This is London, 1939
Convoy, 1940
Secret Mission, 1942
Thursday's Child, 1943
The Lamp Still Burns, 1943
The Man in Grey, 1943
Fanny By Gaslight, 1944
Love Story, 1944
Madonna of the Seven Moons,
    1944
Waterloo Road, 1945
Caesar and Cleopatra, 1945
Caravan, 1946
The Magic Bow, 1947
Captain Boycott, 1947
Blanche Fury, 1948
Woman Hater, 1948
Saraband For Dead Lovers,
    1949
Adam and Evalyn, 1949
King Solomon's Mines, 1950
The Light Touch, 1951
Soldiers Three, 1951
Scaramouche, 1952
The Prisoner of Zenda, 1952
The Wild North, 1952
Young Bess, 1953
Salome, 1953
All the Brothers Were Valiant,
    1954
Beau Brummell, 1954
Green Fire, 1955
Moonfleet, 1955
Footsteps in the Fog, 1955

Deadlock, 1956
Bhowani Junction, 1956
The Last Hunt, 1956
Gun Glory, 1957
The Little Hut, 1957
Harry Black, 1958
The Whole Truth, 1958
North to Alaska, 1960
The Secret Partner, 1961
Commando, 1962
La Congiura dei Dieci, 1962
Sodom and Gomorrah, 1962
Swordsman of Siena, 1963
The Legion's Lost Patrol, 1963
Il Giorno piu Corto, 1963
The Crooked Road, 1964
Among Vultures, 1964
The Secret Invasion, 1964
Frontier Hellcat, 1964
Der Oelprinz, 1965
Old Shatterhand, 1965
Rampage at Apache Wells, 1965
Flaming Frontier, 1965
Red Dragon, 1965
Requiem For a Secret Agent, 1966
A Target For Killing, 1966
The Trygon Factor, 1967
The Last Safari, 1967
Any Second Now, 1969
Hound of the Baskervilles, 1972
The Wild Geese, 1978

CARY GRANT (1904-)
Stylish, likeable leading actor of stage and screen, long in Hollywood. Cast in sophisticated, witty or debonair roles.

This is the Night, 1932
Sinners in the Sun, 1932
Hot Saturday, 1932
Merrily We Go to Hell, 1932
The Devil and the Deep, 1932
Madame Butterfly, 1933
Blonde Venus, 1933
She Done Him Wrong, 1933
Alice in Wonderland, 1933
The Eagle and the Hawk, 1933
Woman Accused, 1933
Gambling Ship, 1933

I'm No Angel, 1933
Thirty Day Princess, 1934
Born to Be Bad, 1934
Kiss and Make Up, 1934
Enter Madame, 1934
Ladies Should Listen, 1934
Wings in the Dark, 1935
The Last Outpost, 1935
Sylvia Scarlett, 1935
Big Brown Eyes, 1935
Suzy, 1936
Wedding Present, 1936
Amazing Quest of Ernest Bliss, 1936
When You're in Love, 1936
The Awful Truth, 1937
The Toast of New York, 1937
Topper, 1937
Bringing Up Baby, 1938
Holiday, 1938
Gunga Din, 1939
Only Angels Have Wings, 1939
In Name Only, 1939
My Favorite Wife, 1940
The Tree of Liberty, 1940
His Girl Friday, 1940
The Philadelphia Story, 1940
Penny Serenade, 1941
Suspicion, 1941
Talk of the Town, 1942
Once Upon a Honeymoon, 1942
Destination Tokyo, 1943
Mr. Lucky, 1943
Once Upon a Time, 1944
None But the Lonely Heart, 1944
Arsenic and Old Lace, 1944
Night and Day, 1945
Notorious, 1946
Without Reservations, 1946
The Bishop's Wife, 1947
Bachelor and the Bobbysoxer, 1947
Every Girl Should Be Married, 1948
Mr. Blandings Builds His Dream House, 1948
I Was a Male War Bride, 1949
Crisis, 1950
Room For One More, 1952
Monkey Business, 1952
Dream Wife, 1953
To Catch a Thief, 1955

Kiss Them For Me, 1957
An Affair to Remember, 1957
The Pride and the Passion,
   1957
Indiscreet, 1958
Houseboat, 1958
North By Northwest, 1959
Operation Petticoat, 1959
The Grass is Greener, 1960
That Touch of Mink, 1962
Charade, 1963
Father Goose, 1964
Walk Don't Run, 1966

LAWRENCE GRANT (1870-
1952)
Character player of stage and
films, long in Hollywood.

The Great Impersonation, 1921
His Hour, 1924
Happiness, 1924
The Grand Duchess & the
   Waiter, 1926
The Duchess of Buffalo, 1926
Service For Ladies, 1927
Gentleman of Paris, 1927
Serenade, 1927
Doomsday, 1928
Red Hair, 1928
Something Always Happens,
   1928
At Yale, 1928
The Woman From Moscow,
   1928
The Canary Murder Case, 1929
Bulldog Drummond, 1929
The Case of Lena Smith, 1929
Is Everybody Happy?, 1929
The Boudoir Diplomat, 1930
The Cat Creeps, 1930
Daughter of the Dragon, 1931
The Unholy Garden, 1931
The Squaw Man, 1931
Man About Town, 1932
Speak Easily, 1932
Faithless, 1932
Clear All Wires, 1932
Jewel Robbery, 1932
The Mask of Fu Manchu, 1932
Grand Hotel, 1932
Shanghai Express, 1932

Queen Christina, 1933
Looking Forward, 1933
By Candlelight, 1934
Nana, 1934
I'll Tell the World, 1934
The Count of Monte Cristo,
   1934
The Werewolf of London, 1935
The Devil is a Woman, 1935
The Man Who Reclaimed His
   Head, 1935
Vanessa: Her Love Story,
   1935
The Dark Angel, 1935
Three Kids and a Queen, 1935
A Tale of Two Cities, 1935
Little Lord Fauntleroy, 1936
House of a Thousand Candles,
   1936
Mary of Scotland, 1936
Under the Red Robe, 1937
The Prisoner of Zenda, 1937
Service de Luxe, 1938
The Young in Heart, 1938
Bluebeard's Eighth Wife, 1938
Son of Frankenstein, 1939
Women in War, 1940
Dr. Jekyll and Mr. Hyde, 1941
Confidential Agent, 1945

GEORGE GRAVES (1876-1949)
Hearty, good-humored character player of stage (from 1890)
and screen, usually in gentlemanly parts. Occasional films
in the 30s.

The Crooked Lady, 1932
A Sister to Assist 'Er, 1933
Those Were the Days, 1934
Honours Easy, 1935
Royal Cavalcade, 1935
Heart's Desire, 1935
Wolf's Clothing, 1936
The Tenth Man, 1936
Robber Symphony, 1936
A Star Fell From Heaven, 1936

LORD PETER GRAVES
   (1911-   )
Tall, distinguished leading man

and latterly small-part actor of
stage (1934) and screen; former estate agent. Not to be
confused with American film
and tv actor Peter Graves
(1925-).

Kipps, 1941
Ships With Wings, 1941
King Arthur Was a Gentleman,
1942
Miss London Ltd. , 1943
Bees in Paradise, 1944
Give Us the Moon, 1944
I'll Be Your Sweetheart, 1945
Waltz Time, 1945
Gaiety George, 1946
Spring Song, 1946
The Laughing Lady, 1946
Mrs. Fitzherbert, 1947
Spring in Park Lane, 1948
Maytime in Mayfair, 1949
The Lady With a Lamp, 1951
Encore, 1952
Derby Day, 1952
Lilacs in the Spring, 1954
The Admirable Crichton, 1957
Alfie, 1966
The Wrong Box, 1966
The Jokers, 1966
How I Won the War, 1967
I'll Never Forget Whatsisname,
1967
The Assassination Bureau, 1969
The Adventurers, 1970
The Magic Christian, 1970
Paul and Michelle, 1974
The Slipper and the Rose, 1976

CHARLES GRAY (1928-)
Dominant character actor of
stage, films and television,
adept at sinister or unsympathetic characterizations.

The Desperate Man, 1959
The Entertainer, 1960
Man in the Moon, 1961
Masquerade, 1965
Night of the Generals, 1966
You Only Live Twice, 1967
The Man Outside, 1967

Secret War of Harry Frigg,
1968
The Devil Rides Out, 1968
The Devil's Bride, 1968
File of the Golden Goose, 1968
Mosquito Squadron, 1969
The Executioner, 1970
Cromwell, 1970
Diamonds Are Forever, 1971
The Beast Must Die, 1974
The Rocky Horror Show, 1975
Murder On the Midnight Ex-
press, 1975
Seven Nights in Japan, 1976
The Seven Per Cent Solution,
1976
Silver Bears, 1978
Julius Caesar, 1979
Richard II, 1979
Legacy, 1979

DONALD GRAY (1914-)
One-armed leading actor and
character player of stage,
films, and television, famous
in the latter media as "Mark
Saber. " Also former radio
announcer and actor.

Well Done Henry, 1937
Strange Experiment, 1937
Murder in the Family, 1938
Thirteen Men and a Gun, 1938
Sword of Honour, 1939
The Four Feathers, 1939
We'll Meet Again, 1942
Idol of Paris, 1948
Saturday Island, 1952
The Diamond, 1954
Burnt Evidence, 1954
Timeslip, 1955
Satellite in the Sky, 1956
Supersonic Saucer, 1956
The Secret Tent, 1956
Out of the Shadow, 1961

DULCIE GRAY (1919-)
Pleasant, attractive leading
lady of stage (since 1936) and
films, also author and playwright. Married to Michael
Denison.

Two Thousand Women, 1944
Victory Wedding, 1944
Madonna of the Seven Moons,
    1944
A Place of One's Own, 1945
They Were Sisters, 1945
Wanted For Murder, 1946
The Years Between, 1946
A Man About the House, 1946
Mine Own Executioner, 1947
My Brother Jonathan, 1948
The Glass Mountain, 1949
The Franchise Affair, 1950
Angels One Five, 1951
There Was a Young Lady, 1953
A Man Could Get Killed, 1965

EVE GRAY (1904-)
Beautiful blonde leading actress
of the thirties, also on stage
(from 1924).

Daughter of the Night, 1927
Poppies of Flanders, 1927
The Silver Lining, 1927
One of the Best, 1927
Moulin Rouge, 1928
Smashing Through, 1928
The Loves of Robert Burns,
    1930
Why Sailors Leave Home, 1930
Night Birds, 1930
Smithy, 1933
Midnight, 1933
The Flaw, 1933
The Wickham Mystery, 1933
The Bermondsey Kid, 1933
The Crimson Candle, 1934
Womanhood, 1934
Guest of Honour, 1934
Big Business, 1934
What's in a Name, 1934
Murder at Monte Carlo, 1935
Death On the Set, 1935
Three Witnesses, 1935
Just For Tonight, 1935
Scrooge, 1935
Department Store, 1935
The Last Journey, 1935
Twice Branded, 1936
Jury's Evidence, 1936
They Didn't Know, 1936

The Happy Family, 1936
Such is Life, 1936
Pearls Bring Tears, 1937
When the Devil Was Well, 1937
The Vicar of Bray, 1937
Strange Adventures of Mr.
    Smith, 1937
Fifty Shilling Boxer, 1937
The Angelus, 1937
Silver Blaze, 1937
His Lordship Regrets, 1938
The Awakening, 1938
One Good Turn, 1951

NADIA GRAY (1923-)
Russian-born leading actress
of British and international
films, also on stage.

L'Enconnue d'un Soir, 1948
Monseigneur, 1948
The Spider and the Fly, 1949
Night Without Stars, 1951
Valley of the Eagles, 1951
Top Secret, 1952
Wife For a Night, 1952
Gran Varieta, 1953
La Vierge du Rhin, 1953
Neopolitan Fantasy, 1954
Sins of Casanova, 1954
House of Ricordi, 1954
Music in Blue, 1955
Folies Bergere, 1956
Puccini, 1956
Senechal the Magnificent, 1957
Holiday Island, 1958
The Captain's Table, 1959
Parisienne, 1959
La Dolce Vita, 1959
Candide, 1960
Mr. Topaze, 1961
Maniac, 1963
The Crooked Road, 1965
The Naked Runner, 1967
Two For the Road, 1967
The Oldest Profession, 1967
Rue Haute, 1976

SALLY GRAY (1916-)
Well-liked leading lady of the
30s and 40s, on stage also
from 1925.

School For Scandal, 1930
Marry the Girl, 1935
Radio Pirates, 1935
Cross Currents, 1935
Lucky Days, 1935
Checkmate, 1935
Cheer Up, 1936
Calling the Tune, 1936
Honeymoon Merry-Go-Round, 1936
Cafe Colette, 1937
Over She Goes, 1937
Saturday Night Revue, 1937
Mr. Reeder in Room 13, 1938
Hold My Hand, 1938
Lightning Conductor, 1938
The Lambeth Walk, 1939
Sword of Honour, 1939
The Saint in London, 1939
A Window in London, 1939
The Saint's Vacation, 1941
Dangerous Moonlight, 1941
Green For Danger, 1946
Carnival, 1946
They Made Me a Fugitive, 1947
The Mark of Cain, 1948
Silent Dust, 1948
Obsession, 1949
Escape Route, 1953

DANNY GREEN (1903-)
Large, good-humoured character player, often cast as dumb
cockney gangster.

Atlantic, 1929
The Silent House, 1929
The Crooked Billet, 1929
Things Are Looking Up, 1935
Crime Over London, 1936
Gangway, 1937
Midnight Menace, 1937
Fiddlers Three, 1944
The Man Within, 1947
No Orchids For Miss Blandish,
  1948
Someone at the Door, 1950
The Lady Craved Excitement,
  1950
Her Favourite Husband, 1950
A Tale of Five Cities, 1951
Little Big Shot, 1952
Whispering Smith Hits London,

1952
Laughing Anne, 1953
A Kid For Two Farthings,
  1955
The Ladykillers, 1955
Assignment Redhead, 1956
Interpol, 1957
Seven Waves Away, 1957
Beyond This Place, 1959
Hidden Homicide, 1959
Girls of Latin Quarter, 1960
In the Wake of a Stranger,
  1961
The Fast Lady, 1962
The Old Dark House, 1963

HUGHIE GREEN (1920-)
Character actor and former
juvenile performer of stage
(1934) and screen, recently on
television as quizmaster. Also
Hollywood. Films occasional.

Little Friend, 1934
Radio Pirates, 1935
Midshipman Easy, 1935
Melody and Romance, 1937
Down Our Alley, 1939
Music Hall Parade, 1939
Tom Brown's Schooldays, 1940
If Winter Comes, 1948
The Hills of Home, 1948
Paper Orchid, 1949
Crazy Days, 1962

NIGEL GREEN (1924-1972)
Prominent South-African born
leading actor and strong supporting star of stage, films,
and television; adept at sinister
roles. Also in Hollywood.

Death Takes a Holiday, 1953
As Long As They're Happy, 1955
Reach For the Sky, 1956
Bitter Victory, 1957
Corridors of Blood, 1958
Witness in the Dark, 1959
Domino, 1959
The Primitives, 1960
Beat Girl, 1960

The Queen's Guards, 1960
The Criminal, 1960
The Sword of Sherwood Forest, 1960
Blackmail, 1961
Man at the Carlton Tower, 1961
Pit of Darkness, 1961
Mysterious Island, 1961
The Spanish Sword, 1962
Playback, 1962
The Man Who Finally Died, 1962
The Durant Affair, 1962
Jason and the Argonauts, 1963
Zulu, 1964
Masque of the Red Death, 1964
The Ipcress File, 1965
The Face of Fu Manchu, 1965
The Skull, 1965
Let's Kill Uncle, 1966
Khartoum, 1966
Deadlier Than the Male, 1967
Tobruk, 1967
Africa-Texas Style!, 1967
Play Dirty, 1968
The Pink Jungle, 1968
Fraulein Doktor, 1969
The Wrecking Crew, 1969
The Kremlin Letter, 1970
Countess Dracula, 1971
The Ruling Class, 1972

RICHARD GREENE (1918-)
Handsome light leading man of stage and screen, mainly in Hollywood; later well-known on tv as "Robin Hood."

Four Men and a Prayer, 1938
My Lucky Star, 1938
Kentucky, 1938
Submarine Patrol, 1938
Hound of the Baskervilles, 1939
Here I Am a Stranger, 1939
The Little Princess, 1939
Stanley and Livingstone, 1939
Little Old New York, 1940
I Was an Adventuress, 1940
Unpublished Story, 1942
Flying Fortress, 1942
The Yellow Canary, 1943

Don't Take it to Heart, 1944
Gaiety George, 1946
Forever Amber, 1947
Lady Windermere's Fan, 1949
The Fighting O'Flynn, 1949
That Dangerous Age, 1949
Now Barabbas, 1949
My Daughter Joy, 1950
Shadow of the Eagle, 1950
Lorna Doone, 1951
The Desert Hawk, 1952
The Black Castle, 1952
Captain Scarlett, 1952
Rogue's March, 1952
Return of the Corsican Brothers, 1953
Contraband Spain, 1955
Beyond the Curtain, 1960
Sword of Sherwood Forest, 1960
Dangerous Island, 1967
The Blood of Fu Manchu, 1968
The Castle of Fu Manchu, 1968
Tales From the Crypt, 1972

SYDNEY GREENSTREET (1879-1954)
Heavyweight character star of the forties; films in Hollywood where he generally played villainous roles. On stage from 1902. Also on radio.

The Maltese Falcon, 1941
They Died With Their Boots On, 1941
In This Our Life, 1942
Across the Pacific, 1942
Casablanca, 1942
Background to Danger, 1943
The Conspirators, 1944
Passage to Marseilles, 1944
Between Two Worlds, 1944
Mask of Dimitrios, 1944
Hollywood Canteen, 1944
Pillow to Post, 1945
Conflict, 1945
Christmas in Connecticut, 1945
The Verdict, 1946
Three Strangers, 1946
Devotion, 1946

That Way With Women, 1947
The Hucksters, 1947
Woman in White, 1948
The Velvet Touch, 1948
Ruthless, 1948
Flamingo Road, 1949
It's a Great Feeling, 1949
Malaya, 1950

JOAN GREENWOOD (1921-)
Leading lady of the 40s with
refined, elegant voice; also on
stage (from 1938) and in Hollywood.   Married to Andre
Morell.

John Smith Wakes Up, 1940
My Wife's Family, 1941
He Found a Star, 1941
The Gentle Sex, 1942
They Knew Mr. Knight, 1944
Latin Quarter, 1945
Girl in a Million, 1946
The Man Within, 1947
The October Man, 1947
The White Unicorn, 1947
Saraband For Dead Lovers,
   1948
The Bad Lord Byron, 1948
Whiskey Galore, 1948
Kind Hearts and Coronets,
   1949
Flesh and Blood, 1950
The Man in the White Suit,
   1951
Young Wives' Tale, 1951
Mr. Peek-a-Boo, 1951
The Importance of Being
   Earnest, 1952
Knave of Hearts, 1954
Father Brown, 1954
Moonfleet, 1955
Stage Struck, 1958
Mysterious Island, 1961
The Amorous Prawn, 1962
Tom Jones, 1963
The Moonspinners, 1964
Girl Stroke Boy, 1971
The Uncanny, 1977
The Hound of the Baskervilles,
   1978
The Water Babies, 1979

VERNON GREEVES (-)
Character player of small
roles, in occasional films.
Also stage.

Henry V, 1944
Wall of Death, 1956
The Intimate Stranger, 1956
Lady of Vengeance, 1957
Time Without Pity, 1957
Men of Tomorrow, 1959

EVERLY GREGG (-)
Dark-haired second lead and
supporting actress of stage
and films.

The Private Life of Henry
   VIII, 1933
The Scoundrel, 1935
The Ghost Goes West, 1936
Thunder in the City, 1937
Blondes For Danger, 1938
Pygmalion, 1938
Spies of the Air, 1939
The Gentle Sex, 1943
The Demi-Paradise, 1943
The Two Fathers, 1944
Brief Encounter, 1945
Great Expectations, 1946
The Astonished Heart, 1950
The Magic Box, 1951
Worm's Eye View, 1951
Stolen Face, 1952
At Home With the Hardwickes,
   1952
Night of the Full Moon, 1954
Father Brown, 1954
Lost, 1956
Deadly Record, 1956
Room at the Top, 1959

HUBERT GREGG (1914-)
Light actor of stage (from
1933) and screen, also screenwriter and songwriter.   Married to Pat Kirkwood.

In Which We Serve, 1942
29 Acacia Avenue, 1945
The Root of All Evil, 1947
Landfall, 1949

Once Upon a Dream, 1949
Vote For Huggett, 1949
The Third Visitor, 1951
Robin Hood, 1952
Final Appointment, 1954
The Maggie, 1954
Simon and Laura, 1955
Svengali, 1955
Doctor at Sea, 1955
Stars in Your Eyes, 1956

JOHN GREGSON (1919-1975)
Popular, friendly Scottish leading man and character star of
Stage (1947), screen and television, adept at comedy and
dramatic roles alike. On tv
in series "Gideon's Way" (1965),
"Shirley's World" (1971).

Saraband For Dead Lovers, 1948
Scott of the Antarctic, 1948
Whiskey Galore, 1948
Train of Events, 1949
Treasure Island, 1950
Cairo Road, 1950
The Lavender Hill Mob, 1951
Angels One Five, 1951
Submarine Command, 1952
The Brave Don't Cry, 1952
Venetian Bird, 1952
The Holly and the Ivy, 1952
The Titfield Thunderbolt, 1953
Genevieve, 1953
The Weak and the Wicked, 1953
Conflict of Wings, 1954
To Dorothy a Son, 1954
The Crowded Day, 1954
Above Us the Waves, 1955
Value For Money, 1955
Three Cases of Murder, 1955
Jacqueline, 1956
Battle of the River Plate, 1956
True as a Turtle, 1956
Miracle in Soho, 1957
Rooney, 1958
Sea of Sand, 1958
The Captain's Table, 1959
SOS Pacific, 1959
Faces in the Dark, 1960
Hand in Hand, 1960
Treasure of Monte Cristo, 1961

The Frightened City, 1961
Live Now Pay Later, 1962
The Longest Day, 1962
Tomorrow at Ten, 1962
Night of the Generals, 1966
Fright, 1971
Tiger Lily, 1975

JOYCE GRENFELL (1910-1979)
Character star of stage (since
1939) and films, very adept at
awkward comedy roles; also
formerly on radio. Former
journalist and critic too.

The Lamp Still Burns, 1943
The Demi-Paradise, 1943
While the Sun Shines, 1947
Poet's Pub, 1949
A Run For Your Money, 1949
The Happiest Days of Your
    Life, 1950
Stage Fright, 1950
The Galloping Major, 1951
Laughter in Paradise, 1951
The Magic Box, 1951
The Pickwick Papers, 1952
Genevieve, 1953
The Million Pound Note, 1954
Forbidden Cargo, 1954
The Belles of St. Trinian's,
    1954
The Good Companions, 1957
Blue Murder at St. Trinian's,
    1957
Happy is the Bride, 1958
Pure Hell of St. Trinian's,
    1960
The Old Dark House, 1963
The Yellow Rolls-Royce, 1964
The Americanization of Emily,
    1964

ETHEL GRIFFIES (1878-1975)
Character actress of stage
(from 1881) and films, long in
Hollywood where she played
elderly women for many years.

The Cost of a Kiss, 1917
Old English, 1930

Changes, 1930
Stepdaughters, 1930
Waterloo Bridge, 1931
The Road to Singapore, 1931
Once a Lady, 1931
Manhattan Parade, 1931
Of Human Bondage, 1931
Love Me Tonight, 1932
The Impatient Maiden, 1932
Westward Passage, 1932
Tonight is Ours, 1933
A Lady's Profession, 1933
Alice in Wonderland, 1933
Bulldog Drummond Strikes
  Back, 1934
House of Rothschild, 1934
We Live Again, 1934
Vanessa: Her Love Story,
  1935
Hold 'Em Yale, 1935
The Werewolf of London, 1935
Anna Karenina, 1935
The Return of Peter Grimm,
  1935
The Mystery of Edwin Drood,
  1935
Not So Dusty, 1936
Guilty Melody, 1936
Twice Branded, 1936
Kathleen Mavourneen, 1937
Crackerjack, 1938
I'm From Missouri, 1939
We Are Not Alone, 1939
Vigil in the Night, 1940
Anne of Windy Poplars, 1940
Stranger On the Third Floor,
  1940
Irene, 1940
Great Guns, 1941
Time to Kill, 1941
Dead Men Tell, 1941
A Yank in the RAF, 1941
How Green Was My Valley,
  1941
Between Us Girls, 1942
Son of Fury, 1942
Holy Matrimony, 1943
Jane Eyre, 1944
The White Cliffs of Dover,
  1944
Music For Millions, 1944
The Thrill of Romance, 1945
Molly and Me, 1945

The Horn Blows at Midnight,
  1945
Uncle Harry, 1945
Saratoga Trunk, 1945
Devotion, 1946
The Homestretch, 1947
The Birds, 1963
Billy Liar, 1963
Don't Shake the Family Tree,
  1963

JOSEPHINE GRIFFIN (1928-)
Leading and supporting actress
who had a brief career in films
of the mid-fifties.

The House of the Arrow, 1953
The Crowded Day, 1954
The Weak and the Wicked, 1954
The Purple Plain, 1954
Room in the House, 1955
Portrait of Alison, 1955
On Such a Night, 1956
The Extra Day, 1956
The Man Who Never Was,
  1956
The Spanish Gardener, 1956

HUGH GRIFFITH (1912-)
Enthusiastic, colorful Welsh
actor of stage (since 1939) and
screen, also in Hollywood.
Former bank clerk.

Neutral Port, 1940
The Silver Darlings, 1947
London Belongs to Me, 1948
So Evil My Love, 1948
The First Gentleman, 1948
The Three Weird Sisters, 1948
Dr. Morelle, 1949
The Last Days of Dolwyn, 1949
A Run For Your Money, 1949
Kind Hearts and Coronets, 1949
The Wild Heart, 1950
Laughter in Paradise, 1951
The Galloping Major, 1951
The Titfield Thunderbolt, 1953
The Beggar's Opera, 1953
The Million Pound Note, 1954
The Sleeping Tiger, 1954

The Good Companions, 1955
Passage Home, 1955
Lucky Jim, 1957
Ben Hur, 1959
The Day They Robbed the Bank
of England, 1960
Exodus, 1960
The Story On Page One, 1960
The Counterfeit Traitor, 1962
The Inspector, 1962
Term of Trial, 1962
Mutiny On the Bounty, 1962
Tom Jones, 1963
Hide and Seek, 1964
The Bargee, 1964
Moll Flanders, 1965
Dare I Weep, Dare I Mourn,
1966
The Poppy is Also a Flower,
1966
Brown Eye, Evil Eye, 1966
How to Steal a Million, 1966
Oh Dad Poor Dad, 1967
The Chastity Belt, 1967
Sailor From Gibraltar, 1967
Oliver, 1968
The Fixer, 1968
On My Way to the Crusades...,
1969
Start the Revolution Without
Me, 1970
Cry of the Banshee, 1970
Wuthering Heights, 1970
The Abominable Dr. Phibes,
1971
Whoever Slew Auntie Roo?, 1971
Dr. Phibes Rises Again, 1972
Take Me High, 1973
What?, 1973
Legend of the Werewolf, 1974
Luther, 1974
Craze, 1974
Canterbury Tales, 1974
The Final Programme, 1974
Loving Cousins, 1976
The Passover Plot, 1977
Last Remake of Beau Geste,
1977
Casanova and Co., 1977
Hound of the Baskervilles, 1978

KENNETH GRIFFITH (1921-   )

Sharp-featured Welsh character
player of stage and screen,
generally cast in jealous, cov-
etous, or sniveling roles.

Love On the Dole, 1941
The Farmer's Wife, 1941
The Shop at Sly Corner, 1945
Bond Street, 1948
Forbidden, 1949
Blue Scar, 1949
Waterfront, 1950
High Treason, 1951
The Starfish, 1952
The Green Buddha, 1954
36 Hours, 1954
The Prisoner, 1955
Track the Man Down, 1955
Private's Progress, 1956
1984, 1956
Baby and the Battleship, 1956
Tiger in the Smoke, 1956
Lucky Jim, 1957
Brothers in Law, 1957
Blue Murder at St. Trinian's,
1957
A Night to Remember, 1958
The Naked Truth, 1958
The Two-Headed Spy, 1958
Chain of Events, 1958
Libel, 1958
I'm All Right, Jack, 1959
The Man Upstairs, 1959
Tiger Bay, 1959
Carlton Browne of the F.O.,
1959
Expresso Bongo, 1959
A French Mistress, 1960
Snowball, 1960
Suspect, 1960
Circus of Horrors, 1960
Rag Doll, 1961
The Frightened City, 1961
Payroll, 1961
Only Two Can Play, 1962
The Painted Smile, 1962
We Joined the Navy, 1962
Heavens Above, 1963
Rotten to the Core, 1965
The Bobo, 1967
The Whisperers, 1967
Great Catherine, 1967
Decline and Fall, 1968

The Lion in Winter, 1968
The Assassination Bureau,
  1969
Jane Eyre, 1970
Revenge, 1971
The House in Nightmare Park,
  1973
SPYS, 1974
Skyriders, 1976
The Wild Geese, 1978

ROBERT GRIFFITH (-)
Welsh character player of occasional films, mainly on
stage.

The Night Club, 1925
A Night of Magic, 1944
For Those in Peril, 1944
Painted Boats, 1945
For You Alone, 1945

JANE GRIFFITHS (1930-)
Leading actress of the fifties,
former child player.

The Derelict, 1937
Pandemonium, 1939
The Gambler and the Lady,
  1952
The Million Pound Note, 1954
The Green Scarf, 1955
Shadow of a Man, 1955
The Traitors, 1957
Three Sundays to Live, 1957
Tread Softly Stranger, 1958
The Impersonator, 1961
The Durant Affair, 1962
Dead Man's Evidence, 1962
The Double, 1963

FRED GROVES (1880-1955)
Star of silent films and later
competent character actor,
also on stage (since 1906).

Maria Marten, 1913
Bridegrooms Beware, 1913
Popsy Wopsy, 1913
The Cup Final Mystery, 1914

Inquisitive Ike, 1914
Blackeyed Susan, 1914
The Suicide Club, 1914
Loss of the Birkenhead, 1914
Beautiful Jim, 1914
Her Luck in London, 1914
The Idol of Paris, 1914
There's Good in Everyone,
  1915
Honeymoon For Three, 1915
Gilbert Gets Tigeritis, 1915
Gilbert Dying to Die, 1915
Midshipman Easy, 1915
London's Yellow Peril, 1915
Florence Nightingale, 1915
The World's Desire, 1915
From Shopgirl to Duchess,
  1915
Another Man's Wife, 1915
Her Nameless Child, 1915
Grip, 1915
Home, 1915
Mr. Lyndon at Liberty, 1915
A Will of Her Own, 1915
Charity Ann, 1915
Fine Feathers, 1915
Yvonne, 1915
The Firm of Girdlestone, 1915
Meg the Lady, 1916
Esther, 1916
Driven, 1916
Mother Love, 1916
The Manxman, 1916
Smith, 1917
Drink, 1917
Castle of Dreams, 1919
Garryowen, 1920
Judge Not, 1920
The Mayor of Casterbridge,
  1921
A Master of Craft, 1922
The Crimson Circle, 1922
Rogues of the Turf, 1923
Squibs MP, 1923
Squibs' Honeymoon, 1923
Memories, 1923
Escape, 1930
Suspense, 1930
Sally in Our Alley, 1931
Out of the Blue, 1931
The World, the Flesh, and
  the Devil, 1932
Puppets of Fate, 1933

A Glimpse of Paradise, 1934
The Old Curiosity Shop, 1934
Royal Cavalcade, 1935
Dance Band, 1935
Beloved Imposter, 1936
The Royal Eagle, 1936
Second Bureau, 1936
The Viper, 1938
The Challenge, 1938
No Parking, 1938
Vessel of Wrath, 1938
21 Days, 1939
An Ideal Husband, 1947
Night Beat, 1948
My Brother's Keeper, 1948
The Girl Who Couldn't Quite,
  1950
Up For the Cup, 1950

SIR ALEC GUINNESS (1914-)
Distinguished, versatile actor
of stage (from 1933), screen
and television, outstanding in
any type of role; also a master
of disguise. Also in Hollywood.

Evensong, 1933
Great Expectations, 1946
Oliver Twist, 1948
Kind Hearts and Coronets, 1949
A Run For Your Money, 1949
Last Holiday, 1950
The Mudlark, 1950
The Man in the White Suit,
  1951
The Lavender Hill Mob, 1951
The Card, 1952
The Captain's Paradise, 1953
The Malta Story, 1953
Father Brown, 1954
To Paris With Love, 1954
The Prisoner, 1955
The Ladykillers, 1955
Rowlandson's England, 1955
The Swan, 1956
Barnacle Bill, 1957
Bridge On the River Kwai, 1957
The Scapegoat, 1958
The Horse's Mouth, 1958
Our Man in Havana, 1959
The Wicked Scheme of Jebal
  Deeks, 1959

Tunes of Glory, 1960
A Majority of One, 1961
HMS Defiant, 1962
Lawrence of Arabia, 1962
Fall of the Roman Empire,
  1964
Situation Hopeless But Not
  Serious, 1965
Dr. Zhivago, 1965
The Quiller Memorandum, 1966
Hotel Paradiso, 1966
The Comedians, 1967
Cromwell, 1970
Scrooge, 1970
Brother Sun, Sister Moon,
  1973
Hitler: The Last Ten Days,
  1973
Caesar and Cleopatra, 1976
Murder By Death, 1976
Star Wars, 1977
Raise the Titanic, 1980
Tinker, Tailor, Soldier, Spy,
  1980
Little Lord Fauntleroy, 1980
The Empire Strikes Back,
  1980

RACHEL GURNEY (-)
Attractive, intelligent actress,
mainly on stage and television,
in occasional films. On tv in
"Upstairs Downstairs. "

Tom Brown's School Days,
  1951
The Blakes Slept Here, 1954
Room in the House, 1955
Port Afrique, 1956
A Touch of Larceny, 1960
Game For Three Losers, 1965
Funeral in Berlin, 1966
I Know What I Want, 1972
The Four Feathers, 1978

EDMUND GWENN (1875-1959)
Veteran Welsh character actor
of stage (1895) and films, in
Hollywood from mid-thirties
where he generally played
kindly, benevolent parts.

The Real Thing at Last, 1916
Unmarried, 1920
The Skin Game, 1920
The Skin Game, 1931
How He Lied to Her Husband,
    1931
Hindle Wakes, 1931
Money For Nothing, 1932
Frail Women, 1932
Condemned to Death, 1932
Love On Wheels, 1932
Tell Me Tonight, 1932
The Good Companions, 1933
Cash, 1933
Early to Bed, 1933
I Was a Spy, 1933
Channel Crossing, 1933
Smithy, 1933
Marooned, 1933
Friday the Thirteenth, 1933
Be Mine Tonight, 1933
Waltzes From Vienna, 1934
The Admiral's Secret, 1934
Passing Shadows, 1934
Warn London, 1934
Java Head, 1934
Father and Son, 1934
Spring in the Air, 1934
The Bishop Misbehaves, 1935
Sylvia Scarlett, 1935
The Walking Dead, 1936
Anthony Adverse, 1936
All American Chump, 1936
Mad Holiday, 1936
Laburnum Grove, 1936
Parnell, 1937
South Riding, 1938
A Yank at Oxford, 1938
Penny Paradise, 1938
Cheer Boys Cheer, 1939
An Englishman's Home, 1939
The Earl of Chicago, 1940
Madmen of Europe, 1940
The Doctor Takes a Wife, 1940
Pride and Prejudice, 1940
Foreign Correspondent, 1940
Scotland Yard, 1941
Cheers For Miss Bishop, 1941
The Devil and Miss Jones,
    1941
Charley's Aunt, 1941
One Night in London, 1941
A Yank at Eton, 1942

Meanest Man in the World,
    1943
Forever and a Day, 1943
Lassie Come Home, 1943
Between Two Worlds, 1944
Keys of the Kingdom, 1944
Bewitched, 1945
Dangerous Partners, 1945
She Went to the Races, 1945
Of Human Bondage, 1946
Undercurrent, 1946
Miracle On 34th Street, 1947
Thunder in the Valley, 1947
Life With Father, 1947
Green Dolphin Street, 1947
Apartment For Peggy, 1948
The Hills of Home, 1948
Challenge to Lassie, 1949
A Woman of Distinction, 1950
Louisa, 1950
Pretty Baby, 1950
Mr. 880, 1950
For Heaven's Sake, 1950
Peking Express, 1951
Sally and St. Anne, 1952
Bonzo Goes to College, 1952
Les Miserables, 1952
Something For the Birds, 1952
Mr. Scoutmaster, 1952
The Bigamist, 1953
Them, 1954
The Student Prince, 1954
The Trouble With Harry, 1955
It's a Dog's Life, 1955
Calabuch, 1957

MICHAEL GWYNN (1916-1976)
Character actor of the 50s and
60s, also on stage and tv.

The Runaway Bus, 1954
The Secret Place, 1957
Revenge of Frankenstein, 1958
Dunkirk, 1958
The Camp On Blood Island,
    1958
The Doctor's Dilemma, 1958
Village of the Damned, 1960
Never Take Sweets From a
    Stranger, 1960
Question Seven, 1961
Barabbas, 1962

Cleopatra, 1962
What a Carve Up!, 1962
Some People, 1962
The Horse Without a Head,
  1963
Jason and the Argonauts, 1963
Fall of the Roman Empire,
  1964
The Crowning Gift, 1967
The Deadly Bees, 1967
The Virgin Soldiers, 1969
Scars of Dracula, 1970

GRETA GYNT (1916-)
Glamorous Norwegian-born
blonde of stage (from 1934) and
films, often seen in adventure
or crime pictures.

The Road Back, 1937
Boys Will Be Girls, 1937
The Last Curtain, 1937
Second Best Bed, 1938
Sexton Blake and the Hooded
  Terror, 1938
The Last Barricade, 1938
Too Dangerous to Live, 1939
Dark Eyes of London, 1939
She Couldn't Say No, 1939
The Arsenal Stadium Mystery,
  1939
The Middle Watch, 1939
Two For Danger, 1940
Bulldog Sees it Through, 1940
Room For Two, 1940
Crooks' Tour, 1940
The Common Touch, 1941
It's That Man Again, 1942
Tomorrow We Live, 1943
Mr. Emmanuel, 1944
London Town, 1946
Take My Life, 1947
Dear Murderer, 1947
Easy Money, 1948
The Calendar, 1948
Mr. Perrin and Mr. Traill,
  1948
Shadow of the Eagle, 1950
I'll Get You For This, 1951
Soldiers Three, 1951
Whispering Smith Hits London,
  1952

I'm a Stranger, 1952
The Ringer, 1952
Three Steps in the Dark, 1953
Forbidden Cargo, 1954
The Devil's Point, 1954
See How They Run, 1955
Blue Peter, 1955
Dead On Time, 1955
My Wife's Family, 1956
Fortune is a Woman, 1957
Morning Call, 1958
The Witness, 1959
The Crowning Touch, 1959
Bluebeard's Ten Honeymoons,
  1960
The Runaway, 1964

PETER HADDON (1898-1962)
Light leading man and character actor of stage and screen,
popular in the thirties. Often
in comedy parts.

Alf's Button, 1930
Greek Street, 1930
Yes Madam, 1933
Death at Broadcasting House,
  1934
The Silent Passenger, 1935
Who's Your Father?, 1935
No Monkey Business, 1935
Don't Rush Me, 1936
Public Nuisance Number One,
  1936
The House of the Spaniard,
  1936
The Secret of Stamboul, 1936
Beloved Vagabond, 1936
Over the Moon, 1937
Kate Plus Ten, 1938
Helter Skelter, 1949
The Second Mrs. Tanqueray,
  1952

KENNETH HAIGH (1929-)
Leading and supporting star of
stage and screen, also on television where he is best known
for series "Man at the Top. "
Films occasional. Also Hollywood.

My Teenage Daughter, 1956
High Flight, 1956
Saint Joan, 1957
Cleopatra, 1962
A Hard Day's Night, 1964
Weekend at Dunkirk, 1966
The Deadly Affair, 1966
A Lovely Way to Die, 1968
Eagle in a Cage, 1971
Man at the Top, 1973
Robin and Marian, 1976

SONNIE HALE (1902-1959)
Intelligent light comedian of
stage (from 1921) and films,
mainly active in the 30s.
Also playwright.   Married to
Jessie Matthews.

The Parting of the Waves,
   1927
On With the Dance, 1927
Happy Ever After, 1932
Tell Me Tonight, 1932
Early to Bed, 1933
Friday the Thirteenth, 1933
Evergreen, 1934
Wild Boy, 1934
Are You a Mason?, 1934
My Song For You, 1934
My Heart is Calling, 1934
Marry the Girl, 1935
First a Girl, 1935
It's Love Again, 1936
The Gaunt Stranger, 1938
Let's Be Famous, 1939
Fiddlers Three, 1944
London Town, 1946

C. M. HALLARD (-)
Character player of silent and
early sound films, also on
stage.

Mrs. Thompson, 1919
Edge O' Beyond, 1919
Love in the Wilderness, 1920
Her Story, 1920
In the Night, 1920
The Case of Lady Camber,
   1920

The Pauper Millionaire, 1922
Carry On, 1927
A Light Woman, 1928
Knowing Men, 1930
The W Plan, 1930
Compromising Daphne, 1930
Two Worlds, 1930
Almost a Honeymoon, 1930
The Rasp, 1931
Tell England, 1931
The Woman Between, 1931
Strictly Business, 1932
The Chinese Puzzle, 1932
On Secret Service, 1933
The Third Clue, 1934
Rolling in Money, 1934
Night Mail, 1935
Royal Cavalcade, 1935
Moscow Nights, 1935
Jack of All Trades, 1936
King of the Damned, 1936
The Live Wire, 1937
The Sky's the Limit, 1937

MAY HALLATT (1882-)
Character actress of stage
and films, usually in cameo
roles.   Films occasional.

No Funny Business, 1933
Important People, 1934
The Lambeth Walk, 1939
Painted Boats, 1945
Black Narcissus, 1947
The Spider and the Fly, 1949
The Pickwick Papers, 1952
The Stateless Man, 1955
Separate Tables, 1958
Make Mine Mink, 1960
Dangerous Afternoon, 1961

ARTHUR HAMBLING (1888-)
Distinguished, classical small-
part character star of stage
and screen, active in the 30s
and 40s.

A Night in Montmartre, 1931
The Scoop, 1934
French Leave, 1937
A Romance in Flanders, 1937

Almost a Honeymoon, 1938
Lightning Conductor, 1938
Many Tanks Mr. Atkins, 1938
The Secret Four, 1940
Three Silent Men, 1940
Bulldog Sees it Through, 1940
Hard Steel, 1942
Wings and the Woman, 1942
Browned Off, 1944
Henry V, 1944
Johnny Frenchman, 1945
Odd Man Out, 1947
Daughter of Darkness, 1948
The Lavender Hill Mob, 1951

GERALD HAMER (1886-1973)
Talented character actor of
stage and screen, long in
Hollywood. Best seen in dis-
guised roles.

Swing Time, 1936
Bulldog Drummond's Bride,
   1939
Sherlock Holmes in Washington,
   1943
Sherlock Holmes Faces Death,
   1943
The Scarlet Claw, 1944
Enter Arsene Lupin, 1944
Terror By Night, 1946
The Sign of the Ram, 1948

KAY HAMMOND (1909-)
Attractive leading lady of the
thirties, also on stage (from
1927). Father: Sir Guy Standing; married to Sir John
Clements. Also in Hollywood.

Her Private Affair, 1929
The Trespasser, 1929
Abraham Lincoln, 1930
Children of Chance, 1930
Fascination, 1931
A Night in Montmartre, 1931
Almost a Divorce, 1931
Out of the Blue, 1931
Carnival, 1931
Chance of a Night-Time, 1931
The Third String, 1932

A Night Like This, 1932
Nine Till Six, 1932
Money Means Nothing, 1932
Sally Bishop, 1932
Racetrack, 1933
Double Harness, 1933
Yes Madam, 1933
The Sleeping Car, 1933
Britannia of Billingsgate, 1933
Bitter Sweet, 1933
The Umbrella, 1933
Eight Girls in a Boat, 1934
Bypass to Happiness, 1934
Two On a Doorstep, 1936
Jeannie, 1941
Blithe Spirit, 1945
Call of the Blood, 1948
Five Golden Hours, 1961

PETER HAMMOND (1923-)
Youthful character actor and
light supporting star of the
40s and 50s; latterly a director of films and television.

They Knew Mr. Knight, 1945
Holiday Camp, 1947
Here Come the Huggetts, 1948
Fly Away Peter, 1948
Fools Rush In, 1949
The Huggetts Abroad, 1949
Helter Skelter, 1949
Vote For Huggett, 1949
Morning Departure, 1950
The Reluctant Widow, 1950
The Adventurers, 1951
Come Back Peter, 1952
Father's Doing Fine, 1952
Alf's Baby, 1953
Confession, 1955
The Secret Tent, 1956
Soho Incident, 1956
It's Never Too Late, 1956
X The Unknown, 1956
Model For Murder, 1959

SUSAN HAMPSHIRE (1938-)
Pretty blonde leading actress
of stage (1957), screen and
television; notable in tv series
"The Forsyte Saga" and "The
Pallisers."

The Woman in the Hall, 1947
Upstairs and Downstairs, 1959
During One Night, 1961
The Long Shadow, 1961
Three Lives of Thomasina, 1963
Night Must Fall, 1964
Wonderful Life, 1964
Fighting Prince of Donegal, 1966
The Trygon Factor, 1967
Paris in the Month of August,
   1968
Violent Enemy, 1969
Monte Carlo or Bust, 1969
David Copperfield, 1969
An Ideal Husband, 1971
A Time For Loving, 1972
Living Free, 1972
Baffled, 1972
Neither the Sea Nor the Sand,
   1972
Malpertuis, 1972
Cry Terror, 1975
The Lonely Woman, 1975
Bang, 1977

SHEILA HANCOCK (1935-)
Supporting actress of stage,
films, and television, usually
seen in comedic roles.

Light Up the Sky, 1958
The Girl On the Boat, 1961
Twice Round the Daffodils, 1962
Night Must Fall, 1964
Carry On Cleo, 1964
The Moonspinners, 1964
The Anniversary, 1967
How I Won the War, 1967
The Magnificent $6\frac{1}{2}$, 1969
Take a Girl Like You, 1970

TONY HANCOCK (1924-1968)
Popular comedy star of radio
(1946), films, and television
whose brand of humor was not
for all tastes.   Few films.

Orders Are Orders, 1954
The Rebel, 1961
The Punch and Judy Man, 1963
Those Magnificent Men in

Their Flying Machines, 1965
The Wrong Box, 1966

IRENE HANDL (1901-)
Character comedienne of stage
(from 1937), films and television who began in small roles
and eventually rose to stardom.
Often seen as charlady or maid.

Missing Believed Married, 1937
Strange Boarders, 1938
Mrs. Pym of Scotland Yard,
   1939
George and Margaret, 1940
Dr. O'Dowd, 1940
The Girl in the News, 1940
Night Train to Munich, 1940
Gasbags, 1940
Pimpernel Smith, 1941
Mr. Proudfoot Shows a Light,
   1941
Partners in Crime, 1942
Uncensored, 1942
Get Cracking, 1943
I'll Walk Beside You, 1943
Rhythm Serenade, 1943
The Flemish Farm, 1943
Millions Like Us, 1943
Dear Octopus, 1943
It's In the Bag, 1943
Mr. Emmanuel, 1944
Welcome Mr. Washington, 1944
Give Us This Day, 1944
Kiss the Bride Goodbye, 1944
For You Alone, 1945
Brief Encounter, 1945
The Shop at Sly Corner, 1945
I'll Turn to You, 1946
Temptation Harbour, 1947
The Hills of Donegal, 1947
Woman Hater, 1948
The Fool and the Princess,
   1948
Silent Dust, 1948
Cardboard Cavalier, 1949
For Them That Trespass, 1949
Adam and Evalyn, 1949
The Perfect Woman, 1949
Dark Secret, 1949
The History of Mr. Polly, 1949
One Wild Oat, 1951

Young Wives' Tale, 1951
Top Secret, 1952
Wedding of Lilli Marlene, 1953
Burnt Evidence, 1954
The Belles of St. Trinian's,
  1954
Mad About Men, 1954
A Kid For Two Farthings, 1955
Who Done It, 1956
It's Never Too Late, 1956
The Silken Affair, 1956
Brothers in Law, 1957
Small Hotel, 1957
Happy is the Bride, 1958
The Key, 1958
Law and Disorder, 1958
Next to No Time, 1958
Carry On Nurse, 1959
The Crowning Touch, 1959
Carlton Browne of the F.O.,
  1959
I'm All Right, Jack, 1959
Desert Mice, 1959
Left, Right, and Centre, 1959
Two-Way Stretch, 1960
Carry On Constable, 1960
Inn For Trouble, 1960
School For Scoundrels, 1960
Make Mine Mink, 1960
Doctor in Love, 1960
A French Mistress, 1960
The Night We Got the Bird,
  1960
No Kidding, 1960
Pure Hell of St. Trinian's,
  1960
The Rebel, 1961
Double Bunk, 1961
A Weekend With Lulu, 1961
Watch it Sailor, 1961
Nothing Barred, 1961
Heavens Above, 1963
Just For Fun, 1963
You Must Be Joking!, 1965
Morgan, 1966
The Wrong Box, 1966
Smashing Time, 1967
Wonderwall, 1968
Lionheart, 1968
The Italian Job, 1969
Doctor in Trouble, 1970
The Private Life of Sherlock
  Holmes, 1970

On a Clear Day You Can See
  Forever, 1970
For the Love of Ada, 1972
The Chiffy Kids, 1972
Confessions of a Driving In-
  structor, 1974
Come Play With Me, 1977
Last Remake of Beau Geste,
  1977
Stand Up Virgin Soldiers, 1977
Adventures of a Private Eye,
  1977
Hound of the Baskervilles, 1978

TOMMY HANDLEY (1894-1949)
Comedian of stage and, occasionally, screen; best remembered for his radio work, notably "Itma" programme during
WWII.

Elstree Calling, 1930
Making a Christmas Pudding,
  1933
A Tale of Tails, 1933
Leslie Jeffries and His Orches-
  tra, 1936
Two Men in a Box, 1938
Pathetone Parade of 1940, 1940
It's That Man Again, 1943
Pictorial Revue of 1943, 1943
Time Flies, 1944
Tom Tom Topia, 1946
Making the Grade, 1947

JIMMY HANLEY (1918-1970)
Light leading actor of stage (since
1930) and films, former child star
who became the typical boy next
door or friend of the hero. Married to Dinah Sheridan.

Those Were the Days, 1934
Little Friend, 1934
Red Wagon, 1934
Royal Cavalcade, 1935
Forever England, 1935
Boys Will be Boys, 1935
The Tunnel, 1935
Landslide, 1937
Cotton Queen, 1937

Night Ride, 1937
Housemaster, 1938
Coming of Age, 1938
Beyond Our Horizon, 1939
There Aint No Justice, 1939
Gaslight, 1940
Salute John Citizen, 1942
The Gentle Sex, 1943
Henry V, 1944
The Way Ahead, 1944
Kiss the Bride Goodbye, 1944
For You Alone, 1945
29 Acacia Avenue, 1945
Murder in Reverse, 1945
The Captive Heart, 1946
Holiday Camp, 1947
The Master of Bankdam, 1947
It Always Rains On Sunday,
  1947
Here Come the Huggetts, 1948
It's Hard to Be Good, 1948
The Huggetts Abroad, 1949
Don't Ever Leave Me, 1949
Boys in Brown, 1949
The Blue Lamp, 1950
Room to Let, 1950
The Galloping Major, 1951
Radio Cab Murder, 1954
The Black Rider, 1954
The Deep Blue Sea, 1955
Satellite in the Sky, 1956
Look This Way, 1956
The Lost Continent, 1968

NICHOLAS HANNEN (-)
Character player of stage and
screen who has appeared in a
number of first-rate pictures.

The Man They Could Not Arrest,
  1931
F. P. One, 1933
Murder at the Inn, 1934
Love Affair of the Dictator, 1935
Hail and Farewell, 1936
Who Killed John Savage?, 1937
Marigold, 1938
Spy For a Day, 1940
Fear and Peter Brown, 1940
The Prime Minister, 1941
Henry V, 1944
The Winslow Boy, 1948

Quo Vadis, 1951
Hell is Sold Out, 1951
Three Steps in the Dark, 1953
Quentin Durward, 1955
Richard III, 1955
Seawife, 1957
Family Doctor, 1958
Dunkirk, 1958
Term of Trial, 1962

LAWRENCE HANRAY (-)
Light character actor and occasional leading man of stage
and films, very active through-
out the thirties.

The Pipes of Pan, 1923
Beyond the Cities, 1930
Her Reputation, 1931
Love on Wheels, 1932
That Night in London, 1932
There Goes the Bride, 1932
Faithful Heart, 1932
Leap Year, 1932
Private Life of Henry VIII,
  1933
The Good Companions, 1933
A Dickensian Fantasy, 1933
The Man From Toronto, 1933
His Grace Gives Notice, 1933
Catharine the Great, 1934
Those Were the Days, 1934
What Happened Then, 1934
The Great Defender, 1934
Adventure Limited, 1934
Chu Chin Chow, 1934
Loyalties, 1934
Easy Money, 1934
The Scarlet Pimpernel, 1935
Brewster's Millions, 1935
Mimi, 1935
Expert's Opinion, 1935
Lorna Doone, 1935
Murder at Monte Carlo, 1935
Street Song, 1935
The Lonely Road, 1936
Whom the Gods Love, 1936
Someone at the Door, 1936
As You Like It, 1936
Rembrandt, 1936
The Man Who Could Work
  Miracles, 1936

Beloved Imposter, 1936
Night Without Armour, 1937
Moonlight Sonata, 1937
It's Never Too Late to Mend,
 1937
Midnight Menace, 1937
The Girl in the Taxi, 1937
The Last Chance, 1937
Smash and Grab, 1937
21 Days, 1938
A Royal Divorce, 1938
Hatter's Castle, 1941
Hotel Reserve, 1944
On Approval, 1944
Nicholas Nickleby, 1947
Mine Own Executioner, 1947

LYN HARDING (1867-1952)
Welsh actor of the twenties and
thirties, also on stage (from
1890); used to best advantage in
villainous roles.

The Barton Mystery, 1920
Bachelor Husband, 1920
When Knighthood Was in Flower,
 1921
Les Miserables, 1922
Yolanda, 1924
Land of Hope and Glory, 1927
Further Adventures of the Flag
 Lieutenant, 1927
Sleeping Partners, 1930
The Speckled Band, 1931
The Barton Mystery, 1932
The Constant Nymph, 1933
The Man Who Changed His
 Name, 1934
The Lash, 1934
Wild Boy, 1934
The Triumph of Sherlock
 Holmes, 1935
Escape Me Never, 1935
The Invader, 1936
Spy of Napoleon, 1936
The Man Who Changed His
 Mind, 1936
Fire Over England, 1937
Underneath the Arches, 1937
Please Teacher, 1937
Knight Without Armour, 1937
Silver Blaze, 1937

Mutiny of the Elsinore, 1937
Pearls of the Crown, 1938
The Missing People, 1938
Goodbye Mr. Chips, 1939
The Prime Minister, 1941

SIR CEDRIC HARDWICKE
 (1893-1964)
Distinguished star character
actor of stage and screen, primarily in Hollywood where he
was often cast in villainous or
commanding parts.

Riches and Rogues, 1913
Nelson, 1926
Dreyfus, 1931
Rome Express, 1932
Orders is Orders, 1933
The Ghoul, 1933
The Lady is Willing, 1934
Bella Donna, 1934
Nell Gwyn, 1934
Jew Suss, 1934
King of Paris, 1934
Peg of Old Drury, 1935
Les Miserables, 1935
Becky Sharp, 1935
Tudor Rose, 1936
Laburnum Grove, 1936
Things to Come, 1936
Green Light, 1936
Calling the Tune, 1936
King Solomon's Mines, 1937
On Borrowed Time, 1939
The Hunchback of Notre Dame,
 1939
Stanley and Livingstone, 1939
The Invisible Man Returns,
 1940
Tom Brown's Schooldays, 1940
The Howards of Virginia, 1940
Victory, 1940
Suspicion, 1941
Sundown, 1941
Valley of the Sun, 1942
Ghost of Frankenstein, 1942
Invisible Agent, 1942
Forever and a Day, 1943
Commandos Strike at Dawn,
 1943
The Moon is Down, 1943

The Cross of Lorraine, 1943
The Lodger, 1944
Wilson, 1944
Wing and a Prayer, 1944
The Keys of the Kingdom, 1944
The Picture of Dorian Gray,
    (voice), 1945
Tragic Symphony, 1946
Sentimental Journey, 1946
Beware of Pity, 1946
The Imperfect Lady, 1947
Ivy, 1947
Lured, 1947
Tycoon, 1947
Nicholas Nickleby, 1947
The Winslow Boy, 1948
Song of My Heart, 1948
A Woman's Vengeance, 1948
I Remember Mama, 1948
Rope, 1948
Now Barabbas, 1949
A Connecticut Yankee in King
    Arthur's Court, 1949
The White Tower, 1950
Mr. Emperium, 1951
The Desert Fox, 1951
The Green Glove, 1952
Caribbean, 1952
War of the Worlds (voice),
    1953
Salome, 1953
Botany Bay, 1953
Bait, 1954
Richard III, 1955
Diane, 1956
Helen of Troy, 1956
Gaby, 1956
The Vagabond King, 1956
Power and the Prize, 1956
The Ten Commandments, 1956
Around the World in 80 Days,
    1956
The Story of Mankind, 1957
Baby Face Nelson, 1957
The Magic Fountain, 1961
Five Weeks in a Balloon, 1962
The Pumpkin Eater, 1964

ROBERT HARDY (1925-)
Character actor of stage, films,
and tv, usually seen in strong
roles; films fairly occasional.

Notable on television in "Elizabeth R" (1971) and "Edward
VII. "

Torpedo Run, 1958
The Spy Who Came in From
    the Cold, 1965
How I Won the War, 1967
Berserk!, 1967
10 Rillington Place, 1971
Dark Places, 1974
Escape to Nowhere, 1974
The Death Wheelers, 1974
The Gathering Storm, 1974
Demons of the Mind, 1975
Twelfth Night, 1980

LUMSDEN HARE (1875-1964)
Irish character player of stage
and screen, long in Hollywood.

Avalanche, 1919
On the Banks of the Wabash,
    1923
Second Youth, 1924
Girls Gone Wild, 1929
The Black Watch, 1929
Salute, 1929
The Sky Hawk, 1929
So This is London, 1930
Scotland Yard, 1930
Charlie Chan Carries On, 1931
Svengali, 1931
Always Goodbye, 1931
The Road to Singapore, 1931
Arrowsmith, 1931
The Silent Witness, 1932
International House, 1933
His Double Life, 1933
Man of Two Worlds, 1934
The House of Rothschild, 1934
Black Moon, 1934
The World Moves On, 1934
Outcast Lady, 1934
The Little Minister, 1934
Lives of a Bengal Lancer, 1935
Clive of India, 1935
Folies Bergere, 1935
Cardinal Richelieu, 1935
Lady Tubbs, 1935
She, 1935
The Crusades, 1935

Freckles, 1935
The Three Musketeers, 1935
The Great Impersonation, 1935
Professional Soldier, 1936
Under Two Flags, 1936
The Princess Comes Across,
   1936
Charge of the Light Brigade,
   1936
Lloyds of London, 1936
The Last of Mrs. Cheyney,
   1936
The Life of Emile Zola, 1937
Gunga Din, 1939
Captain Fury, 1939
Northwest Passage, 1940
Rebecca, 1940
A Dispatch From Reuters,
   1940
Hudson's Bay, 1940
Dr. Jekyll and Mr. Hyde, 1941
Suspicion, 1941
Random Harvest, 1942
The Gorilla Man, 1943
Mission to Moscow, 1943
The Lodger, 1944
The Canterville Ghost, 1944
Three Strangers, 1946
The Swordsman, 1947
The Exile, 1947
Mr. Peabody & the Mermaid,
   1948
Hills of Home, 1948
The Fighting O'Flynn, 1949
Challenge to Lassie, 1950
Fortunes of Captain Blood,
   1950
David and Bathsheba, 1951
My Cousin Rachel, 1952
Young Bess, 1953
Julius Caesar, 1953
Count Your Blessings, 1959
The Four Skulls of Jonathan
   Drake, 1959

On Approval, 1930
Tons of Money, 1931
Plunder, 1931
A Night Like This, 1932
Thark, 1932
Just My Luck, 1933
It's a Boy, 1933
A Cuckoo in the Nest, 1933
Friday the 13th, 1933
Turkey Time, 1933
A Cup of Kindness, 1934
Dirty Work, 1934
Are You a Mason?, 1934
Oh Daddy, 1935
Fighting Stock, 1935
Stormy Weather, 1935
Car of Dreams, 1935
Foreign Affair, 1935
Jack of All Trades, 1936
Pot Luck, 1936
You Must Get Married, 1936
Aren't Men Beasts?, 1937
A Spot of Bother, 1938
So This is London, 1939
Yesterday is Over Your
   Shoulder, 1940
Banana Ridge, 1941
Women Aren't Angels, 1942
He Snoops to Conquer, 1944
Things Happen at Night, 1948
One Wild Oat, 1951
The Magic Box, 1951
Our Girl Friday, 1954
Three Men in a Boat, 1956
My Wife's Family, 1956
The Night We Got the Bird,
   1960
The Young Ones, 1961
Out of the Shadow, 1961
Seven Keys, 1962
Crooks Anonymous, 1962
Hotel Paradiso, 1966
Salt and Pepper, 1968
Raising the Roof, 1971

ROBERTSON HARE (1891-)
Bald-headed comedian of stage
(from 1911) and screen, immensely popular during the
20s and 30s.

Rookery Nook, 1930

GORDON HARKER (1885-1967)
Cockney comic actor of stage
(from 1903) and films; portrayed characters from both
sides of the law.

The Ring, 1927

The Farmer's Wife, 1928
The Wrecker, 1928
Champagne, 1928
Return of the Rat, 1929
The Crooked Billet, 1929
Taxi For Two, 1929
The Cockney Spirit in War, 1930
Elstree Calling, 1930
The W Plan, 1930
The Squeaker, 1930
Escape, 1930
Third Time Lucky, 1931
The Stronger Sex, 1931
The Sport of Kings, 1931
Shadows, 1931
The Ringer, 1931
The Man They Could Not Arrest, 1931
The Calendar, 1931
The Professional Guest, 1931
Condemned to Death, 1932
Whiteface, 1932
The Frightened Lady, 1932
Love On Wheels, 1932
Rome Express, 1932
Criminal at Large, 1933
Lucky Number, 1933
Britannia of Billingsgate, 1933
This is the Life, 1933
Friday the 13th, 1933
My Old Dutch, 1934
Road House, 1934
Dirty Work, 1934
The Phantom Light, 1935
The Lad, 1935
Admirals All, 1935
Boys Will Be Boys, 1935
Hyde Park Corner, 1935
Squibs, 1936
The Amateur Gentleman, 1936
Wolf's Clothing, 1936
Two's Company, 1936
Millions, 1936
The Story of Papworth, 1936
Beauty and the Barge, 1937
The Frog, 1937
Blondes For Danger, 1938
No Parking, 1938
Lightning Conductor, 1938
Return of the Frog, 1938
Inspector Hornleigh, 1939
Inspector Hornleigh On

Holiday, 1939
Saloon Bar, 1940
Channel Incident, 1940
Inspector Hornleigh Goes to It, 1941
Once a Crook, 1941
Warn That Man, 1943
29 Acacia Avenue, 1945
Things Happen at Night, 1948
Her Favourite Husband, 1950
The Second Mate, 1951
Derby Day, 1952
Bang You're Dead, 1954
Out of the Clouds, 1955
A Touch of the Sun, 1956
Small Hotel, 1957
Left, Right, and Centre, 1959

GERALD HARPER (1929-)
Character actor of stage and screen, also well-known on television in "AdamAdamant" and "Hadleigh. " Films occasional but memorable.

The Admirable Crichton, 1957
A Night to Remember, 1958
The League of Gentlemen, 1959
Tunes of Glory, 1960
The Punch and Judy Man, 1963
Wonderful Life, 1964
Strangler's Web, 1966
The Shoes of the Fisherman, 1968
If It's a Man, Hang Up, 1975

RICHARD HARRIS (1932-)
Tough, gaunt Irish star of the 60s and 70s, generally cast as the unconventional hero or rebel. Also in Hollywood; now seen in international films.

Alive and Kicking, 1958
Shake Hands With the Devil, 1959
The Wreck of the Mary Deare, 1959
A Terrible Beauty, 1960

The Long & the Short & the
  Tall, 1961
The Guns of Navarone, 1961
All Night Long, 1961
Mutiny On the Bounty, 1962
This Sporting Life, 1963
Three Faces of a Woman, 1965
The Red Desert, 1965
Major Dundee, 1965
The Heroes of Telemark, 1965
The Bible, 1966
Hawaii, 1966
Caprice, 1966
Camelot, 1967
Cromwell, 1970
The Molly Maguires, 1970
A Man Called Horse, 1970
The Snow Goose, 1971
Bloomfield, 1971
Man in the Wilderness, 1971
The Deadly Trackers, 1973
Juggernaut, 1974
99 44/100% Dead, 1974
Gulliver's Travels, 1976
Robin and Marian, 1976
Echoes of a Summer, 1976
Return of a Man Called Horse,
  1976
Orca, 1977
The Cassandra Crossing, 1977
The Golden Rendezvous, 1977
The Wild Geese, 1978
The Number, 1979
Game For Vultures, 1979

ROBERT HARRIS (1900-)
Dignified character actor,
mainly on stage. Occasional
films from 1930. Not to be
confused with American actor
Robert H. Harris (1909-).

The W Plan, 1930
How He Lied to Her Husband,
  1931
Undercover, 1943
Life & Death of Colonel Blimp,
  1943
The Bad Lord Byron, 1948
For Them That Trespass, 1950
Laughing Anne, 1953
That Lady, 1955

Seven Waves Away, 1957
No Down Payment, 1957
The Big Caper, 1958
Oscar Wilde, 1960
The Model Murder Case, 1964
Decline and Fall, 1968
Lady Caroline Lamb, 1972
Tales That Witness Madness,
  1973
The Terrorists, 1975
Love Among the Ruins, 1975
Henry V, 1980

KATHLEEN HARRISON
  (1898-)
Accomplished character actress of stage (from 1926),
films, and television; often
cast as cockney mum or charlady.

Our Boys, 1915
Hobson's Choice, 1931
The Man From Toronto, 1933
The Ghoul, 1933
The Great Defender, 1934
Line Engaged, 1935
Dandy Dick, 1935
Broken Blossoms, 1936
The Tenth Man, 1936
Everybody Dance, 1936
Night Must Fall, 1937
Aren't Men Beasts?, 1937
Wanted, 1937
Bank Holiday, 1938
Convict 99, 1938
Almost a Gentleman, 1938
I've Got a Horse, 1938
Home From Home, 1939
A Girl Must Live, 1939
I Killed the Count, 1939
The Outsider, 1939
Discoveries, 1939
They Came By Night, 1940
Tilly of Bloomsbury, 1940
The Flying Squad, 1940
Salvage With a Smile, 1940
The Girl in the News, 1940
Gaslight, 1940
The Ghost Train, 1941
Major Barbara, 1941
Kipps, 1941

Once a Crook, 1941
I Thank You, 1941
Much Too Shy, 1941
In Which We Serve, 1942
Dear Octopus, 1943
Meet Sexton Blake, 1944
It Happened One Sunday, 1944
Great Day, 1945
Waterloo Road, 1945
I See a Dark Stranger, 1946
Wanted For Murder, 1946
Temptation Harbour, 1947
Holiday Camp, 1947
Bond Street, 1948
Oliver Twist, 1948
The Winslow Boy, 1948
Here Come the Huggetts, 1948
Vote For Huggett, 1949
The Huggets Abroad, 1949
Now Barabbas, 1949
Landfall, 1949
Golden Arrow, 1949
Double Confession, 1950
Waterfront, 1950
Trio, 1950
The Magic Box, 1951
Scrooge, 1951
The Happy Family, 1952
The Pickwick Papers, 1952
Turn the Key Softly, 1953
The Dog and the Diamonds,
   1954
Lilacs in the Spring, 1954
Where There's a Will, 1955
Cast a Dark Shadow, 1955
All For Mary, 1955
It's a Wonderful World, 1956
Home and Away, 1956
The Big Money, 1956
Seven Thunders, 1957
A Cry From the Streets, 1958
Alive and Kicking, 1958
On the Fiddle, 1961
Mrs. Gibbons' Boys, 1962
The Fast Lady, 1962
West Eleven, 1963
Lock Up Your Daughters, 1969
The London Affair, 1979

REX HARRISON (1908-   )
Pleasant, charming light leading man of stage (1924) and

films, also in Hollywood.
Formerly married to Lilli
Palmer, Kay Kendall, Rachel
Roberts.

The Great Game, 1930
School For Scandal, 1930
Get Your Man, 1934
Leave it to Blanche, 1934
All at Sea, 1935
Men Are Not Gods, 1936
Storm in a Teacup, 1937
School For Husbands, 1937
St. Martin's Lane, 1938
Over the Moon, 1938
The Citadel, 1938
The Silent Battle, 1939
Ten Days in Paris, 1939
Night Train to Munich, 1940
Major Barbara, 1941
Journey Together, 1944
I Live in Grosvenor Square,
   1945
The Rake's Progress, 1945
Blithe Spirit, 1945
Anna and the King of Siam,
   1946
The Ghost and Mrs. Muir,
   1947
The Foxes of Harrow, 1947
Unfaithfully Yours, 1948
Escape, 1948
The Long Dark Hall, 1951
The Fourposter, 1952
Main Street to Broadway, 1953
King Richard and the Crusaders,
   1954
The Constant Husband, 1955
The Reluctant Debutante, 1958
Midnight Lace, 1960
The Happy Thieves, 1962
Cleopatra, 1962
My Fair Lady, 1964
The Yellow Rolls-Royce, 1964
The Agony and the Ecstasy,
   1965
The Honey Pot, 1967
Dr. Dolittle, 1967
Think 20th, 1967
A Flea in Her Ear, 1968
Staircase, 1969
Platanov, 1971
Don Quixote, 1972

Man in the Iron Mask, 1977
Crossed Swords, 1978
Shalimar, 1978
Ashanti, 1979
The Fifth Musketeer, 1979
Six Graves For Rogan, 1980

WILLIAM HARTNELL (1908-
1975)
Tough character star of stage
(1924) and screen, often seen
as gruff army sergeant or other
no-nonsense characters. Attained star status in the mid-
40s and proved effective at portraying characters from both
sides of the law.

I'm An Explosive, 1933
Follow the Lady, 1933
The Lure, 1933
Seeing is Believing, 1934
The Perfect Flaw, 1934
Swinging the Lead, 1935
While Parents Sleep, 1935
Nothing Like Publicity, 1936
Midnight at Madame Tussaud's,
1936
Farewell Again, 1937
Murder Will Out, 1939
They Drive By Night, 1939
Flying Fortress, 1939
Too Dangerous to Live, 1939
They Came By Night, 1940
Sabotage at Sea, 1942
Suspected Person, 1942
The Peterville Diamond, 1942
The Goose Steps Out, 1942
The Bells Go Down, 1943
The Dark Tower, 1943
Headline, 1943
Cockpit, 1944
The Way Ahead, 1944
The Agitator, 1945
Murder in Reverse, 1945
Strawberry Roan, 1946
Appointment With Crime, 1946
Odd Man Out, 1947
Temptation Harbour, 1947
Brighton Rock, 1947
Escape, 1948
Now Barabbas, 1949
The Lost People, 1949

Double Confession, 1950
The Dark Man, 1951
The Magic Box, 1951
The Pickwick Papers, 1952
The Holly and the Ivy, 1952
The Ringer, 1952
Will Any Gentleman, 1953
Seagulls Over Sorrento, 1954
Footsteps in the Fog, 1955
Josephine and Men, 1955
Deadlock, 1955
Ring For Catty, 1956
Private's Progress, 1956
Doublecross, 1956
Tons of Trouble, 1956
Date With Disaster, 1957
The Hypnotist, 1957
Hell Drivers, 1957
Yangtse Incident, 1957
The Vice Play, 1958
On the Run, 1958
Carry On Sergeant, 1958
Strictly Confidential, 1959
Shake Hands With the Devil,
1959
The Mouse That Roared, 1959
The Desperate Man, 1959
Night We Dropped a Clanger,
1960
Jackpot, 1960
And the Same to You, 1960
Piccadilly Third Stop, 1960
Tomorrow at Ten, 1962
This Sporting Life, 1963
Heavens Above, 1963
The World Ten Times Over,
1963
To Have and to Hold, 1963

FORRESTER HARVEY (1890-
1945)
Irish character player of stage
and screen, primarily in Hollywood.

London Pride, 1920
The Glad Eye, 1920
The Lilac Sunbonnet, 1922
The Man Who Liked Lemons,
1923
Somebody's Darling, 1925
Nell Gwyn, 1926

If Youth But Knew, 1926
The Flag Lieutenant, 1926
Cash On Delivery, 1926
The Ring, 1927
The Farmer's Wife, 1928
The White Sheik, 1928
Toni, 1928
Glorious Youth, 1928
Spangles, 1928
That Brute Simmons, 1928
Ringing the Changes, 1929
Tailor-Made Man, 1931
Man in Possession, 1931
Guilty Hands, 1931
Devotion, 1931
Shanghai Express, 1932
Sky Devils, 1932
Tarzan the Ape Man, 1932
But the Flesh is Weak, 1932
The Wet Parade, 1932
Mystery Ranch, 1932
Smilin' Through, 1932
Red Dust, 1932
Kongo, 1932
Destination Unknown, 1933
The Eagle and the Hawk, 1933
The Invisible Man, 1933
Man of Two Worlds, 1933
The Mystery of Mr. X, 1933
Tarzan and His Mate, 1934
Menace, 1934
The Painted Veil, 1934
Limehouse Blues, 1934
China Seas, 1935
A Tale of Two Cities, 1935
David Copperfield, 1935
The Best Man Wins, 1935
The Mystery of Edwin Drood,
  1935
Vagabond Lady, 1935
Jalna, 1935
The Perfect Gentleman, 1935
Captain Blood, 1935
Petticoat Fever, 1936
White Hunter, 1936
Lloyds of London, 1936
Personal Property, 1937
The Prince and the Pauper,
  1937
Thoroughbreds Don't Cry,
  1937
Kidnapped, 1938
Bulldog Drummond in Africa,

1938
Mr. Moto of Devil's Island,
  1938
Bulldog Drummond's Secret
  Police, 1939
The Lady's From Kentucky,
  1939
The Witness Vanishes, 1939
The Invisible Man's Return,
  1940
A Chump at Oxford, 1940
Rebecca, 1940
Tom Brown's Schooldays, 1940
Little Nellie Kelly, 1940
Free and Easy, 1941
Dr. Jekyll and Mr. Hyde,
  1941
The Wolf Man, 1941
This Above All, 1942
Mrs. Miniver, 1942
Mysterious Doctor, 1943
Devotion, 1945

LAURENCE HARVEY (1928-
1973)
Tall, dark Lithuanian-born
leading actor of stage (from
1947), films and television;
also in Hollywood. Often cast
in sullen roles. Formerly
married to Margaret Leighton.

House of Darkness, 1948
Man On the Run, 1949
Landfall, 1949
Man From Yesterday, 1949
Cairo Road, 1950
The Black Rose, 1950
There is Another Sun, 1951
Scarlet Thread, 1951
I Believe in You, 1951
A Killer Walks, 1952
Women of Twilight, 1952
Innocents in Paris, 1953
The Good Die Young, 1954
Romeo and Juliet, 1954
King Richard and the Crusaders,
  1954
I Am a Camera, 1955
Storm Over the Nile, 1955
Three Men in a Boat, 1956
After the Ball, 1957

The Truth About Women, 1958
The Silent Enemy, 1958
Room at the Top, 1959
Expresso Bongo, 1959
The Alamo, 1960
Butterfield 8, 1960
Two Loves, 1961
Summer and Smoke, 1961
The Long & the Short & the
   Tall, 1961
A Walk On the Wild Side, 1962
The Manchurian Candidate, 1962
A Girl Named Tamiko, 1963
The Ceremony, 1963
The Running Man, 1963
Wonderful World of the
   Brothers Grimm, 1963
Of Human Bondage, 1964
The Outrage, 1964
Darling, 1965
Life at the Top, 1965
The Spy With a Cold Nose,
   1966
A Dandy in Aspic, 1968
Kampf un Rom, 1968
L'Assolute Naturale, 1969
A Winter's Tale, 1969
He and She, 1969
The Magic Christian, 1970
WUSA, 1970
Escape to the Sun, 1972
Night Watch, 1973
Welcome to Arrow Beach,
   1973

JEREMY HAWK (1918-   )
Character actor of small roles,
primarily on stage; films occasional.

In Which We Serve, 1942
The Goose Steps Out, 1942
The Stranger Came Home,
   1954
Mask of Dust, 1954
Who Done It, 1956
Lucky Jim, 1957
Left, Right, and Centre, 1959
Dentist in the Chair, 1960
Dentist On the Job, 1961
Mystery Submarine, 1963
The Return of the Pink

Panther, 1974
Eskimo Nell, 1976

JACK HAWKINS (1910-1973)
Strong, prominent actor of
stage (since 1923) and screen,
mainly seen as tough, dependable hero; latterly character
star after loss of voice in
1966.   Also in Hollywood.

Birds of Prey, 1930
The Lodger, 1932
The Good Companions, 1933
The Lost Chord, 1933
I Lived With You, 1933
The Jewel, 1933
A Shot in the Dark, 1933
Autumn Crocus, 1934
Death at Broadcasting House,
   1934
Peg of Old Drury, 1935
The Frog, 1937
Beauty and the Barge, 1937
Who Goes Next?, 1938
A Royal Divorce, 1938
Murder Will Out, 1939
The Flying Squad, 1940
Next of Kin, 1942
The Fallen Idol, 1948
Bonnie Prince Charlie, 1948
The Small Back Room, 1948
State Secret, 1950
The Black Rose, 1950
The Elusive Pimpernel, 1950
The Adventurers, 1951
No Highway, 1951
Home at Seven, 1952
Angels One Five, 1952
Mandy, 1952
The Planter's Wife, 1952
The Cruel Sea, 1953
Twice Upon a Time, 1953
The Malta Story, 1953
The Intruder, 1953
Front Page Story, 1954
The Seekers, 1954
The Prisoner, 1955
Touch and Go, 1955
Land of the Pharaohs, 1955
The Long Arm, 1956
Man in the Sky, 1956

Caesar and Cleopatra, 1956
Fortune is a Woman, 1957
The Bridge On the River Kwai,
 1957
Battle For Britain (voice), 1957
Gideon's Day, 1958
The Two-Headed Spy, 1958
The League of Gentlemen, 1959
Ben Hur, 1959
The Fallen Idol, 1959
Spinster, 1960
Two Loves, 1961
Lawrence of Arabia, 1962
Five Finger Exercise, 1962
Lafayette, 1963
Rampage, 1963
Zulu, 1964
The Third Secret, 1964
Guns at Batasi, 1964
Masquerade, 1965
Judith, 1965
Lord Jim, 1965
The Poppy is Also a Flower,
 1966
Shalako, 1968
Great Catherine, 1968
Twinky, 1969
Monte Carlo or Bust, 1969
Oh What a Lovely War, 1969
Waterloo, 1970
The Adventures of Gerard, 1970
Jane Eyre, 1970
When Eight Bells Toll, 1971
Kidnapped, 1971
Nicholas and Alexandra, 1971
Young Winston, 1972
Escape to the Sun, 1972
Restless, 1973
Tales That Witness Madness,
 1973
Theatre of Blood, 1973
QB VII, 1974

JILL HAWORTH (1945-)
Light leading actress in occasional films of the 60s and 70s;
mainly in Hollywood.

Exodus, 1960
The Cardinal, 1963
Your Shadow is Mine, 1963
In Harm's Way, 1965

It, 1966
Horror House, 1970
Home For the Holidays, 1972
The Mutations, 1974

CHARLES HAWTREY (1914-)
Gangly, bespectacled character
comedian of stage (from 1925)
and films, adept at prissy
comedy roles. One of the
mainstays of the "Carry On"
team.

Marry Me, 1932
Melody Maker, 1933
Kiddies On Parade, 1935
Sabotage, 1936
Well Done Henry, 1937
Good Morning Boys, 1937
East of Ludgate Hill, 1937
Where's That Fire?, 1939
Jailbirds, 1939
The Ghost of St. Michael's,
 1941
The Black Sheep of Whitehall,
 1941
Let the People Sing, 1942
The Goose Steps Out, 1942
A Canterbury Tale, 1944
End of the River, 1947
Passport to Pimlico, 1949
Room to Let, 1950
The Galloping Major, 1951
Brandy For the Parson, 1952
Hammer the Toff, 1952
You're Only Young Twice,
 1952
Five Days, 1954
As Long As They're Happy,
 1955
Man of the Moment, 1955
Simon and Laura, 1955
Who Done It, 1956
The March Hare, 1956
I Only Arsked, 1958
Carry On Sergeant, 1958
Carry On Nurse, 1959
Carry On Teacher, 1959
Please Turn Over, 1959
Carry On Constable, 1960
Inn For Trouble, 1960
Carry On Regardless, 1961

Dentist On the Job, 1961
What a Whopper, 1961
Carry On Cabby, 1963
Carry On Jack, 1963
Carry On Spying, 1964
Carry On Cleo, 1964
Carry On Cowboy, 1965
Carry On Screaming, 1966
Carry On Don't Lose Your
  Head, 1966
The Terrornauts, 1967
Carry On Follow That Camel,
  1967
Carry On Doctor, 1968
Carry On Up the Khyber, 1968
Carry On Camping, 1969
Carry On Again Doctor, 1969
Zeta One, 1969
Carry On Up the Jungle, 1970
Carry On Loving, 1970
Carry On Henry VIII, 1971
Carry On Matron, 1972
Carry On Abroad, 1972
Carry On at Your Convenience,
  1972

WILL HAY (1888-1949)
Popular comedian of the thirties and forties with music hall
experience (from 1909); typically portrayed the seedy
schoolmaster. One of the top
box-office stars of the 30s.

Know Your Apples, 1933
Those Were the Days, 1934
Radio Parade of 1935, 1935
Dandy Dick, 1935
Boys Will Be Boys, 1935
Where There's a Will, 1936
Windbag the Sailor, 1936
Good Morning Boys, 1937
Convict 99, 1938
Oh Mr. Porter, 1938
Hey Hey USA, 1938
Old Bones of the River, 1938
Ask a Policeman, 1939
Where's That Fire?, 1939
The Ghost of St. Michael's,
  1941
The Black Sheep of White-
  hall, 1941

The Big Blockade, 1942
Go To Blazes, 1942
The Goose Steps Out, 1942
My Learned Friend, 1944

RICHARD HAYDN (1905-)
Inimitable character star with
unique voice, in Hollywood from
1941. Also on radio, stage
and television, specializing in
aged, eccentric comedy characters. Also author and film
director.

Charley's Aunt, 1941
Ball of Fire, 1941
Are Husbands Necessary?, 1942
Thunder Birds, 1942
No Time For Love, 1943
Forever and a Day, 1943
Henry Aldrich-Boy Scout, 1944
Adventure, 1945
And Then There Were None,
  1945
Cluny Brown, 1946
The Late George Apley, 1947
The Beginning or the End,
  1947
The Green Years, 1947
Singapore, 1947
Forever Amber, 1947
The Foxes of Harrow, 1947
Sitting Pretty, 1948
The Emperor Waltz, 1948
Miss Tatlock's Millions, 1948
Mr. Music, 1950
The Merry Widow, 1952
A Quarter For Your Trouble,
  1952
Never Let Me Go, 1953
Her Twelve Men, 1954
Alice in Wonderland, 1954
Money From Home, 1954
Jupiter's Darling, 1955
The King and Mrs. Candle, 1955
The Toy Tiger, 1956
Charley's Aunt, 1957
Heart of Darkness, 1958
Twilight For the Gods, 1958
The Emperor's New Clothes,
  1958
This Will Do Nicely, 1959

The Ugly Duckling, 1960
The Lost World, 1960
Please Don't Eat the Daisies, 1960
Let's Make Love (voice), 1960
Mutiny On the Bounty, 1962
Five Weeks in a Balloon, 1962
The Sound of Music, 1965
Clarence the Cross-Eyed Lion, 1966
Adventures of Bullwhip Griffin, 1966
The Return of Charlie Chan, 1971
McCloud: Fifth Man in a String Quartet, 1972
Young Frankenstein, 1974

HELEN HAYE (1874-1957)
Eminent character actress of stage (from 1898) and films, often cast as kindly, elderly spinster.

The Skin Game, 1920
Bleak House, 1920
Tilly of Bloomsbury, 1921
Atlantic, 1930
Beyond the Cities, 1930
The Nipper, 1930
Knowing Men, 1930
Congress Dances, 1931
The Skin Game, 1931
The Officer's Mess, 1931
Brown Sugar, 1931
Her First Affaire, 1932
Monte Carlo Madness, 1932
It's a Boy, 1933
This Week of Grace, 1933
Crazy People, 1934
Money Mad, 1934
The Thirty-Nine Steps, 1935
Love Affair of the Dictator, 1935
Drake of England, 1935
Wolf's Clothing, 1936
Everybody Dance, 1936
Interrupted Honeymoon, 1936
Wings of the Morning, 1937
Remember When, 1937
Cotton Queen, 1937
The Girl in the Taxi, 1937

St. Martin's Lane, 1938
A Girl Must Live, 1939
The Spy in Black, 1939
Case of the Frightened Lady, 1940
Kipps, 1941
The Man in Grey, 1943
Dear Octopus, 1943
Fanny By Gaslight, 1944
A Place of One's Own, 1944
Mine Own Executioner, 1947
Mrs. Fitzherbert, 1947
Anna Karenina, 1948
Third Time Lucky, 1949
Conspirator, 1950
An Inspector Calls, 1954
Lilacs in the Spring, 1954
Hobson's Choice, 1954
Front Page Story, 1954
Richard III, 1955
My Teenage Daughter, 1956
Action of the Tiger, 1957
The Gypsy and the Gentleman, 1958

JAMES HAYTER (1907-)
Robust, cheerful character star of stage (from 1925) and films, typically portraying genial fellows but also equally adept at occasional sinister parts. Also Hollywood.

Sensation, 1937
Big Fella, 1937
Marigold, 1938
Murder in Soho, 1939
Come On George, 1939
Sailors Three, 1940
School For Secrets, 1946
Nicholas Nickleby, 1947
End of the River, 1947
Captain Boycott, 1947
Vice Versa, 1948
My Brother Jonathan, 1948
Song For Tomorrow, 1948
The Fallen Idol, 1948
Bonnie Prince Charlie, 1948
Once a Jolly Swagman, 1948
No Room at the Inn, 1949
All Over Town, 1949
Silent Dust, 1949

The Blue Lagoon, 1949
Passport to Pimlico, 1949
For Them That Trespass, 1949
Dear Mr. Prohack, 1949
The Spider and the Fly, 1949
Morning Departure, 1950
Your Witness, 1950
Night and the City, 1950
Waterfront, 1950
The Woman With No Name,
   1950
Trio, 1950
Flesh and Blood, 1951
Tom Brown's School Days,
   1951
Calling Bulldog Drummond,
   1951
The Story of Robin Hood, 1952
I'm a Stranger, 1952
The Crimson Pirate, 1952
The Pickwick Papers, 1952
The Great Game, 1953
Four Sided Triangle, 1953
Will Any Gentleman, 1953
Always a Bride, 1953
For Better, For Worse, 1954
A Day to Remember, 1954
Beau Brummell, 1954
Land of the Pharaohs, 1955
See How They Run, 1955
Touch and Go, 1955
Keep it Clean, 1956
Port Afrique, 1956
It's a Wonderful World, 1956
The Big Money, 1956
Seven Waves Away, 1957
Hell Drivers, 1957
The Heart Within, 1957
Sail Into Danger, 1957
Carry On Admiral, 1958
Gideon's Day, 1958
The Key, 1958
I Was Monty's Double, 1958
The Captain's Table, 1959
The 39 Steps, 1959
The Boy and the Bridge, 1959
Go To Blazes, 1962
Out of the Fog, 1962
Stranger in the House, 1967
Challenge to Robin Hood, 1967
Oliver, 1968
David Copperfield, 1969
Song of Norway, 1970

Scramble, 1970
The Firechasers, 1970
Not Tonight Darling, 1971
Blood On Satan's Claw, 1971
Bawdy Adventures of Tom
   Jones, 1975

JOAN HAYTHORNE (1915-   )
Character actress primarily
seen on stage; occasional films
generally cast in patrician roles.

School For Secrets, 1946
Jassy, 1947
Highly Dangerous, 1950
Svengali, 1954
The Weak and the Wicked, 1954
Dry Rot, 1956
The Feminine Touch, 1956
Three Men in a Boat, 1956
Shakedown, 1959
So Evil So Young, 1961
The Battleaxe, 1962
Very Important Person, 1962
Star!, 1968
Decline and Fall, 1968
Murder is a One-Act Play, 1974

LOUIS HAYWARD (1909-   )
South-African born light leading man and latterly character
star of stage, screen, and tv,
usually seen as the amiable
and occasionally swashbuckling
hero. On tv in series "The
Lone Wolf" (1954), "The Pursuers" (1962), "The Survivors"
(1969).

The Thirteenth Candle, 1931
The Man Outside, 1931
The Love Test, 1932
I'll Stick to You, 1932
Self-Made Lady, 1932
Chelsea Life, 1933
Sorrell and Son, 1934
A Feather in Her Hat, 1935
The Flame Within, 1935
The Suicide Club, 1935
Anthony Adverse, 1936
Absolute Quiet, 1936

The Woman I Love, 1937
Luckiest Girl in the World, 1937
Midnite Intruder, 1938
The Rage of Paris, 1938
The Duke of West Point, 1938
Condemned Women, 1938
The Saint in New York, 1938
Man in the Iron Mask, 1939
My Son, My Son, 1940
The Son of Monte Cristo, 1940
Dance, Girl, Dance, 1940
Electric Man, 1941
Ladies in Retirement, 1941
The Magnificent Ambersons, 1942
And Then There Were None, 1945
The Return of Monte Cristo, 1946
The Young Widow, 1946
The Strange Woman, 1946
Repeat Performance, 1947
Ruthless, 1948
The Black Arrow, 1948
Walk a Crooked Mile, 1948
Captain Sirocco, 1949
Pirates of Capri, 1949
Fortunes of Captain Blood, 1950
The House By the River, 1950
The Lady and the Bandit, 1951
The Son of Dr. Jekyll, 1951
Captain Pirate, 1952
Lady in the Iron Mask, 1952
Royal African Rifles, 1953
Duffy of San Quentin, 1954
The Saint's Return, 1954
So Evil My Love, 1955
The Search For Bridey Murphy, 1956
Camelot, 1957
Road Show, 1958
The Picture of Dorian Gray, 1961
The Christmas Kid, 1966
Chuka, 1967
The Phynx, 1969
Last of the Powerseekers, 1969
Terror in the Wax Museum, 1973

HY HAZELL (1922-1970)
Blonde actress of stage (since

1937) and screen; former singer and dancer.

The Dummy Talks, 1943
My Learned Friend, 1944
Meet Me at Dawn, 1947
Just William's Luck, 1947
Paper Orchid, 1949
Celia, 1949
The Body Said No, 1950
Dance Hall, 1950
The Lady Craved Excitement, 1950
The Franchise Affair, 1951
The Night Won't Talk, 1952
The Yellow Balloon, 1952
Forces' Sweetheart, 1953
Stolen Assignment, 1955
Up in the World, 1956
Anastasia, 1956
The Key Man, 1957
Light Fingers, 1957
Mail Van Murder, 1957
The Whole Truth, 1958
The Trouble With Eve, 1960
What Every Woman Wants, 1962
Every Home Should Have One, 1970

RICHARD HEARNE (1909-)
Acrobatic comedy star with music hall experience; formerly in the circus (1918). Best known for his character "Mr. Pastry."

Give Her a Ring, 1934
Dance Band, 1935
No Monkey Business, 1935
Millions, 1936
Splinters in the Air, 1937
Miss London Ltd., 1943
The Butler's Dilemma, 1943
One Night With You, 1948
Woman Hater, 1948
Helter Skelter, 1949
Something in the City, 1950
Mr. Pastry Does the Laundry, 1950
Captain Horatio Hornblower, 1951

Madame Louise, 1951
What a Husband, 1952
Miss Robin Hood, 1952
The Time of His Life, 1955
Tons of Trouble, 1956
The King's Breakfast, 1963

CLIFFORD HEATHERLEY
(-)
Popular character player and
supporting star of the 20s and
30s.

The Tavern Knight, 1920
Bleak House, 1920
Autumn Pride, 1921
Yellow Face, 1921
The Mystery of Bernard Brown,
     1921
Mademoiselle From Armen-
     tieres, 1926
Beating the Book, 1926
Boadicea, 1926
The Sea Urchin, 1926
The King's Highway, 1927
The Rolling Road, 1927
Roses of Picardy, 1927
The Passing of Mr. Quin,
     1928
Champagne, 1928
Tesha, 1928
The Constant Nymph, 1928
High Treason, 1929
The W Plan, 1930
The Compulsory Husband, 1930
Symphony in Two Flats, 1930
My Old China, 1931
The Love Habit, 1931
Glamour, 1931
Who Killed Doc Robin?, 1931
A Letter of Warning, 1932
Help Yourself, 1932
Brother Alfred, 1932
Indiscretions of Eve, 1932
After the Ball, 1932
Fires of Fate, 1932
Goodnight Vienna, 1932
Forging Ahead, 1933
I Adore You, 1933
Yes Mr. Brown, 1933
Bitter Sweet, 1933
Happy Ever After, 1933

The Little Damozel, 1933
Discord, 1933
Beware of Women, 1933
Cash, 1933
Catherine the Great, 1934
Private Life of Don Juan,
     1934
Trouble in Store, 1934
The Queen's Affair, 1934
The Church Mouse, 1934
Adventure Limited, 1934
A Little Bit of Bluff, 1935
Abdul the Damned, 1935
Our Husband, 1935
No Monkey Business, 1935
Reasonable Doubt, 1936
Show Flat, 1936
Cafe Mascot, 1936
The Invader, 1936
If I Were Rich, 1936
Don't Get Me Wrong, 1937
Feather Your Nest, 1937
It's Not Cricket, 1937
There Was a Young Man, 1937

JACK HEDLEY (1930-)
Likeable actor of stage, screen
and television, well-known in
the latter media as "Tim
Fraser."

Behind the Mask, 1958
Room at the Top, 1959
Left, Right, and Centre, 1959
Make Mine Mink, 1960
Never Back Losers, 1961
Lawrence of Arabia, 1962
In the French Style, 1963
The Very Edge, 1963
The Scarlet Blade, 1963
Of Human Bondage, 1964
Witchcraft, 1964
The Secret of Blood Island,
     1965
The Anniversary, 1967
How I Won the War, 1967
Goodbye Mr. Chips, 1969
Brief Encounter, 1975
Hindle Wakes, 1976
Cat On a Hot Tin Roof, 1976

GERARD HEINZ (1903-1972)
German-born character player
of British films, also occasionally in Hollywood; mainly in
subsidiary roles.

Thunder Rock, 1942
Went the Day Well, 1942
Caravan, 1946
Broken Journey, 1948
Portrait From Life, 1948
The Fallen Idol, 1948
The First Gentleman, 1948
Sleeping Car to Trieste, 1948
Traveller's Joy, 1949
That Dangerous Age, 1949
The Lost People, 1949
State Secret, 1950
The Clouded Yellow, 1950
White Corridors, 1951
Private Information, 1952
His Excellency, 1952
Top Secret, 1952
Desperate Moment, 1953
The Prisoner, 1955
You Pay Your Money, 1957
Accused, 1957
Mark of the Hawk, 1958
The Man Inside, 1958
House of the Seven Hawks,
   1959
I Aim at the Stars, 1960
The Guns of Navarone, 1961
Highway to Battle, 1961
The Cardinal, 1963
Devils of Darkness, 1964
Boy With a Flute, 1964
The Heroes of Telemark, 1965
The Projected Man, 1966
The Dirty Dozen, 1967

TOM HELMORE (-)
Light leading man of stage and
films, latterly in Hollywood in
character parts.

White Cargo (silent), 1929
White Cargo (sound), 1929
Young Woodley, 1930
Leave it to Me, 1930
House of Unrest, 1931
My Wife's Family, 1931

Above Rubies, 1932
The Barton Mystery, 1932
The King's Cup, 1933
Up For the Derby, 1933
Song at Eventide, 1934
Virginia's Husband, 1934
The Scoop, 1934
The Feathered Serpent, 1934
The Right Age to Marry, 1935
Riverside Murder, 1935
The Secret Agent, 1936
Luck of the Turf, 1936
Not Wanted On Voyage, 1936
The House of Silence, 1937
Merry Comes to Town, 1937
Easy Riches, 1938
Paid in Error, 1938
Shadowed Eyes, 1939
Three Daring Daughters, 1948
Malaya, 1950
Shadow On the Wall, 1950
Trouble Along the Way, 1953
Let's Do it Again, 1953
Lucy Gallant, 1955
The Tender Trap, 1955
This Could Be the Night, 1957
Designing Woman, 1957
Vertigo, 1958
Count Your Blessings, 1959
Man in the Net, 1959
The Time Machine, 1960
Advise and Consent, 1962
Flipper's New Adventure, 1964

SIR ROBERT HELPMANN
   (1909-)
Distinguished Australian character actor and ballet star, in
occasional films; also stage
star and choreographer.

One of Our Aircraft is Missing,
   1942
Henry V, 1944
Caravan, 1946
The Red Shoes, 1948
Tales of Hoffman, 1951
The Iron Petticoat, 1956
The Big Money, 1956
55 Days at Peking, 1962
The Soldier's Tale, 1964
The Quiller Memorandum, 1966

Chitty Chitty Bang Bang, 1968
Alice's Adventures in Wonder-
land, 1972
Don Quixote, 1973
The Mango Tree, 1977
Patrick, 1979

DAVID HEMMINGS (1941-)
Slight, sensitive light leading
man of the 60s and 70s, also
on stage and television; now
seen in international films.
Former singer and artist.

Saint Joan, 1957
The Heart Within, 1957
Five Clues to Fortune, 1957
No Trees in the Street, 1958
Men of Tomorrow, 1959
Some People, 1960
The Wind of Change, 1961
The Painted Smile, 1962
Two Left Feet, 1963
Live it Up, 1963
The System, 1964
Be My Guest, 1965
Dateline Diamonds, 1965
Eye of the Devil, 1966
Camelot, 1967
Blow Up, 1967
Charge of the Light Brigade,
1968
Only When I Larf, 1968
Barbarella, 1968
The Long Day's Dying, 1968
The Best House in London,
1969
Alfred the Great, 1969
The Walking Stick, 1970
Fragment of Fear, 1970
Unman Wittering and Zigo,
1970
The Love Machine, 1971
Voices, 1973
Don't Worry Momma, 1973
Juggernaut, 1974
Mr. Quilp, 1975
Deep Red, 1976
The Squeeze, 1977
Islands in the Stream, 1977
Crossed Swords, 1977
The Disappearance, 1977

Blood Relatives, 1978
Squadra Antiruffa, 1978
Power Play, 1978
Just a Gigolo, 1978
The Rime of the Ancient
Mariner, 1978
Thirst, 1979
Murder By Decree, 1979
Harlequin, 1980

IAN HENDRY (1931-)
Masculine, forceful leading
man and supporting player of
stage, films, and television.
Married to Janet Munro.

Room at the Top, 1959
In the Nick, 1960
Live Now Pay Later, 1962
Girl in the Headlines, 1963
This is My Street, 1963
Children of the Damned, 1963
The Beauty Jungle, 1964
Repulsion, 1965
The Hill, 1965
The Sandwich Man, 1966
Casino Royale, 1967
Cry Wolf, 1968
Vendetta For the Saint, 1968
Doppelganger, 1969
Southern Star, 1969
The Mackenzie Break, 1970
Get Carter, 1970
All Coppers Are, 1971
Tales From the Crypt, 1972
The Jerusalem File, 1972
Captain Kronos Vampire Hunter,
1972
Assassin, 1973
Theatre of Blood, 1973
The Internecine Project, 1974
The Passenger, 1975
Intimate Games, 1976
Damien: Omen II, 1978

BOBBY HENREY (1939-)
Child performer whose few film
appearances were exceptional.

The Fallen Idol, 1948
The Wonder Kid, 1950

GLADYS HENSON (1897-)
Irish character player of stage
(from 1910) and films, usually
seen as charlady or homely
mum.

The Captive Heart, 1946
Frieda, 1947
It Always Rains On Sunday,
    1947
Counterblast, 1948
The Weaker Sex, 1948
London Belongs to Me, 1948
The History of Mr. Polly,
    1949
Train of Events, 1949
The Blue Lamp, 1950
The Cure For Love, 1950
Dance Hall, 1950
Highly Dangerous, 1950
The Magnet, 1950
The Happiest Days of Your
    Life, 1950
Cage of Gold, 1950
Lady Godiva Rides Again, 1951
Happy Go Lovely, 1951
Derby Day, 1952
I Believe in You, 1952
Those People Next Door, 1953
Cockleshell Heroes, 1955
Doctor at Large, 1957
Davy, 1957
The Prince and the Showgirl,
    1957
Clue of the Twisted Candle,
    1960
The Trials of Oscar Wilde,
    1960
Double Bunk, 1961
No Love For Johnnie, 1961
Dangerous Afternoon, 1961
Stork Talk, 1962
Death Trap, 1962
The Leather Boys, 1963
Go Kart Go!, 1964
First Men in the Moon, 1964
The Legend of Young Dick
    Turpin, 1965
Bawdy Adventures of Tom
    Jones, 1975

LESLIE HENSON (1891-1957)

Pop-eyed character comedian
of stage (from 1910) and films;
father of Nicky Henson.   Film
appearances sporadic.

Wanted a Widow, 1916
The Real Thing at Last, 1916
The Lifeguardsman, 1916
Broken Bottles, 1920
Alf's Button, 1920
Tons of Money, 1924
On With the Dance, 1927
A Warm Corner, 1930
The Sport of Kings, 1931
It's a Boy, 1933
The Girl From Maxim's, 1933
Oh Daddy, 1935
The Demi-Paradise, 1943
Home and Away, 1956

NICKY HENSON (1945-)
Supporting actor of the 60s
and 70s; son of Leslie Henson.

Here We Go Round the Mul-
    berry Bush, 1967
Witchfinder General, 1968
Mosquito Squadron, 1969
Crooks and Coronets, 1969
There's a Girl in My Soup,
    1970
All Coppers Are, 1971
Penny Gold, 1972
Vampira, 1974
The Death Wheelers, 1974
Bawdy Adventures of Tom
    Jones, 1975
Old Dracula, 1975

AUDREY HEPBURN (1929-)
Beautiful, delicate leading lady
of stage and screen, usually
cast in graceful roles.   Also
in Hollywood.

One Wild Oat, 1951
Young Wives' Tale, 1951
Laughter in Paradise, 1951
The Lavender Hill Mob, 1951
Monte Carlo Baby, 1951
The Secret People, 1952

Roman Holiday, 1953
Sabrina, 1954
War and Peace, 1956
Funny Face, 1957
Love in the Afternoon, 1957
Green Mansions, 1959
The Nun's Story, 1959
The Unforgiven, 1960
Breakfast at Tiffany's, 1961
The Children's Hour, 1962
Charade, 1963
Paris When It Sizzles, 1964
My Fair Lady, 1964
How To Steal a Million,
   1966
Two For the Road, 1967
Wait Until Dark, 1967
Robin and Marian, 1976
Bloodline, 1979
They All Laughed, 1980

HOLMES HERBERT (1882-
   1956)
Distinguished, soft-spoken leading man and latterly character
actor of stage (1890) and films,
in Hollywood from 1917.

A Doll's House, 1918
The Whirlpool, 1918
Market of Souls, 1919
The White Heather, 1919
Black is White, 1920
His House in Order, 1920
My Lady's Garter, 1920
The Right to Love, 1920
Lady Rose's Daughter, 1920
Dead Men Tell No Tales, 1920
Her Lord and Master, 1921
The Family Closet, 1921
The Heedless Moth, 1921
The Wild Goose, 1921
Any Wife, 1922
A Strange Romance, 1922
Divorce Coupons, 1922
A Woman's Woman, 1922
Toilers of the Sea, 1923
Enchanted Cottage, 1924
Sinners in Heaven, 1924
Love's Wilderness, 1924
Daddy's Gone a-Hunting, 1925
Wildfire, 1925

A Woman of the World, 1925
Wreckage, 1925
The Wanderer, 1925
Josselyn's Wife, 1926
The Fire Brigade, 1926
When a Man Loves, 1927
Lovers, 1927
Mr. Wu, 1927
The Heart of Salome,
   1927
The Gay Retreat, 1927
East Side West Side, 1927
The Nest, 1927
Slaves of Beauty, 1927
Sporting Age, 1928
Through the Breakers, 1928
The Silver Slave, 1928
Gentlemen Prefer Blondes,
   1928
The Terror, 1928
On Trial, 1928
The Charlatan, 1929
Madam X, 1929
Careers, 1929
Say it With Songs, 1929
Her Private Life, 1929
The Careless Age, 1929
The Kiss, 1929
Untamed, 1929
The Ship From Shanghai, 1930
The Hot Heiress, 1931
The Single Sin, 1931
Chances, 1931
Daughter of the Dragon, 1931
Dr. Jekyll & Mr. Hyde, 1932
Miss Pinkerton, 1932
Central Park, 1932
Mystery of the Wax Museum,
   1933
The Invisible Man, 1933
House of Rothschild, 1934
The Count of Monte Cristo,
   1934
The Pursuit of Happiness,
   1934
Sons of Steel, 1935
Mark of the Vampire, 1935
Accent On Youth, 1935
Captain Blood, 1935
The Country Beyond, 1936
15 Maiden Lane, 1936
Lloyds of London, 1936
Charge of the Light Brigade,

1936
The Life of Emile Zola, 1937
Slave Ship, 1937
House of Secrets, 1937
The Thirteenth Chair, 1937
Love Under Fire, 1937
Lancer Spy, 1937
Adventures of Robin Hood, 1938
The Black Doll, 1938
Say it in French, 1938
The Sun Never Sets, 1939
The Little Princess, 1939
Juarez, 1939
Stanley and Livingstone, 1939
Adventures of Sherlock Holmes,
  1939
We Are Not Alone, 1939
Everything Happens at Night,
  1939
Foreign Correspondent, 1940
British Intelligence, 1940
Man Hunt, 1941
International Squadron, 1941
The Ghost of Frankenstein, 1942
This Above All, 1942
Invisible Agent, 1942
Sherlock Holmes and the
  Secret Weapon, 1942
Sherlock Holmes and the Voice
  of Terror, 1942
Corvette K-225, 1943
Two Tickets to London, 1943
Sherlock Holmes in Washington,
  1943
The Uninvited, 1944
Calling Dr. Death, 1944
Our Hearts Were Young and
  Gay, 1944
Enter Arsene Lupin, 1944
The House of Fear, 1945
The Mummy's Curse, 1945
Confidential Agent, 1945
The Verdict, 1946
Dressed to Kill, 1946
Singapore, 1947
The Swordsman, 1947
This Time For Keeps, 1947
Johnny Belinda, 1948
Jungle Jim, 1949
Barbary Pirate, 1949
David and Bathsheba, 1951
Anne of the Indies, 1951
The Brigand, 1952

PERCY HERBERT (1925-)
Character actor of films and
television, often cast as soldier or sailor. On tv in
series "Cimarron Strip" (1967).

The Green Buddha, 1954
Cockleshell Heroes, 1955
A Hill in Korea, 1956
The Baby and the Battleship,
  1956
A Child in the House, 1956
Barnacle Bill, 1957
Bridge On the River Kwai, 1957
  1957
Quatermass II, 1957
Steel Bayonet, 1957
The Safecracker, 1958
No Time to Die, 1958
Sea Fury, 1958
Sea of Sand, 1958
Serious Charge, 1959
Yesterday's Enemy, 1959
Don't Panic Chaps, 1959
A Touch of Larceny, 1959
Tunes of Glory, 1960
The Challenge, 1960
There Was a Crooked Man,
  1960
The Guns of Navarone, 1961
Mysterious Island, 1961
Mutiny On the Bounty, 1962
Call Me Bwana, 1963
The Cracksman, 1963
Carry On Jack, 1963
The Counterfeit Constable, 1964
Becket, 1964
Guns at Batasi, 1964
Joey Boy, 1965
Bunny Lake is Missing, 1965
Carry On Cowboy, 1965
One Million Years BC, 1966
Tobruk, 1966
Night of the Big Heat, 1967
The Viking Queen, 1967
Casino Royale, 1967
The Royal Hunt of the Sun,
  1969
Too Late the Hero, 1969
One More Time, 1970
Man in the Wilderness, 1971
Captain Apache, 1971
Doomwatch, 1972

Sweet Suzy, 1973
Craze, 1973
The Mackintosh Man, 1973
The Wild Geese, 1978
The London Affair, 1979

EILEEN HERLIE (1919-   )
Scottish actress, mainly on
stage; film roles occasional
but impressive.

Hungry Hill, 1947
Hamlet, 1948
The Angel With the Trumpet, 1950
Gilbert and Sullivan, 1953
Isn't Life Wonderful, 1953
For Better, For Worse, 1954
She Didn't Say No, 1958
Freud, 1962
Hamlet, 1964
The Seagull, 1968
Lemonade, 1971

CHARLES HESLOP (1884-1966)
Comedy character actor in occasional films; best remembered
for his prolific stage farces.

Hobson's Choice, 1920
This is the Life, 1933
Waltzes From Vienna, 1934
Charing Cross Road, 1935
Crackerjack, 1938
The Lambeth Walk, 1939
Flying Fortress, 1942
The Peterville Diamond, 1942
Never Say Die, 1950
The Late Edwina Black, 1951
The Second Mate, 1951
Hello London, 1958
Follow a Star, 1959
Nothing Barred, 1961
A Pair of Briefs, 1962

ANNE HEYWOOD (1932-   )
Lovely, dark-haired leading
lady, also in Hollywood.
Former beauty contest winner.
Married to producer Raymond
Stross (1916-   ).

Find the Lady, 1956
Checkpoint, 1956
Doctor at Large, 1957
Dangerous Exile, 1957
The Depraved, 1957
Violent Playground, 1958
Floods of Fear, 1958
Heart of a Man, 1959
Upstairs and Downstairs, 1959
A Terrible Beauty, 1960
Carthage in Flames, 1961
Petticoat Pirates, 1961
Stork Talk, 1962
Vengeance, 1962
The Very Edge, 1963
Ninety Degrees in the Shade,
    1966
The Fox, 1968
Midas Run, 1969
The Lady of Monza, 1969
Most Dangerous Man in the
    World, 1969
I Want What I Want, 1971
Trader Horn, 1973
The Nun and the Devil, 1973
Love Under the Elms, 1975

PAT HEYWOOD (1927-   )
Character actress of stage and
screen; films rare.

Romeo and Juliet, 1968
All the Way Up, 1969
Mumsy, Nanny, Sonny and
    Girly, 1969
10 Rillington Place, 1971
Whoever Slew Auntie Roo?,
    1971

GEOFFREY HIBBERT (1922-
1969)
Light actor who began by playing inexperienced juvenile
parts; latterly in character
roles.

Love On the Dole, 1941
The Common Touch, 1941
Next of Kin, 1942
The Shipbuilders, 1943
The Secret People, 1952

Emergency Call, 1952
The End of the Line, 1957
Orders to Kill, 1958
The Links of Justice, 1958
The Great Van Robbery, 1959
Crash Drive, 1959
Johann Sebastian Bach, 1961
Gaolbreak, 1962

SIR SEYMOUR HICKS (1871-
  1949)
Light comedy star of stage
(1887) who became an excellent
supporting star of films. Also
author, producer, director,
screenwriter and playwright.
Married to Ellaline Terriss.

Seymour Hicks and Ellaline
  Terriss, 1913
David Garrick, 1913
Scrooge, 1913
Always Tell Your Wife, 1914
A Prehistoric Love Story,
  1915
Always Tell Your Wife, 1923
Telltales, 1930
Sleeping Partners, 1930
The Love Habit, 1931
Glamour, 1931
Money For Nothing, 1932
The Secret of the Loch, 1934
Royal Cavalcade, 1935
Mr. What's His Name, 1935
Vintage Wine, 1935
Scrooge, 1935
Eliza Comes to Stay, 1936
It's You I Want, 1936
Change For a Sovereign, 1937
The Lambeth Walk, 1939
Young Man's Fancy, 1939
Pastor Hall, 1940
Busman's Honeymoon, 1940
Fame is the Spur, 1947
Silent Dust, 1949

JOAN HICKSON (1906-)
Character actress of stage and
screen, often seen in dithery
or eccentric parts. Also on
television.

Trouble in Store, 1934
Widow's Might, 1935
The Man Who Could Work
  Miracles, 1936
The Lilac Domino, 1937
Love From a Stranger, 1937
Second Thoughts, 1938
Don't Take it to Heart, 1944
I See a Dark Stranger, 1946
This Was a Woman, 1948
The Guinea Pig, 1948
Seven Days to Noon, 1950
High Treason, 1951
Hell is Sold Out, 1951
No Haunt For a Gentleman,
  1952
Hindle Wakes, 1952
The Card, 1952
Curtain Up, 1953
Deadly Nightshade, 1953
Doctor in the House, 1954
Mad About Men, 1954
What Every Woman Wants,
  1954
Dance Little Lady, 1954
Value For Money, 1955
A Time to Kill, 1955
Simon and Laura, 1955
Jumping For Joy, 1955
The Man Who Never Was, 1956
Port of Escape, 1956
A Child in the House, 1956
Happy is the Bride, 1957
No Time For Tears, 1957
Law and Disorder, 1958
Carry On Nurse, 1959
Upstairs and Downstairs, 1959
The 39 Steps, 1959
Carry On Constable, 1960
No Kidding, 1960
Carry On Regardless, 1961
His and Hers, 1961
In the Doghouse, 1961
Murder She Said, 1962
Nurse On Wheels, 1963
Heavens Above, 1963
The Secret of My Success,
  1965
A Day in the Death of Joe Egg,
  1970
Theatre of Blood, 1973
Confessions of a Window
  Cleaner, 1974
Yanks, 1979

BENNY HILL (1925-)
Comedy actor of stage (from
1946) and films, very popular
in television. Adept at make-
up and disguises.

Who Done It, 1956
Light Up the Sky, 1960
Those Magnificent Men in
    Their Flying Machines, 1965
Chitty Chitty Bang Bang, 1968
The Italian Job, 1969
The Waiters, 1969
The Best of Benny Hill, 1974

DAME WENDY HILLER
    (1912-)
Distinguished, outstanding actress primarily on stage (since
1920); films fairly rare but
always superior. Also in
Hollywood. Married to author
Ronald Gow.

Lancashire Luck, 1937
Pygmalion, 1938
Major Barbara, 1941
I Know Where I'm Going, 1945
An Outcast of the Islands,
    1952
Singlehanded, 1953
How to Murder a Rich Uncle,
    1957
Separate Tables, 1958
Something of Value, 1958
Sons and Lovers, 1960
Toys in the Attic, 1963
A Man For All Seasons, 1966
When We Dead Awaken, 1968
David Copperfield, 1969
Peer Gynt, 1972
Clochemerle, 1973
Murder On the Orient Express,
    1974
Voyage of the Damned, 1976
The Cat and the Canary, 1977
Last Wishes, 1978
Richard II, 1979
The Curse of King Tut's Tomb,
    1980
The Elephant Man, 1980

THORA HIRD (1914-)
Character actress of stage,
films and television, usually
cast in comedy roles. Mother
of Janette Scott.

The Black Sheep of Whitehall,
    1941
Went the Day Well, 1942
Two Thousand Women, 1944
The Courtneys of Curzon
    Street, 1947
Corridor of Mirrors, 1947
The Weaker Sex, 1948
The Blind Goddess, 1948
Portrait From Life, 1948
Once a Jolly Swagman, 1948
Fools Rush In, 1949
A Boy, a Girl, and a Bike,
    1949
Maytime in Mayfair, 1949
Madness of the Heart, 1949
Boys in Brown, 1949
Conspirator, 1950
The Magnet, 1950
The Cure For Love, 1950
Once a Sinner, 1950
The Frightened Man, 1952
Emergency Call, 1952
Time Gentlemen Please, 1952
The Lost Hours, 1952
Personal Affair, 1953
The Great Game, 1953
Background, 1953
Street Corner, 1953
A Day to Remember, 1953
The Long Memory, 1953
Turn the Key Softly, 1953
Edge of Divorce, 1954
Don't Blame the Stork, 1954
The Crowded Day, 1954
One Good Turn, 1954
For Better, For Worse, 1954
The Quatermass Experiment,
    1955
Shop Soiled, 1955
The Love Match, 1955
Tiger By the Tail, 1955
Simon and Laura, 1955
Women Without Men, 1956
Sailor Beware, 1956
Lost, 1956
Home and Away, 1956

The Good Companions, 1957
These Dangerous Years, 1957
A Clean Sweep, 1958
Further Up the Creek, 1958
The Entertainer, 1960
Over the Odds, 1961
A Kind of Loving, 1962
Term of Trial, 1962
Bitter Harvest, 1963
Rattle of a Simple Man, 1964
Some Will, Some Won't, 1970
The Nightcomers, 1971

HALLIWELL HOBBES (1877-
1962)
Impeccable small-part character player of stage (from 1898)
and screen, in U.S. from 1923.
Usually played butlers and the
like.

Jealousy, 1929
Lucky in Love, 1929
Grumpy, 1930
Scotland Yard, 1930
Charley's Aunt, 1930
Bachelor Father, 1931
The Right of Way, 1931
Five and Ten, 1931
The Woman Between, 1931
The Sin of Madelon Claudet, 1931
Platinum Blonde, 1931
Dr. Jekyll and Mr. Hyde, 1932
Forbidden, 1932
The Menace, 1932
Lovers Courageous, 1932
Devil's Lottery, 1932
Man About Town, 1932
Weekends Only, 1932
Six Hours to Live, 1932
Payment Deferred, 1932
Looking Forward, 1933
A Study in Scarlet, 1933
The Masquerader, 1933
Should Ladies Behave?, 1933
I Am Suzanne, 1934
Mandalay, 1934
Riptide, 1934
Double Door, 1934
The Key, 1934
Bulldog Drummond Strikes
   Back, 1934

British Agent, 1934
Madame DuBarry, 1934
Menace, 1934
Folies Bergere, 1935
Cardinal Richelieu, 1935
Jalna, 1935
Charlie Chan in Shanghai, 1935
Millions in the Air, 1935
The Story of Louis Pasteur,
   1936
Dracula's Daughter, 1936
Hearts Divided, 1936
The White Angel, 1936
Spendthrift, 1936
Give Me Your Heart, 1936
Maid of Salem, 1937
The Prince and the Pauper,
   1937
Varsity Show, 1937
Fit For a King, 1937
The Jury's Secret, 1938
Bulldog Drummond's Peril,
   1938
Kidnapped, 1938
Service de Luxe, 1938
You Can't Take it With You,
   1938
Storm Over Bengal, 1938
Meet Maxwell Archer, 1939
Pacific Liner, 1939
Remember, 1939
The Hardys Ride High, 1939
Nurse Edith Cavell, 1939
Tell No Tales, 1939
Naughty But Nice, 1939
The Light That Failed, 1939
The Sea Hawk, 1940
The Earl of Chicago, 1940
Third Finger Left Hand, 1940
That Hamilton Woman, 1941
Here Comes Mr. Jordan, 1941
Son of Fury, 1942
To Be Or Not to Be, 1942
War Against Mrs. Hadley, 1942
Journey For Margaret, 1942
Forever and a Day, 1943
Sherlock Holmes Faces Death,
   1943
Gaslight, 1944
Mr. Skeffington, 1944
The Invisible Man's Revenge,
   1944
Casanova Brown, 1944

Canyon Passage, 1946
If Winter Comes, 1947
The Black Arrow, 1948
You Gotta Stay Happy, 1948
That Forsyte Woman, 1949
Miracle in the Rain, 1956
Flower of Pride, 1956
Mrs. Gilling & the Skyscraper,
   1957

JACK HOBBS (1893-1968)
Light leading actor of stage
(1906) and films, often cast in
friendly, cheerful parts.

Love's Legacy, 1915
Tom Brown's School Days, 1916
The Lady Clare, 1919
The Face at the Window, 1920
The Inheritance, 1920
The Shuttle of Life, 1920
The Skin Game, 1921
The Naval Treaty, 1922
Lonely Lady of Grosvenor
   Square, 1922
The Crimson Circle, 1922
The Crooked Man, 1923
The Eleventh Commandment, 1924
The Happy Ending, 1925
Love Lies, 1931
Never Trouble Trouble, 1931
Mischief, 1931
Dr. Josser KC, 1931
The Love Race, 1931
The Last Coupon, 1932
His Wife's Mother, 1932
Josser Joins the Navy, 1932
Josser in the Army, 1932
A Honeymoon in Devon, 1932
Double Wedding, 1933
Too Many Wives, 1933
Beware of Women, 1933
Trouble in Store, 1934
Oh No Doctor, 1934
Handle With Care, 1935
Car of Dreams, 1935
No Limit, 1935
Interrupted Honeymoon, 1936
All That Glitters, 1936
Millions, 1936
When the Devil Was Well, 1937
The Show Goes On, 1937

Fine Feathers, 1937
Why Pick On Me?, 1937
Leave it to Me, 1937
Intimate Relations, 1937
Make it Three, 1938
It's in the Air, 1938
Miracles Do Happen, 1938
Let George Do It, 1940
Behind These Walls, 1948
Worm's Eye View, 1951

VALERIE HOBSON (1917-)
Refined leading lady of stage
(since 1932) and films, cast
usually in aristocratic, well-
bred roles.   Also in Hollywood.

Eyes of Fate, 1933
Path of Glory, 1934
Two Hearts in Waltz Time,
   1934
Badger's Green, 1934
Oh What a Night, 1935
Tugboat Princess, 1935
The Great Impersonation, 1935
Rendezvous at Midnight, 1935
Chinatown Squad, 1935
Bride of Frankenstein, 1935
The Werewolf of London, 1935
The Mystery of Edwin Drood,
   1935
The Secret of Stamboul, 1936
No Escape, 1936
Jump For Glory, 1937
The Drum, 1938
This Man is News, 1938
Q Planes, 1939
The Spy in Black, 1939
The Silent Battle, 1939
This Man in Paris, 1939
Contraband, 1940
Atlantic Ferry, 1941
Unpublished Story, 1942
The Adventures of Tartu, 1943
The Years Between, 1946
Great Expectations, 1946
Blanche Fury, 1948
The Small Voice, 1948
Kind Hearts and Coronets,
   1949
Train of Events, 1949
Interrupted Journey, 1949

The Rocking Horse Winner,
  1950
The Card, 1952
Who Goes There?, 1952
Meet Me Tonight, 1952
The Voice of Merrill, 1952
Background, 1953
Knave of Hearts, 1954

DENNIS HOEY (1893-1960)
Character actor of stage (from
1918) and screen, in Hollywood
from the late 30s; memorable
as Inspector Lestrade in the
Sherlock Holmes series starring
Basil Rathbone and Nigel Bruce.

Tiptoes, 1927
The Man From Chicago, 1930
Tell England, 1931
Never Trouble Trouble, 1931
Love Lies, 1931
Love in Morocco, 1931
Life Goes On, 1932
Barould, 1932
Maid of the Mountains, 1932
I Spy, 1933
Maid Happy, 1933
Facing the Music, 1933
Oh What a Duchess, 1933
The Good Companions, 1933
The Wandering Jew, 1933
Jew Suss, 1934
Lily of Killarney, 1934
Chu Chin Chow, 1934
Brewster's Millions, 1935
Maria Marten, 1935
Mystery of the Mary Celeste,
  1935
Honeymoon For Three, 1935
Immortal Gentleman, 1935
Did I Betray, 1936
Faust, 1936
Uncivilized, 1937
How Green Was My Valley,
  1941
Cairo, 1942
This Above All, 1942
Son of Fury, 1942
Sherlock Holmes and the Secret
  Weapon, 1942
Sherlock Holmes Faces Death,

1943
Frankenstein Meets the Wolf
  Man, 1943
They Came to Blow Up Amer-
  ica, 1943
Bomber's Moon, 1943
Uncertain Glory, 1944
National Velvet, 1944
The Pearl of Death, 1944
The Spider Woman, 1944
The House of Fear, 1945
1001 Nights, 1945
Tarzan and the Leopard
  Woman, 1946
She-Wolf of London, 1946
Anna and the King of Siam,
  1946
The Strange Woman, 1946
Terror By Night, 1946
Kitty, 1946
Where There's Life, 1947
If Winter Comes, 1947
Second Chance, 1947
The Foxes of Harrow, 1947
The Crimson Key, 1947
Christmas Eve, 1947
Golden Earrings, 1947
Ruthless, 1948
Joan of Arc, 1948
Wake of the Red Witch, 1948
The Kid From Texas, 1950
David and Bathsheba, 1951
Caribbean, 1952
The Plymouth Adventure, 1952
The Vase, 1952

IRIS HOEY (1885-   )
Character actress of stage and
films, mainly active in the 30s.

East Lynne, 1922
Her Reputation, 1931
Those Were the Days, 1934
Once in a Million, 1936
A Star Fell From Heaven,
  1936
Living Dangerously, 1936
The Limping Man, 1936
The Tenth Man, 1936
The Perfect Crime, 1937
Let's Make a Night of It, 1937
Pygmalion, 1938

Jane Steps Out, 1938
The Terror, 1938
Just William, 1939
The Midas Touch, 1939
Poet's Pub, 1949
The Girl Who Couldn't Quite,
   1950

ANTHONY HOLLES (1901-
   1950)
Character player of stage and
screen, often seen as eccentric
foreigners or other exasperated
characters.

The Will, 1921
The Star Reporter, 1931
Once Bitten, 1932
Hotel Splendide, 1932
Life Goes On, 1932
Watch Beverly, 1932
Reunion, 1932
The Lodger, 1932
The Missing Rembrandt, 1932
The Midshipmaid, 1933
She Was Only a Village Maiden,
   1933
Forging Ahead, 1933
Cash, 1933
Britannia of Billingsgate, 1933
That's a Good Girl, 1933
Borrowed Clothes, 1934
The Green Pack, 1934
Gentleman's Agreement, 1935
Brewster's Millions, 1935
Limelight, 1936
Things to Come, 1936
Seven Sinners, 1936
The Tenth Man, 1936
This'll Make You Whistle,
   1936
Public Nuisance Number One,
   1936
Millions, 1936
The Gay Adventure, 1936
Dark Journey, 1937
Glamorous Night, 1937
Action For Slander, 1937
Smash and Grab, 1937
The Sky's the Limit, 1937
Paradise For Two, 1937
Mademoiselle Docteur, 1937

Gaiety Girls, 1938
Dangerous Medicine, 1938
Romance a la Carte, 1938
His Lordship Regrets, 1938
They Drive By Night, 1938
Weddings Are Wonderful, 1938
Miracles Do Happen, 1938
The Missing People, 1939
Down Our Alley, 1939
Ten Days in Paris, 1939
The Spider, 1939
Blind Folly, 1939
Neutral Port, 1940
Larceny Street, 1941
Front Line Kids, 1942
Talk About Jacqueline, 1942
Lady From Lisbon, 1942
Old Mother Riley Overseas,
   1943
It's In the Bag, 1943
Up With the Lark, 1943
Battle For Music, 1943
Warn That Man, 1943
Give Me the Stars, 1944
Gaiety George, 1946
Carnival, 1946
The Magic Bow, 1947
Fortune Lane, 1947
The Dark Road, 1948
Bonnie Prince Charlie, 1948
The Rocking Horse Winner,
   1949

JULIAN HOLLOWAY (-)
Small-part character player,
usually seen in comedy parts;
films occasional. Son of Stanley Holloway.

Carry On Doctor, 1968
Carry On Up the Khyber, 1968
Carry On Camping, 1969
Scream and Scream Again,
   1969
The Last Shot You Hear, 1970
Carry On Henry VIII, 1971
Young Winston, 1972
Rebecca, 1980
Rough Cut, 1980

STANLEY HOLLOWAY
(1890-)
Outstanding star of stage (from
1919), screen and television;
also singer, monologuist and
former music hall performer.
Usually seen in vigorous comedy characterizations, but also
a fine dramatic actor as well.
Also in Hollywood. Autobiography 1967 (Wiv a Little Bit
O' Luck). Tv series: "Our
Man Higgins" (1962). Father
of Julian Holloway.

The Rotters, 1921
The Co-Optimists, 1930
The Sleeping Car, 1933
The Girl From Maxim's, 1933
Lily of Killarney, 1934
Love at Second Sight, 1934
Sing As We Go, 1934
Road House, 1934
D'Ye Ken John Peel?, 1935
In Town Tonight, 1935
Squibs, 1935
Play Up the Band, 1936
Sam Cartoons (voice), 1936
Song of the Forge, 1937
The Vicar of Bray, 1937
Cotton Queen, 1937
Sam Small Leaves Town, 1937
Our Island Nation, 1938
Co-Operette, 1939
Albert's Savings, 1940
Father O'Flynn, 1940
Major Barbara, 1941
Salute John Citizen, 1942
The Way Ahead, 1944
This Happy Breed, 1944
Champagne Charlie, 1944
The Way to the Stars, 1945
Brief Encounter, 1945
Caesar and Cleopatra, 1945
Wanted For Murder, 1946
Carnival, 1946
Meet Me at Dawn, 1947
Nicholas Nickleby, 1947
Snowbound, 1948
Noose, 1948
One Night With You, 1948
The Winslow Boy, 1948
Another Shore, 1948

Hamlet, 1948
Passport to Pimlico, 1949
The Perfect Woman, 1949
Midnight Episode, 1950
One Wild Oat, 1951
The Lavender Hill Mob, 1951
The Magic Box, 1951
Lady Godiva Rides Again, 1951
Sailor's Consolation (voice),
1951
The Happy Family, 1952
Meet Me Tonight, 1952
The Titfield Thunderbolt, 1953
The Beggar's Opera, 1953
A Day to Remember, 1953
Meet Mr. Lucifer, 1953
Fast and Loose, 1954
An Alligator Named Daisy,
1955
Jumping For Joy, 1955
Alive and Kicking, 1958
No Trees in the Street, 1959
Hello London, 1960
No Love For Johnnie, 1961
On the Fiddle, 1961
My Fair Lady, 1964
Ten Little Indians, 1965
In Harm's Way, 1965
The Sandwich Man, 1966
The Fantasticks, 1966
Mrs. Brown, You've Got a
Lovely Daughter, 1968
Run a Crooked Mile, 1969
What's in it For Harry?, 1969
Blanding Castle, 1969
Private Life of Sherlock
Holmes, 1970
Flight of the Doves, 1971
Up the Front, 1972
Dr. Jekyll and Mr. Hyde,
1973
Journey Into Fear, 1975

IAN HOLM (1931-)
Leading actor and strong supporting player of stage (since
1954) and films.

The Bofors Gun, 1968
A Midsummer Night's Dream,
1968
The Fixer, 1968

Oh What a Lovely War, 1969
A Severed Head, 1971
Mary Queen of Scots, 1971
Nicholas and Alexandra, 1971
Young Winston, 1972
Regan, 1973
The Homecoming, 1973
Juggernaut, 1974
Robin and Marian, 1976
Shout at the Devil, 1976
Man in the Iron Mask, 1976
March Or Die, 1977
Jesus of Nazareth, 1977
Alien, 1979
All Quiet On the Western
    Front, 1979
SOS Titanic, 1979

SONIA HOLM (-)
Character actress who had a
brief career in supporting roles
of the 40s and 50s.

When the Bough Breaks, 1947
The Loves of Joanna Godden, 1947
Broken Journey, 1948
Miranda, 1948
The Calendar, 1948
Warning to Wantons, 1949
The Bad Lord Byron, 1949
13 East Street, 1952
The Crowded Day, 1954

PATRICK HOLT (1912-)
Dependable leading man of the
40s and latterly character actor, often seen in second features.   On tv in "Lillie."
Married to Sandra Dorne.

The Return of the Frog, 1938
Sword of Honour, 1939
Dangerous Comment, 1940
Convoy, 1941
Hungry Hill, 1947
Frieda, 1947
The Master of Bankdam, 1947
The October Man, 1947
When the Bough Breaks, 1947
Good Time Girl, 1948
The Mark of Cain, 1948

My Sister and I, 1948
Fly Away Peter, 1948
Portrait From Life, 1948
A Boy, a Girl, and a Bike,
    1949
Boys in Brown, 1949
Marry Me, 1949
Guilt is My Shadow, 1950
13 East Street, 1952
Circumstantial Evidence, 1952
Come Back Peter, 1952
Ivanhoe, 1952
The Unholy Four, 1954
The Stranger Came Home,
    1954
The Golden Link, 1954
Men of Sherwood Forest, 1954
The Dark Avenger, 1955
Miss Tulip Stays the Night,
    1955
Stolen Assignment, 1955
The Gelignite Gang, 1956
Alias John Preston, 1956
Operation Murder, 1957
Girl in the Picture, 1957
Suspended Alibi, 1957
Fortune is a Woman, 1957
There's Always a Thursday,
    1957
Murder Reported, 1957
I Was Monty's Double, 1958
Further Up the Creek, 1958
The Challenge, 1960
Too Hot to Handle, 1960
Dentist On the Job, 1961
The Frightened City, 1961
Serena, 1962
Flight From Singapore, 1962
Night of the Prowler, 1963
Girl in the Headlines, 1963
Guns at Batasi, 1964
Genghis Kahn, 1965
Thunderball, 1965
Murderer's Row, 1966
The Vulture, 1967
Hammerhead, 1968
The Magic Christian, 1970
Cromwell, 1970
When Dinosaurs Ruled the
    Earth, 1970
No Blade of Grass, 1971
Young Winston, 1972
Psychomania, 1972

Diamonds On Wheels, 1973
The Amorous Milkman, 1974
Legend of the Werewolf, 1974

VIDA HOPE (1918-1962)
Comedy character actress of
stage and screen who usually
portrayed the lower classes;
also stage director.

English Without Tears, 1944
The Way to the Stars, 1945
While the Sun Shines, 1946
Nicholas Nickleby, 1947
It Always Rains On Sunday,
  1947
They Made Me a Fugitive, 1947
The Mark of Cain, 1948
Vice Versa, 1948
For Them That Trespass, 1949
Interrupted Journey, 1949
Paper Orchid, 1949
Double Confession, 1950
The Woman in Question, 1950
The Man in the White Suit,
  1951
Cheer the Brave, 1951
Green Grow the Rushes, 1951
Angels One Five, 1952
Women of Twilight, 1952
Hundred Hour Hunt, 1953
The Long Memory, 1953
The Broken Horseshoe, 1953
Marilyn, 1953
Fast and Loose, 1954
Lease of Life, 1954
Family Doctor, 1958
In the Doghouse, 1961

ANTHONY HOPKINS (1937-)
Versatile Welsh leading actor
of stage and films; latterly taking on ambitious portrayals.
Also in Hollywood.

The White Bus, 1967
The Lion in Winter, 1968
Hamlet, 1970
The Looking Glass War, 1970
When Eight Bells Toll, 1971
Young Winston, 1972

A Doll's House, 1973
QB VII, 1974
The Girl From Petrovka, 1974
Juggernaut, 1974
All Creatures Great and Small,
  1975
Three Sisters, 1975
The Lindbergh Kidnapping Case,
  1976
Dark Victory, 1976
Victory at Entebbe, 1976
Audrey Rose, 1977
A Bridge Too Far, 1977
International Velvet, 1978
Magic, 1978
Mayflower: The Pilgrim Ad-
  venture, 1979
A Change of Seasons, 1980
The Bunker, 1980
Consenting Adults, 1980
The Acts of Peter and Paul, 1980
The Elephant Man, 1980

MICHAEL HORDERN (1911-)
Distinguished character player
of stage (from 1937), films,
and tv; often cast as haggard
military officer and the like.
Former schoolmaster; also in
Hollywood.

Girl in the News, 1939
School For Secrets, 1946
Mine Own Executioner, 1947
Good Time Girl, 1948
Passport to Pimlico, 1949
Train of Events, 1949
Trio, 1950
The Astonished Heart, 1950
Highly Dangerous, 1950
Flesh and Blood, 1951
Scrooge, 1951
Tom Brown's School Days,
  1951
The Story of Robin Hood, 1952
The Card, 1952
The Hour of Thirteen, 1952
Personal Affair, 1953
Street Corner, 1953
The Heart of the Matter, 1953
Grand National Night, 1953
The Beachcomber, 1954

Forbidden Cargo, 1954
You Know What Sailors Are, 1954
The Dark Avenger, 1955
Storm Over the Nile, 1955
The Constant Husband, 1955
The Night My Number Came Up, 1955
Alexander the Great, 1956
The Baby and the Battleship, 1956
The Spanish Gardener, 1956
The Man Who Never Was, 1956
Pacific Destiny, 1956
No Time For Tears, 1957
Windom's Way, 1957
I Was Monty's Double, 1958
The Spaniard's Curse, 1958
Moment of Danger, 1959
Girls at Sea, 1959
Sink the Bismarck, 1960
Man in the Moon, 1961
Macbeth, 1961
El Cid, 1961
Cleopatra, 1962
The VIPs, 1963
Dr. Syn Alias the Scarecrow, 1963
The Yellow Rolls-Royce, 1964
The Spy Who Came in From the Cold, 1965
Genghis Khan, 1965
Cast a Giant Shadow, 1966
A Funny Thing Happened On the Way to the Forum, 1966
Khartoum, 1966
The Jokers, 1966
I'll Never Forget Whatsisname, 1967
The Taming of the Shrew, 1967
How I Won the War, 1967
Prudence and the Pill, 1968
Where Eagles Dare, 1968
The Bed Sitting Room, 1969
Girl Stroke Boy, 1970
Futtock's End, 1970
Some Will, Some Won't, 1970
Anne of the Thousand Days, 1970
Up Pompeii, 1970
The Pied Piper, 1971
Possession of Joel Delany, 1972
England Made Me, 1972
Alice's Adventures in Wonderland, 1972
Theatre of Blood, 1973
The Mackintosh Man, 1973
Demons of the Mind, 1974
Mr. Quilp, 1975
Barry Lyndon (voice), 1975
Lucky Lady, 1975
Royal Flash, 1975
The Slipper and the Rose, 1976
Joseph Andrews, 1977
Watership Down (voice), 1978
The Medusa Touch, 1978
Romeo and Juliet, 1979
Richard II, 1979
Gauguin the Savage, 1980
The Tempest, 1980
All's Well That Ends Well, 1980
Shogun, 1980

DAVID HORNE (1898-1970)
Corpulent character actor, also on stage; often cast in pompous or ostentatious roles.

General John Regan, 1933
Lord of the Manor, 1933
Badger's Green, 1934
The Case For the Crown, 1934
That's My Uncle, 1935
The Village Squire, 1935
Gentleman's Agreement, 1935
Late Extra, 1935
Doomed Cargo, 1935
It's Love Again, 1936
Under Proof, 1936
A Touch of the Moon, 1936
Debt of Honour, 1936
Interrupted Honeymoon, 1936
House of the Spaniard, 1936
Seven Sinners, 1936
The First and the Last, 1937
The Mill On the Floss, 1937
Farewell Again, 1937
The Wrecker, 1938
Four Dark Hours, 1938
21 Days, 1939
Blind Folly, 1939

The Stars Look Down, 1939
Crimes at the Dark House,
  1940
Return to Yesterday, 1940
The Door With Seven Locks,
  1940
Adventure in Blackmail, 1941
Breach of Promise, 1941
Inspector Hornleigh Goes to It,
  1941
They Flew Alone, 1942
The First of the Few, 1942
The Day Will Dawn, 1942
San Demetrio-London, 1943
The Yellow Canary, 1943
Don't Take it to Heart, 1944
The Hundred Pound Window,
  1944
The Seventh Veil, 1945
The Rake's Progress, 1945
The Wicked Lady, 1945
They Were Sisters, 1945
The Man From Morocco, 1945
Spring Song, 1946
Men of Two Worlds, 1946
Gaiety George, 1946
Caravan, 1946
The Man Within, 1947
The Magic Bow, 1947
Easy Money, 1948
It's Hard to Be Good, 1948
The Winslow Boy, 1948
Saraband For Dead Lovers,
  1949
Once Upon a Dream, 1949
The History of Mr. Polly, 1949
Madeleine, 1950
Appointment With Venus, 1951
Five Pound Note, 1951
Wedding Gift, 1952
Street Corner, 1953
Martin Luther, 1953
The Intruder, 1953
Spaceways, 1953
Police Woman, 1953
Beau Brummell, 1954
Three Cases of Murder, 1955
Lust For Life, 1956
The Last Man to Hang, 1956
The Prince and the Showgirl,
  1957
Sheriff of Fractured Jaw, 1958
The Safecracker, 1958

The Devil's Disciple, 1959
Goodbye Again, 1961
Dentist On the Job, 1961
Clue of the New Pin, 1961
Nurse On Wheels, 1963
The Big Job, 1965
Diamonds For Breakfast, 1968

GEOFFREY HORNE (-)
Supporting actor in occasional
films; also Hollywood.

The Bridge On the River Kwai,
  1957
The Strange One, 1957
Bonjour Tristesse, 1958
Tempest, 1958
The Story of Joseph and His
  Brethren, 1962
Two People, 1973

BERNARD HORSFALL (-)
General purpose character
player in occasional films.

Man in the Moon, 1961
Guns at Batasi, 1964
On Her Majesty's Secret Ser-
  vice, 1968
Gold, 1974
Shout at the Devil, 1976

JOHN HORSLEY (-)
Character actor of the fifties,
generally portraying businessmen or police detectives.

Highly Dangerous, 1950
The Quiet Woman, 1951
The Frightened Man, 1952
Encore, 1952
Recoil, 1953
Time Bomb, 1953
Singlehanded, 1953
Deadly Nightshade, 1953
Wheel of Fate, 1953
The Long Memory, 1953
Meet Mr. Malcolm, 1954
Delayed Action, 1954
The Runaway Bus, 1954

Father Brown, 1954
Night People, 1954
Above Us the Waves, 1955
Little Red Monkey, 1955
Barbados Quest, 1955
A Time To Kill, 1955
The Weapon, 1956
Breakaway, 1956
Circus Friends, 1956
Bond of Fear, 1956
Stranger in Town, 1957
Man in the Shadow, 1957
Operation Amsterdam, 1958
Sink the Bismarck, 1960

DONALD HOUSTON (1923-   )
Virile Welsh leading man and
latterly character star, also
on stage (since 1940). Brother:
Glyn Houston.

A Girl Must Live, 1941
The Blue Lagoon, 1949
A Run For Your Money, 1949
Dance Hall, 1950
My Death is a Mockery, 1952
Crow Hollow, 1952
The Red Beret, 1953
Small Town Story, 1953
The Large Rope, 1953
Point of No Return, 1953
Doctor in the House, 1954
The Devil's Pass, 1954
The Happiness of Three Women,
   1954
The Flaw, 1955
Find the Lady, 1956
Double Cross, 1956
The Surgeon's Knife, 1957
Every Valley, 1957
Yangtse Incident, 1957
Girl in the Picture, 1957
A Question of Adultery, 1958
The Man Upstairs, 1958
Room at the Top, 1959
Danger Within, 1959
Jessy, 1959
The Mark, 1961
The 300 Spartans, 1962
The Longest Day, 1962
Twice Round the Daffodils,
   1962

The Prince and the Pauper,
   1962
Maniac, 1962
Doctor in Distress, 1963
Carry On Jack, 1963
633 Squadron, 1964
A Study in Terror, 1965
The Viking Queen, 1967
Where Eagles Dare, 1968
My Lover My Son, 1970
The Bush Baby, 1970
Sunstruck, 1972
Tales That Witness Madness,
   1973
Voyage of the Damned, 1976

GLYN HOUSTON (1926-   )
Imperturbable Welsh character
player of stage, films and television; excellent as Bunter, the
manservant, in several adapta-
tions of Dorothy L. Sayers'
novels starring Ian Carmichael
as Lord Peter Wimsey. Brother of Donald Houston.

Trio, 1950
The Blue Lamp, 1950
Girdle of Gold, 1952
The Great Game, 1953
The Cruel Sea, 1953
Turn the Key Softly, 1953
River Beat, 1954
The Sleeping Tiger, 1954
The Happiness of Three Women,
   1954
The Long Arm, 1956
Tiger Bay, 1959
Payroll, 1960
The Wind of Change, 1961
Flame in the Streets, 1961
Emergency, 1962
Solo For Sparrow, 1962
Mix Me a Person, 1962
Panic, 1963
A Stitch in Time, 1963
One Way Pendulum, 1964
The Brigand of Kandahar, 1965
The Secret of Blood Island,
   1965
Invasion, 1966
Headline Hunters, 1968

Clouds of Witness, 1973
The Nine Tailors, 1974
Five Red Herrings, 1975

RENE HOUSTON (1902-)
Character actress of stage
(since 1916), films, and television, also singer and dancer.
Married to Patrick Aherne.

The Houston Sisters, 1926
Come Into My Parlour, 1932
Their Night Out, 1933
Radio Parade, 1933
Lost in the Legion, 1934
Mr. Cinders, 1934
Variety, 1935
No Monkey Business, 1935
Happy Days Are Here Again,
    1936
Fine Feathers, 1937
A Girl Must Live, 1939
Old Bill and Son, 1940
The Peterville Diamond, 1942
Down Melody Lane, 1943
Two Thousand Women, 1944
Lady Godiva Rides Again, 1951
The Belles of St. Trinian's,
    1954
Track the Man Down, 1955
The Big Money, 1956
A Town Like Alice, 1956
Time Without Pity, 1957
Them Nice Americans, 1958
The Horse's Mouth, 1959
The Flesh and the Fiends,
    1960
And The Same to You, 1960
Three on a Spree, 1961
Watch it Sailor, 1961
No My Darling Daughter, 1961
Twice Round the Daffodils,
    1962
Phantom of the Opera, 1962
Tomorrow at Ten, 1962
Out of the Fog, 1962
Nurse On Wheels, 1963
Carry On Spying, 1964
Repulsion, 1965
Cul de Sac, 1966
The Idol, 1966
Secrets of a Windmill Girl, 1966

River Rivals, 1967
Carry On at Your Convenience,
    1971
Legend of the Werewolf, 1974

ARTHUR HOWARD (1910-)
Character actor, often seen in
cameo comedy roles or as butlers, schoolmasters, etc.
Brother of Leslie Howard,
uncle of Ronald Howard.

The Lady is Willing, 1934
London Belongs to Me, 1948
The Passionate Friends, 1948
Passport to Pimlico, 1949
The Happiest Days of Your
    Life, 1950
Stage Fright, 1950
Never Look Back, 1952
Glad Tidings, 1953
The Intruder, 1953
The Belles of St. Trinian's,
    1954
One Way Out, 1955
One Wish Too Many, 1956
Nowhere to Go, 1958
I Only Arsked, 1958
Bottoms Up, 1960
Watch it Sailor, 1961
Kill Or Cure, 1963
Ladies Who Do, 1963
Joy House, 1965
The Ghost Goes Clear, 1966
The Shoes of the Fisherman,
    1968
The Best House in London, 1969
Jane Eyre, 1970
My Lover My Son, 1970
Hoverbug, 1970
Zeppelin, 1971
Steptoe and Son, 1972
One of Our Dinosaurs is Miss-
    ing, 1975
Bawdy Adventures of Tom
    Jones, 1975
Moonraker, 1979

JOYCE HOWARD (1922-)
Blonde leading lady of the forties; married to Basil Sydney.

Freedom Radio, 1941
Love On the Dole, 1941
The Common Touch, 1941
Back Room Boy, 1942
The Night Has Eyes, 1942
Talk About Jacqueline, 1942
The Gentle Sex, 1943
They Met in the Dark, 1943
They Knew Mr. Knight, 1945
Appointment With Crime, 1946
Woman to Woman, 1946
Mrs. Fitzherbert, 1947
Shadow of the Past, 1950

LESLIE HOWARD (1890-1943)
Distinguished, debonair leading
man of stage (1917) and screen,
typically cast as the intellectual
romantic; popular on both sides
of the Atlantic. Son: Ronald
Howard; Brother: Arthur
Howard. Also director.

The Heroine of Mons, 1914
The Happy Warrior, 1917
The Lackey and the Lady, 1919
The £5 Reward, 1920
Bookworms, 1920
Outward Bound, 1930
Never the Twain Shall Meet,
    1931
A Free Soul, 1931
Five and Ten, 1931
Devotion, 1931
Service For Ladies, 1932
Smilin' Through, 1932
The Animal Kingdom, 1932
Secrets, 1933
Captured, 1933
Berkeley Square, 1933
The Lady is Willing, 1934
Of Human Bondage, 1934
British Agent, 1934
The Scarlet Pimpernel, 1935
The Petrified Forest, 1936
Romeo and Juliet, 1936
It's Love I'm After, 1937
Stand-in, 1937
Intermezzo, 1938
Pygmalion, 1938
Gone With the Wind, 1939
Pimpernel Smith, 1941

49th Parallel, 1941
From the Corners, 1941
The First of the Few, 1942

RONALD HOWARD (1918-)
Actor of stage, films and tele-
vision; son of Leslie Howard,
nephew of Arthur Howard.
Famous on tv as "Sherlock
Holmes" (1958). Also former
sailor and journalist. Also
Hollywood.

Pimpernel Smith, 1941
While the Sun Shines, 1946
My Brother Jonathan, 1948
Night Beat, 1948
Bond Street, 1948
The Queen of Spades, 1949
Now Barabbas, 1949
Double Confession, 1950
Portrait of Clare, 1950
Flesh and Blood, 1950
The Browning Version, 1951
Tom Brown's School Days,
    1951
Assassin For Hire, 1951
Night Was Our Friend, 1951
Wide Boy, 1952
Street Corner, 1952
Black Orchid, 1952
Noose For a Lady, 1953
Glad Tidings, 1953
Flannelfoot, 1953
The World's a Stage, 1954
Rustle of Silk, 1955
Hideout, 1956
Drango, 1956
Light Fingers, 1957
Gideon's Day, 1957
The House in the Woods, 1957
Moment of Indiscretion, 1958
I Accuse, 1958
No Trees in the Street, 1958
Man Accused, 1959
Come September, 1960
Babette Goes to War, 1960
The Spider's Web, 1960
The Malpas Mystery, 1960
Compelled, 1960
The Monster of Highgate Ponds,
    1961

The Naked Edge, 1961
Bomb in the High Street, 1961
Murder She Said, 1962
The Spanish Sword, 1962
Fate Takes a Hand, 1962
Kil-1, 1962
Live Now Pay Later, 1962
Nurse On Wheels, 1963
The Bay of St. Michel, 1963
Siege of the Saxons, 1963
Curse of the Mummy's Tomb, 1964
You Must Be Joking!, 1965
Weekend at Dunkirk, 1966
Africa-Texas Style!, 1967
Run a Crooked Mile, 1969
The Hunting Party, 1971
Persecution, 1974
Take a Hard Ride, 1975

SYDNEY HOWARD (1884-1946)
Portly character comedian famous for unique gestures and stately manner, also on stage (since 1912). No relation to American playwright Sidney Howard (1891-1939).

Splinters, 1929
French Leave, 1930
Tilly of Bloomsbury, 1931
Almost a Divorce, 1931
Up For the Cup, 1931
Splinters in the Navy, 1931
The Mayor's Nest, 1932
It's a King, 1932
Up For the Derby, 1933
Night of the Garter, 1933
Trouble, 1933
Girls Please, 1934
Transatlantic Merry-Go-Round, 1934
It's a Cop, 1934
Where's George?, 1935
Fame, 1936
Chick, 1936
What a Man, 1937
Splinters in the Air, 1937
Shipyard Sally, 1939
Tilly of Bloomsbury, 1940
Once a Crook, 1941
Mr. Proudfoot Shows a Light, 1941

When We Are Married, 1943
Flight From Folly, 1945

TREVOR HOWARD (1916-)
Distinguished star and latterly character star of stage (from 1934) and films, usually seen as tough, reliable hero. Also in Hollywood. Married to Helen Cherry.

The Way Ahead, 1944
The Way to the Stars, 1945
Brief Encounter, 1945
I See a Dark Stranger, 1946
Green For Danger, 1946
They Made Me a Fugitive, 1947
So Well Remembered, 1947
The Passionate Friends, 1948
The Third Man, 1949
The Golden Salamander, 1950
Odette, 1950
The Clouded Yellow, 1951
Lady Godiva Rides Again, 1951
An Outcast of the Islands, 1952
The Gift Horse, 1952
The Heart of the Matter, 1953
The Lovers of Lisbon, 1954
The Stranger's Hand, 1954
Les Amants du Tage, 1955
Cockleshell Heroes, 1955
April in Portugal, 1955
Run For the Sun, 1956
Around the World in 80 Days, 1956
Interpol, 1957
Manuela, 1957
The Key, 1958
The Roots of Heaven, 1958
Moment of Danger, 1959
Sons and Lovers, 1960
The Lion, 1962
Mutiny On the Bounty, 1962
Man in the Middle, 1963
The Invincible Mr. Disraeli, 196
Father Goose, 1964
The Saboteur: Code Name Morituri, 1965
Von Ryan's Express, 1965
Operation Crossbow, 1965
Eagle in a Cage, 1965
The Poppy is Also a Flower,

1966
The Liquidator, 1966
Triple Cross, 1967
The Long Duel, 1967
Pretty Polly, 1967
Charge of the Light Brigade,
  1968
The Battle of Britain, 1969
Twinky, 1969
Ryan's Daughter, 1970
Catch Me a Spy, 1971
Mary Queen of Scots, 1971
The Night Visitor, 1971
Kidnapped, 1971
Something Like the Truth, 1972
Pope Joan, 1972
The Offence, 1972
Ludwig, 1972
Craze, 1973
Catholics, 1973
A Doll's House, 1973
Persecution, 1974
11 Harrowhouse, 1974
The Count of Monte Cristo,
  1975
Conduct Unbecoming, 1975
Hennessey, 1975
Who?, 1975
Bawdy Adventures of Tom
  Jones, 1975
Whispering Death, 1976
Eliza Fraser, 1976
Aces High, 1976
Last Remake of Beau Geste,
  1977
Slavers, 1977
Night of the Askari, 1978
Stevie, 1978
Superman, 1978
The Hurricane, 1979
Meteor, 1979
The Sea Wolves, 1980
Arch of Triumph, 1980
Sir Henry at Rawlinson End, 1980
The Wind Walker, 1980
Staying On, 1980

URSULA HOWELLS (1922-)
Character actress and supporting player of stage, films and
television, most active in the
fifties.

Flesh and Blood, 1951
I Believe in You, 1952
The Oracle, 1953
The Weak and the Wicked,
  1954
The Blakes Slept Here, 1954
The Gilded Cage, 1955
Track the Man Down, 1955
The Constant Husband, 1955
They Can't Hang Me, 1955
The Long Arm, 1956
Keep it Clean, 1956
Account Rendered, 1957
West of Suez, 1957
Death and the Sky Above, 1959
Two Letter Alibi, 1962
80,000 Suspects, 1963
The Sicilians 1964
Dr. Terror's House of Hor-
  rors, 1965
Assignment K, 1967
Mumsy, Nanny, Sonny and
  Girly, 1969
Crossplot, 1969

FRANKIE HOWERD (1921-)
Comic of stage (since 1935),
screen and television who
revels in eccentricity; also
famous on radio since 1946
(Variety Bandbox). In "The
Frankie Howerd Show," "That
Was the Week That Was," and
"Up Pompeii" on tv.

The Runaway Bus, 1954
An Alligator Named Daisy,
  1955
The Ladykillers, 1955
Jumping For Joy, 1955
A Touch of the Sun, 1956
Further Up the Creek, 1958
Watch it Sailor, 1961
The Fast Lady, 1962
The Cool Mikado, 1963
Mouse On the Moon, 1963
The Great St. Trinian's Train
  Robbery, 1966
Carry On Doctor, 1968
Carry On Up the Jungle, 1970
Up Pompeii, 1970
Up the Chastity Belt, 1971

Up the Front, 1972
The House in Nightmare Park,
   1973
Sergeant Pepper's Lonely
   Hearts Club Band, 1978

BOBBY HOWES (1895-1972)
Small, retiring actor and
singer of the thirties; former
acrobat (1909).   Father of
Sally Ann Howes.

On With the Dance, 1927
The Guns of Loos, 1928
Third Time Lucky, 1931
Lord Babs, 1932
For the Love of Mike, 1932
Over the Garden Wall, 1934
Please Teacher, 1937
Sweet Devil, 1938
Yes Madam, 1938
The Trojan Brothers, 1946
Happy Go Lovely, 1951
The Good Companions, 1957
Watch it Sailor, 1961

SALLY ANN HOWES (1930-)
Attractive leading lady and
former teenage performer of
the 40s, also on stage and tv.
Also in Hollywood.   Daughter
of Bobby Howes.

Thursday's Child, 1943
Halfway House, 1944
Dead of Night, 1945
Pink String and Sealing Wax,
   1945
Nicholas Nickleby, 1947
My Sister and I, 1948
Anna Karenina, 1948
The History of Mr. Polly,
   1949
Fools Rush In, 1949
Stop Press Girl, 1950
Honeymoon Deferred, 1951
The Admirable Crichton, 1957
Chitty Chitty Bang Bang, 1968
Hound of the Baskervilles,
   1972
Death Ship, 1980

NOEL HOWLETT (1901-)
Character actor of stage and
screen, typically seen in
cameo roles.   On tv in "The
Forsyte Saga."

Men Are Not Gods, 1936
A Yank at Oxford, 1938
George and Margaret, 1940
Corridor of Mirrors, 1947
This Was a Woman, 1947
Scott of the Antarctic, 1948
The Blind Goddess, 1949
Saraband For Dead Lovers,
   1949
Once Upon a Dream, 1949
Eyewitness, 1950
Father Brown, 1954
Lust For Life, 1956
The Scapegoat, 1959
Battle of the Sexes, 1959
Serious Charge, 1959
You'll Never See Me Again,
   1959
Victim, 1961
Kiss of the Vampire, 1962
Woman of Straw, 1964
Some Will, Some Won't, 1970

WALTER HUDD (1898-1963)
Character actor and occasional
leading man, also on stage;
generally portrayed indifferent
characters.

Moscow Nights, 1935
Rembrandt, 1936
Elephant Boy, 1937
Black Limelight, 1938
The Housemaster, 1938
The Outsider, 1939
Two Minutes, 1939
Dead Man's Shoes, 1939
Dr. O'Dowd, 1940
Major Barbara, 1941
Uncensored, 1942
Love Story, 1944
I Know Where I'm Going, 1945
I Live in Grosvenor Square,
   1945
A Lady Surrenders, 1947
Escape, 1948

Paper Orchid, 1949
Landfall, 1949
The Importance of Being
  Earnest, 1952
Cosh Boy, 1953
All Hallowe'en, 1953
The Good Die Young, 1954
Cast a Dark Shadow, 1955
The Last Man to Hang, 1956
Satellite in the Sky, 1956
Loser Takes All, 1956
Reach For the Sky, 1956
Further Up the Creek, 1958
The Two-Headed Spy, 1958
The Man Upstairs, 1959
Two-Way Stretch, 1960
Sink the Bismarck, 1960
Life For Ruth, 1962
The Prince and the Pauper,
  1962
The Punch and Judy Man, 1963
It's All Happening, 1963

RODDY HUGHES (1891-)
Portly Welsh character star of
stage and films, often seen in
comedy characterizations.

A Glimpse of Paradise, 1934
Kentucky Minstrels, 1934
Lest We Forget, 1934
The Old Curiosity Shop, 1934
Breakers Ahead, 1935
The Small Man, 1935
A Real Bloke, 1935
Cock O' the North, 1935
River House Mystery, 1935
Cheer Up, 1936
Men of Yesterday, 1936
The House of Silence, 1937
Captain's Orders, 1937
Confidence Tricksters, 1938
In Your Garden, 1938
The Stars Look Down, 1939
Old Mother Riley in Business,
  1940
The Ghost of St. Michael's,
  1941
Hatter's Castle, 1941
Quiet Wedding, 1941
Here Comes the Sun, 1945
Nicholas Nickleby, 1947

So Well Remembered, 1947
The Dark Road, 1948
The Last Days of Dolwyn, 1949
The Hidden Room, 1950
Scrooge, 1951
The Man in the White Suit,
  1951
Old Mother Riley's Jungle
  Treasure, 1951
Salute the Toff, 1952
Hammer the Toff, 1952
Escape Route, 1953
Alf's Baby, 1953
The Lark Still Sings, 1954
Mystery On Bird Island, 1954
One Jump Ahead, 1955
See How They Run, 1955
Not So Dusty, 1956
Sea Wife, 1957
The Spaniard's Curse, 1958
The House in Marsh Road,
  1960

CLAUDE HULBERT (1900-
  1964)
Popular comedian of the thirties, also on stage (from
1920); brother of Jack Hulbert.

Champagne, 1928
Naughty Husbands, 1930
A Night Like This, 1932
The Mayor's Nest, 1932
Thark, 1932
The Face at the Window, 1932
Let Me Explain Dear, 1933
Their Night Out, 1933
Radio Parade, 1933
Heads We Go, 1933
The Song You Gave Me, 1933
The Girl in Possession, 1934
A Cup of Kindness, 1934
Lillies of the Field, 1934
Big Business, 1934
Bulldog Jack, 1935
Hello Sweetheart, 1935
Man of the Moment, 1935
Wolf's Clothing, 1936
Where's Sally?, 1936
Interrupted Honeymoon, 1936
Hail and Farewell, 1936
Honeymoon Merry-Go-Round,

1936
Take a Chance, 1937
The Vulture, 1937
It's Not Cricket, 1937
Ship's Concert, 1937
You Live and Learn, 1937
Simply Terrific, 1938
The Viper, 1938
It's in the Blood, 1938
His Lordship Regrets, 1938
Many Tanks Mr. Atkins, 1938
Sailors Three, 1940
The Ghost of St. Michael's,
   1941
The Dummy Talks, 1943
My Learned Friend, 1943
London Town, 1946
Ghosts of Berkeley Square,
   1947
Under the Frozen Falls, 1948
Cardboard Cavalier, 1949
Fun at St. Fanny's, 1956
Not a Hope in Hell, 1960

JACK HULBERT (1892-1978)
Popular light comedy star of
the 30s, also on stage (from
1911); long in association with
his wife Dame Cicely Courtneidge. Brother: Claude
Hulbert.

Elstree Calling, 1930
The Ghost Train, 1931
Sunshine Susie, 1931
Jack's the Boy, 1932
Love On Wheels, 1932
Happy Ever After, 1932
Falling For You, 1933
Jack Ahoy, 1934
The Camels Are Coming, 1934
Bulldog Jack, 1935
Jack of All Trades, 1936
Take My Tip, 1937
Paradise For Two, 1937
Kate Plus Ten, 1938
Under Your Hat, 1951
Into the Blue, 1951
The Magic Box, 1951
Miss Tulip Stays the Night,
   1955
Spider's Web, 1960

The Cherry Picker, 1972
Not Now Darling, 1973

BENITA HUME (1906-1967)
Leading actress of the 30s,
also on stage (from 1923). In
Hollywood from 1935. Married
to Ronald Colman; George
Sanders.

The Happy Ending, 1925
Her Golden Hair Was Hanging
   Down, 1925
They Wouldn't Believe Me,
   1925
Second to None, 1926
Easy Virtue, 1927
The Constant Nymph, 1928
The South Sea Bubble, 1928
The Wrecker, 1928
The Light Woman, 1928
Lady of the Lake, 1928
Balaclava, 1928
The Clue of the New Pin, 1929
High Treason, 1929
The House of the Arrow, 1930
Symphony in Two Flats, 1930
The Flying Fool, 1931
A Honeymoon Adventure, 1931
The Happy Ending, 1931
Sally Bishop, 1932
Service For Ladies, 1932
Women Who Play, 1932
Help Yourself, 1932
Men of Steel, 1932
Diamond Cut Diamond, 1932
Lord Camber's Ladies, 1932
Discord, 1933
The Little Damozel, 1933
The Worst Woman in Paris,
   1933
Looking Forward, 1933
Only Yesterday, 1933
Gambling Ship, 1933
Clear All Wires, 1933
The Private Life of Don Juan,
   1934
Jew Suss, 1934
The Divine Spark, 1935
The Gay Deception, 1935
18 Minutes, 1935
The Garden Murder Case, 1936

Tarzan Escapes, 1936
Moonlight Murder, 1936
Suzy, 1936
Rainbow On the River, 1936
The Last of Mrs. Cheyney,
    1937
Peck's Bad Boy With the
    Circus, 1938

MARTITA HUNT (1900-1969)
Classical character actress of
stage (since 1921) and films,
also occasionally in Hollywood.
Memorable in eccentric characterizations.

A Rank Outsider, 1920
Love On Wheels, 1932
Service For Ladies, 1932
I Was a Spy, 1933
Friday the Thirteenth, 1933
Too Many Millions, 1934
Mr. What's His Name, 1935
The Case of Gabriel Perry,
    1935
When Knights Were Bold, 1936
First a Girl, 1936
Pot Luck, 1936
Tudor Rose, 1936
Interrupted Honeymoon, 1936
Sabotage, 1936
Good Morning Boys, 1937
Farewell Again, 1937
The Mill On the Floss, 1937
Second Best Bed, 1938
Strange Boarders, 1938
Prison Without Bars, 1938
Spare a Copper, 1939
The Nursemaid Who Disap-
    peared, 1939
Trouble Brewing, 1939
A Girl Must Live, 1939
The Good Old Days, 1939
Young Man's Fancy, 1939
At the Villa Rose, 1939
Old Mother Riley Joins Up,
    1939
The Middle Watch, 1939
Tilly of Bloomsbury, 1940
Miss Grant Goes to the Door,
    1940
Freedom Radio, 1941

The Seventh Survivor, 1941
They Flew Alone, 1942
Sabotage at Sea, 1942
The Man in Grey, 1943
Welcome Mr. Washington, 1944
The Wicked Lady, 1945
Great Expectations, 1946
The Little Ballerina, 1947
Ghosts of Berkeley Square,
    1947
So Evil My Love, 1948
My Sister and I, 1948
Anna Karenina, 1948
The Fan, 1949
Treasure Hunt, 1952
The Story of Robin Hood, 1952
Meet Me Tonight, 1952
It Started in Paradise, 1952
Folly to Be Wise, 1952
Melba, 1953
King's Rhapsody, 1955
Anastasia, 1956
The March Hare, 1956
Three Men in a Boat, 1956
Dangerous Exile, 1957
The Admirable Crichton, 1957
Bonjour Tristesse, 1958
Me and the Colonel, 1958
Bottoms Up, 1960
The Brides of Dracula, 1960
Song Without End, 1960
Mr. Topaze, 1962
The Wonderful World of the
    Brothers Grimm, 1963
The Unsinkable Molly Brown,
    1964
Becket, 1964
Bunny Lake is Missing, 1965
The Best House in London,
    1969

IAN HUNTER (1900-1976)
South-African born leading
actor of stage (since 1919)
and screen, also quite frequently in Hollywood. Almost
always seen in friendly, dependable roles.

Mr. Oddy, 1922
Not For Sale, 1924
Confessions, 1925

A Girl of London, 1926
Downhill, 1927
Easy Virtue, 1927
The Ring, 1927
His House in Order, 1928
The Physician, 1928
Thoroughbred, 1928
Valley of the Ghosts, 1929
Syncopation, 1929
Escape, 1930
Cape Forlorn, 1931
Sally in Our Alley, 1931
Something Always Happens,
   1931
The Water Gypsies, 1932
The Sign of Four, 1932
Marry Me, 1932
The Man From Toronto, 1933
Orders is Orders, 1933
Skipper of the Osprey, 1933
Silver Spoon, 1934
Night of the Party, 1934
The Church Mouse, 1934
No Escape, 1934
Death at Broadcasting House,
   1934
A Midsummer Night's Dream,
   1935
Jalna, 1935
The Girl From 10th Avenue,
   1935
I Found Stella Parrish, 1935
The Phantom Light, 1935
Lazybones, 1935
The Morals of Marcus, 1935
The White Angel, 1936
To Mary With Love, 1936
The Devil is a Sissy, 1936
Stolen Holiday, 1937
Call it a Day, 1937
Another Dawn, 1937
Confession, 1937
That Certain Woman, 1937
Always Goodbye, 1938
Secrets of an Actress, 1938
The Adventures of Robin Hood,
   1938
52nd Street, 1938
The Sisters, 1938
Comet Over Broadway, 1938
Tower of London, 1939
Yes My Darling Daughter,
   1939

The Little Princess, 1939
Maisie, 1939
Broadway Serenade, 1939
Tarzan Finds a Son, 1939
Broadway Melody of 1940,
   1940
Dulcy, 1940
Gallant Sons, 1940
The Long Voyage Home, 1940
Bittersweet, 1940
Strange Cargo, 1940
Dr. Jekyll and Mr. Hyde,
   1941
Billy the Kid, 1941
Come Live With Me, 1941
Andy Hardy's Private Secre-
   tary, 1941
Ziegfeld Girl, 1941
Smilin' Through, 1941
A Yank at Eton, 1942
It Comes Up Love, 1943
Forever and a Day, 1943
Bedelia, 1946
White Cradle Inn, 1947
The White Unicorn, 1947
Edward My Son, 1949
Hunted, 1951
It Started in Paradise, 1952
Appointment in London, 1953
Don't Blame the Stork, 1953
Eight O'Clock Walk, 1954
Battle of the River Plate, 1956
Door in the Wall, 1956
Fortune is a Woman, 1957
Rockets Galore, 1958
Northwest Frontier, 1959
The Bulldog Breed, 1960
Dr. Blood's Coffin, 1961
The Queen's Guards, 1961
Guns of Darkness, 1962
Treasure of Monte Cristo,
   1963
Act of Love, 1964

RAYMOND HUNTLEY
   (1904-   )
Character star of stage (from
1922), screen, and television;
often cast in haughty or con-
temptuous roles.

Can You Hear Me Mother?,

1935
Rembrandt, 1936
Whom the Gods Love, 1936
Knight Without Armour, 1937
Dinner at the Ritz, 1937
Night Train to Munich, 1940
The Ghost of St. Michael's,
   1941
Freedom Radio, 1941
Inspector Hornleigh Goes to
   It, 1941
The Ghost Train, 1941
Once a Crook, 1941
They Came to a City, 1941
Pimpernel Smith, 1941
When We Are Married, 1943
The Way Ahead, 1944
I See a Dark Stranger, 1946
School For Secrets, 1946
So Evil My Love, 1948
They Gave Him the Works,
   1948
Broken Journey, 1948
It's Hard to Be Good, 1949
Passport to Pimlico, 1949
Mr. Perrin and Mr. Traill,
   1949
Trio, 1950
The Long Dark Hall, 1950
The Dark Page, 1951
The House in the Square, 1951
Mr. Denning Drives North,
   1952
The Last Page, 1952
Laxdale Hall, 1953
Glad Tidings, 1953
Meet Mr. Lucifer, 1953
Hobson's Choice, 1954
The Teckman Mystery, 1954
Orders Are Orders, 1955
The Dam Busters, 1955
The Constant Husband, 1955
The Prisoner, 1955
Doctor at Sea, 1955
Geordie, 1955
The Last Man to Hang, 1956
The Green Man, 1956
Town On Trial, 1957
Brothers in Law, 1957
Next to No Time, 1958
Room at the Top, 1959
Carleton Brown of the FO,
   1959

Innocent Meeting, 1959
The Mummy, 1959
Carry On Nurse, 1959
I'm All Right, Jack, 1959
Bottoms Up, 1960
Sands of the Desert, 1960
Make Mine Mink, 1960
Follow That Horse, 1960
Our Man in Havana, 1960
A French Mistress, 1960
Suspect, 1961
Pure Hell of St. Trinian's,
   1961
Only Two Can Play, 1962
Waltz of the Toreadors, 1962
On the Beat, 1962
Crooks Anonymous, 1962
Nurse On Wheels, 1963
The Yellow Teddybears, 1963
Father Came Too, 1963
The Black Torment, 1964
Rotten to the Core, 1965
The Great St. Trinian's Train
   Robbery, 1966
Hostile Witness, 1968
The Adding Machine, 1969
Destiny of a Spy, 1969
Young Winston, 1972
That's Your Funeral, 1973
Symptoms, 1974

RICHARD HURNDALL (1910-)
Distinctive character player
of stage, films, and tv.
Films very occasional.

Joanna, 1967
Hostile Witness, 1968
Zeppelin, 1971
I Monster, 1971
Lady Caroline Lamb, 1972
Royal Flash, 1975

DAVID HURST (1925-)
Austrian actor of stage and
screen, mainly cast in comedy
roles.

The Perfect Woman, 1949
Tony Draws a Horse, 1950
Mother Riley Meets the

Vampire, 1952
So Little Time, 1952
As Long As They're Happy, 1953
Always a Bride, 1953
Rough Shoot, 1953
River Beat, 1954
Mad About Men, 1954
One Good Turn, 1954
All For Mary, 1955
The Intimate Stranger, 1956
After the Ball, 1957
Hello Dolly, 1969

VERONICA HURST (1931-)
Attractive light leading actress of the fifties, also in Hollywood. Married to William Sylvester.

Laughter in Paradise, 1951
Here's to the Memory, 1951
Angels One Five, 1952
The Yellow Balloon, 1952
Will Any Gentleman, 1953
The Girl On the Pier, 1953
The Maze, 1953
Don't Blame the Stork, 1954
Bang You're Dead, 1954
The Gilded Cage, 1955
Peeping Tom, 1960
Dead Man's Evidence, 1962
Live it Up, 1963
Licensed to Kill, 1965
The Boy Cried Murder, 1966

JOHN HURT (1940-)
Unconventional leading and supporting actor of stage and screen, also on television.

The Wild and the Willing, 1962
This is My Street, 1963
A Man For All Seasons, 1966
Sailor From Gibraltar, 1967
Before Winter Comes, 1968
Sinful Davy, 1969
In Search of Gregory, 1970
10 Rillington Place, 1971
Cry of the Penguins, 1972
The Pied Piper, 1972

Little Malcolm and His Struggle, 1974
The Naked Civil Servant, 1975
The Disappearance, 1977
The Shout, 1978
Midnight Express, 1978
Watership Down (voice), 1978
Alien, 1979
Heaven's Gate, 1980
Crime and Punishment, 1980
The Elephant Man, 1980
A Wind to the West, 1981

OLIVIA HUSSEY (1951-)
Leading lady of the 60s and 70s, also on television. Now in international films.

Battle of the Villa Fiorita, 1965
Cup Fever, 1965
Romeo and Juliet, 1968
All the Right Noises, 1970
Lost Horizon, 1973
Summertime Killer, 1973
Black Christmas, 1974
The Cat and the Canary, 1977
Jesus of Nazareth, 1977
Death On the Nile, 1978
The Man with Bogart's Face, 1980

DAVID HUTCHESON (1905-)
Monocled character of stage and films, primarily in comedy parts.

Fast and Loose, 1930
Romance in Rhythm, 1934
The Love Test, 1935
Wedding Group, 1936
This'll Make You Whistle, 1936
The Sky's the Limit, 1937
A Gentleman's Gentleman, 1939
She Couldn't Say No, 1939
Lucky to Me, 1939
The Middle Watch, 1939
Bulldog Sees it Through, 1940
Convoy, 1940
Sabotage at Sea, 1942
Next of Kin, 1942
The Life & Death of Colonel Blimp, 1943

The Hundred Pound Window,
   1944
School For Secrets, 1946
The Trojan Brothers, 1946
Vice Versa, 1948
Woman Hater, 1948
Sleeping Car to Trieste, 1948
Madness of the Heart, 1949
My Daughter Joy, 1950
The Elusive Pimpernel, 1950
Circle of Danger, 1951
No Highway, 1951
Encore, 1952
Something Money Can't Buy,
   1952
Law and Disorder, 1958
The Evil of Frankenstein, 1964
The National Health, 1973

HARRY HUTCHINSON (1892-)
Irish character player, usually
seen in cameo roles; films
sporadic. Also on stage.

The Silver Greyhound, 1932
The Door With Seven Locks,
   1940
I See a Dark Stranger, 1946
Dublin Nightmare, 1958
Blow Up, 1966
A Clockwork Orange, 1971
Gumshoe, 1971
The Gambler, 1974

HAROLD HUTH (1892-1967)
Suave character actor equally
adept at heroes and villainous
roles alike; former car salesman. Also later director and
producer.

One of the Best, 1927
Sir or Madam, 1928
A South Sea Bubble, 1928
Balaclava, 1928
Triumph of the Scarlet Pimper-
   nel, 1928
The Silver King, 1929
Downstream, 1929
City of Play, 1929
Leave it to Me, 1930

Hours of Loneliness, 1930
An Obvious Situation, 1930
Jaws of Hell, 1931
The Outsider, 1931
Guilt, 1931
Bracelets, 1931
A Honeymoon Adventure, 1931
Down River, 1931
Women Who Play, 1932
The First Mrs. Fraser, 1932
Aren't We All, 1932
Rome Express, 1932
Sally Bishop, 1932
The World, the Flesh & the
   Devil, 1932
The Flying Squad, 1932
Discord, 1933
The Ghoul, 1933
My Lucky Stars, 1933
The Camels Are Coming, 1934
Take My Tip, 1937
This Was Paris, 1942

WILFRID HYDE-WHITE
   (1903-)
Polished, impeccable character
star of stage (from 1922),
screen and television; also in
Hollywood. Equally outstanding
in comedy and villainous characterizations. Latterly seen on
tv in series "The Associates."

Josser On the Farm, 1934
Night Mail, 1935
Admirals All, 1935
Alibi Inn, 1935
Smith's Wives, 1935
Rembrandt, 1936
Servants All, 1936
Murder By Rope, 1937
The Scarab Murder Case, 1937
Bulldog Drummond at Bay, 1937
Elephant Boy, 1937
Change For a Sovereign, 1938
Meet Mr. Penny, 1938
I've Got a Horse, 1938
The Lambeth Walk, 1939
Poison Pen, 1939
Turned Out Nice Again, 1941
Lady From Lisbon, 1942
Asking For Trouble, 1943

The Demi-Paradise, 1943
Night Boat to Dublin, 1946
Appointment With Crime, 1946
Wanted For Murder, 1946
Meet Me at Dawn, 1947
While the Sun Shines, 1947
Ghosts of Berkeley Square,
   1947
Bond Street, 1948
My Brother Jonathan, 1948
My Brother's Keeper, 1948
The Winslow Boy, 1948
Quartet, 1948
The Passionate Friends, 1948
The Bad Lord Byron, 1948
Britannia Mews, 1949
Adam and Evalyne, 1949
That Dangerous Age, 1949
Helter Skelter, 1949
The Third Man, 1949
The Man On the Eiffel Tower,
   1950
Conspirator, 1950
The Golden Salamander, 1950
The Angel With the Trumpet,
   1950
Last Holiday, 1950
Trio, 1950
The Mudlark, 1950
Highly Dangerous, 1950
Midnight Episode, 1950
Blackmailed, 1951
The Browning Version, 1951
Mr. Drake's Duck, 1951
No Highway, 1951
Mr. Denning Drives North,
   1951
An Outcast of the Islands,
   1952
The Card, 1952
Top Secret, 1952
Gilbert and Sullivan, 1953
The Triangle, 1953
The Million Pound Note, 1954
The Rainbow Jacket, 1954
Duel in the Jungle, 1954
Betrayed, 1954
To Dorothy a Son, 1954
See How They Run, 1955
Midnight Escape, 1955
John and Julie, 1955
Quentin Durward, 1955
The March Hare, 1956

My Teenage Daughter, 1956
The Silken Affair, 1956
Mrs. Gilling & the Skyscraper,
   1957
City After Midnight, 1957
That Woman Opposite, 1957
Vicious Circle, 1957
Tarzan and the Lost Safari,
   1957
The Truth About Women, 1958
Up the Creek, 1958
Wonderful Things, 1958
The Lady is a Square, 1959
Carry On Nurse, 1959
Life in Emergency Ward 10,
   1959
Libel, 1959
Northwest Frontier, 1959
Two-Way Stretch, 1960
Let's Make Love, 1960
His and Hers, 1961
On the Fiddle, 1961
On the Double, 1961
Ada, 1961
Crooks Anonymous, 1962
In Search of the Castaways,
   1962
Aliki-My Love, 1963
John Goldfarb Please Come
   Home, 1964
My Fair Lady, 1964
You Must Be Joking!, 1965
Ten Little Indians, 1965
The Liquidator, 1966
Chamber of Horrors, 1966
Our Man in Marrakesh, 1966
The Sandwich Man, 1966
You Only Live Twice, 1967
Sumuru, 1967
P.J., 1968
The Sunshine Patriot, 1968
Gaily, Gaily, 1969
Run a Crooked Mile, 1969
Fear No Evil, 1969
The Magic Christian, 1970
Skullduggery, 1970
Ritual of Evil, 1970
Fragment of Fear, 1970
Cool Million, 1971
The Cherry Picker, 1972
A Brand New Life, 1973
King Solomon's Treasure,
   1976

The Great Houdini, 1976
The Cat and the Canary, 1977
No Longer Alone, 1978
Battlestar Galactica, 1978
The Rebels, 1979
Scout's Honor, 1980
In God We Trust, 1980
Father Damien: The Leper Priest,
    1980

JANE HYLTON (1926-1979)
Attractive actress of stage
(since 1945) and films; married
to Peter Dyneley.

Daybreak, 1946
A Girl in a Million, 1946
Dear Murderer, 1947
The Upturned Glass, 1947
Holiday Camp, 1947
It Always Rains On Sunday,
    1947
When the Bough Breaks, 1947
My Sister and I, 1948
My Brother's Keeper, 1948
Here Come the Huggetts, 1948
Passport to Pimlico, 1949
Dance Hall, 1950
The Quiet Woman, 1951
Out of True, 1951
Tall Headlines, 1952
It Started in Paradise, 1952
The Weak and the Wicked,
    1954
Burnt Evidence, 1954
Secret Venture, 1955
Laughing in the Sunshine, 1955
You Pay Your Money, 1957
Violent Moment, 1957
Deadly Record, 1959
Devil's Bait, 1959
Night Train For Inverness,
    1960
Circus of Horrors, 1960
House of Mystery, 1961
Bitter Harvest, 1963
The Wild Geese, 1978

DOROTHY HYSON (1915-   )
Attractive actress of the 30s,
also much on stage. Married to
Robert Douglas; Anthony Quayle.

Soldiers of the King, 1933
The Ghoul, 1933
That's a Good Girl, 1933
Turkey Time, 1933
Happy, 1934
A Cup of Kindness, 1934
Sing as We Go, 1934
The Woman in Command, 1934
Spare a Copper, 1939
Now You're Talking, 1940
You Will Remember, 1940

OLAF HYTTEN (1888-1955)
Scottish character actor who
began in silent films; went to
Hollywood in the late 20s and
remained to play innumerable
small parts.

Demos, 1921
Knave of Diamonds, 1921
The Girl Who Came Back,
    1921
Sonia, 1921
Money, 1921
Miss Charity, 1921
Knight Errant, 1922
The Wonderful Story, 1922
Trapped By the Mormons,
    1922
The Bride of Lammermoor,
    1922
Sir Rupert's Wife, 1922
The Crimson Circle, 1922
The Missioner, 1922
His Wife's Husband, 1922
The Stockbroker's Clerk, 1922
The Cause of All That Trouble,
    1923
A Gamble With Hearts, 1923
Little Door Into the World,
    1923
Out to Win, 1923
Chu Chin Chow, 1923
The Reverse of the Medal,
    1923
The White Shadow, 1924
It is the Law, 1924
The Salvation Hunters, 1927
Kitty, 1929
Master and Man, 1929
City of Play, 1929
Grumpy, 1930

Daughter of the Dragon, 1931
Berkeley Square, 1933
Becky Sharp, 1935
The Dark Angel, 1935
Les Miserables, 1935
White Hunter, 1936
The Good Earth, 1937
I Cover the War, 1937
First a Lady, 1937
Adventures of Robin Hood,
1938
The Lone Wolf in Paris, 1938
Marie Antoinette, 1938
Andy Hardy Gets Spring Fever,
1939
Our Leading Citizen, 1939
Rulers of the Sea, 1939
Allegheny Uprising, 1939
Our Neighbours the Carters,
1940
That Hamilton Woman, 1941
Washington Melodrama, 1941
The Black Swan, 1942
Bedtime Story, 1942
The Ghost of Frankenstein,
1942
The Great Commandment,
1942
Destination Unknown, 1942
Sherlock Holmes and the Voice
of Terror, 1942
This Above All, 1942
Casablanca, 1942
Eagle Squadron, 1942
Son of Fury, 1942
Sherlock Holmes Faces Death,
1943
The Lodger, 1944
The Scarlet Claw, 1944
My Name is Julia Ross, 1945
The Brighton Strangler, 1945
Pursuit to Algiers, 1945
Black Beauty, 1946
Three Strangers, 1946
Dressed to Kill, 1946
That Way With Women, 1947
Kim, 1950
Perils of the Jungle, 1953

PETER ILLING (1899-1966)
German-born character player,
long in Britain; usually seen

in explosive or easily agitated
roles.

The End of the River, 1946
Eureka Stockade, 1948
Against the Wind, 1948
Madness of the Heart, 1949
Floodtide, 1949
State Secret, 1950
My Daughter Joy, 1950
I'll Get You For This, 1951
Stakes, 1951
24 Hours of a Woman's Life,
1952
An Outcast of the Islands,
1952
Never Let Me Go, 1953
Innocents in Paris, 1953
Mask of Dust, 1954
The Young Lovers, 1954
Flame and the Flesh, 1954
House Across the Lake, 1954
Svengali, 1955
West of Zanzibar, 1955
That Lady, 1955
Battle of the River Plate, 1956
Zarak, 1956
Bhowani Junction, 1956
Passport to Treason, 1956
Loser Takes All, 1956
Miracle in Soho, 1957
Man in the Shadow, 1957
Manuela, 1957
Interpol, 1957
Campbell's Kingdom, 1957
Fire Down Below, 1957
I Accuse, 1958
Escapement, 1958
The Angry Hills, 1959
Friends and Neighbours, 1959
Whirlpool, 1959
Sands of the Desert, 1960
Moment of Danger, 1960
Bluebeard's Ten Honeymoons,
1960
The Middle Course, 1961
The Secret Partner, 1961
Village of Daughters, 1962
The Devil's Daffodil, 1962
Nine Hours to Rama, 1963
Echo of Diana, 1963
Devils of Darkness, 1964
The Secret Door, 1964

A Man Could Get Killed, 1965
The 25th Hour, 1966

FRIEDA INESCORT (1901-
    1976)
Dark-haired leading lady and
supporting star of stage (1922)
and films, usually cast in well-
bred or dignified roles.   Film
career in Hollywood.

If You Could Only Cook, 1935
The Dark Angel, 1935
The Garden Murder Case,
    1936
The King Steps Out, 1936
Mary of Scotland, 1936
Give Me Your Heart, 1936
Hollywood Boulevard, 1936
The Great O'Malley, 1937
Portia On Trial, 1937
Call it a Day, 1937
Another Dawn, 1937
Beauty For the Asking, 1938
Woman Doctor, 1939
Tarzan Finds a Son, 1939
Zero Hour, 1939
A Woman is the Judge, 1939
Pride and Prejudice, 1940
Convicted Woman, 1940
The Letter, 1940
Sunny, 1941
Father's Son, 1941
The Trial of Mary Dugan,
    1941
You'll Never Get Rich, 1941
Remember the Day, 1941
Courtship of Andy Hardy, 1942
Street of Chance, 1942
Sweater Girl, 1942
It Comes Up Love, 1943
Return of the Vampire, 1943
The Amazing Mrs. Halliday,
    1943
Heavenly Days, 1944
The Judge Steps Out, 1947
Underworld Story, 1950
A Place in the Sun, 1951
Never Wave at a Wac, 1953
Casanova's Big Night, 1954
Foxfire, 1955
The Eddie Duchin Story, 1956

Flame of the Islands, 1956
Darby's Rangers, 1958
The Alligator People, 1959
The Crowded Sky, 1960

BARRIE INGHAM (1934-)
Light leading actor and supporting player of stage and
screen in occasional films.

Tiara Tahiti, 1962
Invasion, 1966
Dr. Who and the Daleks, 1966
Challenge For Robin Hood, 1968
Day of the Jackal, 1973

JILL IRELAND (1936-)
Attractive leading lady, now in
international films.   Married:
David McCallum; Charles
Bronson.

Oh Rosalinda, 1955
Three Men in a Boat, 1956
The Big Money, 1956
Hell Drivers, 1957
There's Always a Thursday,
    1957
Robbery Under Arms, 1957
The Desperate Man, 1959
The Ghost Train Murder, 1959
Carry On Nurse, 1959
Girls of Latin Quarter, 1960
Raising the Wind, 1961
So Evil So Young, 1961
Jungle Street, 1961
Twice Round the Daffodils,
    1962
Battleaxe, 1962
Villa Rides, 1968
Rider On the Rain, 1970
The Family, 1970
Cold Sweat, 1970
Someone Behind the Door,
    1971
The Mechanic, 1972
Wild Horses, 1973
Chino, 1973
The Valachi Papers, 1973
Breakout, 1975
Hard Times, 1975

Breakheart Pass, 1976
From Noon Till Three, 1976
Love and Bullets, 1979
The Girl, the Gold Watch, and
    Everything, 1980

ELLIS IRVING (1902-   )
General purpose actor and
character star of stage and
screen, married to Sophie
Stewart.

The Bermondsey Kid, 1933
Nine Forty-Five, 1934
Murder at Monte Carlo, 1935
The Black Mask, 1935
As You Like It, 1936
Member of the Jury, 1937
The Sea Hawk, 1940
Variety Jubilee, 1943
Strawberry Roan, 1945
Murder in Reverse, 1945
I'll Turn to You, 1946
Green Fingers, 1947
Rough Shoot, 1953
Strictly Confidential, 1959

FREDA JACKSON (1909-   )
Melodramatic character actress
of stage (since 1934), films and
television, usually seen in mean
characterizations.

Mountains O' Mourne, 1938
A Canterbury Tale, 1943
Henry V, 1944
Beware of Pity, 1946
Great Expectations, 1946
No Room at the Inn, 1948
Mr. Denning Drives North,
    1951
Flesh and Blood, 1951
Women of Twilight, 1952
The Good Die Young, 1954
The Crowded Day, 1954
The Enchanted Doll, 1955
The Last Man to Hang, 1956
Bhowani Junction, 1956
The Flesh is Weak, 1957
A Tale of Two Cities, 1958
The Brides of Dracula, 1960

Greyfriars Bobby, 1960
Attempt to Kill, 1961
Shadow of the Cat, 1961
Tom Jones, 1963
West Eleven, 1963
The Third Secret, 1964
Boy With a Flute, 1964
Monster of Terror, 1965
The Jokers, 1966
The Valley of Gwangi, 1969
She Fell Among Thieves, 1980

GLENDA JACKSON (1936-   )
Dominant leading lady of stage
(from 1957) and screen, now
in international films. Also
excellent on tv as "Elizabeth
R" (1971).

Marat/Sade, 1966
Benefit of the Doubt, 1967
Tell Me Lies, 1968
Negatives, 1968
Women in Love, 1969
The Music Lovers, 1970
Sunday Bloody Sunday, 1971
The Boy Friend, 1971
Mary Queen of Scots, 1971
Triple Echo, 1972
A Touch of Class, 1972
Bequest to the Nation, 1973
The Maids, 1974
The Tempter, 1974
The Devil is a Woman, 1975
The Romantic Englishwoman,
    1975
Hedda, 1975
Nasty Habits, 1976
The Incredible Sarah, 1976
Stevie, 1978
House Calls, 1978
Lost and Found, 1979
Health, 1979
The Class of Miss MacMichael,
    1979
Hopscotch, 1980

GORDON JACKSON (1923-   )
Friendly Scottish character
star of stage and screen, also
on radio (from 1939). Married

to Rona Anderson. Also popular on television as Hudson, the butler, in "Upstairs Downstairs. "

The Foreman Went to France, 1942
Nine Men, 1943
Millions Like Us, 1943
San Demetrio-London, 1943
Pink String and Sealing Wax, 1945
The Captive Heart, 1946
Against the Wind, 1948
Eureka Stockade, 1948
Whiskey Galore, 1948
Floodtide, 1949
Stop Press Girl, 1949
Bitter Springs, 1950
Happy Go Lovely, 1951
Lady With a Lamp, 1951
Castle in the Air, 1952
Death Goes to School, 1953
Malta Story, 1953
Meet Mr. Lucifer, 1953
The Love Lottery, 1954
The Delavine Affair, 1954
Passage Home, 1955
Windfall, 1955
The Quatermass Experiment, 1955
Pacific Destiny, 1956
Women Without Men, 1956
The Baby & the Battleship, 1956
Sailor Beware, 1956
Seven Waves Away, 1957
Let's Be Happy, 1957
Hell Drivers, 1957
Black Ice, 1957
Man in the Shadow, 1957
Blind Spot, 1958
Rockets Galore, 1958
Three Crooked Men, 1958
Yesterday's Enemy, 1959
The Bridal Path, 1959
Blind Date, 1959
The Navy Lark, 1959
Devil's Bait, 1959
The Price of Silence, 1960
Cone of Silence, 1960
Snowball, 1960
Tunes of Glory, 1960
Greyfriars Bobby, 1960

Two Wives at One Wedding, 1961
Mutiny On the Bounty, 1962
The Great Escape, 1963
The Long Ships, 1964
Daylight Robbery, 1964
Those Magnificent Men in Their Flying Machines, 1965
The Ipcress File, 1965
Cast a Giant Shadow, 1966
Fighting Prince of Donegal, 1966
Night of the Generals, 1966
Triple Cross, 1967
Danger Route, 1967
The Eliminator, 1968
Negatives, 1968
On the Run, 1969
The Prime of Miss Jean Brodie, 1969
Run Wild Run Free, 1969
Hamlet, 1970
Scrooge, 1970
The Music Lovers, 1970
Kidnapped, 1971
Madame Sin, 1972
Russian Roulette, 1975
Spectre, 1977
The Golden Rendezvous, 1977
The Medusa Touch, 1978
The Last Giraffe, 1979

DEREK JACOBI (1939-)
Versatile actor, mainly seen on stage; also notable in "I Claudius" on television.

Othello, 1965
Three Sisters, 1970
Day of the Jackal, 1973
Blue Blood, 1974
The Odessa File, 1974
The Medusa Touch, 1978
Richard II, 1979
The Human Factor, 1980
Philby, Burgess and MacLean, 1980
Hamlet, 1980

HATTIE JACQUES (1924-)
Chubby character actress of

stage, films and tv, frequently
seen in matronly comedy roles.
Also one of the "Carry On"
team.

Nicholas Nickleby, 1947
Oliver Twist, 1948
Trottie True, 1949
Waterfront, 1950
Chance of a Lifetime, 1950
The Pickwick Papers, 1952
No Haunt For a Gentleman,
   1952
Mother Riley Meets the Vam-
   pire, 1953
All Hallowe'en, 1953
Our Girl Friday, 1954
The Love Lottery, 1954
Up to His Neck, 1954
The Square Peg, 1958
Carry On Sergeant, 1958
Carry On Nurse, 1959
Carry On Teacher, 1959
Follow a Star, 1959
The Night We Dropped a
   Clanger, 1959
The Navy Lark, 1959
Make Mine Mink, 1960
Carry On Constable, 1960
Watch Your Stern, 1960
School For Scoundrels, 1960
Carry On Regardless, 1961
She'll Have to Go, 1961
In the Doghouse, 1962
Carry On Cabby, 1963
The Punch and Judy Man, 1963
The Plank, 1967
The Bobo, 1967
Carry On Doctor, 1968
Carry On Again, Doctor, 1969
Carry On Camping, 1969
Monte Carlo or Bust, 1969
Crooks and Coronets, 1969
Carry On Loving, 1970
The Magic Christian, 1970
Rhubarb, 1970

CARL JAFFE (1902-   )
German character player, long
in Britain; often seen as high-
ranking official or aristocrat.

Over the Moon, 1937
Second Best Bed, 1938
The Silent Battle, 1939
An Englishman's Home, 1939
The Saint in London, 1939
The Lion Has Wings, 1939
Law and Disorder, 1940
All Hands, 1940
Gasbags, 1940
Uncensored, 1942
Continental Express, 1942
Life & Death of Colonel Blimp,
   1943
The Night Invader, 1943
Warn That Man, 1943
Two Thousand Women, 1944
I Didn't Do It, 1945
Gaiety George, 1946
The Blind Goddess, 1948
Counterblast, 1948
The Dancing Years, 1950
State Secret, 1950
Lilli Marlene, 1950
A Tale of Five Cities, 1951
Ivanhoe, 1952
Desperate Moment, 1953
Appointment in London, 1953
Park Plaza 605, 1953
Child's Play, 1954
Cross Channel, 1955
Timeslip, 1955
Satellite in the Sky, 1956
House of Secrets, 1956
The Hostage, 1956
The Traitors, 1957
Case of the Smiling Widow,
   1957
Rockets Galore, 1958
Escapement, 1958
Battle of the VI, 1958
Subway in the Sky, 1959
First Man Into Space, 1959
The Roman Spring of Mrs.
   Stone, 1961
Doomsday at Eleven, 1963
Up Jumped a Swagman, 1965
Operation Crossbow, 1965
The Double Man, 1967
Battle Beneath the Earth, 1967

SIDNEY JAMES (1913-1976)
South-African born character

star of stage (from 1937), screen and television, almost always seen in no-nonsense comedy roles; also one of the "Carry On" group.

Black Memory, 1947
Night Beat, 1948
Once a Jolly Swagman, 1948
The Small Back Room, 1948
Paper Orchid, 1949
Give Us This Day, 1949
Salt to the Devil, 1950
Nothing to Lose, 1950
The Man in Black, 1950
Last Holiday, 1950
The Lady Craved Excitement, 1950
Talk of a Million, 1951
The Galloping Major, 1951
The Lavender Hill Mob, 1951
Lady Godiva Rides Again, 1951
I Believe in You, 1951
One Sinner, 1951
Tall Headlines, 1952
Emergency Call, 1952
The Gift Horse, 1952
Time Gentlemen Please, 1952
Father's Doing Fine, 1952
The Venetian Bird, 1952
The Yellow Balloon, 1952
Miss Robin Hood, 1952
Cosh Boy, 1953
The Titfield Thunderbolt, 1953
Wedding of Lilli Marlene, 1953
Will Any Gentleman, 1953
The Square Ring, 1953
The Flanagan Boy, 1953
Park Plaza 605, 1953
Is Your Honeymoon Really Necessary?, 1953
The Malta Story, 1954
Escape By Night, 1954
The Weak and the Wicked, 1954
House Across the Lake, 1954
Rainbow Jacket, 1954
Father Brown, 1954
Seagulls Over Sorrento, 1954
The Belles of St. Trinain's, 1954
The Crowded Day, 1954
Orders Are Orders, 1954

For Better, For Worse, 1954
Aunt Clara, 1954
Out of the Clouds, 1955
A Kid For Two Farthings, 1955
John and Julie, 1955
The Glass Cage, 1955
The Deep Blue Sea, 1955
Joe Macbeth, 1955
A Yank in Ermine, 1955
Trapeze, 1956
It's a Great Day, 1956
The Extra Day, 1956
Ramsbottom Rides Again, 1956
Wicked As They Come, 1956
Dry Rot, 1956
The Iron Petticoat, 1956
Quatermass II, 1957
Interpol, 1957
The Smallest Show On Earth, 1957
The Shiralee, 1957
Hell Drivers, 1957
Story of Esther Costello, 1957
Campbell's Kingdom, 1957
A King in New York, 1957
The Silent Enemy, 1958
Next to No Time, 1958
Another Time Another Place, 1958
The Man Inside, 1958
I Was Monty's Double, 1958
Sheriff of Fractured Jaw, 1958
Too Many Crooks, 1959
The 39 Steps, 1959
Make Mine a Million, 1959
Idol On Parade, 1959
Upstairs and Downstairs, 1959
Tommy the Toreador, 1959
Desert Mice, 1959
Carry On Constable, 1960
And The Same to You, 1960
Watch Your Stern, 1960
Pure Hell of St. Trinian's, 1960
Double Bunk, 1961
Carry On Regardless, 1961
A Weekend With Lulu, 1961
The Green Helmet, 1961
What a Carve Up!, 1961
What a Whopper!, 1961
Raising the Wind, 1961
Carry On Cruising, 1962

We Joined the Navy, 1962
Carry On Cabby, 1963
Tokolshe, 1964
Carry On Cleo, 1964
The Beauty Jungle, 1964
Three Hats For Lisa, 1965
The Big Job, 1965
Carry On Cowboy, 1965
Where the Bullets Fly, 1966
Don't Lose Your Head, 1966
Carry On Doctor, 1967
Carry On Up the Khyber, 1968
Carry On Camping, 1969
Carry On Again Doctor, 1969
Carry On Loving, 1970
Carry On Up the Jungle, 1970
Carry On Henry VIII, 1971
Carry On at Your Convenience, 1971
Carry On Matron, 1972
Carry On Abroad, 1972
Bless This House, 1972
Carry On Girls, 1973
Carry On Dick, 1974

ERNEST JAY (1894-1957)
Character player of stage and screen, often in cameo roles.

Dora, 1912
Tiger Bay, 1933
Checkmate, 1935
The Iron Duke, 1935
Broken Blossoms, 1936
Don't Take it to Heart, 1944
School For Secrets, 1946
Vice Versa, 1947
Blanche Fury, 1948
Death in the Hand, 1948
The History of Mr. Polly, 1949
Edward My Son, 1949
Golden Arrow, 1949
I Believe in You, 1952
The Sword and the Rose, 1953
Top Secret, 1953
Who Done It, 1955
Curse of Frankenstein, 1956
Doctor at Large, 1957

MICHAEL JAYSTON (1936-)
Forceful leading actor of the

70s, also on stage.

A Midsummer Night's Dream, 1968
Cromwell, 1970
Nicholas and Alexandra, 1971
Follow Me, 1972
The Public Eye, 1972
Alice's Adventures in Wonderland, 1972
Bequest to the Nation, 1973
Tales That Witness Madness, 1973
The Homecoming, 1973
Craze, 1973
The Internecine Project, 1974
Death in Small Doses, 1975
She Fell Among Thieves, 1980
Tinker, Tailor, Soldier, Spy, 1980

ISABEL JEANS (1891-)
Talented actress of stage (since 1909), screen and television, mainly seen in aristocratic parts. Formerly married to Claude Rains. Also in Hollywood.

The Profligate, 1917
Tilly of Bloomsbury, 1921
The Rat, 1925
Triumph of the Rat, 1926
Windsor Castle, 1926
Downhill, 1927
Easy Virtue, 1927
Further Adventures of the Flag Lieutenant, 1928
Power Over Men, 1929
Return of the Rat, 1929
Sally Bishop, 1932
Rolling in Money, 1934
Love Affair of the Dictator, 1935
The Crouching Beast, 1935
Tovarich, 1937
Youth Takes a Fling, 1938
Secrets of an Actress, 1938
Hard to Get, 1938
Fools For Scandal, 1938
Garden of the Moon, 1938
Man About Town, 1939

Good Girls Go to Paris, 1939
Banana Ridge, 1941
Suspicion, 1941
Great Day, 1945
Elizabeth of Ladymead, 1949
It Happened in Rome, 1957
Gigi, 1958
A Breath of Scandal, 1960
Heavens Above, 1963
The Magic Christian, 1970
Clouds of Witness, 1973

URSULA JEANS (1906-1973)
Character actress of stage
(since 1925) and films, also
in Hollywood. Married to
Roger Livesey.

The Gypsy Cavalier, 1922
The Virgin Queen, 1923
Silence, 1926
False Colours, 1927
The Fake, 1927
Quinneys, 1927
The Passing of Mr. Quin, 1928
SOS, 1928
The Love Habit, 1931
The Flying Fool, 1931
The Crooked Lady, 1932
Once Bitten, 1932
The Barton Mystery, 1932
I Lived With You, 1933
On Thin Ice, 1933
Cavalcade, 1933
Friday the Thirteenth, 1933
Man in the Mirror, 1936
Dark Journey, 1937
Storm in a Teacup, 1937
Over the Moon, 1937
Life & Death of Colonel Blimp,
  1943
Mr. Emmanuel, 1944
Gaiety George, 1946
The Woman in the Hall, 1947
The Weaker Sex, 1948
Elizabeth of Ladymead, 1949
The Night My Number Came
  Up, 1955
The Dam Busters, 1955
Northwest Frontier, 1959
The Queen's Guards, 1960

The Green Helmet, 1961
Boy With a Flute, 1964
Battle of the Villa Fiorita,
  1965

ALLAN JEAVES (1885-1963)
Stately, solid supporting star
with long and distinguished
stage experience.

Nelson, 1918
Gentleman of France, 1921
The Solitary Cyclist, 1921
Hound of the Baskervilles,
  1922
The Missioner, 1922
Bulldog Drummond's Third
  Round, 1925
The Hate Ship, 1929
The Ghost Train, 1931
Stranglehold, 1931
Woman in Chains, 1932
The Impassive Footman, 1932
Above Rubies, 1932
Anne One Hundred, 1933
Little Napoleon, 1933
Purse Strings, 1933
Paris Plane, 1933
Song of the Plough, 1933
Ask Beccles, 1933
Eyes of Fate, 1933
Catherine the Great, 1934
Colonel Blood, 1934
Red Ensign, 1934
The Scarlet Pimpernel, 1935
Sanders of the River, 1935
Koenigsmark, 1935
Drake of England, 1935
His Lordship, 1936
Forget-Me-Not, 1936
Rembrandt, 1936
Things To Come, 1936
Seven Sinners, 1936
House of the Spaniard, 1936
Crown v Stevens, 1936
Public Nuisance, 1936
The Squeaker, 1937
The Green Cockatoo, 1937
Elephant Boy, 1937
The High Command, 1937
Return of the Scarlet Pim-

pernel, 1938
A Royal Divorce, 1938
They Drive By Night, 1938
Thirteen Men and a Gun, 1938
Dangerous Medicine, 1938
The Good Old Days, 1939
The Spider, 1939
The Four Feathers, 1939
The Stars Look Down, 1939
The Thief of Bagdad, 1940
Spy For a Day, 1940
Sailors Three, 1940
You Will Remember, 1940
Convoy, 1941
The Proud Valley, 1941
Pimpernel Smith, 1941
At Dawn We Die, 1942
The Shipbuilders, 1943
Perfect Strangers, 1945
Dead of Night, 1945
Lisbon Story, 1946
The Man Within, 1947
Blanche Fury, 1948
Saraband For Dead Lovers,
1948
The Reluctant Widow, 1950
Waterfront, 1950
The Hidden Room, 1950
Reach For Glory, 1962

BARBARA JEFFORD (1931-)
Stage and screen actress,
mainly seen in subsidiary parts.
Films occasional.

Ulysses, 1967
The Bofors Gun, 1968
A Midsummer Night's Dream,
1968
The Shoes of the Fisherman,
1968
Lust For a Vampire, 1970
Hitler: The Last Ten Days,
1973

PETER JEFFREY (1929-)
Supporting player of the seventies, also on stage.

Becket, 1964
If, 1968

Anne of a Thousand Days,
1970
The Abominable Dr. Phibes,
1971
The Horsemen, 1971
Dr. Phibes Rises Again, 1972
O Lucky Man, 1973
The Odessa File, 1974
Return of the Pink Panther,
1974
Come Out, Come Out Where-
ever You Are, 1974
Midnight Express, 1978

LIONEL JEFFRIES (1926-)
Bald character star, almost
always seen in comedy roles;
also in Hollywood. Latterly
director as well.

Stage Fright, 1950
Will Any Gentleman, 1953
The Black Rider, 1954
Windfall, 1955
The Colditz Story, 1955
The Quatermass Experiment,
1955
No Smoking, 1955
All For Mary, 1955
Jumping For Joy, 1955
Bhowani Junction, 1956
Lust For Life, 1956
The Baby and the Battleship,
1956
The High Terrace, 1956
Up in the World, 1956
Man in the Sky, 1956
Doctor at Large, 1957
The Hour of Decision, 1957
Vicious Circle, 1957
Barnacle Bill, 1957
Blue Murder at St. Trinian's,
1957
Revenge of Frankenstein, 1958
Orders to Kill, 1958
Dunkirk, 1958
Up the Creek, 1958
Law and Disorder, 1958
Girls at Sea, 1958
Further Up the Creek, 1958
Behind the Mask, 1958
Nowhere to Go, 1958

The Nun's Story, 1959
Life is a Circus, 1959
Idol On Parade, 1959
Bobbikins, 1959
Please Turn Over, 1959
Two-Way Stretch, 1960
Jazzboat, 1960
Let's Get Married, 1960
The Trials of Oscar Wilde,
   1960
Tarzan the Magnificent, 1960
Fanny, 1961
The Hellions, 1961
Operation Snatch, 1962
Mrs. Gibbons' Boys, 1962
The Wrong Arm of the Law,
   1962
Notorious Landlady, 1962
Kill or Cure, 1963
Call Me Bwana, 1963
The Scarlet Blade, 1963
The Long Ships, 1964
First Men in the Moon, 1964
Murder Ahoy, 1964
The Truth About Spring, 1965
You Must Be Joking!, 1965
The Secret of My Success,
   1965
Spy With a Cold Nose, 1966
Drop Dead Darling, 1966
Camelot, 1967
Oh Dad Poor Dad, 1967
Rocket to the Moon, 1967
Chitty Chitty Bang Bang, 1968
Twinky, 1969
Eyewitness, 1970
Whoever Slew Auntie Roo?, 1971
What Changed Charley Farthing,
   1974
Royal Flash, 1975
Wombling Free, 1977
The Water Babies, 1978
The Prisoner of Zenda, 1979

MEGS JENKINS (1917-   )
Pleasant character actress,
also on stage (from 1933),
usually seen in kindly, serene
characterizations.

The Silent Battle, 1939

Continental Express, 1942
Millions Like Us, 1943
The Lamp Still Burns, 1943
It's in the Bag, 1943
Painted Boats, 1945
29 Acacia Avenue, 1945
Green For Danger, 1946
The Brothers, 1947
The Monkey's Paw, 1948
The History of Mr. Polly,
   1949
Saraband For Dead Lovers,
   1949
A Boy, a Girl, and a Bike,
   1949
No Place For Jennifer, 1950
White Corridors, 1951
Ivanhoe, 1952
Secret People, 1952
Rough Shoot, 1953
Personal Affair, 1953
Trouble in Store, 1953
The Cruel Sea, 1953
The Gay Dog, 1954
John and Julie, 1955
Out of the Clouds, 1955
Man in the Sky, 1957
The Passionate Stranger, 1957
The Story of Esther Costello,
   1957
Indiscreet, 1958
Tiger Bay, 1959
Friends and Neighbours, 1959
Jet Storm, 1959
Conspiracy of Hearts, 1960
The Green Helmet, 1961
Macbeth, 1961
The Innocents, 1961
Life For Ruth, 1962
The Barber of Stamford Hill,
   1962
The Wild and the Willing,
   1962
Bunny Lake is Missing, 1965
Murder Most Foul, 1965
Walk in the Shadow, 1966
Stranger in the House, 1967
Oliver, 1968
David Copperfield, 1969
The Smashing Bird I Used to
   Know, 1969
Asylum, 1972

MARY JERROLD (1877-1955)
Character actress of stage and films, mainly seen as kindly old woman.

Sinless Sinners, 1919
Candytuft, I Mean Veronica, 1921
The W Plan, 1930
Alibi, 1931
The Shadow Between, 1931
The Sport of Kings, 1931
Blind Spot, 1932
The Last Coupon, 1932
Perfect Understanding, 1933
Friday the Thirteenth, 1933
The Lash, 1934
The Great Defender, 1934
Doctor's Orders, 1934
Spring in the Air, 1934
The Price of Wisdom, 1935
Fighting Stock, 1935
Jack of All Trades, 1936
Saturday Night Revue, 1937
The Man at the Gate, 1941
Talk About Jacqueline, 1942
The Gentle Sex, 1943
The Flemish Farm, 1943
The Way Ahead, 1944
The Magic Bow, 1947
Ghosts of Berkeley Square, 1947
Colonel Bogey, 1948
Woman Hater, 1948
Bond Street, 1948
Mr. Perrin and Mr. Traill, 1948
The Queen of Spades, 1949
Marry Me, 1949
She Shall Have Murder, 1950
Meet Me Tonight, 1952
Top of the Form, 1953

PATRICIA JESSEL (1921-1968)
Character actress and supporting player of stage and films, also in Hollywood.

Quo Vadis, 1951
The Flesh is Weak, 1957
Model For Murder, 1959
The Man Upstairs, 1959

No Kidding, 1960
City of the Dead, 1961
Horror Hotel, 1963
A Jolly Bad Fellow, 1964
A Funny Thing Happened On the Way to the Forum, 1966

ROSAMUND JOHN (1913-)
Pleasant red-headed leading lady of the forties, also on stage (since 1931).

Secret of the Loch, 1934
The First of the Few, 1942
The Gentle Sex, 1943
The Lamp Still Burns, 1943
Tawny Pipit, 1944
Soldier Soldier, 1945
The Way to the Stars, 1945
Green For Danger, 1946
The Upturned Glass, 1947
Fame is the Spur, 1947
When the Bough Breaks, 1947
No Place For Jennifer, 1949
She Shall Have Murder, 1950
Never Look Back, 1952
Street Corner, 1953
Operation Murder, 1956

GLYNIS JOHNS (1923-)
Welsh actress of stage (from 1935) and screen with unique voice; former child actress. Also in Hollywood. Daughter of Mervyn Johns.

South Riding, 1938
Prison Without Bars, 1938
Murder in the Family, 1938
On the Night of the Fire, 1939
The Briggs Family, 1940
Under Your Hat, 1940
The Prime Minister, 1941
49th Parallel, 1941
The Adventures of Tartu, 1943
Halfway House, 1944
Perfect Strangers, 1945
This Man is Mine, 1946
Frieda, 1947
An Ideal Husband, 1947

Miranda, 1948
Third Time Lucky, 1948
Dear Mr. Prohack, 1949
Helter Skelter, 1949
State Secret, 1950
Flesh and Blood, 1950
No Highway, 1951
Appointment With Venus, 1951
Encore, 1951
The Magic Box, 1951
The Card, 1952
The Sword and the Rose, 1953
Personal Affair, 1953
Rob Roy, 1953
The Weak and the Wicked,
   1954
The Seekers, 1954
The Beachcomber, 1954
Mad About Men, 1954
Josephine and Men, 1955
Loser Takes All, 1956
The Day They Gave Babies
   Away, 1956
The Court Jester, 1956
Around the World in 80 Days,
   1956
All Mine to Give, 1957
Another Time Another Place,
   1958
Shake Hands With the Devil,
   1959
The Spider's Web, 1960
The Sundowners, 1960
The Cabinet of Dr. Caligari,
   1961
The Chapman Report, 1962
Papa's Delicate Condition, 1963
Mary Poppins, 1964
Dear Brigitte, 1965
Don't Just Stand There, 1968
Lock Up Your Daughters, 1969
Under Milk Wood, 1971
Vault of Horror, 1973

MERVYN JOHNS (1899-)
Veteran Welsh actor of stage
(from 1923) and screen, typically cast in amiable roles.
Father of Glynis Johns; married to Diana Churchill. Former dentist.

Lady in Danger, 1934
Pot Luck, 1935
The Guvnor, 1935
Everything is Thunder, 1936
In the Soup, 1936
Dishonour Bright, 1936
Storm in a Teacup, 1937
Almost a Gentleman, 1938
Jamaica Inn, 1939
The Midas Touch, 1939
Saloon Bar, 1940
Convoy, 1940
The Girl in the News, 1941
The Foreman Went to France,
   1942
Next of Kin, 1942
Went the Day Well, 1942
The Bells Go Down, 1943
My Learned Friend, 1943
San Demetrio-London, 1943
Halfway House, 1944
Twilight Hour, 1944
They Knew Mr. Knight, 1945
Dead of Night, 1945
Pink String and Sealing Wax,
   1945
The Captive Heart, 1946
Captain Boycott, 1947
Easy Money, 1948
Counterblast, 1948
Quartet, 1948
Edward My Son, 1949
Helter Skelter, 1949
Diamond City, 1949
Tony Draws a Horse, 1950
Scrooge, 1951
The Magic Box, 1951
Tall Headlines, 1952
Valley of Song, 1953
The Oracle, 1953
Devil's Plot, 1953
Master of Ballantrae, 1953
Romeo and Juliet, 1954
Blue Peter, 1955
1984, 1956
Intimate Stranger, 1956
Shield of Faith, 1956
Moby Dick, 1956
Find the Lady, 1956
The Tunnel, 1957
The Counterfeit Plan, 1957
Doctor at Large, 1957

Danger List, 1957
Vicious Circle, 1957
My Friend Charles, 1957
The Surgeon's Knife, 1957
The Gypsy and the Gentleman,
 1958
The Devil's Disciple, 1959
Moment of Truth, 1959
Once More With Feeling, 1960
Never Let Go, 1960
The Sundowners, 1960
Francis of Assisi, 1961
No Love For Johnnie, 1961
Echo of Barbara, 1961
The Rebel, 1961
55 Days at Peking, 1962
Day of the Triffids, 1963
The Old Dark House, 1963
80,000 Suspects, 1963
The Victors, 1963
A Jolly Bad Fellow, 1964
The Heroes of Telemark, 1965
Who Killed the Cat?, 1966
The National Health, 1973
House of Mortal Sin, 1975
The Confessional, 1977

CELIA JOHNSON (1908-)
Distinguished, aristocratic
leading actress of stage (since
1928) and films; pictures relatively few but always excellent.

Dirty Work, 1934
A Letter From Home, 1941
In Which We Serve, 1942
Dear Octopus, 1943
This Happy Breed, 1944
Brief Encounter, 1945
The Astonished Heart, 1949
I Believe in You, 1951
The Distaff Side, 1952
The Holly and the Ivy, 1952
The Captain's Paradise, 1953
A Kid For Two Farthings, 1955
The Good Companions, 1957
The Prime of Miss Jean
 Brodie, 1969
Romeo and Juliet, 1979
The Hostage Tower, 1980
All's Well That Ends Well, 1980
Staying On, 1980

KATIE JOHNSON (1878-1957)
Character actress who achieved
stardom in her later years after having played small roles
for a number of years.

After Office Hours, 1932
Strictly in Confidence, 1933
A Glimpse of Paradise, 1934
Laburnum Grove, 1936
Dusty Ermine, 1936
The Last Adventurers, 1937
Marigold, 1938
Jeannie, 1941
Freedom Radio, 1941
Talk About Jacqueline, 1942
The Years Between, 1946
I See a Dark Stranger, 1946
The Shop at Sly Corner, 1946
Meet Me at Dawn, 1947
I Believe in You, 1952
Death of an Angel, 1952
Three Steps in the Dark, 1953
The Delavine Affair, 1954
The Ladykillers, 1955
How to Murder a Rich Uncle,
 1956
Studs Lonigan, 1957

RICHARD JOHNSON (1927-)
Tall, handsome leading man of
stage (since 1944) and screen,
latterly seen in international
productions.

Captain Horatio Hornblower,
 1951
Saadia, 1953
Never So Few, 1959
La Strega in Amore, 1962
Cairo, 1963
The Haunting, 1963
80,000 Suspects, 1963
The Pumpkin Eater, 1964
Moll Flanders, 1965
Operation Crossbow, 1965
Khartoum, 1966
Deadlier Than the Male, 1967
The Rover, 1967
Danger Route, 1967
Lady Hamilton, 1968
Oedipus the King, 1968

Twist of Sand, 1968
Some Girls Do, 1969
Trajan's Column, 1969
Julius Caesar, 1970
Restless, 1973
Perche, 1975
Beyond the Door, 1975
Hennessy, 1975
Aces High, 1976
Night Child, 1976
Four Feathers, 1978
Take All of Me, 1978
The Comeback, 1978
The Fish Men, 1979
Portrait of a Rebel: Margaret
    Sanger, 1980
Haywire, 1980
Zombie, 1980

MARGARET JOHNSTON
    (1918-)
Attractive Australian character
actress and former leading
lady of the 40s, also on stage
(from 1936).

The Prime Minister, 1941
The Rake's Progress, 1945
A Man About the House, 1947
Portrait of Clare, 1950
The Magic Box, 1951
Knave of Hearts, 1954
Touch and Go, 1955
Night of the Eagle, 1962
The Model Murder Case, 1963
The Nose On My Face, 1964
Life at the Top, 1965
The Psychopath, 1966
Schizo, 1966
Sebastian, 1967

OLIVER JOHNSTON (1888-1966)
General purpose character
actor, mainly active in the
50s and 60s.

Stolen Life, 1939
Room in the House, 1955
A King in New York, 1957
The Hypnotist, 1957

Hello London, 1958
Indiscreet, 1958
A Touch of Larceny, 1959
Kidnapped, 1960
Francis of Assisi, 1961
Cleopatra, 1962
Dr. Crippen, 1962
Backfire, 1962
Tomb of Ligeia, 1963
A Countess From Hong Kong,
    1967

BARRY JONES (1893-)
Character star of stage (1921)
and screen, also in Hollywood.
Equally skillful at displaying
evil and kindly characterizations.

Number Seventeen, 1932
Women Who Play, 1932
Arms and the Man, 1932
The Gay Adventure, 1936
Murder in the Family, 1938
Squadron Leader X, 1942
Dancing With Crime, 1947
Frieda, 1947
The Calendar, 1948
Uneasy Terms, 1948
The Bad Lord Byron, 1949
That Dangerous Age, 1949
Seven Days to Noon, 1950
Madeleine, 1950
The Clouded Yellow, 1950
White Corridors, 1951
Appointment With Venus, 1951
The Plymouth Adventure, 1952
Return to Paradise, 1953
Prince Valiant, 1954
Demetrius and the Gladiator,
    1954
Brigadoon, 1955
The Glass Slipper, 1955
Alexander the Great, 1956
War and Peace, 1956
Saint Joan, 1957
The Safecracker, 1958
The 39 Steps, 1959
A Study in Terror, 1965
The Heroes of Telemark,
    1965

DUDLEY JONES (1914-   )
Small-part character actor,
mainly on stage and tv.   Films
very rare.

Once a Jolly Swagman, 1949
On Her Majesty's Secret Ser-
    vice, 1968
How Green Was My Valley,
    1975

EMRYS JONES (1915-1972)
Character actor of the forties,
also on stage.

The Shipbuilders, 1941
Tired Men, 1942
One of Our Aircraft is Missing,
    1942
Information Please, 1943
Give Me the Stars, 1944
The Rake's Progress, 1945
The Wicked Lady, 1945
Beware of Pity, 1946
Nicholas Nickleby, 1947
Holiday Camp, 1947
This Was a Woman, 1948
The Small Back Room, 1948
Blue Scar, 1949
Dark Secret, 1949
Miss Pilgrim's Progress, 1950
Deadly Nightshade, 1953
Three Cases of Murder, 1955
The Shield of Faith, 1956
The Trials of Oscar Wilde,
    1960
Ticket to Paradise, 1961
Serena, 1962
On the Run, 1963

FREDDIE JONES (1927-   )
Character star of the 60s and
70s with a penchant for nervous
characterizations.

Marat /Sade, 1967
Accident, 1967
Far From the Madding Crowd,
    1967
The Bliss of Mrs. Blossom,
    1968

Otley, 1969
The Man Who Haunted Himself,
    1970
Doctor in Trouble, 1970
Goodbye Gemini, 1970
Frankenstein Must Be Destroyed,
    1970
Kidnapped, 1971
Sitting Target, 1972
Satanic Rites of Dracula, 1973
Antony and Cleopatra, 1973
All Creatures Great and Small,
    1973
Son of Dracula, 1974
In the Devil's Garden, 1974
Juggernaut, 1974
Old Dracula, 1975
Appointment With a Killer,
    1975
Never Too Young to Rock, 1976
Zulu Dawn, 1980
The Elephant Man, 1980

GRIFFITH JONES (1910-   )
Heroic leading man of stage
(from 1930) and screen, latterly in character parts.

The Faithful Heart, 1932
Money Talks, 1932
Catherine the Great, 1934
Leave it to Blanche, 1934
Escape Me Never, 1935
First a Girl, 1935
Line Engaged, 1935
The Mill On the Floss, 1937
The Wife of General Ling, 1937
Return of a Stranger, 1937
A Yank at Oxford, 1938
Four Just Men, 1939
Young Man's Fancy, 1939
Atlantic Ferry, 1941
This Was Paris, 1942
The Day Will Dawn, 1942
Uncensored, 1942
Henry V, 1944
The Wicked Lady, 1945
The Rake's Progress, 1945
They Made Me a Fugitive,
    1947
Miranda, 1948
Good Time Girl, 1948

Look Before You Love, 1948
Once Upon a Dream, 1949
Honeymoon Deferred, 1951
Star of My Night, 1954
The Scarlet Web, 1954
The Sea Shall Not Have Them,
    1955
Face in the Night, 1957
Account Rendered, 1957
Not Wanted On Voyage, 1957
Kill Her Gently, 1957
The High Wall, 1958
The Truth About Women, 1958
Hidden Homicide, 1959
The Crowning Touch, 1959
Strangler's Web, 1965
Decline and Fall, 1968

PETER JONES (1920-)
Character actor of stage and
screen, primarily in comic
parts.

Fanny By Gaslight, 1944
Vice Versa, 1948
The Blue Lagoon, 1949
Chance of a Lifetime, 1950
The Browning Version, 1951
The Franchise Affair, 1951
Home to Danger, 1951
The Magic Box, 1951
Time Gentlemen Please, 1952
Miss Robin Hood, 1952
24 Hours of a Woman's Life,
    1952
Elstree Story, 1952
Yellow Balloon, 1953
Albert RN, 1953
The Long Memory, 1953
Innocents in Paris, 1953
The Good Beginning, 1953
A Day to Remember, 1953
For Better, For Worse, 1954
Charley Moon, 1956
Private's Progress, 1956
Blue Murder at St. Trinian's,
    1957
Operation Bullshine, 1959
Danger Within, 1959
Never Let Go, 1960
School For Scoundrels, 1960
The Bulldog Breed, 1960

Nearly a Nasty Accident, 1961
Romanoff and Juliet, 1961
A Stitch in Time, 1963
Father Came Too, 1963
Press For Time, 1966
Just Like a Woman, 1966
Smashing Time, 1967
Hot Millions, 1968
Carry On Doctor, 1968

PATRICK JORDAN (-)
Character player of stage,
screen, and television.

Cloak Without Dagger, 1956
The Man Upstairs, 1959
Man Detained, 1961
Bunny Lake is Missing, 1965
The Heroes of Telemark, 1965
Robbery, 1967
Play Dirty, 1968
Gold is Where You Find It,
    1968
Too Late the Hero, 1969
Jane Eyre, 1970
Sitting Target, 1972
In the Devil's Garden, 1974
The Slipper and the Rose, 1976
The Pink Panther Strikes
    Again, 1976

YOOTHA JOYCE (1927-)
Comedy character actress,
mainly popular on television.

Sparrows Can't Sing, 1962
The Pumpkin Eater, 1964
Fanatic, 1965
Catch Us if You Can, 1965
Having a Wild Weekend, 1965
A Man For All Seasons, 1966
Kaleidoscope, 1966
Stranger in the House, 1967
Our Mother's House, 1967
All the Right Noises, 1969
Twenty-Nine, 1969
Fragment of Fear, 1970
Burke and Hare, 1971
The Night Digger, 1971
Frankenstein: The True Story,
    1973

EDWARD JUDD (1932-   )
Light leading man and character actor, often seen in horror
productions.

X The Unknown, 1956
Carry On Sergeant, 1958
I Was Monty's Double, 1958
Subway in the Sky, 1958
The Man Upstairs, 1959
No Safety Ahead, 1959
Shakedown, 1959
The Challenge, 1960
The Criminal, 1960
The Day the Earth Caught
    Fire, 1961
Mystery Submarine, 1962
Stolen Hours, 1963
The World 10 Times Over,
    1963
The Long Ships, 1964
First Men in the Moon, 1964
Strange Bedfellows, 1965
The Invasion, 1965
Island of Terror, 1966
Vengeance of She, 1967
Think 20th, 1967
Universal Soldier, 1971
Living Free, 1972
O Lucky Man, 1973
The Vault of Horror, 1973
Assassin, 1973
Feelings, 1975
Whose Child am I?, 1975
The Incredible Sarah, 1976

JAMES ROBERTSON JUSTICE
    (1905-1975)
Bluff, bearded, bearlike Scottish actor, familiar in comedy
roles, especially that of Sir
Lancelot Spratt, senior surgeon
in the "Doctor" films. Also
in Hollywood.   Former naturalist and journalist; also an
expert in falconry.

For Those in Peril, 1944
Fiddlers Three, 1944
Vice Versa, 1948
Scott of the Antarctic, 1948
My Brother Jonathan, 1948

Against the Wind, 1948
Quartet, 1948
Whiskey Galore, 1948
Stop Press Girl, 1949
Christopher Columbus, 1949
Poet's Pub, 1949
Private Angelo, 1949
Prelude to Fame, 1950
My Daughter Joy, 1950
The Black Rose, 1950
Blackmailed, 1951
Pool of London, 1951
Circle of Danger, 1951
David and Bathsheba, 1951
Anne of the Indies, 1951
Captain Horatio Hornblower,
    1951
The Story of Robin Hood, 1952
The Lady Says No, 1952
The Voice of Merrill, 1952
Miss Robin Hood, 1952
Les Miserables, 1952
The Sword and the Rose, 1953
Rob Roy, 1953
Doctor in the House, 1954
Out of the Clouds, 1955
Land of the Pharaohs, 1955
Above Us the Waves, 1955
Doctor at Sea, 1955
Storm Over the Nile, 1955
An Alligator Named Daisy,
    1955
The Iron Petticoat, 1956
Moby Dick, 1956
Checkpoint, 1956
Doctor at Large, 1957
Campbell's Kingdom, 1957
Seven Thunders, 1957
The Living Idol, 1957
Orders to Kill, 1958
Revenge of Frankenstein, 1958
Upstairs and Downstairs, 1959
Doctor in Love, 1960
A French Mistress, 1960
A Foxhole in Cairo, 1960
Very Important Person, 1961
The Guns of Navarone, 1961
Raising the Wind, 1961
Murder She Said, 1962
A Pair of Briefs, 1962
Crooks Anonymous, 1962
Guns of Darkness, 1962
Dr. Crippen, 1962

The Fast Lady, 1962
Love On a Pillow, 1963
Mystery Submarine, 1963
Doctor in Distress, 1963
Father Came Too, 1963
Up From the Beach, 1965
Those Magnificent Men in
    Their Flying Machines
    (voice), 1965
You Must Be Joking!, 1965
The Face of Fu Manchu, 1965
Doctor in Clover, 1965
The Trygon Factor, 1967
Two Weeks in September, 1967
Hell is Empty, 1967
Mayerling, 1968
Chitty Chitty Bang Bang, 1968
Zeta One, 1969
Some Will, Some Won't, 1970
Doctor in Trouble, 1970

JOHN JUSTIN (1917-)
Handsome leading actor of stage
(since 1933) and screen, latterly
in character parts.   Married to
Barbara Murray.

The Thief of Bagdad, 1940
The Gentle Sex, 1943
Journey Together, 1945
Call of the Blood, 1948
The Angel With the Trumpet,
    1950
The Sound Barrier, 1952
Hot Ice, 1952
The Village, 1952
Melba, 1953
King of the Khyber Rifles, 1953
Seagulls Over Sorrento, 1954
The Teckman Mystery, 1954
The Man Who Loved Redheads,
    1955
Untamed, 1955
Safari, 1956
Guilty, 1956
Crime Passionelle, 1956
Island in the Sun, 1957
The Spider's Web, 1960
Candidate For Murder, 1962
Les Hommes Veluent, 1965
Savage Messiah, 1972
Lisztomania, 1975
Valentino, 1977

The Big Sleep, 1978

ALEXIS KANNER (1942-)
General purpose actor of the
sixties, in occasional pictures.

We Joined the Navy, 1962
Reach For Glory, 1962
Crossplot, 1969
Connecting Rooms, 1969
Twenty-Nine, 1969
Goodbye Gemini, 1970

MIRIAM KARLIN (1925-)
Husky-voiced character actress,
also on stage, frequently seen
in comedy parts.

The Deep Blue Sea, 1955
The Woman For Joe, 1955
Fun at St. Fanny's, 1956
Room at the Top, 1959
The Entertainer, 1960
The Millionairess, 1960
Hand in Hand, 1960
Crossroads to Crime, 1960
On the Fiddle, 1961
Phantom of the Opera, 1962
I Thank a Fool, 1962
Heavens Above, 1963
The Small World of Sammy
    Lee, 1963
The Bargee, 1964
Ladies Who Do, 1964
A Clockwork Orange, 1971
Barry Lyndon, 1975
Mahler, 1975
Dick Deadeye, 1976

BORIS KARLOFF (1887-1969)
Gaunt, mild-mannered character
star who came to Hollywood in
1916 and remained to play in
innumerable films.   Gained
fame for his part as the monster in "Frankenstein" and from
then on played in mainly horror
films.   Also on stage and tv.
TV series: "Colonel March of
Scotland Yard" (1955), "Thriller"
(1958-59).

The Dumb Girl of Portici,
1916
His Majesty the American,
1919
The Prince and Betty, 1919
The Deadlier Sex, 1920
The Courage of Marge O'Doone,
1920
The Last of the Mohicans,
1920
The Hope Diamond Mystery,
1921
Without Benefit of Clergy,
1921
Cheated Hearts, 1921
The Cave Girl, 1921
The Man From Downing Street,
1922
The Infidel, 1922
Altar Stairs, 1922
Omar the Tentmaker, 1922
The Woman Conquers, 1922
The Prisoner, 1923
The Hellions, 1924
Dynamite Dan, 1924
Parisian Nights, 1925
Forbidden Cargo, 1925
The Prairie Wife, 1925
Lady Robin Hood, 1925
Never the Twain Shall Meet,
1925
The Greater Glory, 1926
Her Honor the Governor, 1926
The Nicklehopper, 1926
The Bells, 1926
Eagle of the Sea, 1926
Flames, 1926
The Golden Web, 1926
Flaming Fury, 1926
Valencia, 1926
Man in the Saddle, 1926
Old Ironsides, 1926
Tarzan and the Golden Lion,
1927
Let it Rain, 1927
The Meddlin' Stranger, 1927
Princess From Hoboken, 1927
The Phantom Buster, 1927
Soft Cushions, 1927
Two Arabian Knights, 1927
The Love Mart, 1927
Vultures of the Sea, 1928
The Little Wild Girl, 1928

The Fatal Warning, 1929
Devil's Chaplain, 1929
Two Sisters, 1929
Phantom of the North, 1929
Anne Against the World, 1929
King of the Kongo, 1929
Behind That Curtain, 1929
Unholy Night, 1929
Burning the Wind, 1929
The Band One, 1930
The Sea Bat, 1930
Utah Kid, 1930
Mother's Cry, 1931
The Criminal Code, 1931
Cracked Nuts, 1931
Donovan's Kid, 1931
King of the Wild, 1931
Smart Money, 1931
The Public Defender, 1931
I Like Your Nerve, 1931
Five Star Final, 1931
Pardon Us, 1931
Graft, 1931
The Mad Genius, 1931
The Yellow Ticket, 1931
The Guilty Generation, 1931
Frankenstein, 1931
Tonight or Never, 1931
Business and Pleasure, 1932
Alias the Doctor, 1932
Behind the Mask, 1932
Scarface, 1932
The Miracle Man, 1932
The Cohens and the Kellys in
Hollywood, 1932
Night World, 1932
The Old Dark House, 1932
The Mask of Fu Manchu, 1932
The Mummy, 1932
The Ghoul, 1933
The Lost Patrol, 1934
The House of Rothschild, 1934
The Gift of Gab, 1934
The Black Cat, 1934
Bride of Frankenstein, 1935
The Black Room, 1935
The Raven, 1935
The Invisible Ray, 1936
The Walking Dead, 1936
The Man Who Lived Again,
1936
Juggernaut, 1936
Charlie Chan at the Opera,

1937
Night Key, 1937
West of Shanghai, 1937
The Invisible Menace, 1938
Mr. Wong-Detective, 1938
Tower of London, 1939
The Mystery of Mr. Wong, 1939
Mr. Wong in Chinatown, 1939
Son of Frankenstein, 1939
The Man They Could Not Hang, 1939
The Fatal Hour, 1940
British Intelligence, 1940
Black Friday, 1940
The Man With Nine Lives, 1940
Devil's Island, 1940
Doomed to Die, 1940
Before I Hang, 1940
The Ape, 1940
You'll Find Out, 1940
The Devil Commands, 1941
The Boogie Man Will Get You, 1942
The Climax, 1944
House of Frankenstein, 1944
The Body Snatcher, 1945
Isle of the Dead, 1945
Bedlam, 1946
The Secret Life of Walter Mitty, 1947
Lured, 1947
Unconquered, 1947
Dick Tracy Meets Gruesome, 1947
Tap Roots, 1948
Abbott & Costello Meet the Killer--Boris Karloff, 1949
The Strange Door, 1951
The Black Castle, 1952
Abbott and Costello Meet Dr. Jekyll and Mr. Hyde, 1953
Monster of the Island, 1953
The Hindu, 1953
Voodoo Island, 1957
Grip of the Strangler, 1958
Frankenstein 1970, 1958
Corridors of Blood, 1962
The Raven, 1963
The Terror, 1963
Black Sabbath, 1963
Comedy of Terrors, 1963
Bikini Beach, 1964

Die Monster Die, 1965
Ghost in the Invisible Bikini, 1966
The Daydreamer (voice), 1966
The Venetian Affair, 1967
The Sorcerers, 1967
Mad Monster Party (voice), 1967
Targets, 1968
Curse of the Crimson Altar, 1968
The Snake People, 1969
The Incredible Invasion, 1969
Cauldron of Blood, 1969
The Fear Chamber, 1970
House of Evil, 1970

HAROLD KASKET (1916-)
Character player of stage and screen, former impressionist.

Hotel Sahara, 1951
Moulin Rouge, 1953
House of the Arrow, 1953
One Good Turn, 1954
Beau Brummell, 1954
The Key Man, 1957
Interpol, 1957
Manuela, 1957
The Naked Earth, 1958
Wonderful Things, 1958
The Navy Lark, 1959
Whirlpool, 1959
Heart of a Man, 1959
Tommy the Toreador, 1959
Sands of the Desert, 1960
The Boy Who Stole a Million, 1961
The Greengage Summer, 1961
The Fourth Square, 1961
The Return of Mr. Moto, 1965
Arabesque, 1966
Where's Jack?, 1969

MAURICE KAUFMANN (1928-)
General purpose character player, also on stage.

Secret Venture, 1955
The Love Match, 1955

The Quatermass Experiment,
  1955
It's a Wonderful World, 1956
Find the Lady, 1956
The Girl in the Picture, 1957
Zoo Baby, 1957
Date With Disaster, 1957
Top Floor Girl, 1959
Behemoth the Sea Monster,
  1959
House of Mystery, 1961
Tarnished Heroes, 1961
Play it Cool, 1962
On the Beat, 1962
We Shall See, 1964
A Shot in the Dark, 1964
Fanatic, 1965
Circus of Fear, 1966
Company of Fools, 1966
Cry Wolf, 1968
Man of Violence, 1970
Bloomfield, 1970
The Abominable Dr. Phibes,
  1971

GEOFFREY KEEN (1918-)
Distinctive, versatile character
player, also on stage; son of
Malcolm Keen.

Riders of the New Forest,
  1946
Odd Man Out, 1947
The Fallen Idol, 1948
The Third Man, 1949
Treasure Island, 1950
It's Hard to Be Good, 1950
Seven Days to Noon, 1950
The Clouded Yellow, 1950
Chance of a Lifetime, 1951
High Treason, 1951
Cheer the Brave, 1951
Green Grow the Rushes, 1951
His Excellency, 1952
The Stranger in Between, 1952
Cry the Beloved Country, 1952
Lady in the Fog, 1952
Angels One Five, 1952
The Long Memory, 1953
Rob Roy, 1953
Genevieve, 1953
Face the Music, 1954

Turn the Key Softly, 1954
The Maggie, 1954
Doctor in the House, 1954
The Divided Heart, 1954
Carrington VC, 1955
Storm Over the Nile, 1955
Doctor at Sea, 1955
Passage Home, 1955
The Glass Cage, 1955
Portrait of Alison, 1955
A Town Like Alice, 1956
Zarak, 1956
Loser Takes All, 1956
The Man Who Never Was,
  1956
The Long Arm, 1956
The Spanish Gardener, 1956
Sailor Beware, 1956
The Scamp, 1957
The Birthday Present, 1957
Doctor at Large, 1957
Town On Trial, 1957
The Secret Place, 1957
Yield to the Night, 1957
Triple Deception, 1957
Fortune is a Woman, 1957
Nowhere to Go, 1958
The Scapegoat, 1959
Horrors of the Black Museum,
  1959
Beyond This Place, 1959
Deadly Record, 1959
The Boy and the Bridge, 1959
Devil's Bait, 1959
The Dover Road Mystery, 1960
Sink the Bismarck, 1960
The Angry Silence, 1960
The Malpas Mystery, 1961
No Love For Johnnie, 1961
Spare the Rod, 1961
The Silent Weapon, 1961
Raising the Wind, 1961
Live Now Pay Later, 1962
The Spiral Road, 1962
A Matter of WHO, 1962
The Inspector, 1962
The Prince and the Pauper,
  1962
The Mind Benders, 1962
The Cracksman, 1963
Return to Sender, 1963
Dr. Syn Alias the Scarecrow,
  1963

Torpedo Bay, 1964
Dr. Zhivago, 1965
The Heroes of Telemark, 1965
Born Free, 1966
Berserk!, 1967
Thunderbird 6, 1968
Cromwell, 1970
Taste the Blood of Dracula, 1970
Sacco and Vanzetti, 1971
Living Free, 1972
Doomwatch, 1973
QB VII, 1974
The Spy Who Loved Me, 1977
Moonraker, 1979

MALCOLM KEEN (1887-1970)
Distinguished character star of
stage and screen, also in Hollywood.   Father of Geoffrey
Keen.

Jimmy, 1916
The Lost Chord, 1917
Master of Men, 1917
The Skin Game, 1920
A Bill of Divorcement, 1922
Settled Out of Court, 1925
The Lodger, 1926
Mountain Eagle, 1926
Julius Caesar, 1927
Packing Up, 1928
The Manxman, 1929
Wolves, 1930
The House of Unrest, 1931
Jealousy, 1931
77 Park Lane, 1931
Night of the Party, 1934
Whispering Tongues, 1934
Dangerous Ground, 1934
Wanted Men, 1936
The Lonely Road, 1936
Mr. Reeder in Room 13, 1938
Sixty Glorious Years, 1938
The Great Mr. Handel, 1942
The Mating Season, 1951
Rob Roy, 1953
The Birthday Present, 1957
Fortune is a Woman, 1957
Operation Amsterdam, 1958
Macbeth, 1961
Francis of Assisi, 1961
Life For Ruth, 1962

Two and Two Make Six, 1962
Walk in the Shadow, 1966

ANDREW KEIR (1926-)
Often bearded Scottish charac-
ter star, usually seen in
strong, no-nonsense roles.
Also on tv, notably in series
"The Outsiders" (1977).

The Lady Craved Excitement,
    1950
The Brave Don't Cry, 1952
Laxdale Hall, 1953
The Maggie, 1954
Heart of a Child, 1957
Suspended Alibi, 1957
A Night to Remember, 1958
The Day They Robbed the Bank
    of England, 1960
Cleopatra, 1962
The Pirates of Blood River,
    1962
Torpedo Bay, 1964
Devil Ship Pirates, 1964
Fall of the Roman Empire,
    1964
Lord Jim, 1965
Dracula Prince of Darkness,
    1966
Daleks Invasion Earth 2150 AD,
    1966
Fighting Prince of Donegal,
    1966
The Long Duel, 1967
The Viking Queen, 1967
Quatermass and the Pit, 1967
Attack On the Iron Coast,
    1968
The Royal Hunt of the Sun, 1969
The Last Grenade, 1970
Zeppelin, 1971
Blood From the Mummy's
    Tomb, 1971
The Night Visitor, 1971
Mary Queen of Scots, 1971
Catholics, 1973
The Thirty Nine Steps, 1980

CECIL KELLAWAY (1893-1973)
South-African born character

actor who spent many years in Australia before coming to Hollywood in 1939 where he remained to play a number of warmhearted, roguish parts.

It Isn't Done, 1937
Double Danger, 1938
Tarnished Angel, 1938
We Are Not Alone, 1939
Wuthering Heights, 1939
Intermezzo, 1939
Mexican Spitfire, 1940
The Invisible Man Returns, 1940
House of the Seven Gables, 1940
Brother Orchid, 1940
Phantom Raiders, 1940
The Mummy's Hand, 1940
Diamond Frontiers, 1940
Mexican Spitfire Out West, 1940
The Letter, 1940
Lady With Red Hair, 1940
South of Suez, 1940
West Point Widow, 1941
Burma Convoy, 1941
Appointment For Love, 1941
New York Town, 1941
The Night of January Sixth, 1941
Bahama Passage, 1942
The Lady Has Plans, 1942
Take a Letter Darling, 1942
Are Husbands Necessary?, 1942
I Married a Witch, 1942
My Heart Belongs to Daddy, 1942
The Good Fellows, 1943
Forever and a Day, 1943
The Crystal Ball, 1943
It Aint Hay, 1943
Mrs. Parkington, 1944
Practically Yours, 1944
Frenchman's Creek, 1944
And Now Tomorrow, 1944
Love Letters, 1945
Kitty, 1946
Easy to Wed, 1946
The Cockeyed Miracle, 1946
Monsieur Beaucaire, 1946

The Postman Always Rings Twice, 1946
Always Together, 1947
Unconquered, 1947
Portrait of Jennie, 1948
The Luck of the Irish, 1948
Joan of Arc, 1948
The Decision of Christopher Blake, 1948
Down to the Sea in Ships, 1949
Harvey, 1950
The Reformer and the Redhead, 1950
Kim, 1950
Half Angel, 1951
Francis Goes to the Races, 1951
Just Across the Street, 1952
My Wife's Best Friend, 1952
Thunder in the East, 1953
Young Bess, 1953
Beast From 20,000 Fathoms, 1953
Female On the Beach, 1955
Interrupted Melody, 1955
The Prodigal, 1955
The Toy Tiger, 1956
Proud Rebel, 1958
The Shaggy Dog, 1959
Private Lives of Adam & Eve, 1960
Francis of Assisi, 1961
Tammy Tell Me True, 1961
Zotz, 1962
The Cardinal, 1963
Hush Hush Sweet Charlotte, 1964
Spinout, 1966
Fitzwilly, 1967
Guess Who's Coming to Dinner, 1967
Getting Straight, 1970

PAMELA KELLINO (1916-)
Actress of stage and films, latterly tv personality and writer; married to director Roy Kellino; James Mason. Films occasional.

Jew Suss, 1934
I Met a Murderer, 1939

Prince of Peace, 1939
They Were Sisters, 1945
The Upturned Glass, 1947
Lady Possessed, 1951
Pandora & the Flying Dutch-
    man, 1951

JUDY KELLY (1913-)
Australian leading lady of
films, popular in the thirties.

Adam's Apple, 1928
Money Talks, 1932
Lord Camber's Ladies, 1932
Their Night Out, 1933
Hawleys of High Street, 1933
The Love Nest, 1933
Private Life of Henry VIII,
    1933
Crime On the Hill, 1933
Mannequin, 1933
The Black Abbott, 1934
Four Masked Men, 1934
Anything Might Happen, 1934
It's a Bet, 1935
Things Are Looking Up, 1935
Royal Cavalcade, 1935
Marry the Girl, 1935
Charing Cross Road, 1935
Captain Bill, 1935
Under Proof, 1936
First Offence, 1936
A Star Fell From Heaven,
    1936
The Limping Man, 1936
Aren't Men Beasts?, 1937
Boys Will Be Girls, 1937
Over She Goes, 1937
The Price of Folly, 1937
Make Up, 1937
The Last Chance, 1937
Premiere, 1938
Jane Steps Out, 1938
Queer Cargo, 1938
At the Villa Rose, 1939
Dead Man's Shoes, 1939
The Midas Touch, 1939
George and Margaret, 1940
Tomorrow We Live, 1942
The Butler's Dilemma, 1943
It Happened One Sunday, 1944
Dead of Night, 1945

Dancing With Crime, 1947
Warning to Wantons, 1948

MOULTRIE KELSALL
    (1901-)
Scotch character star of stage
and films, most active during
the 50s.

Landfall, 1949
Last Holiday, 1950
The Franchise Affair, 1951
The Lavender Hill Mob, 1951
Captain Horatio Hornblower,
    1951
Johnny On the Run, 1953
The Master of Ballantrae,
    1953
Albert RN, 1953
The Maggie, 1954
Trouble in the Glen, 1954
The Dark Avenger, 1955
The Man Who Never Was,
    1956
The Barretts of Wimpole Street,
    1957
Seven Waves Away, 1957
The Naked Truth, 1958
Inn of the Sixth Happiness,
    1958
Violent Playground, 1958
Battle of the Sexes, 1959
Beyond This Place, 1959
Light in the Piazza, 1961
The Birthday Party, 1968

JEREMY KEMP (1934-)
Leading actor and strong character star of stage (from 1957),
films, and television, adept at
villainous roles. Tv series:
"Z Cars."

Cleopatra, 1962
Face of a Stranger, 1964
Dr. Terror's House of Horrors,
    1965
Operation Crossbow, 1965
Cast a Giant Shadow, 1966
The Blue Max, 1966
Assignment K, 1968

The Strange Affair, 1968
Twist of Sand, 1968
The Games, 1969
Darling Lili, 1970
Eyewitness, 1970
Pope Joan, 1972
The Belstone Fox, 1973
The Blockhouse, 1974
The Seven Per Cent Solution,
   1976
A Bridge Too Far, 1977
Free Spirit, 1978
Caravans, 1978
Leopard in the Snow, 1978
The Prisoner of Zenda, 1979
The Winter's Tale, 1980

RACHEL KEMPSON (1910-   )
Dignified leading actress of
stage, screen, and television;
married to Sir Michael Redgrave; mother of Vanessa,
Lynn and Corin Redgrave.

Jeannie, 1941
The Captive Heart, 1946
A Woman's Vengeance, 1948
The Sea Shall Not Have Them,
   1955
Tom Jones, 1963
The Third Secret, 1964
Curse of the Fly, 1965
Georgy Girl, 1966
The Jokers, 1966
Charge of the Light Brigade,
   1968
A Touch of Love, 1969
The Virgin Soldiers, 1969
Jane Eyre, 1970
Jennie, 1976

JOAN KEMP-WELCH (1906-   )
Character actress of stage and
screen, usually seen as shy
spinster; turned to tv directing
in the fifties.

Once a Thief, 1935
Girl in the Taxi, 1937
The Girl in the Street, 1938
School For Husbands, 1939

Busman's Honeymoon, 1940
Pimpernel Smith, 1941
Wings and the Woman, 1941
Jeannie, 1941

HENRY KENDALL (1897-1962)
Entertaining light comedian and
revue star of the thirties and
forties, on stage from 1914.

Mr. Pim Passes By, 1921
Tilly of Bloomsbury, 1921
French Leave, 1930
The House Opposite, 1931
The Flying Fool, 1931
Rich and Strange, 1931
Innocents of Chicago, 1932
Watch Beverly, 1932
Mr. Bill the Conqueror, 1932
That's a Good Girl, 1933
The Iron Stair, 1933
The Shadow, 1933
Counsel's Opinion, 1933
King of the Ritz, 1933
Timbuctoo, 1933
The Man Outside, 1933
The Stickpin, 1933
Great Stuff, 1933
The Ghost Camera, 1933
This Week of Grace, 1933
The Flaw, 1933
Without You, 1934
The Man I Want, 1934
Guest of Honour, 1934
The Girl in Possession, 1934
Sometimes Good, 1934
Leave it to Blanche, 1934
Crazy People, 1934
Death at Broadcasting House,
   1934
Death On the Set, 1935
Three Witnesses, 1935
Lend Me Your Wife, 1935
A Wife or Two, 1936
This'll Make You Whistle, 1936
Twelve Good Men, 1936
Amazing Quest of Ernest Bliss,
   1936
Mysterious Mr. Davis, 1936
Ship's Concert, 1937
Take a Chance, 1937
Side Street Angel, 1937

It's Not Cricket, 1937
The Compulsory Wife, 1937
School For Husbands, 1938
The Butler's Dilemma, 1943
29 Acacia Avenue, 1945
Dumb Dora Discovers Tobacco,
   1945
Helter Skelter, 1949
The Voice of Merrill, 1952
An Alligator Named Daisy,
   1955
Shadow of the Cat, 1961
Nothing Barred, 1961

KAY KENDALL (1926-1959)
Beautiful leading lady of the
fifties, former dancer (1941);
also on stage and in Hollywood.
Married: Rex Harrison. Very
adroit at comedy roles.

Fiddlers Three, 1944
Champagne Charlie, 1944
Dreaming, 1944
Caesar and Cleopatra, 1945
Waltz Time, 1945
Spring Song, 1946
London Town, 1946
Dance Hall, 1950
Happy Go Lovely, 1951
Lady Godiva Rides Again, 1951
Wings of Danger, 1952
Curtain Up, 1952
It Started in Paradise, 1952
Mantrap, 1952
Street of Shadows, 1953
The Square Ring, 1953
Meet Mr. Lucifer, 1953
Genevieve, 1953
Fast and Loose, 1954
Doctor in the House, 1954
The Constant Husband, 1955
Simon and Laura, 1955
Quentin Durward, 1955
Abdullah the Great, 1956
Les Girls, 1957
The Reluctant Debutante, 1958
Once More With Feeling, 1960

SUZY KENDALL (1944-   )
Attractive leading actress of

the 60s and 70s; former model.
Also in Hollywood.

Up Jumped a Swagman, 1965
The Liquidator, 1966
Circus of Fear, 1966
The Sandwich Man, 1966
To Sir With Love, 1967
Penthouse, 1967
30 is a Dangerous Age Cynthia,
   1967
Fraulein Doktor, 1968
Up the Junction, 1968
The Gamblers, 1969
The Betrayal, 1969
Assault, 1970
Darker Than Amber, 1970
The Bird With the Crystal
   Plumage, 1970
Fear is the Key, 1972
Craze, 1973
Tales That Witness Madness,
   1973
Diary of a Cloistered Nun,
   1973
Torso, 1974
Spasmo, 1975
To the Bitter End, 1975
Adventures of a Private Eye,
   1977

JAMES KENNEY (1930-   )
Juvenile actor and supporting
player of the 40s and 50s; son
of revue comic Horace Kenney.

Circus Boy, 1947
Vice Versa, 1948
Trapped By the Terror, 1949
Captain Horatio Hornblower,
   1951
The Magic Box, 1951
An Outcast of the Islands,
   1952
The Gentle Gunman, 1952
The Gift Horse, 1952
Cosh Boy, 1953
The Good Die Young, 1954
The Sea Shall Not Have Them,
   1955
Above Us the Waves, 1955
Doctor at Sea, 1955

The Love Match, 1955
The Gelignite Gang, 1956
Yangtse Incident, 1957
Seven Thunders, 1957
Son of a Stranger, 1958
Hidden Homicide, 1959
No Safety Ahead, 1959
Ambush in Leopard Street,
    1962

JEAN KENT (1921-)
Leading lady of the 40s and
50s; also on stage as dancer
from 1932.

The Rocks of Valpre, 1935
Hullo Fame, 1940
It's That Man Again, 1942
Miss London Ltd. , 1943
Warn That Man, 1943
Bees in Paradise, 1944
Fanny By Gaslight, 1944
Two Thousand Women, 1944
Champagne Charlie, 1944
Madonna of the Seven Moons,
    1944
Waterloo Road, 1944
Soldier Soldier, 1944
The Rake's Progress, 1945
Caravan, 1946
Carnival, 1946
The Magic Bow, 1947
The Man Within, 1947
The Loves of Joanna Godden,
    1947
Bond Street, 1948
Sleeping Car to Trieste, 1948
Trottie True, 1949
The Reluctant Widow, 1950
The Woman in Question, 1950
Her Favourite Husband, 1950
The Browning Version, 1951
Before I Wake, 1955
The Prince and the Showgirl,
    1957
Bonjour Tristesse, 1958
Grip of the Strangler, 1958
Beyond This Place, 1959
Please Turn Over, 1959
Bluebeard's Ten Honeymoons,
    1960
Color Him Dead, 1974
Shout at the Devil, 1976

DEBORAH KERR (1921-)
Beautiful, ladylike star of
stage and films; former dancer
(1938).   Often seen in aristocratic or well-bred roles.
Also in Hollywood.

Major Barbara, 1941
Love On the Dole, 1941
Penn of Pennsylvania, 1941
Hatter's Castle, 1941
The Day Will Dawn, 1942
Life & Death of Colonel Blimp,
    1943
Perfect Strangers, 1945
I See a Dark Stranger, 1946
Black Narcissus, 1947
The Hucksters, 1947
If Winter Comes, 1948
Please Believe Me, 1949
Edward My Son, 1949
King Solomon's Mines, 1950
Quo Vadis, 1951
The Prisoner of Zenda, 1952
Dream Wife, 1952
Thunder in the East, 1953
Julius Caesar, 1953
Young Bess, 1953
From Here to Eternity, 1953
The End of the Affair, 1955
The King and I, 1956
The Proud and the Profane,
    1956
Tea and Sympathy, 1956
Heaven Knows Mr. Allison,
    1956
An Affair to Remember, 1957
Separate Tables, 1958
Bonjour Tristesse, 1958
Count Your Blessings, 1959
The Journey, 1959
Beloved Infidel, 1959
The Sundowners, 1960
The Grass is Greener, 1961
The Naked Edge, 1961
The Innocents, 1961
The Chalk Garden, 1964
Night of the Iguana, 1964
Marriage on the Rocks, 1965
Eye of the Devil, 1966
Casino Royale, 1967
Think 20th, 1967
Prudence and the Pill, 1968

The Arrangement, 1969
The Gypsy Moths, 1969

FREDERICK KERR (1858-
1933)
Character player of stage and
screen of the early 30s, primarily cast in doddering or in-
coherent parts. Also Hollywood.

Honour of the Family, 1927
Lady of Scandal, 1930
Raffles, 1930
The Devil to Pay, 1930
Born to Love, 1931
Always Goodbye, 1931
Waterloo Bridge, 1931
Friends and Lovers, 1931
Frankenstein, 1931
Lovers Courageous, 1932
Beauty and the Boss, 1932
But the Flesh is Weak, 1932
The Midshipmaid, 1932
The Man From Toronto,
1933

J. M. KERRIGAN (1885-1964)
Irish character player, formerly
with Abbey Theatre; in Hollywood from 1935.

O'Neill of the Glen, 1916
The Romance of Puck Fair,
1916
Little Old New York, 1923
Lucky in Love, 1929
Song of My Heart, 1930
New Movietone Follies of 1930,
1930
Laughter, 1930
Don't Bet On Women, 1931
The Black Camel, 1931
Merely Mary Ann, 1931
The Rainbow Trail, 1932
Careless Lady, 1932
Rockabye, 1932
Air Hostess, 1933
A Study in Scarlet, 1933
Paddy the Next Best Thing,
1934

The Lost Patrol, 1934
A Modern Hero, 1934
The Key, 1934
The Fountain, 1934
Happiness Ahead, 1934
The Informer, 1935
The Werewolf of London, 1935
Barbary Coast, 1935
A Feather in Her Hat, 1935
Timothy's Quest, 1936
Colleen, 1936
Special Investigator, 1936
Spendthrift, 1936
The General Died at Dawn,
1936
Prisoner of Shark Island, 1936
Lloyds of London, 1936
Plough and the Stars, 1936
Laughing Irish Eyes, 1936
London By Night, 1937
The Barrier, 1937
Vacation From Love, 1938
Ride a Crooked Mile, 1938
Little Orphan Annie, 1939
The Great Man, 1939
Flying Irishman, 1939
Union Pacific, 1939
Six Thousand Enemies, 1939
Zero Hours, 1939
Two Bright Boys, 1939
The Witness Vanishes, 1939
Sabotage, 1939
Gone With the Wind, 1939
Congo Maisie, 1940
Three Cheers For the Irish,
1940
Young Tom Edison, 1940
Untamed, 1940
The Sea Hawk, 1940
One Crowded Night, 1940
No Time For Comedy, 1940
The Long Voyage Home, 1940
Adventure in Washington, 1941
Appointment For Love, 1941
The Wolf Man, 1941
Captain of the Clouds, 1942
The Vanishing Virginian, 1942
Action in the North Atlantic,
1943
Mr. Lucky, 1943
The Fighting Seabees, 1944
Wilson, 1944
Big Bonanza, 1945

Tarzan and the Amazons, 1945
The Great John L, 1945
The Spanish Main, 1945
She Went to the Races, 1946
Black Beauty, 1946
Abie's Irish Rose, 1946
Call Northside 777, 1948
Luck of the Irish, 1948
The Fighting O'Flynn, 1949
Mrs. Mike, 1950
Sealed Cargo, 1951
Park Row, 1952
My Cousin Rachel, 1952
The Wild North, 1952
20,000 Leagues Under the Sea,
    1954
It's a Dog's Life, 1955
The Fastest Gun Alive, 1956

TERRY KILBURN (1926-)
Juvenile player of the thirties
and forties in Hollywood; formerly on radio; latterly stage
director.

Lord Jeff, 1938
A Christmas Carol, 1938
The Boy From Barnardo's,
    1938
Sweethearts, 1939
Goodbye Mr. Chips, 1939
Adventures of Sherlock Holmes,
    1939
They Shall Have Music, 1939
Andy Hardy Gets Spring Fever,
    1939
The Swiss Family Robinson,
    1940
A Yank at Eton, 1942
National Velvet, 1944
Black Beauty, 1946
Song of Scheherazade, 1947
Bulldog Drummond at Bay,
    1947
Only the Valiant, 1951
Fiend Without a Face, 1958

WALTER KINGSFORD (1882-
    1958)
Veteran character actor of
stage and screen; in Hollywood

from the mid-thirties. Usually portrayed benevolent professional men; familiar as
Dr. Carew in the "Dr. Kildare" films.

The Pursuit of Happiness,
    1934
The President Vanishes, 1934
The White Cockatoo, 1935
Mystery of Edwin Drood, 1935
Naughty Marietta, 1935
Shanghai, 1935
I Found Stella Parrish, 1935
The Melody Lingers On, 1935
The Invisible Ray, 1936
Professional Soldier, 1936
The Story of Louis Pasteur,
    1936
Music Goes Round, 1936
Little Lord Fauntleroy, 1936
Trouble For Two, 1936
Hearts Divided, 1936
Meet Nero Wolfe, 1936
Mad Holiday, 1936
Stolen Holiday, 1937
Maytime, 1937
Captains Courageous, 1937
The League of Frightened Men,
    1937
The Devil is Driving, 1937
The Life of Emile Zola, 1937
Double or Nothing, 1937
I'll Take Romance, 1937
Paradise For Three, 1938
A Yank at Oxford, 1938
There's Always a Woman, 1938
Toy Wife, 1938
The Lone Wolf in Paris, 1938
Lord Jeff, 1938
Algiers, 1938
Carefree, 1938
If I Were King, 1938
Young Dr. Kildare, 1938
The Young in Heart, 1938
Say it in French, 1938
Juarez, 1939
Calling Dr. Kildare, 1939
Man in the Iron Mask, 1939
Miracles For Sale, 1939
The Witness Vanishes, 1939
Dancing Co-ed, 1939
Secret of Dr. Kildare, 1939

Adventure in Diamonds, 1940
Dr. Kildare's Strange Case,
   1940
Star Dust, 1940
Lucky Partners, 1940
Dr. Kildare Goes Home, 1940
A Dispatch From Reuters,
   1940
Dr. Kildare's Crisis, 1940
Kitty Foyle, 1940
The Lone Wolf Takes a Chance,
   1941
The People Vs. Dr. Kildare,
   1941
The Devil and Miss Jones,
   1941
Ellery Queen & the Perfect
   Crime, 1941
Dr. Kildare's Wedding Day,
   1941
Unholy Partners, 1941
The Corsican Brothers, 1942
Dr. Kildare's Victory, 1942
My Favorite Blonde, 1942
Fingers at the Window, 1942
Calling Dr. Gillespie, 1942
Loves of Edgar Allan Poe, 1942
Flight For Freedom, 1943
Mr. Lucky, 1943
Bomber's Moon, 1943
Hi Diddle Diddle, 1943
The Hitler Gang, 1944
Mr. Skeffington, 1944
Three Men in White, 1944
Between Two Women, 1945
The Velvet Touch, 1948
The Black Arrow, 1948
Slattery's Hurricane, 1949
My Forbidden Past, 1951
The Desert Fox, 1951
Loose in London, 1953
The Search For Bridey Murphy,
   1956
Merry Andrew, 1958

ROY KINNEAR (1934-)
Rotund comedy character star
and supporting player of the
60s and 70s.

Sparrows Can't Sing, 1962
Tiara Tahiti, 1962

The Boys, 1962
Heavens Above, 1963
The Small World of Sammy
   Lee, 1963
A Place to Go, 1963
The Informers, 1963
French Dressing, 1965
The Hill, 1965
Help!, 1965
The Deadly Affair, 1966
A Funny Thing Happened On
   the Way to the Forum, 1966
Albert Carter QOSO, 1967
How I Won the War, 1967
The Bed Sitting Room, 1969
Lock Up Your Daughters, 1969
Scrooge, 1970
Taste the Blood of Dracula,
   1970
The Firechasers, 1970
Egghead's Robot, 1970
Willie Wonka & the Chocolate
   Factory, 1971
Melody, 1971
The Pied Piper, 1972
The Three Musketeers, 1973
Juggernaut, 1974
One of Our Dinosaurs is Miss-
   ing, 1975
Royal Flash, 1975
Adventures of Sherlock Holmes'
   Smarter Brother, 1975
Herbie Goes to Monte Carlo,
   1977
Last Remake of Beau Geste,
   1977
Eskimo Nell, 1977
Watership Down (voice), 1978
Hound of the Baskervilles, 1978
The London Affair, 1979

PAT KIRKWOOD (1921-)
Ebullient dancer and singer of
stage (since 1936) and screen,
also in Hollywood. Films infrequent. Married to Hubert
Gregg.

Save a Little Sunshine, 1938
Me and My Pal, 1939
Come On George, 1939
Band Wagon, 1940

No Leave No Love, 1942
Flight From Folly, 1945
Once a Sinner, 1950
After the Ball, 1956

ESMOND KNIGHT (1906-)
Welsh star of stage (from
1925) and screen, latterly in
character roles after being
partially blinded in WWII.
Also on tv; married to Nora
Swinburne.

The Blue Peter, 1928
Romany Love, 1931
The Ringer, 1931
77 Park Lane, 1931
Deadlock, 1932
The Bermondsey Kid, 1933
Waltzes From Vienna, 1934
King of Whales, 1934
Lest We Forget, 1934
The Blue Squadron, 1934
Father and Son, 1934
Girls Will Be Boys, 1934
My Old Dutch, 1934
Doctor's Orders, 1934
Womanhood, 1934
Dandy Dick, 1935
Some Day, 1935
Crime Unlimited, 1935
Pagliacci, 1936
Did I Betray, 1936
The Vicar of Bray, 1937
Weddings Are Wonderful, 1938
What Men Live By, 1939
The Arsenal Stadium Mystery,
  1939
Contraband, 1940
Fingers, 1940
This England, 1941
The Silver Fleet, 1943
A Canterbury Tale, 1943
Halfway House, 1944
Henry V, 1944
Black Narcissus, 1947
Uncle Silas, 1947
End of the River, 1947
Holiday Camp, 1947
Hamlet, 1948
The Red Shoes, 1948
Gone to Earth, 1950

The Wild Heart, 1950
Girdle of Gold, 1952
The Steel Key, 1953
Richard III, 1955
Count of Monte Cristo, 1956
OSS, 1956
Sailor of Fortune, 1957
The Prince and the Showgirl,
  1957
Battle of the VI, 1958
Third Man on the Mountain,
  1959
Sink the Bismarck, 1960
Peeping Tom, 1960
The Spy Who Came in From
  the Cold, 1965
A Winter's Tale, 1968
Where's Jack?, 1969
Anne of the Thousand Days,
  1970
The Boy Who Turned Yellow,
  1972
Yellow Dog, 1973
Robin and Marian, 1976
Man in the Iron Mask, 1976
Rebecca, 1980

PATRIC KNOWLES (1911-)
Cultured leading and supporting
star of stage and films, in
Hollywood from 1936. Also
author.

Norah O'Neale, 1934
The Guvnor, 1935
Honours Easy, 1936
Abdul the Damned, 1936
Give Me Your Heart, 1936
The Student's Romance, 1936
Charge of the Light Brigade,
  1936
It's Love I'm After, 1937
Expensive Husbands, 1938
The Patient in Room 18, 1938
Adventures of Robin Hood, 1938
Four's a Crowd, 1938
The Sisters, 1938
Storm Over Bengal, 1938
Heart of the North, 1938
Torchy Blane in Chinatown,
  1939
Beauty For the Asking, 1939

Five Came Back, 1939
The Spellbinder, 1939
Another Thin Man, 1939
The Honeymoon's Over, 1939
Married and in Love, 1940
Women in War, 1940
A Bill of Divorcement, 1940
Anne of Windy Poplars, 1940
How Green Was My Valley,
   1941
The Wolf Man, 1941
Strange Case of Dr. RX, 1942
Eyes of the Underworld, 1942
The Mystery of Marie Roget,
   1942
Lady in a Jam, 1942
Sin Town, 1942
Who Done it?, 1942
Always a Bridesmaid, 1943
Forever and a Day, 1943
Frankenstein Meets the Wolf
   Man, 1943
All By Myself, 1943
Hit the Ice, 1943
Crazy House, 1943
Pardon My Rhythm, 1944
Chip Off the Old Block, 1944
This is the Life, 1944
Masquerade in Mexico, 1945
Kitty, 1946
OSS, 1946
The Bride Wore Boots, 1946
Of Human Bondage, 1946
Monsieur Beaucaire, 1946
Ivy, 1947
Dream Girl, 1948
Isn't it Romantic?, 1948
The Big Steal, 1949
Three Came Home, 1950
Quebec, 1951
Mutiny, 1952
Tarzan's Savage Fury, 1952
No Man's Woman, 1953
Jamaica Run, 1953
Flame of Calcutta, 1953
Khyber Patrol, 1954
World For Ransom, 1956
Band of Angels, 1957
From the Earth to the Moon,
   1958
Auntie Mame, 1958
The Way West, 1967
The Devil's Brigade, 1968

In Enemy Country, 1968
Murder One, 1969
Chisum, 1970
The Man, 1972
Terror in the Wax Museum,
   1973
Arnold, 1973

ALEXANDER KNOX (1907-   )
Canadian character star and
leading actor of stage (from
1929) and screen; film career
divided between Britain and
Hollywood.   Also playwright
and novelist.

The Gaunt Stranger, 1938
The Four Feathers, 1939
Cheer Boys Cheer, 1939
The Sea Wolf, 1941
This Above All, 1942
None Shall Escape, 1943
Wilson, 1944
Over Twenty-One, 1945
Sister Kenny, 1946
The Judge Steps Out, 1947
Sign of the Ram, 1948
Tokyo Joe, 1949
I'd Climb the Highest Moun-
   tain, 1950
Son of Dr. Jekyll, 1951
Two of a Kind, 1951
Saturday's Hero, 1951
Paula, 1952
The Greatest Love, 1952
Commandos Strike at Dawn,
   1954
The Sleeping Tiger, 1954
The Divided Heart, 1954
The Night My Number Came
   Up, 1955
Reach For the Sky, 1956
Alias John Preston, 1956
High Tide at Noon, 1957
Davy, 1957
Operation Amsterdam, 1958
The Two-Headed Spy, 1958
Chase a Crooked Shadow, 1958
The Vikings, 1958
Intent to Kill, 1959
Wreck of the Mary Deare,
   1959

Oscar Wilde, 1960
Crack in the Mirror, 1960
The Damned, 1961
The Shareout, 1962
The Longest Day, 1962
In the Cool of the Day, 1963
Man in the Middle, 1963
Woman of Straw, 1964
Mr. Moses, 1965
Crack in the World, 1965
The Psychopath, 1966
Modesty Blaise, 1966
Khartoum, 1966
Accident, 1967
The 25th Hour, 1967
How I Won the War, 1967
You Only Live Twice, 1967
Villa Rides, 1968
Fraulein Doktor, 1968
Shalako, 1968
Run a Crooked Mile, 1969
Skullduggery, 1970
Nicholas and Alexandra, 1971
Puppet On a Chain, 1971
Meeting at Potsdam, 1976
The Chosen, 1978
Cry of the Innocent, 1980
Tinker, Tailor, Soldier, Spy,
    1980

TEDDY KNOX (1896-1974)
Comedy actor with long stage
and music hall experience; long
teamed with Jimmy Nervo and
member of the "Crazy Gang. "

Nervo and Knox, 1926
The Rising Generation, 1928
Alf's Button, 1930
It's in the Bag, 1936
Skylarks, 1936
Okay For Sound, 1937
Alf's Button Afloat, 1938
Cavalcade of the Stars, 1938
The Frozen Limits, 1939
Gasbags, 1940
Life is a Circus, 1959

HENRY KORRIS (1888-1971)
Popular revue artist and
comedian who made rare film

appearances in the early forties.

Somewhere in England, 1940
Somewhere On Leave, 1942
Somewhere in Camp, 1942
Happidrome, 1943

DAVID KOSSOFF (1919-   )
Character actor of stage (from
1942) and films, former air-
plane designer.   Active in the
50s.

The Good Beginning, 1953
The Young Lovers, 1954
The Angel Who Pawned Her
    Harp, 1955
A Kid For Two Farthings,
    1955
The Bespoke Overcoat, 1955
The Woman For Joe, 1955
Who Done It, 1956
Now and Forever, 1956
Wicked as They Come, 1956
Svengali, 1956
1984, 1956
The Iron Petticoat, 1956
Triple Deception, 1957
Count Five and Die, 1958
Indiscreet, 1958
Innocent Sinners, 1958
Jet Storm, 1959
House of the Seven Hawks,
    1959
The Journey, 1959
The Mouse That Roared, 1959
Inn For Trouble, 1960
Conspiracy of Hearts, 1960
The Two Faces of Dr. Jekyll,
    1960
Freud, 1962
Summer Holiday, 1963
Mouse On the Moon, 1963
Ring of Spies, 1963
Private Life of Sherlock Holmes,
    1970
The London Affair, 1979

KENNETH KOVE (1893-   )
"Silly-ass" comedian of the

thirties, also on stage (from 1913).

Murder, 1930
The Great Game, 1930
Down River, 1931
Chance of a Night Time, 1931
Fascination, 1931
The Man at Six, 1931
Almost a Divorce, 1931
Out of the Blue, 1931
Mischief, 1931
M'Blimey, 1931
Two White Arms, 1932
Help Yourself, 1932
Diamond Cut Diamond, 1932
Pyjamas Preferred, 1932
Her First Affaire, 1932
The Man From Toronto, 1933
Send 'Em Back Half Dead, 1933
Dora, 1933
Crime On the Hill, 1933
Song of the Plough, 1933
The Crimson Candle, 1934
The Life of the Party, 1934
Crazy People, 1934
Youthful Folly, 1934
Radio Pirates, 1935
Marry the Girl, 1935
Look Up and Laugh, 1935
Don't Rush Me, 1936
Cheer Up!, 1936
The Bank Messenger Mystery, 1936
Talking Feet, 1937
Black Eyes, 1939
Asking For Trouble, 1942
They Knew Mr. Knight, 1945
Innocents in Paris, 1953

SAM KYDD (1917-)
Distinctive small-part character player of films and television, often seen in comedy parts.

The Captive Heart, 1946
Scott of the Antarctic, 1948
The Small Back Room, 1948
Movie-Go-Round, 1949
Treasure Island, 1950

The Clouded Yellow, 1950
Pool of London, 1951
High Treason, 1951
Captain Horatio Hornblower, 1951
Penny Points to Paradise, 1951
Secret People, 1952
The Voice of Merrill, 1952
Trent's Last Case, 1952
The Cruel Sea, 1953
Appointment in London, 1953
Death Goes to School, 1953
Singlehanded, 1953
Devil On Horseback, 1954
Radio Cab Murder, 1954
Final Appointment, 1954
They Who Dare, 1954
Storm Over the Nile, 1955
The Quatermass Experiment, 1955
The Ladykillers, 1955
The Long Arm, 1956
Tiger in the Smoke, 1956
Soho Incident, 1956
The Hideout, 1956
Circus Friends, 1956
Yangtse Incident, 1957
Up the Creek, 1958
Further Up the Creek, 1958
Orders to Kill, 1958
I Was Monty's Double, 1958
Law and Disorder, 1958
Hound of the Baskervilles, 1959
The 39 Steps, 1959
Libel, 1959
I'm All Right, Jack, 1959
Sink the Bismarck, 1960
Follow That Horse, 1960
Dead Lucky, 1960
House in Marsh Road, 1960
Treasure of Monte Cristo, 1961
Clue of the Silver Key, 1961
The Iron Maiden, 1962
The Young Detectives, 1963
Smokescreen, 1964
Island of Terror, 1965
The Projected Man, 1966
Gold is Where You Find It, 1968
Till Death Us Do Part, 1968

Too Late the Hero, 1969
10 Rillington Place, 1971
Confessions of a Window
   Cleaner, 1974
Great Expectations, 1975

CATHERINE LACEY (1904-)
Character actress who usually
portrays spinsterish or sympathetic characters, also on
stage.

The Lady Vanishes, 1938
Poison Pen, 1939
All Living Things, 1939
House of the Arrow, 1940
Cottage to Let, 1941
I Know Where I'm Going, 1945
Pink String and Sealing Wax,
   1945
Carnival, 1946
The October Man, 1947
When the Bough Breaks, 1947
The White Unicorn, 1947
Whiskey Galore, 1948
Innocent Sinners, 1953
Man in the Sky, 1957
The Solitary Child, 1958
Rockets Galore, 1958
Crack in the Mirror, 1960
Another Sky, 1960
Shadow of the Cat, 1961
The Servant, 1963
Fighting Prince of Donegal,
   1966
The Sorcerers, 1967
The Mummy's Shroud, 1967
Private Life of Sherlock
   Holmes, 1970

PATRICIA LAFFAN (1919-)
Leading lady and supporting
actress of stage and screen,
also in Hollywood.

The Rake's Progress, 1945
Caravan, 1946
Death in High Heels, 1947
Who Killed Van Loon?, 1948
Hangman's Wharf, 1950
Quo Vadis, 1951

Escape Route, 1953
Rough Shoot, 1953
Don't Blame the Stork, 1954
Devil Girl From Mars, 1954
23 Paces to Baker Street,
   1956
Hidden Homicide, 1959
Crooks in Cloisters, 1963

JENNY LAIRD (1917-)
Character actress and supporting player, also on stage.

Auld Lang Syne, 1937
The House of Silence, 1937
Passenger to London, 1937
The Last Chance, 1937
What a Man, 1937
Lily of Laguna, 1938
Black Eyes, 1939
Just William, 1939
The Lamp Still Burns, 1943
Browned Off, 1944
Painted Boats, 1945
Wanted For Murder, 1946
Beware of Pity, 1946
Making the Grade, 1947
Black Narcissus, 1947
Eyewitness, 1950
The Long Dark Hall, 1951
Life in Her Hands, 1951
Conspiracy of Hearts, 1960
Village of the Damned, 1960
Henry IV Part 2, 1980

JACK LAMBERT (1899-)
Scottish character star of stage
and screen; not to be confused
with American actor Jack Lambert (1920-).

A Honeymoon Adventure, 1931
House Broken, 1936
The Ghost Goes West, 1936
The Spider, 1939
Nine Men, 1943
Hue and Cry, 1946
The Captive Heart, 1946
The Brothers, 1947
Eureka Stockade, 1948
Floodtide, 1949

The Lost Hours, 1952
The Great Game, 1953
The Candlelight Murder, 1953
The Sea Shall Not Have Them,
   1955
Storm Over the Nile, 1955
Cross Channel, 1955
Three Cases of Murder, 1955
Reach For the Sky, 1956
The Little Hut, 1957
Son of Robin Hood, 1958
Greyfriars Bobby, 1960
Bomb in the High Street, 1961
Francis of Assisi, 1961
On the Fiddle, 1961
Cuckoo Patrol, 1965
Modesty Blaise, 1966
Miss MacTaggart Won't Lie
   Down, 1966
Neither the Sea Nor the Sand,
   1972

LLOYD LAMBLE (1914-)
Australian character player
usually cast as policemen, civil
servants, etc. Mainly active
during the 50s.

Lady in the Fog, 1952
Come Back Peter, 1952
Curtain Up, 1952
Gilbert and Sullivan, 1953
Street Corner, 1953
Mantrap, 1953
Three Steps to the Gallows,
   1953
The Mirror and Markheim, 1954
Profile, 1954
The Green Buddha, 1954
Belles of St. Trinian's, 1954
White Fire, 1954
Track the Man Down, 1955
The Gelignite Gang, 1956
The Man Who Never Was, 1956
Suspended Alibi, 1957
Quatermass II, 1957
Barnacle Bill, 1957
Seawife, 1957
There's Always a Thursday,
   1957
Blue Murder at St. Trinian's,
   1958

No Trees in the Street, 1958
The Man Who Wouldn't Talk,
   1958
The Bank Raiders, 1958
The Trials of Oscar Wilde,
   1960
Pure Hell of St. Trinian's,
   1960
Term of Trial, 1962
And Now the Screaming Starts,
   1973

DUNCAN LAMONT (1918-)
Versatile Scottish character
player and general purpose
actor of stage and films; equally
good at sinister or kindly roles.

The Woman in Question, 1950
The Man in the White Suit,
   1951
The Lost Hours, 1952
The Night Won't Talk, 1952
The Intruder, 1953
The Teckman Mystery, 1954
Waterfront, 1954
Meet Mr. Malcolm, 1954
Burnt Evidence, 1954
Time is My Enemy, 1954
The Golden Coach, 1954
End of the Road, 1954
The Passing Stranger, 1954
Passage Home, 1955
Quentin Durward, 1955
The Quatermass Experiment,
   1955
The Baby and the Battleship,
   1956
High Flight, 1957
A Tale of Two Cities, 1958
I Was Monty's Double, 1958
The 39 Steps, 1959
Ben Hur, 1959
A Touch of Larceny, 1959
The Queen's Guards, 1960
Circle of Deception, 1961
Macbeth, 1961
Mutiny On the Bounty, 1962
The Scarlet Blade, 1963
Panic, 1963
Murder at the Gallop, 1963
Devil Ship Pirates, 1964

The Evil of Frankenstein,
1964
The Brigand of Kandahar,
1965
The Murder Game, 1965
The Witches, 1966
Arabesque, 1966
Frankenstein Created Woman,
1967
Quatermass and the Pit, 1967
The Devil's Own, 1967
Dr. Jekyll and Mr. Hyde,
1968
Decline and Fall, 1968
The Battle of Britain, 1969
Pope Joan, 1972
Escape From the Dark, 1976

MOLLY LAMONT (1910-)
Blonde leading lady of the 30s,
former beauty contest winner;
latterly in Hollywood.

The Black Hand Gang, 1930
Uneasy Virtue, 1931
Shadows, 1931
Old Soldiers Never Die, 1931
What a Night, 1931
My Wife's Family, 1931
The House Opposite, 1931
Dr. Josser KC, 1931
Strictly Business, 1932
The Strangler, 1932
Brother Alfred, 1932
Lucky Girl, 1932
The Last Coupon, 1932
Josser On the River, 1932
His Wife's Mother, 1932
Letting in the Sunshine, 1933
Leave it to Me, 1933
Paris Plane, 1933
White Ensign, 1934
Irish Hearts, 1934
The Third Clue, 1934
Wedding Anniversary, 1934
Murder at Monte Carlo, 1935
Alibi Inn, 1935
Oh What a Night, 1935
Handle With Care, 1935
Rolling Home, 1935
Jalna, 1935
Muss 'Em Up, 1936

Mary of Scotland, 1936
Jungle Princess, 1936
A Doctor's Diary, 1937
The Awful Truth, 1937
The Moon and Sixpence, 1942
Mr. Skeffington, 1944
Minstrel Man, 1944
The Suspect, 1945
So Goes My Love, 1946
The Dark Corner, 1946
Ivy, 1947
Christmas Eve, 1947
South Sea Sinner, 1950
The First Legion, 1951

ELSA LANCHESTER (1902-)
Eccentric character star of
stage (1918), screen and tele-
vision; former singer.   Also
Hollywood.   Married to Charles
Laughton.

One of the Best, 1927
The Tonic, 1928
Daydreams, 1928
The Constant Nymph, 1928
Bluebottles, 1928
Mr. Smith Wakes Up, 1929
Comets, 1930
The Love Habit, 1930
The Stronger Sex, 1931
Potiphar's Wife, 1931
The Officer's Mess, 1931
Private Life of Henry VIII,
1933
David Copperfield, 1935
The Bride of Frankenstein,
1935
Naughty Marietta, 1935
Miss Bracegirdle Does Her
Duty, 1936
The Ghost Goes West, 1936
Rembrandt, 1936
Mayflower, 1937
Vessel of Wrath, 1938
Ladies in Retirement, 1941
Tales of Manhattan, 1942
Son of Fury, 1942
Forever and a Day, 1943
Lassie Come Home, 1943
Thumbs Up, 1943
Passport to Adventure, 1944

The Spiral Staircase, 1945
The Razor's Edge, 1946
End of the Rainbow, 1947
Northwest Outpost, 1947
The Bishop's Wife, 1947
The Big Clock, 1948
Come to the Stable, 1949
Secret Garden, 1949
The Inspector General, 1949
Buccaneer's Girl, 1950
Mystery Street, 1950
The Petty Girl, 1950
Frenchie, 1951
Dreamboat, 1952
Les Miserables, 1952
Girls of Pleasure Island,
   1953
Androcles and the Lion, 1953
Hell's Half Acre, 1954
The Glass Slipper, 1955
Three Ring Circus, 1955
Witness For the Prosecution,
   1957
Bell Book and Candle, 1958
Honeymoon Hotel, 1964
Mary Poppins, 1964
Pajama Party, 1964
That Darn Cat, 1965
Blackbeard's Ghost, 1967
Easy Come, Easy Go, 1967
Me Natalie, 1969
Rascal, 1969
Willard, 1971
Arnold, 1973
Terror in the Wax Museum,
   1973
Murder By Death, 1976
Die Laughing, 1980

MARLA LANDI (1937-)
Italian-born leading actress of
British films of the fifites;
former model. Films occasional.

Hornet's Next, 1955
Across the Bridge, 1957
First Man Into Space, 1958
The Dublin Nightmare, 1958
Hound of the Baskervilles, 1959
Pirates of Blood River, 1961
The Murder Game, 1965

AVICE LANDONE (1910-1976)
Unruffled character actress of
stage and screen, often seen
in dignified roles.

My Brother Jonathan, 1948
Guilt is My Shadow, 1950
White Corridors, 1951
The Franchise Affair, 1951
Love in Pawn, 1953
Escape By Night, 1954
The Embezzler, 1954
Windfall, 1955
An Alligator Named Daisy,
   1955
Reach For the Sky, 1956
Eyewitness, 1956
True as a Turtle, 1957
A Cry From the Streets, 1958
Carve Her Name With Pride,
   1958
The Wind Cannot Read, 1958
Family Doctor, 1958
Operation Cupid, 1960
Five Golden Hours, 1961
Gaolbreak, 1962
Nothing But the Best, 1963
The Leather Boys, 1964

LUPINO LANE (1892-1959)
Acrobatic comedy character
star of stage (since 1896) and
films, also in Hollywood.
Brother: Wallace Lupino;
cousins: Barry Lupino, Stanley Lupino.

His Cooling Courtship, 1915
Nipper's Busy Holiday, 1915
Nipper and the Curate, 1915
The Man in Possession, 1915
Nipper's Busy Bee Time,
   1916
A Wife in a Hurry, 1916
The Dummy, 1916
The Missing Link, 1917
Hello, Who's Your Lady
   Friend?, 1917
Splash Me Nicely, 1917
Unexpected Treasure, 1918
Trips and Tribunals, 1918
His Busy Day, 1918

His Salad Days, 1918
Love and Lobster, 1918
A Dreamland Frolic, 1919
Clarence Crooks and Chivalry,
    1919
A Lot About a Lottery, 1920
A Night Out and a Day In,
    1920
The Reporter, 1922
Isn't Life Wonderful?, 1924
The Love Parade, 1929
Show of Shows, 1929
Bride of the Regiment, 1930
The Yellow Mask, 1930
Golden Dawn, 1930
Never Trouble Trouble, 1931
No Lady, 1931
A Southern Maid, 1933
Who's Your Father?, 1935
Trust the Navy, 1935
The Deputy Drummer, 1935
Hot News, 1936
Me and My Gal, 1939
The Lambeth Walk, 1939

HAROLD LANG (1923-1970)
General purpose character
player of the fifties; also drama
instructor.

Floodtide, 1949
The Spider and the Fly, 1949
Cairo Road, 1950
Cloudburst, 1951
Calling Bulldog Drummond, 1951
So Little Time, 1952
Wings of Danger, 1952
It Started in Paradise, 1952
The Saint's Return, 1953
Laughing Anne, 1953
The Long Memory, 1953
Street Corner, 1953
Star of My Night, 1954
Adventure in the Hopfields,
    1954
Dance Little Lady, 1954
36 Hours, 1954
The Passing Stranger, 1954
Men of Sherwood Forest, 1954
Murder By Proxy, 1955
The Quatermass Experiment,
    1955

It's a Wonderful World, 1956
The Hideout, 1956
The Flesh is Weak, 1957
Chain of Events, 1958
Man With a Gun, 1958
The Betrayal, 1958
Carve Her Name With Pride,
    1958
The Nanny, 1965

MATHESON LANG (1879-1948)
Scotch stage (from 1897) and
film actor who despite theatri-
cal style achieved popularity
in the latter media.

The Merchant of Venice, 1916
Masks and Faces, 1917
The Ware Case, 1917
The House Opposite, 1917
Everybody's Business, 1917
Victory and Peace, 1918
Mr. Wu, 1919
Carnival, 1921
Romance of Old Bagdad, 1922
Dick Turpin's Ride to York,
    1922
The Wandering Jew, 1923
Guy Fawkes, 1923
Henry King of Navarre, 1924
Slaves of Destiny, 1924
White Slippers, 1924
The Secret Kingdom, 1925
The Qualified Adventurer, 1925
Island of Despair, 1926
The Chinese Bungalow, 1926
The King's Highway, 1927
Blue Peter, 1928
Triumph of the Scarlet Pim-
    pernel, 1929
The Chinese Bungalow, 1930
Carnival, 1931
Channel Crossing, 1933
Little Friend, 1934
Royal Cavalcade, 1935
Drake of England, 1935
The Cardinal, 1936

ROBERT LANG (1934-   )
Character player of occasional
films; primarily on stage.

Uncle Vanya, 1963
Othello, 1965
Twenty-Nine, 1969
The Dance of Death, 1969
Savage Messiah, 1972
Night Watch, 1973
The Mackintosh Man, 1973
I'm the Girl He Wants to Kill,
    1974
Shout at the Devil, 1976
The Medusa Touch, 1978
The Great Train Robbery, 1979

DAVID LANGTON (-)
Stage and television performer
("Upstairs, Downstairs") in
sporadic, very occasional films.

Seven Waves Away, 1957
A Hard Day's Night, 1964
The Liquidator, 1966
Clouds of Witness, 1973
The Incredible Sarah, 1976

ANGELA LANSBURY (1925-)
Character actress of stage and
screen, in Hollywood from the
mid-forties, usually cast in
domineering or unsympathetic
roles.   Latterly in stage musicals.

Gaslight, 1944
National Velvet, 1944
The Picture of Dorian Gray,
    1945
The Harvey Girls, 1946
The Hoodlum Saint, 1946
Till the Clouds Roll By, 1946
Private Affairs of Bel Ami,
    1947
If Winter Comes, 1948
Tenth Avenue Angel, 1948
State of the Union, 1948
The Three Musketeers, 1948
The Red Danube, 1949
Samson and Delilah, 1949
Kind Lady, 1951
Mutiny, 1952
Remains to be Seen, 1953

Lawless Street, 1955
The Purple Mask, 1955
Please Murder Me, 1956
The Court Jester, 1956
The Key, 1957
The Long Hot Summer, 1958
The Reluctant Debutante, 1958
Summer of the Seventeenth
    Doll, 1959
Dark at the Top of the Stairs,
    1960
A Breath of Scandal, 1960
Blue Hawaii, 1961
All Fall Down, 1962
The Manchurian Candidate,
    1962
In the Cool of the Day, 1963
The World of Henry Orient,
    1964
Dear Heart, 1965
Harlow, 1965
The Greatest Story Ever Told,
    1965
Moll Flanders, 1965
Mr. Buddwing, 1966
Something For Everyone, 1970
Bedknobs and Broomsticks,
    1971
Death On the Nile, 1978
The Lady Vanishes, 1980
The Mirror Crack'd, 1980

HUGH LATIMER (1913-)
Character actor and supporting
star, also seen on stage.

Corridor of Mirrors, 1948
Adventures of PC 49, 1949
Someone at the Door, 1950
Ghost Ship, 1952
Counterspy, 1953
Tim Driscoll's Donkey, 1955
The Last Man to Hang, 1956
Rogue's Yarn, 1956
The Cosmic Monster, 1958
The Gentle Trap, 1960
Night Train to Paris, 1964
Ambush at Devil's Gap, 1966
Talk of the Devil, 1967
School For Sex, 1969
Jane Eyre, 1970

SIR HARRY LAUDER (1870-
1950)
Scottish music hall entertainer
and singer (from 1890) in occasional films; former miner.

Chronophone Shorts, 1907
We Parted On the Shore, 1907
The Wedding of Sandy McNab,
1907
Stop Your Tickling Jock, 1907
She is My Daisy, 1907
Inverary, 1907
I Love a Lassie, 1907
Harry Lauder in a Hurry,
1908
Golfing, 1913
Huntingtower, 1927
Auld Lang Syne, 1930
Harry Lauder Songs, 1931
The End of the Road, 1936
Song of the Road, 1940

CHARLES LAUGHTON (1899-
1962)
Portly, versatile leading man
and character star of stage
(from 1926) and screen, mainly
in Hollywood. Married to Elsa
Lanchester. Also occasional
director.

Wolves, 1927
Bluebottles, 1928
Daydreams, 1928
Piccadilly, 1929
Comets, 1930
Down River, 1930
The Old Dark House, 1932
The Devil and the Deep, 1932
Payment Deferred, 1932
Sign of the Cross, 1932
If I Had a Million, 1932
Island of Lost Souls, 1933
Private Life of Henry VIII,
1933
White Woman, 1933
The Barretts of Wimpole
Street, 1934
Ruggles of Red Gap, 1935
Les Miserables, 1935
Mutiny On the Bounty, 1935

Rembrandt, 1936
I Claudius, 1937
Vessel of Wrath, 1937
St. Martin's Lane, 1938
Jamaica Inn, 1939
The Hunchback of Notre Dame,
1939
They Knew What They Wanted,
1940
It Started With Eve, 1941
The Tuttles of Tahiti, 1941
Tales of Manhattan, 1942
Stand By For Action, 1943
Forever and a Day, 1943
This Land is Mine, 1943
The Man From Down Under,
1943
The Canterville Ghost, 1944
The Suspect, 1945
Captain Kidd, 1945
Because of Him, 1946
The Paradine Case, 1948
The Big Clock, 1948
Arch of Triumph, 1948
Girl From Manhattan, 1949
The Bribe, 1949
Man On the Eiffel Tower, 1950
The Blue Veil, 1951
The Strange Door, 1951
Full House, 1952
Abbott and Costello Meet Cap-
tain Kidd, 1952
Salome, 1953
Young Bess, 1953
Hobson's Choice, 1954
Witness For the Prosecution,
1957
Under Ten Flags, 1960
Spartacus, 1960
Advise and Consent, 1962

JOHN LAURIE (1897-)
Dry, acidulous Scottish character star of stage and screen,
quite frequently seen in stern
or gloomy parts.

Juno and the Paycock, 1929
Red Ensign, 1934
The Thirty-Nine Steps, 1935
Her Last Affaire, 1935
Tudor Rose, 1936

As You Like It, 1936
East Meets West, 1936
Born That Way, 1936
Edge of the World, 1937
Farewell Again, 1937
The Windmill, 1937
Jericho, 1937
There Was a Young Man, 1937
A Royal Divorce, 1938
Q Planes, 1939
The Four Feathers, 1939
The Ware Case, 1939
Convoy, 1940
Laugh it Off, 1940
Sailors Three, 1940
Old Mother Riley's Ghosts, 1941
Old Mother Riley Cleans Up, 1941
The Ghost of St. Michael's, 1941
Ships With Wings, 1941
Dangerous Moonlight, 1941
The Lamp Still Burns, 1943
The Demi-Paradise, 1943
The Gentle Sex, 1943
Life & Death of Colonel Blimp, 1943
Henry V, 1944
The Way Ahead, 1944
Medal For the General, 1944
Fanny By Gaslight, 1944
I Know Where I'm Going, 1945
The World Owes Me a Living, 1945
The Agitator, 1945
Caesar and Cleopatra, 1945
School For Secrets, 1946
Gaiety George, 1946
Jassy, 1947
The Brothers, 1947
Uncle Silas, 1947
Mine Own Executioner, 1947
Bonnie Prince Charlie, 1948
Hamlet, 1948
Floodtide, 1949
No Trace, 1950
Treasure Island, 1950
Madeleine, 1950
Trio, 1950
Happy Go Lovely, 1951
Laughter in Paradise, 1951
Pandora & the Flying Dutch-
man, 1951
Encore, 1952
Potter of the Yard, 1952
Tread Softly, 1952
Saturday Island, 1952
The Fake, 1953
The Great Game, 1953
Too Many Detectives, 1953
Mr. Beamish Goes South, 1953
Love in Pawn, 1953
Strange Stories, 1953
Hobson's Choice, 1954
Devil Girl From Mars, 1954
The Black Knight, 1954
Richard III, 1955
Campbell's Kingdom, 1957
Murder Reported, 1957
Day of Grace, 1957
Rockets Galore, 1958
Next to No Time, 1958
Kidnapped, 1959
Don't Bother to Knock, 1961
Siege of the Saxons, 1963
Ladies Who Do, 1963
Eagle Rock, 1964
The Reptile, 1966
Mr. Ten Per Cent, 1966
Dad's Army, 1971
The Prisoner of Zenda, 1979

JUNE LAVERICK (1932-   )
Leading actress in occasional
films in the late 50s.

Doctor at Large, 1957
Gypsy and the Gentleman, 1957
Son of Robin Hood, 1958
The Duke Wore Jeans, 1958
Follow a Star, 1959

PETER LAWFORD (1923-   )
Light leading actor and latterly
character star of films and
television, in Hollywood from
1938. Tv series: "Dear
Phoebe" (1955), "The Thin
Man" (1958).

Poor Old Bill, 1931
A Gentleman of Paris, 1931

The Boy From Barnardo's,
  1938
Lord Jeff, 1938
Mrs. Miniver, 1942
Random Harvest, 1942
A Yank at Eton, 1942
Thunder Birds, 1942
Girl Crazy, 1943
Immortal Sergeant, 1943
Above Suspicion, 1943
Flesh and Fantasy, 1943
Sahara, 1943
Sherlock Holmes Faces Death,
  1943
Mrs. Parkington, 1944
The White Cliffs of Dover,
  1944
The Canterville Ghost, 1944
Picture of Dorian Gray, 1945
Son of Lassie, 1945
Cluny Brown, 1946
Two Sisters From Boston,
  1946
It Happened in Brooklyn, 1947
My Brother Talks to Horses,
  1947
Good News, 1947
Easter Parade, 1948
On an Island With You, 1948
Julia Misbehaves, 1948
Little Women, 1949
The Red Danube, 1949
Please Believe Me, 1950
Royal Wedding, 1951
Just This Once, 1952
Kangaroo, 1952
You For Me, 1952
The Hour of Thirteen, 1952
Rogue's March, 1953
It Should Happen to You, 1954
Never So Few, 1959
Oceans Eleven, 1960
Pepe, 1960
Exodus, 1960
Sergeants Three, 1961
Advise and Consent, 1962
The Longest Day, 1962
Dead Ringer, 1964
Sylvia, 1965
Harlow, 1965
The Oscar, 1966
A Man Called Adam, 1966
Dead Run, 1967

Skidoo, 1968
Salt and Pepper, 1968
The April Fools, 1969
Hook Line and Sinker, 1969
Buona Sera Mrs. Campbell,
  1969
One More Time, 1970
Ellery Queen: Don't Look
  Behind You, 1971
They Only Kill Their Masters,
  1972
That's Entertainment, 1974
The Phantom of Hollywood,
  1974
Rosebud, 1975
Seven From Heaven, 1979

DELPHI LAWRENCE (1927-)
Anglo-Hungarian actress, popular in British films of the 50s.

Blood Orange, 1953
Meet Mr. Callaghan, 1954
Murder By Proxy, 1955
The Gold Express, 1955
Barbados Quest, 1955
Doublecross, 1956
The Feminine Touch, 1956
It's Never Too Late, 1956
Stranger's Meeting, 1957
Just My Luck, 1957
Blind Spot, 1958
Son of Robin Hood, 1958
Too Many Crooks, 1959
The Man Who Could Cheat
  Death, 1959
Cone of Silence, 1960
The Square Mile Murder, 1961
The Fourth Square, 1961
Seven Keys, 1962
Farewell Performance, 1963
Bunny Lake is Missing, 1965
Pistolero, 1967
The Last Challenge, 1967

GERTRUDE LAWRENCE
  (1898-1952)
Ebullient revue and music hall
star, often in connection with
Noel Coward. Films only occasional. Also Hollywood.

The Battle of Paris, 1929
Aren't We All, 1932
Lord Camber's Ladies, 1932
No Funny Business, 1933
Mimi, 1935
Rembrandt, 1936
Men Are Not Gods, 1937
Stage Door Canteen, 1943
The Glass Menagerie, 1950
Biography, 1950
Skylark, 1951

SARAH LAWSON (1928-)
Leading actress primarily seen
during the fifties.

The Browning Version, 1951
The Night Won't Talk, 1952
Three Steps in the Dark, 1953
Street Corner, 1953
Meet Mr. Malcolm, 1954
You Know What Sailors Are, 1954
Blue Peter, 1955
It's Never Too Late, 1956
Man With a Dog, 1958
The Links of Justice, 1958
Three Crooked Men, 1958
The Solitary Child, 1958
Night Without Pity, 1962
Night of the Big Heat, 1967
The Devil's Bride, 1968

WILFRID LAWSON (1900-1966)
Character actor of stage (from
1916) and screen; seen to best
advantage in eccentric characterizations. Also in Hollywood.

East Lynne, 1931
Strike it Rich, 1933
Turn of the Tide, 1935
Ladies in Love, 1936
White Hunter, 1936
The Man Who Made Diamonds,
   1937
Bank Holiday, 1938
The Terror, 1938
Yellow Sands, 1938
The Gaunt Stranger, 1938
Pygmalion, 1938
Allegheny Uprising, 1939
Stolen Life, 1939

Dead Man's Shoes, 1939
The Long Voyage Home, 1940
Pastor Hall, 1940
Gentleman of Venture, 1940
Danny Boy, 1941
The Man at the Gate, 1941
Jeannie, 1941
The Farmer's Wife, 1941
Tower of Terror, 1941
Hard Steel, 1942
The Night Has Eyes, 1942
The Great Mr. Handel, 1942
Thursday's Child, 1943
Fanny By Gaslight, 1944
Macbeth, 1945
The Turners of Prospect Road,
   1947
Make Me An Offer, 1955
The Prisoner, 1955
An Alligator Named Daisy, 1955
Now and Forever, 1956
War and Peace, 1956
Doctor at Large, 1957
Hell Drivers, 1957
The Naked Truth, 1958
Room at the Top, 1958
Tread Softly Stranger, 1958
Expresso Bongo, 1959
The Naked Edge, 1961
Nothing Barred, 1961
Over the Odds, 1961
Go to Blazes, 1962
Postman's Knock, 1962
Tom Jones, 1963
Becket, 1964
The Wrong Box, 1966
The Viking Queen, 1967

FRANK LAWTON (1904-1969)
Light leading man and latterly
character actor, also in Hollywood. Married to Evelyn Laye.

Young Woodley, 1930
Birds of Prey, 1930
The Skin Game, 1931
The Outsider, 1931
Michael and Mary, 1931
After Office Hours, 1932
Cavalcade, 1933
Heads We Go, 1933
Friday the Thirteenth, 1933
One More River, 1934

David Copperfield, 1935
Invisible Ray, 1936
The Devil Doll, 1936
The Mill On the Floss, 1937
Four Just Men, 1939
Dangerous Comment, 1940
Went the Day Well, 1942
The Winslow Boy, 1948
Rough Shoot, 1953
Doublecross, 1956
The Rising of the Moon, 1957
Gideon's Day, 1957
A Night to Remember, 1958
The Queen's Guards, 1960

EVELYN LAYE (1900-)
Musical comedy actress of
stage (since 1915) and screen,
also in Hollywood. Films
sporadic. Married: Sonnie
Hale; Frank Lawton.

Luck of the Navy, 1927
One Heavenly Night, 1931
Waltz Time, 1933
The Night is Young, 1934
Princess Charming, 1934
Evensong, 1934
Make Mine a Million, 1959
Theatre of Death, 1966
Say Hello to Yesterday, 1970

PHILIP LEAVER (-)
Character player often seen as
continental types, sometimes
villainous.

Too Many Husbands, 1938
The Lady Vanishes, 1938
This Man is News, 1938
Inspector Hornleigh On Holiday,
  1939
Smiling Along, 1939
Alibi, 1942
The Silver Fleet, 1943
Dr. Morelle--Case of the
  Missing Heiress, 1949
Tales of Hoffman, 1951
Mother Riley Meets the Vampire,
  1952
Martin Luther, 1953

The Gamma People, 1956
Spaceways, 1956
The Key Man, 1957
Jack the Ripper, 1959

ANNA LEE (1913-)
Pretty blonde leading lady and
supporting actress, in Hollywood from 1939. Formerly
married to director Robert
Stevenson.

Ebb Tide, 1932
Yes Mr. Brown, 1932
Say it With Music, 1932
King's Cup, 1933
Mayfair Girl, 1933
The Bermondsey Kid, 1933
Mannequin, 1933
Chelsea Life, 1933
Faces, 1934
Lucky Loser, 1934
Rolling in Money, 1934
The Camels Are Coming, 1934
Heat Wave, 1935
First a Girl, 1935
Passing of the Third Floor
  Back, 1936
The Man Who Changed His
  Mind, 1936
OHMS, 1937
King Solomon's Mines, 1937
Non Stop New York, 1937
Four Just Men, 1939
Young Man's Fancy, 1940
Seven Sinners, 1940
Return to Yesterday, 1940
My Life With Caroline, 1941
How Green Was My Valley,
  1941
Flying Tigers, 1942
Flesh and Fantasy, 1942
Hangmen Also Die, 1943
Abroad With Two Yanks, 1944
Summer Storm, 1944
Commandos Strike at Dawn,
  1944
High Conquest, 1945
Bedlam, 1946
The Ghost and Mrs. Muir,
  1947
Fort Apache, 1948

Prison Warden, 1949
The Best Man Wins, 1949
Boots Malone, 1952
Gideon's Day, 1957
The Last Hurrah, 1958
The Horse Soldiers, 1959
This Earth is Mine, 1959
The Big Night, 1960
Two Rode Together, 1961
Whatever Happened to Baby
  Jane?, 1962
Man Who Shot Liberty Valance,
  1962
Jack the Giant Killer, 1962
For Those Who Think Young,
  1964
Unsinkable Molly Brown, 1964
The Sound of Music, 1965
Picture Mommy Dead, 1966
In Like Flint, 1967
Star!, 1968
Scruples, 1980

BELINDA LEE (1935-1961)
Beautiful blonde leading lady
of the fifties, latterly seen in
international films.

The Runaway Bus, 1954
Life With the Lyons, 1954
Meet Mr. Callaghan, 1954
The Belles of St. Trinian's,
  1954
Murder By Proxy, 1955
Footsteps in the Fog, 1955
Man of the Moment, 1955
No Smoking, 1955
Who Done It, 1955
The Feminine Touch, 1956
Eyewitness, 1956
The Secret Place, 1956
The Big Money, 1956
Miracle in Soho, 1957
Dangerous Exile, 1957
Nor the Moon By Night, 1958
Elephant Gun, 1959
Ce Corps Tant Desire, 1959
The Chasers, 1959
Nights of Lucretia Borgia,
  1959
Messalina, 1959
Love the Italian Way, 1960

Joseph and His Brethren,
  1960
Constantine and the Cross,
  1961
Carthage in Flames, 1961

BERNARD LEE (1908-)
Dependable, amiable character actor of stage (from 1914)
and films, generally seen as
police inspector or military
officer. Plays "M" in the
James Bond films.

The Double Event, 1934
River House Mystery, 1935
Rhodes of Africa, 1936
The Black Tulip, 1937
The Terror, 1938
Murder in Soho, 1939
The Frozen Limits, 1939
Let George Do It, 1940
Spare a Copper, 1940
Once a Crook, 1941
This Man is Mine, 1946
The Courtneys of Curzon
  Street, 1947
The Fallen Idol, 1948
Quartet, 1948
Elizabeth of Ladymead, 1949
The Third Man, 1949
The Blue Lamp, 1950
Morning Departure, 1950
Last Holiday, 1950
Odette, 1950
Cage of Gold, 1950
White Corridors, 1951
The Adventurers, 1951
Calling Bulldog Drummond,
  1951
Appointment With Venus, 1951
Mr. Denning Drives North,
  1951
The Gift Horse, 1952
The Yellow Balloon, 1952
Singlehanded, 1952
Beat the Devil, 1953
The Sleeping Partner, 1953
The Rainbow Jacket, 1954
African Story, 1954
Seagulls Over Sorrento, 1954
Father Brown, 1954

The Purple Plain, 1954
Out of the Clouds, 1955
The Ship That Died of Shame, 1955
Battle of the River Plate, 1956
The Spanish Gardener, 1956
Fire Down Below, 1957
Across the Bridge, 1957
High Flight, 1957
Dunkirk, 1958
The Key, 1958
The Man Upstairs, 1958
Nowhere to Go, 1958
Danger Within, 1959
Beyond This Place, 1959
The Angry Silence, 1959
Cone of Silence, 1960
Kidnapped, 1960
Clue of the Twisted Candle, 1960
The Secret Partner, 1961
Fury at Smuggler's Bay, 1961
Partners in Crime, 1961
Whistle Down the Wind, 1961
Clue of the Silver Key, 1961
The Share Out, 1962
Vengeance, 1962
The L-Shaped Room, 1962
Dr. No, 1962
Two Left Feet, 1963
A Place to Go, 1963
From Russia With Love, 1963
Ring of Spies, 1963
Saturday Night Out, 1964
Who Was Maddox?, 1964
Goldfinger, 1964
Dr. Terror's House of Horrors, 1965
Moll Flanders, 1965
Legend of Young Dick Turpin, 1965
The Spy Who Came in From the Cold, 1965
Thunderball, 1965
Operation Kid Brother, 1967
You Only Live Twice, 1967
On Her Majesty's Secret Service, 1968
The Man Who Died Twice, 1970
The Raging Moon, 1970
10 Rillington Place, 1971
Danger Point, 1971
Diamonds Are Forever, 1971
Dulcima, 1972

Live and Let Die, 1973
Frankenstein and the Monster From Hell, 1973
The Man With the Golden Gun, 1974
Percy's Progress, 1975
The Spy Who Loved Me, 1977
Beauty and the Beast, 1977
Moonraker, 1979
Warhead, 1980
For Your Eyes Only, 1981

CHRISTOPHER LEE (1922-)
Tall star of films and television with splendid voice; became famous in horror films during the fifties and has since been seen chiefly in sinister characterizations. Also Hollywood.

Corridor of Mirrors, 1948
Hamlet, 1948
One Night With You, 1948
Penny and the Pownall Case, 1948
Scott of the Antarctic, 1948
A Song For Tomorrow, 1948
Saraband For Dead Lovers, 1948
My Brother's Keeper, 1948
Trottie True, 1949
They Were Not Divided, 1950
Prelude to Fame, 1950
Captain Horatio Hornblower, 1951
Valley of the Eagles, 1951
Top Secret, 1952
Paul Temple Returns, 1952
The Crimson Pirate, 1952
Innocents in Paris, 1953
Moulin Rouge, 1953
The Mirror and Markheim, 1954
The Dark Avenger, 1954
That Lady, 1955
Storm Over the Nile, 1955
Cockleshell Heroes, 1955
Crossroads, 1955
Private's Progress, 1956
Port Afrique, 1956
Beyond Mombasa, 1956
Alias John Preston, 1956

Moby Dick, 1956
Battle of the River Plate, 1956
Ill Met By Moonlight, 1957
Fortune is a Woman, 1957
Curse of Frankenstein, 1957
The Traitor, 1957
The Truth About Women, 1958
A Tale of Two Cities, 1958
Dracula, 1958
Battle of the VI, 1958
Corridors of Blood, 1958
Hound of the Baskervilles, 1959
The Man Who Could Cheat
   Death, 1959
The Mummy, 1959
Treasure of San Teresa, 1959
The Two Faces of Dr. Jekyll,
   1960
Beat Girl, 1960
Too Hot to Handle, 1960
City of the Dead, 1960
The Hands of Orlac, 1960
Taste of Fear, 1961
Terror of the Tongs, 1961
The Longest Day, 1962
The Red Orchid, 1962
The Valley of Fear, 1962
The Devil's Daffodil, 1962
Pirates of Blood River, 1962
The Devil's Agent, 1962
Sherlock Holmes and the Deadly
   Necklace, 1963
What?, 1963
Katharsis, 1963
Faust, 1963
The Virgin of Nuremberg, 1963
The Whip and the Body, 1963
Carmilla, 1963
Devil Ship Pirates, 1963
The Gorgon, 1963
The Sign of Satan, 1964
Horror Castle, 1964
Dr. Terror's House of Horrors,
   1965
She, 1965
The Face of Fu Manchu, 1965
The Skull, 1965
Dracula Prince of Darkness,
   1965
Rasputin the Mad Monk, 1965
House of Blood, 1965
The Dunwich Horror, 1965
Brides of Fu Manchu, 1966

Theatre of Death, 1966
Circus of Fear, 1966
Five Golden Dragons, 1966
Night of the Big Heat, 1967
Vengeance of Fu Manchu, 1967
Diabolica, 1967
The Pendulum, 1968
The Devil Rides Out, 1968
Eve, 1968
Curse of the Crimson Altar,
   1968
Dracula Has Risen From the
   Grave, 1968
Blood of Fu Manchu, 1968
The Castle of Fu Manchu, 1968
The Oblong Box, 1969
Scream and Scream Again, 1969
The Magic Christian, 1970
Julius Caesar, 1970
Taste the Blood of Dracula,
   1970
Private Life of Sherlock Holmes,
   1970
Scars of Dracula, 1970
The House That Dripped Blood,
   1970
One More Time, 1970
I Monster, 1970
Hannie Caulder, 1971
Dracula AD 1972, 1972
Deathline, 1972
The Creeping Flesh, 1972
Nothing But the Night, 1972
Horror Express, 1972
In Search of Dracula, 1973
The Wicker Man, 1973
The Satanic Rites of Dracula,
   1973
Dark Places, 1973
Frankenstein & the Monster
   From Hell, 1973
The Man With the Golden Gun,
   1974
Count Dracula, 1974
Tendre Dracula, 1974
Raw Meat, 1974
The Three Musketeers, 1974
The Four Musketeers, 1975
Diagnosis: Murder, 1975
Killer Force, 1975
To the Devil a Daughter, 1976
The Keeper, 1976
Dracula Pere et Fils, 1976

Airport 77, 1977
Starship Invasions, 1977
End of the World, 1977
Meatcleaver Massacre, 1977
Return From Witch Mountain,
 1978
Count Dracula & His Vampire
 Bride, 1978
Caravans, 1978
Night of the Askari, 1978
The Passage, 1979
The Jaguar Lives, 1979
An Arabian Adventure, 1979
Circle of Iron, 1979
1941, 1979
Serial, 1980
Bear Island, 1980
Once Upon a Spy, 1980

RICHARD LEECH (1922-)
Character player of films and
television; frequently seen in
military roles.

Lease of Life, 1954
Children Galore, 1954
The Dam Busters, 1955
The Long Arm, 1956
It's Never Too Late, 1956
Yangtse Incident, 1957
Night of the Demon, 1957
Time Without Pity, 1957
The Good Companions, 1957
The Moonraker, 1958
Dublin Nightmare, 1958
A Lady Mislaid, 1958
Ice Cold in Alex, 1958
The Horse's Mouth, 1958
A Night to Remember, 1958
The Wind Cannot Read, 1958
Tunes of Glory, 1960
Terror of the Tongs, 1961
The War Lover, 1962
The Wild and the Willing, 1962
I Thank a Fool, 1963
Riccochet, 1963
The Flood, 1963
Walk a Tightrope, 1963
Fighting Prince of Donegal,
 1966
Promenade, 1967
Young Winston, 1972
The Gathering Storm, 1974

ALISON LEGGATT (1904-)
Character actress and supporting player of stage and films.

Nine Till Six, 1932
This Happy Breed, 1944
Waterloo Road, 1945
Marry Me, 1949
A Boy, a Girl, and a Bike,
 1949
The Miniver Story, 1950
The Card, 1952
Encore, 1952
Noose For a Lady, 1953
Touch and Go, 1955
A Woman Possessed, 1958
Never Take Sweets From a
 Stranger, 1960
Day of the Triffids, 1963
Nothing But the Best, 1963
One Way Pendulum, 1964
Far From the Madding Crowd,
 1967
Goodbye Mr. Chips, 1969
The Seven Per Cent Solution,
 1976

BEATRIX LEHMANN (1898-)
Character actress frequently
seen in shy, retiring, or eccentric parts; also on stage
and tv.

Passing of the Third Floor
 Back, 1935
Strangers on a Honeymoon,
 1936
The Rat, 1937
Black Limelight, 1938
Mr. Borland Thinks Again,
 1940
Candles at Nine, 1944
The Key, 1957
On the Fiddle, 1961
Psyche 59, 1964
The Spy Who Came in From
 the Cold, 1964
A Funny Thing Happened On
 the Way to the Forum, 1966
Wonderwall, 1968
Staircase, 1969
Crime and Punishment,
 1980

CARLA LEHMANN (1917-)
Canadian leading actress of
British films of the 40s; also
on stage (from 1935).

So This is London, 1939
Sailors Three, 1940
Cottage to Let, 1941
Once a Crook, 1941
Flying Fortress, 1942
Talk About Jacqueline, 1942
Secret Mission, 1942
Candlelight in Algeria, 1943
Welcome to Britain, 1944
29 Acacia Avenue, 1945
Fame is the Spur, 1947

SUZANNA LEIGH (1945-)
Attractive blonde leading actress
of the sixties; also on television
and in Hollywood.

Oscar Wilde, 1960
Bomb in the High Street, 1961
Boeing Boeing, 1965
The Pleasure Girls, 1965
The Deadly Bees, 1967
Deadlier Than the Male, 1967
Paradise Hawaiian Style, 1967
Subterfuge, 1968
The Lost Continent, 1968
Lust For a Vampire, 1970
The Fiend, 1971
Son of Dracula, 1974

VIVIEN LEIGH (1913-1967)
Beautiful dark-haired leading
lady of stage and screen; gained
fame in Hollywood. Former
wife of Laurence Olivier.

Things Are Looking Up, 1934
The Village Squire, 1935
Gentleman's Agreement, 1935
Look Up and Laugh, 1935
Fire Over England, 1937
Dark Journey, 1937
Storm in a Teacup, 1937
A Yank at Oxford, 1938
21 Days, 1938
St. Martin's Lane, 1938

Guide Dogs For the Blind, 1939
Gone With the Wind, 1939
Waterloo Bridge, 1940
That Hamilton Woman, 1941
Caesar and Cleopatra, 1945
Anna Karenina, 1948
A Streetcar Named Desire,
  1951
The Deep Blue Sea, 1955
The Roman Spring of Mrs.
  Stone, 1961
Ship of Fools, 1965

BARBARA LEIGH-HUNT
  (1941-)
Character actress mainly on
stage and tv. Films few.

A Midsummer Night's Dream,
  1961
Frenzy, 1972
The Six Wives of Henry VIII,
  1972
A Bequest to the Nation, 1973
Oh Heavenly Dog, 1980

RONALD LEIGH-HUNT
  (1916-)
Urbane character player and
supporting star, also on stage
and television.

Paul Temple Returns, 1952
The Broken Horseshoe, 1953
Tiger By the Tail, 1953
Shadow of a Man, 1955
Man On the Cliff, 1955
Hi-Jack, 1957
Zoo Baby, 1957
A Touch of Larceny, 1959
Sink the Bismarck, 1960
Piccadilly Third Stop, 1960
Oscar Wilde, 1960
The Hand, 1960
Very Important Person, 1961
The Invisible Asset, 1963
70 Deadly Pills, 1964
The Third Secret, 1964
Curse of the Voodoo, 1965
The Truth About Spring, 1965
Where the Bullets Fly, 1966

Khartoum, 1966
The Liquidator, 1966
Hostile Witness, 1968
Clegg, 1969
Le Mans, 1969
Baxter, 1973
Mohammed Messenger of God,
    1977

MARGARET LEIGHTON (1922-
    1976)
Polished leading lady and latterly character actress, also
on stage (since 1938) and tv.
Married to Laurence Harvey;
Michael Wilding.   Also in Hollywood.

Bonnie Prince Charlie, 1948
The Winslow Boy, 1948
Under Capricorn, 1949
The Astonished Heart, 1950
The Elusive Pimpernel, 1950
Calling Bulldog Drummond,
    1951
Home at Seven, 1952
The Holly and the Ivy, 1952
The Good Die Young, 1954
The Teckman Mystery, 1954
Carrington VC, 1955
The Constant Husband, 1955
The Passionate Stranger, 1957
The Sound and the Fury, 1959
Waltz of the Toreadors, 1962
The Best Man, 1964
The Third Secret, 1964
The Loved One, 1965
Seven Women, 1966
The Madwoman of Chaillot, 1969
Hamlet, 1970
An Ideal Husband, 1971
The Go-Between, 1971
Zee and Co. , 1971
Lady Caroline Lamb, 1972
Bequest to the Nation, 1973
From Beyond the Grave, 1973
Frankenstein: The True Story,
    1973
Galileo, 1975
Great Expectations, 1975
Dirty Knight's Work, 1976
A Choice of Weapons, 1976

FREDERICK LEISTER (1885-   )
Distinguished character player
of stage (since 1906) and films,
often cast as friendly doctor,
lawyer, etc.

The Message, 1930
Dreyfus, 1931
Bracelets, 1931
Down River, 1931
The World, the Flesh & the
    Devil, 1932
The Iron Duke, 1935
Whom the Gods Love, 1936
OHMS, 1937
The Show Goes On, 1937
Dinner at the Ritz, 1937
King Solomon's Mines, 1937
Sixty Glorious Years, 1938
Goodbye Mr. Chips, 1939
The Outsider, 1939
On the Night of the Fire, 1939
Spellbound, 1940
Atlantic Ferry, 1941
The Prime Minister, 1941
Next of Kin, 1942
We'll Meet Again, 1942
The Shipbuilders, 1943
Dear Octopus, 1943
The Gentle Sex, 1943
One Exciting Night, 1944
Kiss the Bride Goodbye, 1944
The Hundred Pound Window,
    1944
The Agitator, 1945
The Captive Heart, 1946
So Well Remembered, 1947
Mrs. Fitzherbert, 1947
Escape, 1948
Quartet, 1948
Night Beat, 1948
Forbidden, 1949
Paper Orchid, 1949
For Them That Trespass, 1949
Landfall, 1949
All Over Town, 1949
The 20 Questions Murder Mys-
    tery, 1950
The Rossiter Case, 1951
Green Grow the Rushes, 1951
Top Secret, 1952
The Crimson Pirate, 1952
Circumstantial Evidence, 1952

The End of the Affair, 1955
Before I Wake, 1955
The Time of His Life, 1955
Footsteps in the Fog, 1955
Souls in Conflict, 1955
The Dam Busters, 1955
Dangerous Exile, 1957
Family Doctor, 1958
Left, Right, and Centre, 1959
A French Mistress, 1960

JOHN LE MESURIER (1912-)
Character star of films and
television; a master of the quiz-
zical comedy expression. Often in cameo roles as professional man. Tv series: "Dad's
Army" (1968-77).

Death in the Hand, 1948
Escape From Broadmoor, 1948
A Matter of Murder, 1949
Mother Riley's New Venture,
  1949
Dark Interval, 1950
Blind Man's Bluff, 1952
The Drayton Case, 1953
The Blue Parrott, 1953
Black Thirteen, 1953
Dangerous Cargo, 1954
Beautiful Stranger, 1954
Police Dog, 1955
Josephine and Men, 1955
A Time to Kill, 1955
The Baby and the Battleship,
  1956
Battle of the River Plate, 1956
Private's Progress, 1956
Happy is the Bride, 1957
Brothers in Law, 1957
The Good Companions, 1957
These Dangerous Years, 1957
High Flight, 1957
Law and Disorder, 1958
I Was Monty's Double, 1958
The Moonraker, 1958
The Man Who Wouldn't Talk,
  1958
Blind Spot, 1958
Man With a Gun, 1958
Blood of the Vampire, 1958
I'm All Right, Jack, 1959

Too Many Crooks, 1959
A Touch of Larceny, 1959
Carleton Browne of the FO,
  1959
Hound of the Baskervilles,
  1959
The Captain's Table, 1959
Our Man in Havana, 1959
Shake Hands With the Devil,
  1959
Jack the Ripper, 1960
Follow a Star, 1960
School For Scoundrels, 1960
Day They Robbed the Bank of
  England, 1960
Let's Get Married, 1960
Never Let Go, 1960
Dead Lucky, 1960
Doctor in Love, 1960
The Night We Got the Bird,
  1960
Pure Hell of St. Trinian's,
  1960
The Bulldog Breed, 1960
The Rebel, 1961
Invasion Quartet, 1961
Five Golden Hours, 1961
Don't Bother to Knock, 1961
On the Fiddle, 1961
Very Important Person, 1961
Mr. Topaze, 1962
Jigsaw, 1962
Hair of the Dog, 1962
Go To Blazes, 1962
Flat Two, 1962
Village of Daughters, 1962
Waltz of the Toreadors, 1962
Mrs. Gibbons' Boys, 1962
Only Two Can Play, 1962
Wrong Arm of the Law, 1962
We Joined the Navy, 1962
The Punch and Judy Man, 1963
The Pink Panther, 1963
In the Cool of the Day, 1963
Never Put it in Writing, 1963
Hot Enough For June, 1963
The Mouse On the Moon, 1963
The Main Attraction, 1963
The Moonspinners, 1964
The Early Bird, 1965
City Under the Sea, 1965
Cuckoo Patrol, 1965
Masquerade, 1965

Where the Spies Are, 1965
Those Magnificent Men in
   Their Flying Machines, 1965
The Sandwich Man, 1966
Eye of the Devil, 1966
The Liquidator, 1966
Finders Keepers, 1966
Mr. Ten Per Cent, 1966
The Wrong Box, 1966
Our Man in Marrakesh, 1966
Casino Royale, 1967
Salt and Pepper, 1968
The Undertakers, 1969
The Italian Job, 1969
Midas Run, 1969
The Magic Christian, 1970
Doctor in Trouble, 1970
Dad's Army, 1971
The Alf Garnett Saga, 1972
Au Pair Girls, 1973
File It Under Fear, 1973
Confessions of a Window
   Cleaner, 1974
Brief Encounter, 1974
The Adventures of Sherlock
   Holmes' Smarter Brother,
   1975
Stand Up Virgin Soldiers, 1977
Jabberwocky, 1977
Who's Killing the Great Chefs
   of Europe?, 1978
The Spaceman & King Arthur, 1979
The Fiendish Plot of Dr. Fu Man-
   chu, 1980

QUEENIE LEONARD (-)
Charming, inimitable small-
part character actress, usually
seen as maids or the like; in
Hollywood from early 40s.
Also on tv.

Who Killed Doc Robin?, 1931
Pity the Poor Rich, 1935
Limelight, 1936
Skylarks, 1936
Moonlight Sonata, 1937
Kate Plus Ten, 1938
Ladies in Retirement, 1941
Confirm or Deny, 1941
Eagle Squadron, 1942
This Above All, 1942
Thumbs Up, 1943

Forever and a Day, 1943
Our Hearts Were Young and
   Gay, 1944
The Lodger, 1944
Molly and Me, 1945
My Name is Julia Ross, 1945
And Then There Were None,
   1945
Cluny Brown, 1946
The Locket, 1946
Life With Father, 1947
The Lone Wolf in London,
   1947
The Black Arrow, 1948
Thunder On the Hill, 1951
Lorna Doone, 1951
Alice in Wonderland, 1951
Les Miserables, 1952
The Narrow Margin, 1952
Thunder in the East, 1953
The King's Thief, 1955
23 Paces to Baker Street,
   1956
D-Day, the Sixth of June, 1956
A Hundred and One Dalmations
   (voice), 1961
Hatari!, 1962
Notorious Landlady, 1962
The Prize, 1963
Mary Poppins, 1964
My Fair Lady, 1964
What a Way to Go!, 1964
Doctor Dolittle, 1967
Star!, 1968
Bedknobs and Broomsticks,
   1971

CAROLE LESLEY (1935-1974)
Leading actress who attained
brief stardom during the 50s;
films fairly rare.

The Silver Darlings, 1947
Trottie True, 1949
These Dangerous Years, 1957
Woman in a Dressing Gown,
   1957
No Trees in the Street, 1958
Operation Bullshine, 1959
Doctor in Love, 1960
Three On a Spree, 1961
What a Whopper, 1962
The Pot Carriers, 1962

MARK LESTER (1958-   )
Juvenile player of the sixties
and seventies who gained recog-
nition in the role of "Oliver."

Allez France, 1964
Spaceflight IC-1, 1965
Fahrenheit 451, 1966
Our Mother's House, 1967
Oliver!, 1968
Run Wild Run Free, 1969
Eyewitness, 1970
Melody, 1971
Black Beauty, 1971
Night Hair Child, 1971
Whoever Slew Auntie Roo?,
   1972
Scalawag, 1973
Redneck, 1975
Little Adventurer, 1975
Crossed Swords, 1978

HUMPHREY LESTOCQ (-)
Character actor and supporting
star of the 50s and 60s.

Stop Press Girl, 1949
Once a Sinner, 1950
Two On the Tiles, 1951
Angels One Five, 1952
Come Back Peter, 1952
The Good Beginning, 1953
Meet Mr. Lucifer, 1953
Son of Robin Hood, 1958
Not a Hope in Hell, 1960
The Unstoppable Man, 1960
The Long Shadow, 1960
Two Wives at One Wedding,
   1961
The Third Alibi, 1961
Pit of Darkness, 1961
The Court Martial of Major
   Keller, 1961
Bomb in the High Street, 1961
The Golden Rabbit, 1962
Design For Living, 1962
Waltz of the Toreadors, 1962

FIONA LEWIS (1946-   )
Brunette leading actress of the
70s, also on television. Latterly in Hollywood.

The Fearless Vampire Killers,
   1967
Joanna, 1968
Otley, 1968
Where's Jack?, 1969
Villain, 1971
Dr. Phibes Rises Again, 1972
Dracula, 1973
Lisztomania, 1975
Drum, 1976
Stunts, 1977
The Fury, 1978
Tintorera, 1978
Wanda Nevada, 1979

RONALD LEWIS (1928-   )
Welsh leading man of the fif-
ties, also on stage (from 1951).
Also in Hollywood.

The Square Ring, 1953
The Beachcomber, 1954
The Prisoner, 1955
Storm Over the Nile, 1955
A Hill in Korea, 1956
Sailor Beware, 1956
The Secret Place, 1957
Robbery Under Arms, 1957
The Wind Cannot Read, 1958
Bachelor of Hearts, 1958
Conspiracy of Hearts, 1960
Stop Me Before I Kill, 1961
The Full Treatment, 1961
Taste of Fear, 1961
Billy Budd, 1962
Jigsaw, 1962
Twice Round the Daffodils,
   1962
Nurse On Wheels, 1963
Mr. Sardonicus, 1963
Siege of the Saxons, 1963
The Brigand of Kandahar, 1965
Friends, 1971
Paul and Michelle, 1974

EDWARD LEXY (1897-   )
Popular character player of
the 30s and 40s, generally
seen in military or detective
roles.

Farewell Again, 1937

Smash and Grab, 1937
Mademoiselle Docteur, 1937
The Terror, 1938
The Drum, 1938
South Riding, 1938
This Man is News, 1938
Kate Plus Ten, 1938
Second Best Bed, 1938
St. Martin's Lane, 1938
Many Tanks Mr. Atkins, 1938
Night Journey, 1938
Too Dangerous to Live, 1939
The Gang's All Here, 1939
The Outsider, 1939
This Man in Paris, 1939
Mrs. Pym of Scotland Yard,
   1939
The Spider, 1939
Traitor Spy, 1939
Laugh it Off, 1940
Spare a Copper, 1940
Convoy, 1940
The Proud Valley, 1940
Larceny Street, 1941
Medal For the General, 1944
Girl in a Million, 1946
Piccadilly Incident, 1946
School For Secrets, 1946
While I Live, 1947
Captain Boycott, 1947
Blanche Fury, 1948
The Mark of Cain, 1948
The Winslow Boy, 1948
It's Not Cricket, 1949
Children of Chance, 1949
Three Men and a Girl, 1949
The 20 Questions Murder
   Mystery, 1950
Cloudburst, 1951
Smart Alec, 1951
Night Was Our Friend, 1951
You're Only Young Twice, 1952
Miss Robin Hood, 1952
Orders Are Orders, 1954
Where There's a Will, 1955
The Rising of the Moon, 1957
The Man Who Wouldn't Talk,
   1958

JOHN LEYTON (1939-   )
Pop singer and occasional
actor of the sixties, primarily
in subsidiary roles.

The Johnny Leyton Touch,
   1961
It's Trad, Dad, 1962
The Great Escape, 1963
Guns at Batasi, 1964
Every Day's a Holiday, 1964
Von Ryan's Express, 1965
The Idol, 1966
Krakatoa, 1968
Schizo, 1978

ALBERT LIEVEN (1906-1971)
German-born character actor
of stage (from 1928) and films,
primarily in Britain. Also in
international films. Formerly
married to Susan Shaw.

I By Day and You By Night,
   1932
Lower Rhine Folkes, 1933
Reifende Jugend, 1933
Charley's Aunt, 1934
Gluckspilze, 1934
Fraulein Liselott, 1934
Krach um Iolanthe, 1934
Die Klugen Frauen, 1935
Kater Lampe, 1936
Victoria the Great, 1937
Eine Frau Ohne Bedeutung,
   1938
Night Train to Munich, 1940
Convoy, 1940
For Freedom, 1940
Spy For a Day, 1940
Neutral Port, 1940
Jeannie, 1941
The Big Blockade, 1942
The Young Mr. Pitt, 1942
Life and Death of Colonel
   Blimp, 1943
The Yellow Canary, 1943
English Without Tears, 1944
The Seventh Veil, 1945
Beware of Pity, 1946
Frieda, 1947
Sleeping Car to Trieste, 1948
Hotel Sahara, 1948
The Dark Light, 1951
The Rose From Stamboul, 1953
Geleibtes Leben, 1953
Desperate Moment, 1953
The Devil's General, 1955

Reifende Jugend, 1955
Loser Takes All, 1955
House of Intrigue, 1956
Subway in the Sky, 1959
Conspiracy of Hearts, 1960
The Royal Game, 1960
A Foxhole in Cairo, 1961
The Devil's Daffodil, 1961
The Guns of Navarone, 1961
Death Trap, 1962
The Victors, 1963
Mystery Submarine, 1963
Sanders of the River, 1963
Traitor's Gate, 1964
Ride the High Wind, 1965
City of Fear, 1966
The Gorilla Gang, 1968

GILLIAN LIND (1904-)
Character actress, also on
stage; married to Cyril Raymond.

Condemned to Death, 1932
The Man Outside, 1933
Dick Turpin, 1933
Open All Night, 1934
Death Croons the Blues, 1937
The Oracle, 1953
The Heart of the Matter, 1953
Aunt Clara, 1954
Don't Talk to Strange Men, 1962
And Now the Screaming Starts,
1973

JEANNIE LINDEN (1939-)
Leading and supporting actress
in occasional films of the 60s
and 70s.

Nightmare, 1963
Dr. Who and the Daleks, 1966
Women in Love, 1969
A Severed Head, 1971
Hedda, 1975
Old Dracula, 1975
Valentino, 1977

CEC LINDER (-)
Canadian character player,
long resident in Britain.

Crack in the Mirror, 1959
Jet Storm, 1959
Subway in the Sky, 1959
SOS Pacific, 1959
Too Young to Love, 1960
Lolita, 1962
Goldfinger, 1964
The Verdict, 1964
Explosion, 1971
Innocent Bystanders, 1972
A Touch of Class, 1973
Sunday in the Country, 1975
Why Rock the Boat?, 1975
Arthur Miller on Home Ground,
1979
Lost and Found, 1979
City on Fire, 1979

OLGA LINDO (1898-1968)
Anglo-Norwegian character
actress long in British films;
also on stage. Sometimes
seen as landlady or maid.

The Shadow Between, 1931
Dark World, 1935
The Last Journey, 1935
Royal Cavalcade, 1935
The Case of Gabriel Perry,
1935
A Romance in Flanders, 1937
Luck of the Navy, 1938
What Men Live By, 1939
The Stars Look Down, 1939
Return to Yesterday, 1940
Alibi, 1942
When We Are Married, 1943
Time Flies, 1944
Give Me the Stars, 1944
Night Boat to Dublin, 1946
Bedelia, 1946
I See a Dark Stranger, 1946
The Phantom Shot, 1947
Things Happen at Night, 1948
Obsession, 1949
Train of Events, 1949
The 20 Questions Murder
Mystery, 1950
An Inspector Calls, 1954
Raising a Riot, 1955
The Extra Day, 1956
Yield to the Night, 1956
Woman in a Dressing Gown,

1957
Sapphire, 1959
Make Mine a Million, 1959
Dr. Crippen, 1962
Out of the Fog, 1962

FRANCIS LISTER (1899-1951)
Elegant character star of the
thirties and forties, also in
Hollywood. Married to Nora
Swinburne.

Branded, 1920
Old Wives' Tale, 1921
The Fortune of Christina
McNab, 1921
Should a Doctor Tell?, 1923
Boden's Boy, 1923
The Unwanted, 1924
Comin' Thro' the Rye, 1924
Atlantic, 1929
At the Villa Rose, 1930
Uneasy Virtue, 1931
Brown Sugar, 1931
Jack's the Boy, 1932
Night and Day, 1933
Counsel's Opinion, 1933
Hawleys of High Street, 1933
Up to the Neck, 1933
Clive of India, 1935
Cardinal Richelieu, 1935
Living Dangerously, 1936
Sensation, 1937
Return of the Scarlet Pimpernel,
1937
Murder in Soho, 1939
Henry V, 1944
The Hundred Pound Window,
1944
The Wicked Lady,
Christopher Columbus, 1949
Home to Danger, 1951

MOIRA LISTER (1923-)
Pretty South-African born leading lady and latterly character
actress; also on stage as child
from 1929.

The Shipbuilders, 1943
Love Story, 1944

My Ain Folk, 1944
Don Chicago, 1945
The Agitator, 1945
Wanted For Murder, 1946
Mrs. Fitzherbert, 1947
Uneasy Terms, 1948
So Evil My Love, 1948
Another Shore, 1948
Once a Jolly Swagman, 1948
A Run For Your Money, 1949
Pool of London, 1951
Files From Scotland Yard,
1951
White Corridors, 1951
Something Money Can't Buy,
1952
The Cruel Sea, 1953
Grand National Night, 1953
Trouble in Store, 1953
The Limping Man, 1953
John and Julie, 1955
The Deep Blue Sea, 1955
Seven Waves Away, 1957
The Yellow Rolls-Royce, 1964
Joey Boy, 1965
The Double Man, 1967
Stranger in the House, 1967
Not Now Darling, 1973

JACK LIVESEY (1901-1961)
Welsh character actor active
during the thirties; brother of
Roger Livesey, son of Sam
Livesey.

The Wandering Jew, 1933
Song of the Plough, 1933
Husbands Are So Jealous, 1934
The End of the Act, 1934
The Passing of the Third Floor
Back, 1935
Variety, 1935
The Howard Case, 1936
Rembrandt, 1936
It's Never Too Late To Mend,
1937
Behind Your Back, 1937
When the Poppies Bloom Again,
1937
First Night, 1937
Murder Tomorrow, 1938
Bedtime Story, 1938

Penny Paradise, 1938
Old Bones of the River, 1938
Old Bill and Son, 1940
The World Owes Me a Living,
  1945
The First Gentleman, 1948
Murder at the Windmill, 1949
Paul Temple's Triumph, 1950
That Touch of Mink, 1962

ROGER LIVESEY (1906-1976)
Distinguished, inimitable Welsh
star and character actor of
stage (1917) and films, also
notable on tv in "The Pallisers."
Son of Sam Livesey, brother of
Jack Livesey. Married: Ursula Jeans.

The Old Curiosity Shop, 1920
Where the Rainbow Ends, 1921
The Four Feathers, 1921
Married Love, 1923
East Lynne, 1931
A Veteran of Waterloo, 1933
A Cuckoo in the Nest, 1933
Blind Justice, 1934
Lorna Doone, 1935
The Price of Wisdom, 1935
Midshipman Easy, 1935
Rembrandt, 1936
The Drum, 1938
Keep Smiling, 1938
Spies of the Air, 1939
Rebel Son, 1939
The Girl in the News, 1940
Life and Death of Colonel
  Blimp, 1943
I Know Where I'm Going, 1945
A Matter of Life and Death,
  1946
Vice Versa, 1948
That Dangerous Age, 1949
Green Grow the Rushes, 1951
The Master of Ballantrae, 1953
The Intimate Stranger, 1956
It Happened in Broad Daylight,
  1958
The League of Gentlemen, 1959
The Entertainer, 1960
No My Darling Daughter, 1961
Of Human Bondage, 1964

Moll Flanders, 1965
Oedipus the King, 1968
Hamlet, 1970
Futtock's End, 1970

SAM LIVESEY (1873-1936)
Welsh character actor of the
thirties. Sons: Jack Livesey,
Roger Livesey.

Victory and Peace, 1918
The Chinese Puzzle, 1919
Sinless Sinners, 1919
The Black Spider, 1920
Burnt In, 1920
All the Winners, 1920
Marriage Line, 1921
Married Love, 1923
Zero, 1928
Wait and See, 1928
The Forger, 1928
Blackmail, 1929
Young Woodley, 1929
Young Woodley (remake), 1930
Raise the Roof, 1930
One Family, 1930
Dreyfus, 1931
The Girl in the Night, 1931
Up For the Cup, 1931
Many Waters, 1931
The Wickham Mystery, 1931
Hound of the Baskervilles, 1931
Jealousy, 1931
Mr. Bill the Conqueror, 1932
Insult, 1932
The Wonderful Story, 1932
The Flag Lieutenant, 1932
The Shadows, 1933
Commissionaire, 1933
The Private Life of Henry VIII,
  1933
Jew Suss, 1934
Tangled Evidence, 1934
The Great Defender, 1934
Turn of the Tide, 1935
Variety, 1935
Royal Cavalcade, 1935
Drake of England, 1935
Where's George?, 1935
Calling the Tune, 1936
Men of Yesterday, 1936
Rembrandt, 1936

Wings of the Morning, 1937
The Mill On the Floss, 1937
Dark Journey, 1937

DESMOND LLEWELYN (-)
Welsh character actor of films
and tv, best recognized as "Q,"
the gadget man, in the James
Bond films.

They Were Not Divided, 1950
Bunty Wins a Pup, 1953
Sword of Sherwood Forest, 1960
Cleopatra, 1962
Dr. No, 1962
From Russia With Love, 1963
The Silent Playground, 1963
Goldfinger, 1964
Thunderball, 1965
Operation Kid Brother, 1967
You Only Live Twice, 1967
On Her Majesty's Secret Ser-
    vice, 1968
Diamonds Are Forever, 1971
Live and Let Die, 1973
The Man With the Golden Gun,
    1974
The Nine Tailors, 1974
The Spy Who Loved Me, 1977
Moonraker, 1979
Warhead, 1980
For Your Eyes Only, 1981

FEWLASS LLEWELYN (-)
Welsh character actor of the
30s; often seen as titled gentlemen.

The Lady Clare, 1919
A Bill For Divorcement, 1922
This Freedom, 1923
The Flag Lieutenant, 1926
Further Adventures of the Flag
    Lieutenant, 1927
Virginia's Husband, 1928
Afterwards, 1928
The Outsider, 1931
The Officer's Mess, 1931
Ask Beccles, 1933
Red Ensign, 1934
Seeing is Believing, 1934

The Phantom Light, 1935
Stormy Weather, 1935
On Top of the World, 1936
Jack of All Trades, 1936
All In, 1936
Good Morning Boys, 1937
It's a Grand Old World, 1937
Brief Ecstasy, 1937
Special Edition, 1938
A Spot of Bother, 1938

DORIS LLOYD (1899-1968)
Character actress of stage and
screen, in Hollywood from the
20s; often seen in aristocratic
parts.

The Lady, 1925
The Black Bird, 1926
The Midnight Kiss, 1926
Exit Smiling, 1926
Is Zat So?, 1927
Lonesome Ladies, 1927
Two Girls Wanted, 1927
Come to My House, 1928
The Careless Age, 1928
The Drake Case, 1929
Disraeli, 1929
Sarah and Son, 1930
Old English, 1930
Reno, 1930
Charley's Aunt, 1930
Way For a Sailor, 1930
Transgression, 1931
Bought, 1931
Once a Lady, 1931
Waterloo Bridge, 1931
Devotion, 1931
Bachelor Father, 1931
Tarzan the Ape Man, 1932
Back Street, 1932
Secrets, 1933
Oliver Twist, 1933
Looking Forward, 1933
Peg O' My Heart, 1933
A Study in Scarlet, 1933
Voltaire, 1933
Tarzan and His Mate, 1934
She Was a Lady, 1934
Glamour, 1934
Sisters Under the Skin, 1934
Kiss and Make Up, 1934

British Agent, 1934
Clive of India, 1935
Becky Sharp, 1935
Peter Ibbetson, 1935
The Woman in Red, 1935
A Shot in the Dark, 1935
The Perfect Gentleman, 1935
Don't Get Personal, 1936
Mary of Scotland, 1936
Plough and the Stars, 1936
Tovarich, 1937
The Soldier and the Lady, 1937
Alcatraz Island, 1937
Vigil in the Night, 1939
I'm From Missouri, 1939
The Under Pup, 1939
Barricade, 1939
The Letter, 1940
The Great Plane Robbery, 1940
Shining Victory, 1941
The Great Lie, 1941
Ghost of Frankenstein, 1942
Night Monster, 1942
Journey For Margaret, 1942
Mission to Moscow, 1943
The Constant Nymph, 1943
The Lodger, 1944
Phantom Lady, 1944
Molly and Me, 1945
My Name is Julia Ross, 1945
Devotion, 1946
Holiday in Mexico, 1946
Of Human Bondage, 1946
The Secret Life of Walter
    Mitty, 1947
Sign of the Ram, 1948
Kind Lady, 1951
Young Bess, 1953
A Man Called Peter, 1955
The Swan, 1956
The Time Machine, 1960
Midnight Lace, 1960
Notorious Landlady, 1962
Mary Poppins, 1964
The Sound of Music, 1965
Rosie, 1967

FREDERICK LLOYD (-)
Character actor of the thirties,
also on stage.

The W Plan, 1930

The Temporary Widow, 1930
Hound of the Baskervilles,
    1931
The Perfect Lady, 1931
The Great Gay Road, 1931
A Gentleman of Paris, 1931
The Beggar Student, 1931
Tell England, 1931
Sleepless Nights, 1932
Arms and the Man, 1932
The Crime at Blossom's, 1933
The Song You Gave Me, 1933
Mixed Doubles, 1933
Up For the Derby, 1933
Blossom Time, 1934
Radio Pirates, 1935
Royal Cavalcade, 1935
Lieutenant Daring RN, 1935
Everything is Thunder, 1936
Secret Lives, 1937
Mademoiselle Docteur, 1937
April Romance, 1937
Weddings Are Wonderful, 1938
21 Days, 1939
Oliver Twist, 1948

JEREMY LLOYD (-)
Supporting actor of the 60s,
mainly seen in comedy characterizations. Also on tv.

Very Important Person, 1961
Operation Snatch, 1962
We Joined the Navy, 1962
Just For Fun, 1963
Death Drums Along the River,
    1963
Three Hats For Lisa, 1965
Doctor in Clover, 1965
Those Magnificent Men in Their
    Flying Machines, 1965
The Liquidator, 1966
The Wrong Box, 1966
Smashing Time, 1967
The Assassination Bureau, 1969
Games That Lovers Play, 1970
The Magic Christian, 1970
Murder On the Orient Express,
    1974
Bawdy Adventures of Tom
    Jones, 1975

NORMAN LLOYD (1914-)
Character player mainly seen
in Hollywood; often cast as
weakling or villain; latterly tv
producer, notably on the Alfred
Hitchcock program.

Saboteur, 1942
Within These Walls, 1945
The Unseen, 1945
The Southerner, 1945
Spellbound, 1945
A Letter For Eve, 1946
The Young Widow, 1946
A Walk in the Sun, 1946
The Green Years, 1946
The Beginning or the End,
1947
No Minor Vices, 1948
Scene of the Crime, 1949
Calamity Jane and Sam Bass,
1949
The Black Book, 1949
Buccaneer's Girl, 1950
The Flame and the Arrow,
1950
M, 1951
He Ran All the Way, 1951
The Light Touch, 1952
Limelight, 1952
Audrey Rose, 1977
FM, 1978
The Nude Bomb, 1980

SUE LLOYD (1939-)
Attractive leading lady of the
60s and 70s.

Who Was Maddox?, 1964
Hysteria, 1964
The Return of Mr. Moto, 1965
The Ipcress File, 1965
That Riviera Touch, 1966
The Champagne Murders, 1967
Attack On the Iron Coast, 1968
Corruption, 1968
Where's Jack?, 1969
Ned Kelly, 1970
Percy, 1971
Innocent Bystanders, 1972
Go For a Take, 1972
That's Your Funeral, 1973

Penny Gold, 1973
Spanish Fly, 1976
The Happy Housewives, 1976
Revenge of the Pink Panther,
1978
Rough Cut, 1980

CHARLES LLOYD-PACK
(1905-)
Stage and screen character
player, mainly seen in humble
roles.

High Treason, 1951
I'm a Stranger, 1952
The Importance of Being
Earnest, 1952
Noose For a Lady, 1953
River Beat, 1954
Conflict of Wings, 1954
The Constant Husband, 1955
Loser Takes All, 1956
The Scamp, 1957
Night of the Demon, 1957
Alive On Saturday, 1957
Quatermass II, 1957
Stranger in Town, 1957
Revenge of Frankenstein, 1958
Dracula, 1958
Bobbikins, 1959
The Three Worlds of Gulliver,
1960
Circle of Deception, 1961
Terror of the Tongs, 1961
Victim, 1961
The Kitchen, 1961
Flat Two, 1962
Crooks Anonymous, 1962
Siege of the Saxons, 1963
The Third Secret, 1964
Every Day's a Holiday, 1964
The Reptile, 1965
Sebastian, 1967
If, 1968
Diamonds For Breakfast, 1968
Song of Norway, 1970
The Man Who Haunted Himself,
1970
Madame Sin, 1972

HARRY LOCKE (-)
Small-part character actor,

almost always in comedy characterizations.

Panic at Madame Tussaud's,
  1948
Private Angelo, 1949
Treasure Island, 1950
Tread Softly, 1952
Judgement Deferred, 1952
Angels One Five, 1952
The Teckman Mystery, 1954
Doctor in the House, 1954
A Yank in Ermine, 1955
Yield to the Night, 1956
The Baby and the Battleship,
  1956
Town On Trial, 1957
Woman in a Dressing Gown,
  1957
Nowhere to Go, 1958
Upstairs and Downstairs, 1959
Carry On Nurse, 1959
Light Up the Sky, 1960
Never Back Losers, 1961
The Man in the Back Seat, 1961
The Girl On the Boat, 1961
On the Fiddle, 1961
She'll Have to Go, 1962
The Amorous Prawn, 1962
The L-Shaped Room, 1962
Kill Or Cure, 1963
The Small World of Sammy
  Lee, 1963
Go Kart Go!, 1964
A Home of Your Own, 1964
The Legend of Young Dick
  Turpin, 1965
The Early Bird, 1965
The Family Way, 1966
Arabesque, 1966
The Sky Bike, 1967
Carry On Again Doctor, 1969
On the Run, 1969
Oh What a Lovely War, 1969
Tales From the Crypt, 1972
The Creeping Flesh, 1972

JULIA LOCKWOOD (1941-)
Leading actress of occasional
films of the 50s; daughter of
Margaret Lockwood.

The Flying Eye, 1955

My Teenage Daughter, 1956
The Solitary Child, 1958
Please Turn Over, 1959
No Kidding, 1960

MARGARET LOCKWOOD
  (1916-)
Beautiful dark-haired leading
lady of stage, films, and television; also in Hollywood.
Daughter: Julia Lockwood.

Lorna Doone, 1934
The Case of Gabriel Perry,
  1935
Some Day, 1935
Honours Easy, 1935
Midshipman Easy, 1935
Man of the Moment, 1935
Jury's Evidence, 1936
The Amateur Gentleman, 1936
Beloved Vagabond, 1936
Irish For Luck, 1936
The Street Singer, 1937
Who's Your Lady Friend?, 1937
Dr. Syn, 1937
Melody and Romance, 1937
Owd Bob, 1938
Bank Holiday, 1938
The Lady Vanishes, 1938
A Girl Must Live, 1939
The Stars Look Down, 1939
Suzannah of the Mounties,
  1939
Rulers of the Sea, 1939
Night Train to Munich, 1940
The Girl in the News, 1940
Quiet Wedding, 1941
Alibi, 1942
The Man in Grey, 1943
Dear Octopus, 1943
Give Us the Moon, 1944
Love Story, 1945
A Place of One's Own, 1945
I'll Be Your Sweetheart, 1945
The Wicked Lady, 1945
Bedelia, 1946
Hungry Hill, 1946
Jassy, 1947
The White Unicorn, 1947
Look Before You Love, 1948
Cardboard Cavalier, 1949
Madness of the Heart, 1949

Highly Dangerous, 1950
Trent's Last Case, 1952
Laughing Anne, 1953
Trouble in the Glen, 1954
Cast a Dark Shadow, 1955
The Slipper and the Rose, 1976

JOHN LODER (1898-   )
Handsome leading man and latterly supporting actor of stage
and screen, also in Hollywood;
former soldier.

Madame Wants No Children,
   1926
The Firstborn, 1928
A Doctor's Secret, 1929
Sunset Pass, 1929
Her Private Affair, 1929
Unholy Night, 1929
The Racketeer, 1929
Rich People, 1930
Lillies of the Field, 1930
Man Hunter, 1930
Sweethearts and Wives, 1930
Second Story Murder, 1930
One Night at Susie's, 1930
Seas Beneath, 1931
Wedding Rehearsal, 1932
Money Means Nothing, 1932
Money For Speed, 1933
Paris Plane, 1933
The Private Life of Henry VIII,
   1933
You Made Me Love You, 1933
Love, Life, and Laughter, 1933
The Battle, 1934
Rolling in Money, 1934
Warn London, 1934
Java Head, 1934
Sing as We Go, 1934
My Song Goes Round the World,
   1934
Lorna Doone, 1935
The Silent Passenger, 1935
It Happened in Paris, 1935
Eighteen Minutes, 1935
Queen of Hearts, 1936
Whom the Gods Love, 1936
Ourselves Alone, 1936
The Guilty Melody, 1936
The Man Who Changed His

Mind, 1936
Sabotage, 1936
King Solomon's Mines, 1937
Dr. Syn, 1937
Non Stop New York, 1937
Mademoiselle Docteur, 1937
River of Unrest, 1937
Owd Bob, 1938
Anything to Declare, 1938
To the Victor, 1938
Katie, 1939
The Silent Battle, 1939
Murder Will Out, 1939
Meet Maxwell Archer, 1939
Mozart, 1940
Adventure in Diamonds, 1940
Diamond Frontier, 1940
Tin Pan Alley, 1940
Confirm Or Deny, 1941
How Green Was My Valley,
   1941
Scotland Yard, 1941
One Night in Lisbon, 1941
Eagle Squadron, 1942
Now Voyager, 1942
Gentleman Jim, 1942
The Gorilla Man, 1942
Mysterious Doctor, 1943
Murder On the Waterfront,
   1943
Old Acquaintance, 1943
Passage to Marseille, 1944
Abroad With Two Yanks, 1944
The Hairy Ape, 1944
Jealousy, 1945
Game of Death, 1945
The Fighting Guardsman, 1945
The Brighton Strangler, 1945
One More Tomorrow, 1946
Wife of Monte Cristo, 1946
Dishonoured Lady, 1947
Dead On Time, 1955
Small Hotel, 1957
The Woman and the Hunter,
   1957
The Story of Esther Costello,
   1957
Gideon's Day, 1957
The Secret Man, 1958
The Firechasers, 1970

DAVID LODGE (1922-   )
Character actor of stage and

films, equally adept at both comedy and dramatic parts.

Cockleshell Heroes, 1955
Private's Progress, 1956
Battle of the River Plate, 1956
The Intimate Stranger, 1956
The Counterfeit Plan, 1957
These Dangerous Years, 1957
Stranger's Meeting, 1957
No Time to Die, 1958
Up the Creek, 1958
Further Up the Creek, 1958
Ice Cold in Alex, 1958
The Crossroad Gallows, 1958
I Only Arsked, 1958
Girls at Sea, 1958
Life in Emergency Ward 10,
   1959
Idol On Parade, 1959
The Ugly Duckling, 1959
The League of Gentlemen, 1959
Two-Way Stretch, 1960
Jazzbot, 1960
The Running, Jumping, and
   Standing Still Film, 1960
Watch Your Stern, 1960
The Bulldog Breed, 1960
Never Let Go, 1960
Yesterday's Enemy, 1961
The Hellfire Club, 1961
No My Darling Daughter, 1961
Raising the Wind, 1961
Carry On Regardless, 1961
Go To Blazes, 1962
Mrs. Gibbons' Boys, 1962
The Pirates of Blood River,
   1962
Trial and Error, 1962
Captain Clegg, 1962
Time to Remember, 1962
On the Beat, 1962
Two Left Feet, 1963
Kill Or Cure, 1963
A Shot in the Dark, 1964
Guns at Batasi, 1964
The Long Ships, 1964
Saturday Night Out, 1964
The Intelligence Men, 1965
Moll Flanders, 1965
Cup Fever, 1965
San Ferry Ann, 1965
Having a Wild Weekend, 1965
Catch Us if You Can, 1965

Press For Time, 1966
Smashing Time, 1967
The Sky Bike, 1967
Headline Hunters, 1968
What's Good For the Goose,
   1969
Crooks and Coronets, 1969
The Smashing Bird I Used to
   Know, 1969
Bachelor of Arts, 1969
Scream and Scream Again,
   1969
Oh What a Lovely War, 1969
Corruption, 1969
Scramble, 1970
Doctors Wear Scarlet, 1970
Eyewitness, 1970
Crime Doesn't Pay, 1970
Incense For the Damned, 1970
Hoffman, 1970
The Railway Children, 1971
Go For a Take, 1972
The Amazing Mr. Blunden,
   1972
Charley One-Eye, 1973
Return of the Pink Panther, 1974
QB VII, 1974

CECELIA LOFTUS (1876-1943)
Character actress of stage and
films, in U.S. from 1895.

East Lynne, 1931
Doctors' Wives, 1931
Young Sinners, 1931
Once in a Blue Moon, 1936
The Old Maid, 1939
The Bluebird, 1940
Lucky Partners, 1940
It's a Date, 1940
The Black Cat, 1941

MARIE LOHR (1890-1975)
Australian actress of stage
(from 1901) and screen, usually
seen in dignified or aristocratic
roles.

The Real Thing at Last, 1916
Aren't We All, 1932
Road House, 1934
My Heart is Calling, 1934

Lady in Danger, 1934
Foreign Affaires, 1935
Royal Cavalcade, 1935
Fighting Stock, 1935
Cock O' the North, 1935
Whom the Gods Love, 1936
It's You I Want, 1936
Dreams Come True, 1936
Reasonable Doubt, 1936
Oh Daddy, 1936
South Riding, 1938
Pygmalion, 1938
A Gentleman's Gentleman, 1939
George and Margaret, 1940
Major Barbara, 1941
Went the Day Well, 1942
Twilight Hour, 1944
Kiss the Bride Goodbye, 1944
The Rake's Progress, 1945
The Magic Bow, 1947
Ghosts of Berkeley Square,
   1947
Counterblast, 1948
Anna Karenina, 1948
The Winslow Boy, 1948
Silent Dust, 1949
Treasure Hunt, 1950
Playbill, 1951
Little Big Shot, 1952
The Devil's Plot, 1953
Always a Bride, 1953
Out of the Clouds, 1955
Escapade, 1955
A Town Like Alice, 1956
On Such a Night, 1956
Seven Waves Away, 1957
Small Hotel, 1957
Carleton Browne of the FO,
   1959
Great Catherine, 1968

HERBERT LOM (1917-   )
Versatile Czech actor of stage
(from 1936), films and television, in England since 1939.
Equally skilled at dramatic or
comedy roles; also adept at
portraying kindliness as well as
villainy.   Also Hollywood.   Tv
series: "The Human Jungle."

Mein Kampf My Crimes, 1940

Tomorrow We Live, 1941
Secret Mission, 1942
The Young Mr. Pitt, 1942
The Dark Tower, 1943
Hotel Reserve, 1944
The Seventh Veil, 1945
Night Boat to Dublin, 1946
Appointment With Crime, 1946
Dual Alibi, 1947
Snowbound, 1948
Good Time Girl, 1948
Portrait From Life, 1948
The Lucky Mascot, 1948
The Lost People, 1949
The Golden Salamander, 1950
Night and the City, 1950
State Secret, 1950
The Black Rose, 1950
Cage of Gold, 1950
Hell is Sold Out, 1951
Two On the Tiles, 1951
Mr. Denning Drives North,
   1951
The Ringer, 1952
Whispering Smith Hits London,
   1952
The Net, 1953
Paris Express, 1953
Rough Shoot, 1953
The Love Lottery, 1954
Beautiful Stranger, 1954
Star of India, 1954
The Brass Monkey, 1954
The Ladykillers, 1955
War and Peace, 1956
Fire Down Below, 1957
Hell Drivers, 1957
Action of the Tiger, 1957
The Assignment, 1958
Chase a Crooked Shadow, 1958
Intent to Kill, 1958
I Accuse!, 1958
The Roots of Heaven, 1958
No Trees in the Street, 1959
Third Man On the Mountain,
   1959
The Big Fisherman, 1959
Northwest Frontier, 1959
Passport to Shame, 1959
Spartacus, 1960
I Aim at the Stars, 1960
El Cid, 1961
The Frightened City, 1961

Mr. Topaze, 1961
Mysterious Island, 1961
Phantom of the Opera, 1962
Tiara Tahiti, 1962
The Horse Without a Head,
    1963
A Shot in the Dark, 1964
Return From the Ashes, 1965
The Treasure of Silver Lake,
    1965
Our Man in Marrakesh, 1966
Uncle Tom's Cabin, 1966
Gambit, 1966
The Karate Killers, 1967
Eve, 1968
Villa Rides, 1968
Assignment to Kill, 1968
Doppelganger, 1969
99 Women, 1969
Mr. Jerico, 1970
Dorian Gray, 1970
Count Dracula, 1970
Murders in the Rue Morgue,
    1971
Mark of the Devil, 1972
Asylum, 1972
And Now the Screaming Starts,
    1973
Dark Places, 1973
Return of the Pink Panther, 1974
Ten Little Indians, 1975
Pink Panther Strikes Again, 1976
Bride of Fengriffen, 1976
Revenge of the Pink Panther,
    1978
Charleston, 1978
The Lady Vanishes, 1980
Hopscotch, 1980
The Man With Bogart's Face, 1980

HERBERT LOMAS (1887-1961)
Thin character player most
active in the thirties; also on
stage.

Many Waters, 1931
Frail Women, 1932
The Sign of Four, 1932
When London Sleeps, 1932
The Missing Rembrandt, 1932
The Man From Toronto, 1933
Daughters of Today, 1933

Java Head, 1934
Lorna Doone, 1935
The Phantom Light, 1935
Fighting Stock, 1935
The Black Mask, 1935
Rembrandt, 1936
Fame, 1936
The Ghost Goes West, 1936
Knight Without Armour, 1937
South Riding, 1938
The Lion Has Wings, 1939
Inquest, 1939
Jamaica Inn, 1939
Ask a Policeman, 1939
Mr. Borland Thinks Again,
    1940
The Ghost Train, 1941
Penn of Pennsylvania, 1941
South American George, 1941
They Met in the Dark, 1943
I Know Where I'm Going, 1945
The Master of Bankdam, 1947
The Man Within, 1947
The Guinea Pig, 1948
Bonnie Prince Charlie, 1948
The Magic Box, 1951
The Net, 1953

JOHN LONGDEN (1900-1971)
Tall star of the thirties and
later character actor of stage
(since 1923) and films; former
mining engineer.

Ball of Fortune, 1926
House of Marney, 1926
The Glad Eye, 1927
Flight Commander, 1927
The Arcadians, 1927
Quinneys, 1927
Bright Young Things, 1927
Palais de Danse, 1928
Mademoiselle Parley Voo, 1928
What Money Can Buy, 1928
The Last Post, 1929
The Flying Squad, 1929
Blackmail, 1929
Memories, 1929
Atlantic, 1929
Juno and the Paycock, 1929
Elstree Calling, 1930
Flame of Love, 1930

Two Worlds, 1930
Children of Chance, 1930
The Skin Game, 1931
The Ringer, 1931
Two Crowded Hours, 1931
The Wickham Mystery, 1931
Rynox, 1931
Murder On the Second Floor,
   1932
Lucky Sweep, 1932
Born Lucky, 1932
Jennifer Hale, 1936
French Leave, 1937
Little Miss Somebody, 1937
Young and Innocent, 1937
Dial 999, 1938
Bad Boy, 1938
The Gaunt Stranger, 1938
Q Planes, 1939
Jamaica Inn, 1939
Goodbye Mr. Chips, 1939
The Lion Has Wings, 1939
Contraband, 1940
The Common Touch, 1941
Tower of Terror, 1941
Post 23, 1941
Old Mother Riley's Circus,
   1941
Rose of Tralee, 1942
Unpublished Story, 1942
The Silver Fleet, 1943
Death By Design, 1943
Ghosts of Berkeley Square,
   1947
Dusty Bates, 1947
Anna Karenina, 1948
The Last Load, 1948
Bonnie Prince Charlie, 1948
Trapped By the Terror, 1949
The Lady Craved Excitement,
   1950
The Elusive Pimpernel, 1950
Pool of London, 1951
The Dark Light, 1951
Black Widow, 1951
The Man With the Twisted Lip,
   1951
The Magic Box, 1951
Trek to Mashomba, 1951
The Wallet, 1952
Dangerous Cargo, 1954
Meet Mr. Callaghan, 1954
The Ship That Died of Shame,

1955
Alias John Preston, 1956
Raiders of the River, 1956
Dangerous Exile, 1957
Quatermass II, 1957
Three Sundays to Live, 1957
Broad Waterways, 1959
A Woman's Temptation, 1959
An Honourable Murder, 1960
So Evil So Young, 1961
Lancelot and Guinevere, 1963
Frozen Alive, 1964

TERENCE LONGDEN (1922-)
General purpose actor of the
50s and 60s, often in comedy
films.

Never Look Back, 1952
Appointment in London, 1953
Simon and Laura, 1955
Jumping For Joy, 1955
The Man Who Never Was,
   1956
Doctor at Large, 1957
Another Time Another Place,
   1958
Carry On Sergeant, 1958
The Silent Enemy, 1958
Ben Hur, 1959
Carry On Nurse, 1959
Carry On Constable, 1960
Carry On Regardless, 1961
Out of the Shadow, 1961
On the Fiddle, 1961
What a Whopper, 1961
Clash By Night, 1963
The Return of Mr. Moto, 1965
The Gathering Storm, 1974

ERNIE LOTINGA (1876-1951)
Slapstick comedian of the 20s
and 30s, formerly on stage
and in music halls. Also former baker.

Joining Up, 1928
Nap, 1928
The Orderly Room, 1928
The Raw Recruit, 1928
Doing His Duty, 1929

Spirits, 1929
Josser KC, 1929
Accidental Treatment, 1930
PC Josser, 1931
Josser Joins the Navy, 1932
Josser in the Army, 1932
Josser On the River, 1932
Josser On the Farm, 1934
Smith's Wives, 1935
Love Up the Pole, 1936

BESSIE LOVE (1898-   )
American leading actress of
the 20s; in England since the
mid-30s where she has since
played cameo roles.

Birth of a Nation, 1915
The Flying Torpedo, 1916
The Aryan, 1916
The Good Bad Man, 1916
Acquitted, 1916
Reggie Mixes In, 1916
Stranded, 1916
Hell-to-Pay Austin, 1916
Intolerance, 1916
A Sister of Six, 1916
Nina the Flower Girl, 1917
A Daughter of the Poor, 1917
Cheerful Givers, 1917
The Great Adventure, 1918
How Could You Caroline?,
   1918
The Little Reformer, 1918
Dawn of Understanding, 1918
The Enchanted Barn, 1919
The Yankee Princess, 1919
The Little Boss, 1919
Cupid Forecloses, 1919
Carolyn of the Corners, 1919
Pegeen, 1920
Bonnie May, 1920
Penny of Top High Trail, 1921
The Swamp, 1921
The Sea Lion, 1921
The Vermilion Pencil, 1922
Forget Me Not, 1922
Bulldog Courage, 1922
The Village Blacksmith, 1922
Deserted at the Altar, 1922
Human Wreckage, 1923
The Eternal Three, 1923

St. Elmo, 1923
Slave of Desire, 1923
Gentle Julia, 1923
Torment, 1924
Those Who Dance, 1924
The Silent Watcher, 1924
Sundown, 1924
Tongues of Flame, 1924
Dynamite Smith, 1924
The Lost World, 1925
Soul Fire, 1925
A Son of His Father, 1925
The King on Main Street, 1925
The Song and Dance Man,
   1925
Lovely Mary, 1926
Young April, 1926
Going Crooked, 1926
Rubber Tires, 1927
Dress Parade, 1927
A Harp in Hock, 1927
Matinee Idol, 1928
Sally of the Scandals, 1928
Anybody Here Seen Kelly?,
   1928
Broadway Melody, 1929
Hollywood Revue, 1929
The Idle Rich, 1929
Girl in the Show, 1929
Chasing Rainbows, 1930
Conspiracy, 1930
Good News, 1930
See America Thirst, 1930
Morals For Women, 1931
Live Again, 1935
Atlantic Ferry, 1942
London Scrapbook, 1942
Journey Together, 1945
The Magic Box, 1951
No Highway, 1951
The Weak and the Wicked,
   1952
Beau Brummell, 1954
The Barefoot Contessa, 1954
Touch and Go, 1955
Story of Esther Costello, 1957
Next to No Time, 1958
Nowhere to Go, 1958
Too Young to Love, 1959
The Greengage Summer, 1961
Roman Spring of Mrs. Stone,
   1961
The Wild Affair, 1963

Children of the Damned, 1964
I Think They Call Him John,
    1964
Promise Her Anything, 1965
I'll Never Forget Whatsisname,
    1967
Battle Beneath the Earth, 1967
Isadora, 1968
On Her Majesty's Secret Ser-
    vice, 1968
Sunday Bloody Sunday, 1971
Catlow, 1971
Cat and Mouse, 1974
Mousey, 1974
Vampyres, 1975
The Ritz, 1976
Gulliver's Travels (voice),
    1977

MONTAGU LOVE (1877-1943)
Heavyweight character actor
long in Hollywood; an excellent
silent film villain, later in
character roles.

Hearts in Exile, 1915
A Woman's Way, 1916
The Gilded Cage, 1916
Bought and Paid For, 1916
Rasputin the Mad Monk, 1917
Hands Up, 1917
The Brand of Satan, 1917
The Cross-Bearer, 1918
Vengeance, 1918
The Awakening, 1918
The Grouch, 1918
The Hand Invisible, 1919
The Green Eyes, 1919
A Broadway Saint, 1919
Roughneck, 1919
Him That Hath, 1919
The Steel King, 1919
The World and His Wife, 1920
The Case of Becky, 1921
Peter Ibbetson, 1921
Shams of Society, 1921
Love's Redemption, 1921
The Beauty Shop, 1922
Streets of Paris, 1922
Secrets of Paris, 1923
The Leopardess, 1923
Roulette, 1924

Love of Women, 1924
The Eternal City, 1924
Son of the Sahara, 1924
Sinners in Heaven, 1924
Out of the Storm, 1925
The Ancient Highway, 1925
Hands Up, 1926
The Social Highwayman, 1926
Son of the Sheik, 1926
Don Juan, 1926
The Silent Lover, 1927
A Night of Love, 1927
King of Kings, 1927
The Tender Hour, 1927
Rose of the Golden West,
    1927
Jesse James, 1927
Good Time Charley, 1927
The Haunted Ship, 1928
The Noose, 1928
The Hawk's Nest, 1928
The Wind, 1928
The Haunted House, 1928
The Devil's Skipper, 1928
Midstream, 1929
Her Private Life, 1929
Last Warning, 1929
Synthetic Sin, 1929
The Divine Lady, 1929
Bulldog Drummond, 1929
Charming Sinners, 1929
A Most Immoral Lady, 1929
Mysterious Island, 1929
Love Comes Along, 1930
Notorious Affair, 1930
Double Cross Roads, 1930
Back Pay, 1930
Inside the Lines, 1930
Outward Bound, 1930
Kismet, 1930
Reno, 1930
The Cat Creeps, 1930
Stowaway, 1931
Alexander Hamilton, 1931
Vanity Fair, 1932
The Silver Lining, 1932
The Midnight Lady, 1932
His Double Life, 1933
Limehouse Blues, 1934
Clive of India, 1935
The Crusades, 1935
The Man Who Broke the Bank
    at Monte Carlo, 1935

Country Doctor, 1936
Sutter's Gold, 1936
Sing Baby Sing, 1936
The White Angel, 1936
Champagne Charlie, 1936
Lloyds of London, 1936
Reunion, 1936
One in a Million, 1937
The Prince and the Pauper,
    1937
Parnell, 1937
The Life of Emile Zola, 1937
London By Night, 1937
The Prisoner of Zenda, 1937
Damsel in Distress, 1937
Adventure's End, 1937
Tovarich, 1937
The Buccaneer, 1938
Adventures of Robin Hood, 1938
Kidnapped, 1938
Professor Beware, 1938
If I Were King, 1938
Gunga Din, 1939
Juarez, 1939
Man in the Iron Mask, 1939
Rulers of the Sea, 1939
We Are Not Alone, 1939
The Lone Wolf Strikes, 1940
Northwest Passage, 1940
Dr. Erlich's Magic Bullet, 1940
All This And Heaven Too, 1940
Private Affairs, 1940
The Sea Hawk, 1940
The Mark of Zorro, 1940
Northwest Mounted Police, 1940
Son of Monte Cristo, 1940
A Dispatch From Reuters, 1940
Hudson's Bay, 1941
Shining Victory, 1941
The Devil and Miss Jones, 1941
Lady For a Night, 1942
The Remarkable Andrew, 1942
Sherlock Holmes and the Voice
    of Terror, 1942
Tennessee Johnson, 1943
The Constant Nymph, 1943
Holy Matrimony, 1943
Devotion (release delayed), 1946

RAYMOND LOVELL (1900-1953)
Canadian actor of stage (since
1924) and films, long in Britain;

usually cast in pompous, self-
effacing or sinister roles.
Married to Tamara Desni.

Love, Life, and Laughter,
    1933
The Third Clue, 1934
Warn London, 1934
Some Day, 1935
Sexton Blake and the Made-
    moiselle, 1935
The Case of Gabriel Perry,
    1935
Crime Unlimited, 1935
Gaolbreak, 1935
Troubled Waters, 1936
Not So Dusty, 1936
King of the Damned, 1936
Gypsy Melody, 1936
Fair Exchange, 1936
Secret Lives, 1937
Mademoiselle Docteur, 1937
Glamorous Night, 1937
Behind Your Back, 1937
Midnight Menace, 1937
Murder Tomorrow, 1938
Q Planes, 1939
Contraband, 1940
He Found a Star, 1941
49th Parallel, 1941
The Common Touch, 1941
The Goose Steps Out, 1942
Alibi, 1942
The Young Mr. Pitt, 1942
Uncensored, 1942
The Man in Grey, 1943
Warn That Man, 1943
Candlelight in Algeria, 1943
The Way Ahead, 1944
Hotel Reserve, 1944
Caesar and Cleopatra, 1945
Night Boat to Dublin, 1946
Appointment With Crime, 1946
End of the River, 1947
Who Killed Van Loon?, 1948
Easy Money, 1948
The Three Weird Sisters, 1948
Quartet, 1948
The Blind Goddess, 1948
The Calendar, 1948
But Not in Vain, 1948
My Brother's Keeper, 1948
Snowbound, 1948

So Evil My Love, 1948
The Romantic Age, 1949
The Bad Lord Byron, 1949
Once Upon a Dream, 1949
Madness of the Heart, 1949
Fools Rush In, 1949
The Mudlark, 1950
Time Gentlemen Please, 1952
The Pickwick Papers, 1952
The Steel Key, 1953

ARTHUR LOWE (1904-)
Comedy character of stage
(since 1945) and films, formerly
seen in cameo roles; also popular on tv in "Coronation Street,"
"Dad's Army."

Stormy Crossing, 1948
London Belongs to Me, 1948
Kind Hearts and Coronets, 1949
The Spider and the Fly, 1949
The Mirror and Markheim,
    1954
The Green Man, 1956
This Sporting Life, 1963
The White Bus, 1967
If, 1968
The Bed Sitting Room, 1969
It All Goes to Show, 1969
Spring and Port Wine, 1970
Some Will, Some Won't, 1970
The Rise & Rise of Michael
    Rimmer, 1970
Fragment of Fear, 1970
A Hole Lot of Trouble, 1970
William Webb Ellis You Are
    Mad, 1970
Dad's Army, 1971
The Ruling Class, 1972
Adolf Hitler-My Part in His
    Downfall, 1972
O Lucky Man, 1973
Theatre of Blood, 1973
Man About the House, 1974
No Sex Please We're British,
    1974
Bawdy Adventures of Tom
    Jones, 1975
Royal Flash, 1975

ARTHUR LUCAN (1887-1954)
Comedy character star most
famous as Old Mother Riley,
the Irish washerwoman; also
concert party comedian (from
1900) and music hall performer
(1913).

Stars On Parade, 1936
Kathleen Mavourneen, 1936
Old Mother Riley, 1937
Old Mother Riley in Paris,
    1938
Old Mother Riley MP, 1939
Old Mother Riley Joins Up,
    1939
Old Mother Riley in Business,
    1940
Old Mother Riley's Ghosts,
    1941
Old Mother Riley's Circus,
    1941
Old Mother Riley Detective,
    1943
Old Mother Riley Overseas,
    1944
Old Mother Riley at Home,
    1945
Old Mother Riley's New Ven-
    ture, 1949
Old Mother Riley Headmistress,
    1950
Old Mother Riley's Jungle
    Treasure, 1951
Mother Riley Meets the Vam-
    pire, 1952

WILLIAM LUCAS (1926-)
Leading actor and character
player of stage, films, and
television.

Portrait of Alison, 1955
Timeslip, 1955
X The Unknown, 1956
Up in the World, 1956
Breakout, 1959
The Professionals, 1960
Sons and Lovers, 1960
Crack in the Mirror, 1960
The Devil's Daffodil, 1961
Shadow of the Cat, 1961

Payroll, 1961
Touch of Death, 1962
The Break, 1962
The Very Edge, 1963
Calculated Risk, 1963
Bitter Harvest, 1963
The Marked One, 1963
Dateline Diamonds, 1965
Night of the Big Heat, 1967
The Sky Bike, 1967
Scramble, 1970
Tower of Evil, 1972
Island of the Burning Damned,
    1973
Man at the Top, 1973

CYRIL LUCKHAM (1907-)
Small-part character actor
often seen as persons of some
authority; also on stage and
tv. Notable as Sir Lawrence
Mont in "The Forsyte Saga. "

The Good Die Young, 1954
Stranger From Venus, 1954
The Hostage, 1956
How to Murder a Rich Uncle,
    1957
Invasion Quartet, 1961
Some People, 1962
Position of Trust, 1963
The Pumpkin Eater, 1964
The Alphabet Murders, 1966
A Man For All Seasons, 1966
The Naked Runner, 1967
Happy Deathday, 1969
Anne of the Thousand Days, 1970
Cry of the Penguins, 1972
Providence, 1977

PATRICK LUDLOW (1903-)
Character actor and second
lead of the thirties; also on
stage.

The Ware Case, 1928
The Third Eye, 1929
The Third Gun, 1929
Naughty Husbands, 1930
The Blue Danube, 1932
Bachelor's Baby, 1932

Love On the Spot, 1932
Watch Beverly, 1932
Bitter Sweet, 1933
Chelsea Life, 1933
Evergreen, 1934
Jury's Evidence, 1936
King of Hearts, 1936
They Didn't Know, 1936
Rose of Tralee, 1937
Gangway, 1937
Old Mother Riley, 1937
Old Mother Riley MP, 1939
Modesty Blaise, 1966

IDA LUPINO (1914-)
Dark-haired leading lady; long
in Hollywood.   Later director.
Daughter of Stanley Lupino.
Married: Louis Hayward;
Howard Duff.

Her First Affaire, 1933
Money For Speed, 1933
High Finance, 1933
The Ghost Camera, 1933
I Lived With You, 1934
Prince of Arcadia, 1934
Search For Beauty, 1934
Come On Marines, 1934
Ready For Love, 1934
Paris in Spring, 1935
Smart Girl, 1935
Peter Ibbetson, 1935
Anything Goes, 1936
One Rainy Afternoon, 1936
Yours For the Asking, 1936
The Gay Desperado, 1936
Sea Devils, 1937
Artists and Models, 1937
Let's Get Married, 1937
Fight For Your Lady, 1937
The Lady and the Mob, 1939
The Lone Wolf Spy Hunt, 1939
Adventures of Sherlock Holmes,
    1939
The Light That Failed, 1939
They Drive By Night, 1940
High Sierra, 1941
The Sea Wolf, 1941
Out of the Fog, 1941
Ladies in Retirement, 1941
Moontide, 1942

The Hard Way, 1942
Life Begins at 8:30, 1942
Forever and a Day, 1943
Thank Your Lucky Stars, 1943
In Our Time, 1944
Hollywood Canteen, 1944
Pillow to Paris, 1945
Devotion, 1946
The Man I Love, 1947
The Deep Valley, 1947
Escape Me Never, 1947
Roadhouse, 1948
Lust For Gold, 1949
Woman in Hiding, 1950
On Dangerous Ground, 1951
Beware My Lovely, 1952
Jennifer, 1953
The Bigamist, 1953
Private Hell 36, 1954
Women's Prison, 1955
The Big Knife, 1955
While the City Sleeps, 1956
Strange Intruder, 1956
Backtrack, 1969
Women in Chains, 1971
Junior Bonner, 1972
The Devil's Rain, 1975
Food of the Gods, 1976

STANLEY LUPINO (1895-1942)
Intelligent star of stage (1900)
and films, mainly seen in mu-
sical comedy films during the
30s. Daughter: Ida Lupino;
Cousins: Wallace Lupino,
Lupino Lane; Brother: Barry
Lupino.

Love Lies, 1931
The Love Race, 1931
Sleepless Nights, 1932
King of the Ritz, 1933
You Made Me Love You, 1933
Facing the Music, 1933
Happy, 1934
Honeymoon For Three, 1935
Cheer Up, 1936
Sporting Love, 1936
Over She Goes, 1937
Hold My Hand, 1938
Lucky to Me, 1939

WALLACE LUPINO (-)
Character actor of the thirties;
brother of Lupino Lane, cousin of Stanley Lupino.

The Yellow Mask, 1930
Children of Chance, 1930
Bull Rushes, 1931
Never Trouble Trouble, 1931
Aroma of the South Seas, 1931
No Lady, 1931
Love Lies, 1931
The Love Race, 1931
The Bad Companions, 1932
Innocents of Chicago, 1932
Old Spanish Customers, 1932
Josser On the River, 1932
The Maid of the Mountains,
    1932
The Stolen Necklace, 1933
The Melody Maker, 1933
Forging Ahead, 1933
Song Birds, 1933
Master and Man, 1934
Bagged, 1934
Wishes, 1934
Hyde Park, 1934
The Student's Romance, 1935
The Deputy Drummer, 1935
Trust the Navy, 1935
The Man Who Could Work
    Miracles, 1936
Hot News, 1936
Shipmates O' Mine, 1936
Love Up the Pole, 1936
The First and the Last, 1937
The Lambeth Walk, 1939
Twenty-One Days, 1939
Waterloo Road, 1945

VIOLA LYEL (1900-1972)
Comedy character actress and
occasional lead of the 30s,
also on stage.

SOS, 1928
Lord Richard in the Pantry,
    1930
Thread O'Scarlet, 1930
Hobson's Choice, 1931
After Office Hours, 1932

Marry Me, 1932
Let Me Explain Dear, 1932
Marooned, 1933
Channel Crossing, 1933
A Political Party, 1934
Over the Garden Wall, 1934
Passing Shadows, 1934
Night Mail, 1935
Her Father's Daughter, 1940
The Farmer's Wife, 1941
Quiet Wedding, 1941
The Patient Vanishes, 1941
Wanted For Murder, 1946
Mr. Perrin and Mr. Traill,
  1948
No Place For Jennifer, 1950
Black Thirteen, 1953
Isn't Life Wonderful?, 1953
See How They Run, 1955
The Little Hut, 1957

ALFRED LYNCH (1933-)
Character star of the sixties,
often seen as cockney soldier.

On the Fiddle, 1961
Two and Two Make Six, 1961
55 Days at Peking, 1962
The Password is Courage, 1963
West Eleven, 1963
The Hill, 1965
The Taming of the Shrew, 1967
The Sea Gull, 1969
The Blockhouse, 1974

ANN LYNN (1934-)
Pretty leading actress of the
sixties, also on television;
granddaughter of Ralph Lynn.

Johnny You're Wanted, 1956
Moment of Indiscretion, 1958
Naked Fury, 1959
Piccadilly Third Stop, 1960
Wind of Change, 1961
Strip Tease Murder, 1961
Flame in the Streets, 1961
Strongroom, 1962
A Woman's Privilege, 1962
The Party's Over, 1963
Doctor in Distress, 1963

The System, 1964
The Black Torment, 1964
A Shot in the Dark, 1964
The Uncle, 1965
Four in the Morning, 1965
I'll Never Forget Whatsisname,
  1967
Baby Love, 1968
Separation, 1968
The Spy's Wife, 1971
Hitler: The Last Ten Days,
  1973
The Other Side of the Under-
  neath, 1976

RALPH LYNN (1882-1962)
Monocled "silly ass" comedian
of the thirties, also on stage
(from 1900). Son: Director
Robery Lynn (1918-); Granddaughter: Ann Lynn.

Peace and Quiet, 1929
Rookery Nook, 1930
Plunder, 1931
Tons of Money, 1931
Chance of a Night Time, 1931
Mischief, 1931
A Night Like This, 1932
Thark, 1932
Just My Luck, 1933
A Cuckoo in the Nest, 1933
Summer Lightning, 1933
Up to the Neck, 1933
Turkey Time, 1933
A Cup of Kindness, 1934
Dirty Work, 1934
Fighting Stock, 1935
Stormy Weather, 1935
Foreign Affaires, 1935
In the Soup, 1936
Pot Luck, 1936
All In, 1936
For Valour, 1937
The Adventures of Rex, 1959

CLEMENT McCALLIN (1913-)
Character player mainly on
stage, seen sporadically in
films since 1939.

Stolen Life, 1939
Edward My Son, 1949
Lady With a Lamp, 1951
The Rossiter Case, 1951
Murder in the Cathedral, 1952
Happy Deathday, 1969

DAVID McCALLUM (1933-)
Slight Scottish actor of films
and television, popular in the
latter medium as Ilya Kuryakin
in "The Man From U.N.C.L.E."
Also latterly in international
films; formerly married to Jill
Ireland.

Prelude to Fame, 1950
Last Holiday, 1950
The Secret Place, 1957
Hell Drivers, 1957
Robbery Under Arms, 1957
Violent Playground, 1958
A Night to Remember, 1958
The Long & the Short & the
    Tall, 1961
Jungle Street, 1961
Billy Budd, 1962
Freud, 1962
The Great Escape, 1963
The Greatest Story Ever Told,
    1965
One Spy Too Many, 1966
The Spy With My Face, 1966
Around the World Under the
    Sea, 1966
The Karate Killers, 1967
To Trap a Spy, 1967
Three Bites of the Apple, 1967
Mosquito Squadron, 1969
Frankenstein: The True Story,
    1973
Dogs, 1976
The Kingfisher Caper, 1976
A Watcher in the Woods, 1980

JOHN McCALLUM (1918-)
Australian leading actor of
stage (from 1934) and films,
married to Googie Withers.

Joe Goes Back, 1944

Australia is Like This, 1944
A Son is Born, 1944
Bush Christmas, 1947
The Root of All Evil, 1947
The Loves of Joanna Godden,
    1947
It Always Rains On Sunday,
    1947
Miranda, 1948
The Calendar, 1948
A Boy, a Girl, and a Bike,
    1949
Traveller's Joy, 1949
The Woman in Question, 1950
Valley of the Eagles, 1951
The Magic Box, 1951
Lady Godiva Rides Again, 1951
Derby Day, 1952
Trent's Last Case, 1952
The Long Memory, 1953
Melba, 1953
Devil On Horseback, 1954
Trouble in the Glen, 1954
Port of Escape, 1955
Smiley, 1956
Safe Harbour, 1957

NEIL McCALLUM (1929-1976)
Portly Canadian character actor,
in British films of the 50s and
60s.

On the Run, 1958
The Siege of Pinchgut, 1959
The Devil's Disciple, 1959
Jet Storm, 1959
The Inspector, 1962
The Longest Day, 1962
Night Without Pity, 1962
The War Lover, 1963
Witchcraft, 1964
The Woman Who Wouldn't Die,
    1965
Lost Continent, 1968
Quest For Love, 1971

NEIL McCARTHY (-)
Character star of films and
television who usually plays
characters of brawn rather
than brain.

Sands of the Desert, 1960
Offbeat, 1961
The Young Detectives, 1963
The Cracksman, 1963
Zulu, 1964
Where Eagles Dare, 1968
Project Z, 1968
The Public Eye, 1972
The Nine Tailors, 1974
Dirty Knight's Work, 1976
The Incredible Sarah, 1976
The Thief of Baghdad, 1979
Shogun, 1980

SEAN McCLORY (1923-)
Irish character actor long in
Hollywood; formerly with the
Abbey Theatre. Also much on
television.

Beyond Glory, 1949
The Daughter of Rosie O'Grady,
     1950
Rommel, the Desert Fox, 1951
Lorna Doone, 1951
Anne of the Indies, 1951
Les Miserables, 1952
The Quiet Man, 1952
The Secret Sharer, 1953
Niagara, 1953
Plunder in the Sun, 1953
Island in the Sky, 1953
Ring of Fear, 1954
Them, 1954
Moonfleet, 1955
The Long Grey Line, 1955
Diane, 1956
Cheyenne Autumn, 1964
Follow Me Boys, 1966
The Gnome-Mobile, 1967
Bandolero, 1968
Kate McShane, 1975
Roller Boogie, 1979

F. J. McCORMICK (1891-1947)
Irish character star and member of the Abbey Theatre; films
very rare.

Plough and the Stars, 1936
Hungry Hill, 1946
Odd Man Out, 1947

ALEC McCOWEN (1925-)
Star character actor of stage,
films, and television, also in
Hollywood.

The Cruel Sea, 1953
The Divided Heart, 1954
The Deep Blue Sea, 1955
The Long Arm, 1956
The Good Companions, 1957
The One That Got Away, 1957
Time Without Pity, 1957
Town On Trial, 1957
The Silent Enemy, 1958
A Night to Remember, 1958
The Doctor's Dilemma, 1959
A Midsummer Night's Dream,
     1961
The Loneliness of the Long
     Distance Runner, 1962
In the Cool of the Day, 1963
The Agony and the Ecstasy,
     1965
The Witches, 1966
The Devil's Own, 1967
The Hawaiians, 1970
Frenzy, 1972
Travels With My Aunt, 1972
Stevie, 1978
Hanover Street, 1979
Twelfth Night, 1980
Henry V, 1980

HUGH McDERMOTT (1908-
     1972)
Scotch light actor of stage and
films, often seen as Americans;
also in Hollywood.

The Captain's Table, 1936
David Livingstone, 1936
The Wife of General Ling,
     1937
Well Done Henry, 1937
Where's That Fire?, 1939
Neutral Port, 1940
For Freedom, 1940
Spring Meeting, 1941
Pimpernel Smith, 1941
The Young Mr. Pitt, 1942
The Seventh Veil, 1945
This Man is Mine, 1946
Good Time Girl, 1948

No Orchids For Miss Blandish,
1948
The Huggetts Abroad, 1949
Four Days, 1951
Trent's Last Case, 1952
Two On the Tiles, 1952
Lilli Marlene, 1953
The Love Lottery, 1954
Night People, 1954
Fire Over Africa, 1954
Johnny On the Spot, 1954
As Long as They're Happy,
1955
You Pay Your Money, 1956
A King in New York, 1957
The Man Who Wouldn't Talk,
1958
The Cillini Cup, 1959
Follow the Boys, 1962
First Men in the Moon, 1964
Delayed Flight, 1966
File of the Golden Goose,
1969
The Adding Machine, 1969
Guns in the Heather, 1969
The Games, 1970
Lawman, 1971
Captain Apache, 1971
Chato's Land, 1972

RODDY McDOWALL (1928-)
Popular child actor of the forties in Hollywood, also on
stage and television. Also
latterly photographer.

Murder in the Family, 1936
Just William, 1937
Scruffy, 1937
Hey Hey USA, 1938
Poison Pen, 1939
The Outsider, 1939
Dead Man's Shoes, 1939
Saloon Bar, 1940
This England, 1940
Man Hunt, 1941
How Green Was My Valley,
1941
Confirm Or Deny, 1941
Son of Fury, 1942
On the Sunny Side, 1942
The Pied Piper, 1942

My Friend Flicka, 1943
Lassie Come Home, 1943
The White Cliffs of Dover,
1944
The Keys of the Kingdom, 1944
Molly and Me, 1945
Thunderhead, 1945
Holiday in Mexico, 1946
Rocky, 1948
Kidnapped, 1948
Tuna Clipper, 1949
Black Midnight, 1949
Macbeth, 1950
Killer Shark, 1950
The Steel Fist, 1952
Midnight Lace, 1960
The Subterraneans, 1960
The Longest Day, 1962
Cleopatra, 1962
Shock Treatment, 1964
The Loved One, 1965
That Darn Cat, 1965
The Greatest Story Ever Told,
1965
The Third Day, 1965
Inside Daisy Clover, 1966
The Defector, 1966
Adventures of Bullwhip Griffin,
1966
Lord Love a Duck, 1966
The Cool Ones, 1967
It, 1967
Planet of the Apes, 1968
Five Card Stud, 1968
Angel Angel Down You Go,
1969
Hello Down There, 1969
Midas Run, 1969
Beneath the Planet of the
Apes, 1970
Escape From the Planet of
the Apes, 1971
Bedknobs and Broomsticks,
1971
Pretty Maids All in a Row,
1971
Conquest of the Planet of the
Apes, 1972
The Poseidon Adventure, 1972
Life & Times of Judge Roy
Bean, 1972
The Legend of Hell House,
1973

Arnold, 1973
Battle For the Planet of the
    Apes, 1973
Dirty Mary Crazy Larry, 1974
Funny Lady, 1975
Embryo, 1976
Mean Johnny Barrows, 1976
The Rhinemann Exchange,
    1977
Sixth and Main, 1977
Laserblast, 1978
The Cat From Outer Space,
    1978
Circle of Iron, 1979
Scavenger Hunt, 1979
The Immigrants, 1979
The Memory of Eva Ryker, 1980
Charlie Chan and the Curse of
    the Dragon Queen, 1980

MALCOLM McDOWELL
    (1944-)
Fashionable young star of the
70s; also on stage and television.

Poor Cow, 1967
If, 1968
The Raging Moon, 1970
Figures in a Landscape, 1970
A Clockwork Orange, 1971
O Lucky Man, 1973
Royal Flash, 1975
Aces High, 1976
Voyage of the Damned, 1976
Caligula, 1977
The Passage, 1979
Time After Time, 1979
She Fell Among Thieves, 1980
Look Back in Anger, 1980

JOHN McENERY (1945-)
Light leading actor of stage
and screen, popular during the
70s.

The Other People, 1968
Romeo and Juliet, 1968
The Lady in the Car, 1970
Bartleby, 1971
Nicholas and Alexandra, 1971

Days of Fury, 1973
The Land That Time Forgot,
    1974
Little Malcolm, 1974
Galileo, 1975
The Duellists, 1977
Schizo, 1978

PETER McENERY (1940-)
Supporting player and occasional leading man of the 60s,
also on television.

Beat Girl, 1960
Tunes of Glory, 1960
Victim, 1961
The Moonspinners, 1963
Fighting Prince of Donegal,
    1966
The Game is Over, 1966
I Killed Rasputin, 1967
The Other People, 1968
Negatives, 1968
Entertaining Mr. Sloane, 1970
The Adventures of Gerard,
    1970
Tales That Witness Madness,
    1973

GERALDINE McEWAN
    (1933-)
Attractive leading lady, primarily seen on stage; films
infrequent.

There Was a Young Lady,
    1953
No Kidding, 1960
The Dance of Death, 1969
Bawdy Adventures of Tom
    Jones, 1975
Escape From the Dark, 1976

NIALL MacGINNIS (1913-)
Versatile Irish character actor, on stage from 1931;
films from 1934.

Egg and Butter Man, 1934
Turn of the Tide, 1935

Ourselves Alone, 1936
The Crimson Circle, 1936
Debt of Honour, 1936
Edge of the World, 1937
The Last Adventurers, 1937
Luck of the Irish, 1937
River of Unrest, 1937
Mountains O'Mourne, 1938
East of Piccadilly, 1941
49th Parallel, 1941
The Avengers, 1942
Undercover, 1943
We Dive at Dawn, 1943
The Hundred Pound Window, 1944
Tawny Pipit, 1944
Henry V, 1944
Captain Boycott, 1947
Hamlet, 1948
Anna Karenina, 1948
No Room at the Inn, 1948
Diamond City, 1949
Christopher Columbus, 1949
Which Will You Have?, 1949
Chance of a Lifetime, 1950
No Highway, 1951
Talk of a Million, 1951
Murder in the Cathedral, 1952
Martin Luther, 1953
Hell Below Zero, 1954
Betrayed, 1954
Special Delivery, 1954
Conflict of Wings, 1954
Knights of the Round Table, 1954
Helen of Troy, 1955
Alexander the Great, 1956
Battle of the River Plate, 1956
Lust For Life, 1956
The Shiralee, 1957
Night of the Demon, 1957
She Didn't Say No, 1958
Behind the Mask, 1958
Shake Hands With the Devil, 1959
The Nun's Story, 1959
Tarzan's Greatest Adventure, 1959
This Other Eden, 1960
Never Take Sweets From a Stranger, 1960
Kidnapped, 1960
A Terrible Beauty, 1960

In the Nick, 1960
A Foxhole in Cairo, 1960
Sword of Sherwood Forest, 1961
Johnny Nobody, 1961
The Prince and the Pauper, 1962
Face in the Rain, 1962
The Webster Boy, 1962
Playboy of the Western World, 1962
Billy Budd, 1962
The Devil's Agent, 1962
The Man Who Finally Died, 1962
Jason and the Argonauts, 1963
Becket, 1964
The Truth About Spring, 1965
The Spy Who Came in From The Cold, 1965
The War Lord, 1965
A Man Could Get Killed, 1965
Island of Terror, 1966
The Viking Queen, 1966
Torture Garden, 1967
Shoes of the Fisherman, 1968
Sinful Davy, 1969
River of Mystery, 1969
The Mackintosh Man, 1973

PATRICK McGOOHAN (1928-)
American-born leading actor of
British films, also on stage
(since 1953) and tv. Television
series: "Danger Man" (1960-
66), "The Prisoner" (1967).

Passage Home, 1955
I Am a Camera, 1955
High Tide at Noon, 1956
Zarak, 1957
Hell Drivers, 1957
The Gypsy and the Gentleman, 1957
Nor the Moon By Night, 1958
Two Living One Dead, 1961
All Night Long, 1962
The Quare Fellow, 1962
Life For Ruth, 1963
Dr. Syn Alias the Scarecrow, 1963
The Three Lives of Thomasina,

1964
Walk in the Shadow, 1966
Ice Station Zebra, 1968
The Moonshine War, 1970
Mary Queen of Scots, 1971
The Genius, 1975
Silver Streak, 1976
Brass Target, 1978
Escape From Alcatraz, 1979
The Hard Way, 1979

JACK MacGOWRAN (1916-1973)
Irish character actor of stage,
screen and television, often seen
in waspish roles. Also Hollywood.

No Resting Place, 1951
The Quiet Man, 1952
The Gentle Gunman, 1952
The Titfield Thunderbolt, 1953
Raiders of the River, 1956
Sailor Beware, 1956
Manuela, 1957
The Rising of the Moon, 1957
Rooney, 1958
She Didn't Say No, 1958
The Boy and the Bridge, 1959
Behemoth the Sea Monster,
  1959
Darby O'Gill and the Little
  People, 1959
Blind Date, 1960
Mix Me a Person, 1961
Two and Two Make Six, 1962
Vengeance, 1962
Tom Jones, 1963
The Ceremony, 1964
Young Cassidy, 1965
Dr. Zhivago, 1965
Lord Jim, 1965
Cul de Sac, 1966
The Fearless Vampire Killers,
  1967
How I Won the War, 1967
Wonderwall, 1968
King Lear, 1970
The Exorcist, 1973

TUCKER McGUIRE (-)
Character actress of stage and

screen; films sporadic.

Stranger on a Honeymoon, 1936
Clothes and the Woman, 1937
Climbing High, 1938
Shipyard Sally, 1939
The Night Has Eyes, 1942
King of the Underworld, 1952
Murder at Scotland Yard, 1952
A Ghost For Sale, 1952
The Net, 1953
A Night to Remember, 1958

BARRY MacKAY (1906-)
Leading actor of stage and
screen, latterly in character
roles; also singer.

Evergreen, 1934
Passing Shadows, 1934
Forbidden Territory, 1934
Private Life of Don Juan, 1934
Oh Daddy, 1935
Forever England, 1935
Me and Marlborough, 1935
Private Secretary, 1935
Glamorous Night, 1937
Gangway, 1937
The Great Barrier, 1937
Who Killed John Savage?, 1937
Sailing Along, 1938
A Christmas Carol, 1938
Smuggled Cargo, 1940
The Pickwick Papers, 1952
Grand National Night, 1953
Orders Are Orders, 1954

JAMES McKECHNIE (-)
Light supporting actor and character player of the 40s.

San Demetrio-London, 1943
Life & Death of Colonel Blimp,
  1943
Two Thousand Women, 1944
Caesar and Cleopatra, 1945
Painted Boats, 1945
The Years Between, 1947
Scott of the Antarctic, 1948
Bond Street, 1948
Madeleine, 1950

IAN McKELLIN (1935-)
Stage actor in very occasional
films of the late 60s.

Alfred the Great, 1969
A Touch of Love, 1969
The Promise, 1969

SIOBHAN McKENNA (1923-)
Irish actress of stage (since
1940), films, and tv; films
rare. Married to Denis O'Dea.

Hungry Hill, 1946
Daughter of Darkness, 1948
The Lost People, 1949
The Adventurers, 1951
King of Kings, 1960
Playboy of the Western World,
1962
Of Human Bondage, 1964
Dr. Zhivago, 1965
Philadelphia Here I Come, 1975

T. P. McKENNA (1931-)
Irish stage and film character
player of the 60s and 70s.

Freedom to Die, 1962
The Girl With Green Eyes, 1964
Downfall, 1964
Ferry Cross the Mersey, 1964
Young Cassidy, 1965
Ulysses, 1967
Charge of the Light Brigade,
1968
Anne of the Thousand Days, 1970
The Beast in the Cellar, 1970
Perfect Friday, 1970
Villain, 1971
The Death Policy, 1973
All Creatures Great and Small,
1975
Portrait of the Artist as a
Young Man, 1979

VIRGINIA McKENNA (1931-)
Leading actress of stage (from
1950) and films; married: Denholm Elliott, Bill Travers.

Father's Doing Fine, 1952
The Second Mrs. Tanqueray,
1952
The Cruel Sea, 1953
The Oracle, 1953
Simba, 1954
The Ship That Died of Shame,
1955
A Town Like Alice, 1956
The Barretts of Wimpole Street,
1957
The Smallest Show On Earth,
1957
Carve Her Name With Pride,
1958
The Passionate Summer, 1958
The Wreck of the Mary Deare,
1959
Two Living One Dead, 1961
Born Free, 1966
Ring of Bright Water, 1969
An Elephant Called Slowly,
1970
Waterloo, 1970
The Lion at World's End, 1971
Swallows and Amazons, 1974
The Gathering Storm, 1974
Christian the Lion, 1976
Disappearance, 1976
Holocaust 2000, 1977

LEO McKERN (1920-)
Canny, corpulent Australian
character star of stage (1944)
and screen, also in Hollywood.
Also outstanding on television
as lawyer Horace Rumpole on
"Rumpole of the Bailey."

Murder in the Cathedral, 1952
All For Mary, 1955
X The Unknown, 1956
Time Without Pity, 1957
A Tale of Two Cities, 1958
Beyond This Place, 1959
Yesterday's Enemy, 1959
The Mouse That Roared, 1959
Scent of Mystery, 1960
Jazzboat, 1960
The Running, Jumping, and
Standing Still Film, 1960
The Day the Earth Caught

Fire, 1961
Mr. Topaze, 1962
The Inspector, 1962
The Horse Without a Head,
  1963
Doctor in Distress, 1963
Hot Enough For June, 1963
A Jolly Bad Fellow, 1964
King and Country, 1964
Moll Flanders, 1965
Help!, 1965
A Man For All Seasons, 1966
Assignment K, 1967
Decline and Fall, 1968
The Shoes of the Fisherman,
  1968
Nobody Runs Forever, 1969
Ryan's Daughter, 1970
Massacre in Rome, 1973
The Adventures of Sherlock
  Holmes Smarter Brother,
  1975
The Omen, 1976
Candleshoe, 1978
The Blue Lagoon, 1980

CYRIL McLAGLEN (1899-)
Leading actor and supporting
player of early sound films,
also in Hollywood. Brother of
Victor McLaglen.

Call of the Road, 1920
Mademoiselle From Armen-
  tieres, 1926
Island of Despair, 1926
Boadicea, 1926
Hindle Wakes, 1927
Quinneys, 1927
Flight Commander, 1927
The Arcadians, 1927
Madame Pompadour, 1927
Balaclava, 1928
Underground, 1928
You Know What Sailors Are,
  1928
The Lost Patrol, 1929
Suspense, 1930
Bed and Breakfast, 1930
Alf's Button, 1930
No Lady, 1931
Down River, 1931

Josser Joins the Navy, 1932
Verdict of the Sea, 1932
Money For Speed, 1933
The Fear Ship, 1933
A Royal Demand, 1933
A Tale of Two Cities, 1935
Mary of Scotland, 1936
Plough and the Stars, 1936
Toilers of the Sea, 1936
Wee Willie Winkie, 1937
The Long Voyage Home, 1940
The Black Swan, 1942

VICTOR McLAGLEN (1883-
  1959)
Tough star of silent films,
later in Hollywood; former
soldier (1897).   Brother of
Cyril McLaglen; father of director Andrew McLaglen
(1925-).

The Call of the Road, 1920
Carnival, 1921
Corinthian Jack, 1921
Prey of the Dragon, 1921
The Sport of Kings, 1921
The Glorious Adventure, 1921
Romance of Old Bagdad, 1922
The Crimson Circle, 1922
Little Brother of God, 1922
The Sailor Tramp, 1922
The Romany, 1923
Heartstrings, 1923
M'Lord of the White Road,
  1923
Beloved Brute, 1923
In the Blood, 1923
The Boatswain's Mate, 1924
Women and Diamonds, 1924
The Gay Corinthian, 1924
The Passionate Adventure,
  1924
Percy, 1925
The Fighting Heart, 1925
The Unholy Three, 1925
Winds of Chance, 1925
Men of Steel, 1925
Isle of Retribution, 1926
Beau Geste, 1926
What Price Glory, 1926
Captain Lash, 1927

The Loves of Carmen, 1927
A Girl in Every Port, 1928
Hangman's House, 1928
River Pirate, 1928
Mother Macree, 1928
The Cockeyed World, 1929
Strong Boy, 1929
The Black Watch, 1929
Hot For Paris, 1930
Happy Days, 1930
On the Level, 1930
Dishonoured, 1930
Wicked, 1931
A Devil With Women, 1931
Three Rogues, 1931
Women of All Nations, 1931
Annabelle's Affairs, 1931
The Gay Caballero, 1932
The Devil's Lottery, 1932
Guilty as Hell, 1932
Rackety Rax, 1932
Hot Petters, 1933
Dick Turpin, 1933
Laughing at Life, 1933
The Lost Patrol, 1934
No More Women, 1934
Wharf Angel, 1934
Murder at the Vanities, 1934
Under Pressure, 1934
The Captain Hates the Sea,
  1934
The Informer, 1935
The Great Hotel Murder, 1935
Under Two Flags, 1936
Professional Soldier, 1936
Klondike Annie, 1936
Nancy Steele is Missing, 1937
Sea Devils, 1937
This is My Affair, 1937
The Magnificent Brute, 1937
Wee Willie Winkie, 1937
Battle of Broadway, 1938
The Devil's Party, 1938
We're Going to Be Rich, 1938
Gunga Din, 1939
Pacific Liner, 1939
Let Freedom Ring, 1939
Ex-Champ, 1939
Captain Fury, 1939
Full Confession, 1939
Rio, 1939
The Big Guy, 1940
South of Pago Pago, 1940

Diamond Frontiers, 1940
Broadway Limited, 1941
Call Out the Marines, 1942
Powder Town, 1942
China Girl, 1943
Princess and the Pirate, 1944
Tampico, 1944
Roger Toughy, Gangster, 1944
Rough, Tough, and Ready,
  1945
Love, Honour and Goodbye,
  1945
Whistle Stop, 1946
The Michigan Kid, 1947
The Foxes of Harrow, 1947
Fort Apache, 1948
She Wore a Yellow Ribbon,
  1949
Rio Grande, 1950
The Quiet Man, 1952
Fair Wind to Java, 1953
Trouble in the Glen, 1954
Prince Valiant, 1954
Lady Godiva, 1955
Many Rivers to Cross, 1955
Bengazi, 1956
Around the World in 80 Days,
  1956
The Abductors, 1957
Sea Fury, 1958

GIBB McLAUGHLIN (1884-
  197*)
Emaciated character star of
stage (since 1911) and screen;
a master of disguise who was
sometimes cast in sinister
roles or as Chinaman.

Beyond the Dreams of Avarice,
  1920
The Road to London, 1921
Carnival, 1921
Bohemian Girl, 1922
The Pointing Finger, 1922
Three to One Against, 1923
The Only Way, 1925
Somebody's Darling, 1925
Nell Gwyn, 1926
London, 1926
The House of Marney, 1926
Madame Pompadour, 1927

The Arcadians, 1927
Poppies of Flanders, 1927
The White Sheik, 1928
The Farmer's Wife, 1928
Not Quite a Lady, 1928
Glorious Youth, 1928
The Price of Divorce, 1928
Kitty, 1929
The Silent House, 1929
Power Over Men, 1929
Woman From China, 1930
The W Plan, 1930
The Brat, 1930
School For Scandal, 1930
Third Time Lucky, 1931
Sally in Our Alley, 1931
My Old China, 1931
Jealousy, 1931
The Temperance Fete, 1932
Goodnight Vienna, 1932
Whiteface, 1932
The Love Contract, 1932
Money Means Nothing, 1932
Where is This Lady?, 1932
Congress Dances, 1932
The Thirteenth Candle, 1933
King of the Ritz, 1933
No Funny Business, 1933
High Finance, 1933
Britannia of Billingsgate, 1933
Bitter Sweet, 1933
The Private Life of Henry VIII,
 1933
Dick Turpin, 1933
Friday the 13th, 1933
Magic Night, 1933
Catherine the Great, 1934
The Queen's Affair, 1934
The Church Mouse, 1934
Blossom Time, 1934
Little Friend, 1934
There Goes Susie, 1934
Jew Suss, 1934
The Old Curiosity Shop, 1934
The Scarlet Pimpernel, 1935
The Iron Duke, 1935
Swinging the Lead, 1935
Love Affair of the Dictator,
 1935
Bulldog Jack, 1935
Drake of England, 1935
Me and Marlborough, 1935

I Give My Heart, 1935
Hyde Park Corner, 1935
Two's Company, 1936
Broken Blossoms, 1936
Where There's a Will, 1936
Juggernaut, 1936
All In, 1936
Irish For Luck, 1936
You Live and Learn, 1937
Mr. Reeder in Room 13, 1938
Almost a Gentleman, 1938
Break the News, 1938
Thirteen Men and a Gun, 1938
Hold My Hand, 1938
Hey Hey USA, 1938
The Loves of Madame DuBarry,
 1938
Inspector Hornleigh, 1939
Confidential Lady, 1939
Come On George, 1939
Spy For a Day, 1940
Spellbound, 1941
Freedom Radio, 1941
Penn of Pennsylvania, 1941
Much Too Shy, 1942
Tomorrow We Live, 1942
The Young Mr. Pitt, 1942
My Learned Friend, 1943
Give Us the Moon, 1944
Caesar and Cleopatra, 1945
Oliver Twist, 1948
The Queen of Spades, 1948
Once Upon a Dream, 1949
Night and the City, 1950
The Black Rose, 1950
The Lavender Hill Mob, 1951
The House in the Square, 1951
The Pickwick Papers, 1952
The Card, 1952
Grand National Night, 1953
Paris Express, 1953
Hobson's Choice, 1954
The Brain Machine, 1955
The Deep Blue Sea, 1955
Who Done It, 1956
The Man Who Never Was, 1956
Seawife, 1957

IAN MacLEAN (-)
General purpose and supporting
actor of the thirties.

Brewster's Millions, 1935
Jack of All Trades, 1936
Mayfair Melody, 1937
The Street Singer, 1937
The Singing Cop, 1938
Quiet Please, 1938
Simply Terrific, 1938
Thistledown, 1938
The Return of Carol Deane,
   1938
Marigold, 1938
The Nursemaid Who Disap-
   peared, 1939
A Gentleman's Gentleman, 1939
Murder Will Out, 1939
The Arsenal Stadium Mystery,
   1939
Two For Danger, 1940
That's the Ticket, 1940
The Young Mr. Pitt, 1942
Twilight Hour, 1944
Dreaming, 1944

GORDON McLEOD (-)
Character star of the thirties
and forties, sometimes seen
in evil or menacing roles.

The Only Way, 1925
David Garrick, 1928
There Goes the Bride, 1932
Chelsea Life, 1933
Mixed Doubles, 1933
Lucky Losers, 1934
The Primrose Path, 1934
Brides to Be, 1934
The Case For the Crown, 1934
Borrow a Million, 1934
To Catch a Thief, 1936
The Crimson Circle, 1936
Nothing Like Publicity, 1936
Not Wanted On Voyage, 1936
Talk of the Devil, 1936
Victoria the Great, 1937
The Squeaker, 1937
The Frog, 1937
The Rat, 1937
Sixty Glorious Years, 1938
Thistledown, 1938
I See Ice, 1938
Double Or Quits, 1938
Dangerous Medicine, 1938

Q Planes, 1939
The Saint in London, 1939
Confidential Lady, 1939
Hoots Mon, 1939
That's the Ticket, 1940
Crooks' Tour, 1940
Two For Danger, 1940
The Saint's Vacation, 1941
The Patient Vanishes, 1941
The Prime Minister, 1941
Facing the Music, 1941
The Saint Meets the Tiger,
   1941
Hatter's Castle, 1941
The First of the Few, 1942
We'll Smile Again, 1942
The Balloon Goes Up, 1942
Meet Sexton Blake, 1944
He Snoops to Conquer, 1944
Easy Money, 1948
Corridor of Mirrors, 1948
The Winslow Boy, 1948
Chance of a Lifetime, 1950
A Case For PC 49, 1951
Four Days, 1951

GUS McNAUGHTON (1884-1969)
Comedy supporting star of the
30s, formerly in music halls;
also on stage (from 1899).

Murder, 1930
Comets, 1930
Children of Chance, 1930
Lucky Girl, 1932
The Last Coupon, 1932
Maid of the Mountains, 1932
Money Talks, 1932
His Wife's Mother, 1932
Their Night Out, 1933
Leave it to Me, 1933
Heads We Go, 1933
The Love Nest, 1933
Song Birds, 1933
Radio Parade, 1933
Crime On the Hill, 1933
Happy, 1934
Bagged, 1934
Seeing is Believing, 1934
Master and Man, 1934
Luck of a Sailor, 1934
There Goes Susie, 1934

Crazy People, 1934
Spring in the Air, 1934
The Charming Deceiver, 1935
Barnacle Bill, 1935
Royal Cavalcade, 1935
The Thirty-Nine Steps, 1935
Joy Ride, 1935
Music Hath Charms, 1935
Invitation to the Waltz, 1935
The Crouching Beast, 1935
Not So Dusty, 1936
Keep Your Seats Please, 1936
Southern Roses, 1936
Busman's Holiday, 1936
The Heirloom Mystery, 1936
You Must Get Married, 1936
Strange Adventures of Mr.
    Smith, 1937
Keep Fit, 1937
Storm in a Teacup, 1937
Action For Slander, 1937
South Riding, 1938
The Divorce of Lady X, 1938
Easy Riches, 1938
We're Going to Be Rich, 1938
St. Martin's Lane, 1938
You're the Doctor, 1938
Keep Smiling, 1938
Q Planes, 1939
Trouble Brewing, 1939
I Killed the Count, 1939
There Aint No Justice, 1939
All at Sea, 1939
What Would You Do Chums?,
    1939
Blind Folly, 1939
Two For Dinner, 1940
That's the Ticket, 1940
George and Margaret, 1940
Old Bill and Son, 1940
Facing the Music, 1941
Penn of Pennsylvania, 1941
Jeannie, 1941
South American George, 1941
Let the People Sing, 1942
The Day Will Dawn, 1942
Much Too Shy, 1942
Rose of Tralee, 1942
The Shipbuilders, 1943
Demobbed, 1943
A Place of One's Own, 1944
Here Comes the Sun, 1945
The Trojan Brothers, 1946

The Turners of Prospect Road,
    1947
This Was a Woman, 1948
The Lucky Mascot, 1948

PATRICK MacNEE (1922-   )
Dark-haired leading actor of
stage and screen, probably
best known as John Steed in
the tv show "The Avengers"
(1960-68). Also on tv in "The
New Avengers" (1976).

The Life and Death of Colonel
    Blimp, 1943
Hamlet, 1948
The Fatal Night, 1948
The Girl is Mine, 1950
Flesh and Blood, 1951
Scrooge, 1951
Three Cases of Murder, 1955
Battle of the River Plate, 1956
Les Girls, 1958
Mr. Jerico, 1970
Incense For the Damned, 1970
Sherlock Holmes in New York,
    1976
Billion Dollar Threat, 1979
The Sea Wolves, 1980

NORMAN MacOWAN (1877-
    1961)
Scottish character actor mainly
seen during the fifties.

Whiskey Galore, 1948
Valley of the Eagles, 1951
Laxdale Hall, 1953
Where There's a Will, 1955
X The Unknown, 1956
Heart of a Child, 1958
Tread Softly Stranger, 1958
The Boy and the Bridge, 1959
Kidnapped, 1959
Battle of the Sexes, 1959
City of the Dead, 1960

DUNCAN MacRAE (1905-
    1967)
Rugged-looking Scottish charac-

ter star, often seen in stern roles.

The Brothers, 1947
Whiskey Galore, 1948
The Woman in Question, 1950
You're Only Young Twice, 1952
The Kidnappers, 1953
The Maggie, 1954
Geordie, 1955
Rockets Galore, 1957
The Bridal Path, 1958
Kidnapped, 1959
Our Man in Havana, 1959
Tunes of Glory, 1960
Greyfriars Bobby, 1960
The Best of Enemies, 1961
A Jolly Bad Fellow, 1964
The Model Murder Case, 1964
Casino Royale, 1967
30 is a Dangerous Age, Cynthia, 1967

IAN McSHANE (1942-)
Leading and supporting actor of the 60s and 70s, also in Hollywood.

The Wild and the Willing, 1962
The Pleasure Girls, 1965
Sky West and Crooked, 1965
The Battle of Britain, 1969
If It's Tuesday, This Must Be Belgium, 1969
Pussycat Pussycat I Love You, 1970
Tam Lin, 1971
Villain, 1971
Sitting Target, 1972
The Last of Sheila, 1973
Ransom, 1974
The Terrorists, 1975
Journey Into Fear, 1975
Jesus of Nazareth, 1977
The Fifth Musketeer, 1979
Disraeli: Portrait of a Romantic, 1980
The Miracle Named Louise, 1980

PETER MADDEN (1910-)
Thin character player of films and television; active in the 60s.

Counterblast, 1948
A Matter or Murder, 1949
Tom Brown's School Days, 1951
Battle of the VI, 1958
Fiend Without a Face, 1958
Floods of Fear, 1958
Hell is a City, 1960
Saturday Night & Sunday Morning, 1960
Exodus, 1960
Loneliness of the Long Distance Runner, 1962
The Road to Hong Kong, 1962
A Kind of Loving, 1962
From Russia With Love, 1963
The Very Edge, 1963
Nothing But the Best, 1964
Woman of Straw, 1964
Dr. Zhivago, 1965
He Who Rides a Tiger, 1966
Vendetta For the Saint, 1968
Henry VIII and His Six Wives, 1972
Mohammed Messenger of God, 1977

VICTOR MADDERN (1926-)
Cockney character actor of stage and films, formerly on radio; also seen on tv in series "Fair Exchange" (1962).

Seven Days to Noon, 1950
Morning Departure, 1950
His Excellency, 1952
Sailor of the King, 1953
Time Bomb, 1953
Street of Shadows, 1953
Footsteps in the Fog, 1955
Josephine and Men, 1955
Cockleshell Heroes, 1955
Carrington VC, 1955
The Night My Number Came Up, 1955
Private's Progress, 1956
It's a Great Day, 1956

Child in the House, 1956
A Hill in Korea, 1956
The Last Man to Hang, 1956
Seven Waves Away, 1957
Saint Joan, 1957
Barnacle Bill, 1957
Man in the Sky, 1957
Face in the Night, 1957
Stranger's Meeting, 1957
Son of a Stranger, 1957
Dunkirk, 1958
Happy is the Bride, 1958
The Safecracker, 1958
Blood of the Vampire, 1958
Cat and Mouse, 1958
I Was Monty's Double, 1958
I'm All Right, Jack, 1959
The Siege of Pinchgut, 1959
Please Turn Over, 1959
Exodus, 1960
Sink the Bismarck, 1960
Let's Get Married, 1960
Light Up the Sky, 1960
Watch Your Stern, 1960
Crossroads to Crime, 1960
On the Fiddle, 1961
Petticoat Pirates, 1961
Carry On Regardless, 1961
HMS Defiant, 1962
Carry On Cleo, 1964
Carry On Spying, 1964
Rotten to the Core, 1965
Bunny Lake is Missing, 1965
Cuckoo Patrol, 1965
Circus of Fear, 1966
The Magnificent Two, 1967
Talk of the Devil, 1967
The Lost Continent, 1968
Chitty Chitty Bang Bang, 1968
The Magic Christian, 1970
A Hole Lot of Trouble, 1970
Digby, the Biggest Dog in the
   World, 1974

PATRICK MAGEE (1924-)
Incisive character actor of
stage and films, often seen in
sinister roles.

The Criminal, 1960
Never Back Losers, 1961
Rag Doll, 1961

The Boys, 1962
A Prize of Arms, 1962
The Servant, 1963
Dementia 13, 1963
The Young Racers, 1963
Riccochet, 1963
The Very Edge, 1963
Zulu, 1964
Masque of the Red Death,
   1964
Seance On a Wet Afternoon,
   1964
The Skull, 1965
Monster of Terror, 1965
Marat/Sade, 1967
Decline and Fall, 1968
The Birthday Party, 1968
King Lear, 1970
Cromwell, 1970
You Can't Win Them All, 1971
The Fiend, 1971
A Clockwork Orange, 1971
The Trojan Women, 1971
Young Winston, 1972
Asylum, 1972
Beware of the Brethren, 1972
Lady Ice, 1973
And Now the Screaming Starts,
   1973
The Final Programme, 1974
Luther, 1974
Demons of the Mind, 1974
Galileo, 1975
Barry Lyndon, 1975
Telefon, 1977
Rough Cut, 1980

MARNE MAITLAND (1920-)
Anglo-Indian character player
long in British pictures; often
seen in evil or sinister parts.
Also on television.

Cairo Road, 1950
An Outcast of the Islands,
   1952
The Golden Mask, 1952
Father Brown, 1954
The Flame and the Flesh,
   1954
Diplomatic Passport, 1954
Bhowani Junction, 1956

I Was Monty's Double, 1958
I Only Arsked, 1958
The Camp On Blood Island,
  1958
Mark of the Hawk, 1958
Windom's Way, 1958
The Wind Cannot Read, 1958
Stranglers of Bombay, 1959
I'm All Right, Jack, 1959
Carleton Browne of the FO,
  1959
Visa to Canton, 1960
Cone of Silence, 1960
Sands of the Desert, 1960
The Middle Course, 1961
Terror of the Tongs, 1961
Phantom of the Opera, 1962
Cleopatra, 1962
Nine Hours to Rama, 1962
Master Spy, 1963
Panic, 1963
First Men in the Moon, 1964
The Return of Mr. Moto, 1965
Lord Jim, 1965
The Reptile, 1965
Khartoum, 1966
The Bobo, 1967
Duffy, 1968
Shoes of the Fisherman, 1968
Anne of the Thousand Days,
  1970
The Statue, 1971
Shaft in Africa, 1973
Man With the Golden Gun, 1974
The Anonymous Avenger, 1976
The Pink Panther Strikes
  Again, 1976
March Or Die, 1977
The Day Christ Died, 1980

ELIOT MAKEHAM (1882-1956)
Character star of the 30s and
40s, often seen as accountants,
clerks, or other small roles.
Also on stage.

Rome Express, 1932
Orders Are Orders, 1933
Friday the 13th, 1933
Forging Ahead, 1933
I'm an Explosive, 1933
I Lived With You, 1933

Little Napoleon, 1933
Home Sweet Home, 1933
The Laughter of Fools, 1933
The Roof, 1933
Unfinished Symphony, 1934
The Crimson Candle, 1934
Bypass to Happiness, 1934
Lorna Doone, 1935
The Last Journey, 1935
Once in a New Moon, 1935
Peg of Old Drury, 1935
Her Last Affaire, 1935
Two Hearts in Harmony, 1935
To Catch a Thief, 1936
The Brown Wallet, 1936
A Star Fell From Heaven,
  1936
Born That Way, 1936
Calling the Tune, 1936
East Meets West, 1936
Tomorrow We Live, 1936
The Mill On the Floss, 1937
Take My Tip, 1937
Racing Romance, 1937
East of Ludgate Hill, 1937
Dark Journey, 1937
Farewell Again, 1937
Head Over Heels, 1937
Storm in a Teacup, 1937
Coming of Age, 1938
Vessel of Wrath, 1938
Darts Are Trumps, 1938
Merely Mr. Hawkins, 1938
Bedtime Story, 1938
You're the Doctor, 1938
Anything to Declare, 1938
What Men Live By, 1939
Four Just Men, 1939
Inspector Hornleigh, 1939
Me and My Pal, 1939
Spare a Copper, 1940
Spy For a Day, 1940
Saloon Bar, 1940
Night Train to Munich, 1940
Busman's Honeymoon, 1940
Pastor Hall, 1940
All Hands, 1940
Food For Thought, 1940
John Smith Wakes Up, 1940
The Common Touch, 1941
Facing the Music, 1941
They Flew Alone, 1942
Suspected Person, 1942

Uncensored, 1942
Bell Bottom George, 1943
A Canterbury Tale, 1943
Halfway House, 1944
Give Us the Moon, 1944
Candles at Nine, 1944
I'll Be Your Sweetheart, 1945
Perfect Strangers, 1945
Daybreak, 1946
The Magic Bow, 1947
Frieda, 1947
The Little Ballerina, 1947
Jassy, 1947
Call of the Blood, 1948
Forbidden, 1949
Murder at the Windmill, 1949
Children of Chance, 1949
Trio, 1950
Night and the City, 1950
Scrooge, 1951
Scarlet Thread, 1951
Green Grow the Rushes, 1951
Decameron Nights, 1952
The Yellow Balloon, 1952
The Crimson Pirate, 1952
The Fake, 1953
Doctor in the House, 1954
Sailor Beware, 1956

ANDREA MALANDRINOS
(-)
Greek actor of British films,
often in cameo roles.

The Golden Cage, 1933
Two Wives For Henry, 1933
Send 'Em Back Half Dead,
1933
Broken Melody, 1934
How's Chances, 1934
The Admiral's Secret, 1934
Virginia's Husband, 1934
The Invader, 1936
Secret Agent, 1936
Prison Breaker, 1936
The Price of Folly, 1937
Gypsy, 1937
The Last Barricade, 1938
Take Cover, 1938
Two Days to Live, 1939
Room For Two, 1940
Champagne Charlie, 1944

The Lavender Hill Mob, 1951
Night Plane to Amsterdam,
1955
Stolen Time, 1955
The Prince and the Showgirl,
1957
The Boy and the Bridge, 1959
The Boy Who Stole a Million,
1961
The Magnificent Two, 1967
The Magus, 1968
Man of Violence, 1970

AUBREY MALLALIEU (-)
Small-part character player of
the thirties and forties.

What Happened to Harkness?,
1934
The Riverside Murder, 1935
Cross Currents, 1935
Music Hath Charms, 1935
Prison Breaker, 1936
Nothing Like Publicity, 1936
A Touch of the Moon, 1936
Such is Life, 1936
All That Glitters, 1936
Love at Sea, 1936
The Black Tulip, 1937
Holiday's End, 1937
Patricia Gets Her Man, 1937
Pearls Bring Tears, 1937
When the Devil Was Well,
1937
Keep Fit, 1937
The Strange Adventures of
Mr. Smith, 1937
Fifty Shilling Boxer, 1937
Change For a Sovereign, 1937
East of Ludgate Hill, 1937
His Lordship Regrets, 1938
Thank Evans, 1938
Easy Riches, 1938
The Reverse By My Lot, 1938
Paid in Error, 1938
Simply Terrific, 1938
Coming of Age, 1938
The Claydon Treasure Mystery,
1938
Almost a Honeymoon, 1938
The Gables Mystery, 1938
Dangerous Medicine, 1938

The Return of Carol Deane,
 1938
Save a Little Sunshine, 1938
You're the Doctor, 1938
His Lordship Goes to Press,
 1938
Return of the Frog, 1938
Miracles Do Happen, 1938
21 Days, 1939
Me and My Pal, 1939
Dead Men Are Dangerous, 1939
So This is London, 1939
The Face at the Window, 1939
I Killed the Count, 1939
All at Sea, 1939
The Stars Look Down, 1939
Busman's Honeymoon, 1940
The Briggs Family, 1940
Bulldog Sees it Through, 1940
The Door With Seven Locks,
 1940
Salvage With a Smile, 1940
Wings and the Woman, 1941
The Fine Feathers, 1941
Gert and Daisy's Weekend, 1941
Breach of Promise, 1941
Penn of Pennsylvania, 1941
Hatter's Castle, 1941
Unpublished Story, 1942
Let the People Sing, 1942
The Goose Steps Out, 1942
Asking For Trouble, 1942
My Learned Friend, 1943
The Yellow Canary, 1943
The Demi-Paradise, 1943
Kiss the Bride Goodbye, 1944
He Snoops to Conquer, 1944
Murder in Reverse, 1945
I Live in Grosvenor Square,
 1945
Under New Management, 1946
Meet Me at Dawn, 1947
The Fatal Night, 1948
Counterblast, 1948
The Facts of Love, 1949
A Girl in a Million, 1949

MILES MALLESON (1888-1969)
Distinguished actor of stage
(1911) and screen, often in
flustered comedy roles; also
director, screenwriter, and
playwright.

The Headmaster, 1921
The W Plan, 1930
Two Worlds, 1930
The Yellow Mask, 1930
Night Birds, 1930
Children of Chance, 1930
City of Song, 1931
The Woman Between, 1931
Sally in Our Alley, 1931
A Night in Montmartre, 1931
The Blue Danube, 1932
The Water Gypsies, 1932
The Sign of Four, 1932
The Mayor's Nest, 1932
The Love Contract, 1932
Love on Wheels, 1932
Money Means Nothing, 1932
Frail Women, 1932
Strange Evidence, 1933
Perfect Understanding, 1933
Summer Lightning, 1933
Bitter Sweet, 1933
The Queen's Affair, 1934
Nell Gwyn, 1934
Falling in Love, 1934
The Thirty-Nine Steps, 1935
Lorna Doone, 1935
Lazybones, 1935
Vintage Wine, 1935
Peg of Old Drury, 1935
Rhodes of Africa, 1936
Tudor Rose, 1936
Knight Without Armour, 1937
Action For Slander, 1937
Victoria the Great, 1937
The Rat, 1937
Sixty Glorious Years, 1938
A Royal Divorce, 1938
For Freedom, 1940
The Thief of Bagdad, 1940
Spellbound, 1941
Major Barbara, 1941
This Was Paris, 1942
Unpublished Story, 1942
They Flew Alone, 1942
The First of the Few, 1942
Thunder Rock, 1942
World of Plenty, 1943
The Demi-Paradise, 1943
The Yellow Canary, 1943
The Gentle Sex, 1943
The Adventures of Tartu, 1943
Mr. Emmanuel, 1944
Dead of Night, 1945

While the Sun Shines, 1946
Idol of Paris, 1948
One Night With You, 1948
Saraband For Dead Lovers,
   1948
Woman Hater, 1948
The History of Mr. Polly, 1949
Cardboard Cavalier, 1949
The Queen of Spades, 1949
The Perfect Woman, 1949
Train of Events, 1949
Kind Hearts and Coronets, 1949
The Golden Salamander, 1950
Stage Fright, 1950
The Magic Box, 1951
Scrooge, 1951
The Man in the White Suit,
   1951
The Woman's Angle, 1952
The Happy Family, 1952
The Importance of Being Earn-
   est, 1952
Treasure Hunt, 1952
Venetian Bird, 1952
Trent's Last Case, 1952
Folly to Be Wise, 1952
The Captain's Paradise, 1953
King's Rhapsody, 1955
Geordie, 1955
The Man Who Never Was, 1956
Private's Progress, 1956
The Silken Affair, 1956
Dry Rot, 1956
Three Men in a Boat, 1956
Brothers in Law, 1957
The Admirable Crichton, 1957
Barnacle Bill, 1957
Campbell's Kingdom, 1957
Happy is the Bride, 1958
Gideon's Day, 1958
Dracula, 1958
Bachelor of Hearts, 1958
The Naked Truth, 1958
The Captain's Table, 1959
Carleton Browne of the FO,
   1959
Hound of the Baskervilles, 1959
I'm All Right, Jack, 1959
Kidnapped, 1959
And the Same to You, 1960
The Day They Robbed the
   Bank of England, 1960
Brides of Dracula, 1960

Peeping Tom, 1960
The Hellfire Club, 1961
Fury at Smuggler's Bay, 1961
Double Bunk, 1961
Postman's Knock, 1962
Phantom of the Opera, 1962
Go to Blazes, 1962
Vengeance, 1962
Heavens Above, 1963
Call Me Bwana, 1963
First Men in the Moon, 1964
A Jolly Bad Fellow, 1964
Circus World, 1964
Murder Ahoy, 1964
The Magnificent Showman, 1964
You Must Be Joking, 1965

H. F. MALTBY (1880-1963)
Comedy character actor of
stage (from 1899) and screen;
also playwright and screen
writer.

The Rotters, 1921
Facing the Music, 1933
Home Sweet Home, 1933
A Political Party, 1933
I Spy, 1933
Those Were the Days, 1934
Luck of a Sailor, 1934
Freedom of the Seas, 1934
Over the Garden Wall, 1934
Lost in the Legion, 1934
Falling in Love, 1934
Josser On the Farm, 1934
Girls Will Be Boys, 1934
A Little Bit of Fluff, 1935
The Right Age to Marry, 1935
It Happened in Paris, 1935
Vanity, 1935
The Morals of Marcus, 1935
Emil and the Detectives, 1935
King of the Castle, 1935
Queen of Hearts, 1936
A Touch of the Moon, 1936
Trouble Ahead, 1936
Jack of All Trades, 1936
Sweeney Todd, 1936
Fame, 1936
The Howard Case, 1936
The Crimes of Stephen Hawke,
   1936

Not So Dusty, 1936
To Catch a Thief, 1936
Where There's a Will, 1936
Calling the Tune, 1936
Everything is Thunder, 1936
Nothing Like Publicity, 1936
Head Office, 1936
Busman's Holiday, 1936
The Heirloom Mystery, 1936
Everything in Life, 1936
Reasonable Doubt, 1936
Secret Agent, 1936
Wake Up Famous, 1937
Song of the Road, 1937
Pearls Bring Tears, 1937
Never Too Late to Mend, 1937
Farewell Cinderella, 1937
Okay For Sound, 1937
Take My Tip, 1937
Strange Adventures of Mr.
   Smith, 1937
Boys Will Be Girls, 1937
Why Pick On Me, 1937
Mr. Smith Carries On, 1937
Sing as You Swing, 1937
Ticket of Leave Man, 1937
Live Wire, 1937
Paradise For Two, 1937
The Sky's the Limit, 1937
Young and Innocent, 1937
Captain's Orders, 1937
What a Man, 1937
To the Victor, 1938
Owd Bob, 1938
Paid in Error, 1938
Darts Are Trumps, 1938
His Lordship Regrets, 1938
Weddings Are Wonderful, 1938
You're the Doctor, 1938
His Lordship Goes to Press,
   1938
Pygmalion, 1938
Everything Happens to Me, 1938
A Yank at Oxford, 1938
The Good Old Days, 1939
Old Mother Riley Joins Up,
   1939
Blind Folly, 1939
The Gang's All Here, 1939
Crimes at the Dark House,
   1940
Garrison Follies, 1940
Under Your Hat, 1940

Facing the Music, 1941
Gert and Daisy's Weekend,
   1941
Bob's Your Uncle, 1941
Front Line Kids, 1942
Gert and Daisy Clean Up, 1942
Old Mother Riley Detective,
   1943
Somewhere in Civvies, 1943
A Canterbury Tale, 1943
Medal For the General, 1944
Home Sweet Home, 1945
Caesar and Cleopatra, 1945
The Trojan Brothers, 1946

EILY MALYON (1879-1961)
Character actress of stage and
films, long in Hollywood; char-
acteristically played dry, acidulous roles.

His Greatest Gamble, 1934
The Little Minister, 1934
Romance in Manhattan, 1935
Clive of India, 1935
Les Miserables, 1935
The Florentine Dagger, 1935
The Flame Within, 1935
The Melody Lingers On, 1935
A Tale of Two Cities, 1935
One Rainy Afternoon, 1936
Dracula's Daughter, 1936
The White Angel, 1936
Anthony Adverse, 1936
A Woman Rebels, 1936
Three Men On a Horse, 1936
Night Must Fall, 1937
Kidnapped, 1938
Rebecca of Sunnybrook Farm,
   1938
The Young in Heart, 1938
On Borrowed Time, 1938
The Little Princess, 1939
Hound of the Baskervilles,
   1939
Confessions of a Nazi Spy, 1939
We Are Not Alone, 1939
Barricade, 1939
Young Tom Edison, 1940
Untamed, 1940
Foreign Correspondent, 1940
Man Hunt, 1941

Man in the Trunk, 1942
I Married a Witch, 1942
Going My Way, 1944
The Seventh Cross, 1944
Paris Underground, 1945
She Wolf of London, 1946
The Secret Heart, 1946

MILES MANDER (1888-1946)
Character actor of stage and
screen, sometimes seen in
villainous roles; also in Hollywood; former farmer, aviator,
theatre manager, film exhibitor.
Also director and writer.

Once Upon a Time, 1918
Testimony, 1920
The Children of Gideon, 1920
The Old Arm Chair, 1920
A Rank Outsider, 1920
The Road to London, 1921
Place of Honour, 1921
A Temporary Lady, 1921
Half a Truth, 1922
Open Country, 1922
Lovers in Araby, 1924
The Prude's Fall, 1924
The Painted Lady, 1925
The Lady in Furs, 1925
Riding For a King, 1926
The Pleasure Garden, 1926
London Love, 1926
Sentence of Death, 1927
Women of Paris, 1928
Tiptoes, 1928
The Fake, 1928
The Physician, 1928
The First Born, 1928
Balaclava, 1928
The Crooked Billet, 1929
Loose Ends, 1930
Murder, 1930
Frail Women, 1932
The Missing Rembrandt, 1932
Lily Christine, 1932
That Night in London, 1932
The Lodger, 1932
Matinee Idol, 1933
Loyalties, 1933
Don Quixote, 1933
Bitter Sweet, 1933

The Private Life of Henry
  VIII, 1933
Four Masked Men, 1934
The Battle, 1934
The Case For the Crown,
  1934
Death Drives Through, 1935
Here's a Romance, 1935
The Flying Doctor, 1936
The Three Musketeers, 1936
Lloyds of London, 1936
Slave Ship, 1937
Wake Up and Live, 1937
Kidnapped, 1938
Suez, 1938
The Mad Miss Manton, 1938
Wuthering Heights, 1939
Tower of London, 1939
The Three Musketeers, 1939
The Little Princess, 1939
Man in the Iron Mask, 1939
Stanley and Livingstone, 1939
Captain Caution, 1940
South of Suez, 1940
The Primrose Path, 1940
The Road to Singapore, 1940
House of the Seven Gables,
  1940
Lady Hamilton, 1941
Dr. Kildare's Wedding Day,
  1941
To Be Or Not to Be, 1942
This Above All, 1942
Fingers at the Window, 1942
Tarzan's New York Adventure,
  1942
The War Against Mrs. Hadley,
  1942
Mrs. Miniver (voice), 1942
Madame Curie, 1943
Five Graves to Cairo, 1943
Phantom of the Opera, 1943
Gaudalcanal Diary, 1943
Return of the Vampire, 1943
Assignment in Brittainy, 1943
Four Jills in a Jeep, 1944
Enter Arsene Lupin, 1944
The White Cliffs of Dover,
  1944
Farewell My Lovely, 1944
The Scarlet Claw, 1944
The Pearl of Death, 1944
The Brighton Strangler, 1945

The Picture of Dorian Gray,
1945
Confidential Agent, 1945
The Imperfect Lady, 1946
Bandit of Sherwood Forest,
1946
The Walls Came Tumbling
Down, 1946

LUCIE MANNHEIM (1895-
1976)
German character actress,
long in Britain; wife of Marius
Goring.

Danton, 1931
Madam Wants No Children, 1933
The Thirty-Nine Steps, 1935
East Meets West, 1936
The High Command, 1937
The Yellow Canary, 1943
Hotel Reserve, 1944
Tawny Pipit, 1944
So Little Time, 1952
Paris Express, 1953
Beyond the Curtain, 1960
Confess Dr. Corda, 1960
Bunny Lake is Missing, 1965

HUGH MANNING (1920-)
Character actor with distinctive
speaking voice; mainly seen on
stage.

The Dam Busters, 1955
The Secret Place, 1956
Our Man in Havana, 1959
A Midsummer Night's Dream,
1961
The Honey Pot, 1967
The Mackintosh Man, 1973
The Elephant Man, 1980

ANDRE MARANNE (-)
Character actor of the 60s and
70s, often seen as Frenchman
or other continental types.

The Middle Course, 1961
The Greengage Summer, 1961

Two Wives at One Wedding,
1961
HMS Defiant, 1962
The Silent Invasion, 1962
Night Train to Paris, 1964
A Shot in the Dark, 1964
Return From the Ashes, 1965
Duffy, 1968
The Battle of Britain, 1969
Bequest to the Nation, 1973
Gold, 1974
Paul and Michelle, 1974
Return of the Pink Panther,
1974
The Pink Panther Strikes
Again, 1976
Revenge of the Pink Panther,
1978
The London Affair, 1979

ARTHUR MARGETSON (1897-
1951)
Supporting player of stage and
screen, in Hollywood from
1940; former stockbroker's
clerk.

Wolves, 1930
Other People's Sins, 1931
Many Waters, 1931
Flat No. 9, 1932
His Grave Gives Notice, 1933
Little Friend, 1934
The Great Defender, 1934
Royal Cavalcade, 1935
The Divine Spark, 1935
Music Hath Charms, 1935
The Mystery of the Mary
Celeste, 1935
I Give My Heart, 1935
Broken Blossoms, 1936
Wanted Men, 1936
Juggernaut, 1936
Pagliacci, 1936
Head Office, 1936
Action For Slander, 1937
Smash and Grab, 1937
The Loves of Madame DuBarry,
1938
The Return of Carol Deane,
1938
The Nursemaid Who Disap-

peared, 1939
Me and My Pal, 1939
Return to Yesterday, 1940
Larceny Street, 1941
Random Harvest, 1942
Commandos Strike at Dawn,
1943
Sherlock Holmes Faces Death,
1943

HOWARD MARION-CRAWFORD
(1914-1969)
Robust, jovial, good-natured
character star of stage and
screen, also excellent on tv
as Dr. Watson in "The Adventures of Sherlock Holmes"
(1955) with Ronald Howard.

Forever England, 1935
Thirteen Men and a Gun, 1938
Freedom Radio, 1941
The Rake's Progress, 1945
The Phantom Shot, 1947
The Hasty Heart, 1949
Mr. Drake's Duck, 1950
The Man in the White Suit,
1951
His Excellency, 1952
Where's Charley?, 1952
Top of the Form, 1953
Don't Blame the Stork, 1954
Rainbow Jacket, 1954
Five Days, 1954
West of Zanzibar, 1954
Reach For the Sky, 1956
The Silken Affair, 1956
Man in the Sky, 1957
The Birthday Present, 1957
The Tyburn Case, 1957
Nowhere to Go, 1958
The Silent Enemy, 1958
Virgin Island, 1958
Gideon's Day, 1958
Next to No Time, 1958
Life in Danger, 1959
Model For Murder, 1959
A Foxhole in Cairo, 1960
Othello, 1960
Carry On Regardless, 1961
Lawrence of Arabia, 1962
Tamahine, 1963

Man in the Middle, 1964
The Face of Fu Manchu, 1965
Secrets of a Windmill Girl,
1966
The Brides of Fu Manchu,
1966
Vengeance of Fu Manchu, 1968
Charge of the Light Brigade,
1968
Kiss and Kill, 1970
The Castle of Fu Manchu, 1972

ALFRED MARKS (1921-)
Bald character star, also seen
on stage and tv; often in comedy parts.

Penny Points to Paradise, 1951
Johnny You're Wanted, 1956
Desert Mice, 1959
There Was a Crooked Man,
1960
The Frightened City, 1961
She'll Have to Go, 1962
A Weekend With Lulu, 1962
Scramble, 1970
Scream and Scream Again,
1970
Our Miss Fred, 1972
Valentino, 1977

ARNOLD MARLE (-)
Character actor of the 40s and
50s, almost always seen as
kindly father or elderly gentleman.

One of Our Aircraft is Missing,
1942
Mr. Emmanuel, 1944
Men of Two Worlds, 1946
White Cradle Inn, 1947
Portrait From Life, 1948
The Glass Mountain, 1949
The Floating Dutchman, 1953
The Green Buddha, 1954
Little Red Monkey, 1955
Break in the Circle, 1955
Cross Channel, 1955
The Glass Cage, 1955
The Abominable Snowman, 1957

The Man Who Could Cheat
   Death, 1959
The Snake Woman, 1961
The Password is Courage,
   1962

ANTHONY MARLOWE (1913-)
Stage actor seen very rarely in
films.

The Great Commandment, 1942
Saadia, 1954
Room in the House, 1955

PATRICIA MARMONT (-)
Supporting actress in occasional
films; daughter of Percy Marmont.

Loyal Heart, 1946
Front Page Story, 1954
The Crowded Day, 1954
No Time For Tears, 1957
The Tyburn Case, 1957
Suddenly Last Summer, 1959
Mary Had a Little, 1961

PERCY MARMONT (1883-1977)
Romantic Lead of early Holly-
wood silent films, then back to
England where he played char-
acter parts from the late 20s.
Also on stage (from 1900).
Daughter: Patricia Marmont.

The Lie, 1918
Rose of the World, 1918
Turn of the Wheel, 1918
Three Men and a Girl, 1919
The Climbers, 1919
The Vengeance of Durand, 1919
The Branded Woman, 1920
Dead Men Tell No Tales, 1920
What's Your Reputation Worth?,
   1921
Love's Penalty, 1921
Wife Against Wife, 1921
The First Woman, 1922
Married People, 1922
If Winter Comes, 1923

The Midnight Alarm, 1923
Broadway Broke, 1923
The Light That Failed, 1923
The Man Life Passed By, 1923
The Shooting of Dan McGrew,
   1924
The Enemy Sex, 1924
The Marriage Cheat, 1924
The Legend of Hollywood, 1924
The Clean Heart, 1924
K The Unknown, 1924
Broken Laws, 1924
Idle Tongues, 1924
Daddy's Gone a Hunting, 1925
Just a Woman, 1925
Street of Forgotten Men, 1925
Fine Clothes, 1925
Lord Jim, 1925
Infatuation, 1925
The Miracle of Life, 1926
Mantrap, 1926
Fascinating Youth, 1926
Aloma of the South Seas, 1926
The Stronger Will, 1927
San Francisco Nights, 1928
Sir Or Madam, 1928
The Warning, 1928
Yellow Stockings, 1928
The Lady of the Lake, 1928
The Silver King, 1929
The Squeaker, 1930
Cross Roads, 1930
Rich and Strange, 1931
The Loves of Ariane, 1931
The Written Law, 1931
The Silver Greyhound, 1932
Blind Spot, 1932
Say it With Music, 1932
Her Imaginary Lover, 1933
White Lilac, 1935
Vanity, 1935
David Livingstone, 1936
The Captain's Table, 1936
Secret Agent, 1936
Conquest of the Air, 1936
Young and Innocent, 1937
Action For Slander, 1937
Pearls of the Crown, 1938
Bringing it Home, 1940
Penn of Pennsylvania, 1941
Those Kids From Town, 1942
I'll Walk Beside You, 1943
Loyal Heart, 1946

Swiss Honeymoon, 1947
No Orchids For Miss Blandish,
   1948
Dark Secret, 1949
The Gambler and the Lady,
   1952
Four Sided Triangle, 1953
Knave of Hearts, 1954
Footsteps in the Fog, 1955
Lisbon, 1956
Hostile Witness, 1968

MOORE MARRIOTT (1885-1949)
Character star of stage (from
1892) and films who specialized
in portraying ancient country
folk; best remembered as Jere-
miah Harbottle in the Will Hay
comedies.

Dick Turpin, 1908
His Sister's Honour, 1914
By the Shortest of Hairs, 1915
The Grip of Iron, 1920
Mary Latimer Nun, 1920
The Winding Road, 1920
Four Men in a Van, 1921
Head of the Family, 1922
The Monkey's Paw, 1923
The Odd Freak, 1923
Lawyer Quince, 1924
The Long Hole, 1924
Dixon's Return, 1924
The Conspirators, 1924
The Affair at the Novelty
   Theatre, 1924
The Mating of Marcus, 1924
The Clicking of Cuthbert, 1924
Ordeal By Golf, 1924
Not For Sale, 1924
Madonna of the Cells, 1925
Afraid of Love, 1925
There's Many a Slip, 1925
King of the Castle, 1925
The Qualified Adventurer, 1925
The Cold Cure, 1925
The Only Man, 1925
Every Mother's Son, 1926
London Love, 1926
The Happy Rascals, 1926
Second to None, 1926
Cash On Delivery, 1926

The Greater War, 1926
Passion Island, 1927
The Silver Lining, 1927
Carry On, 1927
Huntingtower, 1927
Victory, 1928
The Burglar and the Girl, 1928
Toni, 1928
The King's Breakfast, 1928
Sweeney Todd, 1928
Widecombe Fair, 1928
Mr. Smith Wakes Up, 1929
The Flying Scotsman, 1929
The Lady From the Sea, 1929
Kissing Cup's Race, 1930
Aroma of the South Seas, 1931
The Lyon's Mail, 1931
Up For the Cup, 1931
Dance Pretty Lady, 1932
The Crooked Lady, 1932
The Water Gypsies, 1932
Nine Till Six, 1932
Mr. Bill the Conqueror, 1932
Heroes of the Mine, 1932
The Wonderful Story, 1932
Little Waitress, 1932
Moorland Tragedy, 1933
Crime at Blossom's, 1933
Money For Speed, 1933
Hawleys of High Street, 1933
Dora, 1933
Love's Old Sweet Song, 1933
Lucky Blaze, 1933
The House of Trent, 1933
A Political Party, 1934
Faces, 1934
The Black Skull, 1934
Girls Please, 1934
Nell Gwyn, 1934
The Feathered Serpent, 1934
Dandy Dick, 1935
Drake of England, 1935
The Halfday Excursion, 1935
The Man Without a Face, 1935
His Apologies, 1935
Turn of the Tide, 1935
Gay Old Dog, 1935
What the Puppy Said, 1936
When Knights Were Bold, 1936
Strange Cargo, 1936
Wednesday's Luck, 1936
Accused, 1936
Luck of the Turf, 1936

Talk of the Devil, 1936
Windbag the Sailor, 1936
As You Like It, 1936
Amazing Quest of Ernest Bliss,
    1936
Feather Your Nest, 1937
Fifty Shilling Boxer, 1937
The Fatal Hour, 1937
Night Ride, 1937
Oh Mr. Porter, 1937
Intimate Relations, 1937
Dreaming Lips, 1937
To the Victor, 1938
Owd Bob, 1938
Convict 99, 1938
Old Bones of the River, 1938
Ask a Policeman, 1939
A Girl Must Live, 1939
Where's That Fire?, 1939
Cheer Boys Cheer, 1939
The Frozen Limits, 1939
Band Wagon, 1940
Charley's Big-Hearted Aunt,
    1940
Gasbags, 1940
I Thank You, 1941
Back Room Boy, 1942
Hi Gang, 1942
Millions Like Us, 1943
Time Flies, 1944
It Happened One Sunday, 1944
Don't Take it to Heart, 1944
A Place of One's Own, 1944
The Agitator, 1945
I'll Be Your Sweetheart, 1945
Green For Danger, 1946
The Root of All Evil, 1947
Green Fingers, 1947
The Hills of Donegal, 1947
The History of Mr. Polly, 1949
Hi Jinks in Society, 1949

BETTY MARSDEN (1919-)
Character actress and supporting player, also quite frequently
on stage. Films sporadic.

Sky Raiders, 1938
Ships With Wings, 1941
Night Comes Too Soon, 1948
The Young Lovers, 1954
Ramsbottom Rides Again, 1956

Let's Get Married, 1960
The Big Day, 1960
Carry On Regardless, 1961
The Boys, 1962
The Leather Boys, 1963
The Wild Affair, 1963
Carry On Camping, 1969
The Best House in London,
    1969
Eyewitness, 1970

CAROL MARSH (1929-)
Leading lady of the forties and
fifties, also on stage (from
1946).

Brighton Rock, 1947
Alice in Wonderland, 1948
Marry Me, 1949
Helter Skelter, 1949
The Romantic Age, 1949
Scrooge, 1951
Salute the Toff, 1952
Private Information, 1952
Mysterious Bullet, 1955
Dracula, 1958
Man Accused, 1959

GARRY MARSH (1902-)
Hearty, balding character actor
of stage (since 1917) and screen,
often cast in robust or explosive roles, sometimes comical.
On tv in "The Forsyte Saga. "

Night Birds, 1930
PC Josser, 1931
The Eternal Flame, 1931
Third Time Lucky, 1931
Uneasy Virtue, 1931
Dreyfus, 1931
Keepers of Youth, 1931
The Man They Could Not Ar-
    rest, 1931
Stranglehold, 1931
Stamboul, 1931
Star Reporter, 1931
COD, 1932
Postal Orders, 1932
Number Seventeen, 1932
After Office Hours, 1932

Fires of Fate, 1932
Maid of the Mountains, 1932
Don't Be a Dummy, 1932
Taxi to Paradise, 1933
The Lost Chord, 1933
Falling For You, 1933
The Love Nest, 1933
That's a Good Girl, 1933
Ask Beccles, 1933
Two Wives For Henry, 1933
The Silver Spoon, 1934
It's a Cop, 1934
Rolling in Money, 1934
Warn London, 1934
Lord Edgware Dies, 1934
Bella Donna, 1934
Are You a Mason?, 1934
Gay Love, 1934
Money Mad, 1934
The Green Pack, 1934
Josser On the Farm, 1934
Widow's Might, 1935
Death On the Set, 1935
Three Witnesses, 1935
Inside the Room, 1935
Mr. What's His Name, 1935
Full Circle, 1935
Night Mail, 1935
Department Store, 1935
Charing Cross Road, 1935
Scrooge, 1935
A Wife Or Two, 1936
When Knights Were Bold, 1936
Debt of Honour, 1936
Amazing Quest of Ernest Bliss,
   1936
The Man in the Mirror, 1936
All In, 1936
It's a Grand Old World, 1937
The Vicar of Bray, 1937
The Angelus, 1937
Romance in Flanders, 1937
Leave it to Me, 1937
Intimate Relations, 1937
Melody and Romance, 1937
Meet Mr. Penny, 1938
Dark Stairway, 1938
Bank Holiday, 1938
I See Ice, 1938
The Claydon Treasure Mystery,
   1938
Convict 99, 1938
Break the News, 1938

This Man is News, 1938
It's in the Air, 1938
Let's Be Famous, 1939
Trouble Brewing, 1939
Four Just Men, 1939
This Man in Paris, 1939
Hoots Mon, 1939
Old Mother Riley Joins Up,
   1939
Let George Do It, 1939
Return to Yesterday, 1940
Dead of Night, 1945
I'll Be Your Sweetheart, 1945
The Rake's Progress, 1945
Pink String & Sealing Wax,
   1945
Girl in a Million, 1946
I See a Dark Stranger, 1946
Dancing With Crime, 1947
The Shop at Sly Corner, 1947
While the Sun Shines, 1947
Frieda, 1947
Double Pursuit, 1948
Just William's Luck, 1948
Good Time Girl, 1948
My Brother's Keeper, 1948
Things Happen at Night, 1948
William Comes to Town, 1948
Badger's Green, 1949
Forbidden, 1949
Paper Orchid, 1949
Murder at the Windmill, 1949
Miss Pilgrim's Progress, 1950
Someone at the Door, 1950
Something in the City, 1950
Mr. Drake's Duck, 1950
The Big Frame, 1951
Worm's Eye View, 1951
Old Mother Riley's Jungle
   Treasure, 1951
Madame Louise, 1951
The Magic Box, 1951
The Voice of Merrill, 1952
The Lost Hours, 1952
Those People Next Door, 1953
Double Exposure, 1954
Aunt Clara, 1954
Man of the Moment, 1955
Who Done it, 1956
Johnny You're Wanted, 1956
The Trouble With Eve, 1960
Ring of Spies, 1963
Where the Bullets Fly, 1966

Camelot, 1967
Ouch!, 1968

ALAN MARSHALL (1909-1961)
Australian light romantic lead-
ing man of the 30s and 40s in
Hollywood, also on stage.

The Garden of Allah, 1936
After the Thin Man, 1936
Night Must Fall, 1937
Parnell, 1937
Conquest, 1937
Robber Symphony, 1937
The Road to Reno, 1938
Dramatic School, 1938
Invisible Enemy, 1938
I Met My Love Again, 1938
The Hunchback of Notre Dame,
   1939
The Adventures of Sherlock
   Holmes, 1939
Exile Express, 1939
Four Girls in White, 1939
Tom, Dick, and Harry, 1940
Married and in Love, 1940
Irene, 1940
The Howards of Virginia, 1940
He Stayed For Breakfast, 1940
Lydia, 1941
Bride By Mistake, 1944
The White Cliffs of Dover, 1944
The Barkleys of Broadway, 1948
The Opposite Sex, 1956
The House On Haunted Hill,
   1959
Day of the Outlaw, 1959

HERBERT MARSHALL (1890-
1966)
Suave leading actor of stage
(since 1911) and screen, in
Hollywood from early 30s; lost
leg during WWI. Formerly
married to Edna Best.

Mumsie, 1927
Dawn, 1928
The Letter, 1929
Murder, 1930
Michael and Mary, 1931

The Calendar, 1931
Secrets of a Secretary, 1931
The Faithful Heart, 1932
Blonde Venus, 1932
Trouble in Paradise, 1932
Evenings For Sale, 1932
I Was a Spy, 1933
Clear All Wires, 1933
The Solitaire Man, 1933
Four Frightened People, 1934
Riptide, 1934
Outcast Lady, 1934
Painted Veil, 1934
The Good Fairy, 1935
The Flame Within, 1935
Accent On Youth, 1935
The Dark Angel, 1935
If You Could Only Cook, 1935
The Lady Consents, 1936
Till We Meet Again, 1936
Forgotten Faces, 1936
Girls' Dormitory, 1936
A Woman Rebels, 1936
Make Way For a Lady, 1936
Angel, 1937
Breakfast For Two, 1937
Mad About Music, 1938
Always Goodbye, 1938
Woman Against Woman, 1938
Zaza, 1939
A Bill of Divorcement, 1940
Foreign Correspondent, 1940
The Letter, 1940
Adventure in Washington, 1941
The Little Foxes, 1941
When Ladies Meet, 1941
Kathleen, 1941
The Moon and Sixpence, 1942
Forever and a Day, 1943
Flight For Freedom, 1943
Young Ideas, 1943
Andy Hardy's Blonde Trouble,
   1944
The Unseen, 1945
The Enchanted Cottage, 1945
Crack Up, 1946
The Razor's Edge, 1946
Duel in the Sun, 1947
Ivy, 1947
High Wall, 1948
The Secret Garden, 1949
Underworld Story, 1950
Anne of the Indies, 1951

Captain Blackjack, 1952
Angel Face, 1953
Riders to the Stars, 1954
The Black Shield of Falworth,
    1954
Gog, 1954
The Virgin Queen, 1955
The Weapon, 1957
Stage Struck, 1958
The Fly, 1958
Wicked As They Come, 1958
College Confidential, 1959
Midnight Lace, 1960
Fever in the Blood, 1961
Five Weeks in a Balloon, 1962
The List of Adrian Messenger,
    1963
The Caretakers, 1964
The Third Day, 1965

ZENA MARSHALL (1927-)
Attractive dark-haired leading
lady, also on stage.

Caesar and Cleopatra, 1945
End of the River, 1947
Snowbound, 1948
Sleeping Car to Trieste, 1948
Miranda, 1948
Good Time Girl, 1948
The Bad Lord Byron, 1949
Marry Me, 1949
The Lost People, 1949
Meet Simon Cherry, 1949
Morning Departure, 1950
So Long at the Fair, 1950
Soho Conspiracy, 1950
Dark Interval, 1950
Hell is Sold Out, 1951
Blind Man's Bluff, 1952
Love's a Luxury, 1952
Deadly Nightshade, 1953
The Caretaker's Daughter, 1953
The Scarlet Web, 1954
The Embezzler, 1954
The Bermuda Affair, 1956
My Wife's Family, 1956
Let's Be Happy, 1957
A Story of David, 1960
Backfire, 1962
Crosstrap, 1962
Dr. No, 1962

Guilty Party, 1962
The Switch, 1963
The Verdict, 1964
Those Magnificent Men in Their
    Flying Machines, 1965
The Terrornauts, 1967

EDIE MARTIN (1880-1964)
Character actress of stage
(since 1886) and films, typically
seen in cameos as frail, dainty
old ladies.

Servants All, 1936
Farewell Again, 1937
Bad Boy, 1938
Old Mother Riley in Business,
    1940
The Demi-Paradise, 1943
A Place of One's Own, 1944
They Were Sisters, 1945
Here Comes the Sun, 1945
Great Expectations, 1946
The History of Mr. Polly, 1949
The Lavender Hill Mob, 1951
The Man in the White Suit, 1951
Time Gentlemen Please, 1952
The Titfield Thunderbolt, 1953
Genevieve, 1953
End of the Road, 1954
Lease of Life, 1954
The Ladykillers, 1955
Too Many Crooks, 1959

MILLICENT MARTIN (1934-)
Vibrant singer and actress of
stage, films, and television;
popular in the sixties.

Libel, 1959
The Girl On the Boat, 1961
The Horsemasters, 1961
Invasion Quartet, 1961
Nothing But the Best, 1963
Those Magnificent Men in Their
    Flying Machines, 1965
Stop the World I Want to Get
    Off, 1966
Alfie, 1966

MICHAEL MARTIN-HARVEY
(-)
Stage and screen character actor, sometimes seen in eccentric parts; son of stage star Sir John Martin-Harvey.

The Only Way, 1925
Robber Symphony, 1936
Drums, 1938
Mutiny of the Elsinore, 1939
Berlin Express, 1948
The Monkey's Paw, 1948
Torment, 1949
The Case of Charles Peace, 1949
The Third Visitor, 1951
Judgement Deferred, 1952
The Long Memory, 1953

ORLANDO MARTINS (1899-)
West African actor who has been appearing in British films since the mid-thirties.

Sanders of the River, 1935
Jericho, 1937
The Man From Morocco, 1945
Men of Two Worlds, 1946
End of the River, 1947
Good Time Girl, 1948
The Hasty Heart, 1949
American Guerilla in the Phillippines, 1950
Where No Vultures Fly, 1951
Cry the Beloved Country, 1952
The Heart of the Matter, 1953
West of Zanzibar, 1954
Simba, 1955
Safari, 1956
Tarzan and the Lost Safari, 1957
Seven Waves Away, 1957
The Naked Earth, 1958
Killers of Kilimanjaro, 1959
Sapphire, 1959
The Nun's Story, 1959
Sammy Going South, 1963
Call Me Bwana, 1963
Mister Moses, 1965
Frankie and Johnnie, 1966

VIRGINIA MASKELL (1936-1968)
Pretty, intelligent leading lady of the 50s and 60s.

Happy is the Bride, 1957
Virgin Island, 1958
The Man Upstairs, 1959
Jet Storm, 1959
Suspect, 1960
Doctor in Love, 1960
Only Two Can Play, 1962
The Wild and the Willing, 1962
Interlude, 1968

ELLIOTT MASON (1897-1949)
Scotch character actress of the thirties and forties, also on stage.

Born That Way, 1936
Gaolbreak, 1936
The Ghost Goes West, 1936
Black Limelight, 1938
Owd Bob, 1938
Marigold, 1938
The Ware Case, 1938
Blind Folly, 1939
21 Days, 1939
Return to Yesterday, 1940
The Ghost of St. Michael's, 1941
Turned Out Nice Again, 1941
The Gentle Sex, 1943
On Approval, 1944
The Agitator, 1945
Perfect Strangers, 1945
The Captive Heart, 1946

JAMES MASON (1909-)
Versatile leading actor of stage (from 1931) and films, adept at any type of role; now an international star. Formerly married to Pamela Kellino. No relation to the American small-part player (1890-1959) of the same name.

Late Extra, 1935
Twice Branded, 1936

Troubled Waters, 1936
Prison Breaker, 1936
Blind Man's Bluff, 1936
The Secret of Stamboul, 1936
The Mill On the Floss, 1937
Fire Over England, 1937
The High Command, 1937
Catch as Catch Can, 1937
Return of the Scarlet Pimpernel,
  1937
I Met a Murderer, 1939
This Man is Dangerous, 1941
Hatter's Castle, 1941
The Night Has Eyes, 1942
Alibi, 1942
Secret Mission, 1942
Thunder Rock, 1942
The Bells Go Down, 1943
The Man in Grey, 1943
They Met in the Dark, 1943
Candlelight in Algeria, 1943
Fanny By Gaslight, 1944
Hotel Reserve, 1944
A Place of One's Own, 1944
They Were Sisters, 1945
The Seventh Veil, 1945
The Wicked Lady, 1945
Odd Man Out, 1947
The Upturned Glass, 1947
Caught, 1949
Madame Bovary, 1949
The Reckless Moment, 1949
East Side, West Side, 1949
One Way Street, 1950
Pandora & the Flying Dutchman,
  1951
Rommel-Desert Fox, 1951
Five Fingers, 1952
Lady Possessed, 1952
The Prisoner of Zenda, 1952
Face to Face, 1952
The Tell-Tale Heart, 1953
Charade, 1953
The Man Between, 1953
The Story of Three Loves, 1953
The Desert Rats, 1953
Julius Caesar, 1953
Botany Bay, 1953
The Child, 1954
Prince Valiant, 1954
A Star is Born, 1954
20,000 Leagues Under the Sea,
  1954

Forever Darling, 1956
Bigger Than Life, 1956
Island in the Sun, 1957
Cry Terror, 1958
The Decks Ran Red, 1959
North By Northwest, 1959
Journey to the Center of the
  Earth, 1959
A Touch of Larceny, 1959
The Trials of Oscar Wilde,
  1960
The Marriage Go Round, 1961
Escape From Zahrain, 1961
Lolita, 1962
Rebecca, 1962
Hero's Island, 1962
Tiara Tahiti, 1963
John Brown's Raid, 1963
The Hiding Place, 1963
Torpedo Bay, 1964
Fall of the Roman Empire,
  1964
The Pumpkin Eater, 1964
Lord Jim, 1965
Genghis Khan, 1965
The Uninhibited, 1965
Player Pianos, 1965
The Blue Max, 1966
Georgy Girl, 1966
The Deadly Affair, 1966
Stranger in the House, 1967
The London Nobody Knows,
  1967
Duffy, 1968
Mayerling, 1968
Subterfuge, 1968
Age of Consent, 1969
The Sea Gull, 1969
Spring and Port Wine, 1970
Cold Sweat, 1971
Bad Man's River, 1972
Kill Kill Kill, 1972
Child's Play, 1973
The Last of Sheila, 1973
The Mackintosh Man, 1973
Frankenstein: The True Story,
  1973
11 Harrowhouse, 1974
Trikimia, 1974
What Are Friends For?, 1974
Nostro Nero in Casa Nichols,
  1974
The Marseille Contract, 1974

The Deal, 1975
The Left Hand of the Law, 1975
Mandingo, 1975
Great Expectations, 1975
Inside Out, 1975
The Schoolmistress and the
Devil, 1975
Autobiography of a Princess,
1975
Voyage of the Damned, 1976
La Polezei Interveiene Ordine
di Uccidere, 1976
People of the Wind (voice),
1976
Homage to Chagall (voice),
1976
Cross of Iron, 1977
Hot Stuff, 1977
Jesus of Nazareth, 1977
Fear in the City, 1978
Heaven Can Wait, 1978
The Boys From Brazil, 1978
Salem's Lot, 1979
The Passage, 1979
Murder By Decree, 1979
Bloodline, 1979
The Water Babies, 1979
Ffolkes, 1980
Masada, 1980

ANNA MASSEY (1937-)
Supporting actress of stage
and screen; daughter of Raymond Massey and Adrienne
Allen; sister of Daniel Massey.

Gideon's Day, 1958
Peeping Tom, 1960
Bunny Lake is Missing, 1965
De Sade, 1967
David Copperfield, 1969
The Looking Glass War, 1970
Frenzy, 1972
A Doll's House, 1973
Vault of Horror, 1973
The Corn is Green, 1979
Rebecca, 1980

DANIEL MASSEY (1933-)
Tall actor of stage and screen;
son of Raymond Massey and

Adrienne Allen; sister: Anna
Massey. Married to Adrienne
Corri.

In Which We Serve, 1942
Girls at Sea, 1958
Upstairs and Downstairs, 1959
Operation Bullshine, 1959
The Entertainer, 1960
The Queen's Guards, 1960
Go To Blazes, 1962
Moll Flanders, 1965
The Jokers, 1966
Star!, 1968
Fragment of Fear, 1970
Mary Queen of Scots, 1971
Vault of Horror, 1973
The Incredible Sarah, 1976
Warlords of Atlantis, 1978
The Cat and the Canary, 1978
Illusions, 1979

RAYMOND MASSEY (1896-)
Canadian actor of stage (1922)
and films, in England in the
20s and 30s, also later in
Hollywood. Adept at kindly
as well as villainous roles.
Married: Adrienne Allen;
children: Daniel Massey, Anna
Massey. Also seen on tv as
Dr. Gillespie in the "Dr. Kildare" series (1961-65).

The Speckled Band, 1931
The Face at the Window, 1932
The Old Dark House, 1932
The Scarlet Pimpernel, 1935
Things to Come, 1936
Fire Over England, 1937
Dreaming Lips, 1937
Under the Red Robe, 1937
The Prisoner of Zenda, 1937
The Hurricane, 1937
The Drum, 1938
Black Limelight, 1938
Abe Lincoln in Illinois, 1939
Santa Fe Trail, 1940
49th Parallel, 1941
Reap the Wild Wind, 1942
Dangerously They Live, 1942
Desperate Journey, 1942

Action in the North Atlantic,
1943
Arsenic and Old Lace, 1944
The Woman in the Window,
1944
Hotel Berlin, 1945
God is My Co-Pilot, 1945
A Matter of Life and Death,
1946
Possessed, 1947
Mourning Becomes Electra,
1947
The Fountainhead, 1949
Roseanna McCoy, 1949
Chain Lightning, 1950
Barricade, 1950
Dallas, 1950
Sugarfoot, 1951
David and Bathsheba, 1951
Come Fill the Cup, 1951
Carson City, 1952
The Desert Song, 1953
Prince of Players, 1954
Battle Cry, 1955
East of Eden, 1955
Seven Angry Men, 1955
Omar Khayyam, 1957
The Naked and the Dead, 1958
The Queen's Guards, 1960
The Great Imposter, 1961
The Fiercest Heart, 1961
How the West Was Won, 1962
MacKenna's Gold, 1969
All My Darling Daughters,
1972
My Darling Daughters' Anni-
versary, 1973

PAUL MASSIE (1932-   )
Canadian leading actor and supporting player of stage and
screen; films fairly occasional.

High Tide at Noon, 1957
Orders to Kill, 1958
Sapphire, 1959
Libel, 1959
The Two Faces of Dr. Jekyll,
1960
The Rebel, 1961
The Pot Carriers, 1962
Raising the Wind, 1962

AUBREY MATHER (1885-1958)
Friendly, bald-headed character actor of stage (from 1905)
and films, also in Hollywood.

Young Woodley, 1930
Tell Me Tonight, 1932
Aren't We All, 1932
Woman in Chains, 1932
Love On the Spot, 1932
The Impassive Footman, 1932
The Man Who Changed His
Name, 1934
Red Wagon, 1934
The Admiral's Secret, 1934
The Lash, 1934
Anything Might Happen, 1934
The Silent Passenger, 1935
Ball at Savoy, 1936
The Man in the Mirror, 1936
Sabotage, 1936
Chick, 1936
As You Like It, 1936
When Knights Were Bold, 1936
Night Must Fall, 1937
Underneath the Arches, 1937
Just William, 1939
No No Nanette, 1940
A Rage in Heaven, 1941
Ball of Fire, 1941
Suspicion, 1941
Mrs. Miniver, 1942
Random Harvest, 1942
The Wife Takes a Flyer, 1942
Forever and a Day, 1943
Heaven Can Wait, 1943
The Song of Bernadette, 1943
Jane Eyre, 1944
The Lodger, 1944
Wilson, 1944
The Keys of the Kingdom,
1944
National Velvet, 1944
The House of Fear, 1945
Temptation, 1946
The Hucksters, 1947
It Happened in Brooklyn, 1947
The Mighty McGurk, 1947
Julia Misbehaves, 1948
Joan of Arc, 1948
The Adventures of Don Juan,
1948
Everybody Does It, 1949

The Secret Garden, 1949
That Forsyte Woman, 1949
The Importance of Being
  Earnest, 1952
The Golden Mask, 1952
To Dorothy a Son, 1954
Fast and Loose, 1954

MURRAY MATHESON (1910-)
Quiet, pleasant-mannered character actor primarily seen on
television; in Hollywood from
early 50s.

The Secret Tunnel, 1947
The Fool and the Princess,
  1948
Hurricane Smith, 1952
The Plymouth Adventure, 1952
Botany Bay, 1953
King of the Khyber Rifles,
  1953
Love is a Many Splendored
  Thing, 1955
Wall of Noise, 1963
Signpost to Murder, 1965
Assault On a Queen, 1966
How to Succeed in Business, 1967
Detour to Nowhere, 1972

A. E. MATTHEWS (1869-1960)
Suave early romantic lead of
stage (from 1886) and films
who is best remembered for a
gallery of whimsical, crotchety,
ancient gentlemen.

Highwayman's Honour, 1914
Wanted a Widow, 1916
The Real Thing at Last, 1916
The Lifeguardsman, 1917
Once Upon a Time, 1918
The Lackey and the Lady, 1919
Castle of Dreams, 1919
The Iron Duke, 1935
Men Are Not Gods, 1936
Quiet Wedding, 1941
Pimpernel Smith, 1941
Surprise Broadcast, 1941
Thunder Rock, 1942
The Great Mr. Handel, 1942

Life and Death of Colonel
  Blimp, 1943
The Man in Grey, 1943
Escape to Danger, 1943
The Way Ahead, 1944
They Came to a City, 1944
Love Story, 1944
Twilight Hour, 1944
Flight From Folly, 1945
Piccadilly Incident, 1946
Ghosts of Berkeley Square,
  1947
Just William's Luck, 1948
William Comes to Town, 1948
Whiskey Galore, 1948
Britannia Mews, 1949
The Chiltern Hundreds, 1949
Landfall, 1949
Mr. Drake's Duck, 1950
The Galloping Major, 1951
Laughter in Paradise, 1951
The Magic Box, 1951
Who Goes There?, 1952
Castle in the Air, 1952
Penny Princess, 1952
Something Money Can't Buy,
  1952
Made in Heaven, 1952
Skid Kids, 1953
The Million Pound Note, 1954
The Weak and the Wicked,
  1954
Happy Ever After, 1954
Aunt Clara, 1954
Miss Tulip Stays the Night,
  1955
Around the World in 80 Days,
  1956
Loser Takes All, 1956
Three Men in a Boat, 1956
Doctor at Large, 1957
Carry On Admiral, 1957
Inn For Trouble, 1960

FRANCIS MATTHEWS (1927-)
Light leading man of the 50s
and 60s, also on stage and television.

Bhowani Junction, 1956
Small Hotel, 1957
Accused, 1957

Revenge of Frankenstein, 1957
A Woman Possessed, 1958
I Only Arsked, 1958
Corridors of Blood, 1958
Sentenced For Life, 1960
Treasure of Monte Cristo,
1961
The Hellfire Club, 1961
The Pursuers, 1961
The Lamp in Assassin Mews,
1962
The Battleaxe, 1962
A Stitch in Time, 1963
The Beauty Jungle, 1964
Murder Ahoy, 1964
The Intelligence Men, 1965
Rasputin the Mad Monk, 1965
Dracula Prince of Darkness,
1965
That Riviera Touch, 1966
Just Like a Woman, 1966
Crossplot, 1969
Taste of Excitement, 1969

JESSIE MATTHEWS (1907-)
Vibrant, graceful singing and
dancing star of stage (from
1917) and screen, popular in
musicals of the thirties.

Beloved Vagabond, 1923
Straws in the Wind, 1924
Out of the Blue, 1931
There Goes the Bride, 1932
The Midshipmaid, 1932
The Man From Toronto, 1933
The Good Companions, 1933
Friday the Thirteenth, 1933
Waltzes From Vienna, 1934
Evergreen, 1934
First a Girl, 1935
It's Love Again, 1936
Head Over Heels, 1936
Gangway, 1937
Sailing Along, 1938
Climbing High, 1939
Victory Wedding, 1940
Forever and a Day, 1943
Candles at Nine, 1944
Life's Nothing Without Music, 1947
Making the Grade, 1947
Tom Thumb, 1958
Hound of the Baskervilles, 1978

LESTER MATTHEWS (1900-
1975)
Leading actor and latterly
character player of stage
(1916) and films, in Hollywood
from 1934.

The Lame Duck, 1931
Creeping Shadows, 1931
The Man at Six, 1931
The Wyckham Mystery, 1931
Gypsy Blood, 1931
The Old Man, 1931
Her Night Out, 1932
Indiscretions of Eve, 1932
Fires of Fate, 1932
House of Dreams, 1933
Their Night Out, 1933
Stolen Necklace, 1933
Out of the Past, 1933
Called Back, 1933
She Was Only a Village
Maiden, 1933
Melody Maker, 1933
Facing the Music, 1933
The Song You Gave Me, 1933
On Secret Service, 1933
Borrowed Clothes, 1934
Boomerang, 1934
Song at Eventide, 1934
Blossom Time, 1934
Irish Hearts, 1934
The Poisoned Diamond, 1934
The Werewolf of London, 1935
The Raven, 1935
Professional Soldier, 1936
Spy 77, 1936
Song and Dance Man, 1936
Thank You Jeeves, 1936
15 Maiden Lane, 1936
Lloyds of London, 1936
Crack Up, 1937
The Prince and the Pauper,
1937
Lancer Spy, 1937
There's Always a Woman,
1938
Adventures of Robin Hood,
1938
Three Loves Has Nancy,
1938
Mr. Moto On Devil's Island,
1938
If I Were King, 1938

Time Out For Murder, 1938
The Three Musketeers, 1939
Susannah of the Mounties, 1939
Conspiracy, 1939
Rulers of the Sea, 1939
Everything Happens at Night,
  1939
British Intelligence, 1940
Northwest Passage, 1940
The Biscuit Eater, 1940
Women in War, 1940
Man Hunt, 1941
The Lone Wolf Keeps a Date,
  1941
A Yank in the RAF, 1941
Son of Fury, 1942
The Pied Piper, 1942
Across the Pacific, 1942
Desperate Journey, 1942
Manila Calling, 1942
The Mysterious Doctor, 1943
Four Jills in a Jeep, 1944
Between Two Worlds, 1944
The Story of Dr. Wassell, 1944
The Invisible Man's Revenge,
  1944
Shadows in the Night, 1944
Objective Burma, 1945
Two O'clock Courage, 1945
The Exile, 1947
Dark Delusion, 1947
Fighting Father Dunne, 1948
Her Wonderful Lie, 1950
Lorna Doone, 1951
Lady in the Iron Mask, 1952
Les Miserables, 1952
Operation Secret, 1952
Stars and Stripes Forever, 1952
Niagara, 1953
Trouble Along the Way, 1953
Young Bess, 1953
Fort Ti, 1953
Bad For Each Other, 1953
Flame of the Islands, 1956
Mary Poppins, 1964

LOIS MAXWELL (1927-)
Canadian leading lady and latterly supporting actress; also
in Hollywood. Probably best
known as Miss Moneypenny in
the James Bond films.

Spring Song, 1946
That Hagen Girl, 1947
Corridor of Mirrors, 1948
The Decision of Christopher
  Blake, 1948
The Dark Past, 1948
Kazan, 1949
Crime Doctor's Diary, 1949
Brief Rapture, 1950
Tomorrow is Too Late, 1950
The Woman's Angle, 1952
Lady in the Fog, 1952
Women of Twilight, 1952
Aida, 1953
Mantrap, 1953
Passport to Treason, 1956
The High Terrace, 1956
Satellite in the Sky, 1956
Kill Me Tomorrow, 1957
Time Without Pity, 1957
The Unstoppable Man, 1960
Lolita, 1962
Dr. No, 1962
Come Fly With Me, 1963
The Haunting, 1963
From Russia With Love, 1963
Goldfinger, 1964
Thunderball, 1965
Operation Kid Brother, 1966
You Only Live Twice, 1967
On Her Majesty's Secret Ser-
  vice, 1968
The Adventurers, 1970
Diamonds Are Forever, 1971
Live and Let Die, 1973
The Man With the Golden Gun,
  1974
The Spy Who Loved Me, 1977
Moonraker, 1979
Warhead, 1980

JACK MAY (1922-)
Supporting actor who is mainly
seen on stage.

Brief Encounter, 1945
Behind the Headlines, 1953
Cat Girl, 1957
A Prize of Arms, 1962
Solo For Sparrow, 1962
Goodbye Mr. Chips, 1969
Trog, 1970

Night After Night, 1970
Big Zipper, 1974
The Man Who Would Be King,
1975
The Seven Per Cent Solution,
1976

FERDY MAYNE (1916-)
German character star, long
resident in Britain; specializes
in sly or villainous roles.

Old Mother Riley Overseas,
1943
Meet Sexton Blake, 1944
The Echo Murders, 1945
The Temptress, 1949
Prelude to Fame, 1950
Night and the City, 1950
Hotel Sahara, 1951
Made in Heaven, 1952
The Blue Parrot, 1953
Marilyn, 1953
Paris Express, 1953
Desperate Moment, 1953
The Captain's Paradise, 1953
The Broken Horseshoe, 1953
Three Steps to the Gallows,
1953
All Hallowe'en, 1953
You Know What Sailors Are,
1954
White Fire, 1954
Beautiful Stranger, 1954
Malaga, 1954
The Divided Heart, 1954
Third Party Risk, 1955
Storm Over the Nile, 1955
Crossroads, 1955
Gentlemen Marry Brunettes,
1955
The Narrowing Circle, 1956
Find the Lady, 1956
Seven Waves Away, 1957
You Pay Your Money, 1957
The Big Chance, 1957
The End of the Line, 1957
Blue Murder at St. Trinian's,
1958
Woman of Mystery, 1958
Next to No Time, 1958
Deadly Record, 1959

Tommy the Toreador, 1959
Ben Hur, 1959
Third Man On the Mountain,
1959
Our Man in Havana, 1959
The Spider's Web, 1960
Crossroads to Crime, 1960
Frederic Chopin, 1961
The Green Helmet, 1961
Highway to Battle, 1961
Three Spare Wives, 1962
Masters of Venus, 1962
Freud, 1962
The Counterfeit Constable, 1964
Promise Her Anything, 1965
Operation Crossbow, 1965
The Bobo, 1967
The Fearless Vampire Killers,
1967
Where Eagles Dare, 1968
The Limbo Line, 1968
Gates to Paradise, 1968
The Magic Christian, 1970
The Walking Stick, 1970
The Vampire Lovers, 1970
The Adventurers, 1970
Von Richtofen and Brown, 1971
When Eight Bells Toll, 1971
Eagle in a Cage, 1971
Innocent Bystanders, 1972
Au Pair Girls, 1973
Barry Lyndon, 1975
A Man Called Intrepid, 1979

PATRICIA MEDINA (1921-)
Dark-haired leading lady of the
40s and 50s, also in Hollywood.
Married: Richard Greene;
Joseph Cotten.

Simply Terrific, 1938
Double Or Quits, 1938
Secret Journey, 1939
The Day Will Dawn, 1942
The First of the Few, 1942
They Met in the Dark, 1943
Hotel Reserve, 1944
Don't Take it to Heart, 1944
Kiss the Bride Goodbye, 1944
Waltz Time, 1945
The Secret Heart, 1946
Moss Rose, 1947

The Foxes of Harrow, 1947
The Three Musketeers, 1948
Francis, 1949
Fighting O'Flynn, 1949
Children of Chance, 1949
Fortunes of Captain Blood, 1950
Abbott & Costello in the Foreign Legion, 1950
The Jackpot, 1950
The Lady and the Bandit, 1951
Valentino, 1951
Magic Carpet, 1951
Lady in the Iron Mask, 1952
Desperate Search, 1952
Sangaree, 1953
Plunder of the Sun, 1953
Botany Bay, 1953
Siren of Bagdad, 1953
The Black Knight, 1954
Phantom of the Rue Morgue, 1954
Drums of Tahiti, 1954
The Red Cloak, 1955
Mr. Arkadin, 1955
Uranium Boom, 1955
Pirates of Tripoli, 1955
Stranger at My Door, 1956
The Beast of Hollow Mountain, 1956
Duel On the Mississippi, 1956
Buckskin Lady, 1957
Battle of the VI, 1958
Count Your Blessings, 1959
Snow White & the Three Stooges, 1961
The Killing of Sister George, 1968
Latitude Zero, 1969

MICHAEL MEDWIN (1923-)
Light character actor of stage (from 1940) and films, often seen in cheerful Cockney characterizations. Also producer.

Piccadilly Incident, 1946
The Root of All Evil, 1946
Woman Hater, 1947
Black Memory, 1947
The Courtneys of Curzon Street, 1947

An Ideal Husband, 1948
Call of the Blood, 1948
Night Beat, 1948
Anna Karenina, 1948
My Sister and I, 1948
Another Shore, 1948
Look Before You Love, 1948
Operation Diamond, 1948
William Comes to Town, 1948
The Queen of Spades, 1948
For Them That Trespass, 1949
Forbidden, 1949
Trottie True, 1949
Boys in Brown, 1949
Shadow of the Past, 1950
Someone at the Door, 1950
Trio, 1950
The Lady Craved Excitement, 1950
Four in a Jeep, 1951
The Long Dark Hall, 1951
Kathy's Love Affair, 1952
Curtain Up, 1952
Top Secret, 1952
Hindle Wakes, 1952
Love's a Luxury, 1952
Miss Robin Hood, 1952
The Caretaker's Daughter, 1953
The Oracle, 1953
Street Corner, 1953
Genevieve, 1953
The Intruder, 1953
Malta Story, 1953
Spaceways, 1953
Bang You're Dead, 1954
The Harassed Hero, 1954
Conflict of Wings, 1954
The Teckman Mystery, 1954
The Green Scarf, 1955
Above Us the Waves, 1955
Doctor at Sea, 1955
Man On the Beach, 1956
A Hill in Korea, 1956
Checkpoint, 1956
Man in the Road, 1956
Doctor at Large, 1957
Steel Bayonet, 1957
The Duke Wore Jeans, 1958
The Wind Cannot Read, 1958
I Only Arsked, 1958
Carry On Nurse, 1959
Heart of a Man, 1959

Crooks Anonymous, 1962
It's All Happening, 1963
The Dream Maker, 1964
Night Must Fall, 1964
Rattle of a Simple Man, 1964
I've Gotta Horse, 1965
24 Hours to Kill, 1965
The Sandwich Man, 1966
A Countess From Hong Kong,
    1967
Scrooge, 1970
O Lucky Man, 1973
Law and Disorder, 1974

JOHN MEILLON (1933-)
Australian character actor and
supporting player of the sixties.

On the Beach, 1959
The Sundowners, 1960
The Long & the Short & the
    Tall, 1961
Offbeat, 1961
Watch It Sailor, 1961
Operation Snatch, 1962
Billy Budd, 1962
Death Trap, 1962
The Valiant, 1962
The Running Man, 1963
Cairo, 1963
Guns at Batasi, 1964
633 Squadron, 1964
Dead Man's Chest, 1965
They're a Weird Mob, 1966
Walkabout, 1971
The Dove, 1974
Sidecar Racers, 1975
Ride a Wild Pony, 1975
The Cars That Eat People, 1976
Picture Show Man, 1978

JACK MELFORD (-)
Character actor and supporting
star, in films since 1931.

The Sport of Kings, 1931
Night of the Garter, 1933
Bargain Basement, 1935
Look Up and Laugh, 1935
Honeymoon For Three, 1935
Birds of a Feather, 1935

If I Were Rich, 1936
Find the Lady, 1936
Luck of the Turf, 1936
Radio Lover, 1936
Jump For Glory, 1937
Let's Make a Night of It, 1937
Command Performance, 1937
It's in the Air, 1938
Scruffy, 1938
Coming of Age, 1938
Hold My Hand, 1938
Many Tanks Mr. Atkins, 1938
Too Many Husbands, 1938
The Spider, 1939
The Briggs Family, 1940
Spare a Copper, 1940
Theatre Royal, 1943
The October Man, 1947
When You Come Home, 1947
The Laughing Lady, 1947
No Room at the Inn, 1948
Warning to Wantons, 1949
Up For the Cup, 1950
Heights of Danger, 1953
Background, 1953
Fatal Journey, 1954
The Ladykillers, 1955
End of the Line, 1957
Bluebeard's Ten Honeymoons,
    1960
Feet of Clay, 1960
Compelled, 1960
Follow That Man, 1961
Transatlantic, 1961
The Gentle Terror, 1962
A Home of Your Own, 1964
Lust For a Vampire, 1970

MURRAY MELVIN (1932-)
Character player of the 60s and
70s who graduated to films
through Theatre Workshop.

The Criminal, 1960
Petticoat Pirates, 1961
A Taste of Honey, 1961
Solo For Sparrow, 1962
HMS Defiant, 1962
Sparrows Can't Sing, 1963
The Ceremony, 1964
Alfie, 1966
Kaleidoscope, 1966

A Day in the Death of Joe
Egg, 1970
The Boy Friend, 1971
The Devils, 1971
Ghost Story, 1974
Barry Lyndon, 1975
Bawdy Adventures of Tom
Jones, 1975
Shout at the Devil, 1976
Crossed Swords, 1978

VIVIEN MERCHANT (1929-)
Leading lady of stage (since
1943) and television; films infrequent but memorable. Formerly married to playwright
Harold Pinter.

The Way Ahead, 1944
Alfie, 1966
Accident, 1967
Alfred the Great, 1969
Under Milk Wood, 1971
Frenzy, 1972
The Offence, 1972
The Homecoming, 1973
The Maids, 1975
Man in the Iron Mask, 1976

PHILIP MERIVALE (1886-
1946)
Stage and film actor of the
thirties and forties, mainly in
Hollywood.

The Passing of the Third Floor
Back, 1935
Give Us This Night, 1936
Mr. and Mrs. Smith, 1941
A Rage in Heaven, 1941
Pacific Blackout, 1942
Lady For a Night, 1942
This Above All, 1942
Crossroads, 1942
This Land is Mine, 1943
Lost Angel, 1944
The Hour Before the Dawn,
1944
Nothing But Trouble, 1945
The Stranger, 1946
Sister Kenny, 1946

MARY MERRALL (1890-1973)
Character actress of stage
(since 1907) and screen, adept
at eccentric or absent-minded
parts; wife of Franklyn Dyall,
mother of Valentine Dyall.

The Manxman, 1916
Duke's Son, 1920
Men of Steel, 1932
You Will Remember, 1939
Dr. O'Dowd, 1940
Love On the Dole, 1941
Squadron Leader X, 1942
Dead of Night, 1945
Pink String and Sealing Wax,
1945
This Man is Mine, 1946
They Made Me a Fugitive, 1947
Nicholas Nickleby, 1947
Badger's Green, 1948
The Three Weird Sisters, 1948
Scott of the Antarctic, 1948
For Them That Trespass,
1949
Trio, 1950
Obsessed, 1951
The Late Edwina Black, 1951
Out of True, 1951
A Tale of Five Cities, 1951
Encore, 1952
Judgement Deferred, 1952
Meet Me Tonight, 1952
The Pickwick Papers, 1952
Duel in the Jungle, 1954
The Belles of St. Trinian's,
1954
The Weak and the Wicked,
1954
The Green Buddha, 1954
Payroll Robbery, 1955
It's Great to Be Young, 1956
Campbell's Kingdom, 1957
The Camp On Blood Island,
1958
Family Doctor, 1958
Spare the Rod, 1961
Everything I Have, 1962
Bitter Harvest, 1963
Beware of the Dog, 1964
Moll Flanders, 1965
Who Killed the Cat?, 1966
Futtock's End, 1970

GEORGE MERRITT (1890-
1977)
Durable, dependable character
actor, usually seen as solid
citizens. Also on stage; on
tv in "The Forsyte Saga."

The W Plan, 1930
Thread O' Scarlet, 1930
A Gentleman of Paris, 1931
Dreyfus, 1931
Bracelets, 1931
Blind Spot, 1932
The Lodger, 1932
Little Fella, 1932
F P One, 1933
White Face, 1933
I Was a Spy, 1933
Mr. Quincy of Monte Carlo,
1933
Going Straight, 1933
Double Bluff, 1933
The Ghost Camera, 1933
The Fire Raisers, 1933
Crime On the Hill, 1933
Jew Suss, 1934
No Escape, 1934
My Song For You, 1934
The Silver Spoon, 1934
Nine Forty-Five, 1934
Forever England, 1935
Mr. Cohen Takes a Walk,
1935
Ten Minute Alibi, 1935
Emil and the Detectives, 1935
Drake of England, 1935
Me and Marlborough, 1935
Crime Unlimited, 1935
Line Engaged, 1935
Everything is Thunder, 1936
Rembrandt, 1936
Ticket of Leave, 1936
Prison Breaker, 1936
The Man Behind the Mask, 1936
Educated Evans, 1936
Love at Sea, 1936
Dr. Syn, 1937
Young and Innocent, 1937
The Rat, 1937
Return of the Scarlet Pim-
pernel, 1937
The Vicar of Bray, 1937
The Compulsory Wife, 1937

Dangerous Fingers, 1937
The Vulture, 1937
The Gaunt Stranger, 1938
Mr. Reeder in Room 13, 1938
A Window in London, 1939
Q Planes, 1939
All at Sea, 1939
Meet Maxwell Archer, 1939
The Proud Valley, 1940
The Frightened Lady, 1940
They Came By Night, 1940
Two For Danger, 1940
Four Just Men, 1940
Spare a Copper, 1940
Breach of Promise, 1941
He Found a Star, 1941
Hatter's Castle, 1941
Back Room Boy, 1942
Alibi, 1942
They Flew Alone, 1942
I'll Walk Beside You, 1943
A Canterbury Tale, 1943
Demobbed, 1944
Quiet Weekend, 1944
Don't Take it to Heart, 1944
Waterloo Road, 1944
For You Alone, 1945
Home Sweet Home, 1945
The Voice Within, 1945
I'll Be Your Sweetheart, 1945
I'll Turn to You, 1946
Nicholas Nickleby, 1947
The Man Within, 1947
The Root of All Evil, 1947
Love in Waiting, 1948
Dark Secret, 1949
Marry Me, 1949
Something in the City, 1950
Noose For a Lady, 1953
Small Town Story, 1953
Night of the Full Moon, 1954
End of the Road, 1954
The Green Scarf, 1955
Quatermass II, 1957
Tread Softly Stranger, 1958
The Full Treatment, 1961
What Every Woman Wants, 1962
I Monster, 1970
Cromwell, 1970

JANE MERROW (1941-)
Attractive leading lady of the

60s and 70s; also on stage
and tv.

Why Bother to Knock?, 1961
The Wild and the Willing, 1962
The System, 1963
Catacombs, 1964
The Woman Who Wouldn't Die,
  1965
Assignment K, 1967
Night of the Big Heat, 1967
The Lion in Winter, 1968
Hands of the Ripper, 1971
The Horror at 37,000 Feet,
  1973
Island of the Burning Damned,
  1973
Diagnosis Murder, 1975

WILLIAM MERVYN (1912-
1976)
Tubby character comedian with
inimitable voice and manner;
also frequently on television.

The Blue Lamp, 1950
Conflict of Wings, 1954
The Long Arm, 1956
Carve Her Name With Pride,
  1958
Battle of the Sexes, 1959
A Touch of Larceny, 1959
Circus of Horrors, 1960
Invasion Quartet, 1961
Murder Ahoy, 1964
The Legend of Young Dick
  Turpin, 1965
The Jokers, 1966
Deadlier Than the Male, 1967
Carry On Follow That Camel,
  1967
Salt and Pepper, 1968
Hammerhead, 1968
Incense For the Damned, 1970
Carry On Henry VIII, 1971
The Railway Children, 1971
The Ruling Class, 1972
Up the Front, 1972
Charley One-Eye, 1973
Bawdy Adventures of Tom
  Jones, 1975

RALPH MICHAEL (1907-)
Character star of stage, films,
and television; often seen in
sturdy, dependable characterizations.

False Evidence, 1937
John Halifax, Gentleman, 1938
The Girl Who Forgot, 1939
Front Line Kids, 1942
Gert and Daisy Clean Up,
  1942
Women Aren't Angels, 1942
San Demetrio-London, 1943
For Those in Peril, 1944
Dead of Night, 1945
Johnny Frenchman, 1945
The Captive Heart, 1946
Eureka Stockade, 1948
Penny and the Pownall Case,
  1948
A Song For Tomorrow, 1948
The Hasty Heart, 1949
The Astonished Heart, 1950
The Sound Barrier, 1952
King's Rhapsody, 1955
Women Without Men, 1956
Seven Waves Away, 1957
A Night to Remember, 1958
Date at Midnight, 1960
A Taste of Money, 1960
The Court Martial of Major
  Keller, 1961
Private Potter, 1962
The Valiant, 1962
Children of the Damned, 1963
A Jolly Bad Fellow, 1964
Murder Most Foul, 1965
He Who Rides a Tiger, 1965
The Heroes of Telemark, 1965
Khartoum, 1966
House of Cards, 1968
The Assassination Bureau, 1969
The Count of Monte Cristo, 1975
Henry IV Part 2, 1980

KEITH MICHELL (1928-)
Australian leading man of stage
(1947), screen, and television;
former art teacher.

True as a Turtle, 1957

Dangerous Exile, 1957
The Gypsy and the Gentleman, 1958
The Hellfire Club, 1961
All Night Long, 1962
Seven Seas to Calais, 1963
House of Cards, 1968
Prudence and the Pill, 1968
The Executioner, 1970
Henry VIII and His Six Wives, 1972
Moments, 1973
Julius Caesar, 1979
The Tenth Month, 1979
The Day Christ Died, 1980

GUY MIDDLETON (1907-1973)
Moustached character star and
occasional leading man of stage
(from 1928), screen and television; typically portrayed the
smooth but likable cad or other
hearty comedy characters.
Also Hollywood. Former
Stock Exchange broker.

A Woman Alone, 1932
Jimmy Boy, 1935
Two Hearts in Harmony, 1935
Trust the Navy, 1935
Under Proff, 1936
Fame, 1936
The Gay Adventure, 1936
Mysterious Mr. Davis, 1936
A Woman Alone, 1936
Keep Fit, 1937
Take a Chance, 1937
Break the News, 1938
Goodbye Mr. Chips, 1939
French Without Tears, 1939
For Freedom, 1940
Dangerous Moonlight, 1941
Talk About Jacqueline, 1942
The Demi-Paradise, 1943
English Without Tears, 1944
Halfway House, 1944
Champagne Charlie, 1944
29 Acacia Avenue, 1945
The Rake's Progress, 1945
Night Boat to Dublin, 1946
The Captive Heart, 1946
A Man About the House, 1947

The White Unicorn, 1947
Snowbound, 1948
One Night With You, 1948
Once Upon a Dream, 1949
Marry Me, 1949
The Facts of Love, 1949
No Place For Jennifer, 1950
The Happiest Days of Your Life, 1950
Laughter in Paradise, 1951
The Third Visitor, 1951
Young Wives' Tale, 1951
Never Look Back, 1952
The Fake, 1953
Albert RN, 1953
Malaga, 1954
Front Page Story, 1954
The Belles of St. Trinian's, 1954
Make Me An Offer, 1954
Conflict of Wings, 1954
The Harassed Hero, 1954
The Sea Shall Not Have Them, 1955
Break in the Circle, 1955
A Yank in Ermine, 1955
Gentlemen Marry Brunettes, 1955
Now and Forever, 1956
Alive On Saturday, 1957
Doctor at Large, 1957
Let's Be Happy, 1957
The Passionate Summer, 1958
Escort For Hire, 1960
Waltz of the Toreadors, 1962
What Every Woman Wants, 1962
The Fur Collar, 1962
Oh What a Lovely War, 1969
The Magic Christian, 1970
Does Your Nanny Come From Bergen?, 1970

JOSEPHINE MIDDLETON
(-)
Character actress in very occasional films.

The Demi-Paradise, 1943
A Lady Surrenders, 1947
The Browning Version, 1951
Before I Wake, 1955

NOELLE MIDDLETON
(1928-   )
Leading lady of a few films
of the fifties.

Happy Ever After, 1954
Carrington VC, 1955
The Iron Petticoat, 1956
Three Men in a Boat, 1956
John and Julie, 1956
Vicious Circle, 1957

LORD BERNARD MILES
(1907-   )
Distinguished actor of stage
(from 1930) and screen; specializes in kindly rural characters. Former schoolmaster.
Also founder of London's Mermaid Theatre (1959).

Channel Crossing, 1933
The Love Test, 1935
Twelve Good Men, 1936
Midnight at Madame Tussaud's,
    1936
The Challenge, 1938
The Citadel, 1938
Thirteen Men and a Gun, 1938
The Spy in Black, 1938
The Lion Has Wings, 1939
Rebel Son, 1939
Pastor Hall, 1940
Dawn Guard, 1941
Freedom Radio, 1941
Quiet Wedding, 1941
Home Guard, 1941
The Common Touch, 1941
The Big Blockade, 1942
This Was Paris, 1942
One of Our Aircraft is Miss-
    ing, 1942
The Day Will Dawn, 1942
In Which We Serve, 1942
The First of the Few, 1942
The Goose Steps Out, 1942
Two Fathers, 1944
Tawny Pipit, 1944
Tunisian Victory, 1944
Carnival, 1946
Great Expectations, 1946
Nicholas Nickleby, 1947

Fame is the Spur, 1947
The Guinea Pig, 1948
Bernard Miles On Gun Dogs,
    1948
Chance of a Lifetime, 1950
The Magic Box, 1951
Never Let Me Go, 1953
Tiger in the Smoke, 1956
Moby Dick, 1956
The Man Who Knew Too Much,
    1956
Zarak, 1956
Fortune is a Woman, 1957
The Smallest Show On Earth,
    1957
Saint Joan, 1957
Tom Thumb, 1958
The Vision of William Blake,
    1958
Sapphire, 1959
Heavens Above, 1963
The Specialist, 1966
Baby Love, 1968
Run Wild Run Free, 1969

SARAH MILES (1941-   )
Attractive leading lady of the
60s and 70s, also in Hollywood.
Married: Robert Bolt; sister
of director Christopher Miles
(1939-   ).

Term of Trial, 1962
Six Sided Triangle, 1963
The Servant, 1963
The Ceremony, 1964
Those Magnificent Men in
    Their Flying Machines, 1965
I Was Happy Here, 1965
Blow Up, 1966
Ryan's Daughter, 1970
Lady Caroline Lamb, 1972
The Hireling, 1973
The Man Who Loved Cat Danc-
    ing, 1973
Bride to Be, 1975
Great Expectations, 1975
Pepita Jiminez, 1976
The Sailor Who Fell From
    Grace With the Sea, 1976
Dynasty, 1976
The Big Sleep, 1978

RAY MILLAND (1905-)
Handsome Welsh light leading
man and occasionally latterly
director; primarily in Hollywood. Former seaman and
soldier. Tv series: "Mark-
ham" (1959).

The Plaything, 1929
The Informer, 1929
The Flying Scotsman, 1929
The Lady From the Sea, 1929
Way For a Sailor, 1930
The Passion Flower, 1930
Bachelor Father, 1931
Just a Gigolo, 1931
Bought, 1931
Ambassador Bill, 1931
Blonde Crazy, 1931
Polly of the Circus, 1932
The Man Who Played God,
    1932
Payment Deferred, 1932
Orders is Orders, 1933
This is the Life, 1933
Bolero, 1934
We're Not Dressing, 1934
Many Happy Returns, 1934
Charlie Chan in London, 1934
Menace, 1934
One Hour Late, 1935
The Gilded Lily, 1935
Four Hours to Kill, 1935
The Glass Key, 1935
Alias Mary Dow, 1935
Next Time We Love, 1936
Return of Sophie Lang, 1936
Jungle Princess, 1936
Three Smart Girls, 1936
Big Broadcast of 1937, 1937
Bulldog Drummond Escapes,
    1937
Wings Over Honolulu, 1937
Ebb Tide, 1937
Easy Living, 1937
Wise Girl, 1937
Her Jungle Love, 1938
Tropic Holiday, 1938
Men With Wings, 1938
Say it in French, 1938
French Without Tears, 1939
Hotel Imperial, 1939
Beau Geste, 1939

Everything Happens at Night,
    1939
Irene, 1940
The Doctor Takes a Wife, 1940
Untamed, 1940
Arise My Love, 1940
I Wanted Wings, 1941
Skylark, 1941
The Lady Has Plans, 1942
Are Husbands Necessary?,
    1942
The Major and the Minor, 1942
Reap the Wild Wind, 1942
Star Spangled Rhythm, 1942
The Crystal Ball, 1943
Forever and a Day, 1943
The Uninvited, 1944
Lady in the Dark, 1944
Till We Meet Again, 1944
Ministry of Fear, 1944
The Lost Weekend, 1945
Kitty, 1946
The Well Groomed Bride, 1946
California, 1946
The Imperfect Lady, 1947
The Trouble With Women, 1947
Variety Girl, 1947
Golden Earrings, 1947
The Big Clock, 1948
So Evil My Love, 1948
Miss Tatlock's Millions, 1948
Sealed Verdict, 1948
Alias Nick Beal, 1949
It Happens Every Spring, 1949
A Woman of Distinction, 1950
A Life of Her Own, 1950
Copper Canyon, 1950
Circle of Danger, 1951
Night Into Morning, 1951
Rhubarb, 1951
Close to My Heart, 1951
Bugles in the Afternoon, 1952
Something to Live For, 1952
The Thief, 1952
Jamaica Run, 1953
Let's Do It Again, 1953
Dial M For Murder, 1954
Girl in the Red Velvet Swing,
    1955
A Man Alone, 1956
Lisbon, 1956
Three Brave Men, 1957
The River's Edge, 1957

High Flight, 1957
The Safecracker, 1958
The Premature Burial, 1962
Panic in the Year Zero, 1962
The Man With the X-Ray Eyes,
    1963
The Confession, 1965
Hostile Witness, 1968
Rose Rosse per il Fuhrer,
    1968
River of Gold, 1969
Daughter of the Mind, 1969
Company of Killers, 1970
Love Story, 1970
Black Noon, 1971
Embassy, 1972
Frogs, 1972
The Big Game, 1972
The Thing With Two Heads,
    1972
The House in Nightmare Park,
    1973
Terror in the Wax Museum,
    1973
Gold, 1974
The Student Connection, 1974
Too Many Suspects, 1975
The Dead Don't Die, 1975
Escape to Witch Mountain, 1976
The Last Tycoon, 1976
Rich Man Poor Man, 1976
Aces High, 1976
Slavers, 1977
Oil, 1977
The Swiss Conspiracy, 1977
The Uncanny, 1977
La Rigazza in Pigiama Giallo,
    1978
Blackout, 1978
Oliver's Story, 1978
Cruise Into Terror, 1978
Spree, 1978
Battlestar Galactica, 1978
Game For Vultures, 1979
Testimony of Two Men, 1979
The Dream Merchants, 1980

HUGH MILLER (1889-197)
Actor of stage (from 1911)
and films; star of silents,
later in character roles.

In His Grip, 1921
The Puppet Man, 1921
The Letters, 1922
Darkness, 1923
Bonnie Prince Charlie, 1923
Claude Duval, 1924
The Prude's Fall, 1924
Venetian Lovers, 1925
Baddeseley Manor, 1926
The Green Pack, 1934
The Divine Spark, 1935
McGlusky the Sea Rover, 1935
I Give My Heart, 1935
The Dominant Sex, 1937
Bulldog Drummond at Bay,
    1937
The Vicar of Bray, 1937
Spring Handicap, 1937
Victoria the Great, 1937
Return of the Scarlet Pimper-
    nel, 1937
The Rat, 1937
I'll Walk Beside You, 1943
My Sister and I, 1948
Lovers Happy Lovers, 1954
Before I Wake, 1955
The Gelignite Gang, 1956
Behind the Mask, 1958
Lawrence of Arabia, 1962

MANDY MILLER (1944-)
Talented child performer of the
fifties.

The Man in the White Suit,
    1951
Mandy, 1952
Background, 1953
Adventure in the Hopfields,
    1954
Dance Little Lady, 1954
Raising a Riot, 1955
The Secret, 1955
The Feminine Touch, 1956
A Child in the House, 1956
The Snorkel, 1958
Kill Or Cure, 1963

MARTIN MILLER (1899-)
Czechoslovakian character

player long in Britain, generally seen as kindly old gentleman. Also on television in
"The Forsyte Saga. "

Squadron Leader X, 1942
The Adventures of Tartu, 1943
English Without Tears, 1944
Hotel Reserve, 1944
Latin Quarter, 1945
Night Boat to Dublin, 1946
Woman to Woman, 1946
Ghosts of Berkeley Square,
  1947
Mine Own Executioner, 1947
Counterblast, 1948
Bonnie Prince Charlie, 1948
The Huggetts Abroad, 1949
Man On the Run, 1949
Encore, 1951
Where's Charley?, 1952
Front Page Story, 1954
You Know What Sailors Are,
  1954
To Dorothy a Son, 1954
Mad About Men, 1954
The Woman For Joe, 1955
Man of the Moment, 1955
A Child in the House, 1956
The Gamma People, 1956
Seven Thunders, 1957
Mark of the Phoenix, 1958
Violent Moment, 1959
The Rough and the Smooth,
  1959
Libel, 1959
Expresso Bongo, 1959
Exodus, 1960
Peeping Tom, 1960
Phantom of the Opera, 1962
55 Days at Peking, 1962
Incident at Midnight, 1963
The VIPs, 1963
The Pink Panther, 1963
Children of the Damned, 1964
Up Jumped a Swagman, 1965

MAX MILLER (1895-1963)
Popular music hall comedian
("The Cheekie Chappie") and
film performer of the thirties;
former circus performer (1903).

Friday the 13th, 1933
Channel Crossing, 1933
The Good Companions, 1933
Princess Charming, 1934
Things Are Looking Up, 1935
Get Off My Foot, 1935
Educated Evans, 1936
Take it From Me, 1937
Don't Get Me Wrong, 1937
Transatlantic Trouble, 1937
Everything Happens to Me, 1938
The Good Old Days, 1939
Hoots Mon, 1939
Asking For Trouble, 1943

SPIKE MILLIGAN (1918-)
Irish comedy character star of
stage, films and television;
also a popular radio performer
since 1949 ("The Goon Show, "
etc.)

Let's Go Crazy, 1951
Penny Points to Paradise, 1951
London Entertains, 1951
Down Among the Z Men, 1952
Super Secret Service, 1953
The Case of the Mukkinese
  Battlehorn, 1956
The Running, Jumping, and
  Standing Still Film, 1960
Watch Your Stern, 1960
Suspect, 1960
Invasion Quartet, 1961
What a Whopper, 1961
Postman's Knock, 1962
Fish and Milligan, 1966
The Bed Sitting Room, 1969
The Undertakers, 1969
The Magic Christian, 1970
Magnificent Seven Deadly Sins,
  1971
Rentadick, 1972
Alice's Adventures in Wonder-
  land, 1972
The Cherry Picker, 1972
Adolf Hitler--My Part in His
  Downfall, 1973
Digby, the Biggest Dog in the
  World, 1973
Man About the House, 1974
The Great McGonagall, 1974

The Three Musketeers, 1974
The Last Remake of Beau
    Geste, 1977
Hound of the Baskervilles, 1978
The Life of Brian, 1979

HAYLEY MILLS (1946-)
Precocious juvenile actress of
the sixties; also in Hollywood.
Daughter of Sir John Mills,
sister of Juliet Mills.

Tiger Bay, 1959
Pollyanna, 1960
The Parent Trap, 1960
Whistle Down the Wind, 1961
In Search of the Castaways,
    1962
Summer Magic, 1962
The Moonspinners, 1963
The Chalk Garden, 1964
The Truth About Spring, 1964
Sky West and Crooked, 1965
The Daydreamer, 1965
That Darn Cat, 1965
The Trouble With Angels, 1966
The Family Way, 1966
Pretty Polly, 1967
Africa-Texas Style!, 1967
Twisted Nerve, 1968
Take a Girl Like You, 1969
Endless Night, 1971
Cry of the Penguins, 1972
Deadly Strangers, 1974
Only a Scream Away, 1974
The Kingfish Caper, 1976
What Changed Charley Farth-
    ing?, 1976

SIR JOHN MILLS (1908-)
Distinguished, outstanding star
of the forties and latterly character star of great versatility;
also on stage (from 1930) and
tv. Also in Hollywood. Former clerk (1924) and chorus
boy (1928). Daughters: Hayley Mills, Juliet Mills.

The Midshipmaid, 1932
The Ghost Camera, 1933

Britannia of Billingsgate, 1933
River Wolves, 1934
A Political Party, 1934
Those Were the Days, 1934
The Lash, 1934
Blind Justice, 1934
Doctor's Orders, 1934
Royal Cavalcade, 1935
Forever England, 1935
Charing Cross Road, 1935
Car of Dreams, 1935
First Offence, 1936
Tudor Rose, 1936
OHMS, 1937
The Green Cockatoo, 1937
Goodbye Mr. Chips, 1939
All Hands, 1940
Old Bill and Son, 1940
Cottage to Let, 1941
The Black Sheep of Whitehall,
    1941
The Big Blockade, 1942
The Young Mr. Pitt, 1942
In Which We Serve, 1942
We Dive at Dawn, 1943
This Happy Breed, 1944
Victory Wedding, 1944
Waterloo Road, 1944
The Way to the Stars, 1945
Land of Promise, 1945
Great Expectations, 1946
So Well Remembered, 1947
The October Man, 1947
Scott of the Antarctic, 1948
Friend of the Family, 1949
The History of Mr. Polly, 1949
The Rocking Horse Winner,
    1950
Morning Departure, 1950
Mr. Denning Drives North,
    1951
The Gentle Gunman, 1952
The Long Memory, 1953
Hobson's Choice, 1954
The Colditz Story, 1954
The End of the Affair, 1955
Above Us the Waves, 1955
Escapade, 1955
War and Peace, 1956
Around the World in 80 Days,
    1956
It's Great to Be Young, 1956
The Baby and the Battleship,

1956
Town On Trial, 1957
Vicious Circle, 1957
Dunkirk, 1958
Ice Cold in Alex, 1958
I Was Monty's Double, 1958
Tiger Bay, 1959
Summer of the Seventeenth
  Doll, 1960
Tunes of Glory, 1960
Flame in the Streets, 1961
The Swiss Family Robinson,
  1961
The Singer Not the Song, 1961
The Valiant, 1962
Tiara Tahiti, 1963
The Chalk Garden, 1964
The Truth About Spring, 1964
Operation Crossbow, 1965
King Rat, 1965
The Wrong Box, 1966
The Family Way, 1966
Chuka, 1967
Africa-Texas Style!, 1967
Showdown, 1968
Emma Hamilton, 1968
A Black Veil For Lisa, 1969
Run Wild Run Free, 1969
Oh What a Lovely War, 1969
Ryan's Daughter, 1970
Adam's Woman, 1970
Return of the Boomerang, 1970
Dulcima, 1971
Young Winston, 1972
Lady Caroline Lamb, 1972
Zoo Gang, 1972
Tom Brown's Schooldays, 1973
Oklahoma Crude, 1973
The Human Factor, 1975
A Choice of Weapons, 1976
Dirty Knight's Work, 1976
The Devil's Advocate, 1977
The Big Sleep, 1978
Dr. Strange, 1978
The Water Babies, 1979
The Thirty-Nine Steps, 1980
Zulu Dawn, 1980

JULIET MILLS (1941-)
Attractive leading actress of
films and tv, also in Hollywood. Father: Sir John
Mills, sister: Hayley Mills.

Television series: "Nanny and
the Professor" (1970-71).

In Which We Serve, 1942
So Well Remembered, 1947
The October Man, 1947
The History of Mr. Polly, 1949
No My Darling Daughter, 1961
Twice Round the Daffodils, 1962
Nurse On Wheels, 1963
Carry On Jack, 1963
The Rare Breed, 1966
Oh What a Lovely War, 1969
Avanti, 1972
Les Galets D'Etrata, 1972
Les Portes de Feu, 1972
Riata, 1973
Jonathan Livingston Seagull,
  1973
Beyond the Door, 1975
El Segundo Poder, 1977
Alexander: The Other Side of
  Dawn, 1977

BILLY MILTON (1905-)
Light actor of stage and screen,
popular in the thirties; latterly
seen in cameo roles. Also
pianist, singer, and composer.

The Flag Lieutenant, 1926
Young Woodley, 1930
The Man From Chicago, 1930
Bull Rushes, 1931
Who Killed Doc Robin?, 1931
The Great Gay Road, 1931
Three Men in a Boat, 1933
Aunt Sally, 1933
Music Hath Charms, 1935
King of the Castle, 1936
Once in a Million, 1936
Someone at the Door, 1936
A Star Fell From Heaven, 1936
No Escape, 1936
Aren't Men Beasts?, 1937
The Dominant Sex, 1937
Spring Handicap, 1937
Saturday Night Revue, 1937
The Last Chance, 1937
Oh Boy, 1938
Yes Madam, 1938
The Set-Up, 1963
Who Was Maddox?, 1964

Personal and Confidential,
1965
Monster of Terror, 1965
Licensed to Kill, 1965
Hot Millions, 1967
Mrs. Brown, You've Got a
Lovely Daughter, 1968
The Black Windmill, 1974

JULIEN MITCHELL (1884-
1954)
Character player of stage and
films, often seen in small but
telling parts.

The Last Journey, 1935
Educated Evans, 1936
The Frog, 1937
Double Exposures, 1937
Mr. Smith Carries On, 1937
It's In the Air, 1938
The Drum, 1938
Quiet Please, 1938
The Sea Hawk, 1940
Vigil in the Night, 1940
The Goose Steps Out, 1942
Rhythm Serenade, 1943
Schweik's New Adventures,
1943
Hotel Reserve, 1944
The Echo Murders, 1945
Bedelia, 1946
Bonnie Prince Charlie, 1948
A Boy, a Girl, and a Bike,
1949
Chance of a Lifetime, 1950
The Magnet, 1950
The Galloping Major, 1951
Hobson's Choice, 1954

WARREN MITCHELL (1926-)
Comedy character star of the
sixties, also seen on television,
notably in series "Till Death
Us Do Part."

Manuela, 1957
Barnacle Bill, 1957
Man With a Gun, 1958
Three Crooked Men, 1958
The Crawling Eye, 1959

Tommy the Toreador, 1959
Surprise Package, 1960
The Boy Who Stole a Million,
1961
Curse of the Werewolf, 1961
Postman's Knock, 1962
The Roman Spring of Mrs.
Stone, 1962
Village of Daughters, 1962
The Main Attraction, 1962
The Small World of Sammy
Lee, 1963
Where Has Poor Mickey Gone?,
1963
Incident at Midnight, 1963
Calculated Risk, 1963
The King's Breakfast, 1963
Unearthly Stranger, 1963
70 Deadly Pills, 1964
The Sicilians, 1964
Carry On Cleo, 1964
The Intelligence Men, 1965
San Ferry Ann, 1965
The Spy Who Came in From the
Cold, 1965
Help!, 1965
Promise Her Anything, 1965
The Night Caller, 1965
Drop Dead Darling, 1966
The Sandwich Man, 1966
The Jokers, 1966
Till Death Us Do Part, 1968
Diamonds For Breakfast, 1968
Moon Zero Two, 1969
The Assassination Bureau, 1969
The Best House in London, 1969
All the Way Up, 1970
Innocent Bystanders, 1972
The Alf Garnett Saga, 1972
Stand Up Virgin Soldiers, 1977
Jabberwocky, 1977
Meetings with Remarkable Men,
1979

YVONNE MITCHELL (1925-1979)
Prominent, intelligent actress
of stage (since 1939) and films,
also playwright and novelist.

The Queen of Spades, 1948
Children of Chance, 1949
Turn the Key Softly, 1953

The Divided Heart, 1954
Escapade, 1955
Yield to the Night, 1956
Woman in a Dressing Gown, 1957
The Passionate Summer, 1958
Tiger Bay, 1959
Sapphire, 1959
Conspiracy of Hearts, 1960
The Trials of Oscar Wilde,
    1960
Johnny Nobody, 1961
The Main Attraction, 1963
Genghis Khan, 1965
The Corpse, 1970
Demons of the Mind, 1971
The Great Waltz, 1972
The Incredible Sarah, 1976
Widow's Nest, 1977

DONALD MOFFAT (1930-)
Supporting player of Hollywood
films, also on stage and tv.

Battle of the River Plate, 1956
Rachel Rachel, 1968
The Great Northfield Minnesota
    Raid, 1972
Trial of the Catonsville Nine, 1972
Showdown, 1973
The Terminal Man, 1974
Earthquake, 1974
Call of the Wild, 1976
The Long Days of Summer,
    1980
Popeye, 1980

GRAHAM MOFFATT (1919-
    1965)
Comedy character star, best
remembered as Albert, the fat
boy of the Will Hay comedies
of the 30s.

A Cup of Kindness, 1934
Stormy Weather, 1935
The Clairvoyant, 1935
Where There's a Will, 1936
Windbag the Sailor, 1936
Good Morning Boys, 1937
Okay For Sound, 1937
Gangway, 1937

Dr. Syn, 1937
Oh Mr. Porter, 1938
To the Victor, 1938
Owd Bob, 1938
Convict 99, 1938
Old Bones of the River, 1938
Ask a Policeman, 1939
Where's That Fire?, 1939
Cheer Boys Cheer, 1939
Charley's Big-Hearted Aunt,
    1940
I Thank You, 1941
Hi Gang, 1941
Back Room Boy, 1942
Dear Octopus, 1943
Time Flies, 1944
Welcome Mr. Washington, 1944
I Know Where I'm Going, 1945
The Voyage of Peter Joe, 1946
Stage Frights, 1947
Woman Hater, 1948
Three Bags Full, 1949
The Dragon of Pendragon
    Castle, 1950
The Second Mate, 1951
Mother Riley Meets the Vam-
    pire, 1952
Inn For Trouble, 1960
80,000 Suspects, 1963

CLIFFORD MOLLISON (1896-)
Light leading man of the thirties,
also on stage (from 1913); latterly in character parts.

Express Love, 1929
Almost a Honeymoon, 1930
Lucky Number, 1933
Meet My Sister, 1933
A Southern Maid, 1933
Luck of a Sailor, 1934
Freedom of the Seas, 1934
Give Her a Ring, 1934
Mr. Cinders, 1934
Radio Parade of 1935, 1935
Royal Cavalcade, 1935
Blind Folly, 1939
Scrooge, 1951
The Baby and the Battleship,
    1956
Mary Had a Little, 1961
Oh What a Lovely War, 1969

That's Your Funeral, 1972
Love Thy Neighbour, 1973

BOB MONKHOUSE (1928-)
Zany comedian of radio (since 1948), television, and occasional films; former cartoonist (1944) and scriptwriter.

The Secret People, 1952
All in Good Fun, 1956
Carry On Sergeant, 1958
Dentist in the Chair, 1960
Dentist On the Job, 1961
She'll Have to Go, 1962
A Weekend With Lulu, 1962
Thunderbirds Are Go, 1966
The Bliss of Mrs. Blossom, 1968
Up the Junction, 1969
Simon Simon, 1970

LEE MONTAGUE (1927-)
Actor of stage, films and television, mainly seen during the 60s.

Moulin Rouge, 1953
Savage Innocents, 1959
The Secret Partner, 1960
Another Sky, 1960
A Foxhole in Cairo, 1961
The Singer Not the Song, 1961
Billy Budd, 1962
Operation Snatch, 1962
The Horse Without a Head, 1963
You Must Be Joking!, 1965
Deadlier Than the Male, 1967
How I Won the War, 1967
Eagle in a Cage, 1971
Brother Sun, Sister Moon, 1972
Mahler, 1975
Jesus of Nazareth, 1977
Brass Target, 1978
The London Affair, 1979
The Legacy, 1979

RON MOODY (1924-)
Versatile character actor,

also on stage and television; popular in comedy parts. Tv series: "Nobody's Perfect" (1980).

Follow a Star, 1959
Make Mine Mink, 1960
Five Golden Hours, 1961
A Pair of Briefs, 1962
Mouse On the Moon, 1963
Ladies Who Do, 1963
Summer Holiday, 1963
Every Day's a Holiday, 1964
San Ferry Ann, 1965
Murder Most Foul, 1965
The Sandwich Man, 1966
Oliver, 1968
David Copperfield, 1969
The Twelve Chairs, 1970
Flight of the Doves, 1971
Legend of the Werewolf, 1974
Dogpound Shuffle, 1977
The Spaceman and King Arthur, 1979

DUDLEY MOORE (1935-)
Diminutive, talented comedian of films and television, often in association with Peter Cook; also pianist.

The Wrong Box, 1966
Bedazzled, 1967
Think 20th, 1967
30 is a Dangerous Age Cynthia, 1967
Inadmissible Evidence, 1968
Monte Carlo Or Bust, 1969
The Bed Sitting Room, 1969
Staircase, 1969
Alice's Adventures in Wonderland, 1972
Foul Play, 1977
Hound of the Baskervilles, 1978
10, 1979
Wholly Moses, 1980
Arthur, 1980
Dangerously, 1981

EVA MOORE (1870-1955)
Stage and screen actress of the thirties, also in Hollywood.

Chu Chin Chow, 1922
The Other Woman, 1931
Almost a Divorce, 1931
Brown Sugar, 1931
The Old Dark House, 1931
But the Flesh is Weak, 1931
I Was a Spy, 1933
Just Smith, 1933
The Song You Gave Me, 1933
House of Dreams, 1933
A Cup of Kindness, 1934
Little Stranger, 1934
Jew Suss, 1934
Blind Justice, 1934
Annie Leave the Room, 1935
Vintage Wine, 1935
Old Iron, 1938
Of Human Bondage, 1946
The Bandit of Sherwood Forest,
   1946

KEIRON MOORE (1925-)
Handsome Irish star of stage
(since 1942) and screen, also
in Hollywood.

The Voice Within, 1945
A Man About the House, 1947
Mine Own Executioner, 1947
Anna Karenina, 1948
Saints and Sinners, 1949
The Naked Heart, 1950
Honeymoon Deferred, 1951
David and Bathsheba, 1951
Ten Tall Men, 1951
Mantrap, 1952
Recoil, 1953
Conflict of Wings, 1954
The Green Scarf, 1955
Blue Peter, 1955
Satellite in the Sky, 1956
Steel Bayonet, 1957
Three Sundays to Live, 1957
The Key, 1958
The Angry Hills, 1958
The League of Gentlemen, 1959
Darby O'Gill & the Little
   People, 1959
The Day They Robbed the Bank
   of England, 1960
Seige of Sidney Street, 1960
Dr. Blood's Coffin, 1961

Day of the Triffids, 1962
I Thank a Fool, 1962
The 300 Spartans, 1962
The Main Attraction, 1963
Hide and Seek, 1963
Girl in the Headlines, 1963
The Thin Red Line, 1964
Crack in the World, 1965
Arabesque, 1966
Run Like a Thief, 1967
Bikini Paradise, 1967
Custer of the West, 1968

ROGER MOORE (1928-)
Tall, handsome leading man of
stage (1948) and films, also
well-known on tv as "Ivanhoe"
(1956) and "The Saint" (1962);
currently seen as James Bond.
Also Hollywood.

The Fuller Brush Man, 1948
Whirlpool, 1949
As Young as You Feel, 1951
The Last Time I Saw Paris,
   1954
Interrupted Melody, 1955
The King's Thief, 1955
Diane, 1956
The Miracle, 1959
The Sins of Rachel Cade, 1961
Gold of the Seven Saints, 1961
Ille Ratto Delle Sabine, 1962
Vendetta For the Saint, 1968
Crossplot, 1969
The Man Who Haunted Himself,
   1970
Live and Let Die, 1973
Gold, 1974
The Man With the Golden Gun,
   1974
That Lucky Touch, 1975
Street People, 1976
Shout at the Devil, 1976
Sherlock Holmes in New York,
   1976
The Spy Who Loved Me, 1977
The Wild Geese, 1978
Moonraker, 1979
Escape to Athena, 1979
Ffolkes, 1980
The Sea Wolves, 1980

High Road to China, 1980
Cannonball Run, 1980
Sunday Lovers, 1981
For Your Eyes Only, 1981

KENNETH MORE (1914-   )
Pleasant, popular star of the
fifties, also on stage (from
1935). Notable on television
in "The Forsyte Saga" and
"Father Brown" (1973). Adept
at comedy and dramatic characters.

Look Up and Laugh, 1935
Windmill Revels, 1937
Carry On London, 1937
Scott of the Antarctic   1948
Man On the Run, 1949
Now Barabbas, 1949
Stop Press Girl, 1949
Morning Departure, 1950
Chance of a Lifetime, 1950
The Clouded Yellow, 1950
The Franchise Affair, 1950
No Highway, 1951
Appointment With Venus, 1951
The Galloping Major, 1951
Brandy For the Parson, 1952
The Yellow Balloon, 1952
Never Let Me Go, 1953
Genevieve, 1953
Our Girl Friday, 1953
Doctor in the House, 1954
Raising a Riot, 1954
The Deep Blue Sea, 1955
Reach For the Sky, 1956
The Admirable Crichton, 1957
A Night to Remember, 1958
Next to No Time, 1958
The Sheriff of Fractured Jaw,
1958
The 39 Steps, 1959
Northwest Frontier, 1959
Sink the Bismarck, 1960
Man in the Moon, 1960
The Greengage Summer, 1961
Some People, 1962
We Joined the Navy, 1962
The Longest Day, 1962
The Comedy Man, 1963
The Mercenaries, 1967
Fraulein Doktor, 1968
Dark of the Sun, 1968

Oh What a Lovely War, 1969
The Battle of Britain, 1969
Scrooge, 1970
The Slipper and the Rose, 1976
Journey to the Center of the
Earth, 1977
Leopard in the Snow, 1978
The Spaceman and King Arthur,
1979
A Tale of Two Cities, 1980

ERIC MORECAMBE (1926-   )
Music hall comedian later famous on television in the sixties
with partner Ernie Wise; films
rare.

The Intelligence Men, 1965
That Riviera Touch, 1966
The Magnificent Two, 1967
Simon Simon, 1970

ANDRE MORELL (1909-1978)
Distinguished, intelligent character star of stage (since 1930)
and films, also in Hollywood.
Married to Joan Greenwood.

On Top of the Underworld, 1938
Thirteen Men and a Gun, 1938
Ten Days in Paris, 1939
Three Silent Men, 1940
The Case of Lady Brook, 1940
Unpublished Story, 1942
Against the Wind, 1948
No Place For Jennifer, 1950
Stage Fright, 1950
Trio, 1950
Madeleine, 1950
Seven Days to Noon, 1950
So Long at the Fair, 1950
The Clouded Yellow, 1950
High Treason, 1951
Flesh and Blood, 1951
Stolen Face, 1952
Tall Headlines, 1952
His Majesty O'Keefe, 1954
The Black Knight, 1954
The Golden Link, 1954
The Secret, 1955
They Can't Hang Me, 1955
The Black Tent, 1955

Three Cases of Murder, 1955
Summertime, 1955
The Man Who Never Was,
1956
The Baby and the Battleship,
1956
Zarak, 1957
Bridge On the River Kwai,
1957
Interpol, 1957
Paris Holiday, 1958
The Camp On Blood Island,
1958
Ben Hur, 1959
Hound of the Baskervilles,
1959
The Giant Behemoth, 1959
Cone of Silence, 1960
Mysterious Island, 1961
Shadow of the Cat, 1961
Cash On Demand, 1962
The Gold Inside, 1963
Woman of Straw, 1964
The Moonspinners, 1964
She, 1965
Judith, 1965
Plague of the Zombies, 1966
The Wrong Box, 1966
The Mummy's Shroud, 1967
The Vengeance of She,
1968
The Mercenaries, 1968
Julius Caesar, 1970
10 Rillington Place, 1971
Pope Joan, 1972
Barry Lyndon, 1975
The Slipper and the Rose,
1976
Mohammed Messenger of God,
1977
The Great Train Robbery,
1978

TERENCE MORGAN (1921-)
Handsome leading man of
stage (from 1943), films and
television. Tv series: "Sir
Francis Drake" (1962).

Hamlet, 1948
Shadow of the Past, 1950
Captain Horatio Hornblower,

1951
Encore, 1951
Mandy, 1952
It Started in Paradise, 1952
Street Corner, 1953
Turn the Key Softly, 1953
The Steel Key, 1953
Always a Bride, 1953
Forbidden Cargo, 1954
Dance Little Lady, 1954
Svengali, 1955
They Can't Hang Me, 1955
The March Hare, 1956
It's a Wonderful World, 1956
The Scamp, 1957
Tread Softly Stranger, 1958
The Shakedown, 1959
Piccadilly Third Stop, 1960
Curse of the Mummy's Tomb,
1964
Femina, 1965
Surcouf le Retour, 1965
The Penthouse, 1967
Hide and Seek, 1972

ROBERY MORLEY (1908-)
Portly, jovial, witty character
star of stage (from 1928), films
and tv, also in Hollywood.
Equally good in comedy or dramatic parts. Also playwright
(since 1935).

Marie Antoinette, 1938
You Will Remember, 1940
Major Barbara, 1941
This Was Paris, 1942
The Big Blockade, 1942
The Foreman Went to France,
1942
Partners in Crime, 1942
The Young Mr. Pitt, 1942
I Live in Grosvenor Square,
1945
Ghosts of Berkeley Square,
1947
The Small Back Room, 1948
Edward My Son, 1949
The African Queen, 1951
An Outcast of the Islands, 1952
Curtain Up, 1952
The Final Test, 1953

Gilbert and Sullivan, 1953
Melba, 1953
Beat the Devil, 1953
The Good Die Young, 1954
Rainbow Jacket, 1954
Beau Brummell, 1954
Quentin Durward, 1955
Loser Takes All, 1956
Around the World in 80 Days,
  1956
Law and Disorder, 1958
The Sheriff of Fractured Jaw,
  1958
The Journey, 1959
The Doctor's Dilemma, 1959
Libel, 1959
The Battle of the Sexes, 1959
Oscar Wilde, 1960
The Story of Joseph and His
  Brethren, 1960
The Young Ones, 1961
Go to Blazes, 1962
The Road to Hong Kong,
  1962
The Boys, 1962
Take Her She's Mine, 1963
Nine Hours to Rama, 1963
Murder at the Gallop, 1963
The Old Dark House, 1963
Ladies Who Do, 1963
Hot Enough For June, 1963
Topkapi, 1964
Of Human Bondage, 1964
Rhythm 'n Greens, 1964
The Loved One, 1965
A Study in Terror, 1965
Those Magnificent Men in
  Their Flying Machines,
  1965
The Alphabet Murders, 1965
Life at the Top, 1965
Genghis Khan, 1965
Finders Keepers, 1966
Hotel Paradiso, 1966
Way Way Out, 1966
Tender Scoundrel, 1966
Woman Times Seven, 1967
The Trygon Factor, 1967
Hot Millions, 1968
Some Girls Do, 1969
Sinful Davy, 1969
Twinky, 1969
Cromwell, 1970

Song of Norway, 1970
Doctor in Trouble, 1970
When Eight Bells Toll, 1971
Theatre of Blood, 1973
Great Expectations, 1975
The Blue Bird, 1976
Who's Killing the Great Chefs
  of Europe?, 1978
Scavenger Hunt, 1979
The Human Factor, 1980
Oh Heavenly Dog, 1980

LANA MORRIS (1930-)
Attractive brunette leading lady
of stage (1945) and films, popular in second features of the
fifties.

School For Secrets, 1946
Spring in Park Lane, 1948
The Weaker Sex, 1948
It's Hard to Be Good, 1948
Trottie True, 1949
The Chiltern Hundreds, 1949
Morning Departure, 1950
Guilt is My Shadow, 1950
Trio, 1950
The Reluctant Widow, 1950
The Woman in Question, 1950
A Tale of Five Women, 1951
The Red Beret, 1953
The Good Beginning, 1953
Black Thirteen, 1953
Trouble in Store, 1953
Point of No Return, 1953
Radio Cab Murder, 1954
The Straw Man, 1954
Home and Away, 1955
Man of the Moment, 1955
Moment of Indiscretion, 1958
Passport to Shame, 1959
No Trees in the Street, 1959
Jet Storm, 1959
The October Moth, 1960
I Start Counting, 1969

MARY MORRIS (1915-)
Prominent character actress of
stage (since 1925) and films.

Victoria the Great, 1937

Prison Without Bars, 1938
The Spy in Black, 1939
The Thief of Bagdad, 1940
Pimpernel Smith, 1941
Major Barbara, 1941
Undercover, 1943
The Agitator, 1945
The Man From Morocco, 1945
Train of Events, 1949
High Treason, 1951

PHYLLIS MORRIS (1894-   )
Character actress often seen
in cameo roles; also on stage.

The Life of the Party, 1934
Hyde Park, 1934
The Girl in the Crowd, 1934
Night Journey, 1938
Prison Without Bars, 1938
The Adventures of Tartu,
   1943
Life & Death of Colonel
   Blimp, 1943
Julia Misbehaves, 1948
My Own True Love, 1949
Three Came Home, 1950
Black Hand, 1950
Kind Lady, 1951
Mandy, 1952
Top Secret, 1952
The Devil's Disciple, 1959

BARRY MORSE (1919-   )
Leading and latterly supporting
actor of stage and screen who
went to Canada to become a
popular television personality.

The Goose Steps Out, 1942
Thunder Rock, 1942
When We Are Married, 1943
There's a Future in It, 1943
Late at Night, 1946
This Man is Mine, 1946
Mrs. Fitzherbert, 1947
Daughter of Darkness, 1948
No Trace, 1950
Kings of the Sun, 1963
Justine, 1969
The Telephone Book, 1971

Asylum, 1972
Love at First Sight, 1978
The Changeling, 1980
A Tale of Two Cities, 1980

CLIVE MORTON (1904-1975)
Character star of stage (since
1926) and films, usually seen in
stern or no-nonsense roles. Appeared on tv in "The Forsyte Saga."

The Blarney Stone, 1932
Dead Men Tell No Tales, 1938
While the Sun Shines, 1946
Jassy, 1947
Mine Own Executioner, 1947
Scott of the Antarctic, 1948
The Blind Goddess, 1948
Here Come the Huggetts, 1948
A Run For Your Money, 1949
Kind Hearts and Coronets, 1949
Trio, 1950
The Blue Lamp, 1950
The Lavender Hill Mob, 1951
Night Without Stars, 1951
His Excellency, 1952
Castle in the Air, 1952
Turn the Key Softly, 1953
All Hallowe'en, 1953
Orders Are Orders, 1954
The Harassed Hero, 1954
Carrington VC, 1955
Richard III, 1955
Beyond Mombasa, 1956
Seven Waves Away, 1957
Lucky Jim, 1957
After the Ball, 1957
The Duke Wore Jeans, 1958
The Moonraker, 1958
Next to No Time, 1958
The Safecracker, 1958
Shake Hands With the Devil,
   1959
Make Mine a Million, 1959
Clue of the New Pin, 1961
Lawrence of Arabia, 1962
A Matter of WHO, 1962
I Thank a Fool, 1962
The Alphabet Murders, 1965
Stranger in the House, 1967
Goodbye Mr. Chips, 1969
Jane Eyre, 1970

Zeppelin, 1971
Young Winston, 1972
11 Harrowhouse, 1974

PEGGY MOUNT (1916-)
Character actress of stage
and screen, often in comedy
parts; also on television, notably in "The Larkins" and
"George and the Dragon. "

The Embezzler, 1954
Sailor Beware, 1956
Dry Rot, 1956
The Naked Truth, 1958
Inn For Trouble, 1960
Watch It Sailor, 1961
Ladies Who Do, 1963
One Way Pendulum, 1964
Hotel Paradiso, 1966
Finders Keepers, 1966
Oliver, 1968

ALAN MOWBRAY (1893-1969)
Character star of stage and
screen, long in Hollywood
where he often played characters of pompous or domineering manner. Also on television in series "Colonel Flack"
(1957-58).

God's Gift to Women, 1931
Man in Possession, 1931
Guilty Hands, 1931
Alexander Hamilton, 1931
Honour of the Family, 1931
Leftover Ladies, 1931
The Silent Witness, 1932
Lovers Courageous, 1932
Nice Women, 1932
Hotel Continental, 1932
The World and the Flesh, 1932
Man About Town, 1932
Winner Take All, 1932
The Man From Yesterday,
  1932
The Man Called Back, 1932
Two Against the World, 1932
Sherlock Holmes, 1932
Our Betters, 1933

Peg O' My Heart, 1933
A Study in Scarlet, 1933
Midnight Club, 1933
Voltaire, 1933
Berkeley Square, 1933
The World Changes, 1933
Roman Scandals, 1933
Long Lost Father, 1934
The House of Rothschild, 1934
Cheaters, 1934
Where Sinners Meet, 1934
Little Man What Now, 1934
The Girl From Missouri, 1934
One More River, 1934
Charlie Chan in London, 1934
Night Life of the Gods, 1935
Becky Sharp, 1935
Lady Tubbs, 1935
The Gay Deception, 1935
She Couldn't Take It, 1935
In Person, 1935
Moon Over Her Shoulder, 1936
Rose Marie, 1936
Desire, 1936
Muss 'Em Up, 1936
Give Us This Night, 1936
The Case Against Mrs. Ames,
  1936
Fatal Lady, 1936
Mary of Scotland, 1936
My Man Godfrey, 1936
Ladies in Love, 1936
Rainbow On the River, 1936
On the Avenue, 1937
The King and the Chorus Girl,
  1937
As Good as Married, 1937
Marry the Girl, 1937
Topper, 1937
On Such a Night, 1937
Music For Madame, 1937
Stand In, 1937
Vogues of 1938, 1938
Hollywood Hotel, 1938
Merrily We Live, 1938
There Goes My Heart, 1938
Topper Takes a Trip, 1939
Never Say Die, 1939
Way Down South, 1939
The Villain Still Pursued Her,
  1940
Music in My Heart, 1940
Curtain Call, 1940

The Boys From Syracuse, 1940
The Quarterback, 1940
That Hamilton Woman, 1941
That Uncertain Feeling, 1941
Ice Capades, 1941
I Wake Up Screaming, 1942
Isle of Missing Men, 1942
We Were Dancing, 1942
Panama Hattie, 1942
A Yank at Eton, 1942
The Devil With Hitler, 1942
The Powers Girl, 1943
Slightly Dangerous, 1943
Stage Door Canteen, 1943
Holy Matrimony, 1943
His Butler's Sister, 1943
The Doughgirls, 1944
Phantom of 42nd Street, 1944
Bring On the Girls, 1945
Earl Carroll's Vanities, 1945
Where Do We Go From Here?, 1945
Men in Her Diary, 1945
Terror By Night, 1946
My Darling Clementine, 1946
Sunbonnet Sue, 1946
Prince of Thieves, 1947
Lured, 1947
Merton of the Movies, 1947
Captain From Castile, 1947
An Innocent Affair, 1948
Every Girl Should Be Married, 1948
Main Street Kid, 1949
My Dear Secretary, 1949
You're My Everything, 1949
Abbott and Costello Meet Boris Karloff, 1949
Wagonmaster, 1950
The Jackpot, 1950
Crosswinds, 1951
Dick Turpin's Ride, 1951
Just Across the Street, 1952
Blackbeard the Pirate, 1952
Androcles and the Lion, 1953
Ma and Pa Kettle at Home, 1953
Steel Cage, 1954
The King's Thief, 1955
The King and I, 1956
The Man Who Knew Too Much, 1956

Around the World in 80 Days, 1956
A Majority of One, 1962

LEONARD MUDIE (1884-1965)
Character star of Hollywood films, popular in the thirties.

The Mummy, 1932
Voltaire, 1933
The House of Rothschild, 1934
Mystery of Mr. X, 1934
Cleopatra, 1934
Viva Villa, 1934
Les Miserables, 1935
Clive of India, 1935
Cardinal Richelieu, 1935
Becky Sharp, 1935
Rendezvous, 1935
The Great Impersonation, 1935
Captain Blood, 1935
The Story of Louis Pasteur, 1936
Magnificent Obsession, 1936
Mary of Scotland, 1936
His Brother's Wife, 1936
Anthony Adverse, 1936
Lloyds of London, 1936
The King and the Chorus Girl, 1936
The League of Frightened Men, 1937
They Won't Forget, 1937
London By Night, 1937
Lancer Spy, 1937
The Jury's Secret, 1938
Kidnapped, 1938
When Were You Born?, 1938
Dark Victory, 1939
Arrest Bulldog Drummond, 1939
Man About Town, 1939
Tropic Fury, 1939
Congo Maisie, 1940
British Intelligence, 1940
Devil's Island, 1940
Foreign Correspondent, 1940
Shining Victory, 1941
The Nurse's Secret, 1941
Berlin Correspondent, 1942
Appointment in Berlin, 1943
My Name is Julia Ross, 1945

The Corn is Green, 1945
Song of My Heart, 1948
The Magnetic Monster, 1953
Autumn Leaves, 1956
The Big Fisherman, 1959

G. H. MULCASTER (-)
Character star and occasional
lead of stage and screen, in
films since 1916. Married to
Diana Napier.

God Bless Our Red White &
   Blue, 1916
The Wife Whom God Forgot,
   1920
Wild Heather, 1921
The Pipes of Pan, 1923
Mist in the Valley, 1923
The Squire of Long Hadley,
   1925
The Wonderful Wooing, 1925
A Girl of London, 1925
The Princess in the Tower,
   1928
The Man in the Iron Mask,
   1928
Sacrifice, 1929
Inquest, 1931
Purse Strings, 1933
River House Mystery, 1935
The Iron Duke, 1935
Second Bureau, 1936
The £5 Man, 1937
The Gap, 1937
Old Mother Riley, 1937
Little Dolly Daydream, 1938
Lily of Laguna, 1938
All Living Things, 1939
The Lion Has Wings, 1939
Pack Up Your Troubles, 1940
Sailors Don't Care, 1940
The Patient Vanishes, 1941
Let the People Sing, 1942
The Owner Goes Aloft, 1942
The Dummy Talks, 1943
My Learned Friend, 1943
For You Alone, 1945
Under New Management, 1946
Spring in Park Lane, 1948
Under Capricorn, 1949
That Dangerous Age, 1949

Contraband Spain, 1955
Lady of Vengeance, 1957
Downfall, 1964

BARBARA MULLEN (1914-1979)
Irish actress on stage since
1917, also latterly on television,
notably in "Dr. Findlay's Case-
book." Former dancer.

Jeannie, 1941
Thunder Rock, 1942
Welcome Mr. Washington, 1944
A Place of One's Own, 1944
The Trojan Brothers, 1946
Corridor of Mirrors, 1948
My Sister and I, 1948
Talk of a Million, 1951
The Gentle Gunman, 1952
So Little Time, 1952
The Bosun's Mate, 1953
Innocent Sinners, 1958
The Siege of Pinchgut, 1959
The Challenge, 1960
The Very Edge, 1963
It Takes a Thief, 1963
Miss MacTaggart Won't Lie
   Down, 1966

EDWARD MULHARE (1923-)
Tall Irish leading man of stage,
films and television, also in
Hollywood. Films rare. Tv
series: "The Ghost & Mrs.
Muir" (1968-69).

Hill 24 Doesn't Answer, 1955
Signpost to Murder, 1965
Von Ryan's Express, 1965
Our Man Flint, 1965
Eye of the Devil, 1966
Caprice, 1967
Gidget Grows Up, 1972
Benjamin Franklin: The Ambas-
   sador, 1974

HERBERT MUNDIN (1898-1939)
Character player of the thirties,
also on stage; in Hollywood from
1932. Former navy concert
party comic (1918).

Ashes, 1930
Enter the Queen, 1930
The Wrong Mr. Perkins, 1931
Immediate Possession, 1931
We Dine at Seven, 1931
Peace and Quiet, 1931
East Lynne, 1931
The Silent Witness, 1932
The Devil's Lottery, 1932
The Trial of Vivienne Ware,
    1932
Bachelor's Affairs, 1932
Love Me Tonight, 1932
Life Begins, 1932
Chandu the Magician, 1932
One Way Passage, 1932
Sherlock Holmes, 1932
Cavalcade, 1933
Dangerously Yours, 1933
Pleasure Cruise, 1933
Adorable, 1933
It's Great to Be Alive, 1933
Arizona to Broadway, 1933
The Devil's in Love, 1933
Shanghai Madness, 1933
Hoopla, 1933
Orient Express, 1934
Bottoms Up, 1934
Ever Since Eve, 1934
Such Women Are Dangerous,
    1934
Call it Luck, 1934
Hell in the Heavens, 1934
David Copperfield, 1935
Black Sheep, 1935
Mutiny On the Bounty, 1935
Perfect Gentleman, 1935
Charlie Chan's Secret, 1936
A Message to Garcia, 1936
Under Two Flags, 1936
Champagne Charlie, 1936
Tarzan Escapes, 1937
Another Dawn, 1937
You Can't Beat Love, 1937
Angel, 1937
Invisible Enemy, 1938
Lord Jeff, 1938
Adventures of Robin Hood,
    1938
Exposed, 1938
Society Lawyer, 1938

JANET MUNRO (1934-1972)
Scottish leading lady of stage
(1949) and films, also in Hollywood. Married: Tony Wright;
Ian Hendry.

Small Hotel, 1957
The Trollenberg Terror, 1958
Darby O'Gill & the Little Peo-
    ple, 1959
The Young and the Guilty, 1959
Third Man On the Mountain,
    1959
The Swiss Family Robinson,
    1960
The Horsemasters, 1961
The Day the Earth Caught Fire,
    1961
Life For Ruth, 1962
Bitter Harvest, 1963
Hide and Seek, 1963
A Jolly Bad Fellow, 1964
Daylight Robbery, 1964
Walk in the Shadow, 1966
Sebastian, 1968
Cry Wolf, 1968

RICHARD MURDOCH (1907-)
Comedy star with music hall
experience; also popular on
radio, often in partnership with
Arthur Askey.

Over She Goes, 1937
The Terror, 1938
Band Wagon, 1940
The Ghost Train, 1941
One Exciting Night, 1944
The Gay Adventure, 1945
It Happened in Soho, 1948
Golden Arrow, 1949
She Shall Have Murder, 1950
The Magic Box, 1951
Not a Hope in Hell, 1959
Strictly Confidential, 1959

BARBARA MURRAY (1929-)
Attractive leading actress of
stage (since 1946) and screen;
married to John Justin.

Anna Karenina, 1948
Saraband For Dead Lovers,
1948
Badger's Green, 1949
Passport to Pimlico, 1949
Poet's Pub, 1949
Don't Ever Leave Me, 1949
Boys in Brown, 1949
Tony Draws a Horse, 1950
The Dark Man, 1951
Mystery Junction, 1951
Another Man's Poison, 1951
Hot Ice, 1952
The Frightened Man, 1952
Street Corner, 1953
Death Goes to School, 1953
Meet Mr. Lucifer, 1953
The Teckman Mystery, 1954
Doctor at Large, 1957
Campbell's Kingdom, 1957
A Cry From the Streets, 1958
Operation Bullshine, 1959
Girls in Arms, 1960
Doctor in Distress, 1963
A Dandy in Aspic, 1968
Some Will, Some Won't, 1970
Up Pompeii, 1971
Tales From the Crypt, 1972
The Curse of King Tut's Tomb,
1980

STEPHEN MURRAY (1912-)
Prominent character actor and
sometimes leading man of
stage (1933), films, and television.

Pygmalion, 1938
The Prime Minister, 1941
Next of Kin, 1942
Undercover, 1943
The Master of Bankdam, 1947
My Brother Jonathan, 1947
London Belongs to Me, 1948
Silent Dust, 1948
For Them That Trespass,
1949
Now Barabbas, 1949
The Magnet, 1950
Alice in Wonderland, 1951
24 Hours of a Woman's Life,
1952

Four Sided Triangle, 1953
The Stranger's Hand, 1954
The End of the Affair, 1955
Guilty, 1956
The Door in the Wall, 1956
At the Stroke of Nine, 1957
A Tale of Two Cities, 1958
The Nun's Story, 1959
Master Spy, 1963

PETER MURRAY-HILL (1908-
1957)
Leading actor of the thirties and
forties, also on stage; married
to Phyllis Calvert.

Mr. Reeder in Room 13, 1938
A Yank at Oxford, 1938
Jane Steps Out, 1938
The Outsider, 1939
At the Villa Rose, 1939
The House of the Arrow, 1940
The Ghost Train, 1941
Rhythm Serenade, 1943
Bell Bottom George, 1943
Madonna of the Seven Moons,
1944
They Were Sisters, 1945

LIONEL MURTON (1915-)
Canadian character player long
seen in British films, often in
cameos.

Meet the Navy, 1946
The Girl is Mine, 1950
Dangerous Assignment, 1950
The Long Dark Hall, 1951
The Pickwick Papers, 1952
Our Girl Friday, 1954
Night People, 1954
The Runaway Bus, 1954
Raising a Riot, 1955
The Battle of the River Plate,
1956
Interpol, 1957
Carry On Admiral, 1957
Up the Creek, 1958
Further Up the Creek, 1958
Northwest Frontier, 1959
The Captain's Table, 1959

Make Mine a Million, 1959
Our Man in Havana, 1959
Surprise Package, 1960
Petticoat Pirates, 1961
The Main Attraction, 1962
Summer Holiday, 1963
Man in the Middle, 1964
The Truth About Spring, 1964
The Dirty Dozen, 1967
Patton, 1970
The Last Shot You Hear, 1970
Zeta One, 1970
The Revolutionary, 1970
Welcome to the Club, 1970
Confessions of a Window
    Cleaner, 1974

LAURENCE NAISMITH
(1908-   )
Friendly, likable character
actor of stage and films, also
in Hollywood. Tv series:
"The Persuaders" (1971).

A Piece of Cake, 1948
Trouble in the Air, 1948
Badger's Green, 1949
Train of Events, 1949
The Happiest Days of Your
    Life, 1950
High Treason, 1951
Chelsea Story, 1951
Hell is Sold Out, 1951
A Killer Walks, 1952
I Believe in You, 1952
Penny Princess, 1952
His Excellency, 1952
Rough Shoot, 1953
Love in Pawn, 1953
Cosh Boy, 1953
The Long Memory, 1953
Mogambo, 1953
The Beggar's Opera, 1953
The Million Pound Note, 1954
The Black Knight, 1954
The Dam Busters, 1955
Josephine and Men, 1955
Carrington VC, 1955
Richard III, 1955
Tiger in the Smoke, 1956
The Weapon, 1956
The Extra Day, 1956

The Man Who Never Was, 1956
Lust For Life, 1956
Seven Waves Away, 1957
Boy On a Dolphin, 1957
The Barretts of Wimpole Street,
    1957
Robbery Under Arms, 1957
The Gypsy and the Gentleman,
    1958
The Two-Headed Spy, 1958
Gideon's Day, 1958
Naked Earth, 1958
A Night to Remember, 1958
The Tempest, 1958
I Accuse!, 1958
Solomon and Sheba, 1959
Third Man On the Mountain,
    1959
The Criminal, 1960
The Angry Silence, 1960
Village of the Damned, 1960
Sink the Bismarck, 1960
The Trials of Oscar Wilde,
    1960
The World of Suzie Wong, 1960
Greyfriars Bobby, 1961
The Singer Not the Song, 1961
The 300 Spartans, 1962
We Joined the Navy, 1962
I Thank a Fool, 1962
The Prince and the Pauper,
    1962
Cleopatra, 1962
The Valiant, 1962
Jason and the Argonauts, 1963
The Three Lives of Thomasina,
    1964
Sky West and Crooked, 1965
The Scorpio Letters, 1966
Gypsy Girl, 1966
Camelot, 1967
Deadlier Than the Male, 1967
Fitzwilly, 1967
The Long Duel, 1967
The Valley of Gwangi, 1968
Eye of the Cat, 1969
The Bushbaby, 1970
Scrooge, 1970
Quest For Love, 1971
Diamonds Are Forever, 1971
The Amazing Mr. Blunden, 1972
Young Winston, 1972
Romeo and Juliet, 1979

ALAN NAPIER (1903-)
Tall, stately character actor
of stage and screen, in Hollywood from 1940. Usually cast
in noble parts. Tv series:
"Batman" (1965-67), as Alfred,
the butler.

Nettleford, 1930
Caste, 1930
Stamboul, 1931
In a Monastery Garden, 1932
ATP, 1933
Loyalties, 1933
Bitter Sweet, 1933
Wings Over Africa, 1936
Premier Stafford, 1936
For Valour, 1937
Capitol, 1937
The Wife of General Ling,
    1938
Four Just Men, 1939
We Are Not Alone, 1939
The Invisible Man Returns,
    1940
House of the Seven Gables,
    1940
Confirm or Deny, 1941
A Yank at Eton, 1942
Random Harvest, 1942
Cat People, 1942
Eagle Squadron, 1942
Madame Curie, 1943
Lassie Come Home, 1943
The Song of Bernadette, 1943
Assignment in Brittany, 1943
Appointment in Berlin, 1943
Lost Angel, 1944
Action in Arabia, 1944
Ministry of Fear, 1944
The Hairy Ape, 1944
The Uninvited, 1944
Thirty Seconds Over Tokyo,
    1944
Mademoiselle Fifi, 1945
Hangover Square, 1945
Isle of the Dead, 1945
A Scandal in Paris, 1946
House of Horrors, 1946
Three Strangers, 1946
Dark Waters, 1946
High Conquest, 1946
Driftwood, 1947

The Strange Woman, 1947
Adventure Island, 1947
The Lone Wolf in London, 1947
Sinbad the Sailor, 1947
Forever Amber, 1947
Fiesta, 1947
Ivy, 1947
Unconquered, 1947
Joan of Arc, 1948
Macbeth, 1948
Johnny Belinda, 1948
Criss Cross, 1949
The Red Danube, 1949
Tarzan's Magic Fountain, 1949
My Own True Love, 1949
A Connecticut Yankee in King
    Arthur's Court, 1949
Manhandled, 1949
The Hills of Home, 1949
Challenge to Lassie, 1950
Tripoli, 1950
Double Crossbones, 1950
The Great Caruso, 1951
Across the Wide Missouri,
    1951
The Blue Veil, 1951
The Highwayman, 1951
The Strange Door, 1951
Big Jim McLain, 1952
Young Bess, 1953
Julius Caesar, 1953
Desiree, 1954
Moonfleet, 1955
The Court Jester, 1956
Miami Expose, 1956
The Mole People, 1956
Until They Sail, 1957
Journey to the Center of the
    Earth, 1959
The Premature Burial, 1962
Tender is the Night, 1962
Marnie, 1964
My Fair Lady, 1964
The Loved One, 1965
Signpost to Muder, 1965
36 Hours, 1965
Batman, 1966

DIANA NAPIER (1908-)
Silent film small-part player
who achieved stardom during
the 30s; formerly married to
G. H. Mulcaster.

The Rat, 1925
The Squire of Long Hadley,
1925
The King's Highway, 1927
The Farmer's Wife, 1928
The Guns of Loos, 1930
Shadows, 1931
Sunshine Susie, 1931
The Beggar Student, 1931
Dance Pretty Lady, 1932
Wedding Rehearsal, 1932
Her First Affaire, 1932
Strange Evidence, 1933
For Love of You, 1933
Private Life of Henry VIII,
1933
Catherine the Great, 1934
The Warren Case, 1934
Falling in Love, 1934
Private Life of Don Juan, 1934
Hearts Desire, 1935
Royal Cavalcade, 1935
Mimi, 1935
Pagliacci, 1936
Land Without Music, 1936
I Was a Dancer, 1949
Bait, 1950

RUSSELL NAPIER (1910-
1974)
Australian character star of
the 50s and 60s; often seen as
police inspector or other officials.

Blind Man's Bluff, 1952
Death of An Angel, 1952
Black Orchid, 1953
The Unholy Four, 1954
The Dark Stairway, 1954
The Strange Case of Blondie,
1954
Conflict of Wings, 1954
Little Red Monkey, 1955
The Brain Machine, 1955
Blue Peter, 1955
A Time to Kill, 1955
The Narrowing Circle, 1956
Man in the Road, 1956
Guilty, 1956
The Last Man to Hang, 1956
Destination Death, 1956

Person Unknown, 1956
The Lonely House, 1957
The Shiralee, 1957
Robbery Under Arms, 1957
The White Cliffs Mystery, 1957
Night Crossing, 1957
The Case of the Smiling Widow,
1957
A Night to Remember, 1958
Tread Softly Stranger, 1958
Crime of Honour, 1958
The Unseeing Eye, 1959
The Witness, 1959
The Ghost Train Murder, 1959
The Angry Silence, 1960
Hell is a City, 1960
The Last Train, 1960
Evidence in Concrete, 1960
Francis of Assisi, 1961
The Mark, 1961
The Grand Junction Case, 1961
The Never Never Murder, 1961
HMS Defiant, 1962
Man in the Middle, 1964
Blood Beast Terror, 1968
Twisted Nerve, 1968
Nobody Runs Forever, 1968

CHARLIE NAUGHTON (1887-
1976)
Scottish comedian popular during
the 30s, long teamed with Jimmy Gold; also member of the
"Crazy Gang."

Sign Please, 1933
My Lucky Star, 1933
Cock O' the North, 1935
Highland Fling, 1935
Wise Guys, 1937
Okay For Sound, 1937
Alf's Button Afloat, 1938
The Frozen Limits, 1939
Gasbags, 1940
Down Melody Lane, 1943
Life is a Circus, 1959

DAME ANNA NEAGLE (1904-)
Distinguished leading lady of
stage and screen, former dancer
(1917); also in Hollywood.

Married to director/producer Herbert Wilcox (1891-1977).

Should a Doctor Tell, 1930
The Chinese Bungalow, 1930
Goodnight Vienna, 1932
The Flag Lieutenant, 1932
The Little Damozel, 1933
Bitter Sweet, 1933
The Queen's Affair, 1934
Nell Gwyn, 1934
Peg of Old Drury, 1935
Limelight, 1936
The Three Maxims, 1936
London Melody, 1937
Victoria the Great, 1937
Sixty Glorious Years, 1938
Nurse Edith Cavell, 1939
Irene, 1940
No No Nanette, 1940
Sunny, 1941
They Flew Alone, 1942
Forever and a Day, 1943
The Yellow Canary, 1943
I Live in Grosvenor Square, 1945
Royal Wedding, 1946
Piccadilly Incident, 1946
The Courtneys of Curzon Street, 1947
Spring in Park Lane, 1948
Maytime in Mayfair, 1949
Elizabeth of Ladymead, 1949
Odette, 1950
The Lady With a Lamp, 1951
Derby Day, 1952
Lilacs in the Spring, 1954
King's Rhapsody, 1955
My Teenage Daughter, 1956
The Man Who Wouldn't Talk, 1957
The Lady is a Square, 1958

JIMMY NERVO (1897-1975)
Comedy star of the thirties, teamed with Teddy Knox since 1919; member of the "Crazy Gang." Former juggler (1912).

Nervo and Knox, 1926
The Rising Generation, 1928
Alf's Button, 1930

It's in the Bag, 1936
Skylarks, 1936
Okay For Sound, 1937
Cavalcade of the Stars, 1938
Alf's Button Afloat, 1938
The Frozen Limits, 1939
Gasbags, 1940
Life is a Circus, 1959

CATHLEEN NESBITT (1888-)
Character actress of stage (since 1910), films and television, also in Hollywood. On tv in "The Farmer's Daughter," "Upstairs Downstairs."

Canaries Sometimes Sing, 1930
The Frightened Lady, 1932
Falling in Love, 1934
Passing of the Third Floor Back, 1935
Hearts of Humanity, 1936
Beloved Vagabond, 1936
Well Done Henry, 1937
Against the Tide, 1937
Knights For a Day, 1937
A Dream of Love, 1938
Little Dolly Daydream, 1938
Pygmalion, 1938
Gaslight, 1940
The Door With Seven Locks, 1940
The Lamp Still Burns, 1943
Fanny By Gaslight, 1944
The Agitator, 1945
Macbeth, 1945
Men of Two Worlds, 1946
Jassy, 1947
Nicholas Nickleby, 1947
Madness of the Heart, 1949
So Long at the Fair, 1950
Three Coins in the Fountain, 1954
Black Widow, 1954
Desiree, 1954
An Affair to Remember, 1957
Separate Tables, 1958
The Parent Trap, 1961
Promise Her Anything, 1966
The Trygon Factor, 1967
Staircase, 1969
Villain, 1971

French Connection II, 1975
Family Plot, 1976
Julia, 1977
Abide With Me, 1978

DERREN NESBITT (1932-)
Smiling character actor and
occasional writer/director,
often cast in evil or sinister
roles.

A Night to Remember, 1958
Life in Danger, 1959
The Man in the Back Seat,
  1960
In the Nick, 1960
The Sword of Sherwood
  Forest, 1960
Victim, 1961
Strongroom, 1962
Term of Trial, 1962
Kill Or Cure, 1963
The Informers, 1963
Moll Flanders, 1965
The Blue Max, 1966
Operation Third Form, 1966
The Naked Runner, 1967
Where Eagles Dare, 1968
Nobody Runs Forever, 1968
Monte Carlo Or Bust, 1969
Ooh You Are Awful, 1972
Innocent Bystanders, 1972
Get Charlie Tully, 1977
The House On Garibaldi Street,
  1979

JOHN NETTLETON (1929-)
Strong supporting actor mainly
on stage; films infrequent.

A Man For All Seasons, 1966
And Soon the Darkness, 1970
The Last Shot You Hear, 1970
Black Beauty, 1972
Abide With Me, 1978
The Tempest, 1980

JOHN NEVILLE (1925-)
Leading man of the sixties, primarily seen on stage.

Oscar Wilde, 1960
Mr. Topaze, 1962
Billy Budd, 1962
Unearthly Stranger, 1963
A Study in Terror, 1965
The Adventures of Gerard,
  1970

DEREK NEWARK (-)
Character actor of the 60s and
70s; also on stage and tv.

City Under the Sea, 1965
The Little Ones, 1965
The Blue Max, 1966
Oh What a Lovely War, 1969
Fragment of Fear, 1970
The Offence, 1972
The Unpleasantness at the Bell-
  ona Club, 1973
The Black Windmill, 1974
Escape From the Dark,
  1976

MARY NEWLAND (1905-)
Leading lady of stage (1924),
popular in silent and early
sound films; married to di-
rector/writer Reginald Denham
(1894-).

Bindle Introduced, 1926
Bindle in Charge, 1926
Bindle Millionaire, 1926
Bindle's Cocktail, 1926
Bindle Matchmaker, 1926
Bindle at the Party, 1926
The Flag Lieutenant, 1926
A Daughter in Revolt, 1927
Passion Island, 1927
Further Adventures of the Flag
  Lieutenant, 1927
City of Youth, 1928
Virginia's Husband, 1928
Troublesome Wives, 1929
To Oblige a Lady, 1930
The Officer's Mess, 1931
Jealousy, 1931
The Jewel, 1932
Ask Beccles, 1933
Easy Money, 1934

Death at Broadcasting House,
1934
The Price of Wisdom, 1935
The Small Man, 1935
The Silent Passenger, 1935

ANTHONY NEWLANDS
(1926-   )
Character player of the sixties
primarily seen on tv; often
cast as underhanded characters.

Beyond This Place, 1959
The Trials of Oscar Wilde,
1960
The Fourth Square, 1961
Solo For Sparrow, 1962
The Undesirable Neighbour,
1963
The £20,000 Kiss, 1963
Hysteria, 1964
Circus of Fear, 1966
Theatre of Death, 1967
Vendetta For the Saint, 1968
Scream and Scream Again, 1969
Murder is a One-Act Play, 1974

ANTHONY NEWLEY (1931-   )
Talented actor, singer, composer, director and comedian;
former child performer. Married: Joan Collins; Ann Lynn.

Dusty Bates, 1947
The Little Ballerina, 1947
Vice Versa, 1947
Oliver Twist, 1948
The Guinea Pig, 1948
Vote For Huggett, 1949
A Boy, a Girl, and a Bike,
1949
Don't Ever Leave Me, 1949
Highly Dangerous, 1950
Those People Next Door,
1951
Top of the Form, 1952
Up to His Neck, 1954
Blue Peter, 1955
Cockleshell Heroes, 1955
Above Us the Waves, 1955
The Battle of the River

Plate, 1956
Port Afrique, 1956
Last Man to Hang, 1956
X The Unknown, 1956
The Good Companions, 1956
How to Murder a Rich Uncle,
1957
Fire Down Below, 1957
High Flight, 1957
No Time to Die, 1958
The Man Inside, 1958
The Lady is a Square, 1958
Idol On Parade, 1959
The Bandit of Zhobe, 1959
Heart of a Man, 1959
Killers of Kilimanjaro, 1959
Jazzboat, 1959
In the Nick, 1960
Let's Get Married, 1960
The Small World of Sammy
Lee, 1963
Stop the World I Want to Get
Off, 1966
Think 20th, 1967
Dr. Dolittle, 1967
Sweet November, 1968
Can Heironymous Merkin, 1969
Mr. Quilp, 1974
It Seemed Like a Good Idea at
the Time, 1976

NANETTE NEWMAN (1932-   )
Pretty leading lady of the six-
ties and seventies; married to
Bryan Forbes.

Personal Affair, 1953
The League of Gentlemen, 1959
Faces in the Dark, 1960
House of Mystery, 1961
Pit of Darkness, 1961
The Rebel, 1961
The L-Shaped Room, 1962
The Painted Smile, 1962
The Wrong Arm of the Law,
1963
Twice Round the Daffodils,
1963
Of Human Bondage, 1964
Seance On a Wet Afternoon,
1964
The Wrong Box, 1966

The Whisperers, 1967
Deadfall, 1968
The Madwoman of Chaillot, 1969
Captain Nemo and the Underwater City, 1969
Oh What a Lovely War, 1969
The Raging Moon, 1970
Long Ago Tomorrow, 1971
The Love Ban, 1972
It's a 2' 6" Above the Ground World, 1972
Man at the Top, 1973
The Stepford Wives, 1975
International Velvet, 1978

ROBERT NEWTON (1905-1956)
Delightfully hammy star character actor of stage (since 1920) and films, also in Hollywood. Adept at villainous characters. Tv series: "Long John Silver" (1954).

Reunion, 1932
Dark Journey, 1937
Fire Over England, 1937
Farewell Again, 1937
The Squeaker, 1937
The Green Cockatoo, 1937
I Claudius, 1937
Vessel of Wrath, 1938
Yellow Sands, 1938
21 Days, 1939
Dead Men Are Dangerous, 1939
Jamaica Inn, 1939
Poison Pen, 1939
Hell's Cargo, 1939
Bulldog Sees it Through, 1940
Gaslight, 1940
Busman's Honeymoon, 1940
Channel Incident, 1940
Major Barbara, 1941
Hatter's Castle, 1941
They Flew Alone, 1942
This Happy Breed, 1944
Henry V, 1944
Night Boat to Dublin, 1946
Odd Man Out, 1947
Temptation Harbour, 1947

Snowbound, 1948
Oliver Twist, 1948
Kiss the Blood Off My Hands, 1948
Obsession, 1949
Treasure Island, 1950
Waterfront, 1950
Tom Brown's School Days, 1951
Soldiers Three, 1951
Les Miserables, 1952
Blackbeard the Pirate, 1952
Androcles and the Lion, 1953
The Desert Rats, 1953
The High and the Mighty, 1954
The Beachcomber, 1954
Long John Silver, 1955
Around the World in 80 Days, 1956

MARIE NEY (1895-)
Character actress with long stage experience.

Escape, 1930
Home Sweet Home, 1933
The Wandering Jew, 1933
Scrooge, 1935
Brief Ecstasy, 1937
Jamaica Inn, 1939
Uneasy Terms, 1948
The Romantic Age, 1949
Shadow of the Past, 1950
Seven Days to Noon, 1950
Conspirator, 1950
Night Was Our Friend, 1951
The Lavender Hill Mob, 1951
Simba, 1955
Yield to the Night, 1956
The Surgeon's Knife, 1957
Witchcraft, 1964

ANTHONY NICHOLLS (1902-1977)
Dignified character star of stage and films, usually seen in officious parts.

The Laughing Lady, 1946
The Guinea Pig, 1948
The Hasty Heart, 1949
Man On the Run, 1949

Portrait of Clare, 1950
The Woman With No Name,
1950
The Dancing Years, 1950
No Place For Jennifer, 1950
The Franchise Affair, 1951
High Treason, 1951
The Woman's Angle, 1952
Street Corner, 1953
The House of the Arrow, 1953
The Weak and the Wicked,
1954
Make Me an Offer, 1954
Happy Ever After, 1954
The Green Scarf, 1955
The Safecracker, 1958
Dunkirk, 1958
The Horsemasters, 1961
Victim, 1961
Night of the Eagle, 1962
Seven Keys, 1962
The Pumpkin Eater, 1964
Othello, 1965
Mr. Ten Per Cent, 1966
A Man For All Seasons, 1966
Our Mother's House, 1967
If, 1968
The Battle of Britain, 1969
The Walking Stick, 1970
One More Time, 1970
The Man Who Haunted Him-
self, 1970
The Omen, 1976
Day of the Woman, 1977

DANDY NICHOLS (1907-)
Comedy character actress
often cast as cockney charlady; well-known also on television as Else in "Till Death
Us Do Part" (1966-68).

Hue and Cry, 1946
The Fallen Idol, 1948
The Winslow Boy, 1948
Here Come the Huggetts,
1948
The History of Mr. Polly,
1949
Tony Draws a Horse, 1950
Mr. Lord Says No, 1952
Street Corner, 1953

The Intruder, 1953
The Deep Blue Sea, 1955
Where There's a Will, 1955
Not So Dusty, 1956
Yield to the Night, 1956
Carry On Sergeant, 1958
A Cry From the Streets, 1958
Don't Talk to Strange Men,
1962
Ladies Who Do, 1962
The Leather Boys, 1963
Act of Murder, 1964
The Knack, 1965
Georgy Girl, 1966
How I Won the War, 1967
The Birthday Party, 1968
Till Death Us Do Part, 1968
The Bed Sitting Room, 1969
O Lucky Man, 1973
Confessions of a Window
Cleaner, 1974

NORA NICHOLSON (1892-1973)
Stage and screen character
player who specializes in eccentric or slightly dotty roles.

The Blue Lagoon, 1949
Fools Rush In, 1949
Crow Hollow, 1952
Tread Softly, 1952
Raising a Riot, 1955
Hornet's Nest, 1955
A Town Like Alice, 1956
The Captain's Table, 1959
Upstairs and Downstairs, 1959
Dangerous Afternoon, 1961
The Devil Doll, 1963
Diamonds For Breakfast, 1968
Run a Crooked Mile, 1969
Say Hello to Yesterday, 1970

DEREK NIMMO (1931-)
Comic actor of films and television specializing in humorous
voices. Also on stage.

The Millionairess, 1961
The Amorous Prawn, 1962
Tamahine, 1963
Hot Enough For June, 1963

Murder Ahoy, 1964
The Bargee, 1964
Coast of Skeletons, 1965
Joey Boy, 1965
The Liquidator, 1966
The Yellow Hat, 1966
Mr. Ten Per Cent, 1966
Casino Royale, 1967
A Talent For Loving, 1969
One of Our Dinosaurs is
Missing, 1975

BRIAN NISSEN (1927-)
Small-part character in occasional films; mainly on stage.

The Demi-Paradise, 1943
Henry V, 1944
They Were Sisters, 1945
Badger's Green, 1949
Richard III, 1955
The Dam Busters, 1955
Second Fiddle, 1957
Top Floor Girl, 1959
Man Accused, 1959
The Fur Collar, 1962
The Marked One, 1963
Ring of Spies, 1963

DAVID NIVEN (1909-)
Charming, debonair Scottish
leading man, also in Hollywood. Also novelist. For-
mer soldier.

Mutiny On the Bounty, 1935
Barbary Coast, 1935
Without Regret, 1935
A Feather in Her Hat, 1935
Splendor, 1935
Rose Marie, 1936
Palm Springs, 1936
Thank You Jeeves, 1936
Dodsworth, 1936
Beloved Enemy, 1936
Charge of the Light Brigade,
1936
We Have Our Moments, 1937
The Prisoner of Zenda, 1937
Dinner at the Ritz, 1937
Bluebeard's Eighth Wife, 1938

Four Men and a Prayer, 1938
Three Blind Mice, 1938
The Dawn Patrol, 1938
Wuthering Heights, 1939
Bachelor Mother, 1939
The Real Glory, 1939
Eternally Yours, 1939
Raffles, 1940
The First of the Few, 1942
The Way Ahead, 1944
A Matter of Life and Death,
1946
Magnificent Doll, 1946
The Perfect Marriage, 1947
The Other Love, 1947
The Bishop's Wife, 1947
Bonnie Prince Charlie, 1948
Enchantment, 1948
A Kiss in the Dark, 1949
The Elusive Pimpernel, 1950
A Kiss For Corliss, 1950
The Toast of New Orleans,
1950
Soldiers Three, 1951
Happy Go Lovely, 1951
Appointment With Venus, 1951
The Lady Says No, 1952
The Moon is Blue, 1953
The Love Lottery, 1954
Happy Ever After, 1954
Carrington VC, 1955
The King's Thief, 1955
The Birds and the Bees, 1956
Around the World in 80 Days,
1956
Oh Men Oh Women, 1957
The Little Hut, 1957
My Man Godfrey, 1957
The Silken Affair, 1957
Bonjour Tristesse, 1958
Separate Tables, 1958
Ask Any Girl, 1959
Happy Anniversary, 1959
Please Don't Eat the Daisies,
1960
The Guns of Navarone, 1961
The Best of Enemies, 1961
The Road to Hong Kong, 1962
Guns of Darkness, 1962
Conquered City, 1962
55 Days at Peking, 1963
The Pink Panther, 1963
Bedtime Story, 1964

Lady L, 1965
Where the Spies Are, 1966
Eye of the Devil, 1966
Casino Royale, 1967
Think 20th, 1967
Prudence and the Pill, 1968
The Impossible Years, 1968
The Extraordinary Seaman,
     1969
Before Winter Comes, 1969
The Brain, 1970
The Statue, 1971
King, Queen, Knave, 1972
Paper Tiger, 1975
Old Dracula, 1975
No Deposit No Return, 1976
Murder By Death, 1976
Candleshoe, 1978
Death On the Nile, 1978
A Man Called Intrepid, 1979
Escape to Athena, 1979
A Nightingale Sang in Ber-
     keley Square, 1980
The Sea Wolves, 1980
The Prodigal Son, 1980
Rough Cut, 1980

CHRISTINE NORDEN (1923-)
Leading lady of the late forties
and early fifties; former singer.

Mine Own Executioner, 1947
An Ideal Husband, 1948
Night Beat, 1948
Idol of Paris, 1948
Saints and Sinners, 1949
Interrupted Journey, 1949
Black Widow, 1951
Reluctant Heroes, 1951
A Case For PC 49, 1951

PAT NYE (1908-)
Small-part actress of stage,
seen very rarely in films.

Mr. Perrin and Mr. Traill,
     1949
Rover and Me, 1949
The Adventures of PC 49, 1949
The Mirror Crack'd, 1980

MERLE OBERON (1911-1979)
Beautiful leading lady, former
dance hostess (1928); mainly in
Hollywood from 1936.

Alf's Button, 1930
The W Plan, 1930
Never Trouble Trouble, 1931
Fascination, 1931
Service For Ladies, 1932
For the Love of Mike, 1932
Ebb Tide, 1932
Aren't We All, 1932
Wedding Rehearsal, 1932
Men of Tomorrow, 1932
Private Life of Henry VIII,
     1933
The Battle, 1934
Broken Melody, 1934
Private Life of Don Juan, 1934
The Scarlet Pimpernel, 1935
The Dark Angel, 1935
Folies Bergere, 1935
These Three, 1936
Beloved Enemy, 1936
I Claudius, 1937
Over the Moon, 1937
The Divorce of Lady X, 1938
The Cowboy and the Lady, 1938
Wuthering Heights, 1939
The Lion Has Wings, 1939
Till We Meet Again, 1940
That Uncertain Feeling, 1941
Affectionately Yours, 1941
Lydia, 1941
Forever and a Day, 1943
Stage Door Canteen, 1943
First Comes Courage, 1943
The Lodger, 1944
Dark Waters, 1945
This Love of Ours, 1945
A Song to Remember, 1945
Night in Paradise, 1946
Temptation, 1946
Night Song, 1947
Berlin Express, 1948
Pardon My French, 1951
24 Hours of a Woman's Life,
     1952
All is Possible in Granada,
     1954
Desiree, 1954

Deep in My Heart, 1954
The Price of Fear, 1956
Of Love and Desire, 1963
The Oscar, 1966
Hotel, 1967
Interval, 1973

UNA O'CONNOR (1880-1959)
Diminutive Irish character
actress in Hollywood, typically
seen as maids and the like;
formerly with the Abbey
Theatre.

Dark Red Roses, 1929
Murder, 1930
Timbuctoo, 1933
Mary Stevens MD, 1933
Cavalcade, 1933
Pleasure Cruise, 1933
The Invisible Man, 1933
Orient Express, 1934
Stingaree, 1934
Chained, 1934
The Barretts of Wimpole
    Street, 1934
David Copperfield, 1935
The Bride of Frankenstein,
    1935
The Informer, 1935
The Perfect Gentleman, 1935
Little Lord Fauntleroy, 1936
Rose Marie, 1936
Suzy, 1936
Lloyds of London, 1936
The Plough and the Stars,
    1936
Personal Property, 1937
Call it a Day, 1937
The Return of the Frog, 1938
Adventures of Robin Hood,
    1938
We Are Not Alone, 1939
His Brother's Keeper, 1939
He Stayed For Breakfast, 1940
It All Came True, 1940
Lillian Russell, 1940
The Sea Hawk, 1940
Strawberry Blonde, 1941
How Green Was My Valley,
    1941

Always in My Heart, 1942
My Favorite Spy, 1942
Random Harvest, 1942
This Land is Mine, 1942
Holy Matrimony, 1943
The Canterville Ghost, 1944
My Pal Wolf, 1944
Government Girl, 1944
Christmas in Connecticut, 1945
The Bells of St. Mary's, 1945
Cluny Brown, 1946
Of Human Bondage, 1946
The Return of Monte Cristo,
    1946
Ivy, 1947
Lost Honeymoon, 1947
Adventures of Don Juan, 1948
The Corpse Came COD, 1948
Fighting Father Dunne, 1948
Witness For the Prosectuion,
    1957

JOSEPH O'CONOR (1910-   )
Irish character actor in occasional films, primarily seen on
stage and television. Appeared
as Old Jolyon in "The Forsyte
Saga" (1966).

Stranger at My Door, 1950
Gorgo, 1961
Crooks in Cloisters, 1963
The Gorgon, 1964
Oliver, 1968
Anne of the Thousand Days,
    1970
Doomwatch, 1972
The Black Windmill, 1974

DENIS O'DEA (1903-1978)
Versatile Irish actor of stage
and screen, often cast in likable official roles; married to
Siobhan McKenna. Also Hollywood.

The Informer, 1935
Plough and the Stars, 1936
Odd Man Out, 1947
The Fallen Idol, 1948

The Mark of Cain, 1948
The Bad Lord Byron, 1949
Under Capricorn, 1949
Landfall, 1949
Marry Me, 1949
Treasure Island, 1950
The Long Dark Hall, 1951
Captain Horatio Hornblower,
  1951
Never Take No For An Answer,
  1952
Niagara, 1953
Sea Devils, 1953
Mogambo, 1953
The Rising of the Moon, 1957
The Story of Esther Costello,
  1957
Darby O'Gill and the Little
  People, 1959
Esther and the King, 1960

JIMMY O'DEA (1899-1965)
Irish music hall comic in oc-
casional sporadic films; also
Hollywood.

Casey's Millions, 1922
Cruiskeen Lawn, 1922
Jimmy Boy, 1935
Blarney, 1938
Let's Be Famous, 1938
Penny Paradise, 1938
Cheer Boys Cheer, 1939
Ireland's Border Line, 1939
The Rising of the Moon, 1957
Darby O'Gill and the Little
  People, 1959
Johnny Nobody, 1961

BERNADETTE O'FARRELL
  (1926-)
Irish leading actress in occasional films, married to director Frank Launder (1907-).

Captain Boycott, 1947
The Happiest Days of Your
  Life, 1950
Lady Godiva Rides Again,
  1951
Life in Her Hands, 1951

Lady in the Fog, 1952
The Square Ring, 1953
Gilbert and Sullivan, 1953
The Bridal Path, 1959

IAN OGILVY (1943-)
Good-looking light leading man
of films and television. Tv
series: "The Return of the
Saint" (1977).

The She-Beast, 1966
The Day the Fish Came Out, 1967
Stranger in the House, 1967
The Sorcerers, 1967
Witchfinder General, 1968
Wuthering Heights, 1970
Waterloo, 1970
The Invincible Six, 1970
And Now the Screaming Starts,
  1973
No Sex Please We're British,
  1973
The Gathering Storm, 1974

MAUREEN O'HARA (1920-)
Beautiful red-headed Irish leading lady of stage (since 1934)
and films, mainly in Hollywood.
Also on radio (1932).

My Irish Molly, 1938
Kicking the Moon Around, 1938
Jamaica Inn, 1939
The Hunchback of Notre Dame,
  1939
A Bill of Divorcement, 1940
Dance Girl Dance, 1940
They Met in Argentina, 1941
How Green Was My Valley,
  1941
To the Shores of Tripoli, 1942
Ten Gentlemen From West
  Point, 1942
The Black Swan, 1942
The Immortal Sergeant, 1943
This Land is Mine, 1943
The Fallen Sparrow, 1943
Buffalo Bill, 1944
The Spanish Main, 1945
Sentimental Journey, 1946

Do You Love Me?, 1946
Sinbad the Sailor, 1947
The Homestretch, 1947
Miracle On 34th Street, 1947
The Foxes of Harrow, 1947
Sitting Pretty, 1948
Britannia Mews, 1949
A Woman's Secret, 1949
Father Was a Fullback, 1949
Baghdad, 1949
Comanche Territory, 1950
Tripoli, 1950
Rio Grande, 1950
Flame of Araby, 1951
At Sword's Point, 1952
The Quiet Man, 1952
Kangaroo, 1952
Against All Flags, 1952
Redhead From Wyoming, 1952
War Arrow, 1953
Malaga, 1954
The Long Grey Line, 1955
The Magnificent Matador, 1955
Lady Godiva, 1955
Lisbon, 1956
Everything But the Truth, 1956
The Wings of Eagles, 1957
Our Man in Havana, 1959
The Parent Trap, 1961
The Deadly Companions, 1961
Mr. Hobbs Takes a Vacation, 1962
Spencer's Mountain, 1963
McClintock, 1963
Battle of the Villa Fiorita, 1965
The Rare Breed, 1966
How to Commit Marriage, 1969
How Do I Love Thee, 1970
Big Jake, 1971
The Red Pony, 1972

DAN O'HERLIHY (1919-)
Irish character player and occasional lead of stage, films and tv, also in Hollywood. Tv series: "The Travels of Jamie McPheeters" (1963).

Hungry Hill, 1946
Odd Man Out, 1947

Kidnapped, 1948
Macbeth, 1948
Larceny, 1948
Actors and Sin, 1950
The Desert Fox, 1951
The Blue Veil, 1951
Soldiers Three, 1951
At Sword's Point, 1951
Operation Secret, 1952
The Highwayman, 1952
Adventures of Robinson Crusoe, 1952
Bengal Brigade, 1953
Invasion USA, 1953
The Black Shield of Falworth, 1954
The Purple Mask, 1955
The Virgin Queen, 1955
That Woman Opposite, 1957
Home Before Dark, 1958
Imitation of Life, 1958
City After Midnight, 1959
A Terrible Beauty, 1959
One Foot in Hell, 1960
The Cabinet of Caligari, 1961
King of the Roaring 20s, 1961
Fail Safe, 1964
100 Rifles, 1969
The Big Cube, 1969
Waterloo, 1970
The Carey Treatment, 1972
QB VII, 1973
The Tamarind Seed, 1974
MacArthur, 1977

ANTHONY OLIVER (1923-)
Welsh character actor of the 50s and 60s, also on television.

Once a Jolly Swagman, 1948
The Clouded Yellow, 1950
The Magnet, 1951
Glory at Sea, 1952
Penny Princess, 1952
Street Corner, 1953
The Runaway Bus, 1954
To Dorothy a Son, 1954
They Can't Hang Me, 1955
Lost, 1956
Tears For Simon, 1957
Checkpoint, 1957
The Nudist Story, 1960

Crossroads to Crime, 1960
The Entertainer, 1960
Transatlantic, 1961
The Fourth Square, 1961
Out of the Fog, 1962
Danger By My Side, 1962
HMS Defiant, 1962

CHARLES OLIVER (-)
Character actor and supporting
player of the thirties.

Second Bureau, 1936
Midnight at Madame Tussaud's,
    1936
Wings Over Africa, 1936
The Avenging Hand, 1936
Beloved Imposter, 1936
The Green Cockatoo, 1937
Fifty Shilling Boxer, 1937
If I Were Boss, 1938
The Drum, 1938
The Lady Vanishes, 1938
Mountains O' Mourne, 1938
Sexton Blake & the Hooded
    Terror, 1938
Ask a Policeman, 1939
This Man in Paris, 1939
Under Your Hat, 1940
Crooks' Tour, 1940
Inspector Hornleigh Goes to
    It, 1941

VIC OLIVER (1898-1964)
Popular Austrian comedy star
of radio and films, long in
Britain. Former businessman
and conductor. Married to
Sarah Churchill.

Rhythm in the Air, 1936
Who's Your Lady Friend?,
    1937
Around the Town, 1938
Meet Mr. Penny, 1938
Room For Two, 1940
He Found a Star, 1941
Hi Gang, 1941
Give Us the Moon, 1944
I'll Be Your Sweetheart, 1945
For Old Times' Sake, 1948

LORD LAURENCE OLIVIER
    (1907-)
Distinguished, superior star of
stage (since 1922) and screen,
outstanding in any type of role
and also a master Shakesperian
interpreter.   Also in Hollywood.
Married: Jill Esmond; Vivien
Leigh; Joan Plowright.   Also
producer and director of stage
and films.

Too Many Crooks, 1930
The Temporary Widow, 1930
Murder For Sale, 1930
Friends and Lovers, 1931
Potiphar's Wife, 1931
The Yellow Passport, 1931
Westward Passage, 1932
No Funny Business, 1933
Perfect Understanding, 1933
Moscow Nights, 1935
As You Like It, 1936
Fire Over England, 1937
The Divorce of Lady X, 1938
Q Planes, 1939
Wuthering Heights, 1939
21 Days, 1939
Rebecca, 1940
Conquest of the Air, 1940
Pride and Prejudice, 1940
Words For Battle (voice), 1941
Lady Hamilton, 1941
49th Parallel, 1941
The Demi-Paradise, 1943
Henry V, 1944
This Happy Breed (voice), 1944
Hamlet, 1948
The Magic Box, 1951
Carrie, 1952
The Beggar's Opera, 1953
A Queen is Crowned (voice),
    1953
Richard III, 1955
The Prince and the Showgirl,
    1957
The Devil's Disciple, 1959
The Moon and Sixpence, 1959
The Entertainer, 1960
Spartacus, 1960
The Power and the Glory, 1961
Term of Trial, 1962
Uncle Vanya, 1963

Othello, 1965
Bunny Lake is Missing, 1965
Khartoum, 1966
The Shoes of the Fisherman,
    1968
Romeo and Juliet, 1968
Oh What a Lovely War, 1969
The Battle of Britain, 1969
David Copperfield, 1969
The Dance of Death, 1969
Three Sisters, 1970
Nicholas and Alexandra, 1971
Lady Caroline Lamb, 1972
Sleuth, 1972
The Merchant of Venice, 1972
Long Day's Journey Into
    Night, 1973
The Rehearsal, 1974
Love Among the Ruins, 1975
Cat On a Hot Tin Roof, 1976
Marathon Man, 1976
Hindle Wakes, 1976
The Seven Per Cent Solution,
    1977
A Bridge Too Far, 1977
The Collection, 1977
Jesus of Nazareth, 1977
The Gentleman Tramp (voice),
    1978
Come Back Little Sheba, 1978
The Betsy, 1978
The Boys From Brazil, 1978
A Little Romance, 1979
Dracula, 1979
Inchon, 1980
The Jazz Singer, 1980

J. PAT O'MALLEY (1901-)
Irish character star of stage
and screen, long in Hollywood.
Also latterly on television.

Go and Get It, 1920
The Blooming Angel, 1920
Brothers Under the Skin, 1921
Wandering Daughters, 1923
The Eternal Struggle, 1923
The Man From Brodneys,
    1923
Happiness, 1924
The Fighting American, 1924
Bread, 1924

Worldly Goods, 1924
The Teaser, 1925
Tomorrow's Love, 1925
Proud Flesh, 1925
The White Desert, 1926
Midnight Sun, 1927
Alibi, 1929
The Man I Love, 1929
The Fall Guy, 1930
Mothers Cry, 1931
The Sky Spider, 1932
Frisco Jenny, 1933
Behind the Evidence, 1935
The Perfect Clue, 1935
Hollywood Boulevard, 1936
Beloved Enemy, 1936
Romance of the Redwoods,
    1939
Frontier Marshal, 1939
The Night of Nights, 1939
Captain Caution, 1940
A Little Bit of Heaven, 1940
Meet Boston Blackie, 1941
Paris Calling, 1942
Over My Dead Body, 1942
Lassie Come Home, 1943
The Rugged O'Riordans, 1949
Kind Lady, 1951
Blackjack Ketchum Desperado,
    1956
Witness For the Prosecution,
    1957
The Long Hot Summer, 1958
Blueprint For Robbery, 1960
The Cabinet of Caligari, 1961
A House is Not a Home, 1964
Gunn, 1967
Hello Dolly, 1969
The Cheyenne Social Club, 1970
The Skin Game, 1971
Willard, 1971
Detour to Nowhere, 1972
The Gumball Rally, 1976
A Matter of Life & Death, 1981

KATE O'MARA (1939-)
Leading lady in occasional
films of the 60s and 70s.

Promenade, 1967
Great Catherine, 1968
The Limbo Line, 1968

Corruption, 1968
The Desperados, 1969
Horror of Frankenstein, 1970
The Vampire Lovers, 1970
The Tamarind Seed, 1974
Whose Child Am I?, 1975

MAIRE O'NEILL (1885-1952)
Irish character player, sister
of Sara Allgood; formerly with
the Abbey Theatre.

Juno and the Paycock, 1929
M'Blimey, 1932
Sing As We Go, 1934
Peg of Old Drury, 1935
Come Out of the Pantry, 1935
Fame, 1936
Ourselves Alone, 1936
Farewell Again, 1937
Bulldog Drummond at Bay,
  1937
River of Unrest, 1937
Glamorous Night, 1937
Spring Handicap, 1937
Oh Boy, 1938
Mountains O'Mourne, 1938
Penny Paradise, 1938
My Irish Molly, 1938
St. Martin's Lane, 1938
The Missing People, 1939
Sword of Honour, 1939
The Arsenal Stadium Mystery,
  1939
Dr. O'Dowd, 1940
You Will Remember, 1940
Love On the Dole, 1941
Penn of Pennsylvania, 1941
Those Kids From Town, 1942
Let the People Sing, 1942
Theatre Royal, 1943
Great Day, 1945
Murder in Reverse, 1945
Spring Song, 1946
Send For Paul Temple, 1946
Piccadilly Incident, 1946
Gaiety George, 1946
The Hills of Donegal, 1947
Saints and Sinners, 1949
Stranger at My Door, 1950
Treasure Hunt, 1952
Judgement Deferred, 1952
The Oracle, 1953

JULIAN ORCHARD (1930-1979)
Character player of stage and
films, adept at mournful comedy characterizations.

Vintage '28, 1953
On the Beat, 1960
Three On a Spree, 1961
Crooks Anonymous, 1962
Kill Or Cure, 1963
The Spy With a Cold Nose,
  1966
Stranger in the House, 1967
Carry On Doctor, 1968
Can Heironymous Merkin, 1969
The Nine Ages of Nakedness,
  1969
Perfect Friday, 1970
Futtock's End, 1970
Carry On Henry VIII, 1971
The Slipper and the Rose, 1976
Crossed Swords, 1978
The London Affair, 1979

BREFNI O'ROURKE (1889-1946)
Irish character actor of the
forties, also on stage; former
Abbey Theatre member.

This Man is Dangerous, 1941
Hatter's Castle, 1941
The Ghost of St. Michael's,
  1941
Secret Mission, 1942
They Flew Alone, 1942
Unpublished Story, 1942
The Missing Million, 1942
Next of Kin, 1942
Much Too Shy, 1942
The First of the Few, 1942
We'll Meet Again, 1942
Tomorrow We Live, 1942
King Arthur Was a Gentleman,
  1942
Escape to Danger, 1943
They Met in the Dark, 1943
The Flemish Farm, 1943
The Lamp Still Burns, 1943
Don't Take It to Heart, 1944
Tawny Pipit, 1944
It Happened One Sunday, 1944
Twilight Hour, 1944
The Rake's Progress, 1945

The Voice Within, 1945
Waltz Time, 1945
Perfect Strangers, 1945
They Were Sisters, 1945
Murder in Reverse, 1945
Green Fingers, 1946
The Root of All Evil, 1946
I See a Dark Stranger, 1946
The Upturned Glass, 1947

ANDREW OSBORN (1912-)
Supporting actor of stage and
screen; latterly television
producer for BBC.

Who Goes Next?, 1938
Idol of Paris, 1948
Poet's Pub, 1949
Dark Interval, 1950
Shadow of the Past, 1950
The Woman With No Name,
  1950
Lady With a Lamp, 1951
Angels One Five, 1952
The Second Mrs. Tanqueray,
  1952
Spaceways, 1953
Blood Orange, 1953
Murder By Proxy, 1955

HENRY OSCAR (1891-1970)
Character star of stage (from
1911) and films, primarily
seen in either humble or villainous parts.

After Dark, 1932
I Was a Spy, 1933
Red Ensign, 1934
Brides to Be, 1934
The Man Who Knew Too Much,
  1934
Sexton Blake & the Bearded
  Doctor, 1935
The Case of Gabriel Perry,
  1935
Father O'Flynn, 1935
Night Mail, 1935
Me and Marlborough, 1935
The Tunnel, 1935
The Man Behind the Mask,
  1936

Love in Exile, 1936
Seven Sinners, 1936
Dishonour Bright, 1936
No Escape, 1936
Spy of Napoleon, 1936
Sensation, 1937
Fire Over England, 1937
The Academy Decides, 1937
Dark Journey, 1937
Who Killed John Savage?, 1937
Luck of the Navy, 1938
The Terror, 1938
Black Limelight, 1938
Return of the Scarlet Pimper-
  nel, 1938
Dead Man's Shoes, 1939
On the Night of the Fire, 1939
Hell's Cargo, 1939
The Four Feathers, 1939
The Saint in London, 1939
Spies of the Air, 1939
Tilly of Bloomsbury, 1940
Two For Danger, 1940
The Flying Squad, 1940
Mein Kampf My Crimes, 1940
Atlantic Ferry, 1941
Penn of Pennsylvania, 1941
The Seventh Survivor, 1941
Hatter's Castle, 1941
Squadron Leader X, 1942
The Day Will Dawn, 1942
The Upturned Glass, 1947
They Made Me a Fugitive, 1947
Mrs. Fitzherbert, 1947
Idol of Paris, 1948
House of Darkness, 1948
It Happened in Soho, 1948
Bonnie Prince Charlie, 1948
The Greed of William Hart,
  1948
The Bad Lord Byron, 1949
The Man From Yesterday, 1949
Which Will Ye Have?, 1949
Prelude to Fame, 1950
The Black Rose, 1950
Martin Luther, 1953
Men at Work, 1954
Diplomatic Passport, 1954
Knights of the Round Table,
  1954
Beau Brummell, 1954
Portrait of Alison, 1955
Three Cases of Murder, 1955
Private's Progress, 1956

It's a Great Day, 1956
The Little Hut, 1957
The Spaniard's Curse, 1958
The Secret Man, 1958
Beyond This Place, 1959
Oscar Wilde, 1960
Brides of Dracula, 1960
A Foxhole in Cairo, 1961
Lawrence of Arabia, 1962
The Long Ships, 1964
Murder Ahoy, 1964
City Under the Sea, 1965

MILO O'SHEA (1925-)
Irish character star with long
Abbey Theatre experience;
sometimes seen in comedy roles.

Talk of a Million, 1951
This Other Eden, 1959
Mrs. Gibbons' Boys, 1962
Carry On Cabby, 1963
Down Boy!, 1964
Never Put it in Writing, 1964
Ulysses, 1967
Romeo and Juliet, 1968
Barbarella, 1968
The Adding Machine, 1969
The Angel Levine, 1970
Paddy, 1970
Sacco and Vanzetti, 1971
Loot, 1971
Theatre of Blood, 1973
The Hebrew Lesson, 1973
Digby, the Biggest Dog in the
    World, 1974
Percy's Progress, 1975
Arabian Adventure, 1979
Portrait of a Rebel: Margaret
    Sanger, 1980
The Pilot, 1980

TESSIE O'SHEA (1917-)
Popular stage and music hall
performer, often seen in films
playing herself.

The Way Ahead, 1944
London Town, 1946
Holidays With Pay, 1948
Somewhere in Politics, 1949

The Blue Lamp, 1950
The Shiralee, 1957
The Russians Are Coming, 1966
The Best House in London, 1968
Dr. Jekyll and Mr. Hyde, 1968
Bedknobs and Broomsticks,
    1971

MAUREEN O'SULLIVAN
    (1911-)
Irish actress of Hollywood
films; married to director John
Farrow; mother of Mia Farrow.

Just Imagine, 1930
Song O' My Heart, 1930
So This is London, 1930
Princess and the Plumber,
    1930
A Connecticut Yankee, 1931
Skyline, 1931
The Big Shot, 1932
Tarzan the Ape Man, 1932
Fast Companions, 1932
Information Kid, 1932
The Silver Lining, 1932
Skyscraper Souls, 1932
Strange Interlude, 1932
Okay America, 1932
Payment Deferred, 1932
Robber's Roost, 1933
Tugboat Annie, 1933
The Cohens & Kellys in Trouble,
    1933
Stage Mother, 1933
Tarzan and His Mate, 1934
The Thin Man, 1934
Hideout, 1934
The Barretts of Wimpole Street,
    1934
Woman Wanted, 1934
The Bishop Misbehaves, 1935
David Copperfield, 1935
West Point of the Air, 1935
Cardinal Richelieu, 1935
The Flame Within, 1935
Anna Karenina, 1935
The Voice of Bugle Ann, 1936
The Devil Doll, 1936
Tarzan Escapes, 1936
My Dear Miss Aldrich, 1937
A Day at the Races, 1937

The Emperor's Candlesticks,
1937
Between Two Women, 1937
A Yank at Oxford, 1938
Hold That Kiss, 1938
Port of the Seven Seas, 1938
The Crowd Roars, 1938
Spring Madness, 1938
Let Us Live, 1939
Tarzan Finds a Son, 1939
Sporting Blood, 1940
Pride and Prejudice, 1940
Maisie Was a Lady, 1941
Tarzan's Secret Treasure,
1941
Tarzan's New York Adventure,
1942
The Big Clock, 1948
Where Danger Lives, 1951
No Resting Place, 1952
Bonzo Goes to College, 1952
All I Desire, 1953
Mission Over Korea, 1953
Duffy of San Quentin, 1954
The Steel Cage, 1954
The Tall T, 1957
Wild Heritage, 1958
Never Too Late, 1965
The Phynx, 1970
The Crooked Hearts, 1972
The Great Houdinis, 1976

RICHARD O'SULLIVAN (1943-)
Child actor of the fifties, later
in juvenile supporting roles.

The Stranger's Hand, 1953
The Sleeping Tiger, 1954
Dance Little Lady, 1954
The Secret, 1955
The Green Scarf, 1955
The Dark Avenger, 1955
Dangerous Exile, 1956
It's Great to Be Young, 1956
Raiders of the River, 1956
Jacqueline, 1956
Carry On Teacher, 1959
Witness in the Dark, 1959
A Story of David, 1960
And Women Shall Weep, 1960
Spare the Rod, 1961
The Young Ones, 1961

The Webster Boy, 1962
Cleopatra, 1962
Dr. Syn Alias the Scarecrow,
1963
Every Day's a Holiday, 1964
Wonderful Life, 1964
A Dandy in Aspic, 1968
Au Pair Girls, 1973
Father Dear Father, 1973

PETER O'TOOLE (1932-)
Unconventional Irish leading
man of stage (since 1949) and
films, also in Hollywood.
Married: Sian Phillips.

Kidnapped, 1959
The Savage Innocents, 1960
The Day They Robbed the Bank
of England, 1960
Lawrence of Arabia, 1962
Becket, 1964
Lord Jim, 1965
The Sandpiper (voice), 1965
What's New Pussycat?, 1965
The Bible, 1966
How To Steal a Million, 1966
Night of the Generals, 1966
Casino Royale, 1967
Great Catherine, 1968
The Lion in Winter, 1968
Goodbye Mr. Chips, 1969
Country Dance, 1969
Murphy's War, 1970
Under Milk Wood, 1971
The Ruling Class, 1972
Man of La Mancha, 1972
Rosebud, 1974
Man Friday, 1975
Rogue Male, 1976
Foxtrot, 1976
Caligula, 1977
The Stuntman, 1978
Power Play, 1978
Zulu Dawn, 1980
Masada, 1980

BRIAN OULTON (1908-)
Comic character actor of stage
and films, frequently seen in
smug or self-satisfied roles.

Too Many Husbands, 1938
Miranda, 1948
Last Holiday, 1950
Castle in the Air, 1952
The Dog and the Diamonds,
1953
Will Any Gentleman, 1953
Doctor in the House, 1954
The Million Pound Note, 1954
The Reluctant Bride, 1955
Private's Progress, 1956
Happy is the Bride, 1957
Brothers in Law, 1957
The Spaniard's Curse, 1958
The Silent Enemy, 1958
Carry On Nurse, 1959
The 39 Steps, 1959
There Was a Crooked Man,
1960
A French Mistress, 1961
The Damned, 1961
Kiss of the Vampire, 1962
Hair of the Dog, 1962
The Iron Maiden, 1962
Jigsaw, 1962
Carry On Cleo, 1964
The Intelligence Men, 1965
Carry On Camping, 1969
On the Buses, 1971
Ooh You Are Awful, 1972
Cry of the Penguins, 1972

BILL OWEN (1914-)
Comedy character actor of
stage (since 1934) and films;
former singer and musician.

The Weaker Sex, 1945
The Way to the Stars, 1945
Song of the People, 1945
School For Secrets, 1946
Daybreak, 1946
Dancing With Crime, 1947
When the Bough Breaks, 1947
Easy Money, 1948
Trouble in the Air, 1948
My Brother's Keeper, 1948
Once a Jolly Swagman, 1948
Trottie True, 1949
Diamond City, 1949
Martha, 1949
Parlour Trick, 1949

The Roundabout, 1950
The Girl Who Couldn't Quite,
1950
Hotel Sahara, 1951
You See What I Mean, 1952
The Story of Robin Hood, 1952
There Was a Young Lady, 1953
The Square Ring, 1953
A Day to Remember, 1953
The Rainbow Jacket, 1954
The Ship That Died of Shame,
1955
Not So Dusty, 1956
Davy, 1957
Carve Her Name With Pride,
1958
Carry On Sergeant, 1958
A Night Apart, 1959
Carry On Nurse, 1959
Shakedown, 1960
The Hellfire Club, 1961
Carry On Regardless, 1961
On the Fiddle, 1961
Carry On Cabby, 1963
The Secret of Blood Island,
1965
Georgy Girl, 1966
Fighting Prince of Donegal, 1966
Headline Hunters, 1968
Mischief, 1969
Kadoyng, 1972
O Lucky Man, 1973
In Celebration, 1974
The Comeback, 1979

REGINALD OWEN (1887-1972)
Character actor and occasional
leading man of stage (1905) and
screen, in Hollywood from 1929.

Henry VIII, 1911
The Grass Orphan, 1922
The Letter, 1929
Man in Possession, 1931
Platinum Blonde, 1931
A Woman Commands, 1932
Lovers Courageous, 1932
The Man Called Back, 1932
Downstairs, 1932
Sherlock Holmes, 1932
A Study in Scarlet, 1933
The Narrow Corner, 1933

Double Harness, 1933
The Big Brain, 1933
Voltaire, 1933
Queen Christina, 1933
Fashions of 1934, 1934
Nana, 1934
Mandalay, 1934
The House of Rothschild, 1934
The Count of Monte Cristo,
1934
Stingaree, 1934
Where Sinners Meet, 1934
Of Human Bondage, 1934
The Human Side, 1934
Madame Du Barry, 1934
Music in the Air, 1934
Here is My Heart, 1934
The Good Fairy, 1935
Enchanted April, 1935
Escapade, 1935
Call of the Wild, 1935
Anna Karenina, 1935
A Tale of Two Cities, 1935
Rose Marie, 1936
Petticoat Fever, 1936
The Great Zeigfeld, 1936
Trouble For Two, 1936
Yours For the Asking, 1936
Adventure in Manhattan, 1936
Girl On the Front Page, 1936
Love On the Run, 1936
Dangerous Number, 1937
Personal Property, 1937
The Bride Wore Red, 1937
Madame X, 1937
Conquest, 1937
Rosalie, 1937
Paradise For Three, 1938
Everybody Sing, 1938
Kidnapped, 1938
Three Loves Has Nancy, 1938
Vacation From Love, 1938
A Christmas Carol, 1938
The Girl Downstairs, 1939
Fast and Loose, 1939
Hotel Imperial, 1939
Bridal Suite, 1939
The Real Glory, 1939
Remember, 1939
The Earl of Chicago, 1940
Florian, 1940
Hullabaloo, 1940
Free and Easy, 1941

A Woman's Face, 1941
They Met in Bombay, 1941
Charley's Aunt, 1941
Lady Be Good, 1941
Tarzan's Secret Treasure, 1941
Woman of the Year, 1942
We Were Dancing, 1942
Mrs. Miniver, 1942
I Married An Angel, 1942
Pierre of the Plains, 1942
Somewhere I'll Find You, 1942
Cairo, 1942
White Cargo, 1942
Random Harvest, 1942
Reunion in France, 1943
Assignment in Brittainy, 1943
Three Hearts For Julia, 1943
Above Suspicion, 1943
Salute to the Marines, 1943
Madame Curie, 1943
The Canterville Ghost, 1944
National Velvet, 1944
Valley of Decision, 1945
Captain Kidd, 1945
She Went to the Races, 1946
The Sailor Takes a Wife, 1946
Kitty, 1946
Cluny Brown, 1946
Diary of a Chambermaid, 1946
Monseur Beaucaire, 1946
The Imperfect Lady, 1947
Green Dolphin Street, 1947
Thunder in the Valley, 1947
If Winter Comes, 1948
The Pirate, 1948
Piccadilly Incident, 1948
Julia Misbehaves, 1948
The Three Musketeers, 1948
The Hills of Home, 1948
The Secret Garden, 1949
Challenge to Lassie, 1949
The Miniver Story, 1950
Kim, 1950
Grounds For Marriage, 1951
The Great Diamond Robbery,
1953
Red Garters, 1954
Affairs of State, 1955
The Young Invaders, 1958
Darby's Rangers, 1958
Five Weeks in a Balloon, 1962
Tammy and the Doctor, 1963
The Thrill of It, 1963

Voice of the Hurricane, 1964
Mary Poppins, 1964
Rosie, 1968
Bedknobs and Broomsticks, 1971
Topper Returns, 1973

YVONNE OWEN (-)
Supporting actress and occasional leading lady of the forties. Married to Alan Badel.

The Seventh Veil, 1945
The Years Between, 1946
Girl in a Million, 1946
Holiday Camp, 1947
Easy Money, 1948
My Brother's Keeper, 1948
Miranda, 1948
Portrait From Life, 1948
Silent Dust, 1949
Third Time Lucky, 1949
Marry Me, 1949
Someone at the Door, 1950

PATRICIA OWENS (1925-)
Canadian-born leading lady of the 50s and 60s, also in Hollywood.

Miss London Ltd., 1943
While the Sun Shines, 1946
Panic at Madame Tussaud's, 1948
The Happiest Days of Your Life, 1950
Bait, 1950
Mystery Junction, 1951
Ghost Ship, 1952
Crow Hollow, 1952
House of Blackmail, 1953
The Good Die Young, 1954
The Stranger Came Home, 1954
Windfall, 1955
Island in the Sun, 1957
Alive On Saturday, 1957
Sayonara, 1957
No Down Payment, 1957
The Fly, 1958
The Law and Jake Wade, 1958
The Gunrunners, 1958

These Thousand Hills, 1959
Five Gates To Hell, 1959
Hell To Eternity, 1960
X-15, 1961
Seven Women From Hell, 1962
Walk a Tightrope, 1963
Black Spurs, 1965
The Destructors, 1968

DAVID OXLEY (1929-)
General purpose actor of the 50s and 60s.

The Armchair Detective, 1952
The Black Ice, 1957
Saint Joan, 1957
Ill Met By Moonlight, 1957
Sea Fury, 1958
Night Ambush, 1958
Bonjour Tristesse, 1958
Hound of the Baskervilles, 1959
Yesterday's Enemy, 1960
Life at the Top, 1965
Bunny Lake is Missing, 1965

LILLI PALMER (1914-)
Intelligent Austrian leading lady of stage (since 1932) and films, popular in the 40s and 50s, also in Hollywood; formerly married to Rex Harrison.

Crime Unlimited, 1935
First Offence, 1936
Wolf's Clothing, 1936
Secret Agent, 1936
Good Morning Boys, 1937
The Great Barrier, 1937
Sunset in Vienna, 1937
Command Performance, 1937
Crackerjack, 1938
A Girl Must Live, 1939
Blind Folly, 1939
The Door With Seven Locks, 1940
Thunder Rock, 1942
The Gentle Sex, 1943
Englîgh Without Tears, 1944
The Rake's Progress, 1945
Beware of Pity, 1946
Cloak and Dagger, 1946

My Girl Tisa, 1947
Body and Soul, 1948
No Minor Vices, 1948
Hans Le Marin, 1950
The Long Dark Hall, 1951
The Fourposter, 1952
Main Street to Broadway, 1953
Feverwerk, 1954
Devil in Silk, 1954
Is Anna Anderson Anastasia?,
  1956
Tempestuous Love, 1957
Montparnasse, 1958
La Vie a Deux, 1958
But Not For Me, 1958
The Glass Tower, 1958
Maedchen in Uniform, 1958
Conspiracy of Hearts, 1960
Rendezvous at Midnight, 1960
Leviathan, 1960
The Pleasure of His Company,
  1961
The Counterfeit Traitor,
  1962
Of Wayward Love, 1962
Adorable Julia, 1963
And So to Bed, 1963
Torpedo Bay, 1963
Flight of the White Stallions,
  1964
Le Grain de Sable, 1964
Moll Flanders, 1965
Operation Crossbow, 1965
Jack of Diamonds, 1967
Sebastian, 1968
Nobody Runs Forever, 1968
Oedipus the King, 1968
The Dance of Death, 1968
De Sade, 1969
Hard Contract, 1969
The House That Screamed,
  1970
Murders in the Rue Morgue,
  1971
Night Hair Child, 1971
Zoo Gang, 1972
Lotte in Weimar, 1975
The Boys From Brazil, 1978

CECIL PARKER (1897-1971)
Splendid character star and
occasional leading man of

stage (from 1922) and screen,
typically cast as man of importance or position. Also in
Hollywood.

The Woman in White, 1928
The Golden Age, 1933
A Cuckoo in the Nest, 1933
The Silver Spoon, 1934
Flat No. 3, 1934
Nine Forty-Five, 1934
The Office Wife, 1934
Little Friend, 1934
The Blue Squadron, 1934
Lady in Danger, 1934
Dirty Work, 1934
Me and Marlborough, 1935
Crime Unlimited, 1935
Her Last Affaire, 1935
Foreign Affaires, 1935
Jack of All Trades, 1936
Men of Yesterday, 1936
The Man Who Changed His
  Mind, 1936
Dishonour Bright, 1936
Dark Journey, 1937
Storm in a Teacup, 1937
Housemaster, 1938
The Lady Vanishes, 1938
Old Iron, 1938
Bank Holiday, 1938
The Citadel, 1938
She Couldn't Say No, 1939
The Stars Look Down, 1939
Sons of the Sea, 1939
The Spider, 1939
Two For Danger, 1940
Under Your Hat, 1940
The Saint's Vacation, 1941
Dangerous Moonlight, 1941
Ships With Wings, 1941
Caesar and Cleopatra, 1945
Hungry Hill, 1946
The Magic Bow, 1947
Captain Boycott, 1947
The Woman in the Hall, 1947
The First Gentleman, 1948
The Weaker Sex, 1948
Quartet, 1948
Dear Mr. Prohack, 1949
The Chiltern Hundreds, 1949
Under Capricorn, 1949
Tony Draws a Horse, 1950

The Man in the White Suit,
1951
The Magic Box, 1951
His Excellency, 1952
I Believe in You, 1952
Isn't Life Wonderful, 1953
Father Brown, 1954
For Better, For Worse, 1954
The Constant Husband, 1955
The Ladykillers, 1955
It's Great to Be Young, 1956
The Court Jester, 1956
23 Paces to Baker Street,
1956
True as a Turtle, 1957
The Admirable Crichton, 1957
A Tale of Two Cities, 1958
Happy is the Bride, 1958
I Was Monty's Double, 1958
Indiscreet, 1958
The Wreck of the Mary Deare,
1959
The Night We Dropped a
Clanger, 1959
The Navy Lark, 1959
Under Ten Flags, 1960
Follow That Horse, 1960
A French Mistress, 1960
The Pure Hell of St. Trinian's,
1960
The Swiss Family Robinson,
1960
On the Fiddle, 1961
Petticoat Pirates, 1961
The Amorous Prawn, 1962
Vengeance, 1962
The Iron Maiden, 1962
Heavens Above, 1963
The Comedy Man, 1963
Carry On Jack, 1963
Guns at Batasi, 1964
Moll Flanders, 1965
A Man Could Get Killed, 1965
A Study in Terror, 1965
Lady L, 1965
Circus of Fear, 1966
The Magnificent Two, 1967
Oh What a Lovely War, 1969

NATASHA PARRY (1930-)
Attractive leading lady of
stage and screen, married

to director Sir Peter Brook
(1925-).

Golden Arrow, 1949
Dance Hall, 1950
Midnight Episode, 1950
The Dark Man, 1951
Crow Hollow, 1952
Knave of Hearts, 1954
Windom's Way, 1957
The Rough and the Smooth,
1959
Midnight Lace, 1960
Portrait of a Sinner, 1961
The Fourth Square, 1962
The Girl in the Headlines,
1964
Romeo and Juliet, 1968
Oh What a Lovely War, 1969
Meetings with Remarkable Men,
1979

NICHOLAS PARSONS (1928-)
General purpose actor and showman in occasional films.

The Master of Bankdam, 1947
Eyewitness, 1956
Brothers in Law, 1957
Happy is the Bride, 1958
Too Many Crooks, 1959
Carleton Browne of the F.O.,
1959
Doctor in Love, 1960
The Wrong Box, 1966
Don't Raise the Bridge Lower
the River, 1968

RICHARD PASCO (1926-)
Incisive character actor mainly
seen on stage and television.

Kill Me Tomorrow, 1957
Room at the Top, 1959
Yesterday's Enemy, 1960
Sword of Sherwood Forest, 1960
Six Black Horses, 1962
Hot Enough For June, 1963
The Gorgon, 1964
Rasputin the Mad Monk, 1965
Julius Caesar, 1979

WALLY PATCH (1888-1971)
Stout Cockney character star
of stage and screen with music hall experience from 1912.

Boadicea, 1926
The King's Highway, 1927
Luck of the Navy, 1927
Blighty, 1927
Carry On, 1927
The Guns of Loos, 1928
Shooting Stars, 1928
Dr. Sin Fang, 1928
The Reckless Gamble, 1928
You Know What Sailors Are,
    1928
Warned Off, 1928
The Woman in White, 1928
Dick Turpin, 1929
High Treason, 1929
The Great Game, 1930
Balaclava, 1930
Kissing Cup's Race, 1930
Thread O'Scarlet 1930
The Sport of Kings, 1931
Shadows, 1931
Jaws of Hell, 1931
Tell England, 1931
Never Trouble Trouble, 1931
The Great Gay Road, 1931
Castle Sinister, 1932
Heroes of the Mine, 1932
Here's George, 1932
The Good Companions, 1933
Don Quixote, 1933
Britannia of Billingsgate, 1933
Tiger Bay, 1933
Orders is Orders, 1933
Channel Crossing, 1933
Marooned, 1933
Sorrell and Son, 1933
Trouble, 1933
Scotland Yard Mystery, 1934
The Man I Want, 1934
Those Were the Days, 1934
Passing Shadows, 1934
Music Hall, 1934
The Perfect Flaw, 1934
What Happened to Harkness,
    1934
Scoop, 1934
Virginia's Husband, 1934
Badger's Green, 1934

Crazy People, 1934
A Glimpse of Paradise, 1934
The Old Curiosity Shop, 1934
Borrow a Million, 1934
Lost Over London, 1934
Once in a Blue Moon, 1935
His Majesty and Co, 1935
Public Life of Henry IX, 1935
Dandy Dick, 1935
Death On the Set, 1935
That's My Wife, 1935
Street Song, 1935
Off the Dole, 1935
Marry the Girl, 1935
Half Day Excursion, 1935
Where's George?, 1935
What the Parrot Saw, 1935
Old Faithful, 1935
While Parents Sleep, 1935
Get Off My Foot, 1935
A Wife Or Two, 1936
Ticket of Leave, 1936
On Top of the World, 1936
King of the Castle, 1936
Excuse My Glove, 1936
What the Puppy Said, 1936
Prison Breaker, 1936
A Touch of the Moon, 1936
Not So Dusty, 1936
Interrupted Honeymoon, 1936
Apron Fools, 1936
Man Who Could Work Miracles,
    1936
Luck of the Turf, 1936
Hail and Farewell, 1936
Busman's Holiday, 1936
Men Are Not Gods, 1936
The Scarab Murder Case, 1936
You Must Get Married, 1936
The Inspector, 1937
The Price of Folly, 1937
Holiday's End, 1937
The High Command, 1937
The Street Singer, 1937
Farewell Again, 1937
Night Ride, 1937
Dr. Syn, 1937
Missing Believed Married,
    1937
The Sky's the Limit, 1937
Captain's Orders, 1937
Owd Bob, 1938
Bank Holiday, 1938

Quiet Please, 1938
On Velvet, 1938
Almost a Honeymoon, 1938
Break the News, 1938
Thirteen Men and a Gun, 1938
Alf's Button Afloat, 1938
A Night Alone, 1938
The Lady Vanishes, 1938
Pygmalion, 1938
The Ware Case, 1938
The Mind of Mr. Reeder,
   1939
Inspector Hornleigh, 1939
Home From Home, 1939
Sword of Honour, 1939
Poison Pen, 1939
Down Our Alley, 1939
What Would You Do Chums?,
   1939
Hospital Hospitality, 1939
Inspector Hornleigh On Holiday,
   1939
Return to Yesterday, 1940
Laugh it Off, 1940
Band Wagon, 1940
They Came By Night, 1940
Pack Up Your Troubles, 1940
Charley's Big-Hearted Aunt,
   1940
Night Train to Munich, 1940
Two Smart Men, 1940
Old Mother Riley in Business,
   1940
Henry Steps Out, 1940
Gasbags, 1940
Neutral Port, 1940
Quiet Wedding, 1941
Inspector Hornleigh Goes to It,
   1941
Jeannie, 1941
Once a Crook, 1941
Facing the Music, 1941
Cottage to Let, 1941
I Thank You, 1941
The Seventh Survivor, 1941
The Common Touch, 1941
Gert and Daisy's Weekend,
   1941
Bob's Your Uncle, 1941
Let the People Sing, 1942
Sabotage at Sea, 1942
We'll Smile Again, 1942
Unpublished Story, 1942

Death By Design, 1943
Strange to Relate, 1943
The Butler's Dilemma, 1943
Old Mother Riley at Home,
   1944
Don Chicago, 1945
I Didn't Do It, 1945
Dumb Dora Discovers Tobacco,
   1945
A Matter of Life and Death,
   1946
Gaiety George, 1946
Appointment With Crime, 1946
George in Civvy Street, 1946
Green Fingers, 1947
Dusty Bates, 1947
The Ghosts of Berkeley Square,
   1947
River Patrol, 1948
Calling Paul Temple, 1948
Date With a Dream, 1948
The Guinea Pig, 1948
The History of Mr. Polly, 1949
The Adventures of Jane, 1949
20 Questions Murder Mystery,
   1950
Salute the Toff, 1952
Hammer the Toff, 1952
Wedding of Lilli Marlene, 1953
Will Any Gentleman, 1953
Private's Progress, 1956
Morning Call, 1957
The Naked Truth, 1958
I'm All Right, Jack, 1959
The Millionairess, 1960
Operation Cupid, 1960
Nothing Barred, 1961
Serena, 1962
Sparrows Can't Sing, 1963
A Jolly Bad Fellow, 1964
The Bargee, 1964

CHARLES PATON (-)
Strong supporting player of the
thirties.

In Borrowed Plumes, 1928
Two of a Trade, 1928
Piccadilly, 1929
Blackmail, 1929
The Feather, 1929
The Sleeping Cardinal, 1930

The W Plan, 1930
A Sister to Assist 'Er, 1930
Stepping Stones, 1931
My Wife's Family, 1931
Glamour, 1931
What a Night, 1931
The Speckled Band, 1931
Contraband Love, 1931
The Other Mrs. Phipps, 1931
Rynox, 1931
The Spare Room, 1932
Bachelor's Baby, 1932
The Third String, 1932
A Letter of Warning, 1932
Josser Joins the Navy, 1932
The Iron Stair, 1933
This Acting Business, 1933
The Love Nest, 1933
Freedom of the Seas, 1934
Song at Eventide, 1934
Girls Will Be Boys, 1934
The Girl is Possession, 1934
Royal Cavalcade, 1935
Rembrandt, 1936
Jury's Evidence, 1936
The Vandergilt Diamond Mystery, 1936
Pal O' Mine, 1936
Museum Mystery, 1937
The Dominant Sex, 1937
Double Or Quits, 1938
A Sister to Assist 'Er, 1938
Mother of Men, 1938
Men Without Honour, 1939
Old Mother Riley's Ghosts, 1941
The Demi-Paradise, 1943
The Adventurers, 1950

NIGEL PATRICK (1913-)
Gentlemanly actor of stage
(from 1932) and films, also
occasional director. Married
to Beatrice Campbell. Tv
series: "Zero One" (1962).

Mrs. Pym of Scotland Yard, 1939
Noose, 1948
Spring in Park Lane, 1948
Uneasy Terms, 1948
Silent Dust, 1949

Jack of Diamonds, 1949
The Perfect Woman, 1949
Trio, 1950
Morning Departure, 1950
Pandora and the Flying Dutchman, 1951
The Browning Version, 1951
Young Wives' Tale, 1951
Encore, 1952
Who Goes There?, 1952
The Sound Barrier, 1952
Meet Me Tonight, 1952
The Pickwick Papers, 1952
Grand National Night, 1953
Forbidden Cargo, 1954
The Sea Shall Not Have Them, 1955
A Prize of Gold, 1955
All For Mary, 1955
How To Murder a Rich Uncle, 1957
Raintree County, 1957
Count Five and Die, 1958
The Man Inside, 1958
Sapphire, 1959
The League of Gentlemen, 1959
The Trials of Oscar Wilde, 1960
Johnny Nobody, 1961
The Informers, 1963
The Virgin Soldiers, 1969
The Battle of Britain, 1969
The Executioner, 1970
Tales From the Crypt, 1972
The Great Waltz, 1972
The Mackintosh Man, 1973

LEE PATTERSON (1929-)
Canadian leading man of stage
(1950) and films, popular in
second features of the fifties.
Also Hollywood. Tv series:
"Surfside Six" (1960-61).

36 Hours, 1954
The Good Die Young, 1954
The Passing Stranger, 1954
Above Us the Waves, 1955
Soho Incident, 1956
Reach For the Sky, 1956
Dry Rot, 1956
Checkpoint, 1956

The Counterfeit Plan, 1956
Time Lock, 1957
The Key Man, 1957
The Story of Esther Costello,
   1957
The Flying Scot, 1957
The Golden Disc, 1957
The Spaniard's Curse, 1958
Man With a Gun, 1958
Breakout, 1958
Cat and Mouse, 1958
Deadly Record, 1959
Jack the Ripper, 1959
The White Trap, 1959
Third Man On the Mountain,
   1959
The October Moth, 1960
The Three Worlds of Gulliver,
   1960
The Ceremony, 1963
Valley of Mystery, 1967
Chato's Land, 1971

MURIEL PAVLOW (1921-)
Petite, youthful-looking leading
lady of stage (since 1936) and
films, married to Derek Farr.

Romance in Flanders, 1937
Quiet Wedding, 1941
Night Boat to Dublin, 1946
The Shop at Sly Corner, 1947
Out of True, 1951
It Started in Paradise, 1952
The Net, 1953
Malta Story, 1953
Doctor in the House, 1954
Conflict of Wings, 1954
Simon and Laura, 1955
Eyewitness, 1956
Reach For the Sky, 1956
Tiger in the Smoke, 1956
Doctor at Large, 1957
Rooney, 1958
Whirlpool, 1958
Murder She Said, 1962

LENNOX PAWLE (1872-1936)
Character actor in Hollywood,
mainly on stage; best in eccentric parts. Films sporadic.

All the Sad World Needs,
   1918
The Admirable Crichton,
   1918
The Great Adventure, 1921
Married in Hollywood, 1929
The Sky Hawk, 1929
Hot For Paris, 1930
The Sin of Madelon Claudet,
   1932
David Copperfield, 1935
The Gay Deception, 1935
Sylvia Scarlett, 1935

LAURENCE PAYNE (1919-)
Character actor and occasional
leading man of stage and films.

Train of Events, 1949
Glad Tidings, 1953
Dangerous Exile, 1957
Ill Met By Moonlight, 1957
Night Ambush, 1958
Ben Hur, 1959
The Crawling Eye, 1960
The Telltale Heart, 1961
Court Martial of Major Keller,
   1961
The Singer Not the Song, 1961
The Third Alibi, 1961
Barabbas, 1962
Crosstrap, 1962
Vampire Circus, 1972
One Deadly Owner, 1973

MARY PEACH (1934-)
Leading lady and supporting
actress of the sixties.

Follow That Horse, 1959
Room at the Top, 1959
The Lady is a Square, 1959
On the Fiddle, 1961
No Love For Johnnie, 1961
A Pair of Briefs, 1962
A Gathering of Eagles, 1963
Ballad in Blue, 1965
The Projected Man, 1966
Scrooge, 1970
Disraeli: Portrait of a Roman-
tic, 1980

TREVOR PEACOCK (1931-)
Character actor and singer,
primarily on stage and television; films very infrequent.

The Barber of Stamford Hill,
    1962
Lady Caroline Lamb, 1972
Twelfth Night, 1980

LLOYD PEARSON (1897-1966)
Chubby character star usually
seen as gruff northcountrymen;
also on stage.

The Challenge, 1938
Tilly of Bloomsbury, 1940
Kipps, 1941
When We Are Married, 1943
Rhythm Serenade, 1943
Schweik's New Adventures,
    1943
My Learned Friend, 1943
Mr. Perrin and Mr. Traill,
    1948
Hindle Wakes, 1952
Private Information, 1952
Five O'clock Finish, 1954
The Good Companions, 1957
The Angry Silence, 1960

RICHARD PEARSON (1918-)
Character actor of stage,
films, and television.

The Girl is Mine, 1950
The Blue Parrot, 1953
Dangerous Cargo, 1954
Attempt to Kill, 1961
Guns of Darkness, 1962
The Legend of Young Dick
    Turpin, 1965
Charlie Bubbles, 1967
Macbeth, 1970
Sunday Bloody Sunday, 1971
Pope Joan, 1972
Love Among the Ruins, 1975
One of Our Dinosaurs is
    Missing, 1975
The Blue Bird, 1976
All Things Bright and Beauti-
    ful, 1978

She Fell Among Thieves, 1980
Masada, 1980
The Mirror Crack'd, 1980

FREDERICK PEISLEY (1904-)
Character actor of the 30s, latterly seen on stage.

Frail Women, 1932
Scotland Yard Mystery, 1933
The Secret of the Loch, 1934
Gentleman's Agreement, 1935
Cock O' the North, 1935
The Lonely Road, 1936
Murder at the Cabaret, 1936
Overcoat Sam, 1937
Full Speed Ahead, 1939
Hide and Seek, 1963

RON PEMBER (1934-)
Stage and television actor in occasional films of the 70s.

Oh What a Lovely War, 1969
Julius Caesar, 1970
Young Winston, 1972
Raw Meat, 1973
The Land That Time Forgot,
    1975
Rough Cut, 1980

JOHN PENROSE (1917-)
Supporting player of stage and
screen, sometimes cast as
weakling.

Freedom Radio, 1941
The Adventures of Tartu, 1943
Corridor of Mirrors, 1948
Kind Hearts and Coronets, 1949
The Adventures of PC 49, 1949
Hot Ice, 1952
Mantrap, 1953
Street of Shadows, 1953
The Million Pound Note, 1954

LANCE PERCIVAL (1933-)
Scotch character actor of the
sixties, often seen in comedy
films.

On the Fiddle, 1961
Raising the Wind, 1962
Postman's Knock, 1962
The Devil's Daffodil, 1962
Twice Round the Daffodils, 1962
Carry On Cruising, 1962
The VIPs, 1963
Hide and Seek, 1963
It's All Over Town, 1963
The Yellow Rolls-Royce, 1964
The Big Job, 1965
Joey Boy, 1965
Mrs. Brown, You've Got a Lovely Daughter, 1968
Darling Lili, 1969
Too Late the Hero, 1969
There's a Girl in My Soup, 1970
Up Pompeii, 1971
Our Miss Fred, 1972
Weekend Murders, 1972

ESME PERCY (1887-1957)
Distinguished actor of stage (since 1904) and screen; a master interpreter of Shavian parts.

Murder, 1930
Summer Lightning, 1933
The Lucky Number, 1933
On Secret Service, 1933
Bitter Sweet, 1933
Unfinished Symphony, 1934
Nell Gwyn, 1934
Love, Life and Laughter, 1934
Lord Edgware Dies, 1934
Royal Cavalcade, 1935
It Happened in Paris, 1935
Abdul the Damned, 1935
Invitation to the Waltz, 1935
The Invader, 1936
Land Without Music, 1936
Spy 77, 1936
The Amateur Gentleman, 1936
Accused, 1936
A Woman Alone, 1936
Song of Freedom, 1936
Jump For Glory, 1937
Our Fighting Navy, 1937
The First and the Last, 1937
The Frog, 1937

Return of the Scarlet Pimpernel, 1937
Pygmalion, 1938
21 Days, 1939
Caesar and Cleopatra, 1945
Dead of Night, 1945
Lisbon Story, 1946
Ghosts of Berkeley Square, 1947
Death in the Hand, 1948

LESLIE PERRINS (1902-1962)
Character actor of stage (1922) and films, frequently seen as suave villain.

Silken Threads, 1928
Clue of the Second Goblet, 1928
Blake the Lawbreaker, 1928
Immediate Possession, 1930
The Sleeping Cardinal, 1931
House of Unrest, 1931
We Dine at Seven, 1931
The Rosary, 1931
The Calendar, 1931
Betrayed, 1932
Whiteface, 1932
The Lost Chord, 1933
Early to Bed, 1933
Just Smith, 1933
The Roof, 1933
The Pointing Finger, 1933
Scotland Yard Mystery, 1934
Lord Edgware Dies, 1934
The Man Who Changed His Name, 1934
The Lash, 1934
Song at Eventide, 1934
Gay Love, 1934
Open All Night, 1934
Womanhood, 1934
D'Ye Ken John Peel?, 1935
The Rocks of Valpre, 1935
The Triumph of Sherlock Holmes, 1935
The Village Squire, 1935
White Lilac, 1935
The Silent Passenger, 1935
Lucky Days, 1935
Expert's Opinion, 1935
The Shadow of Mike Emerald, 1935

Line Engaged, 1935
Sunshine Ahead, 1936
They Didn't Know, 1936
Tudor Rose, 1936
Rhythm in the Air, 1936
Southern Roses, 1936
The Limping Man, 1936
No Escape, 1936
High Treason, 1937
Sensation, 1937
The Price of Folly, 1937
Bulldog Drummond at Bay,
  1937
Secret Lives, 1937
The High Command, 1937
Dangerous Fingers, 1937
Mr. Reeder in Room 13, 1938
Romance a la Carte, 1938
The Gables Mystery, 1938
No Parking, 1938
Calling All Crooks, 1938
His Lordship Goes to Press,
  1938
Luck of the Navy, 1938
Old Iron, 1938
I Killed the Count, 1939
The Gang's All Here, 1939
All at Sea, 1939
Blind Folly, 1939
John Smith Wakes Up, 1940
The Prime Minister, 1941
Women Aren't Angels, 1942
Suspected Person, 1942
The Woman's Angle, 1943
Heaven is Round the Corner,
  1944
I'll Turn to You, 1946
The Turners of Prospect
  Road, 1947
Idol of Paris, 1948
Man On the Run, 1949
A Run For Your Money, 1949
Midnight Episode, 1950
The Lost Hours, 1952
Guilty, 1956
Grip of the Strangler, 1957

JON PERTWEE (1919-)
Comedy character star of
stage and screen, son of
Roland Pertwee; brother of

screenwriter Michael Pertwee
(1916-).

Trouble in the Air, 1948
A Piece of Cake, 1948
William Comes to Town, 1949
Helter Skelter, 1949
Murder at the Windmill, 1949
Dear Mr. Prohack, 1949
The Body Said No, 1950
Miss Pilgrim's Progress, 1950
Mr. Drake's Duck, 1950
Will Any Gentleman, 1953
The Gay Dog, 1954
A Yank in Ermine, 1955
It's a Wonderful Life, 1955
The Ugly Duckling, 1958
Just Joe, 1959
Not a Hope in Hell, 1960
Nearly a Nasty Accident, 1961
Ladies Who Do, 1962
Carry On Cleo, 1964
Carry On Cowboy, 1965
How to Undress in Public, 1965
I've Gotta Horse, 1965
Carry On Screaming, 1966
A Funny Thing Happened On the
  Way to the Forum, 1966
Up in the Air, 1969
The House That Dripped Blood,
  1970
One of Our Dinosaurs is Miss-
  ing, 1975

ROLAND PERTWEE (-)
Character actor of the forties,
also on stage. Sons: Michael
Pertwee; Jon Pertwee.

The Second Mrs. Tanqueray,
  1916
Quinneys, 1919
The Four Just Men, 1940
Pimpernel Smith, 1941
Freedom Radio, 1941
Jeannie, 1941
Young Man's Fancy, 1943
Madonna of the Seven Moons, 1944
They Were Sisters, 1945
Caravan, 1946
The Magic Bow, 1947

COLIN PETERSEN (1946-)
Juvenile actor of the fifties
in occasional films.

Smiley, 1956
The Scamp, 1957
A Cry From the Streets, 1958

HAY PETRIE (1895-1948)
Diminutive Scottish actor of
the thirties and forties, also
on stage. At his best in eccentric portrayals.

Suspense, 1930
Night Birds, 1930
Gypsy Blood, 1931
Many Waters, 1932
Help Yourself, 1932
Private Life of Henry VIII,
1933
Daughters of Today, 1933
Lucky Number, 1933
Song of the Plough, 1933
Crime On the Hill, 1933
Matinee Idol, 1933
Nell Gwyn, 1934
The Old Curiosity Shop, 1934
Colonel Blood, 1934
The Queen's Affair, 1934
Private Life of Don Juan,
1934
Blind Justice, 1934
Moscow Nights, 1935
Peg of Old Drury, 1935
Invitation to the Waltz, 1935
I Give My Heart, 1935
Men of Yesterday, 1936
House of the Spaniard, 1936
Conquest of the Air, 1936
Hearts of Humanity, 1936
Not Wanted On Voyage, 1936
The Ghost Goes West, 1936
Forget-Me-Not, 1936
Knight Without Armour, 1937
Secret Lives, 1937
The Last Barricade, 1938
Consider Your Verdict, 1938
Keep Smiling, 1938
The Loves of Madame Du
Barry, 1938
21 Days, 1939

The Four Feathers, 1939
Q Planes, 1939
The Spy in Black, 1939
Jamaica Inn, 1939
Inquest, 1939
Ten Days in Paris, 1939
Trunk Crime, 1939
Spellbound, 1940
Spy For a Day, 1940
Contraband, 1940
Convoy, 1940
Pastor Hall, 1940
Crimes at the Dark House,
1940
The Thief of Bagdad, 1940
Turned Out Nice Again, 1941
The Ghost of St. Michael's,
1941
Cottage to Let, 1941
Freedom Radio, 1941
One of Our Aircraft is Missing,
1942
They Flew Alone, 1942
The Great Mr. Handel, 1942
Hard Steel, 1942
This Was Paris, 1942
Battle For Music, 1943
A Canterbury Tale, 1943
On Approval, 1944
Kiss the Bride Goodbye, 1944
The Voice Within, 1945
Waltz Time, 1945
Great Expectations, 1946
Under New Management,
1946
The Laughing Lady, 1946
The Red Shoes, 1948
The Guinea Pig, 1948
The Lucky Mascot, 1948
Noose, 1948
The Fallen Idol, 1948

FRANK PETTINGELL (1891-
1966)
Character actor of stage (since
1910) and screen, seen in both
comedy and dramatic roles,
generally as Yorkshireman.
Former journalist.

Jealousy, 1931
Hobson's Choice, 1931

Frail Women, 1932
In a Monastery Garden, 1932
The Crooked Lady, 1932
Once Bitten, 1932
Double Dealing, 1932
Tight Corner, 1932
Medicine Man, 1933
Yes Madam, 1933
Excess Baggage, 1933
The Good Companions, 1933
That's My Wife, 1933
Lucky Number, 1933
This Week of Grace, 1933
A Cuckoo in the Nest, 1933
Red Wagon, 1934
Keep it Quiet, 1934
Sing As We Go, 1934
My Old Dutch, 1934
Say it With Diamonds, 1935
The Big Splash, 1935
The Right Age to Marry, 1935
Where's George?, 1935
The Last Journey, 1935
The Amateur Gentleman, 1936
On Top of the World, 1936
Fame, 1936
Millions, 1936
It's a Grand Old World, 1937
Take My Tip, 1937
Spring Handicap, 1937
Sailing Along, 1938
Queer Cargo, 1938
Return to Yesterday, 1940
Gaslight, 1940
Busman's Honeymoon, 1940
This England, 1941
Kipps, 1941
Once a Crook, 1941
The Seventh Survivor, 1941
Ships With Wings, 1941
The Young Mr. Pitt, 1942
The Goose Steps Out, 1942
When We Are Married, 1942
Get Cracking, 1943
Gaiety George, 1946
No Room at the Inn, 1948
Escape, 1948
The Magic Box, 1951
The Card, 1951
Meet Me Tonight, 1952
The Crimson Pirate, 1952
The Great Game, 1953
Meet Mr. Lucifer, 1953

Value For Money, 1955
Up the Creek, 1958
Corridors of Blood, 1958
Term of Trial, 1962
The Dock Brief, 1962
Becket, 1964

CONRAD PHILLIPS (1930-)
Leading actor of the fifties and
sixties, famous on television
as "William Tell" (1958).

The Gentlemen Go By, 1948
A Song For Tomorrow, 1948
The Temptress, 1949
The Last Page, 1952
The Secret Tent, 1956
Stranger's Meeting, 1957
A Question of Adultery, 1958
The White Trap, 1959
The Desperate Man, 1959
Witness in the Dark, 1959
Circus of Horrors, 1960
Sons and Lovers, 1960
The Fourth Square, 1961
No Love For Johnnie, 1961
Shadow of the Cat, 1961
Murder She Said, 1962
The Durant Affair, 1962
Dead Man's Evidence, 1962
Impact, 1963
Heavens Above, 1963
The Switch, 1963
Stopover Forever, 1964
The Murder Game, 1966
Who Killed the Cat?, 1966

LESLIE PHILLIPS (1924-)
Light comedy star popular during the 50s and 60s, also on
stage (since 1935) and tv. Former child actor.

A Lassie From Lancashire,
   1935
The Citadel, 1938
Train of Events, 1949
Pool of London, 1951
The Sound Barrier, 1952
The Limping Man, 1953
Les Girls, 1955

Value For Money, 1955
The Gamma People, 1956
The Big Money, 1956
The Barretts of Wimpole
  Street, 1957
Brothers in Law, 1957
The Smallest Show On Earth,
  1957
High Flight, 1957
Just My Luck, 1957
I Was Monty's Double, 1958
The Man Who Liked Funerals,
  1959
Ferdinand of Naples, 1959
Carry On Nurse, 1959
The Angry Hills, 1959
Carry On Teacher, 1959
This Other Eden, 1959
The Night We Dropped a
  Clanger, 1959
The Navy Lark, 1959
Please Turn Over, 1959
Carry On Constable, 1960
Inn For Trouble, 1960
Doctor in Love, 1960
Watch Your Stern, 1960
No Kidding, 1960
A Weekend With Lulu, 1961
Very Important Person, 1961
Raising the Wind, 1961
In the Doghouse, 1961
The Fast Lady, 1962
Crooks Anonymous, 1962
Father Came Too, 1963
You Must Be Joking!, 1965
Doctor in Clover, 1965
Zabaglione, 1966
Maroc 7, 1966
Some Will, Some Won't, 1970
Doctor in Trouble, 1970
Magnificent Seven Deadly Sins,
  1971
Not Now Darling, 1972
Don't Just Lie There, 1973
Spanish Fly, 1975
Not Now Comrade, 1976

SIAN PHILLIPS (1934-)
Actress primarily on stage,
usually plays haughty or dignified characters. Married:
Peter O'Toole.

Becket, 1964
Young Cassidy, 1965
Goodbye Mr. Chips, 1969
Laughter in the Dark, 1969
Murphy's War, 1970
Under Milk Wood, 1971
Nijinsky, 1980
Crime and Punishment, 1980
Tinker, Tailor, Soldier, Spy, 1980

AMBROSINE PHILPOTTS (1912-)
Character actress in occasional
films of the 50s and 60s; more
often on stage.

This Man is Mine, 1946
The Franchise Affair, 1951
The Captain's Paradise, 1953
Up in the World, 1956
The Truth About Women, 1958
The Duke Wore Jeans, 1958
Room at the Top, 1959
Expresso Bongo, 1959
Doctor in Love, 1960
Carry On Regardless, 1961
Two and Two Make Six, 1962
Carry On Cabby, 1963
Life at the Top, 1965
Berserk!, 1967

NICHOLAS PHIPPS (1913-)
Character actor and screenwriter, often seen in comedy
cameo roles; also on stage
(since 1932).

You Will Remember, 1940
Old Bill and Son, 1940
Piccadilly Incident, 1946
Spring in Park Lane, 1948
Maytime in Mayfair, 1949
Elizabeth of Ladymead, 1949
Madeleine, 1950
Appointment With Venus, 1951
Kathy's Love Affair, 1952
The Captain's Paradise, 1953
The Intruder, 1953
Doctor in the House, 1954
Mad About Men, 1954
Doctor at Sea, 1955
All For Mary, 1955

The Iron Petticoat, 1956
Who Done It, 1956
Doctor at Large, 1957
Orders to Kill, 1958
Rockets Galore, 1958
The Navy Lark, 1959
Don't Panic Chaps, 1959
The Captain's Table, 1959
The Pure Hell of St. Trinian's,
  1960
Doctor in Love, 1960
No Love For Johnnie, 1961
The Wild and the Willing, 1962
A Pair of Briefs, 1962
Doctor in Distress, 1963
Summer Holiday, 1963
Charlie Bubbles, 1967
Some Girls Do, 1969
Monte Carlo Or Bust, 1969
The Rise & Rise of Michael
  Rimmer, 1970

DONALD PICKERING (-)
Dignified actor primarily seen
on stage and television, adept
at kindliness or villainy; films
few but memorable.

Nothing But the Best, 1964
The Unpleasantness at the
  Bellona Club, 1973
A Bridge Too Far, 1977
Yanks, 1979
The Thirty-Nine Steps, 1980
Zulu Dawn, 1980

VIVIAN PICKLES (1933-)
Character actress of stage and
screen, former child actress.

Jean's Plan, 1946
Play Dirty, 1968
The Looking Glass War, 1970
Harold and Maude, 1971
Nicholas and Alexandra, 1971
Sunday Bloody Sunday, 1971
O Lucky Man, 1973
Candleshoe, 1978
Rebecca, 1980

WILFRED PICKLES (1904-)

North-country character star
in occasional films; former radio performer.

The Gay Dog, 1953
Serious Charge, 1959
Billy Liar, 1963
The Family Way, 1966
For the Love of Ada, 1972

RONALD PICKUP (-)
Supporting player in very occasional films.

Three Sisters, 1970
Day of the Jackal, 1973
Mahler, 1975
Nijinsky, 1980
Zulu Dawn, 1980

NOVA PILBEAM (1919-)
Juvenile star of the thirties,
also on stage (from 1931).

Little Friend, 1934
The Man Who Knew Too Much,
  1934
Tudor Rose, 1936
Young and Innocent, 1937
Cheer Boys Cheer, 1939
Pastor Hall, 1940
Spring Meeting, 1941
Banana Ridge, 1941
Next of Kin, 1942
The Yellow Canary, 1943
This Man is Mine, 1946
Green Fingers, 1947
Counterblast, 1948
Three Weird Sisters, 1948
Devil's Plot, 1953

FREDERICK PIPER (1902-)
Character actor of stage and
films, often cast as policeman
or common man.

The Good Companions, 1933
Crown v Stevens, 1936
Jamaica Inn, 1939
Four Just Men, 1939
Spare a Copper, 1940

49th Parallel, 1941
The Big Blockade, 1942
San Demetrio-London, 1943
Nine Men, 1943
Fiddlers Three, 1944
Champagne Charlie, 1944
Pink String and Sealing Wax,
   1945
Johnny Frenchman, 1945
Hue and Cry, 1946
The October Man, 1947
The Loves of Joanna Godden,
   1947
The Master of Bankdam, 1947
It Always Rains On Sunday,
   1947
Fly Away Peter, 1948
Penny and the Pownall Case,
   1948
Escape, 1948
Easy Money, 1948
My Brother's Keeper, 1948
To the Public Danger, 1948
Look Before You Love, 1948
Passport to Pimlico, 1949
Vote For Huggett, 1949
It's Not Cricket, 1949
Don't Ever Leave Me, 1949
The Blue Lamp, 1950
The Lavender Hill Mob, 1951
Home at Seven, 1952
Brandy For the Parson, 1952
Hunted, 1952
Escape Route, 1953
Cosh Boy, 1953
Conflict of Wings, 1954
Rainbow Jacket, 1954
Lease of Life, 1954
Doctor at Sea, 1955
Man in the Road, 1956
The Passionate Stranger, 1956
Suspended Alibi, 1957
Doctor at Large, 1957
Sensation, 1957
A Novel Affair, 1957
Second Fiddle, 1957
The Birthday Present, 1957
Barnacle Bill, 1957
Dunkirk, 1958
A Touch of Larceny, 1959
Dead Lucky, 1960
The Day They Robbed the
   Bank of England, 1960

The Monster of Highgate Ponds,
   1961
The Frightened City, 1961
Very Important Person, 1961
What a Carve Up!, 1961
The Piper's Tune, 1962
Return of a Stranger, 1962
Only Two Can Play, 1962
Postman's Knock, 1962
Reach For Glory, 1963
Ricochet, 1963
Becket, 1964
One Way Pendulum, 1964
Catacombs, 1964
He Who Rides a Tiger, 1966

WENSLEY PITHEY (1914-)
Distinctive character actor seen
sporadically in films since 1950;
frequently on stage and tv.

Guilt is My Shadow, 1950
Kill Me Tomorrow, 1957
Serious Charge, 1959
Snowball, 1960
The Boys, 1962
The Guilty Party, 1962
The Knack, 1965
Oliver, 1968
Oh What a Lovely War, 1969
One of Our Dinosaurs is Miss-
   ing, 1975
Ike, 1979
FDR: The Last Year, 1980

INGRID PITT (1945-)
Polish-born actress of stage and
films, often in horror productions.

The Omegans, 1968
Where Eagles Dare, 1968
The Vampire Lovers, 1970
The House That Dripped Blood,
   1970
Countess Dracula, 1970
Nobody Ordered Love, 1971
The Wicker Man, 1973

DONALD PLEASENCE (1919-)
Bald character star of stage

(from 1939) and films, equally
good in villainous, comedic or
eccentric parts. Also in Hollywood.

The Beachcomber, 1954
Orders Are Orders, 1955
Value For Money, 1955
1984, 1956
The Black Tent, 1956
Man in the Sky, 1957
Manuela, 1957
Barnacle Bill, 1957
A Tale of Two Cities, 1958
The Wind Cannot Read, 1958
Heart of a Child, 1958
The Man Inside, 1958
The Two-Headed Spy, 1958
Look Back in Anger, 1959
Killers of Kilimanjaro, 1959
Battle of the Sexes, 1959
The Shakedown, 1960
The Flesh and the Fiends,
  1960
Hell is a City, 1960
Circus of Horrors, 1960
Sons and Lovers, 1960
The Big Day, 1960
Suspect, 1960
The Hands of Orlac, 1960
A Story of David, 1961
No Love For Johnnie, 1961
The Wind of Change, 1961
Spare the Rod, 1961
The Horsemasters, 1961
What a Carve Up!, 1961
The Inspector, 1962
Dr. Crippen, 1962
The Caretaker, 1963
The Great Escape, 1963
Maniac, 1964
The Hallelujah Trail, 1965
The Greatest Story Ever Told,
  1965
Cul de Sac, 1966
Eye of the Devil, 1966
Fantastic Voyage, 1966
Night of the Generals, 1966
You Only Live Twice, 1967
Matchless, 1968
Will Penny, 1968
Mr. Freedom, 1969
The Madwoman of Chaillot,

1969
Arthur Arthur, 1970
Soldier Blue, 1970
Kidnapped, 1971
Outback, 1971
The Pied Piper, 1971
THX 1138, 1971
Henry VIII and His Six Wives,
  1972
Innocent Bystanders, 1972
The Jerusalem File, 1972
Death Line, 1972
Dr. Jekyll & Mr. Hyde, 1973
From Beyond the Grave, 1973
The Mutations, 1973
Tales That Witness Madness,
  1973
The Seaweed Children, 1973
Wedding in White, 1973
Raw Meat, 1973
The Black Windmill, 1974
Barry Mackenzie Holds His
  Own, 1974
The Count of Monte Cristo, 1975
I Don't Want to Be Born, 1975
Hearts of the West, 1975
Escape to Witch Mountain, 1975
Journey Into Fear, 1975
Hindle Wakes, 1976
A Choice of Weapons, 1976
The Devil's Men, 1976
Watch Out We're Mad, 1976
The Passover Plot, 1976
Dirty Knight's Work, 1976
The Last Tycoon, 1976
Oh God, 1977
Land of the Minotaur, 1977
The Eagle Has Landed, 1977
The Uncanny, 1977
Tomorrow Never Comes, 1977·
Telefon, 1977
Jesus of Nazareth, 1977
Centennial, 1978
Blood Relatives, 1978
L'Ordre et la Securite du
  Monde, 1978
Sergeant Pepper's Lonely Hearts
  Club Band, 1978
Power Play, 1978
Halloween, 1978
The Defection of Simas Kudirka,
  1978
Gold of the Amazon Women, 1979

L'Homme en Colere, 1979
The Jaguar Lives, 1979
Out of the Darkness, 1979
Good Luck Miss Wyckoff, 1979
Dracula, 1979
All Quiet On the Western
Front, 1979
French Atlantic Affair, 1979

JOAN PLOWRIGHT (1929-)
Prominent actress primarily
seen on stage; wife of Laurence
Olivier.

Moby Dick, 1956
Time Without Pity, 1957
The Entertainer, 1960
Uncle Vanya, 1963
Three Sisters, 1970
The Merchant of Venice, 1972
Equus, 1977
The Diary of Anne Frank, 1980

CHRISTOPHER PLUMMER
(1927-)
Canadian leading man of British
and international films, also on
stage (1950) and tv.

Johnny Belinda, 1958
Stage Struck, 1958
Wind Across the Everglades,
1958
Fall of the Roman Empire, 1964
The Sound of Music, 1965
Inside Daisy Clover, 1965
Night of the Generals, 1966
Triple Cross, 1967
Oedipus the King, 1967
Nobody Runs Forever, 1968
Lock Up Your Daughters, 1969
The Royal Hunt of the Sun,
1969
The Battle of Britain, 1969
Waterloo, 1970
The Pyx, 1973
Return of the Pink Panther,
1974
Conduct Unbecoming, 1975
The Man Who Would Be King,
1975
Spiral Staircase, 1975

Aces High, 1976
The Day That Shook the World,
1976
The Assignment, 1977
The Disappearance, 1977
Jesus of Nazareth, 1977
International Velvet, 1978
The Silent Partner, 1978
Riel, 1979
Starcrash, 1979
Hanover Street, 1979
Murder By Decree, 1979
The Shadow Box, 1980
Desperate Voyage, 1980
Somewhere in Time, 1980
When the Circus Came to Town,
1980

PATRICIA PLUNKETT (1928-)
Leading lady and supporting actress of stage (since 1946) and
films.

It Always Rains On Sunday, 1947
Bond Street, 1948
Landfall, 1949
For Them That Trespass, 1949
Murder Without Crime, 1950
Mandy, 1952
The Crowded Day, 1954
The Flesh is Weak, 1957
Dunkirk, 1958
Three Survived, 1960
Escort For Hire, 1960
Identity Unknown, 1960

ERIC POHLMANN (1913-)
Chubby Austrian character long
in Britain, generally in sinister
roles; also Hollywood. Former
stage (1948) and radio (1948) actor

Children of Chance, 1949
Blackout, 1950
Highly Dangerous, 1950
State Secret, 1950
The Clouded Yellow, 1950
The Long Dark Hall, 1951
Chance of a Lifetime, 1951
Hell is Sold Out, 1951
Emergency Call, 1952
His Excellency, 1952

The Woman's Angle, 1952
Penny Princess, 1952
Venetian Bird, 1952
The Gambler and the Lady,
1952
Paris Express, 1953
Blood Orange, 1953
Monsoon, 1953
Mogambo, 1953
Rob Roy, 1953
The Beggar's Opera, 1953
The Flame and the Flesh, 1954
They Who Dare, 1954
Knave of Hearts, 1954
Forbidden Cargo, 1954
36 Hours, 1954
The Belles of St. Trinian's,
1954
A Prize of Gold, 1955
Break in the Circle, 1955
The Glass Cage, 1955
Gentlemen Marry Brunettes,
1955
The Constant Husband, 1955
Quentin Durward, 1955
The Gelignite Gang, 1956
House of Secrets, 1956
Lust For Life, 1956
The High Terrace, 1956
Reach For the Sky, 1956
Anastasia, 1956
The Counterfeit Plan, 1957
Barnacle Bill, 1957
Interpol, 1957
Fire Down Below, 1957
House of Cards, 1957
Across the Bridge, 1957
Further Up the Creek, 1958
The Man Inside, 1958
Life is a Circus, 1958
Mark of the Phoenix, 1958
I Accuse!, 1958
Three Crooked Men, 1958
The Duke Wore Jeans, 1958
A Tale of Two Cities, 1958
Alive and Kicking, 1958
Nor the Moon By Night, 1958
House of the Seven Hawks,
1959
Expresso Bongo, 1959
Snowball, 1960
No Kidding, 1960
Visa to Canton, 1960

Sands of the Desert, 1960
The Man Who Couldn't Walk,
1960
Surprise Package, 1960
The Kitchen, 1961
The Singer Not the Song, 1961
Carry On Regardless, 1961
Village of Daughters, 1962
Mrs. Gibbons' Boys, 1962
The Devil's Agent, 1962
Cairo, 1962
Dr. Syn Alias the Scarecrow,
1963
Shadow of Fear, 1963
Follow the Boys, 1963
55 Days at Peking, 1963
Hot Enough For June, 1963
Carry On Spying, 1964
Night Train to Paris, 1964
The Sicilians, 1964
Joey Boy, 1965
Those Magnificent Men in Their
Flying Machines, 1965
Where the Spies Are, 1965
The Million Dollar Collar, 1967
Inspector Clouseau, 1968
The Horsemen, 1971
Return of the Pink Panther,
1974
Auch Mimosen Wollen Bluhen,
1975
Tiffany Jones, 1976

ELLEN POLLOCK (1903-)
Character actress of stage and
films, active during the thirties.

Moulin Rouge, 1928
Piccadilly, 1929
The Informer, 1929
Too Many Crooks, 1930
Night Birds, 1930
Midnight, 1931
My Wife's Family, 1931
Heads We Go, 1933
Channel Crossing, 1933
Mr. Cinders, 1934
It's a Bet, 1935
Royal Cavalcade, 1935
The Happy Family, 1936
Millions, 1936
Non Stop New York, 1937

The Street Singer, 1937
Aren't Men Beasts, 1937
Splinters in the Air, 1937
Shadow of Death, 1939
Sons of the Sea, 1939
Spare a Copper, 1940
Kiss the Bride Goodbye, 1944
Don Chicago, 1945
Bedelia, 1946
Warning to Wantons, 1949
Something in the City, 1950
To Have and to Hold, 1951
The Galloping Major, 1951
The Fake, 1953
The Golden Link, 1954
The Time of His Life, 1955
Not So Dusty, 1956
The Hypnotist, 1957
The Long Knife, 1958

OLAF POOLEY (-)
Small-part player seen sporadically in films since 1948.

Penny and the Pownall Case,
   1948
The Lost People, 1949
Highly Dangerous, 1950
The Woman's Angle, 1952
Top Secret, 1952
Anastasia, 1956
Windom's Way, 1957
Stars of a Summer Night, 1959
The Battleaxe, 1962
The Assassination Bureau,
   1969
The Corpse, 1970

ERIC PORTER (1928-)
Strong character actor of stage
(from 1945) and screen, adept
at kindly or sinister roles.
Also on tv, notably as Soames
in "The Forsyte Saga. " (1967).

Fall of the Roman Empire,
   1964
The Pumpkin Eater, 1964
The Heroes of Telemark, 1965
Kaleidoscope, 1966
The Lost Continent, 1968
Antony and Cleopatra, 1971

Nicholas and Alexandra, 1971
Hands of the Ripper, 1971
Day of the Jackal, 1973
Hitler: The Last Ten Days,
   1973
The Belstone Fox, 1973
Callan, 1974
Hennessy, 1975
Free Spirit, 1978
The Thirty-Nine Steps, 1980
Little Lord Fauntleroy, 1980
Hamlet, 1980

NYREE DAWN PORTER
   (1940-)
Attractive New Zealand leading
lady of films and television.
Tv series: "The Forsyte Saga"
(1967); "The Protectors" (1972).

Sentenced For Life, 1960
Identity Unknown, 1960
Man at the Carlton Tower, 1961
Part Time Wife, 1961
Live Now Pay Later, 1962
Two Left Feet, 1963
The Cracksman, 1963
Jane Eyre, 1970
The House That Dripped Blood,
   1970
From Beyond the Grave, 1973
Death in Small Doses, 1973

ERIC PORTMAN (1903-1969)
Distinguished leading man and
latterly character actor of stage
(1924) and films, popular in the
40s; personality lent itself to
both kindly and sinister roles.
Also in Hollywood.

Maria Marten, 1935
Old Roses, 1935
Abdul the Damned, 1935
Hyde Park Corner, 1935
The Cardinal, 1936
The Crimes of Stephen Hawke,
   1936
Hearts of Humanity, 1936
Moonlight Sonata, 1937
The Prince and the Pauper,
   1937

49th Parallel, 1941
One of Our Aircraft is Miss-
  ing, 1942
Uncensored, 1942
Squadron Leader X, 1942
We Dive at Dawn, 1943
Escape to Danger, 1943
Millions Like Us, 1943
A Canterbury Tale, 1943
Great Day, 1945
Wanted For Murder, 1946
Men of Two Worlds, 1946
Dear Murderer, 1947
The Mark of Cain, 1947
Corridor of Mirrors, 1948
Daybreak, 1948
The Blind Goddess, 1948
The Spider and the Fly, 1949
Cairo Road, 1950
The Magic Box, 1951
His Excellency, 1952
South of Algiers, 1952
The Colditz Story, 1954
The Deep Blue Sea, 1955
Child in the House, 1956
The Good Companions, 1957
The Naked Edge, 1961
Freud, 1962
The Man Who Finally Died,
  1962
West Eleven, 1963
The Bedford Incident, 1965
The Spy With a Cold Nose,
  1966
The Whisperers, 1967
Think 20th, 1967
Deadfall, 1968
Assignment to Kill, 1968

ADRIENNE POSTA (1948-)
Teenage actress of the sixties
usually seen in impudent
parts.

No Time For Tears, 1959
To Sir With Love, 1967
Here We Go Round the Mul-
  berry Bush, 1967
Up the Junction, 1968
Some Girls Do, 1969
Percy, 1970
Up Pompeii, 1971
Percy's Progress, 1974

ROBERT POWELL (1946-)
Captivating leading actor of the
70s and 80s, also on stage and
television.

Secrets, 1971
Running Scared, 1972
Asylum, 1972
The Asphyx, 1973
The Death Policy, 1973
Tommy, 1975
Mahler, 1975
Jesus of Nazareth, 1977
The Four Feathers, 1978
The Thirty-Nine Steps, 1980
Jane Austen in Manhattan, 1981
Harlequin, 1981

SANDY POWELL (1898-)
Yorkshire comedy star of the
thirties with music hall and
stage experience; also well-
known on radio for catchphrase
"Can You Hear Me Mother?"

Sandy the Fireman, 1930
Sandy the Lost Policeman, 1931
The Third String, 1932
Pathetone Parade, 1934
Can You Hear Me Mother?, 1935
It's a Grand Old World, 1937
Leave it To Me, 1937
I've Got a Horse, 1938
Home From Home, 1939
All at Sea, 1939
Cup Tie Honeymoon, 1948

HARTLEY POWER (1894-1966)
Bald American character actor
in Britain from 1930, seen in
a wide variety of roles, generally comic.

Down River, 1931
Aunt Sally, 1933
Just Smith, 1933
Yes Mr. Brown, 1933
Friday the 13th, 1933
Evergreen, 1934
The Camels Are Coming, 1934
Road House, 1934
Where There's a Will, 1936

Jury's Evidence, 1936
Living Dangerously, 1936
The Return of the Frog, 1938
Just Like a Woman, 1938
Murder Will Out, 1939
A Window in London, 1939
Return to Yesterday, 1940
Atlantic Ferry, 1941
Alibi, 1942
Lady in Distress, 1942
The Way to the Stars, 1945
The Man From Morocco, 1945
Dead of Night, 1945
Girl in a Million, 1946
The Armchair Detective, 1952
Roman Holiday, 1953
The Million Pound Note, 1954
To Dorothy a Son, 1954
Island In the Sun, 1957

DENNIS PRICE (1915-1973)
Tall, suave, elegant leading
man of the forties and latterly
character star of distinction;
adept at smooth villains and
polished comedy roles. Also
on stage (from 1937) and television. Tv series: "The
World of Wooster" (as Jeeves).

A Canterbury Tale, 1943
A Place of One's Own, 1944
The Echo Murders, 1945
Caravan, 1946
Hungry Hill, 1946
The Magic Bow, 1947
Dear Murderer, 1947
Jassy, 1947
Holiday Camp, 1947
The Master of Bankdam, 1947
The White Unicorn, 1947
Easy Money, 1948
Snowbound, 1948
Good Time Girl, 1948
The Bad Lord Byron, 1948
Kind Hearts and Coronets,
    1949
The Lost People, 1949
Helter Skelter, 1949
Cockpit, 1949
The Dancing Years, 1950
Murder Without Crime, 1950

The Adventurers, 1950
The Magic Box, 1951
Lady Godiva Rides Again, 1951
The House in the Square, 1951
Song of Paris, 1952
The Tall Headlines, 1952
Noose For a Lady, 1953
Murder at 3 am, 1953
The Intruder, 1953
Time is My Enemy, 1954
For Better, For Worse, 1954
That Lady, 1955
Oh Rosalinda, 1955
Private's Progress, 1956
Charley Moon, 1956
Port Afrique, 1956
A Touch of the Sun, 1956
The Tommy Steele Story, 1957
Fortune is a Woman, 1957
The Naked Truth, 1958
Hello London, 1958
Danger Within, 1959
I'm All Right, Jack, 1959
Don't Panic Chaps, 1959
School For Scoundrels, 1960
Oscar Wilde, 1960
Piccadilly Third Stop, 1960
Tunes of Glory, 1960
The Millionairess, 1960
The Pure Hell of St. Trinian's,
    1960
No Love For Johnnie, 1961
The Rebel, 1961
Five Golden Hours, 1961
Double Bunk, 1961
Watch it Sailor, 1961
Victim, 1961
What a Carve Up!, 1961
Go To Blazes, 1962
Play It Cool, 1962
Behave Yourself, 1962
The Pot Carriers, 1962
The Amorous Prawn, 1962
The Wrong Arm of the Law,
    1962
Kill Or Cure, 1963
The Cool Mikado, 1963
The VIPs, 1963
The Cracksman, 1963
Doctor in Distress, 1963
Tamahine, 1963
The Comedy Man, 1963
The Dark, 1964

A Jolly Bad Fellow, 1964
Witchcraft, 1964
Wonderful Life, 1964
The Horror of It All, 1964
The Earth Dies Screaming,
1964
You Must Be Joking!, 1965
Eighth Witness, 1965
Murder Most Foul, 1965
Curse of the Voodoo, 1965
A High Wind in Jamaica, 1965
Ten Little Indians, 1965
Just Like a Woman, 1966
The Jewels, 1966
Cochran Story, 1966
Rocket to the Moon, 1967
Dear Brutus, 1967
Age of Abandon, 1968
Rope, 1968
Horror House, 1969
Myself When Young, 1969
Dr. Jekyll and Mr. Hyde,
1970
Venus in Furs, 1970
The Magic Christian, 1970
Some Will, Some Won't, 1970
The Horror of Frankenstein,
1970
Rise & Rise of Michael Rim-
mer, 1970
Twins of Evil, 1971
Eden End, 1971
The Fourposter, 1971
The Invisible Man, 1972
Attempt to Murder, 1972
Pulp, 1972
Alice's Adventures in Wonder-
land, 1972
Go For a Take, 1972
Tower of Evil, 1972
The Adventures of Barry McKen-
zie, 1972
Theatre of Blood, 1973
Horror Hospital, 1973
That's Your Funeral, 1973
Son of Dracula, 1974

NANCY PRICE (1880-1970)
Distinguished character actress of stage (since 1899)
and screen, also an avid
traveler and naturalist.

The Lyons Mail, 1916
Belphegor the Mountebank,
1921
Love, Life, and Laughter, 1923
The Woman Who Obeyed, 1923
Comin' Thro' The Rye, 1923
Bonnie Prince Charlie, 1924
Huntingtower, 1927
His House in Order, 1928
The Price of Divorce, 1928
The Doctor's Secret, 1929
Three Live Ghosts, 1929
The American Prisoner, 1929
The Loves of Robert Burns,
1930
In Gay Madrid, 1930
Caught Short, 1930
The Speckled Band, 1931
Down Our Street, 1932
The Crucifix, 1934
Dead Man's Shoes, 1939
The Stars Look Down, 1939
Secret Mission, 1942
Madonna of the Seven Moons,
1944
I Live in Grosvenor Square,
1945
I Know Where I'm Going, 1945
Carnival, 1946
The Master of Bankdam, 1947
The Three Weird Sisters, 1948
Naked Earth, 1950
Mandy, 1952
The Naked Heart, 1955

BRYAN PRINGLE (1935-)
Character actor of the 60s and
70s; mainly on stage and television.

Saturday Night & Sunday Morn-
ing, 1960
HMS Defiant, 1962
French Dressing, 1964
The Early Bird, 1965
How I Won the War, 1967
Diamonds For Breakfast, 1968
Spring and Port Wine, 1970
The Boy Friend, 1971
Mr. Quilp, 1975
Jabberwocky, 1977
Henry V, 1980

NOEL PURCELL (1900-)
Gaunt, bearded Irish character actor, often seen in comedy roles.

Ireland's Border Line, 1939
Odd Man Out, 1947
Captain Boycott, 1947
The Blue Lagoon, 1949
Saints and Sinners, 1949
Talk of a Million, 1950
No Resting Place, 1951
Appointment With Venus, 1951
Encore, 1952
The Crimson Pirate, 1952
Decameron Nights, 1952
The Pickwick Papers, 1952
Father's Doing Fine, 1952
Grand National Night, 1953
Doctor in the House, 1954
The Seekers, 1954
Mad About Men, 1954
Svengali, 1955
Doctor at Sea, 1955
Lust For Life, 1956
Jacqueline, 1956
Moby Dick, 1956
The Rising of the Moon, 1957
Doctor at Large, 1957
Rockets Galore, 1958
Merry Andrew, 1958
Rooney, 1958
The Key, 1958
Shake Hands With the Devil,
   1959
Tommy the Toreador, 1959
Ferry to Hong Kong, 1959
Man in the Moon, 1960
No Kidding, 1960
Make Mine Mink, 1960
Watch Your Stern, 1960
The Millionairess, 1960
Double Bunk, 1961
Johnny Nobody, 1961
The Iron Maiden, 1962
Mutiny On the Bounty, 1962
The Running Man, 1963
The List of Adrian Messenger,
   1963
Nurse On Wheels, 1963
The Ceremony, 1964
Swingin' Maiden, 1964
Lord Jim, 1965

Doctor in Clover, 1965
Drop Dead Darling, 1966
I Spy, 1967
The Violent Enemy, 1969
Where's Jack?, 1969
Sinful Davy, 1969
The Mackenzie Break, 1971
The Mackintosh Man, 1973

REGINALD PURDELL (1896-
   1963)
Comedy character actor and occasional writer, popular during
the thirties. Also on stage
and radio.

The Middle Watch, 1930
Congress Dances, 1931
A Night in Montmartre, 1932
My Lucky Star, 1933
Strictly in Confidence, 1933
Up to the Neck, 1933
Three Men in a Boat, 1933
Crime On the Hill, 1933
On the Air, 1934
The Queen's Affair, 1934
Luck of a Sailor, 1934
The Old Curiosity Shop, 1934
What's in a Name?, 1934
Radio Parade of 1935, 1935
Key to Harmony, 1935
Royal Cavalcade, 1935
Get Off My Foot, 1935
Crown v Stevens, 1936
Debt of Honour, 1936
Where's Sally?, 1936
Hail and Farewell, 1936
Side Street Angel, 1937
Ship's Concert, 1937
Dark Stairway, 1938
Quiet Please, 1938
Simply Terrific, 1938
The Viper, 1938
It's in the Blood, 1938
Many Tanks Mr. Atkins, 1938
Q Planes, 1939
The Missing People, 1939
His Brother's Keeper, 1939
The Middle Watch, 1939
Pack Up Your Troubles, 1940
Busman's Honeymoon, 1940
Fingers, 1940

Variety Jubilee, 1943
We Dive at Dawn, 1943
Bell Bottom George, 1943
It's in the Bag, 1943
Candles at Nine, 1944
Love Story, 1944
Two Thousand Women, 1944
London Town, 1946
The Root of All Evil, 1947
Man About the House, 1947
Holiday Camp, 1947
Captain Boycott, 1947
Brighton Rock, 1947
Files From Scotland Yard,
  1951

EDMUND PURDOM (1924-)
Light leading man of stage
(since 1945) and screen, in
Hollywood and international
films.

Titanic, 1953
Julius Caesar, 1953
The Student Prince, 1954
The Egyptian, 1954
The Prodigal, 1955
The King's Thief, 1955
Moment of Danger, 1956
Agguato a Tangieri, 1957
Erode il Grande, 1958
The Cossacks, 1959
Herod the Great, 1960
Malaga, 1960
Fury of the Pagan, 1960
Nights of Rasputin, 1961
White Slave Ship, 1961
Queen of the Nile, 1962
Last of the Vikings, 1962
The Comedy Man, 1963
Lafayette, 1963
Suleiman the Conqueror, 1963
Athena, 1964
The Beauty Jungle, 1964
The Yellow Rolls-Royce, 1964
L'Umo Che Ride, 1965
The Black Corsair, 1969
Man in the Golden Mask, 1969
Evil Fingers, 1972
House of Freaks, 1973
Perche, 1975
Povero Cristo, 1975

Night Child, 1976
Mr. Scarface, 1976
Sophia Loren Her Own Story, 1980

ANNA QUAYLE (1937-)
Character actress of the sixties
and seventies, mainly in comedy
parts.

A Hard Day's Night, 1964
Drop Dead Darling, 1966
The Sandwich Man, 1966
Casino Royale, 1967
Smashing Time, 1967
Chitty Chitty Bang Bang, 1968
Up the Chastity Belt, 1971
Mistress Pamela, 1974
The Seven Per Cent Solution,
  1976
Eskimo Nell, 1977
Henry V, 1980

ANTHONY QUAYLE (1913-)
Distinguished, prominent character star of stage (since 1931)
and screen, also in Hollywood;
also author.

Moscow Nights, 1935
Pygmalion, 1938
Saraband For Dead Lovers, 1948
Hamlet, 1948
Oh Rosalinda, 1955
Battle of the River Plate, 1956
No Time For Tears, 1957
Woman in a Dressing Gown,
  1957
The Man Who Wouldn't Talk,
  1957
The Wrong Man, 1957
Ice Cold in Alex, 1958
Tarzan's Greatest Adventure,
  1959
Serious Charge, 1959
The Challenge, 1960
The Guns of Navarone, 1961
Drums For a Queen (voice),
  1961
HMS Defiant, 1962
Lawrence of Arabia, 1962
East of Sudan, 1964

Fall of the Roman Empire, 1964
Operation Crossbow, 1965
A Study in Terror, 1965
The Poppy is Also a Flower, 1966
Before Winter Comes, 1969
Mackenna's Gold, 1969
Island Unknown, 1969
Anne of the Thousand Days, 1970
Everything You Always Wanted to Know About Sex, 1972
Bequest to the Nation, 1973
QB VII, 1973
Jarrett, 1973
The Tamarind Seed, 1974
Great Expectations, 1975
Moses, 1976
Holocaust 2000, 1977
The Eagle Has Landed, 1977
Murder By Decree, 1979
Henry IV Part 1, 1980
Henry IV Part 2, 1980
The Manions of America, 1981

DENIS QUILLEY (1927-)
Character player of small parts, mainly on stage; films rare.

Life at the Top, 1965
Anne of the Thousand Days, 1970
The Black Windmill, 1974
Murder On the Orient Express, 1974
In This House of Brede, 1975

TONY QUINN (-)
Irish character actor, often seen in cameo roles.

Lest We Forget, 1934
Danny Boy, 1941
Thunder Rock, 1942
It's in the Bag, 1943
Hungry Hill, 1946
The Imperfect Lady, 1947
Saints and Sinners, 1949
The Strangers Came, 1949
Never Say Die, 1950
Talk of a Million, 1950

The Lavender Hill Mob, 1951
The Beachcomber, 1954
Shadow of a Man, 1955
Tons of Trouble, 1956
Booby Trap, 1957
The Rising of the Moon, 1957
Undercover Girl, 1958
The Great Van Robbery, 1959
The Trouble With Eve, 1960
The Trunk, 1961
The Runaway, 1964
Murder Ahoy, 1964

RONALD RADD (1924-1976)
Character actor often seen in sinister parts; frequently on tv.

The Camp On Blood Island, 1958
The Small World of Sammy Lee, 1963
Where the Spies Are, 1965
Up Jumped a Swagman, 1965
Mr. Ten Per Cent, 1966
The Double Man, 1967
The Sea Gull, 1969
The Kremlin Letter, 1970
The Offence, 1972
Divorce His, Divorce Hers, 1973
The Spiral Staircase, 1974
Galileo, 1975
Operation Daybreak, 1976

BASIL RADFORD (1897-1952)
Hearty comedy star of stage (1922) and films, often teamed with Naunton Wayne as imperturbable gentleman abroad.

Barnum Was Right, 1929
There Goes the Bride, 1932
Just Smith, 1933
A Southern Maid, 1933
Broken Blossoms, 1936
Dishonour Bright, 1936
Jump For Glory, 1937
Young and Innocent, 1937
Captain's Orders, 1937
Convict 99, 1938
Climbing High, 1938

The Lady Vanishes, 1938
Let's Be Famous, 1939
Trouble Brewing, 1939
Jamaica Inn, 1939
Spies of the Air, 1939
Secret Journey, 1939
Just William, 1939
The Girl Who Forgot, 1939
She Couldn't Say No, 1939
The Flying Squad, 1940
Night Train to Munich, 1940
Room For Two, 1940
Crooks' Tour, 1940
The Girl in the News, 1941
Unpublished Story, 1942
Partners in Crime, 1942
The Flying Fortress, 1943
Dear Octopus, 1943
Millions Like Us, 1943
Twilight Hour, 1944
The Way to the Stars, 1945
Dead of Night, 1945
The Captive Heart, 1946
Girl in a Million, 1947
The Winslow Boy, 1948
Quartet, 1948
Whiskey Galore, 1948
Passport to Pimlico, 1949
Stop Press Girl, 1949
It's Not Cricket, 1949
Chance of a Lifetime, 1950
White Corridors, 1951
The Galloping Major, 1951

CHIPS RAFFERTY (1909-1971)
Tall, lanky Australian leading
man and latterly character star,
also in Hollywood. Frequently
played a variation on a drawl-
ing country type called "Dinkum."

Ants in His Pants, 1938
Dan Rudd, MP, 1939
Forty Thousand Horsemen,
  1940
The Rats of Tobruk, 1944
Bush Christmas, 1945
The Overlanders, 1946
The Loves of Joanna Godden,
  1947
Eureka Stockade, 1948
Bitter Springs, 1951

Kangaroo, 1952
The Desert Rats, 1953
King of the Coral Sea, 1954
Walk Into Hell, 1956
Smiley, 1956
Smiley Gets a Gun, 1958
The Sundowners, 1960
The Wackiest Ship in the Army,
  1960
Mutiny On the Bounty, 1962
They're a Weird Mob, 1966
Double Trouble, 1967
Kona Coast, 1968
Skullduggery, 1970
Outback, 1971

JACK RAINE (1896-1979)
Character player and supporting
actor, latterly seen in Hollywood.

Comets, 1930
Raise the Roof, 1930
Infatuation, 1930
Harmony Heaven, 1930
Suspense, 1930
The Hate Ship, 1930
The Middle Watch, 1930
Night Birds, 1930
Fires of Fate, 1932
Her Night Out, 1932
The Ghoul, 1933
Out of the Past, 1933
The Fortunate Fool, 1933
The House of Trent, 1933
Lillies of the Field, 1934
Little Friend, 1934
Dangerous Ground, 1934
Important People, 1934
Mimi, 1935
The Clairvoyant, 1935
Meet Mr. Penny, 1938
Double Or Quits, 1938
Eyewitness, 1939
Neutral Port, 1940
I Didn't Do It, 1945
Send For Paul Temple, 1946
Holiday Camp, 1947
Just William's Luck, 1947
Mine Own Executioner, 1947
Easy Money, 1948
Good Time Girl, 1948
My Brother's Keeper, 1948

Calling Paul Temple, 1948
The Story of Shirley Yorke,
1948
No Way Back, 1949
The Happy Time, 1952
Above and Beyond, 1953
Julius Caesar, 1953
Dangerous When Wet, 1953
Rhapsody, 1954
Prince of Players, 1954
Not as a Stranger, 1955
The Power and the Prize, 1956
An Affair to Remember, 1957
Woman Obsessed, 1959
My Fair Lady, 1964
Hello Dolly, 1969
Scandalous John, 1971

CLAUDE RAINS (1889-1967)
Cultured, charming actor of
stage (from 1900) and screen,
long resident in U.S. Equally
skillful in kindly or villainous
parts. Formerly married to
Isabel Jeans.

The Invisible Man, 1933
Crime Without Passion, 1934
The Man Who Reclaimed His
Head, 1934
The Clairvoyant, 1935
The Mystery of Edwin Drood,
1935
The Last Outpost, 1935
Anthony Adverse, 1936
Hearts Divided, 1936
Stolen Holiday, 1936
The Prince and the Pauper,
1937
They Won't Forget, 1937
Gold is Where You Find It, 1938
The Adventures of Robin Hood,
1938
White Banners, 1938
Four Daughters, 1938
They Made Me a Criminal,
1939
Juarez, 1939
Mr. Smith Goes to Washington,
1939
Four Wives, 1939
Daughters Courageous, 1939
Saturday's Children, 1939

The Sea Hawk, 1940
Lady With Red Hair, 1940
Four Mothers, 1940
Here Comes Mr. Jordan, 1941
The Wolf Man, 1941
King's Row, 1941
Moon Tide, 1942
Casablanca, 1942
Now Voyager, 1942
Forever and a Day, 1943
Phantom of the Opera, 1943
Passage to Marseilles, 1944
Mr. Skeffington, 1944
This Love of Ours, 1945
Caesar and Cleopatra, 1945
Angel On My Shoulder, 1946
Deception, 1946
Notorious, 1946
The Unsuspected, 1947
Strange Holiday, 1947
The Passionate Friends, 1948
Rope of Sand, 1949
Song of Surrender, 1949
The White Tower, 1950
Where Danger Lives, 1950
Sealed Cargo, 1951
Paris Express, 1952
Lisbon, 1956
This Earth is Mine, 1959
The Lost World, 1960
Battle of the Worlds, 1961
The Pied Piper of Hamlin, 1961
Lawrence of Arabia, 1962
Twilight of Honour, 1963
The Greatest Story Ever Told,
1965

CECIL RAMAGE (1895-   )
Scots character actor of stage
and screen, mainly active in
the 30s; often seen as man of
prominence.

C.O.D., 1932
The Strangler, 1932
Account Rendered, 1932
Britannia of Billingsgate, 1932
On Secret Service, 1933
Blossom Time, 1937
Freedom of the Seas, 1934
The Luck of a Sailor, 1934
What Happened Then, 1934
Be Careful Mr. Smith, 1935

McGlusky the Sea Rover, 1935
Spy 77, 1936
King of the Damned, 1936
Love In Exile, 1936
The Lonely Road, 1936
The Secret of Stamboul, 1936
The Mill On the Floss, 1937
Return of a Stranger, 1937
The Last Rose of Summer, 1937
Black Eyes, 1939
I Live in Grosvenor Square,
1945
Nicholas Nickleby, 1947
Blanche Fury, 1948
Kind Hearts and Coronets, 1949

CHARLOTTE RAMPLING
(1945-)
Leading actress of films and
television, now seen in international productions.

The Knack, 1965
Rotten to the Core, 1965
Georgy Girl, 1966
The Long Duel, 1967
Sequestro di Persona, 1968
The Damned, 1969
How to Make It, 1969
Three, 1969
The Ski Bum, 1971
Tis Pity She's a Whore, 1971
Corky, 1972
Henry VIII and His Six Wives,
1972
Asylum, 1972
Zardoz, 1973
The Night Porter, 1973
Caravan to Vaccares, 1974
Farewell My Lovely, 1975
Yuppi-Du, 1975
Foxtrot, 1976
Sherlock Holmes in New York,
1976
Un Taxi Mauve, 1977
Orca, 1977
Target: Harry, 1979
Stardust Memories, 1980

RON RANDELL (1918-)
Australian leading man and
supporting actor of international
films and television; former radio star.

The Night of Nights, 1939
Pacific Adventure, 1946
It Had to Be You, 1947
Bulldog Drummond at Bay, 1947
Sign of the Ram, 1948
The Mating of Millie, 1948
The Loves of Carmen, 1948
Oomo Oomo the Shark God,
1949
The Lone Wolf and His Lady,
1949
Tyrant of the Sea, 1950
Counterspy Meets Scotland Yard,
1950
The Corsair, 1951
Lorna Doone, 1951
The Brigand, 1952
Captive Women, 1952
Kiss Me Kate, 1953
Mississippi Gambler, 1953
Girl On the Pier, 1953
Desert Sands, 1954
Quincannon Frontier Scout, 1955
I Am a Camera, 1955
Beyond Mombasa, 1956
Golden Virgin, 1956
The Hostage, 1956
Morning Call, 1957
The Story of Esther Costello,
1957
Girl in Black Stockings, 1957
Davy, 1957
Most Dangerous Man Alive, 1961
King of Kings, 1961
The Longest Day, 1962
Follow the Boys, 1963
Gold For the Caesars, 1963
The Phony American, 1963
Savage Pampas, 1966
The Seven Minutes, 1971

FRANK RANDLE (1901-1957)
North-country comedian of the
forties with music hall experience whose low-budget comedies
were immensely popular.

Somewhere in England, 1940

Somewhere in Camp, 1942
Somewhere On Leave, 1942
Somewhere in Civvies, 1943
Home Sweet Home, 1945
When You Come Home, 1947
Holidays With Pay, 1948
Somewhere in Politics, 1949
School For Randle, 1949
It's a Grand Life, 1953

ELSIE RANDOLPH (1904-)
Revue artist of the thirties,
often seen with Jack Buchanan;
films since fairly rare.

Rich and Strange, 1931
Life Goes On, 1932
Rise and Shine, 1932
Brother Alfred, 1932
Yes Mr. Brown, 1933
That's a Good Girl, 1933
Night of the Garter, 1933
This'll Make You Whistle,
    1935
Smash and Grab, 1937
Cheer the Brave, 1951
Frenzy, 1972
Appointment With a Killer,
    1975

BASIL RATHBONE (1892-1967)
Prominent South-African born
actor of stage (since 1911) and
films, fine in villainous roles
but best remembered as an
outstanding Sherlock Holmes
in the series with Nigel Bruce
(1939-46). In Hollywood from
mid-20s.

Innocent, 1921
The Fruitful Vine, 1921
Loves of Mary Queen of Scots,
    1922
School For Scandal, 1923
Trouping With Ellen, 1924
The Masked Bride, 1925
The Great Deception, 1926
The Last of Mrs. Cheyney,
    1929
The Bishop Murder Case,
    1930

Notorious Affair, 1930
Lady of Scandal, 1930
This Mad World, 1930
The Flirting Widow, 1930
A Lady Surrenders, 1930
Sin Takes a Holiday, 1930
A Woman Commands, 1932
One Precious Year, 1933
After the Ball, 1933
Loyalties, 1933
David Copperfield, 1935
Anna Karenina, 1935
The Last Days of Pompeii,
    1935
A Feather in Her Hat, 1935
A Tale of Two Cities, 1935
Captain Blood, 1935
Kind Lady, 1935
Private Number, 1936
Romeo and Juliet, 1936
The Garden of Allah, 1936
Confessions, 1937
Love From a Stranger, 1937
Make a Wish, 1937
Tovarich, 1937
Adventures of Marco Polo,
    1938
Adventures of Robin Hood,
    1938
If I Were King, 1938
The Dawn Patrol, 1938
The Sun Never Sets, 1939
Son of Frankenstein, 1939
Hound of the Baskervilles, 1939
The Adventures of Sherlock
    Holmes, 1939
Rio, 1939
Tower of London, 1939
Rhythm On the River, 1940
The Mark of Zorro, 1940
The Mad Doctor, 1941
The Black Cat, 1941
International Lady, 1941
Paris Calling, 1942
Fingers At the Window, 1942
Crossroads, 1942
Sherlock Holmes and the Voice
    of Terror, 1942
Sherlock Holmes and the Secret
    Weapon, 1942
Sherlock Holmes Faces Death,
    1943
Sherlock Holmes in Washington
    1943

Above Suspicion, 1943
Crazy House, 1943
The Scarlet Claw, 1944
The Pearl of Death, 1944
The Spider Woman, 1944
Bathing Beauty, 1944
Frenchman's Creek, 1944
The House of Fear, 1945
The Woman in Green, 1945
Pursuit to Algiers, 1945
Terror By Night, 1946
Dressed to Kill, 1946
Heartbeat, 1946
Ichabod and Mr. Toad, 1949
Casanova's Big Night, 1954
We're No Angels, 1955
The Court Jester, 1956
The Black Sheep, 1956
The Last Hurrah, 1958
Pontius Pilate, 1960
The Magic Sword, 1962
Tales of Terror, 1962
Two Before Zero, 1962
Comedy of Terrors, 1963
Planet of Blood, 1966
Ghost in the Invisible Bikini,
  1966
Voyage to a Prehistoric Planet,
  1967
Autopsy of a Ghost, 1967
Hillbillys in a Haunted House,
  1967
Soldier in Love, 1967

GERALD RAWLINSON (-)
Supporting actor of the 20s and
30s, also on stage.

You Know What Sailors Are,
  1928
The Hellcat, 1928
The Silent House, 1928
Life's a Stage, 1929
Devil's Maze, 1929
Alf's Carpet, 1929
Young Woodley, 1929
Young Woodley, 1930
The Night Porter, 1930
The Old Man, 1931
Creeping Shadows, 1931
Brown Sugar, 1931
The Man at Six, 1931
Tell England, 1931

Dangerous Seas, 1931
Collision, 1932
Threads, 1932
The Callbox Mystery, 1932
Sleepless Nights, 1932
Daughters of Today, 1933
Excess Baggage, 1933
You Made Me Love You, 1933
Easy Money, 1934
Say it With Diamonds, 1935
When the Devil Was Well, 1937
His Lordship Regrets, 1938

ANDREW RAY (1939-)
Character actor of films and
television who began in juvenile
roles; son of Ted Ray.

The Mudlark, 1950
The Yellow Balloon, 1952
Escape By Night, 1954
Escapade, 1955
A Prize of Gold, 1955
Woman in a Dressing Gown,
  1957
The Young and the Guilty, 1958
Gideon's Day, 1958
Serious Charge, 1959
Twice Round the Daffodils, 1962
The System, 1964
Tarzan and the Wild Girl, 1973
Great Expectations, 1975
Rough Cut, 1980
The Bunker, 1981

RENEE RAY (1912-)
Leading actress of stage and
screen, popular in the thirties;
former child performer. Also
novelist.

Palais de Danse, 1928
High Treason, 1929
Young Woodley, 1930
Varsity, 1930
Peace and Quiet, 1931
Keepers of Youth, 1931
Tonight's the Night, 1932
Dance Pretty Lady, 1932
Two White Arms, 1932
When London Sleeps, 1932
Here's George, 1932

Born Lucky, 1932
Smiling Along, 1932
The Changing Year, 1932
King's Cup, 1933
Excess Baggage, 1933
Tiger Bay, 1933
Rolling in Money, 1934
Nine Forty-Five, 1934
Easy Money, 1934
Once in a New Moon, 1935
Street Song, 1935
Royal Cavalcade, 1935
Full Circle, 1935
Passing of the Third Floor
    Back, 1935
Beloved Imposter, 1936
Crime Over London, 1936
His Lordship, 1936
Please Teacher, 1937
Farewell Again, 1937
Jennifer Hale, 1937
The Rat, 1937
The Green Cockatoo, 1937
The Return of the Frog, 1938
Bank Holiday, 1938
Housemaster, 1938
Mountains O' Mourne, 1938
Weddings Are Wonderful, 1938
Home From Home, 1939
Old Bill and Son, 1940
A Call For Arms, 1940
If Winter Comes, 1947
They Made Me a Fugitive,
    1947
The Galloping Major, 1951
Women of Twilight, 1952
The Good Die Young, 1954
Vicious Circle, 1957
The Strange World of Planet X,
    1958

TED RAY (1909-1977)
Music hall comedian, radio
star and violinist, in occasional
films; father of Andrew Ray.

Elstree Calling, 1930
Radio Parade of 1935, 1935
A Ray of Sunshine, 1950
Meet Me Tonight, 1952
Escape By Night, 1954
My Wife's Family, 1954

The Crowning Touch, 1959
Carry On Teacher, 1959
Please Turn Over, 1959

CAROL RAYE (1923-)
Australian leading actress in
occasional films in the forties.

Strawberry Roan, 1945
Waltz Time, 1945
Spring Song, 1946
While I Live, 1947

CYRIL RAYMOND (1897-1973)
Stage and film actor seen in
leading roles in silents, latterly
in character parts as doctors
or dull husbands. Married:
Gillian Lind.

The Hypocrites, 1916
Disraeli, 1916
I Will, 1919
His Last Defence, 1919
The Scarlet Kiss, 1920
Wuthering Heights, 1920
Moth and Rust, 1921
Sonia, 1921
The Norwood Builder, 1922
Cocaine, 1922
The Faithful Heart, 1922
The Ghost Train, 1931
These Charming People, 1931
The Happy Ending, 1931
Man of Mayfair, 1931
The Frightened Lady, 1932
The Shadow, 1932
Condemned to Death, 1932
Mixed Doubles, 1933
Home Sweet Home, 1933
Strike It Rich, 1933
The Lure, 1933
The Man Outside, 1933
Keep It Quiet, 1934
The Tunnel, 1935
It's Love Again, 1936
Accused, 1936
Tomorrow We Live, 1936
Stardust, 1937
Dreaming Lips, 1937
Thunder In the City, 1937

The Spy in Black, 1938
Night Alone, 1938
Come On George, 1939
Saloon Bar, 1940
Brief Encounter, 1945
Men of Two Worlds, 1946
This Was a Woman, 1948
Jack of Diamonds, 1949
Angels One Five, 1952
Rough Shoot, 1953
The Heart of the Matter, 1953
The Crowded Day, 1954
Lease of Life, 1954
The Gay Dog, 1954
Charley Moon, 1956
The Baby and the Battleship,
    1956
Dunkirk, 1958
No Kidding, 1960
Don't Talk to Strange Men,
    1962
Night Train to Paris, 1964

GARY RAYMOND (1935-)
Supporting player and occasional leading man of stage
and films, also in Hollywood.
Tv series: "The Rat Patrol"
(1965).

The Moonraker, 1958
Look Back in Anger, 1959
Suddnely Last Summer, 1959
The Millionairess, 1960
El Cid, 1961
Playboy of the Western World,
    1962
Jason and the Argonauts, 1963
Traitor's Gate, 1964
The Greatest Story Ever Told,
    1965
Red and Blue, 1967

CORIN REDGRAVE (1939-)
Character and supporting actor
of stage, films, and television;
son of Sir Michael Redgrave
and Rachel Kempson; sisters:
Lynn Redgrave, Vanessa Redgrave.

Crooks in Cloisters, 1963
A Man For All Seasons, 1966
The Deadly Affair, 1966
The Magus, 1968
Charge of the Light Brigade,
    1968
Oh What a Lovely War, 1969
David Copperfield, 1969
Von Richtofen and Brown, 1971
When Eight Bells Toll, 1971
Serail, 1976

LYNN REDGRAVE (1943-)
Leading actress of stage, films
and tv, often seen in awkward
comedy portrayals. Daughter
of Sir Michael Redgrave and
Rachel Kempson; sister of Corin
and Vanessa Redgrave.

Tom Jones, 1963
The Girl With Green Eyes,
    1964
Georgy Girl, 1966
The Deadly Affair, 1966
Smashing Time, 1967
Blood Kin, 1969
The Virgin Soldiers, 1969
Last of the Mobile Hot Shots,
    1970
Killer From Yuma, 1971
Viva la Muerte Tua, 1971
Every Little Crook and Nanny,
    1972
Everything You Always Wanted
    to Know About Sex, 1972
The National Health, 1973
Don't Turn the Other Cheek,
    1974
The Happy Hooker, 1975
The Big Bus, 1976
Centennial, 1978
Gauguin the Savage, 1980
The Seduction of Miss Leona,
    1980
The Miracle Named Louise,
    1980

SIR MICHAEL REDGRAVE
    (1908-)
Distinguished leading man and

latterly character star of great
versatility, also on stage (from
1934). Married to Rachel
Kempson; father of Corin,
Lynn and Vanessa Redgrave.
Former schoolmaster and
journalist. Also in Hollywood.

Secret Agent, 1936
The Lady Vanishes, 1938
Climbing High, 1938
Stolen Life, 1939
A Window in London, 1939
The Stars Look Down, 1939
Kipps, 1941
Jeannie, 1941
Atlantic Ferry, 1941
The Big Blockade, 1942
Thunder Rock, 1942
The Way to the Stars, 1945
Dead of Night, 1945
The Captive Heart, 1946
The Years Between, 1946
The Man Within, 1947
Fame is the Spur, 1947
Mourning Becomes Electra,
1947
The Secret Beyond the Door,
1948
Winter Garden, 1950
The Browning Version, 1951
The Magic Box, 1951
The Importance of Being
Earnest, 1952
The Sea Shall Not Have Them,
1954
The Green Scarf, 1955
The Night My Number Came
Up, 1955
Mr. Arkadin, 1955
Oh Rosalinda, 1955
The Dam Busters, 1955
Kings and Queens (voice),
1956
1984, 1956
Time Without Pity, 1957
The Happy Road, 1957
Law and Disorder, 1958
The Quiet American, 1958
Behind the Mask, 1958
The Immortal Land (voice),
1958
Shake Hands With the Devil,
1959

The Wreck of the Mary Deare,
1959
May Wedding, 1960
No My Darling Daughter, 1960
The Innocents, 1961
Loneliness of the Long Distance
Runner, 1962
Uncle Vanya, 1963
Young Cassidy, 1965
The Hill, 1965
The Heroes of Telemark, 1965
The 25th Hour, 1967
Palaces of a Queen (voice),
1967
Assignment K, 1967
Heidi, 1968
Oh What a Lovely War, 1969
The Battle of Britain, 1969
David Copperfield, 1969
Connecting Rooms, 1969
Goodbye Mr. Chips, 1969
Goodbye Gemini, 1970
The Go-Between, 1971
Nicholas and Alexandra, 1971
A Christmas Carol (voice), 1972
Dr. Jekyll & Mr. Hyde, 1973

VANESSA REDGRAVE (1937-)
Prominent leading lady of stage
(since 1957) and films, also in
Hollywood. Daughter of Michael
Redgrave and Rachel Kempson;
sister of Corin and Lynn Redgrave.

Behind the Mask, 1958
Circus at Clopton Hall, 1961
Morgan, 1965
A Man For All Seasons, 1966
Blow Up, 1966
Sailor From Gibraltar, 1967
Camelot, 1967
Red and Blue, 1967
Tonite Let's All Make Love in
London, 1967
Charge of the Light Brigade,
1968
Isadora, 1968
A Quiet Place in the Country,
1968
Oh What a Lovely War, 1969
Dropout, 1969
The Sea Gull, 1969

Vacation, 1969
The Trojan Women, 1971
The Body, 1971
The Devils, 1971
Mary Queen of Scots, 1971
Murder On the Orient Express,
1974
Out of Season, 1975
The Seven Per Cent Solution,
1976
Julia, 1977
Agatha, 1979
Yanks, 1979
Bear Island, 1980
Playing For Time, 1980

JOYCE REDMAN (1918-)
Irish character actress,
mainly on stage; films infrequent.

One of Our Aircraft is Miss-
ing, 1942
Tom Jones, 1963
Othello, 1965
Think 20th, 1967
Prudence and the Pill, 1968

LIAM REDMOND (1913-)
Irish character star seen in
friendly or sinister roles,
also in Hollywood. Former
member of the Abbey Theatre.

I See a Dark Stranger, 1946
Captain Boycott, 1947
Daughter of Darkness, 1948
Sword in the Desert, 1949
Saints and Sinners, 1949
High Treason, 1951
The Gentle Gunman, 1952
The Cruel Sea, 1953
Devil On Horseback, 1954
The Final Appointment, 1954
The Passing Stranger, 1954
The Divided Heart, 1954
Happy Ever After, 1954
The Glass Cage, 1955
Yield to the Night, 1956
23 Paces to Baker Street,
1956

Safari, 1956
Jacqueline, 1956
The Long Haul, 1957
Night of the Demon, 1957
Rooney, 1958
Ice Cold in Alex, 1958
The Diplomatic Corpse, 1958
She Didn't Say No, 1958
Alive and Kicking, 1958
No Trees in the Street, 1959
The Boy and the Bridge, 1959
Scent of Mystery, 1960
Under Ten Flags, 1960
The Valiant, 1962
Phantom of the Opera, 1962
Playboy of the Western World,
1962
Kid Galahad, 1963
The Luck of Ginger Coffey,
1964
Moll Flanders, 1965
Tobruk, 1966
The Ghost and Mr. Chicken,
1966
The 25th Hour, 1966
Adventures of Bullwhip Griffin,
1966
The Last Safari, 1967
The Sky Bike, 1967
David Copperfield, 1969
Alf 'n' Family, 1972
And No One Could Save Her,
1973
Barry Lyndon, 1975

MOIRA REDMOND (-)
Character actress of stage and
screen in the sixties.

Violent Moment, 1959
Marriage of Convenience, 1960
Doctor in Love, 1960
Partners in Crime, 1961
Pit of Darkness, 1961
The Share Out, 1962
Jigsaw, 1962
Nightmare, 1962
Kill or Cure, 1963
A Shot in the Dark, 1964
The Limbo Line, 1968
A Winter's Tale, 1968

BRIAN REECE (1913-1962)
Light character player of the
fifties, mainly on stage.

A Case For PC 49, 1951
Fast and Loose, 1954
Orders Are Orders, 1954
Geordie, 1955
Carry On Admiral, 1957
Watch It Sailor, 1961

MAXWELL REED (1919-1974)
Handsome Irish light leading
man of the 40s and 50s, also
on stage (1943); former seaman. Also Hollywood. Mar-
ried: Joan Collins.

The Years Between, 1946
Gaiety George, 1946
Daybreak, 1947
The Brothers, 1947
Holiday Camp, 1947
Dear Murderer, 1947
Daughter of Darkness, 1947
Night Beat, 1948
Madness of the Heart, 1949
The Lost People, 1949
The Clouded Yellow, 1950
The Dark Man, 1950
There is Another Sun, 1951
Flame of Araby, 1951
Wall of Death, 1952
Sea Devils, 1953
The Square Ring, 1953
Marilyn, 1953
The Brain Machine, 1955
Before I Wake, 1955
Helen of Troy, 1956
Notorious Landlady, 1962
Picture Mommy Dead, 1966

OLIVER REED (1938-)
Tough, aggressive leading man
of the 60s and 70s, also in
Hollywood and international
films. Sometimes seen in
mean or vicious roles.
Nephew of director Sir Carol
Reed (1906-1976).

The League of Gentlemen, 1959
The Angry Silence, 1960
The Bulldog Breed, 1960
His and Hers, 1960
Beat Girl, 1969
Sword of Sherwood Forest,
   1960
The Two Faces of Dr. Jekyll,
   1960
Curse of the Werewolf, 1961
The Rebel, 1961
No Love For Johnnie, 1961
The Damned, 1961
The Pirates of Blood River,
   1962
Captain Clegg, 1962
Paranoiac, 1963
The Scarlet Blade, 1963
The Party's Over, 1964
The System, 1964
The Brigand of Kandahar, 1965
The Trap, 1966
The Jokers, 1966
The Shuttered Room, 1967
I'll Never Forget Whatsisname,
   1967
Oliver, 1968
The Assassination Bureau, 1969
Hannibal Brooks, 1969
Women in Love, 1969
The Lady in the Car With
   Glasses and a Gun, 1970
The Devils, 1971
The Hunting Party, 1971
Take a Girl Like You, 1971
Sitting Target, 1972
Days of Fury, 1972
Dirty Weekend, 1972
The Carrycot, 1972
Z. P. G. , 1973
Triple Echo, 1973
The McMasters, 1973
One Russian Summer, 1973
Tommy, 1974
Revolver, 1974
The Three Musketeers, 1974
The Four Musketeers, 1975
Mahler, 1975
Ten Little Indians, 1975
The Plumed Serpent, 1975
Blue Blood, 1975
Royal Flash, 1975

Lizstomania, 1975
The Captive, 1976
Great Scout & Cathouse Thursday, 1976
Burnt Offerings, 1976
Blood in the Streets, 1977
Tomorrow Never Comes, 1977
The Sellout, 1977
Crossed Swords, 1978
The Big Sleep, 1978
Assault On Paradise, 1978
Maniac, 1978
The Brood, 1978
The Class of Miss MacMichael, 1979
Dante's Inferno, 1979
The Mad Trapper, 1979
Omar Mukhtar-Lion of the Desert, 1989
Dr. Heckle and Mr. Hype, 1980
Tarzan of the Apes, 1981

ADA REEVE (1874-1966)
Character actress in occasional films of the 40s and 50s, primarily on stage.

They Came to a City, 1944
Meet Me at Dawn, 1947
When the Bough Breaks, 1947
Dear Mr. Prohack, 1949
Night and the City, 1950
I Believe in You, 1952
Time Bomb, 1953
Eyewitness, 1956
The Passionate Stranger, 1957

KYNASTON REEVES (1893-1971)
Distinguished stage and screen character actor, often cast in scholarly parts. On tv in "The Forsyte Saga."

The Lodger, 1932
The Sign of Four, 1932
Puppets of Fate, 1933
Broken Melody, 1934
The Crimson Candle, 1934

Phantom Fiend, 1935
Vintage Wine, 1935
Dark World, 1935
Take a Chance, 1937
Romance in Flanders, 1937
The Housemaster, 1938
The Outsider, 1939
The Stars Look Down, 1939
Dead Men Are Dangerous, 1939
Sons of the Sea, 1939
Inspector Hornleigh On Leave, 1939
Two For Danger, 1940
The Flying Squad, 1940
The Prime Minister, 1941
The Night Invader, 1943
The Rake's Progress, 1945
Strawberry Roan, 1945
The Echo Murders, 1945
Murder in Reverse, 1945
Bedelia, 1946
This Was a Woman, 1947
The Winslow Boy, 1948
Vice Versa, 1948
The Guinea Pig, 1948
The Weaker Sex, 1949
Badger's Green, 1949
Madness of the Heart, 1949
Tony Draws a Horse, 1950
Blackout, 1950
Madeleine, 1950
Trio, 1950
The Mudlark, 1950
The 20 Questions Murder Mystery, 1950
Captain Horatio Hornblower, 1951
Smart Alex, 1951
Top Secret, 1952
Moving House, 1952
Penny Princess, 1952
Four Sided Triangle, 1953
Top of the Form, 1953
Laxdale Hall, 1953
Burnt Evidence, 1954
Eight O'clock Walk, 1954
The Crowded Day, 1954
Guilty, 1956
Fun at St. Fanny's, 1956
High Flight, 1957
Brothers In Law, 1957
Fiend Without a Face, 1958

Family Doctor, 1958
A Question of Adultery, 1958
Carleton Browne of the F. O.,
1959
School For Scoundrels, 1960
In the Nick, 1960
The Night We Got the Bird,
1960
Carry On Regardless, 1961
Shadow of the Cat, 1961
In the Doghouse, 1961
Go To Blazes, 1962
Top Millions, 1962
Hide and Seek, 1963
Anne of the Thousand Days,
1970

BERYL REID (1920-)
Character actress and revue
star (since 1936), also much
on stage; former radio personality. Also Hollywood.

The Belles of St. Trinian's,
1954
The Extra Day, 1956
Two-Way Stretch, 1960
The Dock Brief, 1962
Think 20th, 1967
Inspector Clouseau, 1968
Star!, 1968
The Killing of Sister George,
1968
The Assassination Bureau, 1969
Entertaining Mr. Sloane, 1970
The Beast in the Cellar, 1971
Dr. Phibes Rises Again, 1972
Psychomania, 1972
Father Dear Father, 1972
The Death Wheelers, 1973
No Sex Please We're British,
1973
Joseph Andrews, 1976
Carry On Emmanuelle, 1978
Tinker, Tailor, Soldier, Spy, 1980

MILTON REID (-)
Bald, muscular character
player often seen in heavy
roles.

Ferry to Hong Kong, 1959
The Swiss Family Robinson,
1960
The Wonders of Aladdin, 1961
Captain Clegg, 1962
Deadlier Than the Male, 1967
Berserk!, 1967
The Horsemen, 1971
The Spy Who Loved Me, 1977

GEORGE RELPH (1888-1960)
Character star primarily seen
on stage, in films sporadically
from 1921.   Father of director/
producer Michael Relph (1915-).

The Door That Has No Key,
1921
Candytuft, I Mean Veronica,
1921
Too Dangerous to Live, 1939
Give Us the Moon, 1944
Nicholas Nickleby, 1947
I Believe in You, 1952
The Final Test, 1953
The Titfield Thunderbolt, 1953
Davy, 1957
Doctor at Large, 1957
Ben Hur, 1959

ROBERT RENDEL (-)
Character actor and sometimes
leading man of the thirties.

Babbit, 1924
Her Night of Romance, 1925
Hound of the Baskervilles, 1931
The Wigan Express, 1934
The Way of Youth, 1934
Borrow a Million, 1934
The Price of Wisdom, 1935
Honours Easy, 1935
Did I Betray, 1936
Twice Branded, 1936
Fire Over England, 1937
The Dark Stairway, 1938
The Singing Cop, 1938
Thank Evans, 1938
Mr. Satan, 1938
Glamour Girl, 1938

The Spy in Black, 1939
The Lion Has Wings, 1939
Four Feathers, 1939
Ten Days in Paris, 1939
All at Sea, 1939
Sailors Three, 1940

MICHAEL RENNIE (1909-
1971)
Tall, handsome leading man,
also in Hollywood. Popular
on television in series "The
Third Man" (1960).

Secret Agent, 1936
Gangway, 1937
Bank Holiday, 1938
The Divorce of Lady X, 1938
This Man in Paris, 1939
This Man is Dangerous, 1941
Dangerous Moonlight, 1941
Ships With Wings, 1941
Turned Out Nice Again, 1941
Pimpernel Smith, 1941
Tower of Terror, 1941
The Big Blockade, 1942
I'll Be Your Sweetheart, 1945
The Wicked Lady, 1945
Caesar and Cleopatra, 1946
The Root of All Evil, 1947
White Cardle Inn, 1947
Idol of Paris, 1948
Uneasy Terms, 1948
The Golden Madonna, 1949
Miss Pilgrim's Progress, 1949
The Body Said No, 1950
Trio, 1950
The Black Rose, 1950
The House in the Square, 1951
The Thirteenth Letter, 1951
The Day the Earth Stood Still,
1951
Phone Call From a Stranger,
1952
Five Fingers, 1952
Les Miserables, 1952
Singlehanded, 1953
The Robe, 1953
Dangerous Crossing, 1953
King of the Khyber Rifles,
1954
Princess of the Nile, 1954

Demetrius and the Gladiators,
1954
Desiree, 1955
Soldier of Fortune, 1955
Seven Cities of Gold, 1955
The Rains of Ranchipur, 1955
Teenage Rebel, 1956
Omar Khayyam, 1957
Island in the Sun, 1957
Battle of the VI, 1958
Third Man On the Mountain,
1959
The Lost World, 1960
Mary Mary, 1963
Ride Beyond Vengeance, 1966
Cyborg 2087, 1966
Hotel, 1967
Subterfuge, 1968
The Power, 1968
The Devil's Brigade, 1968
The Young the Evil and the
Savage, 1968
The Battle of El Alamein, 1968
The Search, 1968
Assignment Terror, 1970

CLIVE REVILL (1930-)
New Zealand character actor
of stage, films and television,
seen mainly in comedy roles.
Also in Hollywood.

The Headless Ghost, 1959
Bunny Lake is Missing, 1965
Modesty Blaise, 1966
A Fine Madness, 1966
Kaleidoscope, 1966
Fathom, 1967
The Double Man, 1967
The Shoes of the Fisherman,
1968
Nobody Runs Forever, 1968
The Assassination Bureau,
1969
The Buttercup Chain, 1970
A Severed Head, 1970
Private Life of Sherlock Holmes,
1970
Rum Runner, 1971
Avanti, 1972
Escape to the Sun, 1972
The Legend of Hell House, 1973

The Little Prince, 1974
The Black Windmill, 1974
Galileo, 1975
One of Our Dinosaurs is Missing, 1975
Matilda, 1978
The Scarlett O'Hara War, 1980
The Diary of Anne Frank, 1980
The Empire Strikes Back (voice), 1980

PETER REYNOLDS (1926-1975)
Light character player often seen in shady or shifty characterizations; mainly in second features.

The Captive Heart, 1946
The Guinea Pig, 1948
Adam and Evalyn, 1949
Guilt is My Shadow, 1950
Smart Alec, 1951
The Four Days, 1951
The Magic Box, 1951
The Woman's Angle, 1952
The Last Page, 1952
24 Hours of a Woman's Life, 1952
Black Thirteen, 1953
The Good Beginning, 1953
Devil Girl From Mars, 1954
The Delavine Affair, 1954
You Can't Escape, 1956
The Long Haul, 1957
The Bank Raider, 1958
Shake Hands With the Devil, 1959
Wrong Number, 1959
Your Money Or Your Wife, 1960
The Challenge, 1960
The Man Who Couldn't Walk, 1960
The Hands of Orlac, 1960
The Breaking Point, 1961
Spare the Rod, 1961
Highway to Battle, 1961
A Question of Suspense, 1961
The Painted Smile, 1962
Gaolbreak, 1962
West Eleven, 1963
Nobody Runs Forever, 1968

MARJORIE RHODES (1902-)

Character actress of stage (from 1920) and films, frequently seen as inquisitive neighbour or homely mum.

Poison Pen, 1939
Love On the Dole, 1941
World of Plenty, 1941
Squadron Leader X, 1942
When We Are Married, 1942
Old Mother Riley Detective, 1943
Theatre Royal, 1943
Escape to Danger, 1943
The Butler's Dilemma, 1943
It Happened One Sunday, 1944
Tawny Pipit, 1944
On Approval, 1944
Great Day, 1945
School For Secrets, 1946
Uncle Silas, 1947
This Was a Woman, 1948
Escape, 1948
Enchantment, 1948
Private Angelo, 1949
The Cure For Love, 1950
The Yellow Balloon, 1952
Decameron Nights, 1952
Time Gentlemen Please, 1952
The Girl On the Pier, 1953
Those People Next Door, 1953
Street Corner, 1953
To Dorothy a Son, 1954
Children Galore, 1954
The Weak and the Wicked, 1955
Footsteps in the Fog, 1955
The Case of Diamond Annie, 1955
Room in the House, 1955
Where There's a Will, 1955
Lost, 1956
Now and Forever, 1956
Yield to the Night, 1956
It's a Great Day, 1956
It's Great to Be Young, 1956
Hell Drivers, 1957
The Passionate Stranger, 1957
After the Ball, 1957
No Time For Tears, 1957
There's Always a Thursday, 1957
Gideon's Day, 1958
A Tale of Two Cities, 1958

Just My Luck, 1958
The Naked Truth, 1958
Alive and Kicking, 1958
Over the Odds, 1960
Watch It Sailor, 1961
Those Magnificent Men in
    Their Flying Machines, 1965
I've Gotta Horse, 1965
The Family Way, 1966
Mrs. Brown, You've Got a
    Lovely Daughter, 1968
Spring and Port Wine, 1970
Hands of the Ripper, 1971

JOAN RICE (1930-)
Supporting actress who achieved
brief stardom during the fifties,
latterly in occasional character
roles.

Blackmailed, 1950
One Wild Oat, 1951
The Story of Robin Hood, 1952
Curtain Up, 1952
The Gift Horse, 1952
The Steel Key, 1953
A Day to Remember, 1953
His Majesty O'Keefe, 1954
The Crowded Day, 1954
One Good Turn, 1954
Police Dog, 1955
Women Without Men, 1956
The Long Knife, 1958
Operation Bullshine, 1959
Payroll, 1961
The Horror of Frankenstein,
    1970

CLIFF RICHARD (1940-)
Pop star and teenage idol seen
in occasional films.

Serious Charge, 1959
Expresso Bongo, 1959
The Young Ones, 1961
Summer Holiday, 1963
Rhythm 'n Greens, 1964
Wonderful Life, 1964
Finders Keepers, 1966
Two a Penny, 1967
Take Me High, 1973
Hot Property, 1973

IAN RICHARDSON (1934-)
Strong character actor generally
seen on stage, films few but
impressive.

Marat/Sade, 1967
A Midsummer Night's Dream,
    1968
The Darwin Adventure, 1972
Man of La Mancha, 1972
Ike, 1979
Gauguin the Savage, 1980

JOHN RICHARDSON (1936-)
Leading man of the sixties and
seventies, also on stage.

Bachelor of Hearts, 1958
Black Sunday, 1961
She, 1965
One Million Years B.C., 1966
The Vengeance of She, 1968
The Chastity Belt, 1968
On My Way to the Crusades...,
    1969
On a Clear Day You Can See
    Forever, 1970
Torso, 1974
Duck in Orange Sauce, 1975
Eyeball, 1978

SIR RALPH RICHARDSON
    (1902-)
Distinguished actor of stage
(from 1921) and screen, adept
at whimsical comedy characters
as well as fine dramatic roles.
Former painter. Also Hollywood. Married to Meriel Forbes.

The Ghoul, 1933
Friday the 13th, 1933
The Return of Bulldog Drum-
    mond, 1934
Java Head, 1934
The King of Paris, 1934
Bulldog Jack, 1935
The Man Who Could Work
    Miracles, 1936
Things To Come, 1936
Thunder in the City, 1937
South Riding, 1938

The Divorce of Lady X, 1938
The Citadel, 1938
Smith, 1938
Q Planes, 1939
The Four Feathers, 1939
The Lion Has Wings, 1939
On the Night of the Fire, 1939
Health For the Nation, 1940
The Day Will Dawn, 1942
The Silver Fleet, 1943
The Volunteer, 1943
School For Secrets, 1946
Anna Karenina, 1948
The Fallen Idol, 1948
The Heiress, 1949
An Outcast of the Islands, 1951
Home at Seven, 1952
The Sound Barrier, 1952
The Holly and the Ivy, 1952
Richard III, 1955
Smiley, 1956
The Passionate Stranger, 1957
Our Man in Havana, 1959
Oscar Wilde, 1960
Exodus, 1960
The 300 Spartans, 1962
Long Day's Journey Into Night,
1962
Woman of Straw, 1964
Dr. Zhivago, 1965
Khartoum, 1966
The Wrong Box, 1966
Chimes at Midnight, 1966
Midas Run, 1969
Oh What a Lovely War, 1969
The Battle of Britain, 1969
David Copperfield, 1969
The Bed Sitting Room, 1969
The Looking Glass War, 1970
Eagle in a Cage, 1971
Gingerbread House, 1971
Whoever Slew Auntie Roo?,
1971
Alice's Adventures in Wonder-
land, 1972
Lady Caroline Lamb, 1972
Tales From the Crypt, 1972
Frankenstein: The True Story,
1973
A Doll's House, 1973
O Lucky Man, 1973
Rollerball, 1975
Man in the Iron Mask, 1976
Jesus of Nazareth, 1977

No Man's Land, 1978
Watership Down (voice), 1978
Charlie Muffin, 1980

STANLEY RIDGES (1892-1951)
Distinctive, heavy-set character
actor of Hollywood films, typically seen in dominant characterizations.

Success, 1923
Crime Without Passion, 1934
The Scoundrel, 1934
Winterset, 1936
Sinner Take All, 1937
Interns Can't Take Money, 1937
Yellow Jack, 1938
Mad Miss Manton, 1938
There's That Woman Again,
1938
Let Us Live, 1939
Union Pacific, 1939
If I Were King, 1939
Each Dawn I Die, 1939
Espionage Agent, 1939
Dust Be My Destiny, 1939
Nick Carter, Master Detective,
1939
Black Friday, 1940
Sergeant York, 1941
The Sea Wolf, 1941
Mr. D. A. , 1941
They Died With Their Boots On,
1941
To Be Or Not to Be, 1942
The Big Shot, 1942
The Lady is Willing, 1942
Eyes in the Night, 1942
Air Force, 1943
Tarzan Triumphs, 1943
This is the Army, 1943
The Story of Dr. Wassell, 1944
Wilson, 1944
Sign of the Cross, 1944
The Suspect, 1945
God is My Co-Pilot, 1945
Captain Eddie, 1945
The Master Race, 1945
Because of Him, 1946
Canyon Passage, 1946
Mr. Ace, 1946
Possessed, 1947
Live Today For Tomorrow, 1948

Streets of Laredo, 1949
You're My Everything, 1949
Task Force, 1949
Thelma Jordan, 1949
Paid in Full, 1950
No Way Out, 1950
The Groom Wore Spurs, 1951

EDWARD RIGBY (1879-1951)
Endearing character star of
stage (since 1900) and films,
good in doddering comedy portrayals.

The Blue Bird, 1910
Lorna Doone, 1935
Windfall, 1935
No Limit, 1935
Gay Old Dog, 1935
Queen of Hearts, 1936
This Green Hell, 1936
Land Without Music, 1936
Accused, 1936
The Heirloom Mystery, 1936
Irish For Luck, 1936
Jump For Glory, 1937
The Show Goes On, 1937
The Fatal Hour, 1937
Under a Cloud, 1937
Mr. Smith Carries On, 1937
Young and Innocent, 1937
A Yank at Oxford, 1938
Kicking the Moon Around, 1938
Yellow Sands, 1938
Keep Smiling, 1938
The Ware Case, 1938
There Ain't No Justice, 1939
Poison Pen, 1939
Young Man's Fancy, 1939
The Stars Look Down, 1939
Convoy, 1940
Fingers, 1940
Sailors Don't Care, 1940
Proud Valley, 1940
The Girl in the News, 1940
The Farmer's Wife, 1941
Kipps, 1941
Major Barbara, 1941
Penn of Pennsylvania, 1941
The Common Touch, 1941
Flying Fortress, 1942
Let the People Sing, 1942

Salute John Citizen, 1942
Get Cracking, 1943
A Canterbury Tale, 1943
Don't Take It to Heart, 1944
The Agitator, 1945
I Live in Grosvenor Square,
    1945
Perfect Strangers, 1945
Quiet Weekend, 1946
Piccadilly Incident, 1946
Daybreak, 1946
The Years Between, 1946
Green Fingers, 1947
Temptation Harbour, 1947
The Loves of Joanna Godden,
    1947
The Courtneys of Curzon Street,
    1947
Easy Money, 1948
Three Weird Sisters, 1948
Noose, 1948
It's Hard to Be Good, 1948
Rover and Me, 1949
All Over Town, 1949
Christopher Columbus, 1949
Don't Ever Leave Me, 1949
A Run For Your Money, 1949
The Happiest Days of Your
    Life, 1950
Double Confession, 1950
Tony Draws a Horse, 1950
What the Butler Saw, 1950
The Mudlark, 1950
Into the Blue, 1951
Circle of Danger, 1951
The Man in the Dinghy, 1951

DIANA RIGG (1938-)
Attractive leading lady of stage
and films, famous on television
as Emma Peel in "The Avengers" (1965-67). Also on tv in
series "Diana" (1973). Films
infrequent; also in Hollywood.

A Midsummer Night's Dream,
    1968
On Her Majesty's Secret Ser-
    vice, 1968
The Assassination Bureau, 1969
Julius Caesar, 1970
The Hospital, 1971

Theatre of Blood, 1973
In This House of Brede, 1975
A Little Night Music, 1977

WALTER RILLA (1895-)
German character actor of
stage (from 1921) and screen,
long resident in Britain; also
television director. Father of
director Wolf Rilla (1920-).

Haneles Himmelfahrt, 1922
Fortune's Fool, 1923
Der Geiger Von Florenz, 1926
Das Gefahrliche Alter, 1927
The Last Night, 1928
Sajenko the Soviet, 1929
Veribte Triebe, 1929
Rendezvous, 1930
Zirkus Leben, 1931
Namensheirar, 1933
Ein Gewisser Herr Gran, 1933
La Voce del Sangue, 1933
Lady Windermere's Fan, 1935
The Scarlet Pimpernel, 1935
Abdul the Damned, 1935
Victoria the Great, 1937
Sixty Glorious Years, 1938
At the Villa Rose, 1939
Hell's Cargo, 1939
The Gang's All Here, 1939
Black Eyes, 1939
The Adventures of Tartu, 1942
Candlelight in Algeria, 1943
Mr. Emmanuel, 1944
The Lisbon Story, 1946
State Secret, 1950
The Golden Salamander, 1950
The Eagle and the Lamb, 1950
Shadow of the Eagle, 1950
My Daughter Joy, 1950
I'll Get You For This, 1951
The Assassin, 1952
Desperate Moment, 1953
Senza Bandiera, 1953
Track the Man Down, 1955
Star of India, 1956
Gamma People, 1956
Liszt, 1957
The Confessions of Felix
    Krull, 1957
Rosemary, 1958

Song Without End, 1960
The Gioconda Smile, 1960
Riviera Story, 1960
The Secret Ways, 1961
Sanders of the River, 1961
Dr. Mabuse, 1961
Cairo, 1961
Wonderful World of the Brothers
    Grimm, 1962
Room 13, 1962
The Riverline, 1963
The Testament of Dr. Mabuse,
    1963
The Thousand Eyes of Dr.
    Mabuse, 1963
Table Bay, 1964
Frozen Alive, 1964
Code 7 Victim 5, 1964
The Face of Fu Manchu, 1965
Four Keys, 1965
Martin Soldat, 1966
Day of Anger, 1967

MICHAEL RIPPER (1913-)
Character player frequently seen
in comedy cameo roles and in
horror films.

Busman's Holiday, 1936
Captain Boycott, 1947
Eyewitness, 1950
Treasure Hunt, 1952
Gilbert and Sullivan, 1953
The Belles of St. Trinian's,
    1954
Richard III, 1955
Geordie, 1955
The Green Man, 1956
1984, 1956
Man On the Beach, 1956
Yield to the Night, 1956
X The Unknown, 1956
Steel Bayonet, 1957
Quatermass II, 1957
Woman in a Dressing Gown,
    1957
The Revenge of Frankenstein,
    1958
The Mummy, 1959
The Ugly Duckling, 1959
Jackpot, 1960
Dead Lucky, 1960

Brides of Dracula, 1960
Circle of Deception, 1961
Curse of the Werewolf, 1961
The Pirates of Blood River,
  1962
A Prize of Arms, 1962
Captain Clegg, 1962
Phantom of the Opera, 1962
A Matter of WHO, 1962
Two Left Feet, 1963
The Scarlet Blade, 1963
What a Crazy World, 1963
Devil Ship Pirates, 1964
Curse of the Mummy's Tomb,
  1964
Every Day's a Holiday, 1964
The Secret of Blood Island,
  1965
The Reptile, 1966
Plague of the Zombies, 1966
Where the Bullets Fly, 1966
The Mummy's Shroud, 1967
The Deadly Bees, 1967
Torture Garden, 1967
Inspector Clouseau, 1968
The Lost Continent, 1968
Dracula Has Risen From the
  Grave, 1968
Mumsy, Nanny, Sonny & Girly,
  1969
Moon Zero Two, 1969
Scars of Dracula, 1970
Taste the Blood of Dracula,
  1970
The Creeping Flesh, 1972

ARTHUR RISCOE   (1896-
1954)
Stage comedian seen in very
occasional films from 1920.

Horatio's Deception, 1920
The Other Dog's Day, 1920
Oh Jemimah, 1920
The Bitten Biter, 1920
For the Love of Mike, 1932
For Love of You, 1933
Going Gay, 1933
Public Nuisance Number One,
  1936
Street Singer, 1937
Paradise For Two, 1937
Kipps, 1941

CYRIL RITCHARD   (1896-1977)
Australian musical comedy star
of stage (from 1917) and screen,
also Hollywood.   Films sporadic.
Former medical student.

On With the Dance, 1927
Piccadilly, 1929
Blackmail, 1929
Just For a Song, 1930
Symphony in Two Flats, 1930
Service For Ladies, 1932
Danny Boy, 1934
It's a Grand Old World, 1937
The Show Goes On, 1937
Dangerous Medicine, 1938
I See Ice, 1938
Woman Hater, 1948
Peter Pan, 1955
Peter Pan, 1960
Half a Sixpence, 1967

JUNE RITCHIE   (1939-   )
Attractive leading lady often
seen in realist films of the 60s.

A Kind of Loving, 1961
Threepenny Opera, 1962
Live Now Pay Later, 1963
The Mouse On the Moon, 1963
This is My Street, 1964
The World Ten Times Over,
  1965
The Syndicate, 1968
Hunted, 1971

BRIAN RIX   (1924-   )
Character actor of stage (1942)
and films, mainly in comedy
roles.

Reluctant Heroes, 1951
Up to His Neck, 1954
What Every Woman Wants, 1954
Dry Rot, 1956
Not Wanted On Voyage, 1957
The Night We Dropped a Clanger,
  1959
The Night We Got the Bird, 1960
And the Same to You, 1960
Nothing Barred, 1961
Don't Just Lie There, 1973

EWAN ROBERTS (1914-)
Character actor sometimes
seen in comedy roles, also
frequently on stage.

Castle in the Air, 1952
The Titfield Thunderbolt, 1953
River Beat, 1954
The Ladykillers, 1955
Port of Escape, 1956
Night of the Demon, 1957
Five to One, 1963
The Partner, 1963
Day of the Triffids, 1963
The Traitors, 1963
Hostile Witness, 1968
The Internecine Project, 1974

J. H. ROBERTS (-)
Eminent character actor of the
30s and 40s, often seen in
strong supporting roles.

The Skin Game, 1920
The Constant Nymph, 1928
Alibi, 1931
A Safe Affair, 1931
White Face, 1932
High Finance, 1933
It's a Boy, 1933
The Green Pack, 1934
Royal Cavalcade, 1935
The Morals of Marcus, 1935
Pot Luck, 1936
Accused, 1936
Juggernaut, 1936
Young and Innocent, 1937
Farewell Again, 1937
The Divorce of Lady X, 1938
Charley's Big-Hearted Aunt,
    1940
The Door With Seven Locks,
    1940
He Found a Star, 1941
Dangerous Moonlight, 1941
Penn of Pennsylvania, 1941
The First of the Few, 1942
Uncensored, 1942
The Dark Tower, 1943
The Agitator, 1945
Blanche Fury, 1948
Uneasy Terms, 1948

RACHEL ROBERTS (1927-1980)
Notable Welsh actress of stage
(from 1951), films and television, also in Hollywood. Formerly married to Rex Harrison.

Valley of Song, 1952
The Limping Man, 1953
The Weak and the Wicked, 1954
The Crowded Day, 1955
The Good Companions, 1957
Our Man in Havana, 1959
Saturday Night & Sunday Morn-
    ing, 1960
Girl On Approval, 1962
This Sporting Life, 1963
Think 20th, 1967
A Flea in Her Ear, 1968
The Reckoning, 1970
The Wild Rovers, 1971
Doctors' Wives, 1971
Baffled, 1972
O Lucky Man, 1973
The Belstone Fox, 1973
Alpha Beta, 1973
Murder On the Orient Express,
    1974
Great Expectations, 1975
Picnic at Hanging Rock, 1976
A Circle of Children, 1977
Foul Play, 1978
Free Spirit, 1978
When a Stranger Calls, 1979
Yanks, 1979
The Hostage Tower, 1980
The Wall, 1980
Charlie Chan & the Curse of the
    Dragon Queen, 1981

SIR GEORGE ROBEY (1869-
    1954)
Music hall comedian (1891)
known as "The Prime Minister
of Mirth." Star of silent
comedies, later in character
roles. Former engineer.

The Rats, 1900
And Very Nice Too, 1913
Good Queen Bess, 1913
George Robey Turns Anarchist,
    1914

£66. 13. 9 3/4 For Every Man,
    Woman and Child, 1916
Blood Tells, 1916
Doing His Bit, 1917
George Robey's Day Off, 1918
The Rest Cure, 1923
One Arabian Night, 1923
Don Quixote, 1923
The Prehistoric Man, 1924
The Barrister, 1928
Safety First, 1929
The Bride, 1929
Mrs. Mephistopheles, 1929
Marry Me, 1932
The Temperance Fete, 1932
Don Quixote, 1933
Chu Chin Chow, 1934
Royal Cavalcade, 1935
Birds of a Feather, 1935
Men of Yesterday, 1936
Calling the Tune, 1936
Southern Roses, 1936
A Girl Must Live, 1939
Salute John Citizen, 1942
Variety Jubilee, 1943
They Met in the Dark, 1943
Henry V, 1944
Waltz Time, 1945
The Trojan Brothers, 1946
The Pickwick Papers, 1952

JOHN ROBINSON (1908-)
Character actor mainly seen
on stage, often seen in films
as businessman or heavy
father.

The Scarab Murder Case, 1936
The Heirloom Mystery, 1936
All That Glitters, 1936
Farewell to Cinderella, 1937
The Lion Has Wings, 1939
Uneasy Terms, 1948
The Story of Shirley Yorke,
    1948
Emergency Call, 1952
Ghost Ship, 1952
Hammer the Toff, 1952
The Constant Husband, 1955
Fortune is a Woman, 1957
The Doctor's Dilemma, 1958
And the Same to You, 1960

DAME FLORA ROBSON (1902-)
Distinguished, outstanding character star of stage (from 1921)
and films, also in Hollywood.

Gentleman of Paris, 1931
Dance Pretty Lady, 1932
One Precious Year, 1933
Catherine the Great, 1934
Fire Over England, 1937
Farewell Again, 1937
I Claudius, 1937
Poison Pen, 1939
The Lion Has Wings, 1939
Wuthering Heights, 1939
We Are Not Alone, 1939
Invisible Stripes, 1939
The Sea Hawk, 1940
Smith, 1940
Bahama Passage, 1942
Two Thousand Women, 1944
Great Day, 1945
Caesar and Cleopatra, 1945
Saratoga Trunk, 1946
The Years Between, 1946
Holiday Camp, 1947
Black Narcissus, 1947
Frieda, 1947
Good Time Girl, 1948
Saraband For Dead Lovers,
    1948
Tall Headlines, 1952
Malta Story, 1953
Romeo and Juliet, 1954
High Tide at Noon, 1957
No Time For Tears, 1957
The Gypsy and the Gentleman,
    1958
Innocent Sinners, 1958
55 Days at Peking, 1962
Murder at the Gallop, 1963
Guns at Batasi, 1964
Young Cassidy, 1965
Those Magnificent Men in Their
    Flying Machines, 1965
A King's Story (voice), 1965
Eye of the Devil, 1966
Seven Women, 1966
Cry in the Wind, 1967
The Shuttered Room, 1967
The Beloved, 1970
Fragment of Fear, 1970
The Beast in the Cellar, 1971

Comedy, Tragedy and All
  That, 1972
Alice's Adventures in Wonder-
  land, 1972
Restless, 1972
A Man Called Intrepid, 1979
Gauguin the Savage, 1980
A Tale of Two Cities, 1980

MAY ROBSON (1858-1942)
Australian character actress
of stage and films, long in
Hollywood, where she was
often seen as forceful but
kindly old ladies.

How Molly Made Good, 1915
Pals in Paradise, 1926
A Harp in Hock, 1927
Rubber Tires, 1927
King of Kings, 1927
Rejuvenation of Aunt Mary, 1927
Angel of Broadway, 1927
Chicago, 1927
The Blue Danube, 1928
She-Wolf, 1931
Mother's Millions, 1931
Letty Lynton, 1932
Red-Headed Woman, 1932
Strange Interlude, 1932
If I Had a Million, 1932
Little Orphan Annie, 1932
Men Must Fight, 1933
White Sister, 1933
Reunion in Vienna, 1933
Dancing Lady, 1933
Dinner at Eight, 1933
One Man's Journey, 1933
Lady For a Day, 1933
Beauty For Sale, 1933
The Solitaire Man, 1933
Alice in Wonderland, 1933
You Can't Buy Everything,
  1934
Straight is the Way, 1934
Lady By Choice, 1934
Grand Old Girl, 1935
Vanessa: Her Love Story,
  1935
Reckless, 1935
Age of Indiscretion, 1935
Anna Karenina, 1935

Three Kids and a Queen, 1935
Wife vs. Secretary, 1936
The Baxter Millions, 1936
Rainbow On the River, 1936
Top of the Town, 1937
A Star is Born, 1937
The Perfect Specimen, 1938
Adventures of Tom Sawyer,
  1938
Bringing Up Baby, 1938
The Texans, 1938
Four Daughters, 1938
They Made Me a Criminal,
  1938
Yes My Darling Daughter, 1939
The Kid From Kokomo, 1939
Daughters Courageous, 1939
Nurse Edith Cavell, 1939
That's Right You're Wrong,
  1939
Four Wives, 1939
Granny Get Your Gun, 1940
Irene, 1940
Texas Rangers Ride Again,
  1941
Four Mothers, 1941
Million Dollar Baby, 1941
Playmates, 1941
Joan of Paris, 1942

PATRICIA ROC (1918-)
Beautiful leading lady of the
forties and fifties, also on
stage and in Hollywood.

Rebel Son, 1938
The Gaunt Stranger, 1938
The Mind of Mr. Reeder, 1939
The Missing People, 1939
A Window in London, 1939
Dr. O'Dowd, 1940
Pack Up Your Troubles, 1940
Gentleman of Venture, 1940
Three Silent Men, 1940
The Farmer's Wife, 1941
My Wife's Family, 1941
Let the People Sing, 1942
Suspected Person, 1942
We'll Meet Again, 1942
Millions Like Us, 1943
Two Thousand Women, 1944
Love Story, 1944

Madonna of the Seven Moons,
 1944
Johnny Frenchman, 1945
The Wicked Lady, 1945
Canyon Passage, 1946
The Brothers, 1947
So Well Remembered, 1947
Jassy, 1947
Holiday Camp, 1947
When the Bough Breaks, 1947
One Night With You, 1948
The Perfect Woman, 1949
Man On the Eiffel Tower, 1950
Circle of Danger, 1951
Captain Blackjack, 1952
Something Money Can't Buy,
 1952
The Hypnotist, 1957
The House in the Woods, 1957
Bluebeard's Ten Honeymoons,
 1959

ANTON RODGERS (1927-)
Character actor of stage,
films and television, specializing in comedy parts. Outstanding on tv as Edward
Langtry in "Lillie" (1978).

Crash Drive, 1959
Tarnished Heroes, 1961
Part Time Wife, 1961
Carry On Jack, 1963
Rotten to the Core, 1965
Scrooge, 1970
The Man Who Haunted Him-
 self, 1970
Day of the Jackal, 1973
Disraeli: Portrait of a Roman-
 tic, 1980

NORMAN RODWAY (1929-)
Supporting actor of the sixties,
also on stage.

This Other Eden, 1959
Murder in Eden, 1961
A Question of Suspense, 1961
The Quare Fellow, 1962
Ambush in Leopard Street, 1962
The Webster Boy, 1962

Four in the Morning, 1965
Chimes At Midnight, 1966
The Penthouse, 1967
I'll Never Forget Whatsisname,
 1967
Appointment With a Killer,
 1975

PAUL ROGERS (1917-)
Versatile character star of
stage (since 1938) and screen,
active during the sixties.

Murder in the Cathedral, 1952
A Prince For Cynthia, 1953
The Beachcomber, 1954
Beau Brummell, 1954
Svengali, 1955
Our Man in Havana, 1959
The Trials of Oscar Wilde,
 1960
Circle of Deception, 1961
No Love For Johnnie, 1961
The Mark, 1961
The Pot Carriers, 1962
The Prince and the Pauper,
 1962
Billy Budd, 1962
The Wild and the Willing, 1963
Stolen Hours, 1963
The Third Secret, 1964
He Who Rides a Tiger, 1965
Walk in the Shadow, 1966
The Shoes of the Fisherman,
 1968
A Midsummer Night's Dream,
 1968
Decline and Fall, 1968
The Reckoning, 1969
Three Into Two Won't Go, 1969
The Looking Glass War, 1970
I Want What I Want, 1972
The Homecoming, 1973
The Abdication, 1974
Lost in the Stars, 1974
Mr. Quilp, 1975

MARIA ROHM (1949-)
Austrian-born actress of the
60s and 70s in British and
international films.

24 Hours to Kill, 1965
Our Man in Marrakesh, 1966
Five Golden Dragons, 1966
City of Fear, 1966
Sumuru, 1967
House of a Thousand Dolls,
   1967
Eve, 1968
The Vengeance of Fu Manchu,
   1968
The Blood of Fu Manchu, 1968
99 Women, 1968
Venus in Furs, 1970
Dorian Gray, 1970
Count Dracula, 1970
Eugenie, 1971
Black Beauty, 1972
Treasure Island, 1972
Night of the Blood Monster,
   1972
Call of the Wild, 1972
Justine and Juliet, 1973
Annie, 1974
Ten Little Indians, 1975
The Assassin is Not Alone,
   1976
End of Innocence, 1976
Flight to Hell, 1977

GUY ROLFE (1915-)
Lean, good-looking leading man
and character actor of stage
(since 1936) and films, also in
Hollywood. Former boxer and
race driver.

Hungry Hill, 1946
Odd Man Out, 1947
Uncle Silas, 1947
Nicholas Nickleby, 1947
Meet Me at Dawn, 1947
Easy Money, 1948
Broken Journey, 1948
Saraband For Dead Lovers,
   1948
Portrait From Life, 1948
Fools Rush In, 1949
The Spider and the Fly, 1949
The Reluctant Widow, 1950
Prelude to Fame, 1950
Home to Danger, 1951
Ivanhoe, 1952

Operation Diplomat, 1953
Young Bess, 1953
Veils of Baghdad, 1953
Dance Little Lady, 1954
King of the Khyber Rifles, 1954
You Can't Escape, 1956
It's Never Too Late, 1956
Light Fingers, 1957
Girls at Sea, 1958
Yesterday's Enemy, 1959
Stranglers of Bombay, 1959
Snow White and the Three
   Stooges, 1960
King of Kings, 1961
Mr. Sardonicus, 1961
Taras Bulba, 1963
Fall of the Roman Empire, 1964
The Alphabet Murders, 1965
Land Raiders, 1970
Nicholas and Alexandra, 1971
And Now the Screaming Starts,
   1973
Bloodline, 1979

YVONNE ROMAIN (1938-)
French leading actress in British
films of the 50s and 60s, also
in Hollywood.

The Baby and the Battleship,
   1956
Seven Thunders, 1957
Corridors of Blood, 1958
Circus of Horrors, 1960
Curse of the Werewolf, 1961
Village of Daughters, 1961
Devil Doll, 1963
The Brigand of Kandahar, 1965
The Swinger, 1966
Double Trouble, 1967
The Last of Sheila, 1973

STEWART ROME (1886-1965)
Star of stage (from 1907) and
films, a romantic leading man
of silents who matured into gentlemanly character parts. Former engineer.

A Throw of the Dice, 1913
Justice, 1914

The Whirr of the Spinning
 Wheel, 1914
The Price of Fame, 1914
Thou Shalt Not Steal, 1914
What the Firelight Showed,
 1914
Heart of Midlothian, 1914
The Great Poison Mystery,
 1914
The Girl Who Played the
 Game, 1914
Creatures of Clay, 1914
The Girl Who Lived in
 Straight St. , 1914
Guest of the Evening, 1914
The Breaking Point, 1914
The Stress of Circumstance,
 1914
Terror of the Air, 1914
Only a Flower Girl, 1914
Dr. Fenton's Ordeal, 1914
The Grip of Ambition, 1914
The Schemers, 1914
Chimes, 1914
Unfit, 1914
The Bronze Idol, 1914
So Much Good in the Worst
 of Us, 1914
His Country's Bidding, 1914
The Brothers, 1914
The Awakening of Nora, 1914
The Quarry Mystery, 1914
Time the Great Healer, 1914
Tommy's Money Scheme, 1914
Despised and Rejected, 1914
The Double Event, 1914
The Man From India, 1914
They Say Let Them Say, 1914
John Linworth's Atonement,
 1914
The Lie, 1914
Life's Dark Road, 1914
The Canker of Jealousy, 1915
The Shepherd of Souls, 1915
Barnaby Rudge, 1915
The Man With the Scar, 1915
They Called Him Coward,
 1915
A Lancashire Lass, 1915
Schoolgirl Rebels, 1915
The Confession, 1915
Spies, 1915
Moment of Darkness, 1915

One Good Turn, 1915
Jill and the Old Fiddle, 1915
The Curtain's Secret, 1915
The Incorruptible Crown, 1915
Courtmartialled, 1915
The Bottle, 1915
The Baby On the Barge, 1915
The Sweater, 1915
The Second String, 1915
Her Boy, 1915
Sweet Lavender, 1915
The Golden Pavement, 1915
The White Hope, 1915
Night Birds of London, 1915
The Recalling of John Gray,
 1915
As the Sun Went Down, 1915
Iris, 1915
Face to Face, 1916
Trelawney of the Wells, 1916
The White Boys, 1916
Sowing the Wind, 1916
Annie Laurie, 1916
Partners, 1916
The Marriage of William Ashe,
 1916
Grand Babylon Hotel, 1916
Comin' Thro' the Rye, 1916
Molly Bawn, 1916
The House of Fortescue, 1916
The Cobweb, 1917
Her Marriage Lines, 1917
American Heiress, 1917
The Man Behind the Times,
 1917
Eternal Triangle, 1917
A Grain of Sand, 1917
Touch of a Child, 1918
A Daughter of Eve, 1919
Gentleman Rider, 1919
Snow in the Desert, 1919
The Great Coup, 1919
Her Son, 1920
Romance of a Movie Star, 1920
The Case of Lady Camber,
 1920
The Great Gay Road, 1920
Her Penalty, 1921
The Penniless Millionaire, 1921
Christine Johnstone, 1921
The Imperfect Lover, 1921
Dicky Monteith, 1922
When Greek Meets Greek, 1922

Son of Kissing Cup, 1922
The Prodigal Son, 1923
Fires of Fate, 1923
The Woman Who Obeyed, 1923
Uninvited Guest, 1923
The White Hope, 1923
The Colleen Bawn, 1924
The Eleventh Commandment, 1924
The Stirrup Cup Sensation, 1924
Desert Sheik, 1924
Nets of Destiny, 1925
Thou Fool, 1926
Somehow Good, 1927
Silver Treasure, 1928
The Ware Case, 1928
The Passing of Mr. Quinn, 1928
Zero, 1928
The Man Who Changed His Name, 1928
Dark Red Roses, 1929
The Last Hour, 1930
The Price of Things, 1930
Kissing Cup's Race, 1930
Other People's Sins, 1931
Deadlock, 1931
The Great Gay Road, 1931
Rynox, 1931
Marriage Bond, 1932
Betrayal, 1932
Reunion, 1932
Song of the Plough, 1933
Important People, 1934
Designing Woman, 1934
The Girl in the Flat, 1934
Lest We Forget, 1934
Temptation, 1935
Debt of Honour, 1936
Men of Yesterday, 1936
Wings of the Morning, 1937
The Squeaker, 1937
Dinner at the Ritz, 1937
Dance of Death, 1938
The Warning, 1939
Confidential Lady, 1939
Shadowed Eyes, 1940
Banana Ridge, 1941
One of Our Aircraft is Missing, 1942
Salute John Citizen, 1942
Tom's Ride, 1944

The World Owes Me a Living, 1945
The Magic Bow, 1947
The White Unicorn, 1947
Jassy, 1947
My Sister and I, 1948
Woman Hater, 1948
Let's Have a Murder, 1950

GEORGE ROSE (1920-)
Character actor of stage, films and television, also in Hollywood. Tv series: "Beacon Hill" (1977).

The Pickwick Papers, 1952
Grand National Night, 1953
The Square Ring, 1953
The Beggar's Opera, 1953
Devil On Horseback, 1954
The Sea Shall Not Have Them, 1955
Track the Man Down, 1955
The Night My Number Came Up, 1955
The Last Wagon, 1956
The Long Arm, 1956
Brothers in Law, 1957
The Shiralee, 1957
Barnacle Bill, 1957
A Night to Remember, 1958
Cat and Mouse, 1958
Jack the Ripper, 1959
The Devil's Disciple, 1959
The Heart of a Man, 1959
The Flesh and the Fiends, 1960
Macbeth, 1961
Hamlet, 1964
Hawaii, 1966
The Pink Jungle, 1968
A New Leaf, 1971
From the Mixed-Up Files of Mrs. Basil E. Frankweiler, 1973

MILTON ROSMER (1881-1971)
Leading man of stage (from 1899) and silent films, latterly in character roles. Also occasional director.

The Mystery of a Hansom Cab,
  1915
Whoso is Without Sin, 1916
Cynthia in the Wilderness,
  1916
The Greater Need, 1916
Still Waters Run Deep, 1916
The Man Without a Soul, 1916
Lady Windermere's Fan, 1916
Little Women, 1917
The Chinese Puzzle, 1919
Odds Against Her, 1919
With All Her Heart, 1920
Colonel Newcome, 1920
Wuthering Heights, 1920
The 12 Lock, 1920
The Golden Web, 1920
Torn Sails, 1920
The Diamond Necklace, 1920
The Will, 1921
Belphegor the Mountebank,
  1921
Demos, 1921
The Amazing Partnership,
  1921
Woman of No Importance, 1921
General John Regan, 1921
A Romance of Wastdale, 1921
The Passionate Friends, 1922
David Garrick, 1922
The Pointing Finger, 1922
A Gamble With Hearts, 1923
Shadow of Egypt, 1924
The Woman Juror, 1926
High Treason, 1929
The W Plan, 1930
Grand Prix, 1934
The Phantom Light, 1935
Silent Barriers, 1937
South Riding, 1938
Beyond Our Horizon, 1939
Let's Be Famous, 1939
Goodbye Mr. Chips, 1939
The Lion Has Wings, 1939
The Stars Look Down, 1939
Return to Yesterday, 1940
Dangerous Comment, 1940
Atlantic Ferry, 1941
Hatter's Castle, 1941
You're Telling Me, 1941
Daybreak, 1946
Frieda, 1947
Fame is the Spur, 1947

End of the River, 1947
The Monkey's Paw, 1948
The Small Back Room, 1948
Who Killed Van Loon?, 1948

NORMAN ROSSINGTON
  (1928-   )
Character player of stage,
films and television, almost
always seen in comedy roles.

A Night to Remember, 1958
I Only Arsked, 1958
Carry On Sergeant, 1958
Saturday Night and Sunday
  Morning, 1960
Carry On Regardless, 1961
Go to Blazes, 1962
Nurse On Wheels, 1963
The Comedy Man, 1963
A Hard Day's Night, 1964
Daylight Robbery, 1964
Joey Boy, 1965
Cup Fever, 1965
Those Magnificent Men in Their
  Flying Machines, 1965
The Wrong Box, 1966
Tobruk, 1966
Charge of the Light Brigade,
  1968
Negatives, 1968
The Rise and Rise of Michael
  Rimmer, 1970
Simon Simon, 1970
The Engagement, 1970
The Adventures of Gerard, 1970
Go For a Take, 1972
Deathline, 1972
Young Winston, 1972
Digby, the Biggest Dog in the
  World, 1973
Raw Meat, 1973
The Prisoner of Zenda, 1979

LEONARD ROSSITER (1927-   )
Character actor of stage, screen
and tv, usually seen in comedy
parts.

A Kind of Loving, 1962
This Sporting Life, 1963

Billy Liar, 1963
A Jolly Bad Fellow, 1964
King Rat, 1965
Hotel Paradiso, 1966
The Witches, 1966
The Wrong Box, 1966
Deadlier Than the Male, 1967
The Devil's Own, 1967
The Whisperers, 1967
Otley, 1968
Deadfall, 1968
Diamonds For Breakfast, 1968
2001: A Space Odyssey, 1968
Oliver, 1968
Butley, 1973
Luther, 1974
Barry Lyndon, 1975
Voyage of the Damned, 1976
The Pink Panther Strikes
     Again, 1976

JOHN RUDDOCK (1897-)
Character player mainly seen
on stage; also in Hollywood.
Often cast as elder or man of
significance.

Lancashire Luck, 1938
Strawberry Roan, 1945
Waltz Time, 1945
Night Boat to Dublin, 1946
Lisbon Story, 1946
Wanted For Murder, 1946
The Laughing Lady, 1946
Meet Me at Dawn, 1947
The Fallen Idol, 1948
Under Capricorn, 1949
Quo Vadis, 1951
Ivanhoe, 1952
Secret People, 1952
To the Rescue, 1952
Martin Luther, 1953
Lust For Life, 1956
Treasure at the Mill, 1957
Lawrence of Arabia, 1962
Cromwell, 1970
The Horsemen, 1971
Appointment With a Killer,
     1975

WILLIAM RUSHTON (-)

Comedy character actor in occasional films of the sixties.

It's All Over Town, 1963
Nothing But the Best, 1963
Those Magnificent Men in Their
     Flying Machines, 1965
The Bliss of Mrs. Blossom,
     1968
The Best House in London, 1969
Monte Carlo Or Bust, 1969

DAME MARGARET RUTHER-
     FORD (1892-1972)
Lovable, delightful character
of stage (since 1925) and screen
who revelled in eccentricity.
Excellent as Jane Marple in
several films of the sixties.
Also in Hollywood.   Married
to Stringer Davis.

Dusty Ermine, 1936
Talk of the Devil, 1936
Troubled Waters, 1936
Beauty and the Barge, 1937
Catch as Catch Can, 1937
Missing Believed Married, 1937
Spring Meeting, 1941
Quiet Wedding, 1941
The Yellow Canary, 1943
The Demi-Paradise, 1943
English Without Tears, 1944
Blithe Spirit, 1945
While the Sun Shines, 1946
Meet Me at Dawn, 1947
Miranda, 1948
Passport to Pimlico, 1949
The Happiest Days of Your
     Life, 1950
Her Favourite Husband, 1950
The Magic Box, 1951
Curtain Up, 1952
The Importance of Being Earn-
     est, 1952
Castle in the Air, 1952
Miss Robin Hood, 1952
Innocents in Paris, 1953
Trouble in Store, 1953
The Runaway Bus, 1954
Aunt Clara, 1954
Mad About Men, 1954

An Alligator Named Daisy,
   1955
The Smallest Show On Earth,
   1957
Just My Luck, 1957
Dick and the Duchess, 1958
I'm All Right, Jack, 1959
On the Double, 1961
Murder She Said, 1962
Mouse On the Moon, 1963
The VIPs, 1963
Murder at the Gallop, 1963
Murder Ahoy, 1964
Murder Most Foul, 1965
The Alphabet Murders, 1965
Big Time Operators, 1965
Chimes at Midnight, 1966
A Countess From Hong Kong,
   1966
The Wacky World of Mother
   Goose, 1967
Arabella, 1968

KATHLEEN RYAN (1922-)
Quiet Irish actress of stage
(from 1942) and films, also
in Hollywood.

Odd Man Out, 1947
Captain Boycott, 1947
Esther Waters, 1948
Christopher Columbus, 1949
Give Us This Day, 1949
Prelude to Fame, 1950
Try and Get Me, 1951
The Yellow Balloon, 1952
Laxdale Hall, 1953
Captain Lightfoot, 1955
Reach For the Sky, 1956
Jacqueline, 1956
Sail Into Danger, 1957

JOHN SALEW (-)
Character actor of the forties
and fifties, often seen in
cameo roles.

The Silent Battle, 1939
Sailors Don't Care, 1940
Neutral Port, 1940
Turned Out Nice Again, 1941

Suspected Person, 1942
Secret Mission, 1942
Back Room Boy, 1942
Continental Express, 1942
The Young Mr. Pitt, 1942
Lady in Distress, 1942
The Night Invader, 1943
We Dive at Dawn, 1943
Warn That Man, 1943
Millions Like Us, 1943
Tawny Pipit, 1944
Time Flies, 1944
Murder In Reverse, 1945
Bothered by a Beard, 1946
Bedelia, 1946
Caravan, 1946
Beware of Pity, 1946
Meet Me at Dawn, 1947
Uncle Silas, 1947
Dancing With Crime, 1947
My Brother Jonathan, 1948
Counterblast, 1948
Anna Karenina, 1948
Noose, 1948
Kind Hearts and Coronets, 1949
For Them That Trespass, 1949
All Over the Town, 1949
The Spider and the Fly, 1949
The Bad Lord Byron, 1949
No Way Back, 1949
Dark Secret, 1949
The Lavender Hill Mob, 1951
Night Was Our Friend, 1951
Green Grow the Rushes, 1951
Mystery Junction, 1951
His Excellency, 1952
Father Brown, 1954
Face the Music, 1954
Three Cases of Murder, 1955
It's Great to Be Young, 1956
Rogue's Yarn, 1956
The Good Companions, 1957
Alive On Saturday, 1957
Alive and Kicking, 1958
The Gypsy and the Gentleman,
   1958
The Shakedown, 1960
The Impersonator, 1961

PETER SALLIS (1921-)
Character actor of preoccupied
appearance, also seen on

television and stage, often in comedy characterizations.

Anastasia, 1956
The Doctor's Dilemma, 1958
Saturday Night & Sunday
  Morning, 1960
Curse of the Werewolf, 1961
Clash By Night, 1963
Mouse On the Moon, 1963
The Third Secret, 1964
Charlie Bubbles, 1967
Inadmissible Evidence, 1968
Scream and Scream Again, 1969
Wuthering Heights, 1970
My Lover My Son, 1970
The Reckoning, 1970
Taste the Blood of Dracula, 1970
The Night Digger, 1971
Frankenstein: The True Story, 1973
The Incredible Sarah, 1976
Who's Killing the Great Chefs
  of Europe?, 1978
She Loves Me, 1979

GEORGE SANDERS (1906-72)
Suave star of stage (1924),
films and television, mainly
in Hollywood. Generally cast
as cad or elegant crook, but
also the occasional hero.
Brother of Tom Conway, he
was married to Zsa Zsa Gabor;
Benita Hume; Magda Gabor.
Tv series: "George Sanders
Mystery Theatre" (1958).

Find the Lady, 1936
Strange Cargo, 1936
The Man Who Could Work
  Miracles, 1936
Dishonour Bright, 1936
Lloyds of London, 1936
Love is News, 1937
Slave Ship, 1937
Lancer Spy, 1937
The Lady Escapes, 1937
International Settlement, 1938
Four Men and a Prayer, 1938
Mr. Moto's Last Warning,
  1939
The Saint Strikes Back, 1939

Confessions of a Nazi Spy,
  1939
The Saint in London, 1939
The Outsider, 1939
So This is London, 1939
Nurse Edith Cavell, 1939
Allegheny Uprising, 1939
Rebecca, 1940
House of the Seven Gables,
  1940
The Saint Takes Over, 1940
Foreign Correspondent, 1940
Bitter Sweet, 1940
The Son of Monte Cristo, 1940
The Saint in Palm Springs,
  1941
Rage in Heaven, 1941
Man Hunt, 1941
The Gay Falcon, 1941
Sundown, 1941
A Date With the Falcon, 1941
Son of Fury, 1942
The Falcon Takes Over, 1942
Her Cardboard Lover, 1942
Tales of Manhattan, 1942
The Falcon's Brother, 1942
The Moon and Sixpence, 1942
The Black Swan, 1942
Quiet Please-Murder, 1943
They Came to Blow Up Amer-
  ica, 1943
This Land is Mine, 1943
Appointment in Berlin, 1943
Paris After Dark, 1943
The Lodger, 1944
Action in Arabia, 1944
Summer Storm, 1944
Hangover Square, 1945
The Picture of Dorian Gray,
  1945
The Strange Affair of Uncle
  Harry, 1945
Scandal in Paris, 1946
The Strange Woman, 1946
Private Affairs of Bel Ami,
  1947
The Ghost and Mrs. Muir,
  1947
Lured, 1947
Forever Amber, 1947
The Fan, 1949
Samson and Delilah, 1949
Captain Blackjack, 1950

All About Eve, 1950
I Can Get it For You Whole-
sale, 1951
The Light Touch, 1951
Ivanhoe, 1952
Assignment Paris, 1952
Call Me Madam, 1953
The Lonely Woman, 1953
Witness to Murder, 1954
King Richard and the Cru-
saders, 1954
Jupiter's Darling, 1955
Moonfleet, 1955
The Scarlet Coat, 1955
The King's Thief, 1955
Never Say Goodbye, 1956
While the City Sleeps, 1956
That Certain Feeling, 1956
Death of a Scoundrel, 1956
The Seventh Sin, 1957
The Whole Truth, 1958
From the Earth to the Moon,
1958
That Kind of Woman, 1959
A Touch of Larceny, 1959
Solomon and Sheba, 1959
Bluebeard's Ten Honeymoons,
1959
The Last Voyage, 1959
Cone of Silence, 1960
Village of the Damned, 1960
Five Golden Hours, 1961
The Rebel, 1961
Operation Snatch, 1962
In Search of the Castaways,
1962
Cairo, 1962
Ecco, 1963
The Cracksman, 1963
Dark Purpose, 1964
A Shot in the Dark, 1964
The Golden Head, 1964
Moll Flanders, 1965
Trunk to Cairo, 1966
The Quiller Memorandum,
1966
Warning Shot, 1967
Good Times, 1967
The Jungle Book, 1967
One Step to Hell, 1968
The Candy Man, 1969
The Best House in London,
1969

The Body Stealers, 1969
The Kremlin Letter, 1970
Death Wheelers, 1972
Doomwatch, 1972
Endless Night, 1972

CHRISTOPHER SANDFORD
(1939-)
Thin character player in occasional films.

Half a Sixpence, 1967
Before Winter Comes, 1969
Die Screaming Marianne, 1970
Cool It Carol, 1970
Deep End, 1971
Old Dracula, 1975

MICHAEL SARNE (1939-)
Light character actor of the
60s in occasional films, latterly
director.

Sodom and Gomorrah, 1960
The Guns of Navarone, 1961
A Place to Go, 1964
Every Day's a Holiday, 1965
Two Weeks in September, 1967

H. SAXON-SNELL (-)
Character actor of the 20s and
30s, often in authoritative roles.

Luck of the Navy, 1927
Smashing Through, 1928
The Bondman, 1929
A Peep Behind the Scenes, 1929
Clue of the New Pin, 1929
The Third Gun, 1929
The Loves of Robert Burns,
1930
Deadlock, 1931
My Friend the King, 1931
Josser Joins the Navy, 1932 '
The Return of Raffles, 1932
Verdict of the Sea, 1932
Maid Happy, 1933
The Love Wager, 1933
Murder at the Inn, 1934
The Return of Bulldog Drum-

mond, 1934
Once in a New Moon, 1935
His Majesty and Co, 1935
Royal Cavalcade, 1935
Rolling Home, 1935

PAUL SCOFIELD (1922-)
Distinguished, superior star
of stage (1940) seen too rarely
in films.

That Lady, 1955
Carve Her Name With Pride,
   1958
The Train, 1965
A Man For All Seasons, 1966
Tell Me Lies, 1968
King Lear, 1970
Bartleby, 1971
Scorpio, 1973
A Delicate Balance, 1974
The Curse of King Tut's Tomb
   (voice), 1980

JANETTE SCOTT (1938-)
Leading lady of the fifties and
sixties, former child star.
Daughter of Thora Hird; married to singer Mel Tormé.

Went the Day Well, 1942
The Lamp Still Burns, 1943
Medal For the General, 1944
Two Thousand Women, 1944
Spellbound, 1945
No Place For Jennifer, 1950
The Galloping Major, 1951
No Highway, 1951
The Magic Box, 1951
Background, 1953
As Long as They're Happy,
   1954
Helen of Troy, 1956
Now and Forever, 1956
The Good Companions, 1957
Happy is the Bride, 1957
The Lady is a Square, 1958
The Devil's Disciple, 1959
School For Scoundrels, 1960
His and Hers, 1961
Double Bunk, 1961

Two and Two Make Six, 1962
Day of the Triffids, 1963
A Stitch in Time, 1963
Paranoiac, 1963
The Old Dark House, 1963
Siege of the Saxons, 1963
The Beauty Jungle, 1964
Crack in the World, 1965
White Savage, 1966
Bikini Paradise, 1967

MARGARETTA SCOTT (1912-)
Dark-haired leading lady and
latterly character actress of
stage (from 1926) and screen,
usually seen in patrician roles
or as "other woman."

The Private Life of Don Juan,
   1934
Dirty Work, 1934
Peg of Old Drury, 1935
Things to Come, 1936
Action For Slander, 1937
Return of the Scarlet Pimpernel,
   1937
The Girl in the News, 1940
Quiet Wedding, 1941
Atlantic Ferry, 1941
Sabotage at Sea, 1942
Fanny By Gaslight, 1944
The Man From Morocco, 1945
Mrs. Fitzherbert, 1947
Idol of Paris, 1948
The First Gentleman, 1948
Counterblast, 1948
Calling Paul Temple, 1948
The Story of Shirley Yorke,
   1948
Landfall, 1949
Where's Charley?, 1952
The Last Man To Hang, 1956
Town On Trial, 1957
The Scamp, 1957
A Woman Possessed, 1958
An Honourable Murder, 1960
Crescendo, 1969
Percy, 1970

HEATHER SEARS (1935-)
Pleasant, attractive actress

of stage (1955), television and films.

Dry Rot, 1956
The Story of Esther Costello, 1957
Room at the Top, 1959
The Siege of Pinchgut, 1959
Sons and Lovers, 1960
Phantom of the Opera, 1962
Saturday Night Out, 1964
The Black Torment, 1964
Great Expectations, 1975

HARRY SECOMBE (1921-)
Husky Welsh recording artist and comedian in occasional films; former radio star (from 1945).

Helter Skelter, 1949
Penny Points to Paradise, 1951
London Entertains, 1951
Down Among the Z Men, 1952
Forces' Sweetheart, 1953
Svengali, 1955
Trilby, 1956
Davy, 1957
Jet Storm, 1959
Oliver, 1968
The Bed Sitting Room, 1969
Rhubarb, 1970
Doctor in Trouble, 1970
Song of Norway, 1970
Magnificent Seven Deadly Sins, 1971
Sunstruck, 1972

ERNEST SEFTON (-)
Character player of the thirties, also on stage.

Innocents of Chicago, 1932
Old Spanish Customers, 1932
Little Miss Nobody, 1933
Double Wedding, 1933
Britannia of Billingsgate, 1933
Great Stuff, 1933
I'll Stick to You, 1933
Enemy of the Police, 1933
Strike It Rich, 1933

The Bermondsey Kid, 1933
I Adore You, 1933
The Girl in Possession, 1934
Big Business, 1934
What's in a Name, 1934
The Third Clue, 1934
Strictly Illegal, 1935
Say it With Diamonds, 1935
Millions, 1936
Broken Blossoms, 1936
It's in the Bag, 1936
Cheer Up, 1936
Wolf's Clothing, 1936
Double Alibi, 1937
The Fatal Hour, 1937
Dr. Sin Fang, 1937
Jennifer Hale, 1937
I See Ice, 1938
Bad Boy, 1938
Two Days to Live, 1939
The Body Vanishes, 1939
That's the Ticket, 1940
Old Mother Riley in Business, 1940
Amateur Night, 1946
The Grand Escapade, 1946

ELIZABETH SELLARS
(1923-)
Intelligent Scottish actress, on stage from 1938, also on television and in Hollywood.

Floodtide, 1949
Madeleine, 1950
Guilt is My Shadow, 1950
Cloudburst, 1951
Night Was Our Friend, 1951
Hunted, 1952
The Gentle Gunman, 1952
The Long Memory, 1953
The Broken Horseshoe, 1953
Recoil, 1953
The Barefoot Contessa, 1954
Desiree, 1954
Prince of Players, 1954
Forbidden Cargo, 1954
Three Cases of Murder, 1955
The Last Man to Hang, 1956
Man in the Sky, 1957
The Shiralee, 1957
Law and Disorder, 1958

Jet Storm, 1959
The Day They Robbed the
	Bank of England, 1960
Moment of Truth, 1960
Never Let Go, 1960
Middle of Nowhere, 1961
The Webster Boy, 1962
55 Days at Peking, 1963
The Chalk Garden, 1964
The Mummy's Shroud, 1967
The Prime of Miss Jean
	Brodie, 1969
The Hireling, 1973

PETER SELLERS (1925-1980)
Comedy star now seen in international films, a master of
disguises and funny voices.
Also former radio star (from
1946) and variety artist.

Let's Go Crazy, 1951
London Entertains, 1951
Penny Points to Paradise,
	1952
Down Among the Z Men, 1952
Super Secret Service, 1953
Orders Are Orders, 1954
John and Julie, 1955
The Ladykillers, 1955
The Man Who Never Was
	(voice), 1956
Case of the Mukkinese Battle-
	horn, 1956
Dearth of a Salesman, 1957
Insomnia is Good For You,
	1957
The Smallest Show On Earth,
	1957
The Naked Truth, 1958
Up the Creek, 1958
Tom Thumb, 1958
Cold Comfort, 1958
Carleton Browne of the F. O.,
	1959
The Mouse That Roared, 1959
I'm All Right, Jack, 1959
Battle of the Sexes, 1959
Two-Way Stretch, 1960
Never Let Go, 1960
The Running, Jumping &
	Standing Still Film, 1960

Climb Up the Wall, 1960
The Millionairess, 1960
Mr. Topaze, 1961
Only Two Can Play, 1962
Waltz of the Toreadors, 1962
The Dock Brief, 1962
The Road to Hong Kong, 1962
Lolita, 1962
The Wrong Arm of the Law,
	1963
Heavens Above, 1963
The Pink Panther, 1963
Dr. Strangelove, 1964
Big Time Operations, 1964
The World of Henry Orient,
	1964
A Shot in the Dark, 1964
A Carol For Another Christmas,
	1965
What's New Pussycat, 1965
The Wrong Box, 1966
After the Fox, 1966
Casino Royale, 1967
Woman Times Seven, 1967
The Bobo, 1967
The Party, 1968
I Love You Alice B. Toklas,
	1968
Simon Simon, 1970
Hoffman, 1970
The Magic Christian, 1970
There's a Girl in My Soup,
	1970
A Day at the Beach, 1971
Alice's Adventures in Wonder-
	land, 1972
Where Does it Hurt?, 1972
Ghost in the Noonday Sun, 1973
The Optimists of Nine Elms,
	1973
The Blockhouse, 1973
Undercovers Hero, 1974
The Great McGonagall, 1974
Return of the Pink Panther,
	1974
Murder By Death, 1976
The Pink Panther Strikes Again,
	1976
Revenge of the Pink Panther,
	1978
The Prisoner of Zenda, 1979
Being There, 1980
The Fiendish Plot of Dr. Fu
	Manchu, 1980

MORTON SELTEN (1860-1940)
Character actor of the thirties
normally seen playing judges
or other respected professional
men.

Branded, 1920
Somebody's Darling, 1925
The Shadow Between, 1931
Wedding Rehearsal, 1932
Service For Ladies, 1932
The Love Wager, 1933
Falling For You, 1933
The Ware Case, 1934
How's Chances, 1934
Ten Minute Alibi, 1935
His Majesty and Co., 1935
Once in a New Moon, 1935
Annie Leave the Room, 1935
Moscow Nights, 1935
Dark World, 1935
The Ghost Goes West, 1936
Juggernaut, 1936
Two's Company, 1936
Action For Slander, 1937
Fire Over England, 1937
A Yank at Oxford, 1938
Divorce of Lady X, 1938
Young Man's Fancy, 1939
Shipyard Sally, 1939
The Thief of Bagdad, 1940

BRUCE SETON (1909-1969)
Character actor and sometimes
leading man with military experience; on television as well
in "Fabian of the Yard" (1954).

The Shadow of Mike Emerald,
    1935
Blue Smoke, 1935
Melody of My Heart, 1936
The Beauty Doctor, 1936
Wedding Group, 1936
The Vandergilt Diamond Mys-
    tery, 1936
Sweeney Todd, 1936
The Man Who Changed His
    Mind, 1936
Cocktail, 1936
Annie Laurie, 1936
End of the Road, 1936

Racing Romance, 1937
The Green Cockatoo, 1937
Love From a Stranger, 1937
Cafe Colette, 1937
Fifty Shilling Boxer, 1937
Father Steps Out, 1937
If I Were Boss, 1938
Weddings Are Wonderful, 1938
You're the Doctor, 1938
Miracles Do Happen, 1938
Old Mother Riley Joins Up,
    1939
Lucky To Me, 1939
The Middle Watch, 1939
Song of the Road, 1940
Curse of the Wraydons, 1946
Bonnie Prince Charlie, 1948
Whiskey Galore, 1948
The Story of Shirley Yorke,
    1948
Scott of the Antarctic, 1948
Look Before You Love, 1948
Portrait of Clare, 1950
Paul Temple's Triumph, 1950
The Blue Lamp, 1950
Blackmailed, 1951
Worm's Eye View, 1951
Take Me to Paris, 1951
Emergency Call, 1952
The Second Mrs. Tanqueray,
    1952
The Cruel Sea, 1953
Eight O'clock Walk, 1954
Delayed Action, 1954
Man of the Moment, 1955
Breakaway, 1956
There's Always a Thursday,
    1957
West of Suez, 1957
Morning Call, 1957
The Crooked Sky, 1957
Zoo Baby, 1957
Undercover Girl, 1958
Hidden Homicide, 1959
Make Mine a Million, 1959
John Paul Jones, 1959
Violent Moment, 1959
Life in Danger, 1959
Strictly Confidential, 1959
Carry On Constable, 1960
Just Joe, 1960
Operation Cupid, 1960
Gorgo, 1961

The Frightened City, 1961
Ambush in Leopard Street,
   1962
Freedom to Die, 1962
Dead Man's Evidence, 1962

GEORGE SEWELL (1924-)
Tough character actor of film
and television, popular in the
sixties. Tv series: "Special
Branch."

Sparrows Can't Sing, 1963
This Sporting Life, 1963
Kaleidoscope, 1966
Robbery, 1967
The Vengeance of She, 1968
Doppelganger, 1969
Happy Deathday, 1969
Get Carter, 1971
Barry Lyndon, 1975
Operation Daybreak, 1976
Tinker, Tailor, Soldier, Spy, 1980

ATHENE SEYLER (1889-)
Comedy character star, also
on stage (from 1908).

The Adventures of Mr. Pick-
   wick, 1921
This Freedom, 1923
The Perfect Lady, 1931
Tell Me Tonight, 1932
Early to Bed, 1933
Blossom Time, 1934
The Private Life of Don Juan,
   1934
D'Ye Ken John Peel, 1935
The Rocks of Valpre, 1935
Drake of England, 1935
Royal Cavalcade, 1935
Scrooge, 1935
Moscow Nights, 1935
High Treason, 1936
It's Love Again, 1936
Southern Roses, 1936
Irish For Luck, 1936
The Mill On the Floss, 1937
Sensation, 1937
Lilac Domino, 1937
Non Stop New York, 1937
The Sky's the Limit, 1937

The Citadel, 1938
Sailing Along, 1938
The Ware Case, 1938
Young Man's Fancy, 1939
The Saint in London, 1939
Tilly of Bloomsbury, 1940
Quiet Wedding, 1941
Dear Octopus, 1943
Nicholas Nickleby, 1947
The First Gentleman, 1948
The Queen of Spades, 1949
Young Wives' Tale, 1951
The Franchise Affair, 1951
The Secret People, 1952
Made in Heaven, 1952
The Pickwick Papers, 1952
The Beggar's Opera, 1953
The Weak and the Wicked, 1954
For Better, For Worse, 1954
As Long as They're Happy, 1955
Yield to the Night, 1956
Doctor at Large, 1957
Campbell's Kingdom, 1957
How to Murder a Rich Uncle,
   1957
Night of the Demon, 1957
A Tale of Two Cities, 1958
Happy is the Bride, 1958
Inn of the Sixth Happiness, 1958
Make Mine Mink, 1960
A French Mistress, 1960
Visa to Canton, 1960
The Girl in the Boat, 1961
Francis of Assisi, 1961
Satan Never Sleeps, 1962
Two and Two Make Six, 1962
I Thank a Fool, 1962
Nurse On Wheels, 1963

JANE SEYMOUR (1951-)
Attractive leading lady of the 70s.

The Only Way, 1971
Young Winston, 1972
Live and Let Die, 1973
Frankenstein: The True Story,
   1973
Sinbad and the Eye of the
   Tiger, 1977
The Four Feathers, 1978
Battlestar Galactica, 1978
Dallas Cowboys Cheerleaders,
   1979

Oh Heavenly Dog, 1980
Somewhere in Time, 1980
East of Eden, 1981

DENIS SHAW (-)
Character player of the 50s
and 60s, also on stage.

House of Blackmail, 1953
The Colditz Story, 1955
Who Done It, 1956
The Weapon, 1956
The Flesh is Weak, 1957
The Depraved, 1957
A Woman Possessed, 1958
Soapbox Derby, 1958
Moment of Indiscretion, 1958
The Links of Justice, 1958
The Great Van Robbery, 1959
Passport to Shame, 1959
Innocent Meeting, 1959
The Bandit of Zhobe, 1959
No Safety Ahead, 1959
Jack the Ripper, 1959
The Mummy, 1959
Beyond the Curtain, 1960
The Misfits, 1960
Ticket to Paradise, 1961
The Runaway, 1964
The Deadly Affair, 1966
The Viking Queen, 1967
The Magnificent $6\frac{1}{2}$, 1969

ROBERT SHAW (1927-1978)
Leading man of stage (from
1949) and films, also in Hollywood. Good at heroic and
sinister roles alike. Also in
Hollywood. Married to Mary
Ure. Also novelist and playwright. Tv series: "The
Buccaneers" (1956).

The Dam Busters, 1955
A Hill in Korea, 1956
Sea Fury, 1959
The Valiant, 1961
Tomorrow at Ten, 1962
From Russia With Love, 1963
The Caretaker, 1963
The Luck of Ginger Coffey,

1964
Battle of the Bulge, 1965
A Man For All Seasons, 1966
Custer of the West, 1967
The Birthday Party, 1968
The Battle of Britain, 1969
The Royal Hunt of the Sun,
1969
Figures in a Landscape, 1970
A Town Called Bastard, 1971
Young Winston, 1972
The Sting, 1973
The Hireling, 1973
A Reflection of Fear, 1973
The Taking of Pelham 1-2-3,
1974
Jaws, 1975
Diamonds, 1975
End of the Game, 1975
Murder On the Bridge, 1975
Robin and Marian, 1976
The Deep, 1977
Welcome to Blood City, 1977
Swashbuckler, 1977
Black Sunday, 1977
Force 10 From Navarone, 1978
Avalanche Express, 1979

SEBASTIAN SHAW (1903-)
Handsome star of the thirties,
latterly seen in character parts;
also on stage (from 1913) and
television.

Caste, 1930
Taxi to Paradise, 1933
Little Miss Nobody, 1933
Four Masked Men, 1934
Get Your Man, 1934
Adventure Ltd. , 1934
The Way of Youth, 1934
Brewster's Millions, 1935
The Lad, 1935
Ace of Spades, 1935
Three Witnesses, 1935
Department Store, 1935
Jubilee Window, 1935
Birds of a Feather, 1935
Jury's Evidence, 1936
Tomorrow We Live, 1936
Men are Not Gods, 1936
Farewell Again, 1937

The Squeaker, 1937
Too Dangerous to Live, 1939
The Spy in Black, 1939
Now You're Talking, 1940
The Flying Squad, 1940
Bulldog Sees it Through, 1940
Three Silent Men, 1940
East of Piccadilly, 1941
Journey Together, 1945
The Glass Mountain, 1949
Landfall, 1949
Feature Story, 1950
Laxdale Hall, 1953
It Happened Here, 1964
A Midsummer Night's Dream,
  1968

SUSAN SHAW (1929-1978)
Leading lady of the 40s and
50s, former model.   Married
to Albert Lieven; Bonar
Colleano.

London Town, 1945
Walking On Air, 1946
The Upturned Glass, 1947
Holiday Camp, 1947
Jassy, 1947
It Always Rains On Sunday,
  1947
To the Public Danger, 1948
My Brothers' Keeper, 1948
London Belongs to Me, 1948
Quartet, 1948
Here Come the Huggetts, 1948
Vote For Huggett, 1948
It's Not Cricket, 1949
The Huggetts Abroad, 1949
Marry Me, 1949
Train of Events, 1949
Waterfront, 1950
The Woman in Question, 1950
Pool of London, 1951
There is Another Sun, 1951
Wide Boy, 1952
The Killer Walks, 1952
The Intruder, 1953
Small Town Story, 1953
The Large Rope, 1953
The Good Die Young, 1954
Time is My Enemy, 1954
Stolen Time, 1955

Stock Car, 1955
Fire Maidens From Outer
  Space, 1956
Davy, 1957
The Diplomatic Corpse, 1958
Chain of Events, 1958
Carry On Nurse, 1959
The Big Day, 1960
Stranglehold, 1962
The Switch, 1963
Sitting Target, 1972

MOIRA SHEARER (1926-)
Attractive Scottish ballet dancer
in occasional films.

The Red Shoes, 1948
Tales of Hoffman, 1951
The Story of Three Loves,
  1953
The Man Who Loved Redheads,
  1955
Peeping Tom, 1960
Black Tights, 1960

BARBARA SHELLEY (1933-)
Attractive leading lady seen
also in international films,
mainly of the horror genre.
Also frequently on tv.   Former
model.

Cat Girl, 1957
End of the Line, 1957
The Solitary Child, 1957
The Camp On Blood Island,
  1958
Blood of the Vampire, 1958
Murder at Site Three, 1959
Deadly Record, 1959
Bobbikins, 1959
Village of the Damned, 1960
A Story of David, 1960
Shadow of the Cat, 1961
Postman's Knock, 1962
Death Trap, 1962
Stranglehold, 1962
Blind Corner, 1963
The Gorgon, 1964
The Secret of Blood Island,
  1965

Dracula Prince of Darkness,
1965
Rasputin the Mad Monk, 1965
Quatermass and the Pit, 1967
Ghost Story, 1974

JOY SHELTON (1922-)
Leading lady and supporting
actress, married to Sydney
Tafler.

Millions Like Us, 1943
Bees in Paradise, 1944
Waterloo Road, 1945
Send For Paul Temple, 1946
Uneasy Terms, 1948
No Room at the Inn, 1948
Designing Woman, 1948
Once a Sinner, 1950
Midnight Episode, 1950
A Case For PC 49, 1951
Emergency Call, 1952
Park Plaza 605, 1953
Impulse, 1955
No Kidding, 1960
The Greengage Summer, 1961
HMS Defiant, 1962

MICHAEL SHEPLEY (1907-
1961)
Character actor with stage
experience; often seen as
friendly bumbler.

Black Coffee, 1931
A Shot in the Dark, 1933
Are You a Mason?, 1934
Bella Donna, 1934
Tangled Evidence, 1934
Lord Edgware Dies, 1934
The Green Pack, 1934
Open All Night, 1934
The Rocks of Valpre, 1935
Lazybones, 1935
The Ace of Spades, 1935
The Lad, 1935
That's My Uncle, 1935
Vintage Wine, 1935
Jubilee Window, 1935
Squibs, 1935
Private Secretary, 1935

The Triumph of Sherlock
Holmes, 1935
In the Soup, 1936
Beauty and the Barge, 1937
High Treason, 1937
Crackerjack, 1938
Housemaster, 1938
It's in the Air, 1938
Goodbye Mr. Chips, 1939
Quiet Wedding, 1941
The Great Mr. Handel, 1942
The Demi-Paradise, 1943
Henry V, 1944
A Place of One's Own, 1944
I Live in Grosvenor Square,
1945
Mine Own Executioner, 1947
Maytime in Mayfair, 1949
Elizabeth of Ladymead, 1949
Mr. Denning Drives North, 1951
Secret People, 1952
Home at Seven, 1952
Happy Ever After, 1954
You Know What Sailors Are,
1954
Where There's a Will, 1955
Doctor at Sea, 1955
An Alligator Named Daisy, 1955
My Teenage Daughter, 1956
Dry Rot, 1956
A Novel Affair, 1957
Not Wanted On Voyage, 1957
Gideon's Day, 1958
Just Joe, 1960
Why Bother to Knock?, 1961
Double Bunk, 1961

DINAH SHERIDAN (1920-)
Leading lady of stage (since
1932) and films, married to
Jimmy Hanley.

I Give My Heart, 1935
Irish and Proud of It, 1936
Landslide, 1937
Behind Your Back, 1937
Father Steps Out, 1937
Merely Mr. Hawkins, 1938
Full Speed Ahead, 1939
Salute John Citizen, 1942
Get Cracking, 1943
For You Alone, 1945

29 Acacia Avenue, 1945
Murder in Reverse, 1945
The Hills of Donegal, 1947
Calling Paul Temple, 1948
The Huggetts Abroad, 1949
The Story of Shirley Yorke,
1949
Dark Secret, 1949
The Facts of Love, 1949
No Trace, 1950
Blackout, 1950
Paul Temple's Triumph, 1951
Where No Vultures Fly, 1951
The Sound Barrier, 1952
Appointment in London, 1952
Genevieve, 1953
Gilbert and Sullivan, 1953
The Railway Children, 1971
The Mirror Crack'd, 1980

ARTHUR SHIELDS (1895-1970)
Irish character star long in
Hollywood, formerly with the
Abbey Theatre. Brother of
Barry Fitzgerald.

Rafferty's Rise, 1918
The Plough and the Stars, 1936
Drums Along the Mohawk, 1939
The Long Voyage Home, 1940
Little Nellie Kelly, 1940
Confirm or Deny, 1941
Lady Scarface, 1941
How Green Was My Valley, 1941
Broadway, 1942
This Above All, 1942
Gentleman Jim, 1942
The Black Swan, 1942
Pacific Rendezvous, 1942
Nightmare, 1942
The Man From Down Under,
1943
Lassie Come Home, 1943
Madame Curie, 1943
The Keys of the Kingdom,
1944
The White Cliffs of Dover,
1944
National Velvet, 1944
The Sign of the Cross, 1944
Youth Runs Wild, 1944

Third Avenue, 1945
Too Young to Know, 1945
The Corn is Green, 1945
Roughly Speaking, 1945
Valley of Decision, 1945
Three Strangers, 1946
The Verdict, 1946
Gallant Journey, 1946
Easy Come, Easy Go, 1946
The Shocking Miss Pilgrim,
1947
The Fabulous Dorseys, 1947
Seven Keys to Baldpate, 1947
Tap Roots, 1948
Fighting Father Dunne, 1948
My Own True Love, 1949
The Fighting O'Flynn, 1949
Red Light, 1949
She Wore a Yellow Ribbon,
1949
Challenge to Lassie, 1950
Tarzan and the Slave Girl,
1950
Apache Drums, 1951
The River, 1951
The People Against O'Hara,
1951
Sealed Cargo, 1951
The Quiet Man, 1952
South Sea Woman, 1953
Scandal at Scourie, 1953
The World For Ransom, 1954
Pride of the Blue Grass, 1954
A King and Four Queens, 1956
Daughter of Dr. Jekyll, 1957
Night of the Quarter Moon,
1959
The Pigeon That Took Rome,
1962

BILL SHINE (1911-)
Character player often seen in
cameo roles as friendly, brain-
less characters.

The Flying Scotsman, 1929
Under the Greenwood Tree,
1929
The Last Hour, 1930
The Yellow Mask, 1930
These Charming People, 1931

Verdict of the Sea, 1932
My Old Dutch, 1934
The Scarlet Pimpernel, 1935
Highland Fling, 1936
The Strange Adventures of
    Mr. Smith, 1937
Farewell Again, 1937
The Villiers Diamond, 1938
Let George Do It, 1940
Champagne Charlie, 1944
Perfect Strangers, 1945
Wanted For Murder, 1946
Private Angelo, 1949
Under Capricorn, 1949
The Chiltern Hundreds, 1949
Something in the City, 1950
Love's a Luxury, 1952
Hot Ice, 1952
The Caretaker's Daughter,
    1953
Melba, 1953
There Was a Young Lady,
    1953
Knave of Hearts, 1954
Father Brown, 1954
The Deep Blue Sea, 1955
Richard III, 1955
Not So Dusty, 1956
The House in the Woods, 1957
The Diplomatic Corpse, 1958
Jack the Ripper, 1959
The Boy and the Bridge, 1959
The Sky Bike, 1967
Ouch!, 1967

RONALD SHINER (1903-1966)
Comedy star of the fifties who
rose from minor roles, also
on stage (from 1928); former
Canadian Mountie.

My Old Dutch, 1934
Doctor's Orders, 1934
It's a Bet, 1935
Royal Cavalcade, 1935
Gentleman's Agreement, 1935
Once a Thief, 1935
Squibs, 1935
Line Engaged, 1936
Excuse My Glove, 1936
King of Hearts, 1936
The Black Tulip, 1937

Beauty and the Barge, 1937
Dreaming Lips, 1937
Dinner at the Ritz, 1937
They Drive By Night, 1938
A Yank at Oxford, 1938
Prison Without Bars, 1938
The Mind of Mr. Reeder, 1939
Trouble Brewing, 1939
The Flying 55, 1939
The Missing People, 1939
I Killed the Count, 1939
The Gang's All Here, 1939
Discoveries, 1939
Come On George, 1939
The Middle Watch, 1939
Let George Do It, 1940
Bulldog Sees it Through, 1940
The Frightened Lady, 1940
Salvage With a Smile, 1940
Old Bill and Son, 1940
The Seventh Survivor, 1941
Major Barbara, 1941
The Black Sheep of Whitehall,
    1941
South American George, 1941
The Big Blockade, 1942
They Flew Alone, 1942
Those Kids From Town, 1942
Sabotage at Sea, 1942
King Arthur Was a Gentleman,
    1942
The Balloon Goes Up, 1942
Unpublished Story, 1942
Squadron Leader X, 1942
The Young Mr. Pitt, 1942
Get Cracking, 1943
Thursday's Child, 1943
The Gentle Sex, 1943
Miss London Ltd., 1943
The Butler's Dilemma, 1943
Bees in Paradise, 1944
The Way to the Stars, 1945
I Live in Grosvenor Square,
    1945
Caesar and Cleopatra, 1945
George in Civvy Street, 1946
The Man Within, 1947
Ghosts of Berkeley Square,
    1947
Brighton Rock, 1947
Forbidden, 1949
Rise and Shiner, 1950
Worm's Eye View, 1951

The Magic Box, 1951
Reluctant Heroes, 1952
Little Big Shot, 1952
Top of the Form, 1952
Innocents in Paris, 1953
Laughing Anne, 1953
Up to His Neck, 1954
Aunt Clara, 1954
See How They Run, 1955
Keep it Clean, 1956
Dry Rot, 1956
My Wife's Family, 1957
Carry On Admiral, 1957
Not Wanted On Voyage, 1957
Girls at Sea, 1958
Operation Bullshine, 1959
The Navy Lark, 1959
The Night We Got the Bird,
  1960

WINIFRED SHOTTER (1904-)
Leading lady of the thirties,
popular in the Aldwych farces;
also on stage (since 1918).

Peace and Quiet, 1929
Rookery Nook, 1930
On Approval, 1930
Chance of a Night Time, 1931
Mischief, 1931
A Night Like This, 1932
Jack's the Boy, 1932
The Love Contract, 1932
Night and Day, 1933
Just My Luck, 1933
Night of the Garter, 1933
Summer Lightning, 1933
Up to the Neck, 1933
Sorrell and Son, 1933
Lillies of the Field, 1934
D'Ye Ken John Peel?, 1935
The Rocks of Valpre, 1935
Marry the Girl, 1935
Petticoat Fever, 1936
High Treason, 1937
His Lordship Regrets, 1938
Candles at Nine, 1944
The Body Said No, 1950
John and Julie, 1955

ALASTAIR SIM (1900-1976)

Lugubrious, inimitable Scottish
star of stage (1930) and films,
delightful in eccentric comedy
characterizations as well as
dramatic parts. Former lec-
turer.

Riverside Murder, 1935
Private Secretary, 1935
A Fire Has Been Arranged,
  1935
Late Extra, 1935
Troubled Waters, 1936
Wedding Group, 1936
The Big Noise, 1936
Keep Your Seats Please, 1936
The Man in the Mirror, 1936
Mysterious Mr. Davis, 1936
Strange Experiment, 1937
Clothes and the Woman, 1937
Gangway, 1937
The Squeaker, 1937
Romance in Flanders, 1937
Melody and Romance, 1937
Sailing Along, 1938
The Terror, 1938
Alf's Button Afloat, 1938
This Man is News, 1938
Climbing High, 1938
Inspector Hornleigh, 1939
This Man in Paris, 1939
Inspector Hornleigh on Holiday,
  1939
Law and Disorder, 1940
Her Father's Daughter, 1940
Inspector Hornleigh Goes to It,
  1941
Cottage to Let, 1941
Let the People Sing, 1942
Waterloo Road, 1944
Green For Danger, 1946
Hue and Cry, 1946
Captain Boycott, 1947
London Belongs to Me, 1948
Stage Fright, 1950
The Happiest Days of Your Life,
  1950
Laughter in Paradise, 1951
Scrooge, 1951
Lady Godiva Rides Again, 1951
Folly to Be Wise, 1952
Innocents in Paris, 1953
An Inspector Calls, 1954

The Belles of St. Trinian's,
1954
Escapade, 1955
Geordie, 1955
The Green Man, 1956
Blue Murder at St. Trinian's,
1957
The Doctor's Dilemma, 1959
Left, Right, and Centre, 1959
The Millionairess, 1960
School For Scoundrels, 1960
The Anatomist, 1961
The Ruling Class, 1972
A Christmas Carol, 1972
Cold Comfort Farm, 1972
Royal Flash, 1975
Rogue Male, 1976
Escape From the Dark, 1976

GERALD SIM (1925-)
Character actor of the 60s and
70s, usually seen in cameos
as professional man.

Fame is the Spur, 1947
The L-Shaped Room, 1962
Whistle Down the Wind, 1962
The Wrong Arm of the Law,
1963
The Pumpkin Eater, 1964
Seance On a Wet Afternoon,
1964
King Rat, 1965
The Murder Game, 1966
The Wrong Box, 1966
The Whisperers, 1967
Mischief, 1969
Oh What a Lovely War, 1969
Ryan's Daughter, 1970
The Raging Moon, 1970
The Last Grenade, 1970
Dr. Jekyll and Sister Hyde,
1971
Dr. Phibes Rises Again, 1972
Young Winston, 1972
Frenzy, 1972
No Sex Please We're British,
1973
The Slipper and the Rose,
1976
A Bridge Too Far, 1977

SHEILA SIM (1922-)
Leading lady of occasional films
of the 40s and 50s, wife of Sir
Richard Attenborough; also on
stage (since 1939).

A Canterbury Tale, 1943
Great Day, 1945
Dancing With Crime, 1947
The Guinea Pig, 1948
Dear Mr. Prohack, 1949
Pandora and the Flying Dutch-
man, 1951
The Magic Box, 1951
West of Zanzibar, 1954
The Night My Number Came Up,
1955

JEAN SIMMONS (1929-)
Beautiful leading lady, former
child star, also in Hollywood.
Married: Stewart Granger,
Richard Brooks.

Give Us the Moon, 1943
Mr. Emmanuel, 1944
Meet Sexton Blake, 1944
Kiss the Bride Goodbye, 1944
Sports Day, 1945
The Way to the Stars, 1945
Caesar and Cleopatra, 1945
The Woman in the Hall, 1945
Hungry Hill, 1946
Great Expectations, 1946
Black Narcissus, 1947
Uncle Silas, 1947
Hamlet, 1948
The Blue Lagoon, 1949
Adam and Evalyn, 1949
Trio, 1950
Cage of Gold, 1950
So Long at the Fair, 1950
The Clouded Yellow, 1950
Angel Face, 1952
Androcles and the Lion, 1953
Young Bess, 1953
Affair With a Stranger, 1953
The Robe, 1953
The Actress, 1953
She Couldn't Say No, 1954
The Egyptian, 1954
A Bullet is Waiting, 1954

Desiree, 1954
Footsteps in the Fog, 1955
Guys and Dolls, 1956
Hilda Crane, 1956
This Could Be the Night, 1957
Until They Sail, 1957
The Big Country, 1958
Home Before Dark, 1958
This Earth is Mine, 1959
Elmer Gantry, 1960
Spartacus, 1960
The Grass is Greener, 1961
All the Way Home, 1963
Life at the Top, 1965
Mr. Buddwing, 1966
Rough Night in Jericho, 1967
Divorce American Style, 1967
Heidi, 1968
The Happy Ending, 1969
Say Hello to Yesterday, 1971
Mr. Sycamore, 1975
The Easter Promise, 1975
The Dain Curse, 1978
Golden Gate, 1981

JOAN SIMS (1930-)
Character comedy actress,
also seen on stage and television, frequently in small parts.

Trouble in Store, 1953
The Square Ring, 1953
Will Any Gentleman, 1953
Colonel March Investigates, 1953
Meet Mr. Lucifer, 1953
The Belles of St. Trinian's, 1954
Doctor in the House, 1954
What Every Woman Wants, 1954
To Dorothy a Son, 1954
As Long as They're Happy,
  1955
Doctor at Sea, 1955
Stars in Your Eyes, 1956
Keep it Clean, 1956
The Silken Affair, 1956
Dry Rot, 1956
Off the Record, 1956
No Time For Tears, 1957
Davy, 1957
Carry On Admiral, 1957
The Naked Truth, 1958
Just My Luck, 1958

The Captain's Table, 1959
Passport to Shame, 1959
Life in Emergency Ward 10,
  1959
Carry On Nurse, 1959
Carry On Teacher, 1959
Please Turn Over, 1959
Upstairs and Downstairs, 1959
Watch Your Stern, 1960
Doctor in Love, 1960
Carry On Constable, 1960
Carry On Regardless, 1961
His and Hers, 1961
No My Darling Daughter, 1961
Mr. Topaze, 1961
Twice Round the Daffodils, 1962
A Pair of Briefs, 1962
The Iron Maiden, 1962
Nurse On Wheels, 1963
Strictly For the Birds, 1964
Carry On Cleo, 1964
The Big Job, 1965
San Ferry Ann, 1965
Carry On Cowboy, 1965
Doctor in Clover, 1965
Carry On Screaming, 1966
Don't Lose Your Head, 1967
Follow That Camel, 1967
Up the Khyber, 1968
Carry On Doctor, 1968
Carry On Again Doctor, 1969
Carry On Camping, 1969
Carry On Up the Jungle, 1970
Carry On Loving, 1970
Doctor in Trouble, 1970
Carry On Henry VIII, 1971
The Alf Garnett Saga, 1972
One of Our Dinosaurs is Miss-
  ing, 1975
Don't Just Lie There, 1975
Love Among the Ruins, 1975

HUGH SINCLAIR (1903-1962)
Light leading man of stage (from
1922) and films.

Our Betters, 1933
Escape Me Never, 1935
The Marriage of Corbal, 1936
Strangers On a Honeymoon,
  1936
A Girl Must Live, 1938

Four Just Men, 1939
The Saint's Vacation, 1941
The Saint Meets the Tiger,
   1941
Alibi, 1942
Tomorrow We Live, 1942
Welcome Mr. Washington, 1944
Flight From Folly, 1945
They Were Sisters, 1945
Corridor of Mirrors, 1948
Don't Ever Leave Me, 1949
Trottie True, 1949
The Rocking Horse Winner,
   1949
No Trace, 1950
Circle of Danger, 1951
The Second Mrs. Tanqueray,
   1952
Never Look Back, 1952
Judgement Deferred, 1952
Mantrap, 1952
Three Steps in the Dark, 1953

DONALD SINDEN (1923-)
Likable, dependable leading
man and latterly character star
of stage (since 1941) and screen,
adept at comedy or dramatic
parts.

The Cruel Sea, 1953
A Day to Remember, 1953
Mogambo, 1953
You Know What Sailors Are,
   1954
Doctor in the House, 1954
The Beachcomber, 1954
Mad About Men, 1954
Simba, 1954
Above Us the Waves, 1955
An Alligator Named Daisy,
   1955
Josephine and Men, 1955
The Black Tent, 1956
Eyewitness, 1956
Tiger in the Smoke, 1956
Doctor at Large, 1957
Rockets Galore, 1958
The Captain's Table, 1959
Operation Bullshine, 1959
Your Money Or Your Wife,
   1960

The Siege of Sidney Street, 1960
Twice Round the Daffodils, 1962
Mix Me a Person, 1962
Decline and Fall, 1968
Villain, 1971
Rentadick, 1972
The National Health, 1973
Day of the Jackal, 1973
Island at the Top of the World,
   1974
That Lucky Touch, 1975

CAMPBELL SINGER (1909-
   1976)
Character actor of stage and
screen, often seen as policeman
or in comedy roles. Also on
tv, notably in "The Forsyte
Saga."

Premiere, 1937
Take My Life, 1947
Jim the Penman, 1947
Operation Diamond, 1948
Rover and Me, 1949
The Blue Lamp, 1950
Hangman's Wharf, 1950
Someone at the Door, 1950
Dick Barton at Bay, 1950
The Man With the Twisted Lip,
   1951
The Quiet Woman, 1951
A Case For PC 49, 1951
Lady in the Fog, 1952
The Yellow Balloon, 1952
Home at Seven, 1952
The Ringer, 1952
Appointment in London, 1953
The Titfield Thunderbolt, 1953
Time Bomb, 1953
The Girl On the Pier, 1953
Street Corner, 1953
Simba, 1954
Conflict of Wings, 1954
The Young and the Guilty, 1958
The Square Peg, 1958
No Trees in the Street, 1959
The Hands of Orlac, 1960
Flat Two, 1962
The Pot Carriers, 1962
Go Kart Go!, 1964

JOHN SLATER (1916-1975)
Cockney character player of
stage, films and television,
mainly seen in comedic portrayals.

Gert and Daisy's Weekend,
  1941
Love On the Dole, 1941
Went the Day Well, 1942
A Canterbury Tale, 1943
Deadlock, 1943
Candlelight in Algeria, 1943
The Hundred Pound Window,
  1944
For Those in Peril, 1944
Murder in Reverse, 1945
The Seventh Veil, 1945
Othello, 1946
It Always Rains On Sunday,
  1947
Teheran, 1947
Noose, 1948
Escape, 1948
Against the Wind, 1948
Passport to Pimlico, 1949
Prelude to Fame, 1950
The Third Visitor, 1951
The Ringer, 1952
Faithful City, 1952
The Long Memory, 1953
The Flanagan Boy, 1953
The Million Pound Note, 1954
Dollars For Sale, 1955
Johnny You're Wanted, 1956
Star of India, 1956
The Devil's Pass, 1957
Violent Playground, 1958
Slater's Bazaar, 1959
The Night We Got the Bird,
  1960
Nothing Barred, 1961
Three On a Spree, 1961
A Place to Go, 1963
The Yellow Hat, 1966

TOD SLAUGHTER (1885-1962)
Leading actor of stage (from
1905) and screen who played
the hissable villain during the
30s and 40s in outlandish
Victorian melodramas.

Maria Marten, 1935
Sweeney Todd, 1936
The Crimes of Stephen Hawke,
  1936
Song of the Road, 1937
Darby and Joan, 1937
It's Never Too Late to Mend,
  1937
Ticket of Leave Man, 1937
Sexton Blake & the Hooded
  Terror, 1938
The Face at the Window, 1939
Crimes at the Dark House,
  1940
Bothered By a Beard, 1946
The Curse of the Wraydons,
  1946
The Greed of William Hart,
  1948
King of the Underworld, 1952
Murder at Scotland Yard, 1952
Murder at the Grange, 1952
A Ghost For Sale, 1952

OLIVE SLOANE (1896-1963)
Music hall performer (1904)
and star of silent films, latterly seen in small character
roles.

Greatheart, 1921
The Door That Has No Key,
  1921
Trapped By the Mormons, 1922
Lonesome Farm, 1922
Rogues of the Turf, 1923
The Dream of Eugene Aram,
  1923
Money Isn't Everything, 1925
The Good Companions, 1933
Soldiers of the King, 1933
Sing As We Go, 1934
Faces, 1934
Brides to Be, 1934
Music Hall, 1934
Lily of Killarney, 1935
Key to Harmony, 1935
Alibi Inn, 1935
In the Soup, 1936
Cafe Colette, 1937
Stardust, 1937
Overcoat Sam, 1937

Dreaming Lips, 1937
Consider Your Verdict, 1938
Make it Three, 1938
Make Up, 1938
Inquest, 1939
Tower of Terror, 1941
Those Kids From Town, 1942
Let the People Sing, 1942
Thunder Rock, 1942
They Knew Mr. Knight, 1945
The Voice Within, 1945
Send For Paul Temple, 1946
Bank Holiday Luck, 1947
The Guinea Pig, 1948
Under Capricorn, 1949
Waterfront, 1950
Seven Days to Noon, 1950
The Franchise Affair, 1951
Tall Headlines, 1952
Curtain Up, 1952
My Wife's Lodger, 1952
Alf's Baby, 1953
Meet Mr. Lucifer, 1953
The Golden Link, 1954
The Weak and the Wicked, 1954
A Prize of Gold, 1955
The Last Man to Hang, 1956
Man in the Road, 1956
Brothers in Law, 1957
Serious Charge, 1959
Wrong Number, 1959
The House in Marsh Road, 1960
Your Money Or Your Wife, 1960
The Price of Silence, 1960

SIR C. AUBREY SMITH
(1863-1948)
Tall, distinguished, gentlemanly
character star of stage (from
1892) and screen, primarily in
Hollywood. Typically played
prominent gentlemen or military man. Former champion
cricket player.

The Witching Hour, 1916
Builder of Bridges, 1917

Red Pottage, 1918
World Player, 1919
The Face at the Window, 1920
Castles in Spain, 1920
The Bump, 1920
The Shuttle of Life, 1920
Bohemian Girl, 1922
Flames of Passion, 1922
Temptation of Carlton Earle, 1923
The Unwanted, 1924
Rejected Woman, 1924
Birds of Prey, 1930
Such is the Law, 1930
Contraband Love, 1931
Trader Horn, 1931
The Squaw Man, 1931
The Lie, 1931
Never the Twain Shall Meet, 1931
Bachelor Father, 1931
Daybreak, 1931
Just a Gigolo, 1931
Son of India, 1931
Man in Possession, 1931
The Phantom of Paris, 1931
Guilty Hands, 1931
Surrender, 1931
Polly of the Circus, 1931
Land Sakes, 1932
Tarzan the Ape Man, 1932
But the Flesh is Weak, 1932
Love Me Tonight, 1932
Trouble in Paradise, 1932
No More Orchids, 1932
They Just Had to Get Married, 1932
Over the River, 1933
The Scarlet Empress, 1933
Dancing Partner, 1933
Luxury Liner, 1933
Secrets, 1933
The Barbarian, 1933
Adorable, 1933
The Monkey's Paw, 1933
Morning Glory, 1933
Bombshell, 1933
Queen Christina, 1933
Riptide, 1934
The House of Rothschild, 1934
Gambling Lady, 1934
Curtain at Eight, 1934
Bulldog Drummond Strikes

Back, 1934
Cleopatra, 1934
Madame Du Barry, 1934
One More River, 1934
Caravan, 1934
The Firebird, 1934
The Right to Live, 1935
The Tunnel, 1935
Lives of a Bengal Lancer,
1935
The Florentine Dagger, 1935
The Gilded Lily, 1935
Clive of India, 1935
China Seas, 1935
Jalna, 1935
The Crusades, 1935
The Story of Papworth, 1936
Little Lord Fauntleroy, 1936
Romeo and Juliet, 1936
The Garden of Allah, 1936
Lloyds of London, 1936
Queen of Destiny, 1937
Wee Willie Winkie, 1937
The Prisoner of Zenda, 1937
Thoroughbreds Don't Cry,
1937
The Hurricane, 1937
Kidnapped, 1938
Four Men and a Prayer, 1938
Sixty Glorious Years, 1938
East Side of Heaven, 1939
Five Came Back, 1939
The Four Feathers, 1939
The Sun Never Sets, 1939
Eternally Yours, 1939
Another Thin Man, 1939
The Under-Pup, 1939
Balalaika, 1939
Rebecca, 1940
City of Chance, 1940
A Bill of Divorcement, 1940
Waterloo Bridge, 1940
Beyond Tomorrow, 1940
A Little Bit of Heaven, 1940
Free and Easy, 1941
Maisie Was a Lady, 1941
Dr. Jekyll and Mr. Hyde,
1941
Forever Yours, 1942
Forever and a Day, 1943
Two Tickets to London, 1943
Flesh and Fantasy, 1943
Madame Curie, 1943

The White Cliffs of Dover, 1944
The Adventures of Mark Twain,
1944
Secrets of Scotland Yard, 1944
They Shall Have Faith, 1944
And Then There Were None,
1945
Sensations of 1945, 1945
Scotland Yard Investigator,
1945
Cluny Brown, 1946
Rendezvous With Annie, 1946
High Conquest, 1947
Unconquered, 1947
An Ideal Husband, 1948
Little Women, 1949

CONSTANCE SMITH (1929-   )
Leading lady of the fifties, also
in Hollywood.

Brighton Rock, 1947
Now Barabbas, 1949
Trottie True, 1949
The Perfect Woman, 1949
Murder at the Windmill, 1950
Room to Let, 1950
Don't Say Die, 1950
The Mudlark, 1950
I'll Get You For This, 1951
Blackmailed, 1951
The House in the Square, 1951
The Thirteenth Letter, 1951
Red Skies of Montana, 1952
Lure of the Wilderness, 1952
Smoke Jumpers, 1952
Treasure of the Golden Condor,
1953
Taxi, 1953
Man in the Attic, 1954
The Big Tipoff, 1955
Tiger By the Tail, 1955

CYRIL SMITH (1892-1963)
Small-part character player of
stage (since 1900) and films.

Old St. Paul's, 1914
Pallard the Punter, 1919
Walls of Prejudice, 1920
Sweep, 1920

On the Reserve, 1920
Cupid's Cardinal, 1920
Run! Run!, 1920
A Broken Contract, 1920
Cousin Ebeneezer, 1920
Souveniers, 1920
A Little Bet, 1920
A Pair of Gloves, 1920
Home Influence, 1920
The Lightning Liver Cure,
  1920
The Fordington Twins, 1920
The Way of a Man, 1921
Class and No Class, 1921
Fires of Fate, 1923
His First Car, 1930
The Mayor's Nest, 1932
Innocents of Chicago, 1932
Channel Crossing, 1933
The Good Companions, 1933
Friday the Thirteenth, 1933
The Black Abbott, 1934
Waltzes From Vienna, 1934
It's a Cop, 1934
Wild Boy, 1934
Hello Sweetheart, 1935
Mr. What's His Name, 1935
Lend Me Your Wife, 1935
This England, 1935
Bulldog Jack, 1935
Storm in a Teacup, 1937
OHMS, 1937
The Frog, 1937
No Parking, 1938
The Return of the Frog, 1938
The Challenge, 1938
St. Martin's Lane, 1938
Sword of Honour, 1939
Traitor Spy, 1939
Law and Disorder, 1940
The Flying Squad, 1940
When We Are Married, 1943
One Exciting Night, 1944
Meet Sexton Blake, 1944
The Echo Murders, 1945
Don Chicago, 1945
School For Secrets, 1946
Appointment With Crime, 1946
It's Hard to Be Good, 1948
The Rocking Horse Winner,
  1949
The Body Said No, 1950
Conspirator, 1950

Old Mother Riley Headmistress,
  1950
The Third Visitor, 1951
The Dark Man, 1951
Green Grow the Rushes, 1951
Night Was Our Friend, 1951
Stolen Face, 1952
Mother Riley Meets the Vam-
  pire, 1952
The Last Hours, 1952
Women of Twilight, 1952
Wheel of Fate, 1952
Burnt Evidence, 1954
The Strange Case of Blondie,
  1954
John and Julie, 1955
Sailor Beware, 1956
Light Up the Sky, 1960
Watch it Sailor, 1961
Over the Odds, 1961
On the Fiddle, 1961
She Knows Y'Know, 1962

MAGGIE SMITH (1934-   )
Talented actress sometimes
seen in slightly eccentric roles,
also on stage (since 1952) and
in Hollywood. Married: Robert
Stephens.

Nowhere to Go, 1958
Go to Blazes, 1962
The VIPs, 1963
The Pumpkin Eater, 1964
Young Cassidy, 1965
Othello, 1965
The Honey Pot, 1967
Hot Millions, 1968
The Prime of Miss Jean Brodie,
  1969
Oh What a Lovely War, 1969
Travels With My Aunt, 1972
Love and Pain, 1973
Murder By Death, 1976
Death On the Nile, 1978
California Suite, 1978
Clash of the Titans, 1980

EWEN SOLON (1923-   )
Versatile New Zealand character player of films and televi-

sion, notable as Sergeant
Lucas in tv series "Maigret"
(1970).

Vengeance is Mine, 1949
Assassin For Hire, 1951
Valley of the Eagles, 1951
Crow Hollow, 1952
Rob Roy, 1954
Murder Anonymous, 1955
Jumping For Joy, 1955
The Dam Busters, 1955
1984, 1956
Behind the Headlines, 1956
Yangtse Incident, 1957
The Story of Esther Costello,
1957
There's Always a Thursday,
1957
Account Rendered, 1957
The Black Ice, 1957
Accused, 1957
The Silent Enemy, 1958
Hound of the Baskervilles,
1959
Jack the Ripper, 1959
The Sundowners, 1960
Terror of the Tongs, 1961
Curse of the Werewolf, 1961
Infamous Conduct, 1966
Mohammed Messenger of God,
1977
The Spaceman & King Arthur, 1979

MARIAN SPENCER (1905-)
Character actress frequently
seen in cameo roles; long
stage experience.

The Captain's Table, 1936
The Last Rose of Summer, 1937
Auld Lang Syne, 1937
The Life of David Livingstone,
1937
Spellbound, 1940
This Was Paris, 1942
Let the People Sing, 1942
We'll Meet Again, 1942
When We Are Married, 1943
The Demi-Paradise, 1943
Flight From Folly, 1945
The Weaker Sex, 1948

Bond Street, 1948
Intimate Relations, 1953
The Secret, 1955
Corridors of Blood, 1958
Gulliver's Travels, 1959
The World of Suzie Wong, 1962
Doctor of Seven Dials, 1963
Blaze of Glory, 1963
Seance On a Wet Afternoon,
1964

JEREMY SPENSER (1937-)
Leading actor of stage and
films, former child performer.

Anna Karenina, 1948
The Spider and the Fly, 1949
The Dancing Years, 1950
Prelude to Fame, 1950
Portrait of Clare, 1950
Appointment With Venus, 1951
The Planter's Wife, 1952
Background, 1953
Devil On Horseback, 1954
Edge of Divorce, 1954
The Man Who Loved Redheads,
1955
Summertime, 1955
Escapade, 1955
It's Great to Be Young, 1956
The Prince and the Showgirl,
1957
Ferry to Hong Kong, 1958
Wonderful Things, 1958
The Roman Spring of Mrs.
Stone, 1961
Vengeance, 1962
King and Country, 1964
He Who Rides a Tiger, 1965
Fahrenheit 451, 1966

VICTOR SPINETTI (1932-)
Supporting actor and character
player of stage, films, and
television; usually in comedy
roles.

The Gentle Terror, 1962
A Hard Day's Night, 1964
The Wild Affair, 1964
Help!, 1965

The Taming of the Shrew, 1966
The Biggest Bundle of Them
  All, 1967
A Promise of Bed, 1969
Can Heironymous Merkin, 1969
Unman Wittering and Zigo, 1971
Under Milk Wood, 1971
Digby, the Biggest Dog in the
  World, 1973
The Little Prince, 1974
Return of the Pink Panther, 1974
The Great McGonagall, 1975
Dick Deadeye, 1976
Voyage of the Damned, 1976
Fiona, 1979
Some Like it Cool, 1979

RONALD SQUIRE (1886-1958)
Good-natured character star of
stage (from 1909) and films,
often in comedy parts.

Whoso is Without Sin, 1916
Wild Boy, 1934
Unfinished Symphony, 1934
Forbidden Territory, 1934
Come Out of the Pantry, 1935
Love in Exile, 1936
Dusty Ermine, 1936
Action For Slander, 1937
Freedom Radio, 1941
The Flemish Farm, 1943
Don't Take it to Heart, 1944
Journey Together, 1945
While the Sun Shines, 1946
The First Gentleman, 1948
Woman Hater, 1948
The Rocking Horse Winner,
  1949
No Highway, 1951
Encore, 1952
It Started in Paradise, 1952
Laxdale Hall, 1953
Always a Bride, 1953
My Cousin Rachel, 1953
The Million Pound Note, 1954
Raising a Riot, 1955
Footsteps in the Fog, 1955
Josephine and Men, 1955
Around the World in 80 Days,
  1956
Now and Forever, 1956

The Silken Affair, 1956
Seawife, 1957
Island in the Sun, 1957
Count Your Blessings, 1958
Law and Disorder, 1958
The Sheriff of Fractured Jaw,
  1958
Inn of the Sixth Happiness, 1958

WILLIAM SQUIRE (1920-)
Character actor mainly seen on
stage; films sporadic.

The Long Dark Hall, 1951
Alexander the Great, 1956
Battle of the River Plate, 1956
Challenge For Robin Hood, 1967
Where Eagles Dare, 1968
Anne of the Thousand Days,
  1970
The Thirty-Nine Steps, 1980

PHILIP STAINTON (1908-1963)
Portly character actor of stage
and films, frequently seen as
surprised policeman or official.

Scott of the Antarctic, 1948
Passport to Pimlico, 1949
The Blue Lagoon, 1949
The Spider and the Fly, 1949
Angels One Five, 1952
The Quiet Man, 1952
Made in Heaven, 1952
Innocents in Paris, 1953
Mogambo, 1953
Hobson's Choice, 1954
The Ladykillers, 1955
Cast a Dark Shadow, 1955
The Woman For Joe, 1956
Moby Dick, 1956

TERENCE STAMP (1940-)
Youthful, handsome leading man
of the sixties, also on stage
(from 1958) and in Hollywood.

Term of Trial, 1962
Billy Budd, 1962
The Collector, 1965

Modesty Blaise, 1966
Far From the Madding Crowd, 1967
Poor Cow, 1967
Blue, 1968
Theorum, 1968
Spirits of the Dead, 1968
The Mind of Mr. Soames, 1970
Hu-Nan, 1975
Divine Creature, 1976
Superman, 1978
The Thief of Bagdad, 1979
Meetings With Remarkable Men, 1980

ENID STAMP-TAYLOR (1904-1946)
Attractive blonde actress of the thirties; former beauty contest winner. Also stage dancer (since 1922).

Easy Virtue, 1927
Remembrance, 1927
Land of Hope and Glory, 1927
A Little Bit of Fluff, 1928
Yellow Stockings, 1928
Cocktails, 1928
Broken Melody, 1929
Meet My Sister, 1933
A Political Party, 1934
Gay Love, 1934
Virginia's Husband, 1934
The Feathered Serpent, 1934
Radio Pirates, 1935
So You Won't Talk, 1935
Mr. What's His Name, 1935
Jimmy Boy, 1935
While Parents Sleep, 1935
Two Hearts in Harmony, 1935
Queen of Hearts, 1936
Blind Man's Bluff, 1936
Housebroken, 1936
Take a Chance, 1937
Underneath the Arches, 1937
Feather Your Nest, 1937
Okay For Sound, 1937
Talking Feet, 1937
Action For Slander, 1937
Blondes For Danger, 1938
Stepping Toes, 1938

Old Iron, 1938
Climbing High, 1938
The Lambeth Walk, 1939
The Girl Who Forgot, 1939
The Farmer's Wife, 1941
Spring Meeting, 1941
Hatter's Castle, 1941
South American George, 1941
Alibi, 1942
Candlelight in Algeria, 1943
The Wicked Lady, 1945
Caravan, 1946

SIR GUY STANDING (1873-1937)
Dignified character star in Hollywood, also on stage. Father of Kay Hammond. Grandson: John Standing.

The Story of Temple Drake, 1933
The Eagle and the Hawk, 1933
The Midnight Club, 1933
Cradle Song, 1933
Hell and High Water, 1933
Death Takes a Holiday, 1934
The Witching Hour, 1934
Double Door, 1934
Now and Forever, 1934
Lives of a Bengal Lancer, 1935
Car 99, 1935
Annapolis Farewell, 1935
The Return of Sophie Lang, 1936
I'd Give My Life, 1936
Lloyds of London, 1936
Bulldog Drummond Escapes, 1937

JOHN STANDING (1934-)
Character actor of stage and screen; son of Kay Hammond, grandson of Sir Guy Standing.

The Wild and the Willing, 1962
The Iron Maiden, 1962
A Pair of Briefs, 1963
King Rat, 1965
Walk Don't Run, 1966
The Psychopath, 1966

Torture Garden, 1967
A Touch of Love, 1969
All the Right Noises, 1970
Zee and Co., 1971
Au Pair Girls, 1973
The Eagle Has Landed, 1977
The Class of Miss MacMichael, 1979
Legacy, 1979

FRANK STANMORE (1877-1943)
Silent and early sound film actor specializing in comedy character parts; also on stage. Former medical student.

Nan Good-for-Nothing, 1914
His Reformation, 1914
For the Empire, 1914
Revenge of Mr. Thomas Atkins, 1914
The Middleman, 1915
Brother Officers, 1915
Heart of a Child, 1915
The Christian, 1915
Love in a Wood, 1915
His Lordship, 1915
The Odd Freak, 1916
Mixed Relations, 1916
Motherlove, 1916
Odd Charges, 1916
The Persecution of Bob Pretty, 1916
Marked Man, 1916
A Mother of Dartmoor, 1916
A Mother's Influence, 1916
The Manxman, 1916
The Grit of a Jew, 1917
London Pride, 1920
The Coal Shortage, 1920
The Golden Ballot, 1920
Strike Fever, 1920
Housing, 1920
Control, 1920
The House in the Marsh, 1920
Beyond Dreams of Avarice, 1920
Marzipan of the Shapes, 1920
Great Snakes, 1920
Stop Press Comedies, 1920
Judge Not, 1920

The Upper Hand, 1921
The Wonderful Year, 1921
A Question of Principle, 1922
The Big Strong Man, 1922
Spanish Jade, 1922
A Rogue in Love, 1922
Treasure Trove, 1922
Lily of the Alley, 1923
School For Scandal, 1923
Squibs MP, 1923
The Naked Man, 1923
Squibs' Honeymoon, 1923
Syncopated Picture Plays, 1923
Love Life and Laughter, 1923
God's Prodigal, 1923
Reveille, 1924
Alley of Golden Hearts, 1924
Owd Bob, 1924
The Gayest of the Gay, 1924
Perpetua, 1924
Mrs. May Comedies, 1925
The Blackguard, 1925
Satan's Sister, 1925
The Only Way, 1925
The Little People, 1926
Blinkeyes, 1926
Mumsie, 1927
Mr. Nobody, 1927
Wait and See, 1927
The Hellcat, 1928
What Next?, 1928
Houp-La, 1928
The Bravo, 1928
The Changeling, 1928
That Brute Simmons, 1928
Chamber of Horrors, 1928
Master and Man, 1929
Little Miss London, 1929
Three Men in a Cart, 1929
Life's a Stage, 1929
You'd Be Surprised, 1930
Red Pearls, 1930
We Take Off Our Hats, 1930
The Temporary Widow, 1930
Leave it to Me, 1930
Let's Love and Laugh, 1931
The House Opposite, 1931
My Old China, 1931
The Old Man, 1931
What a Night, 1931
The Great Gay Road, 1931
Lucky Girl, 1932
Don Quixote, 1933

The Love Wager, 1933
That's a Good Girl, 1933
It's a Bet, 1935
The Half-Day Excursion, 1935
Live Again, 1936
The Amazing Quest of Ernest
  Bliss, 1936
No Parking, 1938

DON STANNARD (1916-1949)
Light leading man who attained
brief stardom as "Dick Barton."

Don Chicago, 1945
Caesar and Cleopatra, 1945
They Were Sisters, 1945
Pink String and Sealing Wax,
  1945
I'll Turn to You, 1946
Death in High Heels, 1947
Dick Barton Special Agent,
  1948
The Temptress, 1949
Dick Barton Strikes Back, 1949
Dick Barton at Bay, 1949

GRAHAM STARK (1922-   )
Character actor of stage,
screen and television, practically always seen in comedy
cameos.

Super Secret Service, 1953
Forces' Sweetheart, 1953
Song of Norway, 1955
They Never Learn, 1956
The Running, Jumping, and
  Standing Still Film, 1960
The Millionairess, 1960
Sink the Bismarck, 1960
Dentist On the Job, 1961
Watch It Sailor, 1961
A Weekend With Lulu, 1961
Double Bunk, 1961
On the Fiddle, 1961
She'll Have to Go, 1962
Village of Daughters, 1962
Only Two Can Play, 1962
Operation Snatch, 1962
A Pair of Briefs, 1962
The Wrong Arm of the Law,
  1962

Mouse On the Moon, 1963
Lancelot and Guinevere, 1963
Ladies Who Do, 1963
Strictly For the Birds, 1963
Guns at Batasi, 1964
Becket, 1964
A Shot in the Dark, 1964
Go Kart Go!, 1964
Runaway Railway, 1965
San Ferry Ann, 1965
Those Magnificent Men in Their
  Flying Machines, 1965
Alfie, 1966
Finders Keepers, 1966
The Wrong Box, 1966
Casino Royale, 1967
The Plank, 1967
Rocket to the Moon, 1967
Salt and Pepper, 1968
Ghost of a Chance, 1968
Scramble, 1970
Simon Simon, 1970
Doctor in Trouble, 1970
The Magic Christian, 1970
Rhubarb, 1970
Return of the Pink Panther,
  1974
The Pink Panther Strikes Again,
  1976
Revenge of the Pink Panther,
  1978
Crossed Swords, 1978
The Prisoner of Zenda, 1979
Fiona, 1979
The Sea Wolves, 1980

ANTHONY STEEL (1920-   )
Handsome light leading man of
stage (since 1945), films and
television, also in Hollywood.
Formerly married to Anita
Ekberg.

Saraband For Dead Lovers, 1948
Portrait From Life, 1948
A Piece of Cake, 1948
Christopher Columbus, 1949
Once Upon a Dream, 1949
Helter Skelter, 1949
Marry Me, 1949
Poet's Pub, 1949
Don't Ever Leave Me, 1949
Trottie True, 1949

The Chiltern Hundreds, 1949
The Blue Lamp, 1950
The Wooden Horse, 1950
The Mudlark, 1950
Laughter in Paradise, 1951
Another Man's Poison, 1951
Where No Vultures Fly, 1951
Emergency Call, 1952
Something Money Can't Buy, 1952
The Planter's Wife, 1952
Malta Story, 1953
The Master of Ballantrae, 1953
Albert RN, 1953
West of Zanzibar, 1954
Out of the Clouds, 1954
The Sea Shall Not Have Them,
  1955
Passage Home, 1955
Storm Over the Nile, 1955
The Black Tent, 1956
Checkpoint, 1956
Valerie, 1957
Harry Black, 1958
A Question of Adultery, 1958
Honeymoon, 1960
Tiger of the Seven Seas, 1963
The Switch, 1963
A Matter of Choice, 1963
The Queens, 1966
Hell is Empty, 1967
Anzio, 1968
War Devils, 1970
Massacre in Rome, 1974
I'm the Girl He Wants to Kill,
  1974
Run Rabbit, Run, 1975
The Story of O, 1975
Night of the High Tide, 1976
Hard Core, 1977
The World is Full of Married
  Men, 1979
Fiona, 1979
The Mirror Crack'd, 1980

BARBARA STEELE (1938-)
Leading lady who has appeared
in international films, primarily of the horror genre.

Bachelor of Hearts, 1958
Sapphire, 1959
The Devil's Mask, 1960

Your Money Or Your Wife,
  1960
The Pit and the Pendulum, 1961
The Horrible Dr. Hitchcock,
  1962
$8\frac{1}{2}$, 1963
The Ghost, 1963
Hours of Love, 1963
The Spectre, 1964
White Voices, 1964
Castle of Blood, 1964
Sister of Satan, 1965
Nightmare Castle, 1965
Revenge of the Blood Beast,
  1966
Terror Creatures From the
  Grave, 1966
Young Torless, 1966
The Crimson Cult, 1968
Caged Heat, 1974
They Came From Within, 1976
I Never Promised You a Rose
  Garden, 1977
Pretty Baby, 1978
Piranha, 1978
La Cle Sur la Porte, 1978

TOMMY STEELE (1936-)
Affable cockney entertainer and
pop singer, in occasional films.
Also Hollywood; former seaman
(1952).

Kill Me Tomorrow, 1957
The Tommy Steele Story, 1957
The Duke Wore Jeans, 1958
Tommy the Toreador, 1959
Light Up the Sky, 1960
It's All Happening, 1963
Half a Sixpence, 1967
The Happiest Millionaire, 1967
Where's Jack?, 1968
Finian's Rainbow, 1969

KAREL STEPANEK (1899-)
Czechoslovakian character actor
in British films, often cast as
Nazi officer or in other sinister parts.

Hermine Und die Sieben

Aufrechten, 1935
Stranger Than the Rule, 1937
Hotel Sacher, 1939
Tomorrow We Live, 1942
Secret Mission, 1942
They Met in the Dark, 1943
The Captive Heart, 1946
The Fallen Idol, 1948
Broken Journey, 1948
Counterblast, 1948
Golden Arrow, 1949
Give Us This Day, 1949
State Secret, 1950
Cairo Road, 1950
Conspirator, 1950
The Third Visitor, 1951
Walk East On Beacon, 1952
Affair in Trinidad, 1952
City Beneath the Sea, 1953
Never Let Me Go, 1953
The Devil's Plot, 1953
Rough Shoot, 1953
The Gay Adventure, 1954
Dangerous Cargo, 1954
Secret Venture, 1955
Man of the Moment, 1955
A Prize of Gold, 1955
Cockleshell Heroes, 1955
Anastasia, 1956
Man in the Road, 1956
West of Suez, 1957
The Traitors, 1957
Our Man in Havana, 1959
Sink the Bismarck, 1960
I Aim at the Stars, 1960
Johann Sebastian Bach, 1961
The Devil Doll, 1963
Operation Crossbow, 1965
The Heroes of Telemark, 1965
Licensed to Kill, 1966
The Frozen Dead, 1967
File of the Golden Goose, 1968
Before Winter Comes, 1969
The Games, 1970

SUSAN STEPHEN (1932-)
Pretty leading lady of the
fifties.

Treasure Hunt, 1952
Stolen Face, 1952
His Excellency, 1952

Father's Doing Fine, 1952
The Red Beret, 1953
The Case of the Studio Payroll,
1953
Dangerous Cargo, 1954
The House Across the Lake,
1954
For Better, For Worse, 1954
Golden Ivory, 1954
As Long as They're Happy, 1955
Value For Money, 1955
It's Never Too Late, 1956
Pacific Destiny, 1956
The Barretts of Wimpole Street,
1957
Carry On Nurse, 1959
Court Martial of Major Keller,
1961
Return of a Stranger, 1962
Spare Wives, 1962

MARTIN STEPHENS (1949-)
Juvenile actor of the fifties and
sixties.

The Divided Heart, 1954
Another Time Another Place,
1958
Harry Black, 1958
Count Your Blessings, 1959
The Witness, 1959
A Touch of Larceny, 1959
No Kidding, 1960
Village of the Damned, 1960
The Hellfire Club, 1961
The Innocents, 1961
Battle of the Villa Fiorita, 1965
The Witches, 1966

ROBERT STEPHENS (1931-)
Leading man of stage (since
1944) and screen, also in Hollywood. Married: Maggie Smith.

The Browning Version, 1959
The Queen's Guards, 1960
Circle of Deception, 1961
The Pirates of Tortuga, 1961
A Taste of Honey, 1961
The Inspector, 1962
Cleopatra, 1962

Lunch Hour, 1962
The Small World of Sammy
 Lee, 1963
Morgan, 1966
Romeo and Juliet, 1968
The Prime of Miss Jean
 Brodie, 1969
Private Life of Sherlock
 Holmes, 1970
The Asphynx, 1972
Travels With My Aunt, 1972
Luther, 1974
QB VII, 1974
The Duellists, 1977
The Shout, 1978

HENRY STEPHENSON (1871-
1956)
Stage and screen character
actor long in Hollywood, generally appearing as kindly old
gentlemen.

The Spreading Dawn, 1917
The Black Panther's Cub, 1921
Men and Women, 1925
Wild Wild Susan, 1925
Red Headed Woman, 1932
Guilty as Hell, 1932
A Bill of Divorcement, 1932
Cynara, 1932
The Animal Kingdom, 1932
Tomorrow at Seven, 1933
Double Harness, 1933
Blind Adventure, 1933
My Lips Betray, 1933
Little Women, 1933
If I Were Free, 1934
Man of Two Worlds, 1934
The Mystery of Mr. X, 1934
Thirty Day Princess, 1934
Stingaree, 1934
One More River, 1934
She Loves Me Not, 1934
Richest Man in the World,
 1934
What Every Woman Knows,
 1934
Outcast Lady, 1934
The Night is Young, 1935
Vanessa: Her Love Story,
 1935

Reckless, 1935
The Flame Within, 1935
O'Shaughnessey's Boy, 1935
Rendezvous, 1935
Mutiny On the Bounty, 1935
The Perfect Gentleman, 1935
Captain Blood, 1935
Little Lord Fauntleroy, 1936
Half Angel, 1936
Hearts Divided, 1936
Walking On Air, 1936
Give Me Your Heart, 1936
Charge of the Light Brigade,
 1936
Beloved Enemy, 1936
When You're in Love, 1937
The Prince and the Pauper,
 1937
The Emperor's Candlesticks,
 1937
Conquest, 1937
Wise Girl, 1938
The Baroness and the Butler,
 1938
Marie Antoinette, 1938
Suez, 1938
The Young in Heart, 1938
Dramatic School, 1938
Tarzan Finds a Son, 1939
Elizabeth the Queen, 1939
Adventures of Sherlock Holmes,
 1939
Little Old New York, 1940
It's a Date, 1940
Spring Parade, 1940
Down Argentine Way, 1940
Lady From Louisiana, 1941
Rings On Her Fingers, 1942
This Above All, 1942
Mr. Lucky, 1943
Hour Before the Dawn, 1944
Two Girls and a Sailor, 1944
Tarzan and the Amazons, 1945
The Green Years, 1946
Heartbeat, 1946
Of Human Bondage, 1946
Night and Day, 1946
The Return of Monte Cristo,
 1946
Her Sister's Secret, 1947
The Locket, 1947
The Homestretch, 1947
Time Out of Mind, 1947

Dark Delusion, 1947
Song of Love, 1947
Julia Misbehaves, 1948
Enchantment, 1948
Oliver Twist, 1948
Challenge to Lassie, 1949
Trial of John Peter Zenger, 1951
The Just and the Unjust, 1951
Sara Crew, 1951

JAMES STEPHENSON (1888-
1941)
Elegant, incisive leading man
of stage (1935) and films, in
Hollywood from 1938.

Transatlantic Trouble, 1937
The Perfect Crime, 1937
The Man Who Made Diamonds,
1937
Take It From Me, 1937
You Live and Learn, 1937
Dangerous Fingers, 1937
Dark Stairway, 1938
Mr. Satan, 1938
It's in the Blood, 1938
When Were You Born?, 1938
Boy Meets Girl, 1938
White Banners, 1938
Cowboy From Brooklyn, 1938
Heart of the North, 1938
King of the Underworld, 1939
Confessions of a Nazi Spy, 1939
Beau Geste, 1939
Torchy Blane in Chinatown, 1939
On Trial, 1939
Secret Service of the Air, 1939
The Old Maid, 1939
Espionage Agent, 1939
We Are Not Alone, 1939
Elizabeth the Queen, 1939
Calling Philo Vance, 1940
The Sea Hawk, 1940
The Letter, 1940
Murder in the Air, 1940
Devil's Island, 1940
The River's End, 1940
A Dispatch From Reuters,
1940
South of Suez, 1940
Flight From Destiny, 1941
International Squadron, 1941
Shining Victory, 1941

RONNIE STEVENS (1925-)
Distinctive character player of
stage, television and screen,
mainly in comedy parts.

Made in Heaven, 1952
The Scarlet Web, 1954
An Alligator Named Daisy,
1955
I Was Monty's Double, 1958
I'm All Right, Jack, 1959
Danger Within, 1959
Doctor in Love, 1960
Dentist in the Chair, 1960
Dentist On the Job, 1961
Very Important Person, 1961
Nearly a Nasty Accident, 1961
It's Trad, Dad, 1962
On the Beat, 1962
A Pair of Briefs, 1963
Doctor in Distress, 1963
A Home of Your Own, 1964
Doctor in Clover, 1965
San Ferry Ann, 1965
Those Magnificent Men in Their
Flying Machines, 1965
Give a Dog a Bone, 1966
Smashing Time, 1967
Some Girls Do, 1969
Goodbye Mr. Chips, 1969
Twelfth Night, 1980

ATHOLE STEWART (1879-
1940)
Character star of the thirties,
also on stage.

To What Red Hell, 1930
Canaries Sometimes Sing,
1930
The Temporary Widow, 1930
The Speckled Band, 1931
The Faithful Heart, 1932
Frail Women, 1932
The Little Damozel, 1933
The Constant Nymph, 1933
Loyalties, 1933
Four Masked Men, 1934
Path of Glory, 1934
Too Many Millions, 1934
The Clairvoyant, 1935
While Parents Sleep, 1935
Jack of All Trades, 1936

Where's Sally?, 1936
Accused, 1936
Dusty Ermine, 1936
The Amateur Gentleman, 1936
The Tenth Man, 1936
Return of a Stranger, 1937
Action For Slander, 1937
Dr. Syn, 1937
The Singing Cop, 1938
Break the News, 1938
His Lordship Regrets, 1938
Climbing High, 1938
Thistledown, 1938
The Spy in Black, 1939
Poison Pen, 1939
Meet Maxwell Archer, 1939
I Killed the Count, 1939
Confidential Lady, 1939
Four Just Men, 1939
Tilly of Bloomsbury, 1940
Old Mother Riley in Society,
  1940
Gentleman of Venture, 1940
They Came By Night, 1940

SOPHIE STEWART (1908-
  1977)
Scottish actress of stage and
screen, also radio star; also
in Hollywood. Married to
Ellis Irving.

Maria Marten, 1935
The City of Beautiful Nonsense,
  1935
Her Last Affaire, 1935
As You Like It, 1936
Things To Come, 1936
Under the Red Robe, 1936
The Man Who Could Work
  Miracles, 1936
Return of the Scarlet Pimper-
  nel, 1937
Who Goes Next?, 1938
Marigold, 1938
Nurse Edith Cavell, 1939
My Son My Son, 1940
The Lamp Still Burns, 1943
Strawberry Roan, 1945
Uncle Silas, 1947
Made in Heaven, 1952
Devil Girl From Mars,
  1954

No Time For Tears, 1957
Yangtse Incident, 1957

NIGEL STOCK (1919-)
Character actor of stage, films
and tv; former juvenile player.

Lancashire Luck, 1938
Sons of the Sea, 1938
Goodbye Mr. Chips, 1939
It Always Rains On Sunday,
  1947
Brighton Rock, 1947
Derby Day, 1952
Malta Story, 1953
Aunt Clara, 1954
The Dam Busters, 1955
The Night My Number Came
  Up, 1955
Battle of the River Plate, 1956
Eyewitness, 1956
The Silent Enemy, 1958
Never Let Go, 1960
Victim, 1961
HMS Defiant, 1962
The Great Escape, 1963
The Password is Courage, 1963
To Have and to Hold, 1963
Nothing But the Best, 1963
The High Bright Sun, 1964
Night of the Generals, 1966
The Lion in Winter, 1968
The Lost Continent, 1968
Cromwell, 1970
Bequest to the Nation, 1973
Russian Roulette, 1975
A Man Called Intrepid, 1979

BETTY STOCKFIELD (1905-
  1966)
Australian character actress of
stage (since 1924) and films,
popular during the thirties.

Captivation, 1931
City of Song, 1931
77 Park Lane, 1931
Money For Nothing, 1932
Life Goes On, 1932
The Impassive Footman, 1932
Maid of the Mountains, 1932
King of the Ritz, 1932

Women in Chains, 1932
Farewell to Love, 1933
Lord of the Manor, 1933
Anne One Hundred, 1933
The Man Who Changed His
  Name, 1934
The Battle, 1934
Brides to Be, 1934
The Lad, 1935
Runaway Ladies, 1935
Under Proof, 1936
Beloved Vagabond, 1936
Dishonour Bright, 1936
Who's Your Lady Friend?,
  1937
Club de Femmes, 1937
I See Ice, 1938
The Slipper Episode, 1938
Nine Bachelors, 1941
Hard Steel, 1942
Flying Fortress, 1942
Derriere la Facade, 1942
Edward and Caroline, 1950
The Girl Who Couldn't Quite,
  1950
The Lovers of Lisbon, 1955
Guilty, 1956
True as a Turtle, 1957

JOHN STRATTON (1925-)
Supporting actor of the fifties,
also on stage.

The Small Back Room, 1948
The Cure For Love, 1950
Seven Days to Noon, 1950
Appointment With Venus, 1951
The Happy Family, 1952
The Cruel Sea, 1953
The Long Arm, 1956
Seven Waves Away, 1957
Man in the Sky, 1957
The Challenge, 1960
Strangler's Web, 1966

JOHN STRIDE (1936-)
General purpose actor of
stage, tv and occasional films.
Tv series: "The Main Chance."

Sink the Bismarck, 1960

Bitter Harvest, 1963
Macbeth, 1972
Juggernaut, 1974
Brannigan, 1974
The Omen, 1976
Something to Hide, 1976
A Bridge Too Far, 1977
Oh Heavenly Dog, 1980

JOHN STUART (1898-1979)
Leading man of stage (since
1919) and silent films, latterly
in cameo character roles.
Formerly married to Muriel
Angelus.

Her Son, 1920
The Great Gay Road, 1920
The Lights of Home, 1920
Eileen Alannah, 1921
Sally in Our Alley, 1921
Home Sweet Home, 1921
Leaves From My Life, 1921
Sinister Street, 1922
Little Mother, 1922
A Sporting Double, 1922
If Four Walls Told, 1922
The Extra Knot, 1922
This Freedom, 1923
The Missing Bough, 1923
Little Miss Nobody, 1923
School For Scandal, 1923
The Reverse of the Medal, 1923
Constant Hot Water, 1923
The Loves of Mary Queen of
  Scots, 1923
Claude Duval, 1924
Her Redemption, 1924
His Grace Gives Notice, 1924
Alley of Golden Hearts, 1924
The Gayest of the Gay, 1924
We Women, 1925
Daughter in Love, 1925
Parted, 1925
Venetian Lovers, 1925
Baddeseley Manor, 1926
The Pleasure Garden, 1926
Kenilworth Castle, 1926
Tower of London, 1926
London Love, 1926
Mademoiselle From Armentieres,
  1926

Curfew Shall Not Ring To-
night, 1926
Back to the Tress, 1926
The Woman Juror, 1926
Hindle Wakes, 1927
Roses of Picardy, 1927
The Glad Eye, 1927
Flight Commander, 1927
Woman in Pawn, 1927
Sailors Don't Care, 1928
Mademoiselle Parley Voo,
1928
Smashing Through, 1928
Fanny Hawthorn, 1929
Blackmail, 1929
Atlantic, 1929
Taxi For Two, 1929
Kitty, 1929
High Seas, 1929
Memories, 1929
Eve's Fall, 1930
No Exit, 1930
Children of Chance, 1930
Kissing Cup's Race, 1930
The Nipper, 1930
Elstree Calling, 1930
Midnight, 1931
Hound of the Baskervilles,
1931
Hindle Wakes, 1931
In a Monastery Garden, 1932
Number Seventeen, 1932
Men of Steel, 1932
Verdict of the Sea, 1932
Little Fella, 1932
Women Are That Way, 1933
The Pointing Finger, 1933
Naughty Cinderella, 1933
Mr. Quincy of Monte Carlo,
1933
The Lost Chord, 1933
This Week of Grace, 1933
Love's Old Sweet Song, 1933
Head of the Family, 1933
Mayfair Girl, 1933
Home Sweet Home, 1933
Enemy of the Police, 1933
The Wandering Jew, 1933
The House of Trent, 1933
The Black Abbot, 1934
Four Masked Men, 1934
Grand Prix, 1934
Bella Donna, 1934

The Blue Squadron, 1934
Blind Justice, 1934
The Green Pack, 1934
D'Ye Ken John Peel, 1935
Abdul the Damned, 1935
Royal Cavalcade, 1935
Lend Me Your Husband, 1935
Once a Thief, 1935
The Secret Voice, 1936
Reasonable Doubt, 1936
The Elder Brother, 1937
Pearls Bring Tears, 1937
The Show Goes On, 1937
Talking Feet, 1937
The Claydon Treasure Mystery,
1938
Old Mother Riley in Society,
1940
Old Mother Riley's Ghosts,
1941
Ships With Wings, 1941
The Seventh Survivor, 1941
Penn of Pennsylvania, 1941
The Big Blockade, 1942
Banana Ridge, 1942
Hard Steel, 1942
The Missing Million, 1942
Women Aren't Angels, 1942
Headline, 1943
Candles at Nine, 1944
Madonna of the Seven Moons,
1944
Camera Reflections, 1945
Mrs. Fitzherbert, 1947
The Phantom Shot, 1947
Mine Own Executioner, 1947
House of Darkness, 1948
Third Time Lucky, 1948
Escape From Broadmoor, 1948
The Temptress, 1949
Man on the Run, 1949
The Man From Yesterday,
1949
The Magic Box, 1951
Mr. Denning Drives North,
1951
The Ringer, 1952
Mantrap, 1952
To the Rescue, 1952
Street Corner, 1953
Four Sided Triangle, 1953
Front Page Story, 1954
Mysterious Bullet, 1954

Men of Sherwood Forest, 1954
The Gilded Cage, 1955
John and Julie, 1955
Johnny You're Wanted, 1956
Raiders of the River, 1956
Tons of Trouble, 1956
It's a Great Day, 1956
Alias John Preston, 1956
Eyewitness, 1956
The Last Man to Hang, 1956
Reach For the Sky, 1956
The Secret Place, 1957
Quatermass II, 1957
The Crossroad Gallows, 1958
The Naked Truth, 1958
Chain of Events, 1958
Further Up the Creek, 1958
Blood of the Vampire, 1958
Revenge of Frankenstein, 1958
The Secret Man, 1958
The Mummy, 1959
Too Many Crooks, 1959
Sink the Bismarck, 1960
Bottoms Up, 1960
Village of the Damned, 1960
Danger By My Side, 1962
Paranoiac, 1963
The Scarlet Blade, 1963
Son of the Sahara, 1966
Mary Queen of Scots, 1971
Young Winston, 1972
Superman, 1978

NICHOLAS STUART (-)
General purpose actor of stage;
films very few.

Night Beat, 1948
The Divided Heart, 1954
Joe Macbeth, 1955
High Hell, 1958
The Longest Day, 1962

EDWIN STYLES (-)
Character actor of stage and
screen; film appearances sporadic.

Hell Below, 1933
Road House, 1934
On the Air, 1934
Cedric Sharpe & His Sextette,
  1936

Patricia Gets Her Man, 1937
The £5 Man, 1937
Adam and Evalyn, 1949
The Lady With a Lamp, 1951
Derby Day, 1952
Penny Princess, 1952
Top Secret, 1952
Isn't Life Wonderful, 1953
The Weak and the Wicked, 1954
The Dam Busters, 1955
Up in the World, 1956
The Full Treatment, 1961

JULIE SUEDO (1904-)
Dark-haired leading actress of
silent and early sound films;
also on stage (since 1919).

One Arabian Night, 1923
The Man With the Limp, 1923
Queen of Hearts, 1923
Golden Pomegranates, 1924
The Rat, 1925
One Colombo Night, 1926
Triumph of the Rat, 1926
The Stranger, 1927
The Fake, 1927
The Vortex, 1927
One of the Best, 1927
A Window in Piccadilly, 1928
The White Sheik, 1928
The Physician, 1928
Victory, 1928
Two Little Drummer Boys, 1928
Smashing Through, 1928
Afterwards, 1929
The Woman From China, 1930
Dangerous Seas, 1931
Love's Old Sweet Song, 1933
Paris Plane, 1933
Taking Ways, 1933
The Commissionaire, 1933
Nell Gwyn, 1934
Play Up the Band, 1935
Queen of Hearts, 1936
Dream Doctor, 1936
Our Fighting Navy, 1937
A Dream of Love, 1938
George Bizet, 1938
The Life of Chopin, 1938
If I Were Boss, 1938
Romance of Dancing, 1938

On Velvet, 1938
The Dance of Death, 1938
Blarney, 1938
The Villers Diamond, 1938
A Night Alone, 1938
Dark Eyes of London, 1939
Kiss the Bride Goodbye, 1944

FRANCIS L. SULLIVAN (1903-
   1956)
Obese character star of stage
(from 1921) and screen, often
seen in villainous portrayals.
Also in Hollywood.

The Chinese Puzzle, 1932
The Missing Rembrandt, 1932
When London Sleeps, 1932
Called Back, 1933
F. P. One, 1933
The Stickpin, 1933
The Fire Raisers, 1933
The Right to Live, 1933
The Wandering Jew, 1933
The Red Wagon, 1934
Princess Charming, 1934
Return of Bulldog Drummond,
   1934
Chu Chin Chow, 1934
What Happened Then, 1934
Cheating Cheaters, 1934
Great Expectations, 1935
The Mystery of Edwin Drood,
   1935
Her Last Affaire, 1935
Sabotage, 1936
A Woman Alone, 1936
The Spy of Napoleon, 1936
The Limping Man, 1936
Interrupted Honeymoon, 1936
Fine Feathers, 1937
Non Stop New York, 1937
Action For Slander, 1937
Dinner at the Ritz, 1937
21 Days, 1938
The Gables Mystery, 1938
Kate Plus Ten, 1938
The Drum, 1938
The Citadel, 1938
Climbing High, 1938
The Ware Case, 1938
Four Just Men, 1939

Young Man's Fancy, 1939
Pimpernel Smith, 1941
The Foreman Went to France,
   1942
The Day Will Dawn, 1942
Lady From Lisbon, 1942
The Butler's Dilemma, 1943
Fiddlers Three, 1944
Caesar and Cleopatra, 1945
The Laughing Lady, 1946
Great Expectations, 1946
The Man Within, 1947
Take My Life, 1947
Broken Journey, 1948
Oliver Twist, 1948
The Winslow Boy, 1948
Joan of Arc, 1948
Christopher Columbus, 1949
The Red Danube, 1949
Night and the City, 1950
Plunder in the Sun, 1951
Behave Yourself, 1951
My Favorite Spy, 1951
Caribbean, 1952
Sangaree, 1953
Drums of Tahiti, 1954
The Prodigal, 1955
Hell's Island, 1955
Bounty Court Martial, 1955

ELEANOR SUMMERFIELD
   (1921-)
Character actress of stage
(since 1939) and films, typically
seen in comedy roles.

Take My Life, 1947
London Belongs to Me, 1948
The Weaker Sex, 1948
The Story of Shirley Yorke, 1948
Man On the Run, 1949
All Over Town, 1949
No Way Back, 1949
Laughter in Paradise, 1951
The Third Visitor, 1951
Scrooge, 1951
Mandy, 1952
Top Secret, 1952
The Last Page, 1952
Isn't Life Wonderful, 1953
Street Corner, 1953
Final Appointment, 1954

Blackout, 1954
Face the Music, 1954
Murder By Proxy, 1955
Lost, 1956
Odongo, 1956
It's Great to Be Young, 1956
Tears For Simon, 1957
No Road Back, 1957
A Cry From the Streets, 1958
Dentist in the Chair, 1960
The Millionairess, 1960
Spare the Rod, 1961
Why Bother to Knock?, 1961
Petticoat Pirates, 1961
On the Fiddle, 1961
Act of Mercy, 1962
On the Beat, 1962
The Running Man, 1963
Guns of Darkness, 1963
The Yellow Hat, 1965
Some Will, Some Won't, 1970

GEOFFREY SUMNER (1908-)
Character actor specializing in
silly-ass comedy roles; also
frequently on stage.

Premiere, 1938
Too Many Husbands, 1938
She Couldn't Say No, 1939
Law and Disorder, 1940
While the Sun Shines, 1947
Helter Skelter, 1949
Traveller's Joy, 1949
Dark Secret, 1949
The Dark Man, 1951
A Tale of Five Cities, 1951
Appointment With Venus, 1951
Top Secret, 1952
The Happy Family, 1952
Always a Bride, 1953
The Dog and the Diamonds,
  1953
Those People Next Door, 1953
The Flying Eye, 1955
I Only Arsked, 1958
Band of Thieves, 1962
Cul de Sac, 1966

DUDLEY SUTTON (1933-)
Character player of the 60s

and 70s, sometimes in comedy
parts.

The Boys, 1962
The Leather Boys, 1963
Rotten to the Core, 1965
Crossplot, 1969
The Walking Stick, 1970
One More Time, 1970
A Town Called Hell, 1971
The Devils, 1971
Cry of the Penguins, 1972
Cry Terror, 1975
Great Expectations, 1975
The Pink Panther Strikes Again,
  1976
Casanova, 1977
Valentino, 1977
The Big Sleep, 1978
The London Affair, 1979
The Island, 1980

JOHN SUTTON (1908-1963)
Character actor often seen in
villainous swashbuckling or adventure parts, in Hollywood
from mid-thirties; former hunter and plantation manager.

Bulldog Drummond's Revenge,
  1937
Bulldog Drummond Strikes Back,
  1937
Four Men and a Prayer, 1938
Arrest Bulldog Drummond, 1938
The Adventures of Robin Hood,
  1938
Susannah of the Mounties, 1939
Bulldog Drummond's Bride, 1939
Charlie McCarthy Detective,
  1939
Tower of London, 1939
The Invisible Man Returns, 1940
South to Karanga, 1940
A Yank in the RAF, 1941
Hudson's Bay, 1941
Moon Over Her Shoulder, 1941
Ten Gentlemen From West Point,
  1942
My Gal Sal, 1942
Thunder Birds, 1942
Tonight We Raid Calais, 1943

Jane Eyre, 1944
The Hour Before the Dawn,
  1944
Claudia and David, 1946
Captain From Castile, 1947
Mickey, 1948
Adventures of Casanova, 1948
The Three Musketeers, 1948
The Fan, 1949
Bagdad, 1949
Bride of Vengeance, 1949
Second Face, 1950
Captain Pirate, 1951
The Second Woman, 1951
Payment On Demand, 1951
David and Bathsheba, 1951
The Golden Hawk, 1952
My Cousin Rachel, 1952
Lady in the Iron Mask, 1952
Sangaree, 1953
Thief of Damascus, 1953
East of Sumatra, 1954
Amazon Trader, 1954
Death of a Scoundrel, 1956
The Bat, 1959
Return of the Fly, 1959
Beloved Infidel, 1959
The Canadians, 1961
Shadow of Fear, 1963
Of Human Bondage, 1964

MAUREEN SWANSON (1932-)
Leading actress of the fifties
and sixties; retired after short
career.

Moulin Rouge, 1953
Valley of Song, 1953
Knights of the Round Table,
  1954
Orders Are Orders, 1954
Third Party Risk, 1955
A Town Like Alice, 1956
The Spanish Gardener, 1956
Jacqueline, 1956
Up in the World, 1956
Robbery Under Arms, 1957
The Malpas Mystery, 1960
Clue of the Twisted Candle,
  1961

NORA SWINBURNE (1902-)
Attractive star of stage (since
1914) and films, latterly in
character roles. Married:
Francis Lister; Esmond Knight.

Branded, 1920
Saved From the Sea, 1920
The Fortune of Christina McNab,
  1921
Autumn of Pride, 1921
The Wee MacGregor's Sweet-
  heart, 1922
The Red Trail, 1923
Hornet's Nest, 1923
The Unwanted, 1924
His Grace Gives Notice, 1924
A Girl of London, 1925
One Colombo Night, 1926
Alf's Button, 1930
Caste, 1930
Potiphar's Wife, 1931
These Charming People, 1931
Man of Mayfair, 1931
A Voice Said Goodnight, 1932
Mr. Bill the Conqueror, 1932
Whiteface, 1932
Perfect Understanding, 1933
Too Many Wives, 1933
Boomerang, 1934
The Office Wife, 1934
Lend Me Your Husband, 1935
Jury's Evidence, 1936
The Gay Adventure, 1936
The Lonely Road, 1936
Dinner at the Ritz, 1937
Lily of Laguna, 1938
The Citadel, 1938
Gentleman of Venture, 1940
The Farmer's Wife, 1941
They Flew Alone, 1942
Dear Octopus, 1943
The Man in Grey, 1943
Fanny By Gaslight, 1944
They Knew Mr. Knight, 1945
Jassy, 1947
Good Time Girl, 1948
The Blind Goddess, 1948
Quartet, 1948
The Bad Lord Byron, 1948
Fools Rush In, 1949
Marry Me, 1949
Christopher Columbus, 1949

Landfall, 1949
My Daughter Joy, 1950
Quo Vadis, 1951
The River, 1951
Betrayed, 1954
The End of the Affair, 1955
Helen of Troy, 1956
The Strange Awakening, 1958
Third Man On the Mountain,
    1959
Conspiracy of Hearts, 1960
Decision at Midnight, 1962
Post Mortem, 1965
Interlude, 1968
Anne of the Thousand Days,
    1970
Up the Chastity Belt, 1971

BASIL SYDNEY (1894-1968)
Strong character actor of stage
(1911) and films, best in unsympathetic or villainous roles;
also in Hollywood. Married to
Joyce Howard.

Romance, 1920
The Midshipmaid, 1932
Dirty Work, 1934
The Third Clue, 1934
Riverside Murder, 1935
White Lilac, 1935
The Tunnel, 1935
The Amateur Gentleman, 1936
Blind Man's Bluff, 1936
Rhodes of Africa, 1936
Accused, 1936
Crime Over London, 1936
Dr. Zander, 1936
Talk of the Devil, 1936
Four Just Men, 1939
Shadowed Eyes, 1939
The Farmer's Wife, 1941
Ships With Wings, 1941
Spring Meeting, 1941
The Black Sheep of Whitehall,
    1941
Went the Day Well, 1942
Next of Kin, 1942
Caesar and Cleopatra, 1945
Meet Me at Dawn, 1947
The Man Within, 1947
Jassy, 1947

Hamlet, 1948
Treasure Island, 1950
The Angel With the Trumpet,
    1950
The Magic Box, 1951
Ivanhoe, 1952
Salome, 1953
Hell Below Zero, 1954
Star of India, 1954
Simba, 1954
The Dam Busters, 1955
Around the World in 80 Days,
    1956
Island in the Sun, 1957
Seawife, 1957
A Question of Adultery, 1958
John Paul Jones, 1959
The Devil's Disciple, 1959
The Three Worlds of Gulliver,
    1960
A Story of David, 1960
The Hands of Orlac, 1961

ERIC SYKES (1923-)
Comic actor and character star
of television and films, also occasional director. Former
radio writer (1948).

Orders Are Orders, 1954
Charley Moon, 1956
Watch Your Stern, 1960
Very Important Person, 1961
Invasion Quartet, 1961
Village of Daughters, 1962
Kill Or Cure, 1963
Heavens Above, 1963
The Bargee, 1964
One Way Pendulum, 1964
Those Magnificent Men in Their
    Flying Machines, 1965
Rotten to the Core, 1965
The Liquidator, 1966
The Spy With a Cold Nose, 1966
The Plank, 1967
Shalako, 1968
Monte Carlo Or Bust, 1969
Rhubarb, 1970
The Alf Garnett Saga, 1972
Theatre of Blood, 1973

SYLVIA SYMS (1934-)
Attractive blonde leading lady
of stage (since 1952), television, and films; also occasionally in international films.

My Teenage Daughter, 1956
No Time For Tears, 1957
Woman in a Dressing Gown,
   1957
The Birthday Present, 1957
The Moonraker, 1958
Ice Cold in Alex, 1958
Bachelor of Hearts, 1958
No Trees in the Street, 1959
Ferry to Hong Kong, 1959
Expresso Bongo, 1959
Conspiracy of Hearts, 1960
The World of Suzie Wong, 1960
Virgini di Roma, 1961
Flame in the Streets, 1961
Victim, 1961
The Quare Fellow, 1962
The Punch and Judy Man, 1962
The World Ten Times Over,
   1963
East of Sudan, 1964
Operation Crossbow, 1965
The Big Job, 1966
Danger Route, 1967
Hostile Witness, 1968
Run Wild Run Free, 1969
The Desperados, 1969
Born to Win, 1971
Asylum, 1972
The Tamarind Seed, 1974
There Goes the Bride, 1979

SYDNEY TAFLER (1916-1979)
Character star of stage (since
1936) and screen, married to
Joy Shelton.

The Little Ballerina, 1946
It Always Rains On Sunday,
   1947
No Room at the Inn, 1948
Uneasy Terms, 1948
London Belongs to Me, 1948
Passport to Pimlico, 1949
Dance Hall, 1950
Once a Sinner, 1950

The Galloping Major, 1951
The Lavender Hill Mob, 1951
Assassin For Hire, 1951
There is Another Sun, 1951
Scarlet Thread, 1951
Chelsea Story, 1951
Hotel Sahara, 1951
Mystery Junction, 1951
Blind Man's Bluff, 1952
Secret People, 1952
Wide Boy, 1952
Emergency Call, 1952
Time Gentlemen Please, 1952
Venetian Bird, 1952
There Was a Young Lady, 1953
Johnny On the Run, 1953
The Square Ring, 1953
The Saint's Return, 1953
The Floating Dutchman, 1953
Operation Diplomat, 1953
The Crowded Day, 1954
The Sea Shall Not Have Them,
   1955
A Kid For Two Farthings, 1955
The Glass Cage, 1955
The Woman For Joe, 1955
Dial 999, 1955
Cockleshell Heroes, 1955
The Long Arm, 1956
Guilty, 1956
Reach For the Sky, 1956
Fire Maidens From Outer
   Space, 1956
The Counterfeit Plan, 1957
Interpol, 1957
Booby Trap, 1957
The Surgeon's Knife, 1957
Carve Her Name With Pride,
   1958
The Bank Robbers, 1958
Too Many Crooks, 1959
The Crowning Touch, 1959
Follow a Star, 1959
Sink the Bismarck, 1960
No Kidding, 1960
Let's Get Married, 1960
Bottoms Up, 1960
Make Mine Mink, 1960
Light Up the Sky, 1960
The Bulldog Breed, 1960
Five Golden Hours, 1961
Carry On Regardless, 1961
A Weekend With Lulu, 1962

The Seventh Dawn, 1964
Runaway Railway, 1965
Promise Her Anything, 1965
Alfie, 1966
The Sandwich Man, 1966
Berserk!, 1967
The Birthday Party, 1968
The Adventurers, 1970
Danger Point, 1971
The Spy Who Loved Me, 1977

JESSICA TANDY (1909-)
Character actress of stage and
screen, long in U.S. Films
rare but memorable. Married:
Jack Hawkins; Hume Cronyn.

Indiscretions of Eve, 1932
Murder in the Family, 1938
The Seventh Cross, 1944
The Valley of Decision, 1945
The Green Years, 1946
Dragonwyck, 1946
Forever Amber, 1947
A Woman's Vengeance, 1948
September Affair, 1950
The Desert Fox, 1951
The Light in the Forest, 1958
Hemingway's Adventures of a
    Young Man, 1962
The Birds, 1963
Butley, 1973
The Gin Game, 1981

TONY TANNER (1932-)
Revue artiste and light character
player in films of the 60s.

Strictly For the Birds, 1964
A Home of Your Own, 1964
The Pleasure Girls, 1965
Stop the World I Want to Get
    Off, 1966
The Sandwich Man, 1966

COLIN TAPLEY (1911-)
Sturdy New Zealand character
actor of stage and screen,
often in cameo roles. Also
in Hollywood.

Double Door, 1934
Search For Beauty, 1934
Murder at the Vanities, 1934
The Pursuit of Happiness, 1934
The Black Room, 1935
Lives of a Bengal Lancer, 1935
Becky Sharp, 1935
The Last Outpost, 1935
Peter Ibbetson, 1935
The Crusades, 1935
Early to Bed, 1936
The Return of Sophie Lang, 1936
Till We Meet Again, 1936
The Sky Parade, 1936
Thank You Jeeves, 1936
The Crime Nobody Saw, 1937
King of Gamblers, 1937
Booloo, 1938
If I Were King, 1938
Storm Over Bengal, 1938
The Light That Failed, 1939
Women in War, 1940
Arizona, 1941
Samson and Delilah, 1949
Cloudburst, 1950
Wings of Danger, 1951
Angels One Five, 1952
Wide Boy, 1952
Strange Stories, 1953
Three Steps to the Gallows,
    1953
The Steel Key, 1953
Noose For a Lady, 1953
White Fire, 1954
The Diamond, 1954
Late Night Final, 1954
The Dam Busters, 1955
Little Red Monkey, 1955
Barbados Quest, 1955
Stranger in Town, 1957
Blood of the Vampire, 1958
The Safecracker, 1958
Innocent Meeting, 1959
Man Accused, 1959
Night Train For Inverness,
    1960
An Honourable Murder, 1960
Compelled, 1960
So Evil So Young, 1961
The Lamp in Assassin Mews,
    1962
Emergency, 1962

Strongroom, 1962
Gang War, 1962
Paranoiac, 1963

HARRY TATE (1872-1940)
Music hall comic with movable
moustache; also on stage (from
1895).

Harry Tate Grimaces, 1899
Harry Tate Impersonates, 1899
Motoring, 1927
Her First Affaire, 1932
Counsel's Opinion, 1933
My Lucky Star, 1933
I Spy, 1933
Happy, 1934
Royal Cavalcade, 1935
Look Up and Laugh, 1935
Midshipman Easy, 1935
Hyde Park Corner, 1935
Soft Lights and Sweet Music,
   1936
Keep Your Seats Please, 1936
Variety Parade, 1936
Take a Chance, 1937
Wings of the Morning, 1937
Sam Small Leaves Town, 1937

REGINALD TATE (1896-1955)
General purpose character
player, also seen on stage.

Whispering Tongues, 1934
Tangled Evidence, 1934
The Phantom Light, 1935
Riverside Murder, 1935
The Man Behind the Mask,
   1936
For Valour, 1937
Dark Journey, 1937
Too Dangerous to Live, 1939
Poison Pen, 1939
Gentleman of Venture, 1940
Next of Kin, 1942
The Life & Death of Colonel
   Blimp, 1943
The Way Ahead, 1944
Madonna of the Seven Moons,
   1944

The Man From Morocco, 1945
So Well Remembered, 1947
Uncle Silas, 1947
Noose, 1948
Diamond City, 1949
Midnight Episode, 1950
The Story of Robin Hood, 1952
Secret People, 1952
Escape Route, 1953
Malta Story, 1953
King's Rhapsody, 1955

ROD TAYLOR (1929-)
Australian leading man of stage
and screen, in Hollywood from
1955; usually seen as tough
hero. Also on tv in "Hong
Kong" (1960); "Bearcats" (1971).

King of the Coral Sea, 1954
Long John Silver, 1955
The Virgin Queen, 1955
The Catered Affair, 1956
Giant, 1956
Raintree County, 1957
Separate Tables, 1958
Ask Any Girl, 1959
The Time Machine, 1960
The Birds, 1963
The VIPs, 1963
A Gathering of Eagles, 1963
Sunday in New York, 1964
Fate is the Hunter, 1964
36 Hours, 1965
Young Cassidy, 1965
Do Not Disturb, 1965
The Liquidator, 1966
The Glass Bottom Boat, 1966
Hotel, 1967
Chuka, 1967
Dark of the Sun, 1967
Hell is For Heroes, 1968
Nobody Runs Forever, 1968
Zabriskie Point, 1970
The Man Who Had Power Over
   Women, 1970
Darker Than Amber, 1970
The Train Robbers, 1972
Family Flight, 1972
Trader Horn, 1973
The Deadly Trackers, 1973

Shamus, 1973
Hell River, 1974
The Heroes, 1975
The Picture Show Man, 1977
An Eye For An Eye, 1978
Six Graves For Rogan, 1980
Cry of the Innocent, 1980

SIR GODFREY TEARLE (1884-
1953)
Distinguished star of stage
(from 1892) and character star
of films, equally good in kindly
or villainous roles.

Romeo and Juliet, 1908
The Fool, 1913
Lochinvar, 1915
Sir James Mortimer's Wager,
1916
The Real Thing at Last, 1916
A Sinless Sinner, 1919
The March Hare, 1919
Fancy Dress, 1920
Nobody's Child, 1921
Queen's Evidence, 1923
Salome of the Tenements, 1925
Guy of Warwick, 1926
One Colombo Night, 1926
If Youth But Knew, 1928
Infatuation, 1930
These Charming People, 1931
The Shadow Between, 1931
Puppets of Fate, 1933
Jade, 1934
The Thirty-Nine Steps, 1935
The Last Journey, 1935
East Meets West, 1936
Tomorrow We Live, 1942
One of Our Aircraft is Missing,
1942
Undercover, 1943
The Lamp Still Burns, 1943
Medal For the General, 1944
The Rake's Progress, 1945
The Beginning or the End, 1947
Private Angelo, 1949
White Corridors, 1951
I Believe in You, 1951
Mandy, 1952
Decameron Nights, 1952
The Titfield Thunderbolt,
1953

ELLALINE TERRISS (1871-1971)
Distinguished stage actress in oc-
casional films, married to Sir
Seymour Hicks.

Seymour Hicks & Ellaline Ter-
riss, 1913
Always Tell Your Wife, 1914
Blighty, 1927
Atlantic, 1929
Man of Mayfair, 1931
Glamour, 1931
The Iron Duke, 1935
Royal Cavalcade, 1935
Four Just Men, 1939

TERRY-THOMAS (1911-)
Inimitable gap-toothed comedy
star often cast in villainous
comedy roles; also on stage,
television and in Hollywood.
Former radio star (1938).

The Lucky Mascot, 1948
A Date With a Dream, 1948
Helter Skelter, 1949
Melody Club, 1949
The Queen Steps Out, 1951
Cookery Nook, 1951
Private's Progress, 1956
The Green Man, 1957
Brothers in Law, 1957
Lucky Jim, 1957
The Naked Truth, 1958
Happy is the Bride, 1958
Blue Murder at St. Trinian's,
1958
Tom Thumb, 1958
Too Many Crooks, 1959
Carleton Browne of the F.O.,
1959
I'm All Right, Jack, 1959
School For Scoundrels, 1960
Make Mine Mink, 1960
His and Hers, 1961
A Matter of WHO, 1962
Operation Snatch, 1962
Bachelor Flat, 1962
Strange Bedfellows, 1963
Wonderful World of the Brothers
Grimm, 1963
Kill Or Cure, 1963
Mouse On the Moon, 1963

The Wild Affair, 1963
It's a Mad, Mad, Mad, Mad
World, 1963
How to Murder Your Wife, 1965
Those Magnificent Men in Their
Flying Machines, 1965
You Must Be Joking!, 1965
I Love a Mystery, 1966
The Sandwich Man, 1966
Our Man in Marrakesh, 1966
Munster Go Home, 1966
Kiss the Girls & Make Them
Die, 1966
The Perils of Pauline, 1967
Danger: Diabolik, 1967
Rocket to the Moon, 1967
A Guide For the Married Man,
1967
Where Were You When the
Lights Went Out?, 1968
Don't Raise the Bridge Lower
the River, 1968
Arabella, 1968
Don't Look Now, 1968
It's Your Move, 1968
Seven Times Seven, 1969
Monte Carlo or Bust, 1969
2000 Years Later, 1969
Arthur Arthur, 1970
The Abominable Dr. Phibes, 1971
Dr. Phibes Rises Again, 1972
The Cherry Picker, 1972
Vault of Horror, 1973
Robin Hood (voice), 1973
The Heroes, 1974
Spanish Fly, 1975
Bawdy Adventures of Tom
Jones, 1975
Side By Side, 1976
The Last Remake of Beau
Geste, 1977
Hound of the Baskervilles, 1978
The Tempest, 1979

DESMOND TESTER (1919-)
Juvenile player of the thirties,
latterly in Australia.

Midshipman Easy, 1935
Tudor Rose, 1936
Sabotage, 1936
A Woman Alone, 1936

Beloved Vagabond, 1936
Non Stop New York, 1937
The Drum, 1938
The Stars Look Down, 1939
An Englishman's Home, 1939
The Turners of Prospect Road,
1947
Barry Mackenzie Holds His
Own, 1974

HEATHER THATCHER
(18 -19)
Blonde actress of stage (1916)
and films, first in small roles,
then stardom. Also in Hollywood.

The Prisoner of Zenda, 1915
Altar Chains, 1916
Key of the World, 1918
First Men in the Moon, 1919
Pallard the Punter, 1919
The Green Terror, 1919
A Little Bet, 1920
A Pair of Gloves, 1920
Home Influence, 1920
The Little Hour of Peter Wells,
1920
The Flag Lieutenant, 1926
The Plaything, 1929
Express Love, 1929
Comets, 1930
A Warm Corner, 1930
Stepping Stone, 1931
But the Flesh is Weak, 1932
Loyalties, 1933
It's a Boy, 1933
Private Life of Don Juan, 1934
Love Affair of the Dictator,
1935
The Thirteenth Chair, 1937
Tovarich, 1937
Fools For Scandal, 1938
Girl's School, 1938
If I Were King, 1938
Beau Geste, 1939
Scotland Yard, 1941
Man Hunt, 1941
We Were Dancing, 1942
Son of Fury, 1942
The Moon and Sixpence, 1942
Journey For Margaret, 1942
Gaslight, 1944

Anna Karenina, 1948
Trottie True, 1949
Dear Mr. Prohack, 1949
Encore, 1952
Father's Doing Fine, 1952
The Hour of Thirteen, 1952
Will Any Gentleman, 1953
Duel in the Jungle, 1954
The Deep Blue Sea, 1955
Josephine and Men, 1955

TORIN THATCHER (1905-)
Commanding character star of
stage (from 1923) and films,
latterly in Hollywood.

General John Regan, 1934
Irish Hearts, 1934
School For Stars, 1935
Sabotage, 1936
Knight Without Armour, 1937
Well Done Henry, 1937
Climbing High, 1938
The Spy in Black, 1939
Old Mother Riley MP, 1939
Law and Disorder, 1940
Gasbags, 1940
Let George Do It, 1940
Case of the Frightened Lady,
  1940
Major Barbara, 1941
Next of Kin, 1942
The Captive Heart, 1946
Great Expectations, 1946
I See A Dark Stranger, 1946
Jassy, 1947
When the Bough Breaks, 1947
End of the River, 1947
Bonnie Prince Charlie, 1948
The Fallen Idol, 1948
Lost Illusion, 1949
The Black Rose, 1950
Affair in Trinidad, 1952
The Crimson Pirate, 1952
Snows of Kilimanjaro, 1952
Blackbeard the Pirate, 1952
The Desert Rats, 1953
Houdini, 1953
The Robe, 1953
Knock On Wood, 1954
The Black Shield of Falworth,
  1954
Lady Godiva, 1955

Bengal Brigade, 1955
Love is a Many Splendored
  Thing, 1955
Diane, 1956
Helen of Troy, 1956
Istanbul, 1957
Band of Angels, 1957
Witness For the Prosecution,
  1957
Darby's Rangers, 1958
The Seventh Voyage of Sinbad,
  1958
The Miracle, 1959
The Canadians, 1961
Jack the Giant Killer, 1962
Mutiny On the Bounty, 1962
Drums of Africa, 1963
The Sweet and the Bitter, 1965
The Sandpiper, 1965
Hawaii, 1966
The King's Pirate, 1967
Dr. Jekyll and Mr. Hyde, 1968
Brenda Starr, 1976

ERNEST THESIGER (1879-1961)
Gaunt character star of stage
(1909) and screen, often in eccentric characterizations; also
in Hollywood. Former artist;
also a skilled embroiderer.

The Real Thing at Last, 1916
Nelson, 1918
Life Story of David Lloyd George
  1918
A Little Bit of Fluff, 1919
The Bachelor's Club, 1921
Adventures of Mr. Pickwick,
  1921
Weekend Wives, 1928
The Vagabond Queen, 1929
Ashes, 1930
The Old Dark House, 1932
The Only Girl, 1933
The Ghoul, 1933
Night of the Party, 1934
My Heart is Calling, 1934
The Bride of Frankenstein,
  1935
The Man Who Could Work Mira-
  cles, 1936
Lightning Conductor, 1938
They Drive By Night, 1938

The Ware Case, 1938
The Lamp Still Burns, 1943
Don't Take it to Heart, 1944
Henry V, 1944
A Place of One's Own, 1944
Caesar and Cleopatra, 1945
Beware of Pity, 1946
The Man Within, 1947
Jassy, 1947
Ghosts of Berkeley Square,
  1947
The Winslow Boy, 1948
Quartet, 1948
Portrait From Life, 1948
The Lucky Mascot, 1948
The Bad Lord Byron, 1949
Last Holiday, 1950
Midnight Episode, 1950
Laughter in Paradise, 1951
The Man in the White Suit, 1951
Scrooge, 1951
The Magic Box, 1951
The Woman's Angle, 1952
The Robe, 1953
Meet Mr. Lucifer, 1953
The Million Pound Note, 1954
Make Me An Offer, 1954
Father Brown, 1954
Value For Money, 1955
An Alligator Named Daisy, 1955
Quentin Durward, 1955
Who Done It, 1956
Three Men in a Boat, 1956
Doctor at Large, 1957
The Truth About Women, 1958
The Horse's Mouth, 1959
Battle of the Sexes, 1959
Sons and Lovers, 1960
The Roman Spring of Mrs.
  Stone, 1961

GEORGE THIRLWELL (-)
Character player primarily of
stage, in rare films during the
20s and 30s.

The Chinese Bungalow, 1926
Sailors Don't Care, 1928
The Lyons Mail, 1931
The Laughter of Fools, 1933
Little Napoleon, 1933
Fire Over England, 1937

JAMESON THOMAS (1889-1939)
Moustached leading man of silent
films, latterly in Hollywood in
character parts; also on stage
(from 1910).

Chu Chin Chow, 1923
The Drum, 1924
The Cavern Spider, 1924
Decameron Nights, 1924
The Sins Ye Do, 1924
Chester Forgets Himself, 1924
Daughter of Love, 1925
Afraid of Love, 1925
The Apache, 1925
The Gold Cure, 1925
The Brotherhood, 1926
Jungle Woman, 1926
Pearl of the South Seas, 1926
Blighty, 1927
As We Lie, 1927
Roses of Picardy, 1927
Poppies of Flanders, 1927
The White Sheik, 1928
The Farmer's Wife, 1928
Tesha, 1928
The Rising Generation, 1928
Weekend Wives, 1928
Piccadilly, 1929
Power Over Men, 1929
The Feather, 1929
High Treason, 1929
Memories, 1929
Hate Ship, 1929
Elstree Calling, 1930
Night Birds, 1930
Extravagance, 1930
Lover Come Back, 1931
Three Wise Girls, 1932
The Trial of Vivienne Ware,
  1932
The Phantom President, 1932
No More Orchids, 1933
Brief Moment, 1933
The Scarlet Empress, 1933
Bombay Mail, 1934
It Happened One Night, 1934
Beggars in Ermine, 1934
A Lost Lady, 1934
Now and Forever, 1934
Lives of a Bengal Lancer, 1935
Sing Sing Nights, 1935
The World Accuses, 1935

Mr. Dynamite, 1935
Charlie Chan in Egypt, 1935
The Last Outpost, 1935
Coronado, 1935
Mr. Deeds Goes to Town, 1936
House of Secrets, 1937
The League of Frightened Men,
  1937
100 Men and a Girl, 1937
Death Goes North, 1938

JUNE THORBURN (1931-1967)
Leading lady of the fifties and
sixties, also on stage.

The Pickwick Papers, 1952
The Cruel Sea, 1953
Fast and Loose, 1954
Delayed Action, 1954
Orders Are Orders, 1954
Children Galore, 1954
Hornet's Nest, 1955
Touch and Go, 1955
True As a Turtle, 1957
Rooney, 1958
Tom Thumb, 1958
Broth of a Boy, 1959
The Price of Silence, 1960
Escort For Hire, 1960
Three Worlds of Gulliver, 1960
Fury at Smuggler's Bay, 1961
Transatlantic, 1961
Why Bother to Knock?, 1961
The Spanish Sword, 1962
Design For Loving, 1962
The Scarlet Blade, 1963
Master Spy, 1964

RUSSELL THORNDIKE (-)
Classical star of stage and
screen, later in character parts.
Brother of Dame Sybil Thorndike.

Macbeth, 1922
It's Never Too Late to Mend,
  1922
The Dream of Eugene Aram,
  1923
Scrooge, 1923
The Bells, 1923

The Test, 1923
Sins of a Father, 1923
School For Scandal, 1923
Love in an Attic, 1923
The Audacious Mr. Squire, 1923
Heartstrings, 1923
Miriam Rozella, 1924
Human Desires, 1924
Puppets of Fate, 1933
The Roof, 1933
A Shot in the Dark, 1933
Whispering Tongues, 1934
Fame, 1934
Fiddlers Three, 1944
Henry V, 1944
Caesar and Cleopatra, 1945
Hamlet, 1948
Richard III, 1955

DAME SYBIL THORNDIKE
  (1882-1976)
Distinguished actress of stage
(since 1904) and screen, married to Sir Lewis Casson.
Brother: Russell Thorndike.

Moth and Rust, 1921
Nancy, 1922
Macbeth, 1922
Bleak House, 1922
Jane Shore, 1922
Esmeralda, 1922
Lady of the Camellias, 1922
The Merchant of Venice, 1922
The Scarlet Letter, 1922
Dawn, 1928
To What Red Hell, 1929
Hindle Wakes, 1931
Gentleman of Paris, 1931
Tudor Rose, 1936
Major Barbara, 1941
Nicholas Nickleby, 1947
Britannia Mews, 1949
Gone to Earth, 1950
Stage Fright, 1950
The Magic Box, 1951
Lady With a Lamp, 1951
Melba, 1953
The Weak and the Wicked, 1954
The Prince and the Showgirl, 1957
Alive and Kicking, 1958
Smiley Gets a Gun, 1958

Shake Hands With the Devil,
  1959
Jet Storm, 1959
Hand in Hand, 1961
The Big Gamble, 1961
Uncle Vanya, 1963

FRANK THORNTON (1921-)
Comedy actor of the sixties and
seventies, also on television.

It's Trad, Dad, 1962
The Dock Brief, 1962
The Tomb of Legeia, 1964
Gonks Go Beat, 1965
The Early Bird, 1965
Danny the Dragon, 1967
The Bliss of Mrs. Blossom, 1968
Crooks and Coronets, 1969
The Bed Sitting Room, 1969
The Magic Christian, 1970
All the Way Up, 1970
Our Miss Fred, 1972
No Sex Please We're British,
  1973
Digby, the Biggest Dog in the
  World, 1973
The Three Musketeers, 1974
Old Dracula, 1975
Bawdy Adventures of Tom
  Jones, 1975
The Taming of the Shrew, 1981

FRANK TICKLE (-)
Small-part character player
in occasional films, usually as
man of some importance.

Two On a Doorstep, 1936
The Bank Messenger Mystery,
  1936
Twin Faces, 1937
Henry V, 1944
Anna Karenina, 1948
Escape, 1948
Children of Chance, 1949
Brandy For the Parson, 1952

CHARLES TINGWELL (1917-)
Australian character actor of

television and screen, often
seen as characters of humility.

Always Another Dawn, 1948
Bitter Springs, 1950
Kangaroo, 1952
The Desert Rats, 1953
Smiley, 1956
The Shiralee, 1957
Life in Emergency Ward 10,
  1958
Bobbikins, 1959
Cone of Silence, 1960
Tarzan the Magnificent, 1960
Murder She Said, 1962
Murder at the Gallop, 1963
Murder Ahoy, 1964
Beware of the Dog, 1964
Murder Most Foul, 1965
The Secret of Blood Island,
  1965
Thunderbirds Are Go, 1966
Dracula Prince of Darkness,
  1966
Nobody Runs Forever, 1968
Jock Peterson, 1975

ANN TODD (1909-)
Attractive, intelligent leading
lady of the 30s and 40s; also on
stage (since 1928) and in Hollywood; married to director David
Lean (1908-). Not to be confused with the American child
performer of the same name.

Keepers of Youth, 1931
These Charming People, 1931
The Ghost Train, 1931
The Water Gypsies, 1932
The Return of Bulldog Drum-
  mond, 1934
Things To Come, 1936
Action For Slander, 1937
The Squeaker, 1937
South Riding, 1938
Poison Pen, 1939
Danny Boy, 1941
Ships With Wings, 1941
Perfect Strangers, 1945
The Seventh Veil, 1945
Gaiety George, 1946

Daybreak, 1947
So Evil My Love, 1948
The Passionate Friends, 1948
The Paradine Case, 1948
Madeleine, 1950
The Sound Barrier, 1952
The Green Scarf, 1955
Time Without Pity, 1957
Taste of Fear, 1961
Son of Captain Blood, 1962
Ninety Degrees in the Shade, 1966
The Fiend, 1971
The Human Factor, 1980

BOB TODD (1922-)
Bald-headed character comedian
of the 60s, mainly on tv; a
regular performer on the
"Benny Hill Show." Films few.

The Intelligence Men, 1965
Ouch!, 1967
Hot Millions, 1968
Scars of Dracula, 1969
Digby, the Biggest Dog in the
   World, 1973
The Best of Benny Hill, 1974
The Happy Housewives, 1976

RICHARD TODD (1919-)
Popular Irish leading man of
stage (from 1936) and screen,
also in Hollywood. Mainly in
heroic parts.

For Them That Trespass, 1948
The Last Journey, 1949
The Hasty Heart, 1949
Stage Fright, 1950
Portrait of Clare, 1950
Flesh and Blood, 1951
Lightning Strikes Twice, 1951
The Story of Robin Hood, 1952
24 Hours of a Woman's Life,
   1952
Venetian Bird, 1952
Elstree Calling, 1952
The Sword and the Rose, 1953
Rob Roy, 1953
The Bed, 1954
The Dam Busters, 1955

A Man Called Peter, 1955
The Virgin Queen, 1955
D-Day the Sixth of June, 1956
Saint Joan, 1957
Yangtse Incident, 1957
The Naked Earth, 1957
Chase a Crooked Shadow, 1958
Intent to Kill, 1959
Danger Within, 1959
Never Let Go, 1960
The Long & the Short & the
   Tall, 1961
Why Bother to Knock?, 1961
The Hellions, 1961
The Boys, 1962
The Longest Day, 1962
Crime Doesn't Pay, 1962
The Very Edge, 1963
Death Drums Along the River,
   1963
Coast of Skeletons, 1964
Operation Crossbow, 1965
Battle of the Villa Fiorita, 1965
The Love-Ins, 1967
Last of the Long-Haired Boys,
   1968
Subterfuge, 1968
Dorian Gray, 1970
Asylum, 1972
The Big Sleep, 1978
Home Before Midnight, 1979

JOSEPH TOMELTY (1910-)
Irish character player most
prominent during the fifties;
also on stage.

Odd Man Out, 1947
You're Only Young Twice, 1952
The Sound Barrier, 1952
The Gentle Gunman, 1952
Meet Mr. Lucifer, 1953
The Oracle, 1953
Melba, 1953
Devil Girl From Mars, 1954
Young Lovers, 1954
Front Page Story, 1954
Hell Below Zero, 1954
Happy Ever After, 1954
Hobson's Choice, 1954
Simba, 1954
A Kid For Two Farthings, 1955

Timeslip, 1955
A Prize of Gold, 1955
John and Julie, 1955
Moby Dick, 1956
A Night to Remember, 1958
Life is a Circus, 1958
The Captain's Table, 1959
Upstairs and Downstairs, 1959
The Day They Robbed the Bank
   of England, 1960
Hell is a City, 1961
Lancelot and Guinevere, 1963
The Black Torment, 1964

DAVID TOMLINSON (1917-)
Amiable light leading man and
character actor of stage (1936)
and screen, primarily in comedy
roles; also Hollywood. RAF
Pilot during World War II.

Garrison Follies, 1940
Quiet Wedding, 1941
Pimpernel Smith, 1941
My Wife's Family, 1941
Name Rank and Number, 1941
Journey Together, 1945
The Way to the Stars, 1945
School For Secrets, 1946
The Master of Bankdam, 1947
Fame is the Spur, 1947
Easy Money, 1948
Miranda, 1948
Broken Journey, 1948
Sleeping Car to Trieste, 1948
My Brother's Keeper, 1948
Love in Waiting, 1948
Here Come the Huggetts, 1948
Warning to Wantons, 1949
Vote For Huggett, 1949
Marry Me, 1949
Helter Skelter, 1949
Landfall, 1949
The Chiltern Hundreds, 1949
So Long at the Fair, 1950
The Wooden Horse, 1950
Calling Bulldog Drummond,
   1951
Hotel Sahara, 1951
The Magic Box, 1951
Castle in the Air, 1952
Made in Heaven, 1952

Is Your Honeymoon Really Ne-
   cessary?, 1953
All For Mary, 1955
Three Men in a Boat, 1956
Carry On Admiral, 1957
Up the Creek, 1958
Further Up the Creek, 1958
Follow That Horse, 1960
Tom Jones, 1963
Mary Poppins, 1964
The Truth About Spring, 1964
City Under the Sea, 1965
The Liquidator, 1966
The Love Bug, 1969
Bedknobs and Broomsticks, 1971
Bon Baisers de Hong Kong, 1975
The Water Babies, 1979
The Fiendish Plot of Dr. Fu
   Manchu, 1980

GEOFFREY TOONE (1910-)
Heroic Irish leading man of stage
(from 1931) and films, also in
Hollywood.

Queer Cargo, 1938
Night Journey, 1938
Poison Pen, 1939
Sword of Honour, 1939
An Englishman's Home, 1939
The Woman's Angle, 1952
The Great Game, 1953
The Man Between, 1953
Diane, 1956
The King and I, 1956
Zero Hour, 1957
Murder at Site Three, 1959
Once More With Feeling, 1960
The Entertainer, 1960
Terror of the Tongs, 1961
Echo of Diana, 1963
Blaze of Glory, 1963
Dr. Crippen, 1964
Dr. Who and the Daleks, 1966
Personal and Confidential, 1966

BILL TRAVERS (1922-)
Tall, good-looking leading man
of stage (since 1947) and screen,
also in Hollywood. Married to
Virginia McKenna. Also on tv.

Conspirator, 1950
The Wooden Horse, 1950
The Browning Version, 1951
The Planter's Wife, 1952
Hindle Wakes, 1952
Mantrap, 1953
Street of Shadows, 1953
The Square Ring, 1953
Counterspy, 1953
Romeo and Juliet, 1954
Footsteps in the Fog, 1955
Geordie, 1955
Bhowani Junction, 1956
The Barretts of Wimpole Street, 1957
The Seventh Sin, 1957
The Smallest Show On Earth, 1957
The Passionate Summer, 1958
The Bridal Path, 1959
Two Living One Dead, 1961
The Green Helmet, 1961
Invasion Quartet, 1961
Gorgo, 1962
Born Free, 1966
Duel at Diablo, 1966
A Midsummer Night's Dream, 1968
Ring of Bright Water, 1969
An Elephant Called Slowly, 1970
The Lion at World's End, 1971
Boulevard du Rhum, 1971
The Belstone Fox, 1973
Christian the Lion, 1976

HENRY TRAVERS (1874-1965)
Genial character actor of stage (from 1894) and screen, long in Hollywood.

Reunion in Vienna, 1933
Another Language, 1933
My Weakness, 1933
The Invisible Man, 1933
Death Takes a Holiday, 1934
Born to Be Bad, 1934
Maybe It's Love, 1935
After Office Hours, 1935
Four Hours to Kill, 1935
Escapade, 1935
Seven Keys to Baldpate, 1935

The Sisters, 1938
You Can't Get Away With Murder, 1939
Dodge City, 1939
Dark Victory, 1939
On Borrowed Time, 1939
Stanley & Livingstone, 1939
The Rains Came, 1939
Remember, 1939
Primrose Path, 1940
Edison the Man, 1940
Anne of Windy Poplars, 1940
Wyoming, 1940
High Sierra, 1941
The Bad Man, 1941
A Girl, a Guy and a Gob, 1941
I'll Wait For You, 1941
Ball of Fire, 1941
Mrs. Miniver, 1942
Random Harvest, 1942
Pierre of the Plains, 1942
Shadow of a Doubt, 1943
The Moon is Down, 1943
Madame Curie, 1943
None Shall Escape, 1944
Dragon Seed, 1944
The Very Thought of You, 1944
Thrill of Romance, 1945
The Naughty Nineties, 1945
The Bells of St. Mary's, 1945
Gallant Journey, 1946
It's a Wonderful Life, 1946
The Yearling, 1947
The Flame, 1948
Beyond Glory, 1948
The Girl From Jones Beach, 1949

LINDEN TRAVERS (1913-)
Beautiful brunette leading lady of stage (since 1931) and films.

Children of the Fog, 1935
Wednesday's Luck, 1936
Double Alibi, 1937
Against the Tide, 1937
Brief Ecstasy, 1937
The Last Adventurers, 1937
Bank Holiday, 1938
Almost a Honeymoon, 1938
The Terror, 1938
The Lady Vanishes, 1938

Inspector Hornleigh On Holiday,
    1939
The Stars Look Down, 1939
The Ghost Train, 1941
The Seventh Survivor, 1941
South American George, 1941
The Missing Million, 1942
Beware of Pity, 1946
The Master of Bankdam, 1947
Jassy, 1947
Quartet, 1948
No Orchids for Miss Blandish,
    1948
The Bad Lord Byron, 1949
Don't Ever Leave Me, 1949
Christopher Columbus, 1949
Trio, 1950

ARTHUR TREACHER (1894–
    1975)
Tall character comedian with
stage experience, in Hollywood
since 1933 where he was seen
as the perfect butler.   Latterly
associated with fish and chips
food chain.

The Battle of Paris, 1930
Bordertown, 1933
The Captain Hates the Sea,
    1934
Viva Villa, 1934
Gambling Lady, 1934
The Key, 1934
Madame Du Barry, 1934
Forsaking All Others, 1934
David Copperfield, 1935
Let's Live Tonight, 1935
The Woman in Red, 1935
No More Ladies, 1935
Daring Young Man, 1935
Curly Top, 1935
Orchids to You, 1935
Bright Lights, 1935
A Midsummer Night's Dream,
    1935
I Live My Life, 1935
Remember Last Night, 1935
Splendor, 1935
Magnificent Obsession, 1935
Anything Goes, 1936
The Case Against Mrs. Ames,

1936
Hearts Divided, 1936
Satan Met a Lady, 1936
Thank You Jeeves, 1936
Under Your Spell, 1936
Stowaway, 1936
Step Lively Jeeves, 1937
She Had to Eat, 1937
You Can't Have Everything, 1937
Thin Ice, 1937
Heidi, 1937
Mad About Music, 1938
My Lucky Star, 1938
Always in Trouble, 1938
Up the River, 1938
The Little Princess, 1939
Bridal Suite, 1939
Barricade, 1939
Irene, 1940
Brother Rat and a Baby, 1940
Star Spangled Rhythm, 1942
Forever and a Day, 1943
The Amazing Mrs. Halliday,
    1943
In Society, 1944
Chip Off the Old Block, 1944
National Velvet, 1944
That's the Spirit, 1945
Delightfully Dangerous, 1945
Slave Girl, 1947
The Countess of Monte Cristo,
    1948
That Midnight Kiss, 1949
Love That Brute, 1950
Mary Poppins, 1964

DAVID TREE (1915–)
Comedy actor of the thirties with
stage experience; retired after
losing arm during World War II.

Paradise For Two, 1937
Over the Moon, 1937
Knight Without Armour, 1937
Return of the Scarlet Pimpernel,
    1937
The Drum, 1938
Pygmalion, 1938
Old Iron, 1938
Q Planes, 1939
Goodbye Mr. Chips, 1939
French Without Tears, 1939

Just William, 1939
Return to Yesterday, 1940
Major Barbara, 1941

AUSTIN TREVOR (1897-1978)
Irish character star of stage
(from 1915) and films, often
seen as Frenchman or other
continental types after being
cast as Hercule Poirot.

At the Villa Rose, 1930
The W Plan, 1930
Escape, 1930
The Man From Chicago, 1930
Alibi, 1931
Black Coffee, 1931
A Night in Montmartre, 1931
The Crooked Lady, 1932
The Chinese Puzzle, 1932
A Safe Proposition, 1932
On Secret Service, 1933
The Broken Melody, 1934
Lord Edgware Dies, 1934
Death at Broadcasting House,
    1934
Inside the Room, 1935
Royal Cavalcade, 1935
Mimi, 1935
The Silent Passenger, 1935
As You Like It, 1936
Spy 77, 1936
Beloved Vagabond, 1936
Dusty Ermine, 1936
Rembrandt, 1936
Sabotage, 1936
Dark Journey, 1937
Thunder in the City, 1937
Knight Without Armour, 1937
Goodbye Mr. Chips, 1939
The Lion Has Wings, 1939
The Briggs Family, 1940
Law and Disorder, 1940
Night Train to Munich, 1940
Under Your Hat, 1940
The Seventh Survivor, 1941
The Big Blockade, 1942
The Young Mr. Pitt, 1942
Champagne Charlie, 1944
Heaven is Round the Corner,
    1944
Lisbon Story, 1946

Anna Karenina, 1948
Bonnie Prince Charlie, 1948
The Red Shoes, 1948
So Long at the Fair, 1950
Father Brown, 1954
To Paris With Love, 1955
Tons of Trouble, 1956
Dangerous Exile, 1957
Seven Waves Away, 1957
Horrors of the Black Museum,
    1959
Konga, 1961
The Day the Earth Caught Fire,
    1961
Court Martial of Major Keller,
    1961
Never Back Losers, 1962
The Alphabet Murders, 1965

TOMMY TRINDER (1909-)
Cockney music hall performer
and stage (1921) comedian in
occasional films.

Almost a Honeymoon, 1938
Save a Little Sunshine, 1938
She Couldn't Say No, 1939
Laugh it Off, 1940
Sailors Three, 1940
Eating Out With Tommy, 1941
The Foreman Went to France,
    1942
The Bells Go Down, 1943
Champagne Charlie, 1944
Fiddlers Three, 1944
Bitter Springs, 1949
You Lucky People, 1955
Make Mine a Million, 1959
The Beauty Jungle, 1964
Under the Table You Must Go,
    1970
Barry Mackenzie Holds His Own,
    1974

PATRICK TROUGHTON (1920-)
Character actor primarily on
television; films sporadic.

Hamlet, 1948
Escape, 1948
Treasure Island, 1950

Chance of a Lifetime, 1950
The Woman With No Name,
    1950
The Black Knight, 1954
Richard III, 1955
The Moonraker, 1958
Phantom of the Opera, 1962
The Black Torment, 1964
The Gorgon, 1964
The Viking Queen, 1966
Scars of Dracula, 1970
The Omen, 1976
Sinbad and the Eye of the
    Tiger, 1977

CECIL TROUNCER (1898-1953)
Character player noted for fine
speaking voice; frequently on
stage.

Pygmalion, 1938
While the Sun Shines, 1946
The Guinea Pig, 1948
London Belongs to Me, 1948
Saraband For Dead Lovers,
    1949
Lady With a Lamp, 1951
The Magic Box, 1951
The Pickwick Papers, 1952
Isn't Life Wonderful, 1953
The Weak and the Wicked,
    1954

MICHAEL TRUBSHAWE (-)
Character actor of the 50s and
60s, sometimes in military
roles.

The Magic Box, 1951
The Lavender Hill Mob, 1951
Encore, 1952
Brandy For the Parson, 1952
Meet Me Tonight, 1952
Something Money Can't Buy,
    1953
The Titfield Thunderbolt, 1953
The Rainbow Jacket, 1954
You Lucky People, 1955
Private's Progress, 1956
The Rising of the Moon, 1957
Gideon's Day, 1958

Law and Disorder, 1958
Scent of Mystery, 1960
The Guns of Navarone, 1961
The Best of Enemies, 1962
Operation Snatch, 1962
Mouse On the Moon, 1963
Reach For Glory, 1963
The Pink Panther, 1963
A Hard Day's Night, 1964
The Runaway, 1964
Those Magnificent Men in Their
    Flying Machines, 1965
Bedazzled, 1967
Salt and Pepper, 1968
A Dandy in Aspic, 1968
Monte Carlo Or Bust, 1969
The Magic Christian, 1970

RALPH TRUMAN (1900-1977)
Distinctive, prolific character
actor of stage, films and television.

The Bells, 1931
City of Song, 1931
Partners Please, 1932
The Perfect Flaw, 1934
That's My Uncle, 1935
The Lad, 1935
Three Witnesses, 1935
The Case of Gabriel Perry,
    1935
The Silent Passenger, 1935
Jubilee Window, 1935
Lieutenant Daring RN, 1935
Captain Bill, 1935
Mr. Cohen Takes a Walk, 1935
Father O'Flynn, 1935
East Meets West, 1936
The Crimson Circle, 1936
The Marriage of Corbal, 1936
The Gay Adventure, 1936
It's a Grand Old World, 1937
Change For a Sovereign, 1937
Dinner at the Ritz, 1937
Just Like a Woman, 1938
The Challenge, 1938
Many Tanks Mr. Atkins, 1938
The Saint in London, 1939
The Outsider, 1939
The Seventh Survivor, 1941
Sabotage at Sea, 1942

The Butler's Dilemma, 1943
Henry V, 1944
Lisbon Story, 1946
Beware of Pity, 1946
The Laughing Lady, 1946
Woman to Woman, 1946
The Man Within, 1947
Mrs. Fitzherbert, 1947
Eureka Stockade, 1948
Oliver Twist, 1948
Mr. Perrin and Mr. Traill,
   1948
Christopher Columbus, 1949
The Reluctant Widow, 1950
Interrupted Journey, 1950
Treasure Island, 1950
Quo Vadis, 1951
Master of Ballantrae, 1953
Malta Story, 1953
The Golden Coach, 1954
Beau Brummell, 1954
The Night My Number Came
   Up, 1955
The Ship That Died of Shame,
   1955
The Man Who Knew Too Much,
   1956
The Long Arm, 1956
The Black Tent, 1956
Tons of Trouble, 1956
Wicked As They Come, 1956
The Spaniard's Curse, 1958
Beyond This Place, 1959
Exodus, 1960
El Cid, 1961
Nicholas and Alexandra, 1971
Lady Caroline Lamb, 1972
The Unpleasantness at the
   Bellona Club, 1973

JOHN TURNBULL (-)
Character actor seen in numer-
ous films of the thirties.

Tons of Money, 1931
Rodney Steps In, 1931
77 Park Lane, 1931
Keepers of Youth, 1931
The Man at Six, 1931
The Wickham Mystery, 1931
Lloyd of the C.I.D., 1931
Murder On the Second Floor,
   1932
A Voice Said Goodnight, 1932
The Private Life of Henry VIII,
   1933
Puppets of Fate, 1933
The Iron Stair, 1933
The Shadow, 1933
The Man Outside, 1933
The Umbrella, 1933
Ask Beccles, 1933
The Lady is Willing, 1934
The Case For the Crown, 1934
Badger's Green, 1934
Lord Edgware Dies, 1934
What Happened to Harkness?,
   1934
Passing Shadows, 1934
Warn London, 1934
The Girl in the Flat, 1934
It's a Cop, 1934
Tangled Evidence, 1934
Night of the Party, 1934
The Black Abbot, 1934
The Scarlet Pimpernel, 1935
Once in a New Moon, 1935
The Lad, 1935
Sexton Blake & the Bearded
   Doctor, 1935
Radio Pirates, 1935
Black Mask, 1935
Line Engaged, 1935
Passing of the Third Floor
   Back, 1935
Tudor Rose, 1936
Rembrandt, 1936
The Limping Man, 1936
His Lordship, 1936
Conquest of the Air, 1936
Shipmates O' Mine, 1936
Where There's a Will, 1936
Amazing Quest of Ernest Bliss,
   1936
It's a Grand Old World, 1937
Song of the Road, 1937
Make Up, 1937
Silver Blaze, 1937
Death Croons the Blues, 1937
The Terror, 1938
Stepping Toes, 1938
Star of the Circus, 1938
Night Alone, 1938
Inspector Hornleigh On Holiday,
   1939

Dead Men Are Dangerous, 1939
Spies of the Air, 1939
Three Silent Men, 1940
Spare a Copper, 1940
Hard Steel, 1942
There's a Future in It, 1943
The Shipbuilders, 1943
A Place of One's Own, 1944
Daybreak, 1946
The Hangman Waits, 1947
So Well Remembered, 1947
The Happiest Days of Your
  Life, 1950

GEORGE TURNER (-)
Character actor of the 20s and
30s, also on stage.

The Biter Bit, 1920
The English Rose, 1920
The Croxley Master, 1921
Early Birds, 1923
Woman to Woman, 1923
M'Lord of the White Road,
  1923
Sally Bishop, 1923
The Jail Birds, 1923
The Diamond Man, 1924
The Gay Corinthian, 1924
Q Ships, 1928
White Cargo, 1929
The Lame Duck, 1931
A Safe Affair, 1931
Trouble, 1933
Britannia of Billingsgate, 1933
Forging Ahead, 1933
The Man From Toronto, 1933
In Our Time, 1933
Full Speed Ahead, 1936
Playbox Adventure, 1936
Cafe Mascot, 1936
Twin Faces, 1937
Screen Struck, 1937
The Murdered Constable, 1938
The Kite Mob, 1938
Two Smart Men, 1940
Henry Steps Out, 1940
My Ain Folk, 1944
The Well Groomed Bride,
  1946
Race Street, 1948

JOHN TURNER (1932-)
Leading actor known as tv's
"Knight Errant," also on stage.
Rare films mainly in the 60s.

Behemoth the Sea Monster, 1959
Petticoat Pirates, 1961
Stork Talk, 1962
Sammy Going South, 1962
The Black Torment, 1964
Captain Nemo & the Underwater
  City, 1969
The Slipper and the Rose, 1976

RITA TUSHINGHAM (1942-)
Wide-eyed, offbeat actress of
the sixties, also on stage (from
1958). Latterly in international
productions.

A Taste of Honey, 1961
The Leather Boys, 1963
A Place to Go, 1963
Girl With Green Eyes, 1964
The Knack, 1965
Dr. Zhivago, 1965
The Trap, 1966
Smashing Time, 1967
Diamonds For Breakfast, 1968
The Guru, 1969
The Bed Sitting Room, 1969
The Case of Laura C., 1971
Straight On Till Morning, 1972
Where Do You Go From Here?,
  1972
The Human Factor, 1975
Rachel's Man, 1975
Ragazzo di Borgata, 1976
Gran Bollito, 1977
Green Eyes, 1977
Sotto Choc, 1978
Mysteries, 1979

DOROTHY TUTIN (1930-)
Leading actress of stage (from
1949); films few but memorable.

The Importance of Being Earnest,
  1952
The Beggar's Opera, 1953

A Tale of Two Cities, 1958
Cromwell, 1970
The Spy's Wife, 1971
Savage Messiah, 1972

MARGARET TYZACK (1933-)
Character actress of stage and
films; screen appearances occasional. Notable in tv series
"The Forsyte Saga. "

Highway to Battle, 1961
Ring of Spies, 1963
The Whisperers, 1967
2001: A Space Odyssey, 1968
A Clockwork Orange, 1971
Legacy, 1979

MEIER TZELNIKER (1894-)
Small-part character actor well-
known in the Yiddish theatre;
usually in amiable parts.

Mr. Emmanuel, 1944
It Always Rains On Sunday,
    1947
Last Holiday, 1950
The Teckman Mystery, 1954
Make Me An Offer, 1954
The Woman For Joe, 1955
The Extra Day, 1956
Stars in Your Eyes, 1956
The Long Haul, 1957
A Night to Remember, 1958
Expresso Bongo, 1959
Let's Get Married, 1960
Circle of Deception, 1961
His and Hers, 1961
Jungle Street, 1961
The 25th Hour, 1966
The Sorcerers, 1967

EDWARD UNDERDOWN (1908-)
Thin leading actor of stage (from
1932) and screen; former jockey.

Girls Please, 1934
The Warren Case, 1934
Annie Leave the Room, 1935
Wings of the Morning, 1937

Inspector Hornleigh, 1939
The October Man, 1947
The Woman in the Hall, 1947
The Lucky Mascot, 1948
Man On the Run, 1949
They Were Not Divided, 1950
The Woman With No Name, 1950
The Dark Man, 1951
The Woman's Angle, 1952
The Voice of Merrill, 1952
Street of Shadows, 1953
Recoil, 1953
Beat the Devil, 1953
The Rainbow Jacket, 1954
The Camp On Blood Island, 1958
Heart of a Child, 1958
The Two-Headed Spy, 1958
Information Received, 1961
The Third Alibi, 1961
The Day the Earth Caught Fire,
    1961
Locker 69, 1962
Dr. Crippen, 1962
The Bay of St. Michel, 1963
Man in the Middle, 1963
Woman of Straw, 1964
Traitor's Gate, 1964
Dr. Terror's House of Horrors,
    1965
Thunderball, 1965
Khartoum, 1966
Hand of Night, 1966
The Great Pony Raid, 1968
The Magic Christian, 1970
The Lasy Valley, 1971
Running Scared, 1972
Digby, the Biggest Dog in the
    World, 1973
The Abdication, 1974

MARY URE (1933-1975)
Attractive Scottish leading lady
of stage and occasional films,
married to Robert Shaw.

Storm Over the Nile, 1955
The Lady's Not For Burning, 1958
Windom's Way, 1958
Look Back in Anger, 1959
Sons and Lovers, 1960
The Mind Benders, 1963
The Luck of Ginger Coffey, 1964

Custer of the West, 1967
Where Eagles Dare, 1968
Reflection of Fear, 1973

ROBERT URQUHART (1922-)
Scotch leading actor of the fifties and sixties, also on stage
(from 1946). Also latterly in
character roles.

Tread Softly, 1952
You're Only Young Twice, 1952
Paul Temple Returns, 1952
Isn't Life Wonderful, 1953
The House of the Arrow, 1953
Knights of the Round Table,
    1954
Happy Ever After, 1954
Golden Ivory, 1954
The Dark Avenger, 1955
You Can't Escape, 1956
Yangtse Incident, 1957
The Curse of Frankenstein, 1957
Dunkirk, 1958
Murder in Mind, 1959
The Trouble With Eve, 1960
Danger Tomorrow, 1960
The Bulldog Breed, 1960
A Foxhole in Cairo, 1961
The Break, 1962
Murder at the Gallop, 1963
55 Days at Peking, 1963
The Syndicate, 1968
The Limbo Line, 1968
Mosquito Squadron, 1969
Country Dance, 1969
The Looking Glass War, 1970
A Tale of Two Cities, 1980

PETER USTINOV (1921-)
Portly character comedian of
stage (from 1938), screen and
tv, also in Hollywood; also director, writer, playwright and
author.

Hullo Fame, 1940
Mein Kampf My Crimes, 1940
One of Our Aircraft is Missing,
    1942
The Goose Steps Out, 1942

Let the People Sing, 1942
The Way Ahead, 1944
Private Angelo, 1949
Odette, 1950
Hotel Sahara, 1951
The Magic Box, 1951
Quo Vadis, 1951
House of Pleasure, 1952
Beau Brummell, 1954
The Egyptian, 1954
We're No Angels, 1955
Lola Montez, 1955
I Girovaghi, 1956
The Man Who Wagged His Tail,
    1957
The Spies, 1958
The Sundowners, 1960
Spartacus, 1960
Romanoff and Juliet, 1961
Billy Budd, 1962
Women of the World, 1963
Topkapi, 1964
Peaches, 1964
John Goldfarb, Please Come
    Home, 1964
Lady L, 1965
The Comedians, 1966
Blackbeard's Ghost, 1967
Hot Millions, 1968
Viva Max, 1970
Hammersmith is Out, 1972
Robin Hood (voice), 1973
One of Our Dinosaurs is Miss-
    ing, 1975
Logan's Run, 1976
Treasure of Matecumbe, 1976
Jesus of Nazareth, 1977
The Purple Taxi, 1977
Last Remake of Beau Geste,
    1977
Doppio Delitto, 1978
The Mouse and His Child, 1978
Death On the Nile, 1978
Ashanti, 1979
The Thief of Baghdad, 1979
Charlie Chan and the Curse of
    of the Dragon Queen, 1981

FREDERICK VALK (1901-1956)
Tubby Czechoslovakian character
player in Britain from 1939,
also much on stage.

Gasbags, 1940
Neutral Port, 1940
Night Train to Munich, 1940
The Patient Vanishes, 1941
Dangerous Moonlight, 1941
Thunder Rock, 1942
Hotel Reserve, 1944
Dead of Night, 1945
Latin Quarter, 1945
Mrs. Fitzherbert, 1947
Saraband For Dead Lovers,
  1949
Dear Mr. Prohack, 1949
The Magic Box, 1951
An Outcast of the Islands, 1952
Top Secret, 1952
Never Let Me Go, 1953
Albert RN, 1953
The Flanagan Boy, 1953
The Colditz Story, 1955
I Am a Camera, 1955
Secret Venture, 1955
Zarak, 1957

JOHN VAN EYSSEN (1925-)
South African character actor
of the fifties, latterly agent;
also chief production executive
for Columbia Pictures in Britain, 1969-73.

Four Sided Triangle, 1953
Three Steps in the Dark, 1953
Men of Sherwood Forest, 1954
Cockleshell Heroes, 1955
Quatermass II, 1957
The Traitors, 1957
Account Rendered, 1957
The One That Got Away, 1957
Man With a Dog, 1958
The Whole Truth, 1958
Dracula, 1958
Moment of Indiscretion, 1958
Blind Date, 1959
Carry On Nurse, 1959
Carleton Browne of the F.O.,
  1959
I'm All Right, Jack, 1959
Stars of a Summer Night, 1959
Exodus, 1960
The Criminal, 1960
A Story of David, 1960

Marriage of Convenience,
  1960

DAME IRENE VANBRUGH
  (1872-1949)
Distinguished stage actress
(since 1888) who appeared in
occasional silent and sound films.

The Real Thing at Last, 1916
Masks and Faces, 1917
The Gay Lord Quex, 1917
Head of the Family, 1933
Catherine the Great, 1934
Girls Will be Boys, 1934
The Way of Youth, 1934
Youthful Folly, 1934
Escape Me Never, 1935
Wings of the Morning, 1937
Knight Without Armour, 1937
Moonlight Sonata, 1937
It Happened One Sunday, 1944
I Live in Grosvenor Square,
  1945

NORMA VARDEN (1898-)
Character actress usually cast
in supercilious comedy roles,
also in Hollywood (from early
40s).

A Night Like This, 1932
Turkey Time, 1933
The Iron Duke, 1935
Foreign Affaires, 1935
Boys Will Be Boys, 1935
Get Off My Foot, 1935
East Meets West, 1936
Where There's a Will, 1936
Windbag the Sailor, 1936
Wanted, 1937
The Strange Adventures of Mr.
  Smith, 1937
Make Up, 1937
Rhythm Racketeer, 1937
You're the Doctor, 1938
Everything Happens to Me, 1938
Home From Home, 1939
Shipyard Sally, 1939
The Earl of Chicago, 1940
Scotland Yard, 1941

Random Harvest, 1942
We Were Dancing, 1942
Casablanca, 1942
What a Woman, 1943
Sherlock Holmes Faces Death,
    1943
The White Cliffs of Dover, 1944
National Velvet, 1944
Bring On the Girls, 1945
Hold That Blonde, 1945
The Searching Wind, 1946
The Green Years, 1946
The Trouble With Women, 1947
Thunder in the Valley, 1947
Forever Amber, 1947
Adventure in Baltimore, 1949
Fancy Pants, 1950
Thunder On the Hill, 1951
Strangers On a Train, 1951
Les Miserables, 1952
Young Bess, 1953
Gentlemen Prefer Blondes, 1953
Three Coins in the Fountain, 1954
Jupiter's Darling, 1955
Witness For the Prosecution,
    1957
Thirteen Frightened Girls, 1963
A Very Special Favor, 1965
The Sound of Music, 1965
Dr. Dolittle, 1967

BEATRICE VARLEY (1896-
    1969)
Character actress of stage and
screen who was mainly seen as
worried or frustrated old ladies.

Young and Innocent, 1937
Spring Handicap, 1937
Kipps, 1941
South American George, 1941
Hatter's Castle, 1941
Secret Mission, 1942
Squadron Leader X, 1942
We Dive at Dawn, 1943
The Bells Go Down, 1943
The Man in Grey, 1943
There's a Future in It, 1943
I'll Walk Beside You, 1943
Bees in Paradise, 1944
Welcome Mr. Washington, 1944
Love Story, 1944

Victory Wedding, 1944
Waterloo Road, 1945
The Wicked Lady, 1945
The Agitator, 1945
Johnny Frenchman, 1945
Great Day, 1945
Send For Paul Temple, 1946
Bedelia, 1946
So Well Remembered, 1947
Holiday Camp, 1947
Jassy, 1947
The Little Ballerina, 1947
The Upturned Glass, 1947
The Master of Bankdam, 1947
My Brother Jonathan, 1948
No Room at the Inn, 1948
My Brother's Keeper, 1948
Good Time Girl, 1948
Adam and Evalyn, 1949
Marry Me, 1949
Paul Temple's Triumph, 1950
She Shall Have Murder, 1950
Gone to Earth, 1950
Out of True, 1951
Hindle Wakes, 1952
Melba, 1953
Death Goes to School, 1953
Bang You're Dead, 1954
The Black Rider, 1954
The Feminine Touch, 1956
Tiger in the Smoke, 1956
The Good Companions, 1957
Seawife, 1957
The Surgeon's Knife, 1957
Room at the Top, 1958
The Rough and the Smooth, 1959
Horrors of the Black Museum,
    1959
Identity Unknown, 1960
Echo of Barbara, 1961
Night Without Pity, 1962

REG VARNEY (1922-)
Comedy actor in occasional films,
best known for tv series "The
Rag Trade" and "On the Buses"
during the sixties.

Miss Robin Hood, 1952
The Great St. Trinian's Train
    Robbery, 1966
On the Buses, 1971

Mutiny On the Buses, 1972
The Best Pair of Legs in the
 Business, 1972
Go For a Take, 1972
Holiday On the Buses, 1973

FRANKIE VAUGHAN (1928-)
Pop singer of the fifties in occasional films; also Hollywood.

Ramsbottom Rides Again, 1956
The Dangerous Years, 1957
Wonderful Things, 1958
The Lady is a Square, 1958
Heart of a Man, 1959
Let's Make Love, 1960
The Right Approach, 1962
It's All Over Town, 1964

PETER VAUGHAN (1923-)
Dependable character player of
the 60s and 70s, adept at either
good or evil characters.

Sapphire, 1959
Make Mine Mink, 1960
Village of the Damned, 1960
Two Living One Dead, 1961
The Devil's Agent, 1962
The Punch and Judy Man, 1963
Smokescreen, 1964
Fanatic, 1965
Rotten to the Core, 1965
Twist of Sand, 1967
The Naked Runner, 1967
Hammerhead, 1968
The Bofors Gun, 1968
The Man Outside, 1968
Alfred the Great, 1969
Taste of Excitement, 1969
Eyewitness, 1970
Straw Dogs, 1971
Savage Messiah, 1972
The Pied Piper, 1972
The Mackintosh Man, 1973
11 Harrowhouse, 1974
The Blockhouse, 1974
The Eyes Have It, 1974
Symptoms, 1976
Valentino, 1977
Zulu Dawn, 1980

AMY VENESS (1876-1960)
Character actress of the 30s
and 40s, mainly seen in cheerful roles as governesses, nurses,
grandmothers, etc.

My Wife's Family, 1931
Hobson's Choice, 1931
Money For Nothing, 1932
The Marriage Bond, 1932
Flat No. 9, 1932
Let Me Explain Dear, 1932
Pyjamas Preferred, 1932
Self-Made Lady, 1932
Tonight's the Night, 1932
Hawleys of High Street, 1933
Their Night Out, 1933
A Southern Maid, 1933
The Love Nest, 1933
Red Wagon, 1934
The Old Curiosity Shop, 1934
Royal Cavalcade, 1935
Play Up the Band, 1935
Drake of England, 1935
Brewster's Millions, 1935
Lorna Doone, 1935
Joy Ride, 1935
King of Hearts, 1936
Windbag the Sailor, 1936
Did I Betray?, 1936
Beloved Vagabond, 1936
Skylarks, 1936
The Mill On the Floss, 1937
Aren't Men Beasts, 1937
The Angelus, 1937
The Show Goes On, 1937
Thistledown, 1938
Yellow Sands, 1938
Just William, 1939
Flying Fifty-Five, 1939
John Smith Wakes Up, 1940
Millions Like Us, 1943
The Man in Grey, 1943
Fanny By Gaslight, 1944
Madonna of the Seven Moons,
 1944
This Happy Breed, 1944
Don't Take It To Heart, 1944
They Were Sisters, 1945
Don Chicago, 1945
Carnival, 1946
The Turners of Prospect Road,
 1947

Blanche Fury, 1948
My Brother's Keeper, 1948
Good Time Girl, 1948
Oliver Twist, 1948
Here Come the Huggetts, 1949
Vote For Huggett, 1949
The Huggetts Abroad, 1949
A Boy, a Girl, and a Bike,
   1949
The Astonished Heart, 1950
Madeleine, 1950
The Woman With No Name,
   1950
Chance of a Lifetime, 1951
Tom Brown's Schooldays, 1951
Captain Horatio Hornblower,
   1951
Angels One Five, 1952
Doctor in the House, 1954
The Woman For Joe, 1955

JERRY VERNO (1895-1975)
Music hall entertainer and
revue comedian (from 1907)
who played cockney character
parts in films.

Two Crowded Hours, 1931
My Friend the King, 1931
The Beggar Student, 1931
Hotel Splendide, 1932
His Lordship, 1932
His Wife's Mother, 1932
There Goes the Bride, 1932
Life of the Party, 1934
Royal Cavalcade, 1935
The Thirty-Nine Steps, 1935
Lieutenant Daring RN, 1935
Ourselves Alone, 1936
Broken Blossoms, 1936
Gypsy Melody, 1936
Pagliacci, 1936
Annie Laurie, 1936
Sweeney Todd, 1936
Sensation, 1937
Farewell Again, 1937
Non Stop New York, 1937
River of Unrest, 1937
Young and Innocent, 1937
Oh Boy, 1938
The Gables Mystery, 1938
Mountains O'Mourne, 1938

Queer Cargo, 1938
Old Mother Riley in Paris,
   1938
Anything to Declare?, 1939
Take Cover, 1939
The Chinese Bungalow, 1940
The Common Touch, 1941
Bothered By a Beard, 1946
My Brother's Keeper, 1948
The Red Shoes, 1948
The Belles of St. Trinian's,
   1954
After the Ball, 1957
A Place to Go, 1963

RICHARD VERNON (1907-)
Soft-spoken character actor with
upper-class personality, also on
stage and tv. Excellent in
series "The Duchess of Duke
Street II" (1980).

Village of the Damned, 1960
Clue of the Twisted Candle,
   1960
A Foxhole in Cairo, 1960
The Share Out, 1962
Reach For Glory, 1962
Cash On Demand, 1962
The Servant, 1963
Hot Enough For June, 1963
Just For Fun, 1963
Accidental Death, 1963
Goldfinger, 1964
A Hard Day's Night, 1964
The Tomb of Ligeia, 1964
The Counterfeit Constable, 1964
The Secret of My Success, 1965
The Intelligence Men, 1965
The Early Bird, 1965
One Brief Summer, 1970
Satanic Rites of Dracula, 1973
The Pink Panther Strikes
   Again, 1976
Oh Heavenly Dog, 1980
The Human Factor, 1980

CHARLES VICTOR (1896-1965)
Character actor specializing in
cockney parts; also frequently
on stage.

Laugh it Off, 1940
You Will Remember, 1940
Contraband, 1940
Hell's Cargo, 1940
Dr. O'Dowd, 1940
Old Mother Riley in Society,
1940
Old Mother Riley in Business,
1940
49th Parallel, 1941
Ships With Wings, 1941
This England, 1941
East of Piccadilly, 1941
Atlantic Ferry, 1941
He Found a Star, 1941
The Saint Meets the Tiger,
1941
Breach of Promise, 1941
Seven Day's Leave, 1942
Those Kids From Town, 1942
The Missing Million, 1942
The Foreman Went to France,
1942
They Flew Alone, 1942
Next of Kin, 1942
The Peterville Diamond, 1942
Lady From Lisbon, 1942
Squadron Leader X, 1942
The Silver Fleet, 1943
When We Are Married, 1943
Undercover, 1943
Escape to Danger, 1943
Rhythm Serenade, 1943
My Learned Friend, 1943
They Met in the Dark, 1943
San Demetrio-London, 1943
It Happened One Sunday, 1944
The Man From Morocco, 1945
The Way to the Stars, 1945
I Live in Grosvenor Square,
1945
The Rake's Progress, 1945
While the Sun Shines, 1946
Woman to Woman, 1946
This Man is Mine, 1946
Gaiety George, 1946
While I Live, 1947
Meet Me at Dawn, 1947
Green Fingers, 1947
The Calendar, 1948
Broken Journey, 1948
Vote For Huggett, 1949
Fools Rush In, 1949

Temptation Harbour, 1949
Landfall, 1949
The Cure For Love, 1950
Waterfront, 1950
The Elusive Pimpernel, 1950
The Woman in Question, 1950
The Magic Box, 1951
Calling Bulldog Drummond, 1951
The Galloping Major, 1951
The Man Who Cheated Himself,
1951
Something Money Can't Buy,
1952
The Frightened Man, 1952
Made in Heaven, 1952
Encore, 1952
The Ringer, 1952
The Saint's Return, 1953
Those People Next Door, 1953
Street Corner, 1953
Appointment in London, 1953
Girl On the Pier, 1953
Meet Mr. Lucifer, 1953
Fast and Loose, 1954
The Love Lottery, 1954
The Rainbow Jacket, 1954
For Better, For Worse, 1954
The Embezzler, 1955
Value For Money, 1955
Police Dog, 1955
An Alligator Named Daisy, 1955
Dial 999, 1955
Charley Moon, 1956
The Extra Day, 1956
Eyewitness, 1956
Now and Forever, 1956
Tiger in the Smoke, 1956
Home and Away, 1956
There's Always a Thursday,
1957
After the Ball, 1957
The Prince and the Showgirl,
1957
Forty Pounds of Trouble, 1962
The Wrong Box, 1966

HENRY VICTOR (1898-1945)
Star of silent films who later
played character roles, sometimes villainous; also in Hollywood.

Revolution, 1915
She, 1916
The Picture of Dorian Gray,
    1916
Call of the Sea, 1919
The Old Wives' Tale, 1921
A Bill of Divorcement, 1922
The Crimson Circle, 1922
The Prodigal Son, 1923
Scandal, 1923
Slaves of Destiny, 1924
White Monkey, 1925
Crossed Signals, 1926
The Beloved Rogue, 1927
Topsy and Eva, 1927
The Fourth Commandment, 1927
The Guns of Loos, 1928
Tommy Atkins, 1928
Down Channel, 1929
After the Verdict, 1929
Hate Ship, 1929
Song of Soho, 1930
One Heavenly Night, 1931
The Seas Beneath, 1931
Suicide Fleet, 1931
Freaks, 1932
The Mummy, 1932
I Spy, 1933
Musical Film Reviews, 1933
Tiger Bay, 1933
Scotland Yard Mystery, 1934
The Way of Youth, 1934
Murder at Monte Carlo, 1935
Handle With Care, 1935
Can You Hear Me Mother?, 1935
Fame, 1936
The Secret Voice, 1936
Conquest of the Air, 1936
The Silent Barriers, 1937
Our Fighting Navy, 1937
Holiday's End, 1937
Fine Feathers, 1937
Thunder Afloat, 1939
Hotel Imperial, 1939
Confessions of a Nazi Spy, 1939
Pack Up Your Troubles, 1940
Mystery Sea Raider, 1940
Nick Carter Detective, 1940
Zanzibar, 1940
King of the Zombies, 1941
To Be Or Not to Be, 1942
Desperate Journey, 1942
That Nasty Nuisance, 1943

JAMES VILLIERS (1930-)
Character actor of the sixties
and seventies, also on stage,
sometimes seen in villainous
roles.

The Entertainer, 1960
Clue of the New Pin, 1961
The Damned, 1961
Operation Snatch, 1962
Murder at the Gallop, 1963
Father Came Too, 1963
Nothing But the Best, 1963
King and Country, 1964
The Model Murder Case, 1964
Daylight Robbery, 1964
Eva, 1965
The Alphabet Murders, 1965
Repulsion, 1965
You Must be Joking!, 1965
The Nanny, 1965
The Wrong Box, 1966
Half a Sixpence, 1967
The Touchables, 1968
Otley, 1968
Some Girls Do, 1969
A Nice Girl Like Me, 1969
Blood From the Mummy's Tomb,
    1970
Asylum, 1972
The Ruling Class, 1972
The Double Kill, 1975
Joseph Andrews, 1977
Spectre, 1977
Saint Jack, 1979

FRANK VOSPER (-)
Strong character player of the
thirties, also on stage.

Blinkeyes, 1926
The Woman Juror, 1926
The Last Post, 1929
Rome Express, 1932
Strange Evidence, 1933
Dick Turpin, 1933
Open All Night, 1934
Red Ensign, 1934
Blind Justice, 1934
The Man Who Knew Too Much,
    1934

Jew Suss, 1934
Waltzes From Vienna, 1934
Heart's Desire, 1935
Royal Cavalcade, 1935
Langford Reed's Limericks,
  1935
Spy of Napoleon, 1936
The Secret of Stamboul, 1936

ANTHONY WAGER (1933-)
Juvenile player of the forties,
latterly appearing much on
Australian television.

Hungry Hill, 1946
Great Expectations, 1946
The Secret Tunnel, 1947
Fame is the Spur, 1947
The Guinea Pig, 1948
Above Us the Waves, 1955
The Wind Cannot Read, 1958
Night of the Prowler, 1962
The Hi-Jackers, 1963
Be My Guest, 1965
The Night Caller, 1965

ELSIE WAGSTAFFE (-)
Small-part character actress
mainly on stage; films sporadic.

Apron Fools, 1936
John Halifax Gentleman, 1938
Lassie From Lancashire, 1938
The Balloon Goes Up, 1942
The Dark Tower, 1943
Old Mother Riley at Home,
  1945
Appointment With Crime, 1946
Celia, 1949
The End of the Affair, 1955
The Snake Woman, 1961
Saturday Night & Sunday Morn-
  ing, 1961
Whistle Down the Wind, 1962

HUGH WAKEFIELD (1888-
1971)
Monocled character star of
stage (from 1899) and films,
usually in genial roles.

City of Song, 1931
The Sport of Kings, 1931
The Man They Could Not Arrest,
  1931
Women Who Play, 1932
Life Goes On, 1932
Aren't we All, 1932
Farewell to Love, 1933
The Crime at Blossom's, 1933
King of the Ritz, 1933
The Fortunate Fool, 1933
Luck of a Sailor, 1934
My Heart is Calling, 1934
Lady in Danger, 1934
The Man Who Knew Too Much,
  1934
Marry the Girl, 1935
Eighteen Minutes, 1935
No Monkey Business, 1935
Runaway Ladies, 1935
The Improper Duchess, 1936
The Crimson Circle, 1936
Forget-Me-Not, 1936
Interrupted Honeymoon, 1936
It's You I Want, 1936
The Limping Man, 1936
Dreams Come True, 1936
Forever Yours, 1937
The Street Singer, 1937
Death Croons the Blues, 1937
The Live Wire, 1937
Make it Three, 1938
Blithe Spirit, 1945
Journey Together, 1945
One Night With You, 1948
No Highway, 1951
Love's a Luxury, 1953
The Caretaker's Daughter, 1953
The Million Pound Note, 1954

ANTON WALBROOK (1900-1968)
Austrian romantic leading man
of stage (since 1916) and screen,
also in Hollywood.

Mater Dolorossa, 1922
Trapeze, 1931
Melody of Love, 1932
Waltz Time in Vienna, 1933
Victor and Victoria, 1933
Masquerade in Vienna, 1934
Zigeunerbaron, 1935

The Student of Prague, 1935
Der Kurier des Zaren, 1937
Port Arthur, 1937
The Soldier and the Lady, 1937
Victoria the Great, 1937
The Rat, 1937
Sixty Glorious Years, 1938
Gaslight, 1940
Dangerous Moonlight, 1941
49th Parallel, 1941
Life & Death of Colonel Blimp,
  1943
The Man From Morocco, 1945
The Red Shoes, 1948
The Queen of Spades, 1949
La Ronde, 1950
Vienna Waltzes, 1951
On Trial, 1954
Oh Rosalinda, 1955
Lola Montez, 1955
Saint Joan, 1957
I Accuse!, 1958

SYD WALKER (1887-1945)
Stage monologuist and occasional comedy character actor whose catchphrase was "What Would You Do Chums?"

The Gift of Gab, 1934
Royal Cavalcade, 1935
Let's Make a Night of It, 1937
Over She Goes, 1937
Oh Boy, 1938
Sweet Devil, 1938
Hold My Hand, 1939
What Would You Do Chums?,
  1939
I Killed the Count, 1939
The Gang's All Here, 1939

ZENA WALKER (1935-)
Leading actress of the sixties; also very much on television.

Danger Tomorrow, 1960
Snowball, 1960
The Hellions, 1961
Emergency, 1962
The Traitors, 1963
A Boy Ten Feet Tall, 1963
The Switch, 1963

The Marked One, 1963
The Verdict, 1964
Daylight Robbery, 1964
The Model Murder Case, 1964
Troubled Waters, 1964
Change Partners, 1965
The Reckoning, 1969
One of Those Things, 1969
Cromwell, 1970
The Last Shot You Hear, 1970
Murder in Mind, 1973
Abide With Me, 1978

TOM WALLS (1883-1949)
Comic actor of stage (since 1905) and films, popular in the 30s; also producer and director. Former jockey, policeman and busker.

Rookery Nook, 1930
On Approval, 1930
Canaries Sometimes Sing, 1930
Tons of Money, 1931
Plunder, 1931
A Night Like This, 1932
Thark, 1932
Leap Year, 1932
The Blarney Stone, 1933
Just Smith, 1933
Turkey Time, 1933
A Cuckoo in the Nest, 1933
Lady in Danger, 1934
Dirty Work, 1934
A Cup of Kindness, 1934
Fighting Stock, 1935
Stormy Weather, 1935
Me and Marlborough, 1935
Foreign Affairs, 1935
Pot Luck, 1936
Dishonour Bright, 1936
For Valour, 1937
Strange Boarders, 1938
Crackerjack, 1938
Second Best Bed, 1938
Old Iron, 1938
Undercover, 1943
They Met in the Dark, 1943
Halfway House, 1944
Love Story, 1944
Johnny Frenchman, 1945
This Man is Mine, 1946
The Master of Bankdam, 1947

While I Live, 1947
Spring in Park Lane, 1948
Maytime in Mayfair, 1949
Interrupted Journey, 1949
Derby Day, 1949
Skid Kids (release delayed),
  1953

DERMOT WALSH (1924-)
Irish leading man, primarily
seen in second features; married to Hazel Court.

Hungry Hill, 1946
Jassy, 1947
The Mark of Cain, 1948
My Sister and I, 1948
To the Public Danger, 1948
Third Time Lucky, 1949
Torment, 1949
The Frightened Man, 1952
Ghost Ship, 1952
Counterspy, 1953
The Blue Parrot, 1953
The Straw Man, 1953
The Floating Dutchman, 1954
On the Night of the Full Moon,
  1954
Bond of Fear, 1956
Hideout, 1956
At the Stroke of Nine, 1957
Woman of Mystery, 1958
Sea Fury, 1958
Sea of Sand, 1958
Chain of Events, 1958
The Bandit of Zhobe, 1959
The Crowning Touch, 1959
Crash Dive, 1959
The Witness, 1959
Make Mine a Million, 1959
The Clock Struck Three, 1959
The Challenge, 1960
The Flesh and the Fiends,
  1960
The Telltale Heart, 1960
The Trunk, 1961
Bedelia, 1961
Echo of Diana, 1961
The Breaking Point, 1961
Shoot to Kill, 1961
Tarnished Heroes, 1961
Out of the Shadow, 1961

Emergency, 1962
The Switch, 1963
The Cool Mikado, 1963
It Takes a Thief, 1963
Infamous Conduct, 1966

KAY WALSH (1914-)
Leading lady and latterly character actress, former revue
dancer (1932); married director
David Lean (1908-).

How's Chances, 1934
Get Your Man, 1934
Smith's Wives, 1935
Luck of the Irish, 1935
If I Were Rich, 1936
Secret of Stamboul, 1936
All That Glitters, 1936
Keep Fit, 1937
The Last Adventurers, 1937
I See Ice, 1938
Meet Mr. Penny, 1938
The Mind of Mr. Reeder, 1939
The Missing People, 1939
All at Sea, 1939
The Middle Watch, 1939
Sons of the Sea, 1940
The Chinese Bungalow, 1940
The Second Mr. Bush, 1940
In Which We Serve, 1942
This Happy Breed, 1944
Great Expectations, 1946
The October Man, 1947
Vice Versa, 1947
Oliver Twist, 1948
Last Holiday, 1950
Stage Fright, 1950
The Magnet, 1950
The Magic Box, 1951
Encore, 1951
Hunted, 1952
Meet Me Tonight, 1952
Young Bess, 1953
The Rainbow Jacket, 1954
Lease of Life, 1954
Cast a Dark Shadow, 1955
Now and Forever, 1956
The Horse's Mouth, 1958
Tunes of Glory, 1960
Greyfriars Bobby, 1961
Reach For Glory, 1962

Lunch Hour, 1962
80,000 Suspects, 1963
Dr. Syn Alias the Scarecrow,
    1963
The Beauty Jungle, 1964
Circus World, 1964
He Who Rides a Tiger, 1965
A Study in Terror, 1965
The Witches, 1966
Taste of Excitement, 1969
Connecting Rooms, 1969
The Virgin and the Gypsy, 1970
Scrooge, 1970
The Ruling Class, 1972

PERCY WALSH (-)
Small-part character actor of
the 30s and 40s; also on stage.
Often seen in officious roles.

Enter the Queen, 1930
The Wrong Mr. Perkins, 1931
The Green Pack, 1934
The Office Wife, 1934
How's Chances, 1934
Death Drives Through, 1935
The Case of Gabriel Perry,
    1935
Forever England, 1935
This England, 1935
Admirals All, 1935
Checkmate, 1935
Boys Will be Boys, 1935
King of the Damned, 1936
Educated Evans, 1936
Annie Laurie, 1936
Knights For a Day, 1937
Oh Mr. Porter, 1937
The Gang Show, 1937
It's in the Blood, 1938
Four Just Men, 1939
Pastor Hall, 1940
Let George Do It, 1941
Jeannie, 1941
Inspector Hornleigh Goes to It,
    1941
Dawn Guard, 1941
Pimpernel Smith, 1941
The Common Touch, 1941
Breach of Promise, 1941
Secret Mission, 1942
Thursday's Child, 1943

The Adventures of Tartu, 1943
The Courtneys of Curzon Street,
    1947
Meet Me at Dawn, 1947
Fame is the Spur, 1947
The Guinea Pig, 1948
Scott of the Antarctic, 1948
Train of Events, 1949
Traitor Spy, 1949
Dick Barton at Bay, 1950
The Happiest Days of Your Life,
    1950
The Golden Salamander, 1950

HAL WALTERS (-)
Character actor who appeared in
many films during the 30s, often
in comedy parts.

Tonight's the Night, 1932
Come Into My Parlour, 1932
Old Spanish Customers, 1932
On the Air, 1932
Little Fella, 1932
The River House Ghost, 1932
Women Are That Way, 1932
Yes Madam, 1933
Going Straight, 1933
That's My Wife, 1933
Long Live the King, 1933
Great Stuff, 1933
I'll Stick to You, 1933
Enemy of the Police, 1933
Strike It Rich, 1933
Marooned, 1933
The Man I Want, 1934
Bagged, 1934
The Perfect Flaw, 1934
Virginia's Husband, 1934
Crazy People, 1934
Big Business, 1934
Death On the Set, 1935
Department Store, 1935
The Right Age to Marry, 1935
A Fire Has Been Arranged, 1935
Can You Hear Me Mother?, 1935
Blue Smoke, 1935
Don't Rush Me, 1936
Interrupted Honeymoon, 1936
Where There's a Will, 1936
Apron Fools, 1936
Educated Evans, 1936

The Vulture, 1937
Pearls Bring Tears, 1937
Song of the Forge, 1937
Strange Adventures of Mr.
  Smith, 1937
Keep Fit, 1937
Little Miss Somebody, 1937
Television Talent, 1937
The Viper, 1938
Double Or Quits, 1938
Meet Mr. Penny, 1938
Thank Evans, 1938
Ghost Tales Retold, 1938
The Four Feathers, 1939
The Good Old Days, 1939
Pandemonium, 1939
Hoots Mon, 1939
They Came By Night, 1940
Spies of the Air, 1940
That's the Ticket, 1940
Strange to Relate, 1943

THORLEY WALTERS (1913-)
Character actor of stage (since
1934) and films, often seen in
comedy cameo roles.

Trunk Crime, 1939
Secret Journey, 1939
Gentleman of Venture, 1940
They Were Sisters, 1945
Waltz Time, 1945
Josephine and Men, 1955
You Can't Escape, 1956
Who Done It, 1956
Private's Progress, 1956
The Baby and the Battleship,
  1956
A Novel Affair, 1957
Blue Murder at St. Trinian's,
  1957
Second Fiddle, 1957
The Birthday Present, 1957
Happy is the Bride, 1958
The Truth About Women, 1958
A Lady Mislaid, 1958
Carleton Browne of the FO,
  1959
Don't Panic Chaps, 1959
Two-Way Stretch, 1960
Suspect, 1960
A French Mistress, 1960

The Pure Hell of St. Trinian's,
  1960
Invasion Quartet, 1961
Petticoat Pirates, 1961
Sherlock Holmes and the Deadly
  Necklace, 1962
Phantom of the Opera, 1962
Murder She Said, 1962
Ring of Spies, 1963
Heavens Above, 1963
The Earth Dies Screaming, 1964
A Home of Your Own, 1964
Joey Boy, 1965
Rotten to the Core, 1965
A Study in Terror, 1965
The Psychopath, 1966
The Family Way, 1966
Dracula Prince of Darkness,
  1966
The Wrong Box, 1966
Frankenstein Created Woman,
  1967
Twisted Nerve, 1968
Crooks and Coronets, 1969
Oh What a Lovely War, 1969
Frankenstein Must be Destroyed,
  1969
Bartleby, 1970
The Man Who Haunted Himself,
  1970
The Last Shot You Hear, 1970
Trog, 1970
There's a Girl in My Soup, 1970
Vampire Circus, 1972
Cry of the Penguins, 1972
Young Winston, 1972
Death in Small Doses, 1973
The Gathering Storm, 1974
Adventures of Sherlock Holmes'
  Smarter Brother, 1975
The People That Time Forgot,
  1977
Henry V, 1980
Tinker, Tailor, Soldier, Spy, 1980
Malice Aforethought, 1981

MICHAEL WARD (1915-)
Comedy character actor usually
seen in nervous or worried roles.

An Ideal Husband, 1948
Sleeping Car to Trieste, 1948

Hi Jinks in Society, 1949
What the Butler Saw, 1950
No Trace, 1950
Lilli Marlene, 1950
Chelsea Story, 1951
The Frightened Man, 1952
Trouble in Store, 1953
Street Corner, 1953
Up in the World, 1956
Private's Progress, 1956
Just My Luck, 1959
I'm All Right, Jack, 1959
Doctor in Love, 1960
Mary Had a Little, 1961
Carry On Cleo, 1964
Carry On Screaming, 1966
Carry On Don't Lose Your
    Head, 1966

POLLY WARD (1908-)
Energetic singing and dancing
star of the thirties, also on
stage (from 1920).

This Marriage Business, 1927
Shooting Stars, 1928
Harmony Heaven, 1930
Alf's Button, 1930
His Lordship, 1932
Kentucky Minstrels, 1934
The Old Curiosity Shop, 1934
It's a Bet, 1935
Shipmates O' Mine, 1936
Annie Laurie, 1936
Show Flat, 1936
Television Talent, 1937
Feather Your Nest, 1937
Thank Evans, 1938
St. Martin's Lane, 1938
Hold My Hand, 1938
It's in the Air, 1938
Bulldog Sees it Through, 1940
Women Aren't Angels, 1942
New Faces, 1954

SIMON WARD (1941-)
Ambitious leading man of the
seventies, also on stage.

If, 1968
Frankenstein Must be De-
    stroyed, 1969

I Start Counting, 1971
Young Winston, 1972
Hitler: The Last Ten Days,
    1973
Dracula, 1973
The Three Musketeers, 1974
The Four Musketeers, 1975
Deadly Strangers, 1975
All Creatures Great and Small,
    1975
Aces High, 1976
Children of Rage, 1976
The Four Feathers, 1978
The Chosen, 1978
The Last Giraffe, 1979
Zulu Dawn, 1980

WARWICK WARD (1891-1967)
Elegant leading man of silents
latterly in character roles, on
stage from 1907. Also producer
and in Hollywood.

The Silver Lining, 1919
Mary Latimer Nun, 1920
Wuthering Heights, 1920
Call of the Road, 1920
Build Thy House, 1920
The Manchester Man, 1920
The Diamond Necklace, 1921
Handy Andy, 1921
Belphegor the Mountebank, 1921
Demos, 1921
Corinthian Jack, 1921
The Golden Dawn, 1921
The Mayor of Casterbridge, 1921
Little Meg's Children, 1921
The Lilac Sunbonnet, 1922
Tell Your Children, 1922
Call of the East, 1922
Petticoat Loose, 1922
Bulldog Drummond, 1923
The Lady Owner, 1923
The Hotel Mouse, 1923
The Money Habit, 1924
The Great Turf Mystery, 1924
Southern Love, 1924
Hurricane Hutch in Many Adven-
    tures, 1924
The Prude's Fall, 1925
Human Desires, 1925
Madame Sans Gene, 1925
Variety, 1926

The Woman Tempted, 1926
The White Sheik, 1926
Maria Marten, 1928
Eva and the Grasshopper, 1928
Looping the Loop, 1929
Dance of Barcelona, 1929
After the Verdict, 1929
Three Kings, 1929
The Woman He Scorned, 1929
The Informer, 1929
The Yellow Mask, 1930
Birds of Prey, 1930
Strange Case of District At-
   torney M, 1930
Wonderful Lies of Nova Petrova,
   1930
To Oblige a Lady, 1931
Number Please, 1931
Deadlock, 1931
Stamboul, 1931
Man of Mayfair, 1931
The Callbox Mystery, 1932
Life Goes On, 1932
Blind Spot, 1932
FP One, 1933
Ariane, 1934
Elstree Story, 1952

DAVID WARNER (1941-   )
Tall, intelligent leading man
of stage (since 1962) and films,
good in sinister roles.   Also
in Hollywood.

Tom Jones, 1963
War of the Roses, 1966
Morgan, 1966
The Deadly Affair, 1966
Work is a Four Letter Word,
   1967
The Fixer, 1968
The Bofors Gun, 1968
A Midsummer Night's Dream,
   1968
Michael Kohlhaas, 1969
The Sea Gull, 1969
The Ballad of Cable Hogue, 1970
The Engagement, 1970
Perfect Friday, 1970
Straw Dogs, 1971
A Doll's House, 1973
From Beyond the Grave, 1973

Little Malcolm, 1974
Mr. Quilp, 1975
The Omen, 1976
Cross of Iron, 1977
Age of Innocence, 1977
Providence, 1977
Silver Bears, 1978
The Disappearance, 1978
Nightwing, 1979
The Concorde-Airport 79, 1979
SOS Titanic, 1979
Time After Time, 1979
The Thirty-Nine Steps, 1980
The Island, 1980

H. B. WARNER (1876-1958)
Distinguished character star of
stage (from 1883) and films,
in Hollywood from 1914.

English Nell, 1900
The Lost Paradise, 1914
The Ghost Breaker, 1914
The Raiders, 1915
The Beggar of Cawnpore, 1915
Vagabond Prince, 1916
Market of Vain Desire, 1916
Wrath, 1917
God's Man, 1917
The Man Who Turned White,
   1919
The Pagan God, 1919
One Hour Before Dawn, 1920
The White Dove, 1920
Below the Deadline, 1921
Zaza, 1923
Is Love Everything?, 1924
Whispering Smith, 1926
Silence, 1926
King of Kings, 1927
Sorrell and Son, 1927
French Dressing, 1927
Romance of a Rogue, 1928
Man Made Women, 1928
The Naughty Duchess, 1928
The Argyle Case, 1929
Conquest, 1929
The Doctor's Secret, 1929
Divine Lady, 1929
Stark Mad, 1929
The Trial of Mary Dugan, 1929
The Gamblers, 1929

Show of Shows, 1929
Tiger Rose, 1929
Wedding Rings, 1930
On Your Back, 1930
Princess and the Plumber, 1930
The Green Goddess, 1930
The Furies, 1930
Wild Company, 1930
Liliom, 1930
The Reckless Hour, 1931
Five Star Final, 1931
A Woman of Experience, 1931
Expensive Women, 1931
The Phantom of Crestwood, 1932
Charlie Chan's Chance, 1932
A Woman Commands, 1932
The Menace, 1932
Cross Examination, 1932
Tom Brown of Culver, 1932
The Crusader, 1932
The Son Daughter, 1933
Supernatural, 1933
Jennie Gerhardt, 1933
Christopher Bean, 1933
Sorrell and Son, 1934
Grand Canary, 1934
Behold My Wife, 1935
A Tale of Two Cities, 1935
Rose of the Rancho, 1935
The Garden Murder Case, 1936
Mr. Deeds Goes to Town, 1936
Moonlight Murder, 1936
Lost Horizon, 1937
Victoria the Great, 1937
Army Girl, 1938
Girl of the Golden West, 1938
Kidnapped, 1938
The Toy Wife, 1938
Bulldog Drummond in Africa, 1938
You Can't Take it With You, 1938
Let Freedom Ring, 1939
The Gracie Allen Murder Case, 1939
The Rains Came, 1939
Arrest Bulldog Drummond, 1939
Bulldog Drummond's Secret Police, 1939
Bulldog Drummond's Bride, 1939

Nurse Edith Cavell, 1939
Mr. Smith Goes to Washington, 1939
New Moon, 1940
All That Money Can Buy, 1941
Topper Returns, 1941
Ellery Queen & the Perfect Crime, 1941
South of Tahiti, 1941
The Corsican Brothers, 1941
Crossroads, 1942
Hitler's Children, 1943
Action in Arabia, 1944
Woman in Bondage, 1944
Enemy of Women, 1944
Rogue's Gallery, 1945
Strange Impersonation, 1945
Gentleman Joe Palooka, 1945
Captain Tugboat Annie, 1946
It's a Wonderful Life, 1946
High Wall, 1947
Driftwood, 1947
Prince of Thieves, 1948
El Paso, 1949
Hellfire, 1949
The Judge Steps Out, 1949
Sunset Boulevard, 1950
The First Legion, 1951
Here Comes the Groom, 1951
Savage Drums, 1951
Journey Into Light, 1951
The Ten Commandments, 1956

JACK WARNER (1894-   )
Likable character star and occasional leading man of stage and films, former engineer (1919), comedy singer (1927) and radio star (1940); also famous on television in the popular "Dixon of Dock Green."

The Dummy Talks, 1943
The Captive Heart, 1946
Hue and Cry, 1946
Dear Murderer, 1947
Holiday Camp, 1947
It Always Rains On Sunday, 1947
Easy Money, 1948
Against the Wind, 1948
My Brother's Keeper, 1948

Here Come the Huggetts, 1948
Vote For Huggett, 1948
The Huggetts Abroad, 1949
Train of Events, 1949
Boys in Brown, 1949
The Blue Lamp, 1950
Talk of a Million, 1951
Valley of Eagles, 1951
Scrooge, 1951
Emergency Call, 1952
Meet Me Tonight, 1952
Those People Next Door, 1952
The Final Test, 1953
The Square Ring, 1953
Albert RN, 1953
Bang You're Dead, 1954
Forbidden Cargo, 1954
The Quatermass Experiment, 1955
The Ladykillers, 1955
Now and Forever, 1956
Home and Away, 1956
Carve Her Name With Pride, 1958
Jigsaw, 1962

BETTY WARREN (-)
Supporting actress of the forties and fifties, also on stage.

The Farmer's Wife, 1941
Secret Mission, 1942
Variety Jubilee, 1943
They Met in the Dark, 1943
Champagne Charlie, 1944
The Magic Bow, 1947
Passport to Pimlico, 1949
So Long at the Fair, 1950
Tread Softly Stranger, 1958
Macbeth, 1961

C. DENIER WARREN (1889-1971)
Tubby American-born character player long in Britain; very active in the thirties, mainly in comic parts.

Let Me Explain Dear, 1932
Channel Crossing, 1933
Prince of Arcadia, 1933

Counsel's Opinion, 1933
Two Hearts in Waltz Time, 1934
Music Hall, 1934
Kentucky Minstrels, 1934
A Fire Has Been Arranged, 1935
The Clairvoyant, 1935
Temptation, 1935
The Small Man, 1935
A Real Bloke, 1935
Royal Cavalcade, 1935
Marry the Girl, 1935
Heat Wave, 1935
Be Careful Mr. Smith, 1935
Charing Cross Road, 1935
Heart's Desire, 1935
Birds of a Feather, 1935
The Big Noise, 1936
They Didn't Know, 1936
A Star Fell From Heaven, 1936
It's in the Bag, 1936
Beloved Vagabond, 1936
Spy of Napoleon, 1936
Everybody Dance, 1936
You Must Get Married, 1936
Cotton Queen, 1937
Cafe Colette, 1937
Good Morning Boys, 1937
Rose of Tralee, 1937
Song of the Forge, 1937
Keep Fit, 1937
A Romance in Flanders, 1937
Change For a Sovereign, 1937
Little Miss Somebody, 1937
Who Killed John Savage?, 1937
Melody and Romance, 1937
Captain's Orders, 1937
Make it Three, 1938
Strange Boarders, 1938
Kicking the Moon Around, 1938
Break the News, 1938
Old Mother Riley in Paris, 1938
My Irish Molly, 1938
Take Off That Hat, 1938
Trouble Brewing, 1939
Come On George, 1939
The Body Vanishes, 1939
Trouble For Two, 1939
A Gentleman's Gentleman, 1939
Secret Journey, 1939
It's in the Air, 1940

We'll Smile Again, 1942
Kiss the Bride Goodbye, 1944
Old Mother Riley's New Venture, 1949
Old Mother Riley Headmistress, 1950
The Dragon of Pendragon Castle, 1950
Alf's Baby, 1953
House of Blackmail, 1953
A Taste of Money, 1960
Bluebeard's Ten Honeymoons, 1960
The Silent Invasion, 1962
Lolita, 1962

KENNETH J. WARREN (1926-1973)
Portly character actor of stage and films, sometimes in comedy portrayals.

A Woman's Temptation, 1959
The Siege of Pinchgut, 1959
The Navy Lark, 1959
The Criminal, 1960
On the Fiddle, 1961
Strip Tease Murder, 1961
Part Time Wife, 1961
The Boys, 1962
The Small World of Sammy Lee, 1963
The Informers, 1963
The Invisible Asset, 1963
A High Wind in Jamaica, 1965
The 25th Hour, 1966
The Double Man, 1967
Leo the Last, 1970
The Revolutionary, 1970
I Monster, 1971
Demons of the Mind, 1972
The Creeping Flesh, 1973
Digby, the Biggest Dog in the World, 1973
S. P. Y. S. , 1974

HAROLD WARRENDER (1903-1953)
Genial actor of stage (from 1925) and screen, latterly in character roles; former radio quizmaster.

Daydreams, 1928
Friday the Thirteenth, 1933
I Spy, 1933
Catherine the Great, 1934
Leave it to Blanche, 1934
Lady in Danger, 1934
Lazybones, 1935
Mimi, 1935
Invitation to the Waltz, 1935
Convoy, 1940
Contraband, 1940
Sailors Three, 1941
Under the Frozen Falls, 1948
Scott of the Antarctic, 1948
Warning to Wantons, 1949
Conspirator, 1950
Where No Vultures Fly, 1951
Pandora and the Flying Dutchman, 1951
Six Men, 1951
Ivanhoe, 1952
Time Bomb, 1953
Intimate Relations, 1953

JOHN WARWICK (1905-1972)
Australian leading actor and latterly character player, seen frequently as crooks and policemen alike.

Down On the Farm, 1935
Find the Lady, 1936
Lucky Jade, 1937
Double Alibi, 1937
Catch as Catch Can, 1937
When the Poppies Bloom Again, 1937
Passenger to London, 1937
Ticket of Leave Man, 1937
Riding High, 1937
Bad Boy, 1938
A Yank at Oxford, 1938
John Halifax Gentleman, 1938
This Man is News, 1938
Me and My Pal, 1939
Dead Men Are Dangerous, 1939
The Mind of Mr. Reeder, 1939
The Face at the Window, 1939
The Flying Fifty-Five, 1939
All at Sea, 1939
Case of the Frightened Lady, 1940
Spare a Copper, 1940

The Saint's Vacation, 1941
Danny Boy, 1941
My Wife's Family, 1941
The Missing Million, 1942
The Day Will Dawn, 1942
Talk About Jacqueline, 1942
Woman to Woman, 1946
Dancing With Crime, 1947
Teheran, 1947
While I Live, 1947
The Franchise Affair, 1951
The Lavender Hill Mob, 1951
Never Look Back, 1952
Circumstantial Evidence, 1952
Escape Route, 1953
Trouble in Store, 1953
Street Corner, 1953
Bang You're Dead, 1954
Up to His Neck, 1954
Dangerous Voyage, 1954
Contraband Spain, 1955
The Mysterious Bullet, 1955
The Tyburn Case, 1957
Just My Luck, 1957
Print of Death, 1958
The Crossroad Gallows, 1958
Law and Disorder, 1958
The Square Peg, 1958
Horrors of the Black Museum,
1959
The Desperate Man, 1959
Murder at Site Three, 1959
Adam's Woman, 1970

MONA WASHBOURNE (1903-)
Character actress of stage
(since 1924) and films, sometimes in eccentric or comedic
roles; former pianist.

The Winslow Boy, 1948
Maytime in Mayfair, 1949
Dark Interval, 1950
Wide Boy, 1952
Johnny On the Run, 1953
Adventure in the Hopfields,
1954
Child's Play, 1954
Doctor in the House, 1954
To Dorothy a Son, 1954
Cast a Dark Shadow, 1955
It's Great to Be Young, 1956

The Good Companions, 1957
Stranger in Town, 1957
A Cry From the Streets, 1958
Count Your Blessings, 1959
The Brides of Dracula, 1960
Billy Liar, 1963
My Fair Lady, 1964
Night Must Fall, 1964
Ferry Cross the Mersey, 1964
One Way Pendulum, 1964
The Collector, 1965
The Third Day, 1965
Two a Penny, 1967
If, 1968
Mrs. Brown, You've Got a
Lovely Daughter, 1968
The Bed Sitting Room, 1969
The Games, 1970
Fragment of Fear, 1970
Romeo and Juliet, 1971
What Became of Jack and Jill?,
1972
O Lucky Man, 1973
The Driver's Seat, 1974
Mr. Quilp, 1975
The Blue Bird, 1976
Stevie, 1978
The London Affair, 1979

DENIS WATERMAN (1948-)
Leading juvenile player of the
sixties and seventies, also much
on tv; notable in series "The
Sweeney."

Snowball, 1960
Night Train For Inverness, 1960
The Pirates of Blood River,
1962
Go Kart Go!, 1964
Up the Junction, 1967
The Smashing Bird I Used to
Know, 1969
A Promise of Bed, 1969
My Lover My Son, 1970
Scars of Dracula, 1970
Fright, 1971
Man in the Wilderness, 1971
Alice's Adventures in Wonder-
land, 1972
The Belstone Fox, 1973
The Eyes Have It, 1974

Hell House Girls, 1975
The Sweeney, 1976
Free Spirit, 1978

RUSSELL WATERS (1908-)
Character player primarily
seen in mild, inoffensive type
roles.

Tell Me If It Hurts, 1934
And So to Work, 1936
The Woman in the Hall, 1947
What a Life, 1948
Obsession, 1949
Dear Mr. Prohack, 1949
The Blue Lagoon, 1949
Chance of a Lifetime, 1950
The Cure, 1950
The Happiest Days of Your
 Life, 1950
Seven Days to Noon, 1950
The Browning Version, 1951
Mr. Denning Drives North,
 1951
Green Grow the Rushes, 1951
Death of An Angel, 1952
Saturday Island, 1952
Castle in the Air, 1952
The Brave Don't Cry, 1952
Miss Robin Hood, 1952
Turn the Key Softly, 1953
Rob Roy, 1953
Isn't Life Wonderful, 1953
The Maggie, 1954
Adventure in the Hopfields,
 1954
Lease of Life, 1954
Third Party Risk, 1955
The Key, 1957
Man in the Sky, 1957
Yesterday's Enemy, 1959
Left, Right, and Centre, 1959
Danger Tomorrow, 1960
Marriage of Convenience, 1960
Bomb in the High Street, 1962
I Could Go On Singing, 1962
The Heroes of Telemark, 1965
Kidnapped, 1971
The Wicker Man, 1973

JACK WATLING (1923-)

Youthful-looking character actor of stage and screen; former juvenile performer.

Sixty Glorious Years, 1938
Goodbye Mr. Chips, 1939
We Dive at Dawn, 1942
The Day Will Dawn, 1942
The Demi-Paradise, 1943
The Way Ahead, 1944
Journey Together, 1945
The Courtneys of Curzon Street,
 1947
Quartet, 1948
The Winslow Boy, 1948
Easy Money, 1948
The Facts of Life, 1948
Under Capricorn, 1949
Private Information, 1950
Once a Sinner, 1950
The Naked Earth, 1950
White Corridors, 1951
Kathy's Love Affair, 1952
Father's Doing Fine, 1952
Meet Mr. Lucifer, 1953
Flannelfoot, 1953
Dangerous Cargo, 1954
The Golden Link, 1954
Trouble in the Glen, 1954
The Sea Shall Not Have Them,
 1955
The Naked Heart, 1955
Windfall, 1955
A Time to Kill, 1955
Reach For the Sky, 1956
The Admirable Crichton, 1957
That Woman Opposite, 1957
The Birthday Present, 1957
A Night to Remember, 1958
Gideon's Day, 1958
Chain of Events, 1958
The Links of Justice, 1958
The Solitary Child, 1958
Sink the Bismarck, 1960
The Queen's Guards, 1960
The Night We Sprang a Leak,
 1960
Nothing Barred, 1961
Mary Had a Little, 1961
Nearly a Nasty Accident, 1961
Three On a Spree, 1961
Mr. Arkadin, 1962
Flat Two, 1962

Edgar Wallace, 1963
Who Was Maddox?, 1964
The Nanny, 1965
11 Harrowhouse, 1974

CAVEN WATSON (-)
Friendly Scots character actor
who played small roles in occasional films.

In Which We Serve, 1942
We Dive at Dawn, 1943
San Demetrio-London, 1943
The Way Ahead, 1944
Perfect Strangers, 1945
The Way to the Stars, 1945
The Winslow Boy, 1948
The Net, 1953

JACK WATSON (1921-)
Rugged character star of the
60s and 70s, often seen in
military roles; also on tv.

The Man Who Was Nobody,
1960
Peeping Tom, 1960
The Queen's Guards, 1960
Konga, 1961
Fate Takes a Hand, 1962
Time to Remember, 1962
Out of the Fog, 1962
Five to One, 1963
This Sporting Life, 1963
The Gorgon, 1964
Master Spy, 1964
The Hill, 1965
The Night Caller, 1965
The Idol, 1966
Tobruk, 1966
Grand Prix, 1966
The Strange Affair, 1967
The Devil's Brigade, 1968
Decline and Fall, 1968
Midas Run, 1969
Every Home Should Have One,
1970
The Mackenzie Break, 1971
Kidnapped, 1971
Tower of Evil, 1972
From Beyond the Grave, 1973

Juggernaut, 1974
11 Harrowhouse, 1974
Brannigan, 1974
Treasure Island, 1976
Schizo, 1978
The Wild Geese, 1978
Ffolkes, 1980
The Sea Wolves, 1980
Masada, 1980

WYLIE WATSON (1889-1966)
Scottish character comedian
with music hall experience; former singer (1895). Usually seen
in henpecked characterizations.

For the Love of Mike, 1932
Leave it to Me, 1933
Hawleys of High Street, 1933
The Thirty-Nine Steps, 1935
Black Mask, 1935
Radio Lover, 1936
Please Teacher, 1937
Why Pick On Me?, 1937
Paradise For Two, 1937
Queer Cargo, 1938
Gaiety Girls, 1938
Yes Madam, 1938
Jamaica Inn, 1939
She Couldn't Say No, 1939
Pack Up Your Troubles, 1940
Bulldog Sees It Through, 1940
Danny Boy, 1941
My Wife's Family, 1941
The Saint Meets the Tiger, 1941
Mr. Proudfoot Shows a Light,
1941
The Flemish Farm, 1943
The Lamp Still Burns, 1943
Tawny Pipit, 1944
Kiss the Bride Goodbye, 1944
Don't Take it to Heart, 1944
Waterloo Road, 1945
The World Owes Me a Living,
1945
Strawberry Roan, 1945
Don Chicago, 1945
Waltz Time, 1945
Murder in Reverse, 1945
The Trojan Brothers, 1946
The Years Between, 1946
Girl in a Million, 1946

Temptation Harbour, 1947
Fame is the Spur, 1947
Brighton Rock, 1947
My Brother Jonathan, 1948
London Belongs to Me, 1948
No Room at the Inn, 1948
Things Happen at Night, 1948
Whiskey Galore, 1948
The History of Mr. Polly, 1949
Your Witness, 1950
Morning Departure, 1950
Shadow of the Past, 1950
The Magnet, 1950
Happy Go Lovely, 1951
The Sundowners, 1960

RICHARD WATTIS (1912-1975)
Bespectacled character star
with long stage experience;
nearly always seen in comedy
characterizations.

The Happiest Days of Your
    Life, 1950
The Clouded Yellow, 1950
Appointment With Venus, 1951
Mother Riley Meets the Vam-
    pire, 1952
Made in Heaven, 1952
The Importance of Being Earn-
    est, 1952
Top Secret, 1952
The Intruder, 1953
Background, 1953
Top of the Form, 1953
Appointment in London, 1953
Innocents in Paris, 1953
Blood Orange, 1953
Park Plaza 605, 1953
The Belles of St. Trinian's,
    1954
Lease of Life, 1954
Doctor in the House, 1954
Hobson's Choice, 1954
The Crowded Day, 1954
The Time of His Life, 1955
A Yank in Ermine, 1955
An Alligator Named Daisy,
    1955
I Am a Camera, 1955
Simon and Laura, 1955
The Colditz Story, 1955

See How They Run, 1955
Jumping For Joy, 1955
The Man Who Knew Too Much,
    1956
A Touch of the Sun, 1956
The Iron Petticoat, 1956
The Silken Affair, 1956
The Man Who Never Was, 1956
Eyewitness, 1956
It's a Wonderful World, 1956
The Green Man, 1956
The Prince and the Showgirl,
    1957
The Abominable Snowman, 1957
Second Fiddle, 1957
Barnacle Bill, 1957
Blue Murder at St. Trinian's,
    1958
Inn of the Sixth Happiness, 1958
The Ugly Duckling, 1959
Libel, 1959
The Captain's Table, 1959
Second to Hell, 1959
Left, Right, and Centre, 1959
Your Money Or Your Wife,
    1960
Follow a Star, 1960
Follow That Horse, 1960
Very Important Person, 1961
Dentist On the Job, 1961
Nearly a Nasty Accident, 1961
Play It Cool, 1962
I Thank a Fool, 1962
The VIPs, 1963
Come Fly With Me, 1963
Carry On Spying, 1964
Moll Flanders, 1965
Up Jumped a Swagman, 1965
Battle of the Villa Fiorita, 1965
You Must be Joking!, 1965
Bunny Lake is Missing, 1965
Operation Crossbow, 1965
The Alphabet Murders, 1965
The Liquidator, 1966
The Great St. Trinian's Train
    Robbery, 1966
Casino Royale, 1967
Wonderwall, 1968
Chitty Chitty Bang Bang, 1968
Monte Carlo Or Bust, 1969
Games That Lovers Play, 1970
Egghead's Robot, 1970
Tam Lin, 1972

That's Your Funeral, 1972
Hot Property, 1973
Diamonds On Wheels, 1973
Confessions of a Window
  Cleaner, 1974

DODO WATTS (1910-)
Leading actress of stage (from
1924) and early sound films.

Confessions, 1925
Double Dealing, 1928
Auld Lang Syne, 1929
School For Scandal, 1930
Realities, 1930
Almost a Honeymoon, 1930
The Middle Watch, 1930
The Man From Chicago, 1930
Uneasy Virtue, 1931
My Wife's Family, 1931
Her Night Out, 1932
Honeymoon in Devon, 1932
Little Fella, 1932
Impromptu, 1932
Hundred to One, 1933
Dora, 1933
Eight Cylinder Love, 1934
Wedding Eve, 1935
Sing Along With Me, 1952

NAUNTON WAYNE (1901-1970)
Light comedy actor of stage
(since 1920) and films, long in
partnership with Basil Radord
as traveling Englishmen.

The First Mrs. Fraser, 1932
For the Love of You, 1933
Going Gay, 1933
The Lady Vanishes, 1938
A Girl Must Live, 1939
Night Train to Munich, 1940
Crooks' Tour, 1940
Partners in Crime, 1942
Next of Kin, 1942
Millions Like Us, 1943
Girl in a Million, 1945
Dead of Night, 1945
The Calendar, 1947
Quartet, 1948
It's Not Cricket, 1949

Obsession, 1949
Passport to Pimlico, 1949
Stop Press Girl, 1949
Double Confession, 1950
Trio, 1950
Highly Dangerous, 1950
Circle of Danger, 1951
The Happy Family, 1952
Tall Headlines, 1952
Treasure Hunt, 1952
The Titfield Thunderbolt, 1953
You Know What Sailors Are,
  1954
Operation Bullshine, 1959
Double Bunk, 1961
Nothing Barred, 1961

ALAN WEBB (1906-)
Character player of the 60s and
70s, frequently on stage.

Challenge to Lassie, 1950
The Third Secret, 1964
The Pumpkin Eater, 1964
King Rat, 1965
Chimes at Midnight, 1966
The Taming of the Shrew, 1967
Interlude, 1968
Women in Love, 1969
King Lear, 1970
Entertaining Mr. Sloane, 1970
Nicholas and Alexandra, 1971
The Duellists, 1977
The Great Train Robbery, 1979
Rough Cut, 1980

HARRY WELCHMAN (1886-1966)
Musical comedy star and stage
(from 1904) actor who played
character parts in films.

Verdict of the Heart, 1915
Mr. Lyndon at Liberty, 1915
The Lyons Mail, 1916
Princess of the Blood, 1916
The House On the Marsh, 1920
Holiday Husband, 1920
The Maid of the Mountains, 1932
A Southern Maid, 1933
The Last Waltz, 1936
The Common Touch, 1941
This Was Paris, 1942

The Gentle Sex, 1943
Life and Death of Colonel
Blimp, 1943
Waltz Time, 1945
Lisbon Story, 1946
I'll Turn to You, 1946
Loyal Heart, 1946
Green Fingers, 1947
Judgement Deferred, 1952
Eight O'clock Walk, 1954
Mad About Men, 1954

BEN WELDEN (1901-)
Character actor and supporting
player of the 30s and 40s, also
in Hollywood.

The Man From Chicago, 1930
Big Business, 1930
Who Killed Doc Robin?, 1931
77 Park Lane, 1931
The Missing Rembrandt, 1932
His Lordship, 1932
Born Lucky, 1932
Innocents of Chicago, 1932
Home Sweet Home, 1933
Send 'Em Back Half Dead,
1933
Puppets of Fate, 1933
The Medicine Man, 1933
Mr. Quincey of Monte Carlo,
1933
Their Night Out, 1933
His Grace Gives Notice, 1933
This is the Life, 1933
Pride of the Force, 1933
General John Regan, 1933
Mannequin, 1933
Aunt Sally, 1934
River Wolves, 1934
The Black Abbot, 1934
The Man Who Changed His
Name, 1934
Gay Love, 1934
The Medium, 1934
Annie Leave the Room, 1935
Death On the Set, 1935
Royal Cavalcade, 1935
The Big Splash, 1935
Admirals All, 1935
Alibi Inn, 1935
Come Out of the Pantry, 1935

The Mystery of the Mary
Celeste, 1935
Trust the Navy, 1935
The Triumph of Sherlock
Holmes, 1935
The Avenging Hand, 1936
Hot News, 1936
The Improper Duchess, 1936
She Knew What She Wanted,
1936
Marked Woman, 1937
The Great Barrier, 1937
The King and the Chorus Girl,
1937
Kid Galahad, 1937
Another Dawn, 1937
Confession, 1937
Varsity Show, 1937
That Certain Woman, 1937
Back in Circulation, 1937
Alcatraz Island, 1937
Love is On the Air, 1937
Missing Witness, 1937
Crime Ring, 1938
Happy Landing, 1938
Prison Nurse, 1938
The Saint in New York, 1938
Always Goodbye, 1938
Mystery House, 1938
Smashing the Rackets, 1938
Tenth Avenue Kid, 1938
Straight Place and Show, 1938
Hollywood Cavalcade, 1939
Federal Manhunt, 1939
The Lone Wolf Spy Hunt, 1939
I Was a Convict, 1939
Sergeant Madden, 1939
The Star Maker, 1939
Rose of Washington Square, 1939
It's in the Bag, 1940
Outside the Three Mile Limit,
1940
Passport to Alcatraz, 1940
South of Pago Pago, 1940
City For Conquest, 1940
Men of Boy's Town, 1941
Strange Alibi, 1941
I'll Wait For You, 1941
Manpower, 1941
Nine Lives Are Not Enough,
1941
All Through the Night, 1942
Dangerously They Live, 1942

Bullet Scars, 1942
Stand By For Action, 1943
Appointment With Murder, 1943
The Fighting Seabees, 1944
Shadows in the Night, 1944
Search For Danger, 1945
Circumstantial Evidence, 1945
Angel On My Shoulder, 1945
Fighting Fools, 1946
Anna and the King of Siam,
  1946
The Pretender, 1947
The Noose Hangs High, 1948
Sorrowful Jones, 1949
Mary Ryan, Detective, 1949
Buccaneer's Girl, 1950
The Lemon Drop Kid, 1951
Robin Hood, 1952
All Ashore, 1953
Killers From Space, 1954
Ma and Pa Kettle at Waikiki,
  1955
Steel Cage, 1955
Hidden Guns, 1956

JOHN WELSH (1905-)
Gaunt character actor of stage,
films and television, notable in
series "The Duchess of Duke
Street II" (1980) and "The Forsyte Saga. " Usually plays persons of eminence.

The Divided Heart, 1954
An Inspector Calls, 1954
Confession, 1955
Lucky Jim, 1957
The Counterfeit Plan, 1957
The Long Haul, 1957
Man in the Shadow, 1957
The Surgeon's Knife, 1957
The Birthday Present, 1957
The Man Who Wouldn't Talk,
  1958
Revenge of Frankenstein, 1958
Behind the Mask, 1958
Next to No Time, 1958
Room at the Top, 1958
The Rough and the Smooth,
  1959
The Night We Dropped a
  Clanger, 1959

Beyond the Curtain, 1960
Follow That Horse, 1960
Snowball, 1960
Circle of Deception, 1961
Francis of Assisi, 1961
The Mark, 1961
The Square Mile Murder, 1961
Johnny Nobody, 1961
Playboy of the Western World,
  1962
The Quare Fellow, 1962
The Inspector, 1962
Go to Blazes, 1962
Nightmare, 1963
Dead End Creek, 1964
The Man Who Haunted Himself,
  1970
Cromwell, 1970
Unpleasantness at the Bellona
  Club, 1973
The Thirty-Nine Steps, 1980

LOCKWOOD WEST (1906-)
Friendly, mild-mannered character star mainly on stage;
films sporadic.

Celia, 1949
High Treason, 1951
Hammer the Toff, 1952
The Oracle, 1953
Accused, 1957
The Birthday Present, 1957
The Leather Boys, 1963
Game For Three Losers, 1965
Life at the Top, 1965
Bedazzled, 1967
A Dandy in Aspic, 1968
Jane Eyre, 1970
Clouds of Witness, 1973

TIMOTHY WEST (1934-)
Strong character actor of stage
and screen, also well-known on
television, notably as "Edward
VII. " Films infrequent.

Twisted Nerve, 1968
The Looking Glass War, 1970
Nicholas and Alexandra, 1971
Day of the Jackal, 1973
Hitler: The Last Ten Days, 1973

Hedda, 1976
Agatha, 1979
The Thirty Nine Steps, 1980
Churchill and the Generals, 1980
Rough Cut, 1980
Crime and Punishment, 1980

JOHN WESTBROOK (1922-)
Character actor primarily seen
on stage, films relatively few.

Room at the Top, 1958
A Foxhole in Cairo, 1960
A Prize of Arms, 1962
The Tomb of Ligeia, 1964
Masque of the Red Death, 1964
Ffolkes, 1980

DAVID WESTON (1938-)
General purpose actor of the
sixties, also on television.

Doctor in Distress, 1963
Becket, 1964
Masque of the Red Death, 1964
The Legend of Young Dick Tur-
    pin, 1965
The Heroes of Telemark, 1965
The Red Baron, 1970

VIRGINIA WETHERELL
    (1943-)
Supporting actress of the 60s
and 70s, also on stage.

Ricochet, 1963
Alfie, 1966
The Big Switch, 1967
Mrs. Brown, You've Got a
    Lovely Daughter, 1968
Curse of the Crimson Altar,
    1969
Cause For Alarm, 1970
Man of Violence, 1970
A Clockwork Orange, 1971
Dr. Jekyll and Sister Hyde,
    1971
Demons of the Mind, 1972
Disciple of Death, 1972
Dracula, 1973

ALAN WHEATLEY (1907-)
Character actor of stage, films
and television, well-known in
the latter medium as the Sheriff
of Nottingham in series "Robin
Hood. "

Conquest of the Air, 1936
The Rake's Progress, 1945
Caesar and Cleopatra, 1945
Spring Song, 1946
Appointment With Crime, 1946
Jassy, 1947
Brighton Rock, 1947
End of the River, 1947
Counterblast, 1948
Calling Paul Temple, 1948
Corridor of Mirrors, 1948
Sleeping Car to Trieste, 1948
It's Not Cricket, 1949
For Them That Trespass, 1950
Home to Danger, 1951
Whispering Smith Hits London,
    1952
The Pickwick Papers, 1952
Spaceways, 1953
Devil's Plot, 1953
Small Town Story, 1953
The Limping Man, 1953
The Diamond, 1954
House Across the Lake, 1954
Delayed Action, 1954
Simon and Laura, 1955
The Duke Wore Jeans, 1958
Inn For Trouble, 1960
Shadow of the Cat, 1961
Checkmate, 1961
Frederic Chopin, 1961
Tomorrow at Ten, 1963
Clash By Night, 1963
A Jolly Bad Fellow, 1964

MANNING WHILEY (1915-)
Character actor of the forties,
often cast in ominous or menacing parts.

Consider Your Verdict, 1938
Trunk Crime, 1939
Gasbags, 1940
Contraband, 1940
Pastor Hall, 1940

The Flying Squad, 1940
Saloon Bar, 1940
Pack Up Your Troubles, 1940
Sailors Three, 1940
Old Bill and Son, 1940
Freedom Radio, 1941
Pimpernel Smith, 1941
The Ghost of St. Michael's,
   1941
The Saint's Vacation, 1941
The Dummy Talks, 1943
Bell Bottom George, 1943
Meet Sexton Blake, 1944
The Seventh Veil, 1945
For You Alone, 1945
The Shop at Sly Corner, 1946
Teheran, 1947
Uncle Silas, 1947
Children of Chance, 1949
Little Big Shot, 1952

GWYNNE WHITBY (1903-)
Small-part character actress
of stage and occasional films.

Quiet Weekend, 1946
Mine Own Executioner, 1947
The Blue Lamp, 1950
I Believe in You, 1951
Turn the Key Softly, 1953
Time Without Pity, 1957

BARBARA WHITE (1924-)
Leading actress of occasional
films of the forties.

It Happened One Sunday, 1944
The Voice Within, 1945
Quiet Weekend, 1946
While the Sun Shines, 1947
Mine Own Executioner, 1947
This Was a Woman, 1948
All About Eve, 1950

CAROL WHITE (1941-)
Attractive blonde leading lady
of the 60s and 70s, former
child actress.   Also in Hollywood.

Circus Friends, 1956
Carry On Teacher, 1959
Never Let Go, 1960
Beat Girl, 1960
Linda, 1960
A Matter of WHO, 1961
Man in the Back Seat, 1961
The Boys, 1962
Village of Daughters, 1962
Bon Voyage, 1962
Gaolbreak, 1962
Ladies Who Do, 1963
The Playground, 1965
Slave Girls, 1966
I'll Never Forget Whatsisname,
   1967
The Fixer, 1968
Poor Cow, 1968
Daddy's Gone a Hunting, 1969
The Man Who Had Power Over
   Women, 1970
Dulcima, 1971
Something Big, 1971
Made, 1972
Some Call it Loving, 1973
The Squeeze, 1977
The Spaceman & King Arthur,
   1979

J. FISHER WHITE (-)
Character actor and supporting
player of the twenties and thirties.

Nobody's Child, 1919
Damaged Goods, 1919
The Will, 1921
Diana of the Crossways, 1922
Bentley's Conscience, 1922
Owd Bob, 1924
The Perfect Crime, 1925
The Only Way, 1925
Somebody's Darling, 1925
One Colombo Night, 1926
Island of Despair, 1926
Blinkeyes, 1926
Thou Fool, 1926
Somehow Good, 1927
The Fake, 1927
Triumph of the Scarlet Pimper-
   nel, 1928

Balaclava, 1928
The Last Post, 1928
City of Youth, 1928
Lily of Killarney, 1929
Loose Ends, 1930
Kissing Cup's Race, 1930
Dreyfus, 1931
Madame Guillotine, 1931
Man of Mayfair, 1931
Many Waters, 1931
Betrayal, 1932
The Wonderful Story, 1932
The Good Companions, 1933
Counsel's Opinion, 1933
A Cup of Kindness, 1934
The Great Defender, 1934
What Happened Then, 1934
The Old Curiosity Shop, 1934
The City of Beautiful Nonsense,
  1935
The Turn of the Tide, 1935
Hearts of Humanity, 1936
As You Like It, 1936
Dreaming Lips, 1937
Under the Red Robe, 1937
Moonlight Sonata, 1937
The Man Who Made Diamonds,
  1937
The Bells of St. Mary's, 1937
Little Miss Somebody, 1937
Breakers Ahead, 1938
All Living Things, 1939
Pastor Hall, 1940

VALERIE WHITE (1916-)
Character actress seen in occasional, sporadic productions.

Halfway House, 1944
My Learned Friend, 1944
Hue and Cry, 1946
Home and Away, 1956
Travels With My Aunt, 1972

BILLIE WHITELAW (1932-)
Prominent, intense actress of
stage (since 1950), screen and
television; former radio personality. Formerly married
to Peter Vaughan.

The Fake, 1953
The Sleeping Tiger, 1954
Miracle in Soho, 1957
Small Hotel, 1957
Carve Her Name With Pride,
  1958
Breakout, 1958
Bobbikins, 1959
The Flesh and the Fiends, 1960
Hell is a City, 1960
Make Mine Mink, 1960
No Love For Johnnie, 1961
Mr. Topaze, 1961
Payroll, 1961
The Devil's Agent, 1962
The Comedy Man, 1963
Becket, 1964
Charlie Bubbles, 1967
Twisted Nerve, 1968
Dr. Jekyll and Mr. Hyde, 1968
The Adding Machine, 1969
Leo the Last, 1970
Start the Revolution Without
  Me, 1970
Gumshoe, 1971
Eagle in a Cage, 1971
Frenzy, 1972
Night Watch, 1973
The Omen, 1976
The Water Babies, 1979

JON WHITELEY (1945-)
Juvenile player who gave some
memorable performances in the
fifties.

Hunted, 1952
The Kidnappers, 1953
Moonfleet, 1955
The Weapon, 1956
The Spanish Gardener, 1956
The Capetown Affair, 1967

LEONARD WHITING (1950-)
Youthful leading man of the sixties and seventies.

The Legend of Young Dick Turpin, 1965
Romeo and Juliet, 1968

The Royal Hunt of the Sun, 1969
Young Casanova, 1970
Say Hello to Yesterday, 1971
Frankenstein: The True Story,
1973
Rachel's Man, 1975

PAUL WHITSUN-JONES
(1923-1974)
Portly comedy character
player of the 50s and 60s,
also on stage.

The Passing Stranger, 1954
Stock Car, 1955
The Constant Husband, 1955
The Moonraker, 1958
Room at the Top, 1958
Wrong Number, 1959
Tunes of Glory, 1960
Candidate For Murder, 1962
The £20,000 Kiss, 1963
The Wild Affair, 1963
Masque of the Red Death, 1964
Life at the Top, 1965
What's Good For the Goose,
1969
Simon Simon, 1970
All the Right Noises, 1970
Dr. Jekyll and Sister Hyde,
1971

DAME MAY WHITTY (1865-
1948)
Distinguished, dignified character actress of stage (since
1881) and screen, in Hollywood
from the mid-thirties. Generally cast as authoritative
but kindly old ladies.

Enoch Arden, 1915
Colonel Newcome the Perfect
Gentleman, 1920
Night Must Fall, 1937
The Thirteenth Chair, 1937
Conquest, 1937
I Met My Love Again, 1938
The Lady Vanishes, 1938
Raffles, 1939
A Bill of Divorcement, 1940

One Night in Lisbon, 1941
Suspicion, 1941
Mrs. Miniver, 1942
Thunder Birds, 1942
Forever and a Day, 1943
Slightly Dangerous, 1943
Crash Dive, 1943
Stage Door Canteen, 1943
The Constant Nymph, 1943
Lassie Come Home, 1943
Flesh and Fantasy, 1943
Madame Curie, 1943
The White Cliffs of Dover,
1944
Gaslight, 1944
My Name is Julia Ross, 1945
Devotion, 1946
Green Dolphin Street, 1947
This Time For Keeps, 1947
If Winter Comes, 1948
The Sign of the Ram, 1948
The Return of October, 1948

HENRY WILCOXON (1905-)
Leading man of stage (since
1927) and screen, in Hollywood
from mid-thirties. Former
salesman.

The Perfect Lady, 1931
Two-Way Street, 1931
Self-Made Lady, 1932
The Flying Squad, 1932
Taxi to Paradise, 1933
Lord of the Manor, 1933
Cleopatra, 1934
The Crusades, 1935
Princess Charming, 1935
Last of the Mohicans, 1936
A Woman Alone, 1936
The President's Mystery, 1936
Jericho, 1937
Souls at Sea, 1937
Prison Nurse, 1938
Keep Smiling, 1938
Mysterious Mr. Moto, 1938
Dark Sands, 1938
Five of a Kind, 1938
If I Were King, 1938
Woman Doctor, 1939
Tarzan Finds a Son, 1939
Free, Blonde and 21, 1940

Earthbound, 1940
Mystery Sea Raider, 1940
The Crooked Road, 1940
South of Tahiti, 1941
That Hamilton Woman, 1941
The Lone Wolf Takes a Chance,
 1941
Scotland Yard, 1941
The Corsican Brothers, 1941
The Man Who Wouldn't Die,
 1942
Mrs. Miniver, 1942
Johnny Doughboy, 1943
Unconquered, 1947
The Dragnet, 1947
A Connecticut Yankee in King
 Arthur's Court, 1949
Samson and Delilah, 1949
The Miniver Story, 1950
The Greatest Show On Earth,
 1952
Scaramouche, 1952
The Ten Commandments, 1956
The War Lord, 1965
The Private Navy of Sergeant
 O'Farrell, 1968
Man in the Wilderness, 1971
Against a Crooked Sky, 1975
Pony Express Rider, 1976
When Every Day Was the 4th
 of July, 1978
FIST, 1979

JACK WILD (1952-)
Juvenile actor of the 60s and
70s, also on television in
series "H R Puffenstuff."
(1970).

Danny the Dragon, 1967
Oliver, 1968
Melody, 1970
Flight of the Doves, 1971
The Pied Piper, 1972
The Fourteen, 1973

MICHAEL WILDING (1912-
 1979)
Charming, gentlemanly leading
man of stage (1933) and screen,
also in Hollywood. Married:

Elizabeth Taylor; Margaret
Leighton.

Pastorale, 1933
Wedding Group, 1935
There Ain't No Justice, 1939
Tilly of Bloomsbury, 1940
Sailors Don't Care, 1940
Sailors Three, 1940
Convoy, 1940
The Farmer's Wife, 1941
Mr. Proudfoot Shows a Light,
 1941
Kipps, 1941
Cottage to Let, 1941
Ships With Wings, 1941
Spring Meeting, 1942
The Big Blockade, 1942
Secret Mission, 1942
In Which We Serve, 1942
Undercover, 1943
Dear Octopus, 1943
English Without Tears, 1944
Piccadilly Incident, 1946
Carnival, 1946
The Courtneys of Curzon Street,
 1947
An Ideal Husband, 1948
Spring in Park Lane, 1948
Maytime in Mayfair, 1949
Under Capricorn, 1949
Stage Fright, 1950
Into the Blue, 1951
Lady With a Lamp, 1951
The Law and the Lady, 1951
Derby Day, 1952
Trent's Last Case, 1952
Torch Song, 1953
The Egyptian, 1954
The Glass Slipper, 1955
The Scarlet Coat, 1955
Zarak, 1956
Hello London, 1958
Danger Within, 1959
The World of Suzie Wong, 1960
The Naked Edge, 1961
The Best of Enemies, 1961
A Girl Named Tamiko, 1963
The Fatal Mistake, 1966
The Sweet Ride, 1968
Operation Red Roses, 1968
The Madwoman of Chaillot, 1969
Waterloo, 1970

Lady Caroline Lamb, 1972
Frankenstein: The True Story,
1973

BRANSBY WILLIAMS (1870-
1964)
Eminent actor of stage, music
halls (1896) and films; former
clerk. Father of silent star
Eric Bransby Williams (1900-
19).

Royal England, 1911
The Seven Ages of Man, 1914
Bernardo's Confession, 1914
Grimaldi, 1914
The Street Watchman's Story, 1914
Hard Times, 1915
The Greatest Wish in the World,
1918
Adam Bede, 1918
The Adventures of Mr. Pick-
wick, 1921
Scrooge, 1928
Grandfather Smallweed, 1928
Soldiers of the King, 1933
Hearts of Humanity, 1936
Song of the Road, 1937
The Common Touch, 1941
Those Kids From Town, 1942
Tomorrow We Live, 1942
The Agitator, 1945
The Trojan Brothers, 1946
Judgement Deferred, 1952

D. J. WILLIAMS (-)
Dour, aged character actor of
the thirties, often seen as
curmudgeon.

A Highwayman's Honour, 1914
The Inheritance, 1920
The Pointing Finger, 1933
Doctor's Orders, 1934
The Poisoned Diamond, 1934
River Wolves, 1934
A Glimpse of Paradise, 1934
Lily of Killarney, 1934
The Admiral's Secret, 1934
Anything Might Happen, 1934
The Morals of Marcus, 1935

Scrooge, 1935
Maria Marten, 1935
Look Up and Laugh, 1935
Captain Bill, 1935
Sweeney Todd, 1936
The Crimes of Stephen Hawke,
1936
The Beloved Vagabond, 1936
Wings of the Morning, 1937
Elephant Boy, 1937
The House of Silence, 1937
It's Never Too Late to Mend,
1937
The Fatal Hour, 1937
Boys Will be Girls, 1937
Mr. Reeder in Room 13, 1938
John Halifax Gentleman, 1938
Ghost Tales Retold, 1938
The Ghost Train, 1940
Penn of Pennsylvania, 1941
Those Kids From Town, 1942

EMLYN WILLIAMS (1905-)
Distinguished Welsh actor of
stage (from 1927) and films,
also in Hollywood. Also playwright (The Corn is Green,
Night Must Fall, etc.).

The Frightened Lady, 1932
Men of Tomorrow, 1932
Sally Bishop, 1932
Friday the Thirteenth, 1933
My Song For You, 1933
Evensong, 1933
Roadhouse, 1934
The Iron Duke, 1935
Love Affair of the Dictator,
1935
The City of Beautiful Nonsense,
1935
Broken Blossoms, 1936
I Claudius, 1937
Dead Men Tell No Tales, 1938
A Night Alone, 1938
The Citadel, 1938
They Drive By Night, 1938
Jamaica Inn, 1939
The Stars Look Down, 1939
Mr. Borland Thinks Again,
1940
The Girl in the News, 1940

You Will Remember, 1940
This England, 1941
Hatter's Castle, 1941
Major Barbara, 1941
The Last Days of Dolwyn, 1949
Three Husbands, 1950
The Screen, 1950
The Scarf, 1951
Another Man's Poison, 1951
The Magic Box, 1951
Ivanhoe, 1952
The Deep Blue Sea, 1955
I Accuse!, 1958
Beyond This Place, 1959
Wreck of the Mary Deare,
  1959
The L-Shaped Room, 1962
The Wild Duck, 1962
Eye of the Devil, 1966
David Copperfield, 1969
The Walking Stick, 1970

HARCOURT WILLIAMS (1880-
1957)
Distinguished actor of stage
who played important character
roles in films of the 40s and
50s.

Henry V, 1944
Brighton Rock, 1947
Hamlet, 1948
Third Time Lucky, 1948
Vice Versa, 1948
No Room at the Inn, 1948
For Them That Trespass,
  1949
Trottie True, 1949
Under Capricorn, 1949
The Lost People, 1949
Eye Witness, 1950
Cage of Gold, 1950
The Late Edwina Black, 1951
The Magic Box, 1951
Roman Holiday, 1953
Time Bomb, 1953
The Blakes Slept Here, 1954
The Flying Eye, 1955
Quentin Durward, 1955
Around the World in 80 Days,
  1956

HUGH WILLIAMS (1904-1969)
Suave leading man of stage
(since 1921) and films, also in
Hollywood. Also playwright.
Son: Simon Williams.

Charley's Aunt, 1930
A Night in Montmartre, 1931
Gentleman of Paris, 1931
In a Monastery Garden, 1932
Whiteface, 1932
Down Our Street, 1932
Insult, 1932
After Dark, 1932
Rome Express, 1932
Bitter Sweet, 1933
The Jewel, 1933
Sorrell and Son, 1933
This Acting Business, 1933
Outcast Lady, 1934
Let's Live Tonight, 1935
David Copperfield, 1935
Lieutenant Daring RN, 1935
The Last Journey, 1935
Her Last Affaire, 1935
The Amateur Gentleman, 1936
The Man Behind the Mask, 1936
The Happy Family, 1936
Gypsy, 1937
Side Street Angel, 1937
The Windmill, 1937
The Perfect Crime, 1937
Brief Ecstasy, 1937
The Dark Stairway, 1938
Bank Holiday, 1938
Dead Men Tell No Tales, 1938
Premiere, 1938
His Lordship Goes to Press,
  1938
Inspector Hornleigh, 1939
Dark Eyes of London, 1939
Wuthering Heights, 1939
Ships With Wings, 1941
Secret Mission, 1942
One of Our Aircraft is Missing,
  1942
The Day Will Dawn, 1942
Talk About Jacqueline, 1942
Girl in a Million, 1946
Take My Life, 1947
An Ideal Husband, 1948
The Blind Goddess, 1948

Elizabeth of Ladymead, 1949
Paper Orchid, 1949
The Romantic Age, 1949
The Gift Horse, 1952
The Holly and the Ivy, 1952
The Fake, 1953
The Intruder, 1953
Twice Upon a Time, 1953
Star of My Night, 1954
Khartoum, 1966
Dr. Faustus, 1967

JOHN WILLIAMS (1903-)
Tall, polished character actor
of stage (since 1916), films
and tv, mainly in Hollywood.
Frequently seen as police in-
spectors or in comedy parts.

Next of Kin, 1942
The Foreman Went to France,
  1942
A Woman's Vengeance, 1947
The Paradine Case, 1947
Kind Lady, 1950
Dick Turpin's Ride, 1951
Thunder in the East, 1953
Dial M For Murder, 1954
The Student Prince, 1954
Sabrina, 1954
To Catch a Thief, 1955
D-Day, the Sixth of June, 1956
The Solid Gold Cadillac, 1956
Island in the Sun, 1957
Will Success Spoil Rock Hun-
  ter?, 1957
Witness For the Prosecution,
  1957
The Young Philadelphians,
  1959
Visit to a Small Planet, 1960
Midnight Lace, 1960
Dear Brigitte, 1965
Harlow, 1965
Last of the Secret Agents, 1966
Double Trouble, 1967
The Secret War of Harry Frigg,
  1968
A Flea in Her Ear, 1968
The Hound of the Baskervilles,
  1972
Lost in the Stars, 1974

No Deposit No Return, 1976
Hot Lead and Cold Feet, 1978

KENNETH WILLIAMS (1926-)
Comedy actor of radio (specializing in funny voices), stage,
films and television; a member
of the "Carry On" team.

Trent's Last Case, 1952
Valley of Song, 1953
The Beggar's Opera, 1953
The Seekers, 1954
Carry On Sergeant, 1958
Carry On Nurse, 1959
Carry On Teacher, 1959
Tommy the Toreador, 1959
Carry On Constable, 1960
Make Mine Mink, 1960
His and Hers, 1961
Carry On Regardless, 9161
Raising the Wind, 1961
Twice Round the Daffodils, 1962
Carry On Cruising, 1962
Carry On Jack, 1963
Carry On Spying, 1964
Carry On Cleo, 1964
Carry On Cowboy, 1965
Carry On Screaming, 1966
Carry On Don't Lose Your Head,
  1966
Carry On Follow That Camel,
  1967
Carry On Doctor, 1968
Carry On Up the Khyber, 1968
Carry On Camping, 1969
Carry On Again Doctor, 1969
Carry On Loving, 1970
Carry On Henry VIII, 1970
Carry On at Your Convenience,
  1971
Carry On Matron, 1972
Carry On Abroad, 1972
Carry On Dick, 1974
Carry On Behind, 1975
Carry On England, 1976
Carry On Emmanuelle, 1978
Hound of the Baskervilles, 1978

RHYS WILLIAMS (1897-1969)
Strong-looking Welsh character

actor in Hollywood films; former technical advisor.   Equally
adept at kindly or shady characters.

How Green Was My Valley,
   1941
This Above All, 1942
Remember Pearl Harbor, 1942
Mrs. Miniver, 1942
Cairo, 1942
Gentleman Jim, 1942
Random Harvest, 1942
No Time For Love, 1943
The Corn is Green, 1945
Blood On the Sun, 1945
You Came Along, 1945
The Bells of St. Mary's, 1945
The Spiral Staircase, 1946
So Goes My Love, 1946
Cross My Heart, 1946
Easy Come, Easy Go, 1946
The Strange Woman, 1947
The Farmer's Daughter, 1947
The Imperfect Lady, 1947
Moss Rose, 1947
The Trouble With Women,
   1947
If Winter Comes, 1948
The Black Arrow, 1948
The Hills of Home, 1948
Tenth Avenue Angel, 1948
Bad Boy, 1949
The Crooked Way, 1949
Tokyo Joe, 1949
Fighting Man of the Plains,
   1949
The Inspector General, 1949
Kiss Tomorrow Goodbye, 1950
Devil's Doorway, 1950
California Passage, 1950
The Son of Dr. Jekyll, 1951
Lightning Strikes Twice, 1951
The Sword of Monte Cristo,
   1951
Never Trust a Gambler, 1951
The Law and the Lady, 1951
The Light Touch, 1952
Mutiny, 1952
Okinawa, 1952
Meet Me at the Fair, 1952
The Plymouth Adventure, 1952
Carbine Williams, 1952

Les Miserables, 1952
The World in His Arms, 1952
Julius Caesar, 1953
Scandal at Scourie, 1953
Bad For Each Other, 1953
Man in the Attic, 1954
Johnny Guitar, 1954
The Black Shield of Falworth,
   1954
There's No Business Like Show
   Business, 1954
How to be Very, Very Popular,
   1955
The Scarlet Coat, 1955
Mowhawk, 1955
The King's Thief, 1955
The Kentuckian, 1955
Nightmare, 1956
Fastest Gun Alive, 1956
Raintree County, 1957
Merry Andrew, 1958
Midnight Lace, 1960
The Sons of Katie Elder, 1965
Our Man Flint, 1966
Skullduggery, 1970

SIMON WILLIAMS (-)
Light leading man of stage and
television ("Upstairs Downstairs")
who much resembles his father,
Hugh Williams. Films infrequent.

Blood On Satan's Claw, 1970
The Incredible Sarah, 1976
Jabberwocky, 1977
The Uncanny, 1977
No Longer Alone, 1978
The Prisoner of Zenda, 1979
The Fiendish Plot of Dr. Fu
   Manchu, 1980

NICOL WILLIAMSON (1939-)
Dramatic Scottish leading man
of stage (since 1960) and films.

Six Sided Triangle, 1964
The Bofors Gun, 1968
Inadmissible Evidence, 1968
Hamlet, 1969
Laughter in the Dark, 1969
The Reckoning, 1970

The Jerusalem File, 1972
The Wilby Conspiracy, 1975
Robin and Marian, 1976
The Seven Per Cent Solution,
  1976
The Goodbye Girl, 1977
The Cheap Detective, 1978
The Human Factor, 1980

NOEL WILLMAN (1918-   )
Character actor of stage and
films, often seen in villainous
portrayals. Also stage director.

The Pickwick Papers, 1952
Androcles and the Lion, 1953
The Net, 1953
Beau Brummell, 1954
The Dark Avenger, 1955
The Man Who Knew Too Much,
  1956
Seven Waves Away, 1957
Across the Bridge, 1957
Carve Her Name With Pride, 1958
Cone of Silence, 1960
The Criminal, 1960
Never Let Go, 1960
Two Living One Dead, 1961
The Girl On the Boat, 1961
Kiss of the Vampire, 1963
Dr. Zhivago, 1965
The Reptile, 1965
The Vengeance of She, 1968
The Odessa File, 1974
21 Hours at Munich, 1976

DOUGLAS WILMER (1920-   )
Intense character actor, also
seen on stage and television.

Men of Sherwood Forest, 1954
Richard III, 1955
The Right Person, 1955
Passport to Treason, 1956
Battle of the River Plate, 1956
An Honourable Murder, 1960
El Cid, 1961
Cleopatra, 1962
Jason and the Argonauts, 1963
A Shot in the Dark, 1964

Fall of the Roman Empire,
  1964
One Way Pendulum, 1964
The Brides of Fu Manchu, 1966
Khartoum, 1966
Vengeance of Fu Manchu, 1968
Hammerhead, 1968
A Nice Girl Like Me, 1969
The Vampire Lovers, 1970
The Reckoning, 1970
Patton, 1970
Cromwell, 1970
Unman Wittering and Zigo,
  1971
The Golden Voyage of Sinbad,
  1973
The Adventures of Sherlock
  Holmes' Smarter Brother,
  1975
The Incredible Sarah, 1976
Rough Cut, 1980

SUNDAY WILSHIN (1905-   )
Actress popular during the
thirties; also on stage (from
1915).

Pages of Life, 1922
The Green Caravan, 1922
Champagne, 1928
Hours of Loneliness, 1930
Bedrock, 1930
Michael and Mary, 1931
Chance of a Nighttime, 1931
Collision, 1932
Dance Pretty Lady, 1932
Nine Till Six, 1932
The Love Contract, 1932
Marry Me, 1932
To Brighton With Gladys, 1933
As Good as New, 1933
Borrowed Clothes, 1934
Some Day, 1935
Murder By Rope, 1936

IAN WILSON (-)
Supporting player of the 20s
and 30s, latterly seen in small-
part character roles.

The Master of Craft, 1922

Through Fire and Water, 1923
The Cavern Spider, 1924
The Fighting Gladiator, 1926
Shooting Stars, 1928
What Next?, 1928
The Dizzy Limit, 1930
Splinters in the Navy, 1931
Heroes of the Mine, 1932
The Bailiffs, 1932
Oh For a Plumber!, 1933
The Unholy Quest, 1934
The Broken Rosary, 1934
Polly's Two Fathers, 1936
Song of the Forge, 1937
The Lady Craved Excitement, 1950
How to Murder a Rich Uncle, 1957
Happy is the Bride, 1958
Phantom of the Opera, 1962
Carry On Cabby, 1963
Carry On Jack, 1963
Rotten to the Core, 1965
Ouch!, 1967

BARBARA WINDSOR (1937-)
Blonde comedy actress of the
sixties usually seen in cockney
roles.

Lost, 1955
Too Hot to Handle, 1960
Hair of the Dog, 1962
Death Trap, 1962
Sparrows Can't Sing, 1963
Crooks in Cloisters, 1963
Carry On Spying, 1964
San Ferry Ann, 1965
A Study in Terror, 1965
Chitty Chitty Bang Bang, 1968
Carry On Doctor, 1968
Carry On Camping, 1969
Carry On Again Doctor, 1969
The Boy Friend, 1971
Carry On Henry VIII, 1971
Carry On Matron, 1972

VINCENT WINTER (1947-)
Scottish juvenile actor who
offered some memorable performances in the 50s.

The Kidnappers, 1953
The Witness, 1954

The Dark Avenger, 1955
Day of Grace, 1957
Time Lock, 1957
The Bridal Path, 1959
Beyond This Place, 1959
Greyfriars Bobby, 1960
Gorgo, 1961
Born to Sing, 1961
The Horse Without a Head, 1962
The Three Lives of Thomasina,
   1963

ESTELLE WINWOOD (1882-)
Noted character actress of
stage and screen, long in Hollywood; generally seen as eccentrics.   Films sporadic.

The House of Trent, 1933
Quality Street, 1937
The Glass Slipper, 1955
The Swan, 1956
23 Paces to Baker Street, 1956
This Happy Feeling, 1957
Alive and Kicking, 1958
Darby O'Gill & the Little Peo-
   ple, 1959
The Misfits, 1961
The Cabinet of Caligari, 1962
Notorious Landlady, 1962
Dead Ringer, 1964
Games, 1967
Camelot, 1967
The Producers, 1968
Jenny, 1970
Murder By Death, 1976

NORMAN WISDOM (1918-)
Slapstick comedian of stage
(since 1946), television (1948)
and films; former soldier.

A Date With a Dream, 1948
Trouble in Store, 1953
Meet Mr. Lucifer, 1953
One Good Turn, 1954
As Long as They're Happy,
   1955
Man of the Moment, 1955
Up in the World, 1956
Just My Luck, 1957
The Square Peg, 1958

Follow a Star, 1959
The Bulldog Breed, 1960
There Was a Crooked Man,
1960
The Girl On the Boat, 1961
On the Beat, 1962
A Stitch in Time, 1963
The Early Bird, 1965
The Sandwich Man, 1966
Press For Time, 1966
The Night They Raided Minsky's,
1968
What's Good For the Goose,
1969

ERNIE WISE (1925-)
Music hall comedian teamed
with Eric Morecambe since
1943; became popular on tv
during the 60s. Films infrequent.

The Intelligence Men, 1965
That Riviera Touch, 1966
The Magnificent Two, 1967
Simon Simon, 1970

GOOGIE WITHERS (1917-)
Attractive dark-haired leading
actress of comedies and
dramas; former cabaret star
(1931). Married to John
McCallum.

The Girl in the Crowd, 1934
The Love Test, 1935
Windfall, 1935
Her Last Affaire, 1935
All at Sea, 1935
Dark World, 1935
Crown v Stevens, 1936
King of Hearts, 1936
She Knew What She Wanted,
1936
Accused, 1936
Crime Over London, 1936
Pearls Bring Tears, 1937
Paradise For Two, 1937
Paid in Error, 1938
If I Were Boss, 1938
Kate Plus Ten, 1938

Strange Boarders, 1938
Convict 99, 1938
The Lady Vanishes, 1938
You're the Doctor, 1938
Murder in Soho, 1939
Trouble Brewing, 1939
The Gang's All Here, 1939
She Couldn't Say No, 1939
Bulldog Sees it Through, 1940
Busman's Honeymoon, 1940
Jeannie, 1941
Back Room Boy, 1942
One of Our Aircraft is Missing,
1942
The Silver Fleet, 1943
On Approval, 1944
They Came to a City, 1944
Dead of Night, 1945
Pink String and Sealing Wax,
1945
The Loves of Joanna Godden,
1947
It Always Rains On Sunday,
1947
Miranda, 1948
Once Upon a Dream, 1948
Traveller's Joy, 1949
Night and the City, 1950
The Magic Box, 1951
White Corridors, 1951
Lady Godiva Rides Again, 1951
Derby Day, 1952
Devil On Horseback, 1954
Port of Escape, 1956
The Nickel Queen, 1970

SIR DONALD WOLFIT (1902-
1968)
Distinguished, commanding actor of stage (from 1920) and
screen, seen latterly in strong
character portrayals.

Inasmuch, 1934
The Wigan Express, 1934
Death at Broadcasting House,
1934
Drake of England, 1935
The Silent Passenger, 1935
Sexton Blake & the Bearded
Doctor, 1935
Checkmate, 1935

Late Extra, 1935
Hyde Park Corner, 1935
Calling the Tune, 1936
The Pickwick Papers, 1952
The Ringer, 1952
Isn't Life Wonderful, 1953
Svengali, 1954
A Prize of Gold, 1955
The Man On the Beach, 1956
The Man in the Road, 1956
Satellite in the Sky, 1956
Guilty, 1956
The Traitor, 1957
I Accuse!, 1958
Blood of the Vampire, 1958
Room at the Top, 1958
The Angry Hills, 1959
The Rough and the Smooth, 1959
House of the Seven Hawks, 1959
The Hands of Orlac, 1960
The Mark, 1961
Portrait of a Sinner, 1961
Lawrence of Arabia, 1962
Dr. Crippen, 1962
Becket, 1964
Life at the Top, 1965
Ninety Degrees in the Shade, 1965
The Sandwich Man, 1966
Decline and Fall, 1968
Charge of the Light Brigade, 1968

ARTHUR WONTNER (1875-1960)
Star of stage (1897) and films, quite excellent as Sherlock Holmes in several films of the 30s; latterly in character parts.

Temptation's Hour, 1916
Frailty, 1916
Lady Windermere's Fan, 1916
The Bigamist, 1916
Bonnie Prince Charlie, 1923
Shadow of Death, 1923
The Velvet Woman, 1923
The Battle of Love, 1923
Cage of Despair, 1923

The Last Stake, 1923
Secret Mission, 1923
Eugene Aram, 1924
The Diamond Man, 1924
Infamous Lady, 1928
The Message, 1930
The Sleeping Cardinal, 1931
Gentleman of Paris, 1931
Condemned to Death, 1932
The Missing Rembrandt, 1932
The Sign of Four, 1932
The Triumph of Sherlock Holmes, 1935
Line Engaged, 1935
Dishonour Bright, 1936
Second Bureau, 1936
Thunder in the City, 1937
Storm in a Teacup, 1937
Silver Blaze, 1937
The Live Wire, 1937
Just Like a Woman, 1938
Kate Plus Ten, 1938
The Terror, 1938
Thirteen Men and a Gun, 1938
Old Iron, 1938
The Life & Death of Colonel Blimp, 1943
Blanche Fury, 1948
The Elusive Pimpernel, 1950
Brandy For the Parson, 1952
Sea Devils, 1953
Genevieve, 1953
Three Cases of Murder, 1955

GEORGE WOODBRIDGE (1907-)
Portly, jovial character actor of stage and screen, often seen as policeman or innkeeper.

Tower of Terror, 1941
The Big Blockade, 1942
I See a Dark Stranger, 1946
Green For Danger, 1946
Bonnie Prince Charlie, 1948
Escape, 1948
Blanche Fury, 1948
The Fallen Idol, 1948
Children of Chance, 1949
Silent Dust, 1949
Double Confession, 1950
The Naked Earth, 1950

Cloudburst, 1951
Murder in the Cathedral,
 1952
The Flanagan Boy, 1953
The Bosun's Mate, 1953
Gilbert and Sullivan, 1953
Conflict of Wings, 1954
The Green Buddha, 1954
Third Party Risk, 1955
Richard III, 1955
The Naked Heart, 1955
The Constant Husband, 1955
Day of Grace, 1957
A Novel Affair, 1957
Dracula, 1958
Son of Robin Hood, 1958
Two-Way Stretch, 1960
What a Carve Up!, 1962
Out of the Fog, 1962
Nurse On Wheels, 1963
Carry On Jack, 1963
Heavens Above, 1963
Dead End Creek, 1964
Dracula Prince of Darkness,
 1965
Where's Jack?, 1969
Bachelor of Arts, 1969
David Copperfield, 1969

AUBREY WOODS (1928-)
Character actor who has made
sporadic film appearances
since 1947.

Nicholas Nickleby, 1947
The Queen of Spades, 1948
The Greed of William Hart,
 1948
Father Brown, 1954
School For Scoundrels, 1960
Spare the Rod, 1961
A Home of Your Own, 1964
San Ferry Ann, 1965
Just Like a Woman, 1966
Wuthering Heights, 1970
Loot, 1970
Willy Wonka & the Chocolate
 Factory, 1971
The Abominable Dr. Phibes,
 1971
Up Pompeii, 1971
The Darwin Adventure, 1972
Z. P. G. , 1972

That Lucky Touch, 1975
Operation Daybreak, 1976

PETER WOODTHROPE (1931-)
Supporting actor of the sixties,
mainly on stage. Films few.

Hysteria, 1964
The Evil of Frankenstein, 1964
The Skull, 1965
The Blue Max, 1966
Charge of the Light Brigade,
 1968
The Mirror Crack'd, 1980

JOHN WOODVINE (1929-)
Stage actor who has been in
very occasional films.

Darling, 1965
The Walking Stick, 1970
The Devils, 1971
Assault On Agathon, 1976

EDWARD WOODWARD (1930-)
Leading actor of stage (since
1950) and films, popular on
television as "Callan" (1966-71).
Films fairly infrequent but very
memorable. Also recording
artist.

Where There's a Will, 1955
Becket, 1964
File of the Golden Goose, 1969
Incense For the Damned, 1970
Hunted, 1971
Sitting Target, 1972
Young Winston, 1972
Charley One-Eye, 1973
The Wicker Man, 1973
Callan, 1974
Stand Up Virgin Soldiers, 1977
Breaker Morant, 1980

NORMAN WOOLAND (1910-)
Character actor of stage (from
1926) and films; former radio
announcer.

The Gap, 1937
The Five Pound Man, 1937
Hamlet, 1948
Escape, 1948
Look Before You Love, 1948
All Over Town, 1949
Madeleine, 1950
The Angel With the Trumpet,
  1950
Quo Vadis, 1951
Ivanhoe, 1952
The Ringer, 1952
Background, 1953
The Master Plan, 1954
Romeo and Juliet, 1954
Richard III, 1955
Guilty, 1956
My Teenage Daughter, 1956
No Road Back, 1957
The Flesh is Weak, 1957
The Rough and the Smooth,
  1959
The Bandit of Zhobe, 1959
Night Train For Inverness,
  1960
An Honourable Murder, 1960
Portrait of a Sinner, 1961
The Guns of Navarone, 1961
Barabbas, 1962
Life For Ruth, 1962
Master of Venus, 1962
Fall of the Roman Empire,
  1964
Saul and David, 1965
Walk in the Shadow, 1966
The Projected Man, 1966
Fighting Prince of Donegal,
  1966

RICHARD WORDSWORTH
(-)
Character actor of occasional
films; mainly on stage.

The Quatermass Experiment,
  1955
The Man Who Knew Too Much,
  1956
Time Without Pity, 1957
The Camp On Blood Island,
  1958
Revenge of Frankenstein, 1958

Curse of the Werewolf, 1961
Lock Up Your Daughters, 1969

FREDERICK WORLOCK (1886-
  1973)
Character actor of the forties
in Hollywood following lengthy
stage career.

Miracles For Sale, 1939
Lady of the Tropics, 1939
Balalaika, 1939
The Sea Hawk, 1940
Strange Cargo, 1940
Moon Over Burma, 1940
Rage in Heaven, 1941
Free and Easy, 1941
Man Hunt, 1941
Dr. Jekyll and Mr. Hyde, 1941
A Yank in the RAF, 1941
How Green Was My Valley,
  1941
International Lady, 1941
Hudson's Bay, 1941
Random Harvest, 1942
Captains of the Clouds, 1942
Eagle Squadron, 1942
Pacific Rendezvous, 1942
Pierre of the Plains, 1942
The Black Swan, 1943
Madame Curie, 1943
Air Raid Wardens, 1943
Appointment in Berlin, 1943
Sherlock Holmes Faces Death,
  1943
The Lodger, 1944
Hangover Square, 1945
The Woman in Green, 1945
Pursuit to Algiers, 1945
Terror By Night, 1946
Dressed to Kill, 1946
She Wolf of London, 1946
The Imperfect Lady, 1947
Last of the Redmen, 1947
Singapore, 1947
The Lone Wolf in London, 1947
Love From a Stranger, 1947
Joan of Arc, 1948
The Hills of Home, 1948
Johnny Belinda, 1948
Spartacus, 1960
Notorious Landlady, 1962
Spinout, 1966

BRIAN WORTH (1914-)
Light leading man and latterly
equally light character actor;
also on stage.

The Arsenal Stadium Mystery,
    1939
The Lion Has Wings, 1939
Pastor Hall, 1940
Gentleman of Venture, 1940
One Night With You, 1948
Cardboard Cavalier, 1949
Last Holiday, 1950
The Man in the White Suit, 1951
Scrooge, 1951
Tom Brown's School Days, 1951
Hindle Wakes, 1952
Song of Paris, 1952
Treasure Hunt, 1952
Father's Doing Fine, 1952
It Started in Paradise, 1952
Operation Diplomat, 1953
An Inspector Calls, 1954
Barbados Quest, 1955
Windfall, 1955
Breakaway, 1956
Battle of the River Plate, 1956
Assignment Redhead, 1956
Ill Met By Moonlight, 1957
The Square Peg, 1958
Northwest Frontier, 1959
Sink the Bismarck, 1960
Peeping Tom, 1960
Moment of Danger, 1960
Dead Lucky, 1960
Terror of the Tongs, 1961
On Her Majesty's Secret
    Service, 1968

IRENE WORTH (1916-)
American leading lady in
Britain, mainly on stage and
tv.   Films few but excellent.

One Night With You, 1948
Secret People, 1952
Orders to Kill, 1958
The Scapegoat, 1959
Seven Seas to Calais, 1963
To Die in Madrid (voice), 1963
King Lear, 1970
Nicholas and Alexandra, 1971
Rich Kids, 1979

Happy Days, 1980

BEN WRIGHT (-)
Character actor in Hollywood,
adept at playing Germans as
well as stiff upper-lipped Englishmen.

The Desert Rats, 1953
Prince Valiant, 1954
A Man Called Peter, 1955
23 Paces to Baker Street, 1956
The Power and the Prize, 1956
D-Day, the Sixth of June, 1956
Witness For the Prosecution,
    1957
Kiss Them For Me, 1957
Wreck of the Mary Deare, 1959
Journey to the Centre of the
    Earth, 1959
Operation Bottleneck, 1961
Judgement at Nuremberg, 1961
Mutiny On the Bounty, 1962
A Gathering of Eagles, 1963
My Fair Lady, 1964
The Sound of Music, 1965
The Sand Pebbles, 1966
Munster Go Home, 1966
Raid On Rommel, 1971
Search, 1972
Arnold, 1973
Terror in the Wax Museum,
    1973
Turnover Smith, 1980

HUGH E. WRIGHT (1879-1940)
Character comedy actor of
stage (from 1902) and films;
father of Tony Wright.

The Better 'Ole, 1918
The Kiddies in the Ruins, 1918
Hughie at the Victory Derby,
    1919
Garryowen, 1920
Nothing Else Matters, 1920
The Old Curiosity Shop, 1921
Squibs, 1921
The Corner Man, 1921
The Sailor Tramp, 1922
Squibs Wins the Calcutta Sweep,
    1922

Squibs MP, 1923
Squibs' Honeymoon, 1923
Auld Lang Syne, 1929
The Silver King, 1929
East Lynne, 1931
Lord Camber's Ladies, 1932
Pyjamas Preferred, 1932
The Good Companions, 1933
Cash, 1933
The Love Wager, 1933
Oh What a Duchess, 1933
You Made Me Love You, 1933
A Shot in the Dark, 1934
Radio Parade, 1934
On the Air, 1934
Get Your Man, 1934
Crazy People, 1934
Adventure Ltd., 1934
Widow's Might, 1935
Scrooge, 1935
The Big Splash, 1935
Royal Eagle, 1936

HUMBERSTONE WRIGHT (-)
Strong supporting character
player of the 20s and 30s.

Trapped by the London Sharks, 1916
The Secret Woman, 1918
Thelma, 1918
The Rocks of Valpre, 1919
The Double Life of Alfred
   Burton, 1919
God's Clay, 1919
Garden of Resurrection, 1919
The Little Welsh Girl, 1920
Walls of Prejudice, 1920
The Way of the World, 1920
Uncle Dick's Darling, 1920
The English Rose, 1920
Beside the Bonnie Briar Bush,
   1921
The Peacemaker, 1922
A Sporting Double, 1922
Mystery of Dr. Fu Manchu, 1923
The Sign of Four, 1923
In the Blood, 1923
Sally Bishop, 1923
Henry King of Navarre, 1924
Slaves of Destiny, 1924
The Gay Corinthian, 1924
Love Story of Aliette Brunton,
   1924

Further Mysteries of Dr. Fu
   Manchu, 1924
A Dear Liar, 1925
The Squire of Long Hadley,
   1925
London Love, 1926
Safety First, 1926
Mademoiselle From Armentieres,
   1926
The Flag Lieutenant, 1926
Boadicea, 1926
Miss Bracegirdle Does Her
   Duty, 1926
The Garden of Allah, 1927
Hindle Wakes, 1927
Roses of Picardy, 1927
The Glad Eye, 1927
Bright Young Things, 1927
The Arcadians, 1927
The Flight Commander, 1927
A Sister to Assist 'Er, 1927
Sailors Don't Care, 1928
What Money Can Buy, 1928
Mademoiselle Parley Voo, 1928
The Physician, 1928
Waterloo, 1929
Fanny Hawthorn, 1929
White Cargo, 1929
Master and Man, 1929
High Treason, 1929
Alf's Button, 1930
Thread O' Scarlet, 1930
Lloyd of the C.I.D., 1931
Down River, 1931
Congress Dances, 1931
The Marriage Bond, 1932
In a Monastery Garden, 1932
Commissionaire, 1933
The King of Whales, 1934
Strictly Illegal, 1935
Young and Innocent, 1937
Escape Dangerous, 1947

TONY WRIGHT (1925-)
Leading man of stage (from
1946) and films, usually seen
as masculine hero. Former
sailor. Married: Janet Munro.
Son of Hugh E. Wright.

The Flanagan Boy, 1953
Jumping For Joy, 1955
Jacqueline, 1956

Tiger in the Smoke, 1956
Seven Thunders, 1957
The Spaniard's Curse, 1958
Broth of a Boy, 1959
The Rough and the Smooth,
1959
In the Wake of a Stranger,
1959
And the Same to You, 1960
Faces in the Dark, 1960
The House in Marsh Road,
1960
Attempt to Kill, 1961
Portrait of a Sinner, 1961
Journey to Nowhere, 1962
The Liquidator, 1966
Clinic Exclusive, 1971
All Coppers Are, 1972
The Creeping Flesh, 1972

PATRICK WYMARK (1926-
1970)
Prominent character star of
stage (since 1951), films and
television, well-known for tv
series "The Power Game."

The Criminal, 1960
West Eleven, 1962
A Woman's Privilege, 1962
Dr. Syn Alias the Scarecrow,
1963
The Finest Hours (voice),
1964
The Secret of Blood Island,
1965
A King's Story (voice), 1965
Operation Crossbow, 1965
Repulsion, 1965
The Skull, 1965
The Psychopath, 1966
Woman Times Seven, 1967
Tell Me Lies, 1968
Witchfinder General, 1968
Where Eagles Dare, 1968
The Battle of Britain, 1969
Doppelganger, 1969
Cromwell, 1970
Satan's Skin, 1970

DENNIS WYNDHAM (1887-)
Character actor of stage and

screen; married to silent film
actress Poppy Wyndham.

Lorna Doone, 1920
Twisted Tales, 1926
Juno and the Paycock, 1929
Lily of Killarney, 1929
The Informer, 1929
Who Killed Doc Robin?, 1931
Let's Love and Laugh, 1931
The Man They Could Not Arrest,
1931
Gypsy Blood, 1931
The Face at the Window, 1932
The Stolen Necklace, 1933
Anne One Hundred, 1933
Money Mad, 1934
Immortal Gentleman, 1935
Midshipman Easy, 1935
You Must Get Married, 1936
Windbag the Sailor, 1936
Oh Mr. Porter, 1937
Convict 99, 1938
Old Mother Riley MP, 1939
The Arsenal Stadium Mystery,
1939
Old Mother Riley in Society,
1940
Sailors Don't Care, 1940
Neutral Port, 1940
Old Mother Riley's Ghosts, 1941
Sheepdog of the Hills, 1941
Battle For Music, 1943
Bell Bottom George, 1943
I Didn't Do It, 1945
The Dog and the Diamonds,
1953

ROBERT WYNDHAM (-)
Small-part character actor in
occasional films of the forties.

For Those in Peril, 1944
Champagne Charlie, 1944
Fiddlers Three, 1944
Dead of Night, 1945
The Captive Heart, 1946
Who Killed Van Loon?, 1948

DANA WYNTER (1930-)
Elegant leading lady of stage
and films, in Hollywood from

the mid-fifties; also on television in "The Man Who Never
Was" (1966).

White Corridors, 1951
Lady Godiva Rides Again,
   1951
The Woman's Angle, 1952
The Crimson Pirate, 1952
Colonel March Investigates,
   1953
The View From Pompey's
   Head, 1955
Invasion of the Body Snatchers,
   1956
D-Day, the Sixth of June,
   1956
Something of Value, 1957
Fraulein, 1958
In Love and War, 1958
Shake Hands With the Devil,
   1959
Sink the Bismarck, 1960
On the Double, 1961
The List of Adrian Messenger,
   1963
The Spy With the Perfect
   Cover, 1967
If He Hollers Let Him Go,
   1968
Airport, 1970
Santee, 1973
The Savage, 1975
M Station: Hawaii, 1980

DIANA WYNYARD (1906-
   1964)
Distinguished, graceful leading lady of stage and films,
also in Hollywood.

Rasputin and the Empress, 1932
Cavalcade, 1933
Reunion in Vienna, 1933
Men Must Fight, 1933
Over the River, 1934
Where Sinners Meet, 1934
Let's Try Again, 1934
On the Night of the Fire, 1939
Gaslight, 1940
Freedom Radio, 1941
Kipps, 1941
The Prime Minister, 1941

An Ideal Husband, 1948
Tom Brown's School Days, 1951
The Feminine Touch, 1956
Island in the Sun, 1957
Mayerling, 1957
The Second Man, 1959

MARGARET YARDE (-)
Character actress and supporting player at her peak in the
thirties.

Cigarette-Maker's Romance, 1913
The Unwanted Bride, 1922
Madame Recamier, 1923
Falstaff the Tavern King, 1923
The Only Way, 1925
The Painted Lady, 1925
Lady in Silk Stockings, 1925
Sables of Death, 1925
London, 1926
Night Birds, 1930
Michael and Mary, 1931
Let's Love and Laugh, 1931
Third Time Lucky, 1931
Uneasy Virtue, 1931
The Woman Between, 1931
The Good Companions, 1933
Tiger Bay, 1933
Enemy of the Police, 1933
The Man From Toronto, 1933
Matinee Idol, 1933
Trouble in Store, 1934
Nine Forty-Five, 1934
Father and Son, 1934
Sing As We Go, 1934
A Glimpse of Paradise, 1934
The Broken Rosary, 1934
Guest of Honour, 1934
That's My Uncle, 1935
Scrooge, 1935
It Happened in Paris, 1935
The Crouching Beast, 1935
Widow's Might, 1935
Who's Your Father?, 1935
Full Circle, 1935
Jubilee Window, 1935
Squibs, 1935
Eighteen Minutes, 1935
The Deputy Drummer, 1935
Handle With Care, 1935
In the Soup, 1936
Faithful, 1936

Queen of Hearts, 1936
What the Puppy Said, 1936
Gypsy Melody, 1938
No Escape, 1936
Beauty and the Barge, 1937
Calling All Ma's, 1937
The Compulsory Wife, 1937
French Leave, 1937
You Live and Learn, 1937
You're the Doctor, 1938
Prison Without Bars, 1938
French Without Tears, 1939
The Face at the Window, 1939
Crimes at the Dark House,
   1940
George and Margaret, 1940
Two Smart Men, 1940
Henry Steps Out, 1940
Thursday's Child, 1943
Two Fathers, 1944

MICHAEL YORK (1942-)
Handsome leading actor of
stage (since 1960) and films,
also in Hollywood and international films. On tv in "The
Forsyte Saga."

The Taming of the Shrew, 1967
Accident, 1967
Smashing Time, 1967
Red and Blue, 1967
Romeo and Juliet, 1968
The Strange Affair, 1968
Alfred the Great, 1969
The Guru, 1969
Justine, 1969
Something For Everyone, 1970
Touch and Go, 1971
Zeppelin, 1971
England Made Me, 1972
Cabaret, 1972
Brother Sun, Sister Moon,
   1972
Lost Horizon, 1973
The Three Musketeers, 1974
Murder On the Orient Express,
   1974
The Four Musketeers, 1975
Great Expectations, 1975
Conduct Unbecoming, 1975
Seven Nights in Japan, 1976

Logan's Run, 1976
Last Remake of Beau Geste,
   1977
Jesus of Nazareth, 1977
The Island of Dr. Moreau, 1977
Fedora, 1978
A Man Called Intrepid, 1979
Riddle of the Sands, 1979
White Lions, 1979

SUZANNAH YORK (1941-)
Lovely blonde leading lady of
stage, television (1959) and
films, also in Hollywood.

Tunes of Glory, 1960
There Was a Crooked Man,
   1960
The Greengage Summer, 1961
Freud, 1962
Tom Jones, 1963
The Seventh Dawn, 1964
Scene Nun Take One, 1964
Sands of the Kalahari, 1965
Kaleidoscope, 1966
A Man For All Seasons, 1966
A Game Called Scruggs, 1966
Sebastian, 1967
Duffy, 1968
The Killing of Sister George,
   1968
Lock Up Your Daughters, 1969
The Battle of Britain, 1969
Oh What a Lovely War, 1969
They Shoot Horses Don't They?,
   1969
Country Dance, 1969
Jane Eyre, 1970
Happy Birthday Wanda June, 1971
Zee and Co., 1971
Images, 1972
Gold, 1974
The Maids, 1975
Conduct Unbecoming, 1975
That Lucky Touch, 1975
Sky Riders, 1976
Eliza Fraser, 1976
The Shout, 1978
Superman, 1978
Riddle of the Sands, 1979
The Silent Partner, 1979
Long Shot, 1979

ARTHUR YOUNG (1898-1959)
Rotund character player of
stage and screen, often seen
in self-satisfied parts.

Phototone Reels, 1928
No Limit, 1935
Radio Parade of 1935, 1935
Pity the Poor Rich, 1935
Wedding Group, 1936
The Music Maker, 1936
Servants All, 1936
Victoria the Great, 1937
21 Days, 1939
Murder by Invitation, 1941
San Demetrio-London, 1943
The Two Fathers, 1944
The Root of All Evil, 1947
My Brother Jonathan, 1948
Lady With a Lamp, 1951
John of the Fair, 1952
Isn't Life Wonderful, 1953
Stranger From Venus, 1954
An Inspector Calls, 1954
The Gelignite Gang, 1956

DAN YOUNG (-)
North-country comedy actor
with music hall experience;
often seen with Frank Randle.

The New Hotel, 1932
Off the Dole, 1935
Dodging the Dole, 1936
Calling All Crooks, 1938
Somewhere in England, 1940
Somewhere in Camp, 1942
Somewhere On Leave, 1942
Demobbed, 1944
Under New Management, 1946
Holidays With Pay, 1948
Cup Tie Honeymoon, 1948
School For Randle, 1949
Over the Garden Wall, 1950
It's a Grand Life, 1953

JOAN YOUNG (1903-)
Character actress of the forties and fifties, also on stage.

Victoria the Great, 1937

The Lamp Still Burns, 1943
Strawberry Roan, 1945
School For Secrets, 1946
The Small Voice, 1948
Things Happen at Night, 1948
Vice Versa, 1948
Easy Money, 1948
The Fallen Idol, 1948
Good Time Girl, 1948
Trottie True, 1949
Cardboard Cavalier, 1949
Hell is Sold Out, 1951
The Magic Box, 1951
Time Gentlemen Please, 1952
Fast and Loose, 1954
Child's Play, 1954
All For Mary, 1955
The Admirable Crichton,
   1957
Inn of the Sixth Happiness,
   1958
Suddenly Last Summer, 1959
The Last Shot You Hear, 1970

ROLAND YOUNG (1887-1953)
Character star of stage (from
1908) and screen, long in Hollywood where he was often seen
as whimsical, mild-mannered
characters. The perfect Cosmo
Topper.

Sherlock Holmes, 1922
Grit, 1924
Unholy Night, 1929
Her Private Affairs, 1929
Annabelle's Affairs, 1929
The Bishop Murder Case, 1930
Madame Satan, 1930
New Moon, 1931
The Prodigal, 1931
The Squaw Man, 1931
The Guardsman, 1931
Wise Girl, 1931
The Pagan Lady, 1932
Lovers Courageous, 1932
A Woman Commands, 1932
One Hour With You, 1932
This is the Night, 1932
Wedding Rehearsal, 1932
A Lady's Profession, 1933
Pleasure Cruise, 1933

More Than a Kiss, 1933
His Double Life, 1934
Here is My Heart, 1934
David Copperfield, 1935
Ruggles of Red Gap, 1935
The New Yorker, 1935
Street of Women, 1935
One Rainy Afternoon, 1935
They Just Had to Get Married,
  1935
Lullaby, 1936
Unguarded Hour, 1936
The Man Who Could Work
  Miracles, 1936
King Solomon's Mines, 1937
Topper, 1937
Ali Baba Goes to Town, 1937
Give Me Your Heart, 1937
Gypsy, 1937
Don't Bet On Women, 1937
He Met a French Girl, 1938
Call it a Day, 1938
Sailing Along, 1938
The Young in Heart, 1938
Fog Bound, 1939
Here I Am a Stranger, 1939
Topper Takes a Trip, 1939
Yes My Darling Daughter,
  1939
William and Mary, 1940
He Married His Wife, 1940
Star Dust, 1940
Dulcy, 1940
Irene, 1940
No No Nanette, 1940
Private Affairs, 1940
The Philadelphia Story, 1940
Topper Returns, 1941
The Flame of New Orleans,
  1941
Two-Faced Woman, 1941
The Lady Has Plans, 1942
They All Kissed the Bride,
  1942
Tales of Manhattan, 1942
Forever and a Day, 1943
Standing Room Only, 1944
And Then There Were None,
  1945
Bond Street, 1948
You Gotta Stay Happy, 1948
The Great Lover, 1949
Let's Dance, 1950

St. Benny the Dip, 1951
Mr. Mummery's Suspicion,
  1952
That Man From Tangier, 1953

MAI ZETTERLING (1925-)
Lovely, intelligent Swedish
leading actress of stage (1941)
and films, long in Britian.
Also latterly director.

Lasse-Maja, 1941
Frenzy, 1944
Sunshine Follows Rain, 1946
Iris and the Lieutenant, 1946
Frieda, 1947
Night is My Future, 1948
Quartet, 1948
Portrait From Life, 1948
The Bad Lord Byron, 1949
The Lost People, 1949
The Romantic Age, 1949
Blackmailed, 1951
Tall Headlines, 1952
Desperate Moment, 1953
Knock On Wood, 1954
Dance Little Lady, 1955
A Prize of Gold, 1955
Married Life, 1957
Seven Waves Away, 1957
The Truth About Women, 1958
Jet Storm, 1958
Faces in the Dark, 1959
Piccadilly Third Stop, 1960
Offbeat, 1961
Only Two Can Play, 1962
The Man Who Finally Died,
  1962
The Main Attraction, 1963
The Bay of St. Michel, 1963
The Vine Bridge, 1965

GEORGE ZUCCO (1886-1960)
Character star of stage (from
1908) and screen, long in Hollywood where he was typically
seen in an assortment of evil
or villainous characterizations.

Dreyfus, 1931
There Goes the Bride, 1932

The Midshipmaid, 1932
The Man From Toronto, 1933
The Roof, 1933
The Good Companions, 1933
Autumn Crocus, 1934
What's in a Name?, 1934
What Happened Then, 1934
It's a Bet, 1935
The Man Who Could Work
   Miracles, 1936
After the Thin Man, 1936
Parnell, 1937
Saratoga, 1937
Souls at Sea, 1937
London By Night, 1937
Conquest, 1937
Sinner Take All, 1937
Madame X, 1937
The Bride Wore Red, 1937
The Firefly, 1937
Rosalie, 1937
Arsene Lupin Returns, 1938
Lord Jeff, 1938
Vacation From Love, 1938
Fast Company, 1938
Suez, 1938
Marie Antoinette, 1938
Captain Fury, 1939
The Adventures of Sherlock
   Holmes, 1939
The Cat and the Canary, 1939
Charlie Chan in Honolulu,
   1939
Arrest Bulldog Drummond,
   1939
Here I Am a Stranger, 1939
The Hunchback of Notre Dame,
   1939
New Moon, 1940
The Mummy's Hand, 1940
Arise My Love, 1940
Dark Streets of Cairo, 1940
International Lady, 1941

The Monster and the Girl, 1941
A Woman's Face, 1941
Ellery Queen and the Murder
   Ring, 1941
Topper Returns, 1941
My Favorite Blonde, 1942
The Mummy's Tomb, 1942
The Black Swan, 1942
Sherlock Holmes in Washington,
   1943
The Black Raven, 1943
Dead Men Walk, 1943
The Mad Ghoul, 1943
The Mummy's Ghost, 1944
The Seventh Cross, 1944
Voodoo Man, 1944
Shadows in the Night, 1944
Weekend at the Waldorf, 1945
Midnight Manhunt, 1945
House of Frankenstein, 1945
Having a Wonderful Crime,
   1945
Sudan, 1945
Confidential Agent, 1945
Fog Island, 1945
Dr. Renault's Secret, 1946
Moss Rose, 1947
Lured, 1947
Captain From Castile, 1947
The Imperfect Lady, 1947
Desire Me, 1947
Where There's Life, 1947
Tarzan and the Mermaids, 1948
The Pirate, 1948
Joan of Arc, 1948
Madame Bovary, 1949
The Barkleys of Broadway,
   1949
Let's Dance, 1950
The First Legion, 1951
David and Bathsheba, 1951
Secret Service Investigator,
   1953